D1101454

BEST
BRAND NAME
RECIPES

EDITED BY BRIDGID HERRIDGE

BOOK CLUB ASSOCIATES
London

This edition published by Book Club Associates

By arrangement with William Collins Sons & Co Ltd
London · Glasgow · Sydney
Auckland · Toronto · Johannesburg

First published in Great Britain 1983
Reprinted 1984
© Charles Herridge Limited 1983

All rights reserved. No part of this publication may be
reproduced or transmitted in any form or by any means,
electronic or mechanical, including photo-copying,
recording or any information storage and retrieval system
now known or to be invented without permission in
writing from William Collins Sons & Co Ltd

Jacket photography by Tony Latham
Illustrations by Deborah Bull

Filmset by Devon Print Group, Exeter
Printed in Great Britain by
William Collins Sons & Co Ltd, Glasgow

CONTENTS

INTRODUCTION

For many years Britain's food manufacturers have employed highly skilled home economists and cooks to test their products and create new ways of using them. They have published the results of this work on their packets, jars and tins and in leaflets, books and magazines. Their efforts are appreciated, for food manufacturers receive many letters of congratulation from their customers and they are swamped with requests when they advertise new special publications.

There can be few kitchen drawers which do not contain a collection of these labels, cuttings and leaflets — along with the bottle opener, shopping lists, pieces of string and kitchen scissors! Now, for the first time in Britain, we have collected some of the best of these recipes. We have sifted and sorted the kitchen drawer, choosing both old favourites and some brand new cooking ideas.

Some of the older recipes have become family favourites — perhaps collected by granny and handed down through the generations, their source forgotten. But manufacturers are quick to follow new culinary trends and we have also included in this book many new ideas — international dishes, calorie-counted, high fibre and vegetarian recipes, delicious labour-saving main meals using manufactured sauces — which take account of changes in our life style and the latest nutritional research.

All these recipes have been sorted for easy reference. If you want new ideas for cooking sausages or beef or pasta, you look under the section indicated in the contents list. If you have in your cupboard a tin or jar or packet of a manufactured product that you want to use, you look up that manufacturer in the Brand Name Index. If you want to find the recipe for that delicious soup or casserole or cake you made last month, you will find it in the Recipe Index.

Metric and Imperial Measures

The imperial and metric measures used in this book are those calculated by the manufacturer, where these are available. Do not mix metric and imperial amounts as the conversions are not exact and each set of measurements is appropriate for the individual recipe. Metric measurements were not available for some of the recipes and the following conversion tables were used.

Dry Measures

Ounces	Approx g to nearest whole figure	Recommended conversion to nearest unit of 25
1	28	25
2	57	50
3	85	75
4	113	100
5	142	150
6	170	175
7	198	200
8	227	225
9	255	250
10	283	275
11	312	300
12	340	350
13	368	375
14	396	400
15	425	425
16 (1lb)	454	450
17	482	475
18	510	500
19	539	550
20 (1¼lb)	567	575

Liquid Measures

Imperial	Approx ml to nearest whole figure	Recommended ml
¼ pint	142	150
½ pint	283	300
¾ pint	425	450
1 pint	567	600
1½ pints	851	900
1¾ pints	992	1000 (1 litre)

Acknowledgements

We would like to thank the following companies for their help in the compilation of this book.
Adams Foods Ltd; Appleford Ltd; Armour Foods (UK) Ltd; Batchelors Foods Ltd; W.A. Baxter & Sons Ltd; B.E. International Foods Ltd; Birds Eye Wall's Ltd; Booker Health Foods Ltd; Bovril Ltd; Brooke Bond Oxo Ltd; H.P. Bulmer Ltd; Cadbury Typhoo Ltd; Campbell's Soups Ltd; Carnation Food Co Ltd; The Cirio Co Ltd; Colman Foods; CPC (United Kingdom) Ltd; Del Monte Foods Ltd; Dornay Foods Ltd; Elsenham Quality Foods Ltd; Findus Ltd; General Foods Ltd; Granose Foods Ltd; H.J. Heinz Co Ltd; Hermes Sweeteners; HP Foods Ltd; Itona Products Ltd; Jus-rol Ltd; Kavli Ltd; Kellogg Co of Gt Britain Ltd; Kraft Foods Ltd; Lyons Tetley Ltd; Mapletons Foods Ltd; The Nestlé Co Ltd; Paterson Jenks PLC; Princes-Buitoni Ltd; Rank Hovis McDougall Ltd; Rayner Burgess Ltd; Rowntree Mackintosh Sun-Pat Ltd; Ryvita Co Ltd; St Ivel Ltd; Schwarz Spices Ltd; Schweppes Ltd; C. Shippam Ltd; Slimcea Ltd; Spillers Ltd; Wall's Meat Co Ltd; Wander Ltd; Weetabix Ltd; John West Foods Ltd; Whitworth Holdings Ltd; United Biscuits (UK) Ltd; Van den Bergh's & Jurgens Ltd; Young's Seafoods Ltd.

STARTERS

Light Crab Paté

6 oz (170 g) **Armour** Crabmeat
4 oz (125 g) cream cheese
½ teaspoon (2.5 ml) anchovy
  essence
1 teaspoon (5 ml) lemon juice
1–2 tablespoons (15–30 ml)
  milk *or* cream
1 stuffed green olive, sliced

Drain the crabmeat, keep back
some crab pieces and flake the rest.
Mix the flaked crab with the cream
cheese, anchovy essence, lemon
juice, seasoning and enough milk
or cream to moisten the mixture.
Spread the paté in a serving dish
and garnish with crab pieces and
the sliced olive.
   Serve with melba toast.
Serves 6

Quick Fish Cocktail

shredded lettuce
4½ oz (120 g) **Armour** Sardines
  in Vegetable Oil
2 tablespoons (30 ml)
  mayonnaise plus a little
  lemon juice *or* 2 tablespoons
  (30 ml) salad cream
a little tomato ketchup *or* purée
dash Tabasco sauce *or*
  Worcestershire sauce
2 in (5 cm) length cucumber,
  diced
a little paprika and lemon
  wedges *or* cress to garnish

Put a little shredded lettuce in the
bottom of 4 large wine glasses.
Drain the sardines and flake. Mix
with all the other ingredients, pile
into the glasses, sprinkle with the
paprika and garnish with the
lemon wedges or cress.
   Serve with brown bread and
butter.   **Serves 4**

Blue Band

Quick Liver Paté

4 oz (100 g) continental liver
  sausage
2 oz (50 g) **Blue Band**
  Margarine
2 oz (50 g) cream cheese
1 tablespoon (15 ml) single
  cream *or* top of the milk
squeeze of lemon juice
salt and freshly milled black
  pepper
4 stuffed olives to garnish
  (optional)

Remove the skin from the liver
sausage. Place in a bowl and mix
well with the margarine and cream
cheese. Stir in the cream or top of
the milk, the lemon juice and seasoning and mix well. Transfer to 4
small individual dishes, smooth
the tops and chill. Slice the stuffed
olives thinly and use to garnish
each dish, if wished.
   Serve with thin triangles of toast
spread with Blue Band margarine   **Serves 4**

Chicken Liver Paté

4 oz (100 g) butter
2 cloves garlic, crushed
1 onion, chopped
1 lb (450 g) chicken livers,
  roughly chopped
2 Chicken Cubes from **Bovril**,
  crumbled
2 teaspoons (10 ml) brandy
1 tablespoon (15 ml) cream
salt and pepper
clarified butter if the paté is not
  to be used immediately

Melt the butter and fry the garlic
and onion for 5 minutes. Add the
chicken livers and fry for a further
10 minutes until the livers are
cooked. Liquidise the mixture
with the Bovril cubes, brandy and
cream. Season well.
   Transfer to a serving dish. If the
paté is not for immediate use,
cover with a layer of clarified
butter.   **Serves 8**

Ham Mousse

½ oz (15 g) gelatine
¼ pint (150 ml) stock made
  with ½ Chicken Cube from
  Bovril
2–4 tablespoons (30–60 ml)
  horseradish sauce
2 tablespoons (30 ml)
  mayonnaise
½ teaspoon (2.5 ml) mustard
  powder
8 oz (225 g) cooked ham, finely
  minced
¼ pint (150 ml) double cream
1 egg, hard-boiled and finely
  chopped
mustard and cress to garnish

Stir the gelatine into the stock in a
cup or small basin and stand the
cup in a pan of hot water until the
gelatine becomes syrupy. Cool to
lukewarm. Mix with the horseradish sauce, mayonnaise and
mustard powder and fold in the
ham. Whip the cream to soft peaks
and fold into the mixture. Pour
into a mould rinsed with cold
water and leave in the refrigerator
for 2 hours to set. Unmould on to a
plate.
   Serve with the chopped egg
sprinkled on top and garnished
with the mustard and cress.
Serves 4

BULMER

Smoked Mackerel Paté

8 oz (225 g) smoked mackerel
4 tablespoons (60 ml) **Bulmers**
  No 7 Dry Cider (warmed)
2 tablespoons cream *or* top of
  milk
black pepper
4 oz (100 g) melted butter

Remove the skin from the mackerel and cut them into small pieces. Put the fish with all the other ingredients into a liquidiser and blend until smooth.

Serve in a small dish with lemon slices.   **Serves 4**

Sparkling Grapefruit and Orange Starter

1 grapefruit
2 oranges
Bulmers Pomagne, chilled
glacé cherries

Peel the grapefruit and oranges, removing peel and pith. Carefully cut the fruit into segments. Divide into 3 individual glasses. Pour chilled Pomagne over to just cover the fruit. Decorate each serving with a glacé cherry and serve chilled.   **Serves 3**

Farmhouse Paté

4 large rashers streaky bacon
12 oz (350 g) ox liver, trimmed
  and cut into pieces
1 small onion, peeled and
  roughly chopped
3 oz (75 g) fresh white
  breadcrumbs
12 oz (350 g) sausagemeat
½ level teaspoon (2.5 ml)
  mixed herbs

10½ oz (297 g) can **Campbell's**
  Condensed Consommé
1 tablespoon (15 ml) sherry
  (optional)
1 large egg, beaten

Cut the rinds and any small bones from the bacon, and, using the back of a knife, stretch each rasher so that it becomes quite thin. Use to line the base and sides of a 2 lb (1 kg) loaf tin. Using the medium disc on a mincer, mince the liver and onion into a bowl. Stir the breadcrumbs, sausagemeat, herbs, undiluted soup, sherry and beaten egg into the onion and liver mixture and, when all the ingredients are well mixed, put the mixture into the prepared loaf tin and level the surface. Cover the tin with foil and stand it in a roasting tin of hot water. Bake on the centre shelf of a moderate oven, 350°F, 180°C, Gas Mark 4, for about 2 hours—it is cooked when the mixture feels firm. Leave the paté in the tin to set. When cold, turn out.

Serve with buttered toast.

Potato Soufflés

1 lb (450 g) potatoes, peeled
  and cut into small pieces
salt
1 oz (25 g) butter
10½ oz (297 g) can **Campbell's**
  Condensed Celery Soup
2 large eggs, separated

Boil the potato pieces in salted water for about 20 minutes until they are soft. Drain well, then return to the pan and beat the potatoes to a cream, stir in the butter until it has melted and then mix in the undiluted soup. Stir the egg yolks into the potato mixture. Whisk the egg whites until they are stiff and stand in straight peaks then, using a metal spoon, fold the whites into the potato mixture lightly and quickly and divide the mixture evenly between 6 greased individual ramekin or soufflé dishes. Bake in a pre-heated oven at 375°F, 190°C, Gas Mark 5, for 30–35 minutes, until the soufflés are golden brown and well risen. Serve at once.   **Serves 6**

Smoked Mackerel Creams

1 box **Chef** White Sauce Mix
8 oz (225 g) smoked mackerel
black pepper
1 tablespoon (15 ml) lemon
  juice
1 tablespoon (15 ml) cream
parsley sprigs to garnish

Make up the white sauce as instructed on the box. Remove and discard any skin and bones from the fish. Mash the fish with a fork and add to the sauce. Season with black pepper and stir in the lemon juice and cream. Heat through gently then pour into hot individual dishes and serve immediately with hot, crisp toast or black rye bread.

Serve garnished with sprigs of parsley.   **Serves 4**

Mushrooms à la Greque

1 small onion, peeled and finely
  chopped
1 small carrot, peeled and finely
  chopped
1 clove garlic, crushed
2 tablespoons (30 ml) olive oil
½ teaspoon (2.5 ml) ground
  coriander
4 tablespoons (60 ml) white
  wine
salt and pepper
bouquet garni
1 can **Chesswood** Small Whole
  Mushrooms, drained
1 tablespoon (15 ml) parsley,
  chopped

Fry the onion, carrot and garlic in the oil for a few minutes. Add the coriander, wine, seasoning, bouquet garni and mushrooms. Simmer for 15–20 minutes then allow to cool. Remove the bouquet garni, sprinkle with parsley and serve.   **Serves 4**

Cirio Orange Cups Capri

2 large Jaffa oranges
1 head chicory, washed and sliced into rings
14 oz (396 g) can **Cirio** Peeled Tomatoes
2 dessertspoons (20 ml) salad oil
1 dessertspoon (10 ml) vinegar
¼ teaspoon mustard powder
salt and pepper
½ teaspoon (2.5 ml) sugar
2–3 oz (50–75 g) peeled prawns
watercress to garnish
dash of Worcestershire sauce

Wash and dry the oranges and cut them around the middles into halves. Carefully remove the segments, leaving the orange shells to use as cups. Remove as much pith as possible and place the cut-up orange segments in a bowl with the sliced chicory. Drain the tin of tomatoes, reserving the liquid, cut the tomatoes up neatly and add to the oranges and chicory. Beat together the oil, vinegar, mustard, salt, pepper and sugar until completely blended and stir into the mixture in the bowl. Pile into the orange shells and arrange the prawns on top, garnishing with sprigs of watercress. Serve chilled.

   Beat the liquid from the tomatoes with a little salt, pepper and the Worcestershire sauce. Serve in small, individual glasses as an accompaniment to the Orange Cups Capri.   **Serves 4**

Crab and Tomato Mousse

2 level tablespoons (30 ml) gelatine crystals
½ pint (300 ml) warm water
14 oz (396 g) can **Cirio** Peeled Tomatoes
½ pint (300 ml) double cream
½ teaspoon (2.5 ml) paprika
pinch salt
7 oz (198 g) tin crabmeat
1 breakfastcup cucumber, diced
watercress to garnish

Dissolve the gelatine in the warm water (placed in a basin over a pan of hot water to allow the gelatine to dissolve thoroughly). Drain the liquid from the tomatoes and stir the dissolved gelatine and tomato liquid together. Cool until the mixture begins to thicken. Rinse a 1½ pint (900 ml) mould with cold water, pour a little of the jelly into the base and arrange the drained tomatoes on this. Refrigerate until set. Whip the cream until thick but do not over-whip, stir into the rest of the jelly mixture and season with paprika and salt. Flake the crabmeat, mix with the diced cucumber into the mousse mixture and spoon over the tomatoes in the mould. Leave to set.

   To turn out, wrap a hot, wet tea towel round the mould, and invert on to a serving dish. Decorate with sprigs of watercress.

Eggs Baked in Tomato Purée

1 tablespoon (15 ml) **Cirio** Tomato Purée per person
1–2 eggs per person
a little butter
salt and pepper

Heat the tomato purée to boiling point and put a tablespoonful (15 ml) into individual buttered ramekin dishes. Break an egg or eggs into each dish and add a few small pieces of butter. Sprinkle with salt and pepper. Place the dishes in a shallow baking tin of hot water so that the water level is half way up the dishes, cover with foil or greaseproof paper and bake for 6–7 minutes in a moderately hot oven (375°F, 190°C, Gas Mark 5).

Colman's

Curried Prawn and Apple Starter

1 packet **Colman's** Curry Sauce Mix
½ pint (300 ml) water
8 oz (225 g) peeled prawns
1 green apple, cored and chopped
¼ cucumber, diced
1 teaspoon (5 ml) redcurrant jelly
1 head lettuce, shredded
parsley sprigs to garnish

Make up the curry sauce mix as directed. Cool. When cold add the prawns, apple and cucumber and stir in the redcurrant jelly. Arrange the lettuce in 4 individual glass dishes and spoon the prawn mixture on top. Garnish each dish with a parsley sprig.   **Serves 4**

Seafood Cocktail

1 packet **Colman's** Spaghetti Sauce Mix
½ pint (300 ml) water
8 oz (225 g) dressed crab
4 oz (100 g) cooked prawns
8 oz (225 g) white fish, poached
2 oz (50 g) soft white breadcrumbs
2 oz (50 g) butter, melted
1 lemon, sliced

Grease 4 gratin dishes or scallop shells. Make up the spaghetti sauce mix as directed. Stir in the shellfish and white fish and divide between the 4 shells. Mix the breadcrumbs with the butter and sprinkle over the fish mixture. Put under the grill for a few minutes until golden.

   Serve with lemon slices.
Serves 4

Potted Tuna

6 oz (170 g) can tuna, drained
   and flaked
½ pint (250 ml) white sauce
5¾ oz (163 g) jar **Frank
   Cooper's** Tartare Sauce
5 level teaspoons (25 ml)
   gelatine, dissolved in
   3 teaspoons (15 ml) water
5 oz (142 ml) carton single
   cream
lemon slices to garnish

Mix together the tuna, white
sauce, tartare sauce and gelatine.
Beat in the cream, pour the mixture
into 6 individual ramekin dishes
and allow to set for 2 hours.
Garnish each dish with a twist of
lemon.
   Serve with buttered brown
bread.   **Serves 6**

Scampi Shells

8 oz (200 g) white fish, eg cod
   or coley
2 oz (50 g) frozen prawns,
   thawed and chopped
1 can **Frank Cooper's** Cream of
   Scampi Soup
salt and pepper
mashed potato
prawns and parsley sprigs to
   garnish

Steam the fish until just tender,
flake and mix with the prawns and
soup. Pipe a border of potato,
using a large nozzle, round the
edges of four scallop shells. Place
each shell under a pre-heated grill
until golden brown and keep
warm. Heat the fish in the soup
until piping hot, add seasoning to
taste and divide between the
scallop shells. Garnish with
prawns and parsley.   **Serves 4**

Melon Cocktail

1 large melon, chilled
6 tablespoons (90 ml) **Crosse &
   Blackwell** Mayonnaise
1 tablespoon (15 ml) lemon
   juice
cucumber slices and mint
   sprigs to garnish

Cut the melon into 6 wedge-
shaped pieces. Remove the seeds
and loosen the flesh from the skin.
Cut the flesh at right angles to the
skin to form chunks and leave on
the skin. Mix the mayonnaise and
lemon juice and place a spoonful
on top of each melon wedge.
   Garnish with cucumber slices.
Decorate with small mint
sprigs.   **Serves 6**

Potted Herrings

14 oz (396 g) can **Crosse &
   Blackwell** Herrings in
   Tomato Sauce
4 oz (100 g) butter, melted
4 oz (100 g) fresh white breadcrumbs, finely crumbled
1 dessert apple, peeled and
   grated
½ level teaspoon (2.5 ml)
   paprika
2 teaspoons (10 ml) lemon juice
3 hard-boiled eggs, chopped
½ level teaspoon (2.5 ml) salt
pepper to taste
parsley sprigs and lemon twists
   to garnish

Lightly butter the sides and bases
of 8 small soufflé or ramekin
dishes. Empty the herrings into a
bowl, add the melted butter and
blend well together with a fork.
Add the breadcrumbs, grated
apple, paprika, lemon juice, eggs,
salt and pepper and mix well.
Divide the mixture between the
prepared dishes, press down well
and cover with foil. Leave
overnight in the refrigerator before
serving.

To serve, remove the foil,
garnish with the parsley sprigs
and lemon twists and serve
accompanied by crusty French
bread and butter.
   This mixture will keep up to
4 days in a refrigerator or 1 month
in a freezer.   **Serves 8**

ELSENHAM

Savoury Eggs

6 small hard-boiled eggs
3 level tablespoons (45 g)
   butter, softened
3 level teaspoons (15 ml)
   Elsenham Patum Peperium
   (Gentlemen's Relish)
parsley sprigs to garnish

Cut the eggs in half and remove the
yolks. Place the egg yolks and
softened butter in a small mixing
bowl and blend together with a
wooden spoon until smooth. Add
the Patum Peperium and mix well
together. Pipe into the egg cases
and garnish with parsley
sprigs.

Kipper Paté

1 packet **Findus** Kipper Fillets
3 oz (75 g) butter
1 tablespoon (15 ml) lemon
   juice
¼ teaspoon black pepper
¼ small clove garlic, crushed

Cook the kippers as directed on the
packet. Drain, cool and remove the
skin. Pound, sieve or liquidise the
fish and mix with the remaining
ingredients, beating until smooth.
Cover and chill.
   Serve with toast and butter.
Serves 4–5

Spinach au Gratin

8 oz (227 g) packet **Findus**
   Chopped Spinach

2 tablespoons (30 ml) single
    cream
salt and black pepper
grated nutmeg
2 rashers streaky bacon, finely
    chopped
1 oz (25 g) cheese, grated

Cook the spinach as directed,
drain and stir in the cream,
seasoning and nutmeg. Fry the
bacon until crisp. Place the
spinach mixture in individual
dishes and top with the bacon and
cheese. Brown under a hot grill
until the cheese bubbles.
Serves 2–3

Sweetcorn Savoury

1 packet white sauce mix
½ pint (250 ml) milk
1 teaspoon (5 ml) made
    mustard
6 oz (170 g) packet **Findus**
    Sweetcorn
2 eggs, beaten
salt and pepper
grated nutmeg (optional)

Make up the sauce mix according
to pack directions, using the milk.
Stir in the mustard and sweetcorn.
Add the eggs and season to taste.
Divide the mixture into
6 individual ovenproof dishes and
sprinkle with nutmeg. Cook in a
pre-heated oven, 400°F, 200°C,
Gas Mark 6, for 25 minutes. Serve
immediately.   **Serves 6**

Hummus with Crunchy Vegetables

6 oz (175 g) **Granose** Chick
    Peas, soaked overnight and
    drained
½ pint (300 ml) water
4 tablespoons (60 ml) olive oil
4 cloves garlic, crushed
salt and pepper
fresh coriander leaves *or*
    parsley to garnish
wholemeal pitta bread

crisp carrot, cucumber, celery,
    etc., cut into strips

Put the chick peas into a saucepan
or pressure cooker and cook until
soft and the water is taken up
(about 20 minutes at 15 lbs
pressure in pressure cooker).
When cool, liquidise or grind in a
mortar and pestle until smooth.
Gradually beat in enough olive oil
to produce a moist, smooth paste.
Beat in the crushed garlic and
season well with salt and pepper.
Spoon the mixture into a serving
dish and serve chilled, garnished
with the coriander or parsley
leaves.
    Serve with the crisp vegetables
and warmed pitta bread.

Liver and Walnut Paté

12 oz (325 g) soft liver sausage
3 oz (75 g) butter, softened
1 teaspoon (5 ml) dried sage
salt and pepper
4 **Haywards** Pickled Walnuts,
    finely chopped

Beat the liver sausage and butter
together until smooth. Add the
sage, seasoning and walnuts and
mix thoroughly. Press the mixture
into a serving dish.
    Serve with toast.   **Serves 6**

HELLMANN'S

Avocado and Citrus Cocktail

2 avocados, stoned, peeled and
    cubed
2 oranges, peeled and chopped
1 grapefruit, peeled and
    chopped
2 tablespoons (30 ml)
    Hellmann's Real Mayonnaise

Mix together the avocados,
oranges and grapefruit and stir in
the mayonnaise. Chill before
serving.   **Serves 4**

Minted Melon

1 honeydew melon
1 tablespoon (15 ml) chopped
    fresh mint
1 tablespoon (15 ml)
    Hellmann's Real Mayonnaise

Slice the top off the melon and
scoop out the seeds. Use a melon
baller or teaspoon to remove the
flesh of the melon and drain off the
excess juice. Mix together the balls
of melon, fresh mint and mayonnaise and return to the hollowed
out melon.
    Chill well before serving, if
wished, on a bed of ice.
Serves 4

Salmon Mousse

6 oz (150 g) fresh salmon,
    poached *or* a 7½ oz (212 g)
    can salmon, drained
5 fl oz (125 ml) **Hellmann's**
    Real Mayonnaise
salt and pepper
5 fl oz (125 ml) double cream,
    whipped
5 tablespoons (75 ml) cold
    water
4 teaspoons (20 ml) powdered
    gelatine
1 tablespoon (15 ml) lemon
    juice
a few cucumber slices to
    garnish

Remove any skin or bone from the
salmon and flake, add the
mayonnaise and season well. Fold
the cream into the salmon. Mix the
cold water and gelatine in a cup,
place the cup in a pan of gently
simmering water and stir constantly until the gelatine is
dissolved. Add the lemon juice
and dissolved gelatine to the
salmon and mix well. Pour into a
wetted 1 pint (600 ml) mould and
leave to set in the refrigerator for
1½ hours. Turn out on to a plate
and garnish with thin slices of
cucumber.
    Serve with brown bread and
butter.   **Serves 4–6**

Tuna Surprise

3½ oz (98 g) can tuna, drained and flaked
2 tablespoons (30 ml) **Hellmann's** Real Mayonnaise
black pepper
2 tomatoes, chopped
1 oz (25 g) fresh breadcrumbs
1 oz (25 g) cheese, grated

Blend together the tuna, mayonnaise and black pepper to taste. Divide evenly between 4 individual ramekin dishes and sprinkle tomatoes on top. Mix together the breadcrumbs and cheese and spoon over the dishes. Bake at 350°F, 180°C, Gas Mark 4 for 20 minutes then place under a pre-heated grill for 2–3 minutes until golden brown.   **Serves 4**

Garlic Stuffed Mushrooms

8 oz (200 g) flat mushrooms
½ small onion, finely chopped
2 oz (50 g) fresh white breadcrumbs
2 oz (50 g) **Kraft** Cracker Barrel Cheddar Cheese, grated
salt and pepper
2 tablespoons (30 ml) **Kraft** Italian Garlic Dressing

Wash the mushrooms and remove stalks. Place gill side up on a small, greased baking tray. Chop the mushroom stalks and mix with the onion, breadcrumbs and 1 oz (25 g) of the cheese. Season and add the dressing. Mix well. Divide the mixture between the mushrooms, then top with a little of the remaining cheese. Bake in an oven preheated to 425°F, 220°C, Gas Mark 7 for 15–20 minutes.
Serves 4

Philadelphia Consommé Mousse

2 (3 oz, 85g) packets **Kraft** Philadelphia Soft Cheese
14½ oz (411 g) can consommé
1 tablespoon (15 ml) lemon juice
½–1 teaspoon (2.5–5 ml) curry powder
salt and pepper

Cream the cheese in a basin until soft and gradually mix in the consommé, beating thoroughly to avoid lumps. Add the lemon juice, curry powder and seasonings and pour into individual serving dishes. Alternatively, place all the ingredients in a liquidiser and blend at high speed for 1 minute. Chill until set.   **Serves 4**

Avocado Deluxe

2 ripe avocados
19 oz (539 g) can **Libby's** Grapefruit Segments, drained, with syrup reserved
1 oz (25 g) walnut halves
4 tablespoons (60 ml) oil
1 teaspoon (5 ml) French mustard
salt and pepper

Cut the avocados in half and remove the stones. Brush the flesh with a little grapefruit syrup. Fill the centres of the avocados with grapefruit segments and walnuts. In a bowl place the oil, mustard, seasonings and 6 tablespoons (90 ml) of the grapefruit syrup. Mix thoroughly.

Serve with the dressing and brown bread and butter.
Serves 4

Cheese Creams

1½ oz (40 g) butter
1½ oz (40 g) plain flour
½ pint (300 ml) milk
pinch mustard powder
salt and pepper
½ teaspoon (2.5 ml) **Marmite**
2 eggs, separated
½ oz (15 g) gelatine
3 oz (75 g) Stilton cheese, cut into small pieces
3 oz (75 g) cream cheese, cut into small pieces
chopped chives to garnish

Melt the butter and work in the flour. Cook for 1 minute and add the milk gradually, stirring well. Stir over a low heat and simmer for 5 minutes until thick and smooth. Season with the mustard, salt, pepper and Marmite. Cool slightly and beat in the egg yolks.

Dissolve the gelatine in 2 tablespoons (30 ml) of water in a cup and stand the cup in a pan of hot water until the gelatine is syrupy, then cool to lukewarm. Put the sauce, cheese and gelatine into a liquidiser and blend until quite smooth and creamy. Whisk the egg whites to stiff peaks and fold into the cheese mixture. Pour into individual dishes and put into the refrigerator to set.

Garnish with the chopped chives and serve with brown bread and butter.   **Serves 4**

Ham and Cottage Cheese Cucumber

2 jars **Princes** Ham Spread
1 cucumber
8 oz (227 g) cottage cheese
1 oz (25 g) walnuts, chopped
1 tablespoon (15 ml) parsley, chopped
salt
pinch of paprika pepper

Cut each end off the cucumber and divide into 8 equal sections. Scoop the flesh out of each section to ¼ in (0.5 cm) from the edges. Mix the ham spread with the cottage cheese and add the chopped walnuts and parsley. Chop the cucumber flesh and mix with the rest of the ingredients. Season with salt. Pile the mixture back into the cucumber rounds and sprinkle with the paprika pepper.   **Makes 8**

Emerald Cocktail

½ honeydew melon
½ cucumber, diced
1 dessert apple, cored and
    thinly sliced
3 sticks celery, chopped
6 tablespoons (120 ml) **Rose's**
    Lime Juice Cordial
1 teaspoon (5 ml) fresh herbs,
    chopped
salt and freshly ground black
    pepper

Cut the melon flesh into cubes or
balls. Mix all the vegetables and
fruit together with the lime juice,
herbs, salt and pepper. Chill well
before serving.   **Serves 6**

Sardinesalata

8 oz (225 g) cream cheese
4½ oz (120 g) can sardines in
    tomato sauce
2 spring onions
4 tablespoons (80 ml) **Rose's**
    Lime Juice Cordial
sprig parsley
salt and pepper

Soften the cream cheese in a bowl.
Mash the sardines, chop the spring
onions, mix all the ingredients
together with the lime juice and
season well. Divide the mixture
between individual dishes or put
into one large serving dish, cover
and chill in the refrigerator until
required.

Serve, garnished with a sprig of
parsley, with toast, crispbread or
warm pitta bread. A small amount
of lime pickle may be added to the
mixture to give extra piquancy.
Serves 6–8

SCHWARTZ

Mackerel and Dill Paté

8 oz (227 g) smoked mackerel,
    skin and bones removed
3 teaspoons (15 ml) **Schwartz**
    Dill Weed
1 teaspoon (5 ml) **Borden**
    Lemon Juice
¼ teaspoon **Schwartz** Ground
    White Pepper
¼ teaspoon **Schwartz** Garlic
    Salt
¼ pint (142 ml) double cream,
    lightly whipped
1 egg white, stiffly beaten
lemon and cucumber slices to
    garnish

Place the prepared fish in a bowl
and add the dill weed, lemon juice,
pepper and garlic salt. Mash
together well. Stir in the cream
followed by the beaten egg white.
Spoon into individual ramekin
dishes, scallop shells or into one
large bowl. Chill, preferably overnight. Garnish with slices of lemon
and cucumber twisted together.

Serve with hot toast or savoury
crackers. May be stored in a
refrigerator for up to 2 days or
frozen for up to 1 month.
Serves 4–6

Melon, Orange and Ginger Cocktail

1 teaspoon (5 ml) **Schwartz**
    Ground Ginger
4 oz (113 g) granulated sugar
4 tablespoons (60 ml) water
1 large honeydew melon, with
    skin and seeds removed,
    chopped into chunks or
    shaped into balls.
3 large oranges, segmented,
    with all pith and peel
    removed
3 kiwi fruit, peeled and sliced
    (optional)
1 orange, sliced, to garnish

Place the ginger, sugar and water
in a small saucepan and heat gently
until the sugar dissolves. Boil for
5 minutes to form a syrup. Place
the syrup in the refrigerator until
completely cold. Meanwhile
arrange the prepared fruits in
individual serving dishes. Pour
the cold ginger syrup over the
fruit. Chill before serving, garnished with twists of sliced
orange.   **Serves 4–6**

Special Creamy Potted Prawns

4 oz (113 g) butter
1 lb (454 g) shelled, cooked
    prawns
2 teaspoons (10 ml) **Schwartz**
    Mixed Herbs
2 teaspoons (10 ml) **Schwartz**
    Onion Powder
pinch **Schwartz** Cayenne
    Pepper
2 tablespoons (30 ml) double
    cream
lemon wedges and lettuce to
    garnish

Melt the butter in a saucepan. Stir
in the prawns, mixed herbs, onion
powder and cayenne pepper and
fry gently for approximately
5 minutes. Remove from the heat
and allow to cool slightly before
stirring in the cream. Place in the
refrigerator until completely cold
and the butter has set. Spoon into
scallop shells lined with lettuce.
Alternatively, the mixture may be
divided between ramekin dishes
before the chilling stage.

Serve, garnished with lemon
wedges, accompanied by hot
toast, biscuits or crackers. May be
stored in the refrigerator
overnight. Do not freeze.
    Serves 4–6

Taverna Mushrooms

2 teaspoons (10 ml) oil
1 small onion, peeled and sliced
1 clove garlic, crushed with a
    little salt
4 tomatoes, skinned and
    quartered
8 oz (250 g) button mushrooms,
    wiped but not peeled
¼ pint (150 ml) **Schweppes**
    Ginger Cordial
1 rounded tablespoon (20 ml)
    tomato purée
freshly ground pepper
1 good tablespoon (25 ml)
    parsley *or* chives, chopped

Fry the onion and garlic gently in
the oil for a few minutes until soft,
add the tomatoes and mushrooms
and cook for a further 5 minutes.
Mix in the cordial and tomato
purée and bring to boiling point.
Take the pan off the heat, add a
generous amount of pepper and
half the parsley or chives. Cool for
at least 2 hours or overnight.
Adjust the seasoning if necessary
and sprinkle with the remaining
herbs just before serving.
Serves 6

Stuffed Cucumbers

2 medium cucumbers
1 oz (25 g) **Stork** Margarine
Filling
1 oz (25 g) **Stork** Margarine
1 oz (25 g) flour
scant ½ pint (275 ml) milk
½ teaspoon (2.5 ml) paprika
    pepper
1 tablespoon (15 ml) lemon
    juice
2 oz (50 g) cream cheese
6 oz (175 g) Gouda cheese,
    diced
2 oz (50 g) prawns
chopped parsley to garnish

Wash the cucumbers and cut into
4 in (10 cm) lengths, then slice
through in half. Scoop out the
centres and chop finely. Melt the
margarine in a pan and toss the
cucumber lengths until thoroughly
coated. Keep warm. For the filling,
place the margarine, flour, milk,
paprika and lemon juice in a
saucepan, bring to the boil over
moderate heat, stirring continuously and boil for 2–3 minutes.
Remove from the heat and beat in
the cream cheese. Stir in the Gouda
and prawns. Pile the cheese
mixture into the cucumber slices
and sprinkle with chopped
parsley. Serve immediately.

Terrine

8–10 **Wall's** Streaky Bacon
    Rashers, with rinds removed
6 oz (150 g) pig's liver
6 oz (150 g) lean, boneless pork
6 oz (150 g) pork fat
6 oz (150 g) pork sausagemeat
2 eggs, beaten
2 oz (50 g) fresh breadcrumbs
1 teaspoon (5 ml) mixed herbs
2 tablespoons (30 ml) parsley,
    chopped
salt and pepper
1 tablespoon (15 ml) brandy
    (optional)

Line the bottom and sides of a 1 lb
(450 g) loaf tin with the bacon
rashers, overlapping them.
Coarsely mince together the liver,
pork and pork fat, then mix in the
remaining ingredients with seasoning to taste and the brandy, if
used. Pile the mixture into the loaf
tin and press down firmly into the
corners. Cover the tin with foil and
place it in a roasting tin containing
about 1 in (2.5 cm) of hot water.
Bake at 350°F, 180°C, Gas Mark 4,
for 1¼ hours.

　Remove the tin from the oven
and cover with fresh foil. Place a
1 lb (450 g) weight on top and
leave overnight in the refrigerator.
Next day, turn the terrine out of
the tin and serve, cut into slices.
Serves 6–8

Skipper Gratinée

2 (3¼ oz, 90 g) cans **John West**
    Skippers in Tomato Sauce
8 oz (227 g) can **John West**
    Tomatoes
a good squeeze of lemon juice
1 small onion, peeled and
    finely chopped
pinch of basil
salt and freshly ground pepper
3 tablespoons (45 ml) dried
    breadcrumbs
1 oz (25 g) butter
lemon wedges to garnish

Put the Skippers into a shallow,
ovenproof dish, or individual
scallop shells. Mix together the
tomatoes, onion, basil, lemon
juice and seasoning. Cover the fish
with this mixture. Scatter the
breadcrumbs over the top and dot
with butter. Bake in a hot oven at
400°F, 200°C, Gas Mark 6 for
15–20 minutes until the top is
nicely browned. Garnish with the
lemon wedges. **Serves 4**

Skipper Paté

2 (3¾ oz, 106 g) cans **John West**
    Skippers in oil, drained
4 teaspoons (20 ml) French
    mustard
4 teaspoons (20 ml) lemon juice
3 tablespoons (45 ml) curd or
    cream cheese
salt and pepper
1 small onion, peeled and finely
    chopped

Turn the fish into a mixing bowl
and mash with a fork. Stir the
mustard and lemon juice into the
cheese, then add this to the fish.
Season well with salt and pepper
and beat well. Stir in the onion and
then turn the paté into a suitable
container. Cover and chill until
required. Serve with crusty bread
or biscuits. **Serves 6**

Tuna and Apple Salad

2 (7 oz, 198 g) cans **John West** Tuna Steak in Brine
2 red eating apples, cored and chopped
4 sticks celery, chopped
4 tomatoes, quartered
¼ pint (150 ml) natural yoghurt *or* low calorie mayonnaise
salt and pepper

Drain and break the tuna into large pieces. Place in a large bowl with the apples, chopped celery and tomatoes. Stir in the yoghurt or mayonnaise and season to taste with salt and pepper.

Serve on a bed of crisp lettuce and cucumber. **Serves 4**

whitworths

Apple and Prawn Baskets

1 oz (25 g) **Whitworths** Long Grain Rice
3 tablespoons (45 ml) oil
1 tablespoon (15 ml) vinegar
½ teaspoon (2.5 ml) dried thyme
salt and freshly ground black pepper
6 large, crisp apples
1 tablespoon (15 ml) lemon juice
4 oz (125 g) prawns
1 stick celery, chopped
2 oz (50 g) **Whitworths** Chopped Almonds
1 oz (25 g) **Whitworths** Chopped Almonds, finely chopped and toasted, paprika pepper and shredded lettuce to garnish

Cook the rice as directed on the packet. Meanwhile, mix together the oil, vinegar, thyme and seasonings. When the rice is cooked, fold in the dressing and leave to cool. With a sharp, serrated knife cut off the tops of the apples and carefully cut out the flesh, to leave only the shell. Discard the cores, chop the flesh into small cubes and toss in the

lemon juice. Reserve some of the prawns for decoration and mix the remainder with the rice, apple, celery and chopped almonds. Chill for at least 30 minutes.

Spoon into the apple shells, decorate with the reserved prawns, sprinkle the toasted almonds over the top and dust with paprika pepper. Serve immediately on a bed of lettuce. **Serves 6**

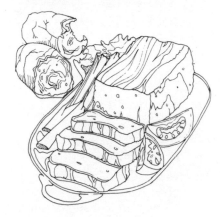

Turkey Paté

10 oz (275 g) turkey meat, uncooked
8 oz (225 g) lean pork
8 oz (225 g) chicken livers
4 tablespoons (60 ml) white wine
2 tablespoons (30 ml) water
2 cloves garlic, crushed
3 oz (75 g) sachet **Whitworths** Country Stuffing Mix
salt and black pepper
4 bay leaves
6 rashers streaky bacon, with rinds removed

Finely mince the turkey, pork and chicken livers. Stir in the wine, water, garlic, stuffing mix and seasoning. Mix thoroughly. Arrange the bay leaves in the base of a 1 lb (450 g) loaf tin. Stretch the bacon rashers slightly with the back of a knife and use to line the loaf tin. Carefully spoon the meat mixture into the prepared tin. Cover with foil and stand the loaf tin in a roasting tin, half-filled with cold water. Bake in a preheated oven at 350°F, 180°C, Gas Mark 4 for 1½–2 hours. Allow to cool, then press with weights and chill until firm.

DIPS

Branston.

Branston Cream Dip

4 oz (100 g) cream cheese
2 tablespoons (30 ml) milk
3 tablespoons (45 ml) **Branston** Pickle
1 clove garlic, crushed (optional)
salt and pepper

Blend together the cream cheese and milk and gradually work in the pickle and garlic. Season to taste and empty into a small dish.

Serve with a selection of raw vegetables and savoury biscuits. This dip will keep, covered, in a refrigerator for 4–5 days.

BURGESS

Tartare Dip

8 oz (225 g) cream cheese
8 heaped teaspoons (60 ml) **Burgess** Sauce Tartare

Mix the cream cheese and Sauce Tartare and chill.

Serve with small savoury biscuits, gristicks, potato crisps or prawns.

FRANK COOPER®

Kashmir Dip

1 can **Frank Cooper's** Kashmir Chicken Soup
8 oz (200 g) cream cheese
2 tablespoons (30 ml) mango chutney

Mix all the ingredients together well. Serve well chilled with sliced peaches, cooked diced chicken, carrot sticks and cocktail biscuits.

Taramasalata

12 slices of white bread, with
 crusts removed
½ pint (275 ml) milk
6 oz (175 g) smoked cod's roe
2 onions, peeled and chopped
juice of 2 lemons
16 tablespoons (240 ml) **Flora**
 Oil

Soak the bread in the milk, then
squeeze the bread dry and place in
a liquidiser, together with the
smoked cod's roe, onion and
lemon juice. Blend until smooth
then gradually add the oil until the
mixture becomes smooth and
creamy. Chill in the refrigerator.
 Serve with hot pitta bread.

HELLMANN'S

Cottage Dip

8 oz (227 g) carton cottage
 cheese
2 tablespoons (30 ml)
 Hellmann's Real Mayonnaise
2 in (5 cm) piece cucumber,
 finely chopped
2 teaspoons (10 ml) parsley,
 chopped
1 small green pepper, de-
 seeded and finely chopped
1 teaspoon (5 ml) lemon juice
black pepper

Blend together the cottage cheese,
mayonnaise, cucumber, parsley,
green pepper and lemon juice.
Add black pepper to taste. Chill.
 Serve with seedless grapes,
chopped red and green peppers,
halved small tomatoes and cocktail
biscuits.

Danish Dip

4 oz (113 g) carton cottage
 cheese
2 tablespoons (30 ml)
 Hellmann's Real Mayonnaise

4 oz (100 g) Danish Blue cheese,
 crumbled

Blend together all ingredients and
serve chilled with celery sticks,
avocado cubes (dipped in lemon
juice), slices of pear (dipped in
lemon juice) and cocktail biscuits.
 Serves 4–6

Egg and Celery Dip

2 hard-boiled eggs, finely
 chopped
2 sticks celery, finely chopped
2 oz (50 g) cream cheese
2 tablespoons (30 ml)
 Hellmann's Real Mayonnaise
1 level teaspoon (5 ml) dry
 mustard
salt and black pepper

Mix together the eggs, celery,
cream cheese, mayonnaise and
mustard. Season to taste then chill
before serving.
 Serve with chicory, strips of
white cabbage, asparagus tips and
cocktail biscuits.

South American Dip

1 small red pepper, de-seeded
 and chopped
1 small green pepper, de-
 seeded and chopped
2 tomatoes, de-seeded and
 chopped
1 oz (25 g) white breadcrumbs
½–1 level teaspoon (2.5–5 ml)
 chilli powder
4 tablespoons (60 ml)
 Hellmann's Real Mayonnaise
2 teaspoons (10 ml) tomato
 purée

Mix together the red and green
peppers, tomatoes, white breadcrumbs and chilli powder. Blend
together the mayonnaise and
tomato purée and add to the
peppers.
 Chill before serving with small
button mushrooms, chicory
leaves, courgette slices and cocktail biscuits. **Serves 4–6**

Kellogg's

Oriental Cheese Dip

4 oz (113 g) carton cottage
 cheese
8 oz (225 g) cream cheese
2 tablespoons (30 ml) mango
 chutney, chopped
1 tablespoon (15 ml) onion,
 finely chopped
1 teaspoon (5 ml) lemon juice
½ teaspoon (2.5 ml) salt
½ teaspoon (2.5 ml) curry
 powder
1 oz (25 g) **Kellogg's** All-Bran
 or Bran Buds

Put the cottage cheese into a sieve
over a bowl and allow the excess
liquid to drain away. Mix the
cottage cheese and cream cheese
together until smooth, then stir in
the chutney, onion, lemon juice,
salt and curry powder. Chill until
the mixture is firm enough to
handle, then shape into a ball and
roll it in the All-Bran. Chill for at
least 1 hour.
 Serve with savoury biscuits.

Knorr

Virginia Dip

6 oz (150 g) cream cheese
2 (5 fl. oz, 142 ml) cartons
 natural yoghurt
1 packet **Knorr** Virginia
 Sweetcorn Soup
1 oz (25·g) peanuts, chopped
peanuts to garnish

Blend together all the ingredients,
cover and leave overnight in a
refrigerator. Garnish with a few
peanuts. Serve with celery and
carrot sticks, cubes of pineapple
and cocktail biscuits.

Welsh Dip

3 oz (75 g) cream cheese
2 (5 fl oz, 142 ml) cartons
    natural yoghurt
1 packet **Knorr** Leek Soup

Blend together the cream cheese
and yoghurt and stir in the soup
mix. Cover and leave overnight in
a refrigerator or cool place.

Serve with carrot and cucumber
sticks, strips of green pepper,
pieces of raw cauliflower and
cocktail biscuits.

Marmite Dip

8 oz (225 g) cottage cheese
2 teaspoons (10 ml) **Marmite**
2 teaspoons (10 ml) chives,
    chopped
salt and pepper
4 medium carrots, peeled and
    cut into thin strips
¼ cucumber, cut into strips,
    but not peeled
3 sticks celery, cut into strips
1 small packet potato crisps

Sieve the cottage cheese and mix
well with the Marmite, chives and
seasoning to taste. Put into a
serving bowl and chill for 1 hour.
Meanwhile, put all the prepared
vegetables into a bowl of salted
water and chill. Drain well and
arrange in a circle on a plate, along
with the potato crisps. Put the
Marmite dip in the centre. Use the
vegetable sticks and crisps to
scoop up the dip.

Cadbury's Marvel

Patio Dip

8 oz (225 g) cottage cheese
4 heaped tablespoons (160 ml)
    dry **Marvel**
1 small onion, peeled
½ teaspoon (2.5 ml) curry paste
1 teaspoon (5 ml) any piquant
    sauce

sprig parsley
2 tablespoons (30 ml) water
salt and pepper
slices of tomato *or* onion rings
    to garnish

Place all the ingredients, with
seasoning to taste, into a liquidiser
or food processor. Blend until
smooth. Turn out into a serving
dish and chill until ready to serve.
Garnish with the tomatoes or
onion rings.

Serve with a selection of fresh
vegetables such as carrots, celery,
cucumber and chicory, plus apples
or pears, cut into slices or sticks.

Crab and Avocado Dip

1 jar **Princes** Crab Paté
1 very soft avocado, mashed
1 clove garlic, crushed
4 oz (100 g) cream cheese
2 tablespoons (30 ml) milk
salt and black pepper

Blend together the paté, avocado,
garlic, cheese and milk and season
to taste.

Serve with radishes and croutons of flaky pastry.

Salmon and Cucumber Dip

1 jar **Princes** Salmon Spread
2 oz (50 g) cream cheese
2 tablespoons (30 ml) natural
    yoghurt
2 oz (50 g) cucumber, unpeeled
    and finely chopped

Blend together the spread, cream
cheese and yoghurt and stir in the
cucumber. Season to taste and
serve with savoury biscuits.

This dip is also delicious served
with scampi.

Avocado Dip

1 ripe avocado
4 tablespoons (80 ml) **Rose's**
    Lime Juice Cordial
4 oz (100 g) cream cheese
2 sticks celery, finely chopped
salt and freshly ground black
    pepper
Tabasco sauce (optional)

Halve the avocado, remove the
stone, scoop out the flesh and
mash it well with the lime juice.
Soften the cheese in a bowl then
gradually beat in the avocado. Stir
in the celery and season well with
salt and pepper, adding a drop of
Tabasco sauce if liked. Place in a
serving dish, cover and chill.

Serve with sticks of fresh, crisp
vegetables, potato crisps or
savoury sticks.

Curried Lentil Dip

1 small onion, peeled and sliced
2 tablespoons (30 ml) **Spry**
    Crisp 'n Dry
1½ tablespoons (22 ml) curry
    powder
1 teaspoon (5 ml) paprika
    pepper
2½ fl. oz (60 ml) tomato juice
1 teaspoon (5 ml) lemon juice
1 dessertspoon (10 ml) apricot
    jam *or* redcurrant jelly
¼ pint (150 ml) mayonnaise *or*
    salad cream
1 oz (25 g) lentils, pre-soaked
    and cooked

Saute the onion in oil, then add the
curry powder and paprika pepper.
Cook for 1 minute, then add the
tomato juice, lemon juice and jam
or jelly. Cover and simmer for 7–
10 minutes. Cool. Mix well with
the mayonnaise and stir in the
lentils.

Tuna Dip

6½ oz (185 g) can **John West**
    Tuna Chunks in Oil
1 oz (25 g) onion, roughly
    chopped
¼ pint (150 ml) mayonnaise
1 tablespoon (15 ml) capers
1 tablespoon (15 ml) vinegar
salt and pepper
celery
cucumber
green pepper
spring onions
cocktail biscuits

Place the tuna, onion, mayonnaise, capers and vinegar in a
liquidiser goblet and blend until
smooth. Adjust the seasoning to
taste. Cut the celery, cucumber,
green pepper and spring onions
into sticks. Pour the Tuna Dip into
a small bowl and surround with
the vegetable sticks and cocktail
biscuits.

COCKTAIL SNACKS

Corned Beef Puffins and Pinwheels

13 oz (368 g) packet puff pastry
1 egg, beaten with 2 teaspoons
    (10 ml) cold water
12 oz (340 g) can **Armour**
    Corned Beef
1 tablespoon (15 ml) bottled
    brown sauce

Divide the pastry in half. Cut the
corned beef into two-thirds and
one-third.

Puffins
Take half the pastry and cut in 3
lengthwise. Roll out each piece to
measure 3 × 10 in (7.5 × 25 cm).
Take the two-thirds piece of

corned beef, cut in 3 slices then
each into 3 again, making 9
fingers. Put these in lines along the
rolled out pastry and brush the
edges with the beaten egg. Roll up
tightly with the joins underneath.
Cut each into 2 in (5 cm) lengths.
Mark the tops with a knife or snip
with pointed scissors and brush
with egg. Put on a baking sheet.
Bake near the top of a pre-heated
oven at 425°F, 220°C, Gas Mark 7,
for 12–15 minutes until browned.

Pinwheels
Take half the pastry and roll to a
rectangle 8 × 10 in (20 × 25 cm).
Cut into 2 strips, each 4 × 10 in
(10 × 25 cm). Take the one-third
piece of corned beef and mash well
with the brown sauce. Spread half
over each pastry strip. Brush the
edges with egg, roll up tightly and
cut into ½ in (1 cm) slices. Put
them flat on a greased baking
sheet. Bake near the top of a pre-
heated oven at 425°F, 220°C, Gas
Mark 7, for 10–12 minutes until
browned. Serve hot or cold.

**Makes about 15 Puffins and
40 Pinwheels**

Savoury Party Snacks

2 sheets **Birds Eye** Puff Pastry,
    thawed

Trim the very outer edges of the
pastry sheets to ensure even
rising. Cut each sheet into three
strips, place on a baking tray and
bake in a preheated oven at 425°F,
220°C, Gas Mark 7 for approximately 10 minutes, or until well
risen and golden brown. Split the
slices in half and leave to dry.
Meanwhile make up the filling.
Sandwich together 2 cooked strips
of pastry with any of the fillings
below or simply spread the
mixture carefully on top of one
slice to make an attractive open
sandwich.

Serve as unusual snacks for
supper or at a party.

Savoury Toppings or Fillings
1 Spread or fill with a soft paté and
garnish with slices of tomato,

cucumber, stuffed olives, or
gherkins.
2 Mash together pilchards or
sardines with a little mayonnaise,
lemon juice, chopped parsley and
chopped cucumber.
3 Pipe or spread with cream or
cottage cheese and garnish with
chopped chives, pieces of pineapple, chopped parsley or paprika.
4 Make a thick white sauce,
season well and stir in cooked
chicken, sweetcorn and prawns
with a touch of cayenne pepper *or*
add to the sauce chopped ham,
chopped cooked mushrooms and
chopped tomato and season with
marjoram.

BURGESS

Vol-au-vents Tartare

½ pint (300 ml) white sauce
4 oz (100 g) smoked haddock,
    cooked and flaked
4 heaped teaspoons (30 ml)
    Burgess Sauce Tartare

Make the vol-au-vent cases out of
puff pastry or buy 12 cases. Cook at
425°F, 220°C, Gas Mark 7 for
15–20 minutes. Remove the caps
and take out the uncooked pastry.
Fill with a mixture of white sauce,
fish and Sauce Tartare. Replace the
caps and serve hot or cold.

Makes 12

Chef

Chicken and Mushroom Vol-au-vents

8 (1½–2 in, 4–5 cm) frozen
    vol-au-vent cases
1 box **Chef** Mushroom Soup
½ pint (300 ml) milk
8 oz (225 g) cooked chicken
parsley sprigs to garnish

Cook the vol-au-vents as instructed on the pack and keep hot.
Meanwhile make up the mushroom soup with the milk, roughly
chop the chicken and stir into the

soup. Heat until simmering. Fill the vol-au-vent cases with the chicken and mushroom mixture, top with the vol-au-vent centres and garnish with the sprigs of parsley. Serve hot.　**Serves 4**

Gentlemen's Snack

7 oz (200 g) best steak, finely minced
1 teaspoon (5 ml) **Elsenham** Mustard
2 egg yolks
1 teaspoon (5 ml) **Elsenham** Seasoned Salt
2 teaspoons (10 ml) small capers
1 tablespoon (15 ml) grape brandy
2 teaspoons (10 ml) **Elsenham** Hot Horseradish
½ oz (15 g) **Elsenham** Patum Peperium
dry breadcrumbs for coating
oil for deep *or* shallow frying

Mix all the ingredients together. Make into small balls, coat with the breadcrumbs and fry. Ideal for party snacks, or make larger, flatter cakes and place on fried bread or toast for a filling supper dish.

HELLMANN'S

Cheese and Onion Vol-au-Vents

1 tablespoon (15 ml) pure corn oil
1 small onion, finely chopped
2 oz (50 g) cheese, grated
3 teaspoons chives *or* spring onion tops, chopped
3 tablespoons (45 ml) **Hellmann's** Real Mayonnaise
seasoning
12 small vol-au-vent cases, cooked

Heat the oil and sauté the onion until golden brown. Mix together the cheese, onion and chives. Stir in the mayonnaise and season to taste. Remove tops from the vol-au-vents. Divide mixture between the vol-au-vent cases and fill. Replace tops.

If wished, the vol-au-vents can be served heated gently in the oven. Place on a baking sheet, cover and heat at 325°F, 170°C, Gas Mark 3 for 15 minutes.
Makes 12 vol-au-vents

Asparagus Tarts

7½ oz (215 g) packet **Jus-Rol** Shortcrust Pastry, thawed
1 egg
¼ pint (150 ml) single cream
1 oz (25 g) Parmesan cheese, grated
10½ oz (298 g) can cut spears asparagus
salt and freshly ground pepper

Roll out the pastry and cut 16 circles using a 2 in (5 cm) plain cutter. Line patty tins with the circles. Beat the egg and cream together, add the cheese and season well. Divide the drained asparagus spears between the pastry cases, pour in the egg mixture and bake in a pre-heated oven at 375°F, 190°C, Gas Mark 5, for 15–20 minutes until set.
Makes 16 tarts

Lemony Haddock Vol-au-Vents

12 **Jus-Rol** Vol-au-Vents
1 oz (25 g) butter
1 oz (25 g) flour
½ pint (300 ml) milk
2 eggs, hard-boiled and chopped
8 oz (225 g) haddock, cooked and flaked
1 level tablespoon (15 ml) parsley, chopped
4 teaspoons (20 ml) lemon juice
salt and freshly ground black pepper

sprigs of parsley to garnish

Prepare the vol-au-vents according to the packet instructions. Make a white sauce in the usual way with the butter, flour and milk; add the eggs, haddock, parsley and lemon juice and season to taste. Carefully remove the centres from the vol-au-vents, scoop out any soft insides and discard. Divide the filling between the cases. Garnish with parsley and serve immediately.
Makes 12 vol-au-vents

Spicy Puffs

½ oz (15 g) butter
1 oz (25 g) onion, peeled and finely chopped
1 level tablespoon (15 ml) medium curry powder
1 level tablespoon (15 ml) flour
4 tablespoons (60 ml) light stock *or* water
2 teaspoons (10 ml) lemon juice
3–4 oz (75–100 g) cooked chicken, finely chopped
1 oz (25 g) sultanas
13 oz (370 g) packet **Jus-Rol** Puff Pastry, thawed
1 egg, beaten

Melt the butter in a saucepan. Add the onion and fry gently until transparent. Add the curry powder and flour, stir well and cook for 1–2 minutes. Stir in the stock and lemon juice, bring to the boil and cook for a further few minutes. Fold in the chicken and sultanas. Season with pepper and salt if desired and spread on a plate to cool.

Roll out the pastry to ⅛ in (0.25 cm) thick. Using a 3 in (8 cm) diameter plain cutter, cut out about 24 rounds, re-rolling the pastry if necessary. Brush lightly with beaten egg. Divide the filling between the pastry rounds. Bring up the edges, seal well and using the fingers flute the top seam (like Cornish pasties). Chill for 30 minutes. Brush with beaten egg and bake in a pre-heated oven at 425°F, 220°C, Gas Mark 7, for 15–20 minutes until golden brown. Serve warm. **Makes about 24 puffs**

Spiced Nuts

2 oz (50 g) **Kellogg's** Special K
2 oz (50 g) **Kellogg's** 30% Bran Flakes
4 oz (100 g) mixed salted nuts
½ (3½ oz, 99 g) packet Pretzel sticks, halved
¼ teaspoon garlic salt
2 teaspoons (10 ml) paprika pepper
pinch pepper
2 oz (50 g) melted butter

Mix all the ingredients together in a roasting tin. Bake in a moderate oven (350°F, 180°C, Gas Mark 4) for 15 minutes. Eat warm or allow to cool and store in an airtight container.

Hot Avocado Canapes

3 small ripe avocados
4 oz (100 g) cooked shoulder ham
6 slices wholemeal bread from a small loaf
a little butter
1 clove garlic (optional)
4 oz (100 g) **Kerrygold** Frozen Double Cream, thawed
3 tablespoons (45 ml) Cheddar cheese, grated

Allow the cream to defrost. Whip the cream lightly, add the grated cheese, salt and pepper. Toast the slices of bread, remove crusts and butter lightly. Rub round the inside of a bowl with a cut clove of garlic. Cut the avocado in quarters and remove the skin. Slice across thickly. Cut the ham in thin strips and place in the bowl with the avocado, add salt and pepper and a squeeze of lemon juice. Mix together and divide between the slices of toast. Put a good spoonful of the cheese cream on top.

Pre-heat the grill for 5 minutes. Just before serving, slip the avocado canapes under the grill to brown quickly. Serve hot as a first course or savoury.   **Serves 6**

Virginia Vol-au-vents

1 packet **Knorr** Virginia Sweetcorn Soup
1 pint (500 ml) milk
4 oz (100 g) cooked ham, diced
4 spring onions, finely chopped
15 small *or* 8 large vol-au-vent cases, cooked

Blend together the soup mix and the milk and bring to the boil, stirring. Add the ham and onions and simmer gently for 5–6 minutes. Divide the mixture between the hot vol-au-vent cases. **Makes 15 small or 8 large vol-au-vents.**

Brisling Roll-ups

4 oz (100 g) frozen puff pastry, thawed
French mustard
1½ oz (42 g) can **John West** Skippers, drained
milk to glaze
sesame *or* poppy seeds to garnish

Roll out the pastry to ⅛ in (0.25 cm) and cut into strips. Spread generously with French mustard. Roll the Skippers up in the strips of pastry. Brush with milk and sprinkle with the sesame or poppy seeds. Bake in a pre-heated oven at 400°F, 200°C, Gas Mark 6, for 10–12 minutes until golden brown. Serve warm.

Brisling and Tomato Puffs

¼ pint (150 ml) water
2 oz (50 g) margarine
8 tablespoons (120 ml) plain flour
2 eggs
2 (3¾ oz, 91 g) cans **John West** Skippers in Tomato Sauce
4 oz (100 g) cheese, grated
Worcestershire sauce
lemon juice
paprika pepper

Put the water and margarine into a saucepan, heat until the fat is melted and then bring to the boil. Take off the heat and beat in the flour. Allow to cool slightly and then beat in the eggs, a little at a time. Pipe or spoon the mixture in small blobs on to greased baking sheets and bake in a pre-heated oven at 400°F, 200°C, Gas Mark 6, for about 15 minutes until golden brown. Mash the Skippers with the grated cheese and season to taste with the Worcestershire sauce and lemon juice and use to fill the puffs. Sprinkle with the paprika pepper.

Skipper Bites

freshly made toast
butter
1 can **John West** Skippers
horseradish relish
parsley sprigs to garnish

Allow the toast to go cold and then spread generously with the butter. Arrange the skippers on the toast leaving a little room between each. Cut the toast into fingers, spoon a small blob of horseradish relish on top and garnish each with a sprig of parsley.

SOUPS

Carrot and Lentil Soup

1 oz (25 g) butter
1 onion, chopped
2 carrots, diced
1 tablespoon (15 g) **Allinson**
    100% Wholewheat Flour
4 oz (100 g) red lentils
2 pints (1.2 litres) stock
1 bay leaf
sea salt and black pepper
1 tablespoon (15 ml) lemon
    juice
chopped parsley to garnish

Melt the butter in a large saucepan,
add the onion, carrots and flour
and cook, stirring occasionally,
until the onion is soft but not
brown. Stir in the lentils and cook
for a further 2–3 minutes, then add
the stock and bay leaf. Simmer for
30–40 minutes, until the lentils
and vegetables are soft. Remove
the bay leaf and rub the soup
through a strainer into a large
mixing bowl, adding the contents
of the strainer, or purée in a
liquidiser. Pour the soup into a
clean pan and add sea salt, black
pepper and lemon juice to taste.
Reheat gently, stirring occasionally.
   Serve garnished with chopped
parsley.   **Serves 6**

Cream of Spinach Soup

1 tablespoon (15 ml) **Allinson**
    100% Wholewheat Flour
2 pints (1.2 litres) stock
2 lb (900 g) spinach, washed
    and steamed
2 tablespoons (30 ml) **Allinson**
    Wheatgerm
1 onion, roughly chopped
1 teaspoon (5 ml) salt
1 tablespoon (15 ml) brewers'
    yeast

4 oz (125 g) milk powder
pinch ground nutmeg
sesame seeds to garnish

Gradually combine all ingredients
in a liquidiser. Empty the mixture
into a saucepan, cover and heat
thoroughly.
   Serve garnished with sesame
seeds.   **Serves 6**

Onion Soup

3 tablespoons (45 ml) oil
4 large Spanish onions,
    chopped
1 clove garlic, finely chopped
1 pint (600 ml) stock
½ teaspoon (2.5 ml) tarragon
4 sprigs parsley, finely
    chopped
¼ pint (150 ml) tomato juice
1 tablespoon (15 ml) **Allinson**
    100% Wholewheat Flour
1 tablespoon (15 ml) brewers'
    yeast
6 slices wholewheat bread,
    toasted
Parmesan cheese, grated

Heat the oil and lightly sauté the
onions and garlic. Add the stock,
tarragon and parsley. Mix the
tomato juice, flour, yeast and salt,
and add to the soup mixture.
Cover and simmer for 15 minutes.
   Serve topped with the toast,
sprinkled with cheese.   **Serves 6**

Potato Soup

¾ pint (400 ml) stock
4 potatoes, peeled and cubed
1 teaspoon (5 ml) dill seeds,
    ground
8 oz (225 g) onions *or* leeks,
    chopped
¾ pint (400 ml) milk
1 tablespoon (15 ml) **Allinson**
    100% Wholewheat Flour
1 tablespoon (15 ml) brewers'
    yeast

½ teaspoon (2.5 ml) salt
chopped chives to garnish

Bring the stock to the boil, add the
potatoes, dill seeds and onions or
leeks. Cover and simmer until the
potatoes are tender. Sieve, or
purée in a liquidiser. Mix the milk
with the flour, yeast and salt and
add to the purée, blending
thoroughly. Return to the saucepan and reheat.
   Serve garnished with chopped
chives.   **Serves 6**

Turkish Yoghurt-Beef Soup

2 oz (50 g) **Allinson** 100%
    Wholewheat Flour
3 pints (1.7 litres) beef stock
½ teaspoon (2.5 ml) salt
1 tablespoon (15 ml) brewers'
    yeast
3 tablespoons (45 ml) oil
2 tablespoons (30 ml) soya flour
1 tablespoon (15 ml) dried mint
    leaves
2 (5 fl oz, 150 ml) cartons natural
    yoghurt

Blend all ingredients together until
smooth. Heat thoroughly but do
not boil or the yoghurt will curdle.
Serves 6

Watercress Soup

1 teaspoon (5 ml) **Allinson**
    100% Wholewheat Flour
2 pints (1.2 litres) stock
2 bunches watercress
1 teaspoon (5 ml) salt
1 tablespoon (15 ml) brewers'
    yeast
5 fl oz (150 ml) carton natural
    yoghurt

Liquidise all ingredients until
smooth. Serve chilled.   **Serves 6**

Corned Beef and Leek Broth

8 oz (225 g) leeks, thinly sliced
1.1 oz (31 g) packet quick dried
   peas or 4 oz (125 g) frozen
   peas
1 pint (500 ml) beef stock
bay leaf
salt and pepper
1 oz (25 g) porridge oats
12 oz (340 g) can **Armour**
   Corned Beef, chopped
8 fl oz (240 ml) milk
a little extra milk or single cream
chopped parsley to garnish

Put the leeks, peas, stock, bay leaf,
salt and pepper into a pan, bring to
the boil, cover and simmer for
10 minutes. Stir in the oats, corned
beef and milk and simmer for a
further 10–15 minutes. Take out
the bay leaf and add a little more
milk or some single cream if liked.
   Sprinkle with parsley and serve
hot.   **Serves 4–6**

ATORA

Chicken Stew Soup with Basil Dumplings

1 chicken carcass
2 onions, peeled, 1 chopped
   and 1 quartered
4 sticks celery, chopped
2 pints (1 litre) water
2 bay leaves
salt and ground black pepper
1 oz (25 g) butter or margarine
1 tablespoon (15 ml) flour
15 oz (425 g) can tomatoes
1 teaspoon (5 ml) fresh basil,
   chopped or ½ teaspoon
   (2.5 ml) dried rubbed basil
1 teaspoon (5 ml) sugar
1 tablespoon (15 ml)
   Worcestershire sauce
10–12 oz (275–400 g) cold,
   cooked chicken, cut into
   chunks

Dumplings
4 oz (100 g) self-raising flour,
   sifted
2 oz (50 g) **Atora** Shredded Suet
1 teaspoon (5 ml) fresh basil,
   chopped or ½ teaspoon
   (2.5 ml) dried rubbed basil
salt and ground black pepper
water to mix

Make a good stock by boiling the
carcass with the quartered onion, 1
stick of celery, the water, bay
leaves, salt and pepper for a good
30 minutes, then strain and
reserve.
   Melt the butter or margarine and
gently fry the remaining onions
and celery for 10 minutes, covered.
The vegetables should be soft and
not at all browned. Stir in the flour
and cook for a minute. Strain in the
juice of the canned tomatoes, then
roughly chop the tomatoes and
add these to the pot together with
the reserved stock. Bring to the
boil, stirring. Add the basil, sugar,
Worcestershire sauce and seasoning. Simmer for 15 minutes, then
stir in the chicken pieces.
   Make the dumplings by mixing
all the ingredients together and
adding enough water to make a
firm dough. Divide into eight
balls. Drop into the pot and
simmer very gently for 20 minutes
until the dumplings are risen and
cooked.
   Serve hot in large soup bowls,
sprinkled with a little fresh or
dried basil, if liked.   **Serves 4**

Bacon and Barley Soup

1 bacon knuckle
2 Red Cubes from **Bovril**
   dissolved in 2½ pints
   (1.5 litres) water
2 oz (50 g) pearl barley, washed
2 medium carrots, peeled and
   diced
1 medium turnip, peeled and
   diced
1 medium onion, peeled and
   chopped

pepper
chopped parsley to garnish

Soak the bacon in cold water for
2 hours if unsmoked, or 6 hours if
smoked. Drain well and put into a
saucepan with the stock. Bring to
the boil, add the barley and return
to the boil. Reduce the heat, cover
with a lid and simmer gently for
40 minutes. Add the carrots,
turnip and onion and continue
simmering for a further 40
minutes. Remove the bacon from
the soup and cut the meat into
small pieces. Add these to the
soup, and continue heating for a
further 10 minutes. Season with
pepper.
   Garnish with parsley to serve.
Serves 6

Carrot Soup

1¾ lb (800 g) carrots, peeled or
   scrubbed and roughly
   chopped
3 sticks celery, chopped
1 large onion, peeled and
   chopped
bouquet garni
2 Chicken Cubes from **Bovril**,
   dissolved in 1½ pints
   (900 ml) water
salt and pepper
good pinch nutmeg
1 tablespoon (15 ml) lemon
   juice
¼ pint (150 ml) single cream
chopped parsley to garnish

Place the carrots, celery, onion,
bouquet garni, stock, nutmeg,
salt, pepper and lemon juice into a
saucepan. Bring to the boil, cover
and simmer for 30 minutes.
Liquidise or rub through a sieve,
pour into a clean saucepan and
reheat, adjusting the seasoning
and adding a little more lemon
juice if required.
   Serve the soup with the cream
swirled over the top, garnished
with the chopped parsley.
Serves 7–8

Cream of Tomato Soup

2 oz (50 g) fat bacon, chopped
1 lb (450 g) tomatoes, sliced

1 medium onion, peeled and
  sliced
1 medium carrot, sliced
1 stick celery, sliced
1 Red Cube from **Bovril**
  dissolved in 1½ pints
  (900 ml) water
salt and pepper
1 bay leaf
1 sprig thyme
1 sprig parsley
1 tablespoon (15 ml) cornflour
½ pint (300 ml) milk
pinch sugar
croutons to garnish

Heat the bacon slowly in a pan
until the fat runs freely, add the
vegetables and fry gently for
10 minutes. Add the stock,
seasoning and herbs, bring to the
boil and simmer for 1 hour. Take
out the herbs and rub the soup
through a fine sieve. Mix the
cornflour with a little of the milk
and stir into the soup with the
remaining milk. Bring just to the
boil, stirring well, and cook gently
for 3 minutes. Check the
seasoning and add the sugar.
  Serve with croutons.
Serves 4

Iced Pea Soup

2 lb (1 kg) shelled fresh *or*
  frozen peas
1 oz (25 g) butter
1 small onion, finely chopped
1 small lettuce, shredded
bunch of fresh mixed herbs
3 Chicken Cubes from **Bovril**,
  dissolved in 3 pints
  (1.75 litres) water
salt and pepper
1 oz (25 g) cooked ham, finely
  chopped
chopped mint to garnish

Put the peas, butter, onion, lettuce
and herbs into a pan with a tight-
fitting lid. Cover and simmer for
10 minutes. Add the stock, salt
and pepper and bring to the boil.
Cover and simmer for 1 hour. Put
through a sieve or liquidise until
smooth. Pour into individual
serving bowls and chill for 1 hour.
  Serve garnished with the ham
and chopped mint.   **Serves 4**

Leek and Potato Soup

4 medium leeks, well cleaned
  and cut into 1 in (2.5 cm)
  rings
1 lb (450 g) potatoes, peeled
  and roughly chopped
2 oz (50 g) butter
2 Chicken Cubes from **Bovril**
  dissolved in 2 pints (1 litre)
  water
salt and pepper
½ pint (300 ml) creamy milk
chopped chives to garnish

Melt the butter and cook the leeks
over a low heat until just soft but
not coloured. Add the potatoes
and continue cooking and stirring
over the low heat for 5 minutes.
Add the stock and season well.
Bring to the boil, then lower the
heat, cover and simmer for 1 hour.
The soup may be blended until
smooth in a liquidiser or served as
it is with pieces of vegetable
visible. Stir the milk into the soup
and reheat gently.
  Serve garnished with chopped
chives.   **Serves 4**

Lettuce Soup

1 oz (25 g) butter
12 oz (350 g) lettuce, shredded,
  using coarse leaves
1 onion, peeled and chopped
4 oz (100 g) potato, peeled and
  cut into small dice
1 Chicken Cube from **Bovril**,
  dissolved in 1 pint (600 ml)
  water
½ pint (300 ml) milk
salt and pepper
1–2 teaspoons (5–10 ml) lemon
  juice
croutons to serve

Melt the butter in a large pan, add
the prepared vegetables and cook
very gently, covered, until tender,
shaking the pan occasionally. Add
the milk and liquidise the soup.
Stir the stock into the puréed mixture, season and simmer gently for
20 minutes. Adjust the seasoning
and add lemon juice to taste.
  Serve with croutons.
Serves 5–6

Mixed Vegetable Soup

1 medium onion, peeled and
  finely diced
1 medium carrot, peeled and
  finely diced
1 medium turnip, peeled and
  finely diced
2 sticks celery, diced
1 oz (25 g) butter
2 Chicken Cubes from **Bovril**
  dissolved in 2 pints (1 litre)
  water
salt and pepper
4 oz (100 g) shelled fresh *or*
  frozen peas
chopped parsley to garnish

Melt the butter and cook the onion,
carrot, turnip and celery over a low
heat until golden. Pour on the
stock and bring to the boil. Season
with salt and pepper, cover and
simmer for 30 minutes. Add the
peas and continue simmering for
10 minutes.
  Serve garnished with chopped
parsley.   **Serves 4**

Jellied Cream of Tomato Soup

½ oz (15 g) gelatine
4 tablespoons (60 ml) water
10½ oz (297 g) can **Campbell's**
  Condensed Cream of Tomato
  Soup
1 teaspoon (5 ml) chopped mint
2 teaspoons (10 ml) vinegar
salt and pepper

Dissolve the gelatine in the water,
in a basin over a pan of hot water.
Empty the can of soup into a basin
and stir in ⅓ can of cold water.
Add the mint and vinegar and
season well. Pour in the dissolved
gelatine, mixing well together,
pour into 4 individual dishes and
chill in the refrigerator until set.
Serves 4

Carnation.

Quick Corn Soup

1½ oz (40 g) butter
1½ oz (40 g) flour
1½ pints (900 ml) stock *or*
  water
1 can (approx 12 oz, 340 g)
  sweetcorn
1 tablespoon green pepper,
  finely chopped (optional)
salt and pepper
1 teaspoon (5 ml)
  Worcestershire sauce
1 small can (5½ fl oz)
  Carnation Evaporated Milk
1–2 rashers bacon

Melt the butter in a saucepan. Stir in the flour, cook for a few minutes. Remove from the heat and gradually stir in the stock, with the sweetcorn, green pepper, seasoning and Worcestershire sauce. Bring to the boil, reduce the heat and simmer for about 10 minutes until the vegetables are soft. Stir in the Carnation and adjust seasoning. Grill the bacon until crisp then serve the soup with the bacon crumbled on top.
Serves 4

Split Pea Soup

2 oz (50 g) dripping
2 medium onions, peeled and
  diced
1–2 sticks celery, sliced
1 large carrot, peeled and diced
1 medium potato, peeled and
  diced
4 oz (100 g) split peas (soaked
  in water 2 hours)
1 bacon knuckle bone
1½ pints (900 ml) water
1 bay leaf
salt and pepper
1 oz (25 g) flour
½ large can **Carnation**
  Evaporated Milk

Melt the dripping in a large saucepan, add the vegetables and fry gently for 10 minutes, stirring occasionally. Add the peas, bacon bone, water, bay leaf and seasoning and bring to the boil, stirring.

Reduce the heat and simmer for about 1½ hours until the peas are soft. Blend the flour with the Carnation and stir into the soup. Adjust the seasoning and simmer for about 5 minutes. Remove the bone and bay leaf before serving.

If made the previous day the soup may need diluting with a little stock or water before re-heating.   **Serves 4**

Chesswood

Tango Soup

1 can **Chesswood** Curry with
  Chicken and Mushrooms
1 large carrot, peeled and finely
  chopped
4 oz (100 g) celery, chopped
8 oz (250 g) tomatoes, skinned
  and chopped
1 teaspoon (5 ml) ground
  ginger
pinch of nutmeg *or* mace
1¼ pints (625 ml) chicken stock
1 cooking apple, peeled and
  finely chopped

Place all the ingredients together in a large saucepan. Bring to the boil and simmer for 25 minutes, stirring occasionally.   **Serves 6**

Iced Pimiento Soup

14 oz (396 g) can **Cirio**
  Pimientos
14 oz (396 g) can **Cirio** Tomato
  Juice
2 teaspoons (10 ml) **Cirio**
  Tomato Purée
salt and pepper
1 teaspoon (5 ml) sugar
2 teaspoons (10 ml) lemon juice
chopped parsley and curls of
  lemon peel to garnish

Drain the pimientos and cut two into very thin slices. Mash the rest

of the pimientos with a fork until puréed. Add the tomato juice and tomato purée, salt, pepper, sugar and lemon juice. Heat gently until boiling. Add the rest of the sliced pimientos, cool and then put into the refrigerator to freeze.

Serve piled in individual soup bowls, garnished with chopped parsley and lemon curls.
Serves 4

Iced Tomato and Avocado Soup

1 avocado pear, peeled and
  roughly chopped
14 oz (396 g) can **Cirio** Peeled
  Tomatoes, roughly chopped
1 small onion, chopped
1 pint (600 ml) stock (stock cube
  can be used)
¼ teaspoon sugar
1 bay leaf *or* ¼ teaspoon
  powdered bayleaf
salt and pepper
watercress to garnish

Place all the ingredients, including the liquid from the can of tomatoes, in a saucepan and bring to the boil, stirring continually. Simmer for 15 minutes, stirring occasionally. Remove the bayleaf, if used, and pass the mixture through a fine sieve or liquidise until smooth.

Serve very well chilled, garnished with watercress.
Serves 4

FRANK COOPER®

Crab Chowder

1 tablespoon (15 ml) corn oil
2 small sticks celery, finely
  chopped
7 oz (198 g) can sweetcorn,
  drained
4 oz (100 g) cod *or* coley, cooked
  and flaked
1 can **Frank Cooper's** Crab
  Bisque

Heat the corn oil and sauté the celery for 3–4 minutes. Stir in the sweetcorn, fish and soup and simmer for 3–4 minutes.

Serve piping hot with fresh, crusty bread.　**Serves 2**

Gazpacho

1 lb (400 g) tomatoes, skinned and chopped
1 small onion, chopped
1 small green pepper, de-seeded and chopped
¼ cucumber, diced
½ level teaspoon (2.5 ml) garlic salt
black pepper to taste
6 tablespoons (90 ml) corn oil
3 tablespoons (45 ml) white wine vinegar
1 can **Frank Cooper's** Vichyssoise
chopped parsley and croutons to garnish

Mix together the tomatoes, onion, green pepper and cucumber. Add the garlic salt and black pepper. Mix together the corn oil and vinegar, pour over the vegetables and marinate for 30 minutes. Add the Vichyssoise and chill before serving. Garnish with the chopped parsley and croutons.　**Serves 4**

Country Mix Soup

1 oz (25 g) butter
1 small onion, peeled and chopped
1 medium potato, peeled and chopped
2 (8 oz, 227 g) packets **Findus** Country Mix
2 pints (1 litre) chicken stock
salt and pepper
croutons and chopped parsley to garnish

Melt the butter in a large saucepan and gently fry the onion and potato for 5 minutes. Add the Country

Mix and chicken stock, bring to the boil and simmer for 20 minutes. Sieve or blend in a liquidiser. Pour back into the saucepan and reheat. Season to taste and garnish with the croutons and parsley.
Serves 6

Cream of Sweetcorn Soup

6 oz (170 g) packet **Findus** Sweetcorn
1 pint (600 ml) chicken stock
2 oz (50 g) butter
2 oz (50 g) flour
1 pint (500 ml) milk
1 tablespoon (15 ml) parsley, chopped
salt and pepper

Cook half the sweetcorn in the chicken stock for 10 minutes. Meanwhile, melt the butter, add the flour and cook over a gentle heat for 2–3 minutes. Remove from the heat and gradually add the milk, stirring continuously. Add the stock and cooked sweetcorn and cook for 5 minutes. Liquidise for 1 minute and sieve. Return the mixture to the pan, add the remaining sweetcorn and the parsley. Cook for 5 minutes until heated through. Season to taste before serving.　**Serves 4**

Creamy Cauliflower Soup with Spicy Croutons

1 oz (25 g) butter
1 oz (25 g) plain flour
1 pint (500 ml) chicken stock
10½ oz (297 g) packet **Findus** Cauliflower Fleurettes
4 tablespoons (60 ml) single cream
salt and pepper
3 tablespoons (45 ml) vegetable oil
2 slices white bread
salt
½ teaspoon (2.5 ml) paprika pepper

Melt the butter in a saucepan. Stir in the flour and cook for 2 minutes. Remove the pan from the heat and gradually stir in the stock. Bring to the boil, stirring constantly. Add the cauliflower and return to the boil. Simmer for 15 minutes. Liquidise, return to the pan and stir in the cream. Season to taste.

To make the croutons, heat the oil in a frying pan. Cut the bread into small cubes and fry until golden brown. Drain well and toss in the salt and paprika.

To serve, garnish the soup with a swirl of cream and paprika. Serve the croutons separately.
Serves 2

Pickled Onion Soup

9½ oz (262.5 g) jar **Haywards** Pickled Onions
2 oz (50 g) margarine
1 oz (25 g) flour
1¼ pints (625 ml) stock made with Red **Oxo** Cubes
1 dessertspoon (10 ml) sugar
4 slices French bread
2 oz (50 g) cheese, grated

Drain the pickled onions and reserve the vinegar. Roughly chop the onions and fry in the margarine for 10 minutes, then stir in the flour. Add the vinegar to the stock to make up to 1½ pints (900 ml) and gradually add to the onions and flour. Add the sugar, bring to the boil and simmer for 15 minutes. Top each slice of bread with grated cheese and grill until golden brown. Float the bread on top of the soup to serve.
Serves 4

Celery Cloud

4 oz (100 g) cream cheese
1 dessertspoon (10 ml) white
  wine
14¾ oz (417 g) can **Heinz**
  Cream of Celery Soup
chopped chives to garnish

Whisk the cream cheese with the
wine and soup and chill thoroughly. Sprinkle with the chives to
serve.   **Serves 2**

Chicken Bisque

1 small can tuna, drained
1 tablespoon (15 ml) can **Heinz**
  Tomato Ketchup
a little milk
onion salt to taste
14¾ oz (417 g) **Heinz** Cream of
  Chicken Soup
lemon slices to garnish

Blend the tuna with the ketchup,
milk, onion salt and soup and chill.
Serve garnished with the lemon
slices.   **Serves 2–3**

HELLMANN'S

Cool Cucumber Soup

1 medium cucumber, coarsely
  sliced
1 medium onion, coarsely
  chopped
1¼ pints (750 ml) chicken stock
salt and pepper
1½ tablespoons (25 ml)
  Hellmann's Real Mayonnaise
1 tablespoon (15 ml) milk

Place the cucumber, onion,
chicken stock and seasoning into a
saucepan, bring to the boil then
simmer gently for 15–20 minutes
until the cucumber and onion are
tender. Liquidise or sieve the soup
until smooth, then chill. Just
before serving, blend the mayonnaise with the milk and swirl on
top of the soup.   **Serves 4**

Creamed Curry Soup with Prawns

2 oz (50 g) **Kerrygold** Butter
2 large onions, peeled and
  chopped
2 large carrots, peeled and
  chopped
1 clove garlic, crushed
1 tablespoon (15 ml) curry
  powder
2 tablespoons (30 ml) plain
  flour
1½ pints (900 ml) chicken stock
4 teaspoons (20 ml) lemon juice
salt and freshly ground pepper
dash of Tabasco sauce
1 bay leaf
½ pint (300 ml) **Kerrygold**
  Whipping Cream, thawed
unpeeled prawns and chopped
  parsley to garnish

Melt the butter in a saucepan. Add
the onion, carrot and garlic and fry
gently until soft but not coloured.
Stir in the curry powder and flour
and cook for 1 minute. Gradually
stir in the stock and bring to the
boil. Add the lemon juice, salt and
pepper to taste, Tabasco and bay
leaf. Cover and simmer gently for
about 20 minutes or until the vegetables are soft. Discard the bay leaf
and cool the soup, then sieve or
liquidise. Adjust the seasoning,
stir in the cream and chill thoroughly. Serve garnished with a
few unpeeled prawns and chopped parsley. A few peeled prawns
may be chopped and added to the
soup before serving.   **Serves 4**

Knorr

Bean and Tomato Soup

4 oz (100 g) haricot beans
1½ pints (750 ml) **Knorr**
  chicken stock
14 oz (397 g) can peeled
  tomatoes, sieved
1 tablespoon (15 ml) cornflour
salt and pepper
chopped chives to garnish

Soak the beans overnight in the
stock. Next day, place the beans,
stock and tomatoes in a large
saucepan, bring to the boil, then
lower the heat and simmer for
1 hour. Blend the cornflour with a
little cold water and add to the
soup, stirring all the time. Bring to
the boil and boil for 1 minute.
Season to taste.
   Serve piping hot, garnished
with the chopped chives and
accompanied by crusty bread.
Serves 4

Potato Soup

1 lb (400 g) potatoes, peeled
  and diced
2 small onions, chopped
1½ pints (750 ml) **Knorr** beef
  stock
¼ pint (142 ml) carton single
  cream
pinch nutmeg
chopped parsley to garnish

Put the potatoes, onions and stock
into a saucepan. Bring to the boil
and simmer until the vegetables
are tender. Rub through a sieve or
liquidise. Stir in the cream and
nutmeg. Reheat before serving,
but do not boil. Garnish with the
parsley.   **Serves 6**

Pot of Goodness

1 packet **Knorr** Highland Lentil
  Soup
1¾ pints (1 litre) water
2 potatoes, peeled and diced
6 oz (175 g) cooked ham, diced
few spring onions, chopped

Blend the soup mix with the water and bring to the boil, stirring. Add the potato, ham and onions, partially cover and simmer for 20 minutes. Serve in bowls with crusty bread.   **Serves 4–6**

LEA & PERRINS

Bacon and Spinach Soup

2 oz (50 g) butter
1 large onion, peeled and chopped
6 oz (150 g) streaky bacon, chopped
1 lb (500 g) frozen spinach
1 oz (25 g) flour
¾ pint (400 ml) chicken stock
¾ pint (400 ml) milk
2 tablespoons (30 ml) **Lea & Perrins** Worcestershire Sauce
¼ pint (150 ml) single cream
salt and pepper

Heat the butter in a large pan, add the onion and bacon and fry gently until soft, about 5 minutes. Add the spinach, cover and heat gently until the spinach has thawed. Stir in the flour and cook for 1 minute. Gradually add the milk and stock, stirring constantly, then add the Worcestershire Sauce. Bring to the boil and simmer for 10 minutes. Pass the soup through a sieve or purée in a liquidiser until smooth. Return to the pan and stir in the cream, reserving 1 tablespoon (15 ml) of cream to garnish. Reheat the soup, but do not boil. Season to taste and serve with the remaining cream swirled on top.   **Serves 6**

Creamed Stilton and Onion Soup

2 oz (50 g) butter
12 oz (300 g) onions, chopped
2 oz (50 g) flour
¾ pint (400 ml) stock
¾ pint (400 ml) milk
6 oz (150 g) Stilton cheese, crumbled
4 teaspoons (20 ml) **Lea & Perrins** Worcestershire Sauce
salt and pepper

chopped chives *or* parsley to garnish

Heat the butter in a large pan, add the onions and fry gently until soft, about 5 minutes. Stir in the flour and cook for 1 minute. Remove from the heat and gradually add the stock and milk, stirring constantly. Return to the heat and bring to the boil, stirring. Reduce the heat and add the cheese, Worcestershire Sauce, salt and pepper, continuing to stir and simmer for 15 minutes. Pass the soup through a sieve, or purée in a liquidiser, until smooth. Reheat gently and season to taste. Garnish with the chopped chives or parsley.   **Serves 6**

Lentil Pottage

1 lb (500 g) ham knuckle, soaked overnight
6 oz (150 g) red lentils
1 medium carrot, peeled and sliced
1 stick celery, chopped
1 medium onion, peeled and sliced
1 tablespoon (15 ml) **Lea & Perrins** Worcestershire Sauce
2½ pints (1.4 litres) water
pepper
4 oz (100 g) frozen peas

Place all the ingredients, except the peas, in a large saucepan and bring slowly to the boil. Skim the surface of the soup with a draining spoon to remove froth. Reduce the heat and simmer gently for about 2 hours, until the ham is cooked. Remove the knuckle from the soup and flake the meat from the bone. Liquidise or sieve the soup and add the meat and peas. Simmer for 10–15 minutes. Adjust the seasoning.
    Serve piping hot with croutons or toast.   **Serves 6–8**

Quick Snack Soup

16 oz (454 g) can baked beans
7 oz (198 g) can corned beef, diced
3 Red **Oxo** Cubes, crumbled and dissolved in 1½ pints (900 ml) hot water
salt and pepper

Put all the ingredients into a saucepan and heat for 10 minutes, stirring occasionally. Season to taste.
    Serve with buttered toast.
Serves 4

Cheese and Vegetable Soup

1 *or* 2 rashers green streaky bacon, with rinds removed, cut into small, thin strips
approx 2 oz (50 g) each of potatoes, carrots, onions, celery and swede *or* turnip, leeks, peeled and finely diced
1 small tomato, cut into 8
a little cabbage, finely shredded *or* a few Brussels sprouts, finely sliced
water to cover
salt and pepper
1–2 oz (25–50 g) macaroni *or* spaghetti, broken into small pieces
Primula Cheese Spread to taste

Put the bacon in a large saucepan with the vegetables and enough water to cover. Season with salt and pepper. Bring to the boil and then reduce the heat and simmer until the vegetables are cooked but not broken up. Add the macaroni or spaghetti and, when the pasta is cooked, flavour with enough cheese spread to taste.   **Serves 4**

Chilled Mushroom Soup with Bacon

2 oz (50 g) **St Ivel** Butter
1 tablespoon (15 ml) flour
1¾ pints (1 litre) chicken stock
8 oz (225 g) button mushrooms
8 oz (250 g) **St Ivel** Natural
   Cottage Cheese
¼ pint (150 ml) **St Ivel** Double
   Cream
1 teaspoon (5 ml) salt
freshly ground black pepper
3 rashers bacon to garnish

Melt the butter in a saucepan and
stir in the flour. Remove from the
heat and blend in approximately a
quarter of the stock. Return to the
heat and bring to the boil. Simmer
for 3 minutes, then remove from
the heat. Stir in the remaining
stock and leave to cool. Wash the
mushrooms and cut the base of the
stems off. Combine the thickened
stock with the mushrooms,
cheese, cream and seasonings.
Blend in a vegetable mouli or
liquidiser and chill for 30 minutes.
Grill the bacon until crisp, then
leave to cool. Snip with scissors to
fine pieces and serve sprinkled on
the soup.   **Serves 6**

Hawaiian Curry Soup

3 tablespoons (45 ml) cooking
   oil
1 large onion, peeled and
   chopped
2 teaspoons (10 ml) curry

1 pint (550 ml) chicken stock
3 (4 fl oz, 114 ml) bottles
   Schweppes Pineapple Juice
2 courgettes, sliced
2 dessertspoons (20 ml) mango
   chutney
juice and grated rind of 1 lemon

5.3 oz (150 g) carton natural
   yoghurt
1 oz (25 g) flaked almonds,
   toasted, to garnish

Heat the oil in a large saucepan and
gently fry the onion and curry
powder for a few minutes. Add the
stock, pineapple juice and courgettes, bring to the boil and
simmer for about 10 minutes, until
the courgettes are tender. Stir in
the chutney then liquidise or sieve
the soup. Season to taste and chill
thoroughly. Add the lemon rind
and juice. Serve with the yoghurt
stirred into the centre and the
almonds sprinkled on top.
Serves 4

Sharwood's

Gazpacho

3 oz (75 g) breadcrumbs
2 cloves garlic, crushed
4 teaspoons (20 ml)
Sharwood's Wine Vinegar
approx 4 tablespoons (60 ml)
   olive oil
1 lb (500 g) tomatoes, skinned
   and chopped
6½ oz (184 g) can **Sharwood's**
   Pimientos, drained and
   chopped
1 large Spanish onion, finely
   chopped
1 cucumber, finely chopped
2 tablespoons (30 ml)
Sharwood's Tomato Purée
Garnish
½ cucumber, chopped
2 small green *or* red peppers,
   de-seeded and chopped
Sharwood's Black Olives,
   stoned
onion rings
croutons

Soak the breadcrumbs and garlic
in the vinegar and add the oil a few
drops at a time until the breadcrumbs are completely saturated.
Stir in the tomatoes, pimientos,
onion, cucumber and tomato
purée. Liquidise the whole mixture to produce a fairly thick purée
and season to taste.

To serve, either dilute the purée
with iced water or ice cubes. Hand
round bowls of the various gar-
nishes for each person to add to
their own bowl of soup.
Serves 6

Chowder

1 onion, peeled and chopped
2 rashers streaky bacon,
   chopped (with rinds
   removed)
1 oz (25 g) margarine
1 pint (500 ml) chicken stock
6 oz (150 g) cooked chicken
8 oz (200 g) cooked mixed
   vegetables (diced carrots,
   swede, turnip, sliced green
   beans etc)
1 medium packet **Cadbury's
Smash** Potato Pieces
¾ pint (125 ml) milk
salt and pepper

Sauté the onion and bacon in the
margarine for a few minutes. Add
the stock, diced chicken and mixed
vegetables. Bring to the boil and
simmer until thoroughly heated.
Stir the Smash into the liquid,
brought up to the boil, then add
the milk and season to taste.

This is a thick, main-course type
of soup, ideal for colder weather
meals.   **Serves 4**

Economy Hustle-up with Potato Rings

1 onion, peeled and chopped
1 rasher bacon, chopped (with
   rind removed)
1 chicken stock cube
1 pint (500 ml) water
1 medium packet **Smash** Potato
   Pieces
approx 8 oz (200 g) cooked
   chicken
¼ pint (125 ml) milk
1 tablespoon (15 ml) parsley,
   chopped

For Potato Rings
1 medium packet **Smash** Potato
    Pieces
knob of butter

Fry the onion and bacon lightly in
the margarine, crumble in the
stock cube and add the water.
Bring to the boil and simmer for
about 10 minutes. Boil fast before
stirring in the potato pieces. Add
the chicken, milk and parsley and
season to taste.

To make the potato rings, make
up the Smash as directed on the
packet and cool slightly before
transferring to a piping bag with a
star pipe attached. Pipe about 9
circles on to greased backing trays.
Brown under the grill or in a fairly
hot oven, about 400°F, 200°C, Gas
Mark 6. The rings freeze well and
should be layered between waxed
paper.

Serve the soup with the potato
rings floated on top.   **Serves 4**

Moorghi Soup

1 large onion, peeled and
    chopped
3 teaspoons (15 ml) curry
    powder
2 oz (50 g) margarine
1 tablespoon (15 ml) tomato
    purée
2 pints (1.2 litres) chicken stock
¼ pint (125 ml) white wine
dried oregano
1 medium packet **Smash** Potato
    Pieces
3 oz (75 g) dry **Marvel**
¼ pint (125 ml) water
4 oz (100 g) cooked chicken
paprika pepper to garnish

In a large saucepan, gently fry the
chopped onion and curry powder
in the margarine for about
10 minutes. Add the tomato
purée, stock, wine, a good pinch of
oregano and seasoning. Cover the
pan and simmer for 15 minutes.
Sieve or liquidise the mixture and
return to a clean pan. Bring to the
boil and add the potato pieces,
stirring continuously. Dissolve the
Marvel in ¼ pint (125 ml) water,
add to the soup with the chicken

and adjust the seasoning if
necessary. Reheat thoroughly.

Sprinkle with the paprika
pepper just before serving.
Serves 6

Minestrone Soup

2 oz (50 g) haricot beans
2 pints (1.1 litres) chicken stock
1 large onion, peeled and
    chopped
1 clove garlic, peeled and
    crushed
2 sticks celery, chopped
2 rashers bacon, diced
1 oz (25 g) **Stork** Margarine
15 oz (425 g) can tomatoes
2 medium carrots, peeled and
    sliced
8 oz (225 g) cabbage, finely
    shredded
2 oz (50 g) wholewheat
    macaroni rings
grated cheese to garnish

Soak the beans overnight in the
stock. Fry the onion, garlic, celery
and bacon in the margarine. Add
the tomatoes, carrots, stock and
beans, season and simmer for
1½ hours. Add the macaroni and
cabbage for the final 15–20
minutes.

Serve with grated cheese.
Serves 4–6

Thick Winter Soup

4 oz (100 g) split peas
4 oz (100 g) **Wall's** Streaky
Bacon Rashers
1 large onion, peeled and
    chopped
6 oz (175 g) packet **Wall's**
Polony
4 oz (100 g) sweetcorn kernels,
    cooked
1 tablespoon (15 ml) cornflour

1½ pints (900 ml) chicken stock
1 bay leaf
1 tablespoon (15 ml) parsley,
    chopped

Put the peas into a bowl, pour over
enough boiling water to cover and
leave overnight to soak. Next day,
cut the rind and any small bones
from the bacon and chop the
rashers into small pieces; fry them
over a medium heat until the fat
starts to run. Add the onion and
cook the two ingredients together
until the onion starts to soften. Cut
the polony into small dice and add
the pieces to the pan with the
sweetcorn. Blend the cornflour to a
smooth paste with a little of the
chicken stock and mix it into the
other ingredients with the rest of
the stock. Bring the soup to the
boil, stirring all the time, then
reduce the heat, add the bay leaf,
cover the pan and simmer the soup
for 1½–2 hours, stirring occasionally until all the ingredients are
cooked. Sprinkle with the chopped
parsley before serving.
Serves 4–6

Golden Corn Soup

1 oz (25 g) butter
2 oz (50 g) onion, grated
8 oz (227 g) can **John West**
    Tomatoes
½ pint (300 ml) chicken stock
11½ oz (326 g) can **John West**
    Sweetcorn
salt and pepper
3–4 tablespoons (45–60 ml)

Melt the butter in a pan, add the
onion and cook until it is soft,
without browning. Add the
tomatoes and break them down
with a spoon. Stir in the stock,
sweetcorn and seasoning. Simmer
for 15 minutes. Stir in the cream
just before serving.   **Serves 4**

FISH AND SEAFOOD

Fisherman's Pie

1 oz (25 g) vegetable margarine
1 oz (25 g) **Allinson** 100%
   Wholewheat Flour
½ pint (300 ml) milk
6 oz (175 g) flaked fish
   (haddock, salmon, tuna *or*
   herring)
salt and pepper
1 teaspoon (5 ml) parsley,
   chopped
squeeze of lemon juice
8 oz (225 g) mashed potato

Melt the margarine and stir in the
flour. Add the milk gradually then
heat, stirring continuously, until
the sauce thickens. Add the flaked
fish, seasoning, parsley, lemon
juice and three-quarters of the
mashed potato. Mix thoroughly
and place in a 1½ pint (900 ml) pie
dish. Cover with the remaining
mashed potato and brown in the
oven (375°F, 190°C, Gas Mark 5)
for 20 minutes.   **Serves 2**

Adriatic Tuna

7 oz (198 g) **Armour** Tuna in Oil
1 medium aubergine, sliced
1 large onion, peeled and sliced
1 clove garlic, chopped
1 small red pepper, de-seeded
   and sliced
2 tablespoons (30 ml) white
   wine
¼ teaspoon thyme
¼ pint (125 ml) chicken stock
salt and pepper
6 oz (175 g) long grain rice

Pour 2 tablespoons (30 ml) of oil
from the tuna into a frying pan.
Add the aubergine, onion, garlic

and pepper. Cover and cook for
about 15 minutes until the vegetables are tender. Mix in the wine,
thyme, stock, and the tuna in
chunks. Continue cooking, uncovered, for about 10 minutes.

   Meanwhile, cook the rice in
boiling, salted water for
10–15 minutes until just tender.
Drain the rice and put on a serving
dish in a ring, with the hot tuna
and vegetables in the centre.
Serves 4

Mediterranean Sardines

2 large aubergines
salt
2 tablespoons (30 ml) oil
1 oz (25 g) butter
1 medium onion, peeled and
   sliced
8 oz (225 g) mushrooms,
   washed and sliced
1 clove garlic, crushed
pepper
2 (4½ oz, 127 g) cans **Armour**
   Sardines in Vegetable Oil,
   drained, reserving oil
lemon juice
8 tablespoons (120 ml) fresh
   breadcrumbs
6 tablespoons (90 ml) fresh
   parsley, chopped

Trim the stalks and ends from the
aubergines, cut into ¼ in (0.5 cm)
slices and spread on kitchen paper.
Sprinkle with salt and leave
30 minutes for the liquid to be
drawn out and to improve the
flavour. Rinse and drain the slices.

   Heat the oil and butter in a large
pan, put in the onion and aubergines and cook gently for about
5 minutes until beginning to
soften. Add the mushrooms, garlic
and pepper, cover and cook for
10 minutes. Arrange the sardines
(with bones removed if wished) on
top of the aubergine mixture,
sprinkle with lemon juice and
continue cooking for another
5 minutes. When the vegetables

are just tender, transfer the mixture, topped with the sardines, to a
serving dish and keep hot. Pour
the oil from the sardines into the
pan and fry the breadcrumbs until
they are lightly browned. Mix in
the parsley and sprinkle over the
sardines.

   Serve hot with boiled rice and
green salad.   **Serves 4–6**

Pilchard Poppers

8 oz (227 g) **Armour** Pilchards
   in Tomato Sauce, drained
2½ oz (64 g) packet instant
   potato reconstituted as
   directed on packet
2 teaspoons (10 ml) onion,
   finely grated
½ teaspoon (2.5 ml) mixed
   herbs
1 teaspoon (5 ml) vinegar
1 egg yolk
salt and pepper
Coating
1 egg beaten with 2 teaspoons
   (10 ml) cold water
about 6 tablespoons (90 ml)
   breadcrumbs
shallow *or* deep oil for frying

Remove the backbones from the
pilchards and mix the fish well
with the potato, onion, herbs,
vinegar, seasonings and egg yolk.
Shape the mixture into 24 small flat
cakes or balls and chill until they
become firm. Dip in the beaten egg
and coat with the breadcrumbs.
Fry in the heated oil for about
4 minutes, turning once if cooked
in a shallow pan, until crisp and
brown. Drain on absorbent paper.

   Serve hot or cold with green
salad.   **Serves 4**

Crab Soufflé

12 oz (350 g) crabmeat
1 tablespoon (15 ml) double
    cream
4 egg yolks
4 spring onions, finely
    chopped
chilli powder *or* cayenne pepper
1 can **Baxters** White Wine Sauce
6 egg whites
browned breadcrumbs and
    grated Parmesan cheese

Put the crabmeat, double cream,
egg yolks and spring onions into a
bowl, season with the chilli or
cayenne pepper and add the can of
White Wine Sauce. Beat well.
Whisk the egg whites until they
form peaks. Fold carefully into the
crab mixture and turn into a
prepared 7 in (18 cm) soufflé dish.
Cook for 25 minutes in a pre-
heated oven at 400°F, 200°C,
Gas Mark 6. Serve immediately,
scattered with browned crumbs
and grated Parmesan cheese.
Serves 4

Fish Casserole Mornay

1 lb (450 g) white fish (cod,
    haddock, monkfish, coley
    etc), skinned and filleted
6 large scallops
12 Mediterranean prawns,
    peeled *or* other shellfish
1 can **Baxters** White Wine Sauce
¼ pint (150 ml) cream
1 dessertspoon (10 ml)
    Parmesan cheese, grated
chopped parsley *or* paprika
    pepper to garnish

Put the fish, divided into 6 equal
pieces, into a casserole dish. Add
the scallops and prawns. Mix the
White Wine Sauce with the cream
and cheese and pour the mixture
over the fish. Cook in a low oven at
350°F, 180°C, Gas Mark 4, for 45
minutes. Garnish with chopped
parsley or paprika.   **Serves 6**

Gratin of Seafood

1¼ lb (575 g) cod fillets *or*
    4 frozen cod steaks, thawed
a little butter
juice of ½ a lemon
4 oz (100 g) shelled prawns
½ tin **Baxters** Lobster Bisque *or*
    Cream of Scampi Soup, made
    up to ½ pint (300 ml) with
    milk
1 oz (25 g) butter
1 oz (25 g) plain flour
salt and pepper
1 tablespoon (15 ml) Parmesan
    cheese, grated

If using fresh cod, discard the skin
and cut the fillets into fine strips.
Butter 4 individual ovenproof
dishes or one large ovenproof
dish, put in the fish and sprinkle
with the lemon juice. Arrange the
prawns on top of the cod. Melt the
butter in a pan and blend in the
flour and the Lobster Bisque (or
Cream of Scampi Soup) with the
milk. Stir over a gentle heat until
boiling then simmer for 1 minute.
Adjust the seasoning. Spoon the
sauce over the fish and sprinkle
with Parmesan cheese. Bake for
20–25 minutes at 350°F, 180°C, Gas
Mark 4 until golden brown.
Serves 4

Tuna and Egg Turnovers

8 oz (250 g) **Be-Ro** Self-raising
    Flour
4 oz (100 g) shredded suet
pinch of salt
1 tablespoon (15 ml) parsley,
    chopped
1 egg, beaten
milk to mix
Filling
7 oz (198 g) can tuna, drained
    and flaked
2 hard-boiled eggs
2 tablespoons (30 ml)
    mayonnaise
cayenne pepper
salt
beaten egg *or* milk to glaze

Mix together the flour, suet, salt
and parsley with the egg and
sufficient milk to make a pliable
dough. Roll out the pastry and cut
into 6 rounds using a saucer.
Combine the filling ingredients
and place a little in the centre of
each pastry round. Damp the
pastry edges, fold over and press
well together. Crimp the edges.
Place on a greased baking tray,
brush with beaten egg or milk and
bake for 30 minutes at 400°F,
200°C, Gas Mark 6.   **Makes 6**

Fish Envelopes

2 sheets **Birds Eye** Puff Pastry,
    thawed
7 oz (198 g) **Birds Eye** Buttered
    Smoked Haddock
3 oz (75 g) **Birds Eye** Sweetcorn
1 teaspoon (5 ml) curry powder
salt and freshly ground black
    pepper
squeeze lemon juice
2 tablespoons (30 ml) double
    cream
2 ripe tomatoes, skinned, de-
    seeded and chopped
1 egg, beaten

Roll each pastry sheet into approximately a 10 in (25 cm) square.
Cook the smoked haddock according to the pack instructions.
Reserve the liquid, skin and flake
the fish. Mix together the smoked
haddock, liquid, sweetcorn and
curry powder. Season to taste and
stir in the lemon juice, cream and
tomatoes. Place equal amounts of
fish on each pastry square. Brush
the edges of the pastry with beaten
egg and fold in the corners to
overlap in the centre, making an
envelope shape. Seal well and
glaze with the remaining egg. Bake
in an oven pre-heated to 425°F,
220°C, Gas Mark 7, for approximately 15–20 minutes or until
golden brown.
Serves 4 (Each envelope serves 2)

Kipper Envelopes

7 oz (198 g) **Birds Eye** Buttered
    Kipper Fillets
2 eggs, hard boiled, shelled and
    chopped
2 tomatoes, skinned and
    chopped
lemon juice
black pepper
1 tablespoon (15 ml) parsley,
    freshly chopped
3 sheets **Birds Eye** Puff Pastry,
    thawed
beaten egg to glaze

Cook the kipper fillets according to
pack instructions, remove from the
bag, reserve the liquor and skin
and flake the fish. Mix the liquor,
kipper, egg and tomatoes together
and flavour with the lemon juice,
seasoning and chopped parsley.
Roll out each pastry sheet to an 8 in
(20 cm) square and dampen the
edges. Pile the filling on one half of
each pastry sheet and fold over the
other half. Seal the edges well and
crimp. Make cuts in the top of the
envelopes and glaze with beaten
egg. Place on a baking sheet and
bake in an oven pre-heated to
425°F, 220°C, Gas Mark 7, for
20–25 minutes or until risen and
golden brown.   **Serves 3**

Cod Provençale

4 cod steaks
½ oz (15 g) **Blue Band**
    Margarine
1 onion, peeled and chopped
½ green pepper, de-seeded
    and sliced
4 oz (125 g) mushrooms,
    washed and sliced
14 oz (396 g) can tomatoes
rind of 1 lemon
1 tablespoon (15 ml) parsley,
    chopped

Place the cod steaks in an ovenproof dish. Melt the margarine in a
pan and sauté the onion, pepper
and mushrooms for 5 minutes.

Add the remaining ingredients.
Pour the mixture over the cod
steaks, cover and bake in a moderately hot oven at 375°F, 190°C,
Gas Mark 5, for 25–30 minutes.
    Can be frozen.   **Serves 4**

Haddock and Tomato Bake

1½ lb (675 g) haddock fillets
salt and pepper
2 onions, peeled and chopped
4 tomatoes, skinned and
    chopped
2 tablespoons (30 ml) tomato
    purée
2 cloves garlic, crushed
2 teaspoons (10 ml) lemon juice
4 tablespoons (60 ml) **Bon**
    White Cooking Wine
3 oz (75 g) fresh white
    breadcrumbs
1 lemon, sliced
sprigs of parsley to garnish

Place the fish in a large, buttered,
ovenproof dish and season well.
Mix together the onion, tomatoes,
tomato purée, garlic, lemon juice
and Bon. Spoon the mixture over
the fish, sprinkle with the breadcrumbs and cook for 35–40
minutes in a pre-heated oven at
400°F, 200°C, Gas Mark 6, until
golden brown.
    Garnish with the slices of lemon
and sprigs of parsley.   **Serves 4**

Baked Trout

4 rainbow trout, approx 6 oz
    (175 g) each
1 oz (25 g) **Bran Fare**
salt and pepper
1 wineglass dry white wine
1 small onion, peeled and sliced
1 bay leaf

little margarine
1 lemon, sliced

Wash and dry the fish. Roll the fish
in the Bran Fare seasoned with salt
and pepper, until well coated.
Place in an ovenproof dish, pour
round the wine and add the onion
rings and bay leaf. Dot the fish
with a little margarine and bake in
the oven set at 350°F, 180°C, Gas
Mark 4, for 20 minutes.
    The crisp skin is delicious and
contrasts well with the delicate
flavour of the flesh. Serve
garnished with lemon slices.
Serves 4

Cider Baked Mackerel

4 medium sized mackerel
salt and pepper
3 bay leaves
2 oranges
½–¾ pint (300–450 ml)
    Bulmers Woodpecker Cider
1 lemon

Clean the mackerel and remove
heads and tails if preferred. Rub
inside and out with salt and
pepper. Place the prepared fish in
an ovenproof dish or casserole
with the bay leaves. Squeeze the
juice from one of the oranges and
mix this with the cider. Pour over
the fish. Slice the other orange and
the lemon and place alternate slices
along each fish. Cover the dish and
bake in a moderately hot oven at
375°F, 190°C, Gas Mark 5 for about
45 minutes.
    The cider takes away the oily
taste and adds a refreshingly sharp
flavour to this dish. It is also
suitable for herrings, making a
cheap fish into something really
special.
    Serve with a green salad and
duchesse potatoes.   **Serves 4**

BURGESS

Supper Kedgeree

1 lb (450 g) smoked haddock
½ pint (300 ml) milk
1 oz (25 g) butter
6 oz (175 g) long grained rice
3 tablespoons (45 ml) **Burgess** Creamed Horseradish
black pepper, freshly ground
salt, if required
parsley, chopped

Put the haddock into a fairly large pan, add milk and simmer very gently until the fish will flake easily. Strain off the milk and put on one side. Turn the fish on to a plate and rinse the pan for cooking the rice. Melt the butter in the pan and add the rice and liquid from the fish. Simmer until the rice is almost tender and the liquid absorbed. Meanwhile, flake the fish and remove the skin and bones. Stir the creamed horseradish in to the rice. Then carefully stir the flaked fish into the mixture. Season with black pepper and salt, if required. Heap kedgeree on a hot dish and sprinkle liberally with chopped parsley.   **Serves 4–6**

Tuna Mousse with Sour Cream Dressing

3 tablespoons (45 ml) water
2 teaspoons (10 ml) sugar
1 teaspoon (5 ml) salt
1 teaspoon (5 ml) dry mustard
3 tablespoons (45 ml) white vinegar
1 packet *or* ½ oz (15 g) gelatine
2–3 sticks celery
3–4 gherkins
2 (7 oz, 198 g) cans tuna
¼ pint (150 ml) cream
Dressing
¼ pint (150 ml) sour cream
½ teaspoon (2.5 ml) celery salt
1 teaspoon (5 ml) **Burgess** Creamed Horseradish

2 teaspoons (10 ml) white vinegar
1 teaspoon (5 ml) instant onion
pepper to taste

Mix together the water, sugar, salt, mustard and vinegar in a small pan. Sprinkle the gelatine over the surface of the liquid and warm over a gentle heat until the gelatine has dissolved. Remove from the heat and allow to cool. Meanwhile, chop the celery and gherkins into small pieces, mash the tuna thoroughly with a fork and whip the cream. Fold the celery, gherkins and tuna into the whipped cream, then fold into the cooled gelatine mixture. Turn into a 1¼ pint (700 ml) mould or dish and chill until set.

To make the dressing, mix all the ingredients in a bowl and chill until required.

Serve with sour cream sauce and green salad.   **Serves 4–6**

Crunchy Fish Pie

4 frozen cod steaks
10½ oz (297 g) can **Campbell's** Condensed Cream of Mushroom Soup
2 oz (50 g) Cheddar cheese, grated
2 oz (50 g) browned breadcrumbs
1 small packet potato crisps, crushed

Place the fish in an ovenproof dish and pour the undiluted soup over. Mix the cheese, crisps and breadcrumbs and sprinkle over the top of the mixture in the dish. Bake at 375°F, 190°C, Gas Mark 5, for 20–25 minutes.   **Serves 4**

Italian Fish Pie

1 lb (450 g) cod *or* coley fillet, cut into 1 in (2.5 cm) squares
10½ oz (297 g) can **Campbell's** Tomato and Mushroom Spaghetti Sauce

1 tablespoon (15 ml) lemon juice
2 tablespoons (30 ml) fresh parsley, chopped *or*
1 tablespoon (15 ml) dried
7½ oz (212 g) packet frozen puff pastry, thawed
milk to glaze

Mix the fish, Spaghetti Sauce, lemon juice and parsley together. Place in a pie dish. Roll out the pastry to fit the dish and place on top of the mixture, sealing the edges well. Glaze with the milk. Bake at 425°F, 220°C, Gas Mark 7, for 20–25 minutes. Turn off the oven and leave to cook for a further 10 minutes.   **Serves 4**

Mackerel Melody

3 mackerel, each weighing about 8 oz (225 g), cleaned
1 egg, hard-boiled, shelled and chopped
10½ oz (297 g) can **Campbell's** Condensed Mushroom Soup
3 oz (75 g) fresh white breadcrumbs
salt and pepper
½ oz (15 g) butter
5 thin slices lemon
a few sprigs watercress

Wash the cleaned mackerel, then make 3 diagonal cuts on each side, to allow the heat to penetrate right to the centre of the fish. Put the hard-boiled egg into a bowl with the breadcrumbs, seasoning and 3 tablespoons (45 ml) of the undiluted soup and stir until well mixed. Rub the butter around the inside of a shallow 3 pint (2 litre) ovenproof dish and lay the fish flat in the base of the dish. Divide the stuffing into three and place a third inside each fish. Stir 3 tablespoons (45 ml) of water into the remaining soup, then heat it to boiling point. Pour the soup around the fish and cover with foil. Bake on the centre shelf of a fairly hot oven, 400°F, 200°C, Gas Mark 6, for 45 minutes, or until the fish is cooked.

To serve, cut the lemon slices in half, arrange 3 on top of each fish and garnish with the watercress sprigs.   **Serves 3**

Mediterranean Herrings

4 herrings, cleaned
1 can **Chesswood** Sliced
   Mushrooms in Creamed
   Sauce
1 small green pepper, de-
   seeded and chopped
2 tomatoes, skinned, de-
   seeded and chopped
1 small onion, peeled and
   chopped
2 teaspoons (10 ml) mixed
   herbs
2 oz (50 g) breadcrumbs

Remove the heads, tails and backbones from the herrings. Heat the
Sliced Mushrooms in Creamed
Sauce in a pan and stir in the
remaining ingredients. Divide the
stuffing into 4 portions and use to
fill the herrings. Place in a greased
ovenproof dish and bake for 30–45
minutes (depending on the size of
the herrings) at 350°F, 180°C, Gas
Mark 4.   **Serves 4**

Smoked Haddock with Mushrooms

1–1¼ lb (500–600 g) smoked
   haddock fillets
¼ pint (125 ml) milk
½ oz (15 g) butter
½ oz (15 g) cornflour
1 can **Chesswood** Button
   Mushrooms
1 tablespoon (15 ml) parsley,
   chopped
salt and pepper

Place the haddock fillets in an
ovenproof dish, pour on the milk
and dot with butter. Cover and
bake for 25 minutes at 375°F,
190°C, Gas Mark 5. Pour off juices
into a saucepan and keep the
haddock warm.

   Drain the brine from the mushrooms and blend with the cornflour. Pour the mixture into the
fish juices and bring to the boil,
stirring continuously. Add the
mushrooms and parsley, season to
taste and heat thoroughly. Arrange
the haddock on a serving dish,
pour over the sauce and serve
immediately.   **Serves 4**

Seafood Creole

1½ tablespoons (25 ml) butter
2 medium onions, peeled and
   chopped
1 clove garlic, minced
   (optional)
½ green pepper, diced
2 oz (50 g) celery, diced
1½ tablespoons (25 ml) flour
28 oz (794 g) can **Cirio** Peeled
   Tomatoes
½–1 teaspoon (2.5–5 ml) salt
1 teaspoon (5 ml) sugar
2 bay leaves
½ teaspoon (2.5 ml) thyme,
   finely chopped
2–4 teaspoons (10–20 ml)
   Worcestershire sauce
½ teaspoon (2.5 ml) Tabasco
   sauce
7 oz (198 g) can tuna, drained
   and flaked
7 oz (198 g) can crabmeat,
   drained and flaked
4½ oz (127 g) can shrimps,
   drained

chopped parsley to garnish
   (optional)

Melt the butter in a frying pan over
low heat, add the onion, garlic,
pepper and celery. Cook gently,
stirring frequently, until the onion
is tender but not brown. Blend in
the flour, then stir in the tomatoes,
salt, sugar, bay leaves, thyme,
Worcestershire and Tabasco
sauces. Increase the heat and bring
to the boil, lower the heat and
simmer slowly for 15 minutes. Stir
in the tuna, crab and shrimp and
continue to simmer for another
15 minutes. Remove the bay
leaves.

   Serve with hot, buttered rice,
garnished with chopped parsley if
liked.   **Serves 4–6**

Colman's

Crusty Roll Bake

4 hard, round rolls
2 oz (50 g) butter, softened
1 lb (450 g) smoked haddock
   fillets
½ pint (300 ml) milk
1 packet **Colman's** Mushroom
   Sauce Mix
8 oz (225 g) frozen mixed
   vegetables, cooked
watercress to garnish

Cut a slice off the top of each roll
and reserve. Scoop out the centres,
spread the insides of the rolls with
the butter, place on a baking sheet
and put into the oven at 350°F,
180°C, Gas Mark 4, for 10 minutes
or until crisp. Simmer the fish in
the milk for 5 minutes. Remove
with a slotted spoon and flake,
discarding all the bones and skin.
Mix the milk, which should have
cooled slightly, with the mushroom sauce mix and cook, stirring,
until thickened. Add the vegetables and cook for another
minute, then add the fish. Fill the
hot rolls with the fish mixture and
serve at once, topped with the lids
of the rolls and garnished with
watercress.   **Serves 4**

Baked Fish Tartare

1 onion, thinly sliced
3 oz (75 g) mushrooms
1 oz (25 g) butter
1 lb (400 g) coley, skinned and boned
4 tablespoons (60 ml) **Frank Cooper's** Tartare Sauce

Sauté the onion and mushrooms in the butter until the onion is soft but not browned. Place the mixture into a casserole dish, add the coley and top with the tartare sauce. Bake at 350°F, 180°C, Gas Mark 4 for 20–25 minutes.
Serves 2–3

Fish Flan

8 oz (200 g) cod fillets, steamed and flaked
3 tablespoons (45 ml) **Frank Cooper's** Tartare Sauce
2 oz (50 g) Cheddar cheese, grated
7 in (18 cm) baked flan case

Combine the fish with the tartare sauce and half of the cheese. Place in the flan case and top with the remaining cheese. Bake at 400°F, 200°C, Gas Mark 6 for 10 minutes, until heated through. **Serves 4**

Tomato and Prawn Baked Cod

1 can **Frank Cooper's** Tomato Soup with Prawns
1 level tablespoon (15 ml) cornflour
1 lb (400 g) cod fillets
chopped parsley to garnish

Blend the cornflour with a little of the cold soup. Heat the remaining soup and add to the cornflour. Return to the heat and bring slowly to the boil. Place the fish in an ovenproof dish. Pour over the soup, cover and bake at 350°F, 180°C, Gas Mark 4 for 20–25 minutes. Garnish with the parsley to serve. **Serves 4**

Russian Baked Potato Cake

1 box **Chef** Parsley Sauce Mix
1 lb (450 g) cooked potatoes
14 oz (396 g) can **Crosse & Blackwell** Herrings in Tomato Sauce
salt and pepper
1 oz (25 g) fresh white breadcrumbs
1 oz (25 g) butter

Butter a 2 pint (1.2 litre) ovenproof dish. Make up the parsley sauce as instructed on the box. Cut the potatoes into thin slices. Remove the herrings from the can and cut lengthways into fillets. Discard the bones if desired. Place the herrings and tomato sauce, the potatoes and prepared parsley sauce in layers in the dish, starting and finishing with the potato. Lightly season each layer. Sprinkle with the breadcrumbs, dot with the butter and bake in the centre of the oven, pre-heated to 400°F, 200°C, Gas Mark 6, for about 40 minutes, until the crumbs are well browned.
Serves 4

Soused Herrings

2 herrings, with bones removed
1 small onion, chopped
1 teaspoon (5 ml) pickling spice
1 teaspoon (5 ml) **Dietade** Fruit Sugar
2 tablespoons (30 ml) water
2 tablespoons (30 ml) golden cider vinegar
¼ teaspoon salt
2 bay leaves

Put all the ingredients in a casserole dish. Bake for 45 minutes in a moderate oven at 325°F, 170°C, Gas Mark 3. Leave to get completely cold.

Serve with a green salad dressed with Appleford's Salad Dressing.
Serves 2

Fish Kaleidoscope

4 cod cutlets
salt and white pepper
2 oz (50 g) mushrooms, sliced
2 large tomatoes, skinned and sliced
1 medium onion, peeled and sliced
¼ pint (125 ml) Dry **Dubonnet**
2 heaped teaspoons (15 ml) cornflour
knob of butter
chopped parsley to garnish

Wipe the fish and remove any bones. Season well with salt and white pepper. Arrange the fish in a 2½ pint (1.4 litre) shallow, ovenproof dish with the mushrooms, tomatoes and onions on top, then season again. Pour over the Dubonnet, cover with a lid or foil and bake in a moderate oven at 350°F, 180°C, Gas Mark 4 for about 45 minutes.

Carefully drain the fish liquid into a saucepan. Blend the cornflour with a little water, add to the liquid and bring to the boil, stirring continuously until thickened. Stir in the butter. Pour the sauce over the fish and sprinkle with the chopped parsley.

Serve with new potatoes.
Serves 4

Fish en Papilotte

1 large packet **Findus** Cod
   Fillets, thawed
salt and pepper
1 tablespoon (15 ml) lemon
   juice
2 oz (50 g) butter
3¾ oz (106 g) crabmeat
1 egg, beaten
4 teaspoons (20 ml) white wine
½ medium onion, chopped
1 oz (25 g) mushrooms,
   chopped
1 tablespoon (15 ml) flour
¼ pint (142 ml) water

Skin the fish and cut into 8 pieces.
Season with the salt and pepper
and sprinkle with the lemon juice.
Fry in 1 oz (25 g) of the butter for
5–10 minutes until golden brown,
remove from the pan and keep
warm. Put the crabmeat into the
same pan with the beaten egg, half
the wine, salt and pepper and stir
well. Fry the onion and mushrooms in the rest of the butter for
5 minutes, until tender, add the
flour and cook for 2–3 minutes.
Remove the pan from the heat and
add the remaining wine and the
water. Bring to the boil, stirring,
until thickened and simmer for
3–5 minutes.

   Butter 4 squares of foil, place a
piece of fish fillet on each, spread
with a layer of the crabmeat mixture then cover with another piece
of fillet. Coat with the sauce and
fold the foil up carefully so that no
juices can escape. Bake at 350°F,
180°C, Gas Mark 4 for 15 minutes.
   Serve the fish in the foil or on
individual warmed plates.
Serves 4

Plaice Marguerite

1 large and 1 small packet
   Findus Plaice Fillets, thawed
1 egg, beaten
1 oz (25 g) browned
   breadcrumbs
½ pint (250 ml) white sauce

5 tablespoons (75 ml) single
   cream
2 egg yolks
4 tablespoons (60 ml) dry
   sherry *or* white wine
1 teaspoon (5 ml) lemon juice
10 mussels, well scrubbed
1 tablespoon (15 ml) lemon
   juice
2 oz (50 g) button mushrooms
1 packet **Findus** Prawns,
   thawed
decorative crouton shapes to
   garnish
oil for deep frying

Skin the plaice fillets, and put 2 or 3
fillets to one side. Poach the remaining fillets in a little salted
water for 5 minutes. Drain, place
the fish on a serving dish and keep
warm. Meanwhile, cut the reserved fish into strips and coat
with egg and breadcrumbs. Make
the white sauce, stir in the cream,
egg yolks, sherry or wine and the
lemon juice. Season with salt and
pepper and reheat, but do not
allow to boil.

   Cook the mussels in a large pan
with 2 tablespoons (30 ml) water
and the lemon juice. Shake the pan
occasionally until the shells open.
Drain. Cook the mushrooms in a
little butter or water. Deep fry the
breaded plaice strips for 2–3
minutes until golden.

   To serve, arrange the mushrooms and prawns on top of the
fish on a large serving dish, coat
with the sauce and garnish with
the mussels, plaice strips and
croutons.   **Serves 4**

Prawn and Mushroom Flambé

10 oz (275 g) long grain rice
2 oz (50 g) butter
8 oz (225 g) mushrooms,
   washed and finely sliced
1 packet **Findus** Peeled Prawns,
   thawed
salt and black pepper
juice of ½ lemon
good pinch of nutmeg
1 small glass brandy
½ pint (250 ml) double cream
1 tablespoon (15 ml) parsley,

chopped

Cook the rice, drain and keep hot.
Melt the butter in a large frying
pan, add the mushrooms and cook
for 2–3 minutes. Stir in the
prawns, nutmeg, seasoning and
lemon juice. Gently warm the
brandy and pour it flaming over
the prawns, shaking the pan so
that the flames spread. When the
flames have died, add the cream
and stir over a gentle heat until the
mixture thickens.

   Serve on a bed of rice, garnished
liberally with the parsley. To save
last-minute cooking, the dish can
be prepared in advance and heated
quickly just before serving.
Serves 6

Prawn Croquettes

¼ oz (7 g) gelatine
¼ pint (142 ml) milk
2 oz (50 g) butter
3 oz (75 g) flour
1 egg, separated
salt and pepper
juice of ½ lemon
pinch dried parsley
2 packets **Findus** Prawns,
   thawed
1 tablespoon (15 ml) vegetable
   oil
2 oz (50 g) browned
   breadcrumbs
fat or oil for frying

Dissolve the gelatine in a lttle of
the milk and add to the rest. Make
a thick white sauce with the butter,
flour and milk, stir in the egg yolk,
salt, pepper, lemon juice, parsley
and prawns. Spread on a plate and
allow to cool.

   When cold, divide the mixture
into 8 and roll each portion into a
cylinder shape. Beat the egg white
and oil together, dip each croquette in this and then coat in the
breadcrumbs. Fry in deep fat or oil
until golden brown.

   Serve hot or cold with a green
salad.   **Serves 4**

Trout Velouté with Grapes

1 packet **Findus** Rainbow
   Trout, thawed

4 tablespoons (60 ml) white
  wine
salt and pepper
1 oz (25 g) butter, melted
4 oz (100 g) black grapes,
  halved and with seeds
  removed
6 green olives, sliced
½ pint (250 ml) home-made or
  packet white sauce, coating
  consistency

Place the trout in a baking tin with
the wine and seasoning. Brush
with the melted butter and cover
with foil. Bake for 30 minutes at
375°F, 190°C, Gas Mark 5. Make
the white sauce, add the liquor
from the fish, season and add the
grapes and olives. Place the fish on
a serving dish and cover with the
sauce.　**Serves 2**

Austrian Fish Cake

8 oz (225 g) smoked haddock,
  cooked and flaked
8 oz (225 g) mashed potatoes
4 oz (100 g) **Haywards** Pickled
  Red Cabbage, drained
2 teaspoons (10 ml) fresh
  parsley, chopped
1 egg, beaten
beaten egg and golden
  breadcrumbs for coating
fat or oil for shallow frying

Mix the fish, potatoes, red cabbage, parsley and egg together and
shape into a large circle. Chill in
the refrigerator for 1 hour, then
coat in egg and breadcrumbs.
Shallow fry for 10 minutes on each
side until golden brown and
warmed through.　**Serves 4**

Homepride

Coat & Cook Plaice Parcels

1 oz (25 g) butter or margarine,
  softened

2 hard-boiled eggs, chopped
7 oz (198 g) can prawns,
  drained and chopped
4 plaice fillets, skinned
salt and pepper
1 sachet **Homepride Coat &
  Cook**, Lemon and Parsley
  Flavour
a few prawns and sprigs of
  watercress to garnish

Mix the fat, eggs and prawns
together to make the stuffing. Dry
the plaice thoroughly on kitchen
paper. Place the fish on a board
and spread with a quarter of the
stuffing mix. Sprinkle with
seasoning. Roll up towards the tail
ends to make 'parcels' and secure
with cocktail sticks. Coat the fish
evenly with the contents of Coat &
Cook sachet. Place the parcels in an
ovenproof dish and bake at 400°F,
200°C, Gas Mark 6, for 12 minutes.
　Serve garnished with prawns
and watercress with boiled new
potatoes, buttered carrot rings and
petit pois.　**Serves 4**

Cod Steaks Spanish Style

4 cod steaks
1 small onion, peeled and
  chopped
a little fat or oil for frying
4 tomatoes, skinned and
  chopped
1 tablespoon (15 ml) parsley,
  chopped
1 oz (25 g) fresh breadcrumbs
salt and pepper
1 can **Homepride** White Wine
  with Cream Cook-in-Sauce

Place the cod steaks in a shallow,
ovenproof dish. Fry the onion in a
little fat or oil until soft, add the
tomatoes, parsley, breadcrumbs
and seasoning, mix well together
and spread over the cod. Pour over
the Cook-in-Sauce, cover and cook
in the oven at 400°F, 200°C, Gas
Mark 6, for 40 minutes.
　Serve with sliced green beans
and sauté potatoes.　**Serves 4**

Seafood Wholewheat Flan

4 oz (100 g) **Harvest Gold**
  Stoneground 100%
  Wholewheat Flour
pinch of salt
1 oz (25 g) lard creamed with
  1 oz (25 g) butter or
  margarine
1 egg, lightly beaten
few drops of iced water
7 oz (198 g) can shrimps
⅓–½ pint (200–300 ml) milk
1 oz (25 g) butter or margarine
1 oz (25 g) **Homepride** Plain
  Flour
7 oz (198 g) can tuna or salmon,
  drained
1 oz (25 g) Cheddar cheese,
  grated
2 eggs, beaten
salt and pepper
cucumber slices to garnish

In a bowl combine the flour and
salt. Rub in the fats until the
mixture resembles fine breadcrumbs. Add the egg and mix to a
firm dough with a round-bladed
knife, adding a little iced water if
necessary. Knead gently, place on
to a lightly floured surface and roll
out to a circle, 2 in (5 cm) larger
than an 8 in (20 cm) fluted flan
ring. Carefully lift and lower the
pastry into the flan ring on a
baking sheet. Prick the base well
and bake 'blind' at 400°F, 200°C,
Gas Mark 6, for 15 minutes. Remove the paper and baking beans.
Return to the oven for a further
5–10 minutes. Cool on a wire tray.
Drain the shrimps, pouring the
juices into a measuring jug. Make
up to ½ pint (300 ml) with milk.
Make a sauce by melting the butter
or margarine, adding the flour and
liquid gradually and stirring
constantly until the sauce has
thickened. Stir in half the shrimps,
all the tuna and the cheese. Stir in
the eggs, remove from the heat and
season if necessary. Leave to cool
slightly, then pour into the flan
case. Sprinkle the flan with the rest
of the shrimps. Arrange overlapping cucumber slices in the
centre. Serve cold.　**Serves 4**

Curried Prawn Milles Feuilles

13 oz (370 g) packet **Jus-rol** Puff
    Pastry, thawed
beaten egg to glaze
3 fl oz (90 ml) double cream
3 fl oz (90 ml) thick
    mayonnaise
grated rind of ½ lemon
1½ level teaspoons (7.5 ml)
    curry powder
4 oz (100 g) peeled prawns
vinegar
black pepper
lemon wedges
parsley sprigs and whole
    prawns (optional) to garnish

Divide the pastry in half and roll
out each piece to an 8½ in (22 cm)
round; place on wetted baking
sheets, brush with the beaten egg
and bake in a pre-heated oven at
450°F, 230°C, Gas Mark 8, for
about 10 minutes, until crisp and
golden. Cool on wire racks. Season
the prawns with vinegar and
pepper and leave to marinate
while the pastry cools then drain
thoroughly on absorbent paper.
Whip the cream very stiffly and
fold in the mayonnaise, lemon
rind and curry powder. Chill. Stir
the prawns through the curry
mixture and sandwich the 2 pastry
layers together with the prawn
filling. Garnish the top with lemon
wedges and parsley sprigs and
whole prawns for special
occasions.   **Serves 6**

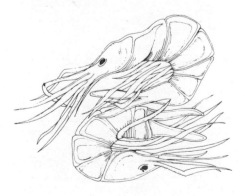

Creamed Baked Trout Parisienne

4 trout, fresh or frozen, cleaned
plain flour with a pinch of salt
    and pepper
2½ oz (62 g) butter
6 oz (150 g) button mushrooms,
    thinly sliced
8 oz (200 g) **Kerrygold** Frozen
    Cream, thawed
2 tablespoons (30 ml) chopped
    parsley *or* chives

Trim the tails of the trout and remove the fins with a pair of kitchen
scissors but leave the heads on.
Wash and dry in kitchen towel.
Melt 2 oz (50 g) of the butter and
pour a little into a large fireproof
dish. Roll the trout in the seasoned
flour and lay in the dish. Spoon
over the remaining melted butter
and bake in a moderately hot oven
for 10–15 minutes, basting
occasionally. Meanwhile, melt the
remaining ½ oz (12 g) butter, add
the thinly sliced mushrooms and
cook briskly. Add the cream and
seasoning and bring to the boil to
thicken slightly. When the trout
are nicely browned and cooked,
add the herbs to the cream, pour
over the trout and serve immediately.

 When watercress is good, use
half a bunch to garnish the dish.

 The cream may still be in a
frozen state when it is added to the
pan. In which case keep the
temperature under the pan low
until the cream has defrosted and
then increase the heat to thicken
the cream slightly.   **Serves 4**

Grilled Fish with Cheese

1 frozen cod steak
melted butter
¼ small onion, peeled and
    grated

3 tablespoons (45 ml)
    Kerrygold Grated Cheddar
    Cheese
2 teaspoons (10 ml) tomato
    ketchup
pinch of dry mustard
salt and pepper

Pre-heat the grill. Place the cod
steak on the grill rack and brush
with the melted butter. Grill for
15 minutes, turning once. Meanwhile, mix the onion with the
cheese, ketchup, mustard and
seasoning to taste. Spread the
cheese mixture over the cod steak
and return to the grill. Cook for
about 5 minutes or until the cheese
topping is melted and bubbling.
Serves 1

LEA & PERRINS

Spiced Lemon Fish Pie

4 frozen cod steaks
1 small onion, chopped
½ pint (300 ml) milk
1 level tablespoon (15 ml)
    cornflour
1 lemon
2 oz (50 g) frozen peas
2 level teaspoons (10 ml) **Lea &
    Perrins** Concentrated Curry
    Sauce
salt and pepper
5–6 serving packet instant
    potato

Place the cod steaks, onion and
milk in a pan, bring to the boil and
simmer for 10 minutes. Drain,
reserving the liquor. Flake the cod.
Blend the cornflour with a little of
the liquor. Heat the remainder, stir
into the cornflour mixture, return
to the pan and bring to the boil,
stirring. Grate the rind from the
lemon and cut away the pith. Cut
between each membrane to
remove segments and chop
roughly. Add the lemon rind and
flesh, peas, fish and onion to the
pan and simmer for 5 minutes. Stir
in the concentrated curry sauce
and seasoning. Turn the mixture
into a 1½ pint (900 ml) pie dish.
Make up the potato following
manufacturer's instructions and

pipe or fork over the pie. Bake at 400°F, 200°C, Gas Mark 6, for 20 minutes. **Serves 4**

Crunchy Herrings

4 fresh herrings
2 oz (50 g) oatmeal
3 oz (75 g) **McVitie's** Digestive
   Biscuits, crushed
salt and pepper
butter to fry
wedges of lemon to serve

Wash and clean the herrings and remove the fins and tail. Slit the fish along the sides and remove the roes. Open each fish out and place, cut side down, on a board and press to flatten. Rinse under cold running water and then dry on kitchen paper.

Blend the oatmeal, biscuits and seasoning together and coat the fish in the mixture. Melt a little butter in a frying pan and fry the fish until golden brown, turning once, for about 8 minutes over a moderate heat. Lift out, drain and serve.

Serve with wedges of lemon.
Serves 4

Salmon Crunch

3 oz (75 g) butter
1 oz (25 g) flour
1 large can evaporated milk
1 teaspoon (5 ml) dry mustard
¼ teaspoon salt
¼ teaspoon pepper
7½ oz (212 g) can pink *or* red
   salmon
a little lemon juice to taste
2–3 sticks celery, finely sliced
4 oz (100 g) **McVitie's** Digestive
   Biscuits, crushed

Melt 1 oz (25 g) of the butter in a saucepan, stir in the flour, cook for 3 minutes, add the milk and bring to the boil, stirring until the sauce has thickened. Season well. Remove the bones and skin from the salmon and flake into a medium

sized dish. Pour over the sauce, adding a little lemon juice and celery and mix thoroughly. Melt the remaining butter and stir in the McVitie's digestive biscuits. Sprinkle on top of the dish and bake in the oven at 350°F, 180°C, Gas Mark 4, for 30 minutes.
Serves 4

Fish Crumble

6 oz (150 g) cooked white fish
1½ oz (40 g) butter
2½ oz (70 g) plain flour
¼ pint (150 ml) milk
½ teaspoon (2.5 ml) **Marmite**
salt and pepper
1 oz (25 g) Cheddar cheese,
   grated

Remove the skin and bones from the fish and flake the flesh. Melt ½ oz (15 g) of the butter and stir in ½ oz (15 g) of the flour. Cook for 1 minute over a low heat and add the milk gradually. Add the Marmite and cook over a low heat, stirring well, until the sauce comes to the boil and thickens. Simmer for 2 minutes and then stir in the fish. Season well and put into a lightly greased 1 pint (600 ml) ovenware dish. Rub the remaining butter into the rest of the flour to make fine crumbs, and stir in the cheese. Sprinkle thickly over the fish and bake at 375°F, 190°C, Gas Mark 5, for 30 minutes.
Serves 2

Cadbury's Marvel

Salmon Special

2 oz (50 g) butter
3 oz (75 g) plain flour
½ pint (275 ml) liquid **Marvel**
3 eggs, separated
salt and pepper
Filling
½ cucumber

1 lemon
6 oz (175 g) cream cheese
salt and freshly ground pepper
8 oz (225 g) salmon
watercress to garnish

Line a 13½ × 9½ in (30 × 22.5 cm) swiss roll tin with greased and floured foil. Melt the butter in a pan and stir in half the flour. Blend in the Marvel, making a smooth sauce. Cool slightly before adding the egg yolks and seasoning, then cool completely. Whisk the egg whites quite stiffly and fold half into the cooled mixture, followed by the flour and then the remaining egg whites. Turn the mixture into the prepared tin and bake in a pre-heated oven at 400°F, 200°C, Gas Mark 6 for 5 minutes, then lower the heat to 300°F, 150°C, Gas Mark 2 for a further 55 minutes until set and golden brown. Turn out on to a piece of greaseproof paper and carefully peel off the foil. Trim the edges with a knife and roll up loosely with the paper in between. Leave to get completely cold.

To make the filling, cut a few thin slices off the lemon and cucumber and set aside for garnishing. Peel and finely chop the remaining cucumber and squeeze the juice from the rest of the lemon. Soften the cream cheese and season well with the lemon juice, salt and pepper. Remove any bones or unsightly skin from the fish and flake into small pieces. Add to the cheese with the cucumber. Carefully unwrap the cooled pastry roll and spread the filling in the centre, taking it right up to the edges. Roll up once again as tightly as possible.

Serve garnished with lemon and cucumber slices, surrounded by sprigs of watercress. **Serves 6**

Spiced Sea Supper

1 lb (450 g) cod *or* haddock
1 pint (550 ml) liquid **Marvel**
1 teaspoon (5 ml) marjoram *or*
    2 bay leaves
2 onions, peeled and chopped
1 clove garlic, peeled and
    crushed
1 green pepper, de-seeded and
    sliced
1 oz (25 g) margarine
1 oz (25 g) flour
2 tablespoons (30 ml) ginger
    wine, cordial or syrup
1½ teaspoons (7.5 ml) ground
    ginger
1 teaspoon (5 ml) turmeric
salt and pepper
1 lemon, sliced
4 black olives

Poach the fish in the Marvel with
the herbs for about 10 minutes.
Lift out the fish and remove any
skin or bones. Soften the
vegetables in the margarine, stir in
the flour and gradually add the
strained fish liquid, ginger liquid
and spices, stirring until blended
and boiling. Adjust the seasoning
to taste and add the fish. Reheat
gently.

    Serve with boiled brown rice,
garnished with slices of lemon and
the olives.   **Serves 4**

Tuna Slice

2 onions, peeled and minced *or*
    grated
3 sticks celery, minced *or* grated
7 oz (198 g) can tuna, drained
2 oz (50 g) fresh breadcrumbs
1½ oz (40 g) dry **Marvel**
1 tablespoon (15 ml) tomato
    purée
2 teaspoons (10 ml)
    Worcestershire sauce
1 egg
salt and pepper

Line a 1 lb (500 g) loaf tin with a
strip of foil to fit the base and ends,
grease the foil and the inside of the
tin. Mix the onion and celery with
the flaked tuna in a bowl, mix in all
the remaining ingredients and
season well. Press the mixture into

the prepared tin and bake at 350°F,
180°C, Gas Mark 4 for 1 hour.
Turn out to serve.

    Serve hot or cold, with vege-
tables or salad. Stuffed tomatoes
are particularly good with this
recipe.   **Serves 4–5**

Mazola

Fish Crispies

1–1¼ lb (400–500 g) cod fillet
juice of 1 orange
salt and pepper
Batter
4 oz (100 g) plain flour
pinch salt
1 egg
¼ pint (125 ml) milk
Mazola pure corn oil for frying

Cut the fish into bite size pieces,
pour over the orange juice and
season well. Sieve together the
flour and salt, add the egg and half
the milk and beat to form a smooth
batter. Stir in the remainder of the
milk. Heat the corn oil in a deep
fryer to 375°F, 190°C. Dip the
pieces of fish in the batter and fry
for 3–4 minutes until crisp and
golden brown. Drain on kitchen
paper.   **Serves 4**

Mariner's Choice

2 lb (1 kg) firm white fish
    fillets, such as halibut
1 onion, peeled and chopped
1 small green pepper, de-
    seeded and cut into strips
4 medium tomatoes, skinned,
    quartered and de-seeded
2 tablespoons (40 ml) oil
½ level teaspoon (2.5 ml)
    cayenne pepper
½ pint (250 ml) **Rose's** Lime
    Juice Cordial
salt and pepper

Wipe the fish and remove any skin
or bones. Cut into 4 pieces. Heat
the oil in a shallow pan and sauté
the onion gently until soft,
sprinkle in the cayenne pepper,
stir in the green pepper and cook
for 5 minutes before adding the
tomatoes and lime juice. Season
well with salt and pepper. Arrange
the fish in a lightly greased,
shallow, ovenproof dish, pour in
the vegetable mixture and bake in
a moderately hot oven, 375°F,
190°C, Gas Mark 5, for about 30
minutes until the fish is cooked.

    Serve with sauté or creamed
potatoes.   **Serves 4**

ROWNTREE'S

Prawn Mould

1 **Rowntree's** Lemon Jelly,
    dissolved in ½ pint (142 ml)
    boiling water
¼ pint (142 ml) mayonnaise
¼ pint (142 ml) cream
salt and pepper
2 tablespoons (30 ml) tarragon
    vinegar
8 oz (225 g) prepared prawns
salad to garnish

When the jelly is cool add the
vinegar. Meanwhile whip the
cream and add the mayonnaise,
salt and pepper. When the jelly
begins to set, whip or liquidise all
together and stir in the prawns.
Pour into a wetted mould and
leave to set. Turn out carefully on
to a dish and surround with salad.

    Serve with brown bread and
butter.

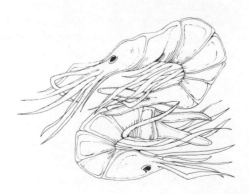

RY·KING

Baked Stuffed Fish

4 fish fillets (plaice, whiting, etc.) skinned and cut in half lengthwise
7 sliced **Ry-King** Wheat, crushed
2 oz (50 g) soft white cheese with chives
juice and rind of 1 lemon
fresh parsley, chopped
salt and pepper
beaten egg to mix

Cream together the cheese and crumbs, add the lemon juice and grated rind (reserve a little for garnish), chopped parsley and seasoning. Blend together with a little beaten egg. Place a spoonful of the mixture on each fillet, roll up and stand each fillet in an oven-proof dish. Cover the dish lightly with foil. Bake for 20–25 minutes in an oven pre-heated to 375°F, 190°C, Gas Mark 5.

Serve sprinkled with lemon rind and parsley. **Serves 4**

Salmon and Soured Cream Pie

1 lb (450 g) salmon, fresh, frozen *or* tinned
water
4 tablespoons (60 ml) white wine
salt and freshly ground black pepper
6½ oz (180 g) **St Ivel** Butter
1½ oz (40 g) plain flour
7 oz (200 g) **St Ivel** Cheddar Cheese, grated
3 hard-boiled eggs, roughly chopped
5 oz (142 ml) carton **St Ivel** Soured Cream
2 tablespoons (50 g) lard
1 lb (450 g) self-raising flour
2 tablespoons (30 ml) **St Ivel** Parmesan Cheese, grated
beaten egg to glaze

Cook the fish with a little cold water, the wine and seasoning. Simmer for about 20 minutes. Reserve the fish stock and flake the fish, removing the bones and skin. Make a sauce from 1½ oz (40 g) of the butter, the plain flour and ½ pint (300 ml) of the fish stock. Remove from the heat, stir in the cheese, eggs, soured cream and parsley. Cool. Prepare shortcrust pastry from the remaining butter with the lard, self-raising flour and Parmesan cheese. Mix with water. Roll out one-third of the pastry to a 4 × 14 in (10 × 35 cm) oblong. Place on a baking sheet. Cover with layers of sauce and salmon. Cover with the remaining pastry and seal the edges well. Garnish with pastry trimmings. Glaze with beaten egg and bake at 375°F, 190°C, Gas Mark 5 for 40 minutes. **Serves 4**

SCHWARTZ

Tuna Plait

2 (8 oz, 227 g) tins tuna in oil
3 sticks celery, thinly sliced
2 oz (50 g) red pepper, finely chopped (optional)
2 tablespoons (30 ml) mayonnaise
1 egg (size 3), beaten
2 teaspoons (10 ml) **Schwartz** Lemon Pepper *or* 2 teaspoons (10 ml) **Schwartz** Seasoning Salt
2 tablespoons (10 ml) **Schwartz** Chives
14 oz (397 g) packet puff pastry
a few **Schwartz** Poppy Seeds for topping
green vegetables *or* salad garnish

Drain the fish and discard the oil. Place the fish in a bowl and add the celery, red pepper, mayonnaise, half the beaten egg, lemon pepper or seasoning salt and chives and mix carefully. Roll out the pastry to an oblong measuring approximately 14 × 12 in (35 × 30 cm). Transfer to a baking tray. Spread the filling lengthwise down the centre third of the pastry. Cut horizontal 1 in (2.5 cm) width strips down each side of the pastry to within 1 in (2.5 cm) of the filling. Fold the end pieces of pastry over the filling and lift strips of pastry over the filling from alternate sides to form a plaited effect. Brush with the remaining beaten egg. Sprinkle with poppy seeds and cook in the oven, pre-heated to 425°F, 220°C, Gas Mark 7 for 25 minutes until golden.

Serve hot or cold, garnished with green vegetables or salad. May be stored in a refrigerator for up to 2 days or frozen for up to 1 month. **Serves 4–6**

Baked Mackerel or Herrings

2 mackerel *or* 4 herrings
1 onion, sliced in rings
1 bottle **Schweppes** Grapefruit Juice

Prepare the fish and remove the backbone with as many bones as possible. Place in a large, shallow, ovenproof dish and season the fish well. Cover with thin onion rings. Pour over the grapefruit juice. Cover the dish and bake in a moderate oven at 350°F, 180°C, Gas Mark 4 for 45 minutes until the fish is cooked.

Serve with new potatoes and green salad. **Serves 2**

Stork

Herby Fish Flan

4 oz (125 g) **Stork** Margarine
6 oz (175 g) plain flour and
   1 teaspoon (5 ml) thyme,
   mixed together
1–2 tablespoons (15–30 ml)
   water

Filling
½ oz (15 g) **Stork** Margarine
1 onion, peeled and finely
   chopped
1 stick celery, washed and
   chopped
7½ oz (210 g) can tuna *or*
   salmon
½ pint (275 ml) milk
1 tablespoon (15 ml) cornflour,
   blended with a little water
3 oz (75 g) Cheddar cheese,
   grated
1 tablespoon (15 ml)
   breadcrumbs
sliced tomato and parsley sprig
   to decorate (optional)

To make the pastry, place the margarine, one-third of the flour mixture and the water in the bowl. Blend with a fork, add the remaining flour and mix to a firm dough. Knead well on a lightly-floured surface and roll out to line a 7 in (18 cm) plain flan ring. Chill. Bake blind in an oven pre-heated to 400°F, 200°C, Gas Mark 6, for 20–25 minutes.

Melt the Stork and fry the onion and celery for 5 minutes. Add the tuna or salmon, milk and blended cornflour and cook, stirring continuously, until thickened. Pour the filling into the pastry case and sprinkle over the cheese and breadcrumbs. Grill for 5 minutes until golden brown.

Serve hot, garnished with the sliced tomato and parsley sprig.
Serves 4

Herring Kebabs

1 oz (25 g) **Stork** Margarine
6 oz (175 g) long grain rice
½ teaspoon (2.5 ml) turmeric
½ teaspoon (2.5 ml) allspice
1 pint (575 ml) water
Kebabs
4 small onions
4 tomatoes
8 button mushrooms
4 herrings
1 oz (25 g) **Stork** Margarine
salt and pepper

Melt 1 oz (25 g) Stork and fry the rice until golden. Add the turmeric, allspice and water, and bring to the boil. Simmer for 15–20 minutes until the rice is tender. Strain. Simmer the onions in salted water until just tender. Strain. To prepare the herrings, remove the heads, split down the stomach and remove the intestines and backbone. Cut each into two fillets. Place the kebab ingredients on skewers, brush with melted stork, season and cook under a hot grill, turning occasionally until cooked. Serve kebabs on a bed of rice.   **Serves 4**

Stuffed Mackerel with Herbs

4 mackerel, each approx 8 oz
   (225 g) in weight
½ small onion, peeled and
   chopped
½ oz (15 g) **Stork** Margarine,
   melted
4 oz (100 g) breadcrumbs
rind of 1 lemon
1 tablespoon (15 ml) fresh
   rosemary, chopped
salt and pepper
1 egg
fresh sprigs of rosemary and
   lemon slices to garnish

Clean the mackerel and remove the backbone. Soften the onion in the Stork and mix with the remaining stuffing ingredients. Stuff the fish and wrap each mackerel in foil. Bake in the centre of the oven, pre-heated to 375°F, 190°C, Gas Mark 5, for 30 minutes. Arrange the mackerel on a warm serving dish and garnish with the sprigs of rosemary and lemon slices.
Serves 4

TREX

Seafood Savoury Flan

6 oz (170 g) plain flour
¼ teaspoon salt
2½ oz (70 g) **Trex** Pure
   Vegetable Fat
1½ tablespoons (20 ml) cold
   water
2–3 scallops
4 oz (100 g) plaice *or* sole fillets
½ pint (300 ml) milk
salt and pepper
1 oz (25 g) butter
1 oz (25 g) flour
2 oz (50 g) shelled prawns
1 oz (25 g) cheese, grated

Prepare the shortcrust pastry by rubbing the Trex into the sifted flour and salt, until the mixture resembles breadcrumbs. Mix to a dough with the water and roll out to line a 7 in (18 cm) flan ring. Bake blind for 10 minutes at 400°F, 200°C, Gas Mark 6, remove the beans and flan ring and return to the oven for a further 10 minutes until brown. Cut the scallops into 4, cut the fish fillets in half and roll up. Poach for 5 minutes in a small pan with the milk and seasonings. Carefully remove from the pan, drain well and arrange in the flan case. Melt the butter in a pan, stir in the flour, gradually add the milk and bring to the boil, stirring. Add the prawns to the sauce and re-heat for 2 minutes. Pour the sauce over the fish, sprinkle with cheese and brown under the grill.
Serves 4–6

Fish Finger Corkscrews

8 fish fingers
4 rashers **Wall's** Streaky Bacon

Cut the rind and any small bones from the bacon and with the back of the knife stretch each rasher to almost twice its length. Cut the rashers in half, wrap a piece around each fish finger and place on a grill pan with the ends underneath. Grill the corkscrews for 5–10 minutes, turning them halfway through the cooking time so they brown and cook evenly.

Serve with chips or baked beans. **Serves 3–4**

Coleslaw Mackerel

7 oz (198 g) can **John West** Mackerel Fillets in Tomato Sauce
2 tablespoons (30 ml) mayonnaise
6 oz (175 g) white cabbage, finely shredded
3 oz (75 g) raw carrot, finely grated
1 oz (25 g) raisins
salt and pepper
4 spring onions, sliced *or* chopped chives to garnish

Mix the tomato sauce from the can of mackerel with the mayonnaise. Add some sauce mixture to the cabbage, carrot and raisins. Season, and place in a dish. Arrange the mackerel on the salad, top with the remaining sauce and sprinkle with the onion or chives. **Serves 2**

Mackerel Crumble

7 oz (198 g) can **John West** Mackerel Steaks in Natural Juices
1 stick celery, trimmed and finely chopped
2 oz (50 g) onion, chopped
1 teaspoon (5 ml) capers
1 teaspoon (5 ml) lemon juice
salt and pepper
2 tablespoons (30 ml) fresh breadcrumbs
1 tablespoon (15 ml) Gouda cheese, grated
½ teaspoon (2.5 ml) lemon rind, grated

Drain the juice from the mackerel and put the juice in a saucepan with the celery and onion. Simmer for 5 minutes. Skin and remove the bones from the mackerel and add the fish to the pan with the capers and the lemon juice. Season to taste. Combine the remaining ingredients together. Spoon the fish mixture into an individual flameproof dish and top with the breadcrumb mixture. Place under a hot grill until golden brown. **Serves 1**

Mackerel and Cheese Baked Potatoes

2–4 hot, freshly baked potatoes
7 oz (198 g) can **John West** Smoked Mackerel Fillets
salt and pepper
chopped parsley
2 oz (50 g) cheese, grated

Cut each potato in half and scoop out most of the inside. Flake the mackerel fillets and mix with the cooked potato, seasoning and chopped parsley. Pile the mixture back into the potato halves and sprinkle liberally with grated cheese. Place under a hot grill until the cheese melts and turns golden. **Serves 2–4**

Savoury Mackerel Pasties

shortcrust pastry made with 6 oz (175 g) flour
7 oz (198 g) can **John West** Mackerel Fillets in Tomato Sauce
1 medium sized carrot, finely grated
1 small onion, finely grated
1 medium potato, peeled and finely grated

salt and pepper
1–2 teaspoons (5–10 ml) bottled tomato sauce

Divide the pastry into 4 and roll into 7 in (18 cm) rounds. Flake and mix the mackerel and tomato sauce with the carrot, onion and potato. Damp the pastry edges, pile the filling in the middle and seal the pastry on top. Bake towards the top of a pre-heated oven at 400°F, 200°C, Gas Mark 6 for 25–30 minutes.

Serve hot or cold with vegetables or salads. **Serves 3–4**

Shamrock Skippers

2 oz (50 g) butter
3 teaspoons (15 ml) lemon juice
2 tablespoons (30 ml) parsley, chopped
4 slices Irish soda bread *or* large granary
1 medium cooked apple, peeled, cored and very thinly sliced or 13½ oz (382 g) can **John West** Apple Slices
1 small onion, finely grated (optional)
1 tablespoon (15 ml) brown sugar
salt and pepper
3¾ oz (106 g) can **John West** Skippers in Oil *or* Tomato
½ oz (15 g) butter cut into small pieces

Blend the butter with the lemon juice and parsley. Toast the bread on one side only. Cover the untoasted side with the apple slices, onion, sugar and seasoning. Arrange the Skippers on top and grill under medium heat about 5 minutes until hot. Dot the prepared butter in a line on top of the Skippers and serve immediately with green salad. **Serves 4**

Prawn Creole

1 oz (25 g) butter
1 onion, peeled and chopped
1 green pepper, de-seeded and
    chopped
1 oz (25 g) flour
15 oz (380 g) can tomatoes
1 tablespoon (15 ml) mixed
    herbs
1 tablespoon (15 ml) sugar
salt and pepper
¼ pint (125 ml) dry white wine
8 oz (225 g) **Young's** North
    Atlantic Prawns

Melt the butter and fry the onion
and green pepper until soft. Add
the flour, then the tomatoes,
herbs, sugar and seasoning. Stir
and simmer for 15 minutes. Stir in
the wine and prawns and allow to
heat through for 5 minutes.

Serve on a bed of savoury rice,
containing chopped celery and
sweetcorn.   **Serves 4–6**

Smoked Haddock Bake

1 lb (450 g) **Young's** Smoked
    Haddock Cutlets
¾ pint (450 ml) milk
black pepper
1½ lb (675 g) cold, cooked
    potatoes
4 eggs, soft-boiled and roughly
    chopped
1 oz (25 g) butter
1 oz (25 g) flour
¼ pint (150 ml) **Young's** Dairy
    Cream
6 oz (175 g) cheese, grated

Poach the fish in the milk with a
little black pepper until just cooked
(about 4 minutes). Cool and flake
the fish, removing the skin and
any small bones. Reserve the milk.
Slice half the potatoes into a large,
greased, ovenproof dish. Put in
half the fish, then the eggs and
cover with the remaining fish.
Layer the rest of the potatoes
neatly on top. Make a sauce by
melting the butter in a pan, add the

flour and cook for 1 minute. Add
the reserved milk, the cream and
4 oz (100 g) of the cheese. Stir until
well blended. Pour over the casserole, coating the top well and
allowing the sauce to trickle
through (shaking the dish gently
will help). Sprinkle the remaining
cheese over the top and bake at
350°F, 180°C, Gas Mark 4 for 45–60
minutes until hot all through and
golden brown.   **Serves 4–6**

Sole and Prawns in the Round

4 oz (100 g) **Young's** North
    Atlantic Prawns
4 oz (100 g) button mushrooms,
    sliced
2 hard-boiled eggs, chopped
seasoning
grated rind of 1 lemon
2 tablespoons (30 ml) double
    cream
12 small lemon sole fillets
¾ pint (450 ml) dry white wine
bay leaf
peppercorns
½ onion
Sauce
1½ oz (40 g) butter
1 oz (25 g) plain flour
salt and pepper
4 fl oz (120 ml) single cream
1 egg yolk

Mix the prawns, mushrooms, hard
boiled eggs, seasoning, lemon
rind and double cream. Divide the
mixture amongst the fish fillets
and roll up carefully. Place in a
large buttered ovenproof dish and
pour over wine, bay leaf,
peppercorns and onion. Cover
with buttered paper and poach in

the oven at 325°F, 160°C, Gas Mark
3, for 10–15 minutes.

To make the sauce, melt the
butter in a saucepan, stir in the
flour off the heat, strain on the
liquor from the fish and stir until
boiling. Season and draw aside.
Mix the cream and egg yolk
together and add to the sauce.
Thicken over the heat without
boiling. Put the sole on a serving
dish and spoon over the sauce.
Serves 6

Sweet and Sour Prawns

8 oz (225 g) **Young's** Peeled
    Prawns
1 tablespoon (15 ml) sherry
salt and pepper
2 tablespoons (30 ml) cooking
    oil
2 onions, peeled and sliced
2 green peppers, de-seeded and
    sliced
¼ pint (150 ml) chicken stock
1 small can pineapple cubes
1 tablespoon (15 ml) cornflour
2 tablespoons (30 ml) soy sauce
4 oz (100 g) sugar

Marinate the prawns in the sherry,
salt and pepper. Heat the oil in a
saucepan and sauté the onions and
peppers until they are tender. Add
the chicken stock and pineapple
cubes. Cover and cook for 3–5
minutes. Blend the cornflour, soy
sauce and sugar and add to the
mixture, stirring until it thickens.
Add the prawns and cook for
30 seconds. Cover the pan, turn off
the heat and leave for 2 minutes
before serving.

Serve with boiled rice.
Serves 4–6

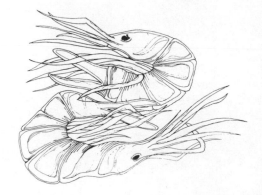

POULTRY and GAME

Devilled Chicken

1 packet **Batchelors** Minestrone
  Soup
4 chicken drumsticks
1 teaspoon (5 ml) mustard
  (made-up)
1 oz (25 g) plain flour
2 oz (50 g) margarine
1 pint (575 ml) water

Wipe the drumsticks and spread
them with mustard. Coat with the
flour and fry in the margarine for
10 minutes, turning them to
brown all over. Remove from the
frying pan and keep hot. Add the
soup mix to the pan and, stirring,
gradually add the water. Bring to
the boil, add the drumsticks and
simmer for 10 minutes.
Serves 4

Chicken à la Crème

4 lb (2 kg) chicken, cut into six
  pieces
1 large green pepper, sliced
4 oz (100 g) button mushrooms,
  sliced
1 can **Baxters** White Wine Sauce
2 tablespoons (30 ml) cream

Place the joints in a casserole with
the pepper and button mushrooms. Cover the mixture with the
White Wine Sauce and the cream.
Cover the casserole and cook for 45
minutes to 1 hour in a preheated
oven at 350°F, 180°C, Gas Mark 4.
Serve with boiled potatoes and
seasonal green vegetables.
Serves 6

Duck Piquant

3 lb (1.3 kg) duck, cooked and
  jointed into 8 equal pieces
1 can **Baxters** Sweet and Sour
  Sauce
1 tablespoon (15 ml) black
  treacle
2 tablespoons (30 ml) tomato
  ketchup
1 dessertspoon (10 ml)
  Worcestershire sauce
raisins and chopped pistachio
  nuts to garnish

Arrange the duck pieces evenly in
a shallow roasting pan or cast iron
casserole. Pour the can of Sweet
and Sour sauce into a bowl and add
the treacle, tomato ketchup and
Worcestershire sauce. Pour this
mixture over the duck and roast for
15–20 minutes at 375°F, 190°C,
Gas Mark 5. Garnish with the
raisins and chopped pistachio nuts
and serve with boiled or fried
rice.   **Serves 4**

Gamekeeper's Stew

6–8 joints of game birds
  (pheasant, partridge, wood
  pigeon), previously roasted
a few sage leaves
2 small oranges, quartered
a few juniper berries
1 bay leaf
1 can **Baxters** Madeira Wine
  Sauce
3 tablespoons (45 ml) **Baxters**
  Cranberry Jelly
forcemeat balls and French
  bread croutons
a little butter for frying
watercress to garnish

Place the game bird joints in a
casserole dish with the sage,
oranges, juniper berries and bay
leaf. Pour the Wine Sauce into a
bowl, melt the Cranberry Jelly and
mix in well. Pour this mixture over
the game and stir in well. Cover
the casserole and cook for 45

minutes at 350°F, 180°C, Gas
Mark 4.
  Just before serving, fry the
forcemeat balls and croutons in the
butter. Add them to the dish and
garnish with the watercress.
  Serve with spiced cabbage,
brussels sprouts and creamed
potatoes.   **Serves 4–6**

Venison in Madeira 'Balmoral Style'

3–4 lb (1.3–1.8 kg) haunch of
  venison, well hung
juniper berries
allspice
peppercorns
cloves
8 oz (225 g) smoked bacon,
  chopped
1 can **Baxters** Madeira Wine
  Sauce
¼ pint (150 ml) sour cream
sprig of thyme

Rub a mixture of the ground
juniper berries, allspice,
peppercorns and cloves into the
venison and place in a deep
casserole. Leave uncovered in the
refrigerator for 2–3 days. The day
before cooking add the bacon and
can of Wine Sauce and leave for a
further night. To cook, cover the
casserole and put in the oven at
325°F, 160°C, Gas Mark 3, for
3 hours. When cooked, remove the
venison and slice on a serving
dish. To the sauce remaining in the
casserole add the sour cream and a
sprig of thyme. Gently reheat and
pour over the sliced venison.
  Serve with rowan jelly, a purée
of potato and celeriac, and fresh
vegetables. Delicious served cold
with spiced plums.   **Serves 6–8**

Bick'n Chicken Crêpes

8 pancakes
2 oz (50 g) butter
8 oz (225 g) cooked chicken, chopped
8 oz (225 g) mushrooms, washed and sliced
1 large onion, peeled and chopped
salt and pepper
1 packet white sauce mix
Bick's Corn Relish
parsley sprigs to garnish

Melt the butter in a saucepan, add the onions and mushrooms and sauté gently for 1–2 minutes. Add the chicken, salt and pepper and leave over a gentle heat until the chicken is warmed through. Prepare the white sauce and mix in some Corn Relish.

Divide the chicken filling between the pancakes, roll up and pour the sauce over. Brown under a hot grill.

Garnish with the parsley sprigs and serve with peas, potatoes, and Corn Relish. **Serves 4**

BIRDS EYE

Chicken and Mushroom Slices

1½ oz (40 g) butter
1½ oz (40 g) flour
½ pint (250 ml) milk
salt and pepper
4 oz (100 g) cooked chicken, diced
1 oz (25 g) cooked ham, chopped
2 oz (50 g) **Birds Eye** Sweetcorn
1 oz (25 g) **Birds Eye** Peas
2 oz (50 g) button mushrooms, sliced
2 sheets **Birds Eye** Puff Pastry, thawed
beaten egg to glaze

Melt the butter in a pan, add the flour and cook for 1 or 2 minutes. Remove from the heat and gradually add the milk, stirring continuously. Bring to the boil and cook for a further 2 minutes, stirring all the time. Season to taste then add the remaining ingredients. Roll out the pastry sheets to 10 in (25 cm) squares and divide the mixture between the two, placing it on one half of the pastry. In the other half of the pastry make diagonal slits about ¼ in (0.5 cm) from the edges. Dampen the edges and fold the slatted half over the filling. Seal well and crimp the edges. Brush with beaten egg, place on a baking tray and bake in an oven pre-heated to 425°F, 220°C, Gas Mark 7, for about 15–20 minutes or until risen and golden brown. **Serves 2**

Chicken Parcels

4 chicken quarters
2 oz (50 g) butter, melted
3 medium onions, peeled and sliced
4 tablespoons (60 ml) demerara sugar
4 oz (100 g) mushrooms, washed and sliced
½ packet (3 oz, 75 g) **Birds Eye** Sweetcorn
2 teaspoons (10 ml) vinegar
paprika pepper
8 oz (227 g) **Birds Eye** Potato Waffles

Cut 4 pieces of foil each large enough to cover a portion of chicken. Brush each piece of chicken with melted butter, dip the slices of onion in the sugar and divide them between the pieces of foil. Cover with mushrooms and sweetcorn. Place the chicken portions on top and sprinkle with vinegar and paprika. Lightly fold the foil over the chicken, place the parcels on a baking tray and bake in the centre of an oven pre-heated to 400°F, 200°C, Gas Mark 6, for about 45 minutes, or until the chicken is tender.

Serve with Potato Waffles, baked in the oven, and a vegetable of your choice.

For variety substitute a pork chop for the chicken. Remove the rind and top with rings of green pepper, onions, tomatoes, salt, pepper, a pinch of sage and slices of mature cheddar cheese. **Serves 4**

Blue Band

Savoury Chicken Crunch

12 oz (350 g) cooked chicken, diced
1 oz (25 g) flaked almonds
Cheese Sauce
2 oz (50 g) **Blue Band** Margarine
2 oz (50 g) plain flour
¾ pint (425 ml) milk
salt and pepper
2 oz (50 g) cheese, grated
Topping
2 oz (50 g) cheese, grated
2 oz (50 g) fresh breadcrumbs
1 teaspoon (5 ml) mixed herbs

Place the chicken and almonds in an ovenproof dish. Place all the ingredients for the sauce, except the cheese, in a saucepan. Stirring continuously, bring to the boil and cook gently until thickened and smooth. Add the cheese and seasoning. Pour the sauce over the chicken and mix together well. Bake in a hot oven at 400°F, 200°C, Gas Mark 6, for 35–40 minutes, until golden and bubbling.

Serve with vegetables or salad. Can be frozen without topping, or reheated. **Serves 4**

Chicken and Ham Pie

shortcrust pastry made with
    12 oz (350 g) flour
1 lb (450 g) raw chicken, cut
    into small cubes
    (approximately 3 chicken
    joints, with bones removed)
4 oz (100 g) lean uncooked
    gammon ham, cubed
2 teaspoons (10 ml) lemon juice
pinch dried thyme
salt and pepper
½ Chicken Cube from **Bovril**
    dissolved in 5 tablespoons
    (75 ml) water
1 egg, beaten

Roll out the pastry and use half to
line an 8 in (20 cm) pie plate. Mix
the chicken and ham with the
lemon juice, thyme, salt and
pepper. Put into the pastry case
and pour in the stock. Cover with
the remaining pastry and seal the
edges well. Use pastry trimmings
to make decorative 'leaves' for the
lid of the pie. Make a small hole in
the lid and brush over the top with
beaten egg. Bake at 400°F, 200°C,
Gas Mark 6, for 20 minutes, then
reduce the heat to 350°F, 180°C,
Gas Mark 4, for a further 40
minutes.

  Serve hot or cold. **Serves 4**

Country Chicken Pie

3 lb (1.4 kg) chicken, cut into
    quarters
bouquet garni
2 Chicken Cubes from **Bovril**,
    crumbled
1 oz (25 g) butter
3 oz (75 g) bacon, with rinds
    removed, chopped
1 large onion, peeled and cut
    into rings
1 oz (25 g) flour
4 sprigs tarragon, chopped
4 oz (100 g) mixed vegetables
8 oz (225 g) frozen puff pastry,
    thawed
beaten egg *or* milk to glaze

Place the chicken, bouquet garni
and 1 crumbled Bovril cube in a
saucepan, cover with water and
slowly bring to the boil. Cover and
simmer for 30 minutes. Remove
the chicken, extract the bones and
cut the flesh into chunks. Reserve
½ pint (300 ml) of the stock. Fry
the bacon and onion in the butter
for 5 minutes. Sprinkle over the
flour and cook for a further minute.
Gradually blend in the reserved
stock, tarragon, the second Bovril
cube and the mixed vegetables.
Bring to the boil, stirring all the
time, add the chicken and season
well. Transfer the mixture to a
2½ pint (1.5 litre) ovenproof dish.
Place a pie funnel in the middle of
the dish.

  Roll out the pastry to 1 in (3 cm)
larger than the dish. Cut off a ½ in
(1 cm) strip and place on the
dampened edge of the dish.
Dampen the edge of the remaining
pastry and place over the filling,
sealing firmly. Decorate the top
with the remaining pastry, cut into
leaf shapes, brush with the egg or
milk and bake at 400°F, 200°C,
Gas Mark 6, for about 20 minutes,
until golden. **Serves 6**

Farmhouse Chicken Bake

2 oz (50 g) butter
1 medium onion, finely
    chopped
2½ lb (1.25 kg) chicken
6 medium carrots, peeled and
    cut into thin strips
1 Chicken Cube from **Bovril**
    dissolved in 1 pint (600 ml)
    water
½ pint (300 ml) dry cider
3 oz (75 g) long grain rice
salt and pepper

Melt the butter and fry the onion
until soft and golden. Add the
chicken and fry until well browned
on all sides. Add the carrots, stock
and cider. Bring to the boil and
then cover and place in the oven at
325°F, 170°C, Gas Mark 3, for
45 minutes. Add the rice and bring
to the boil again. Season well,
cover and return to the oven for a
further 30 minutes. **Serves 4**

Roast Pheasant with Mushrooms

2 medium size pheasants
6–8 oz (175–225 g) mushrooms
4 oz (100 g) butter
6 rashers fat bacon
salt and pepper
1 Red Cube from **Bovril**
    dissolved in ½ pint (300 ml)
    water
1 oz (25 g) day-old
    breadcrumbs
2 oz (50 g) butter

Wipe the mushrooms but do not
wash or peel them. Put them
inside the pheasant with 2 oz
(50 g) butter, salt and pepper. Put
into a roasting tin and place the
bacon rashers over the birds'
breasts. Spread the remaining
butter on a piece of greaseproof
paper and cover the birds. Roast at
400°F, 200°C, Gas Mark 6, for
30 minutes. Remove the paper and
bacon, baste the birds with the pan
juices and continue roasting for a
further 15 minutes.

  When the pheasants are nearly
cooked, fry the breadcrumbs in the
butter over a low heat until crisp
and golden. Place the pheasants
and fried crumbs on a serving dish
and keep warm. Put the roasting
tin on to a low heat and add the
stock. Simmer and scrape the pan
juices until the gravy is richly
brown and hot, then transfer to a
sauceboat.

  Serve the pheasants with this
gravy and give each person a
portion of mushrooms from inside
the bird, and a portion of fried
crumbs. **Serves 6**

Turkey in Red Wine Sauce

1 tablespoon (15 ml) parsley, chopped
grated rind of ½ orange
1 bay leaf
1 sprig thyme
1 oz (25 g) butter
1 small onion, finely chopped
½ oz (15 g) plain flour
1 Red Cube from **Bovril** dissolved in ½ pint (300 ml) water
¼ pint (150 ml) red wine
1 lb (450 g) cold roast turkey slices
salt and pepper

Mix the parsley, orange rind, bay leaf and thyme together. Melt the butter, fry the onion gently, work in the flour and stir and cook over a low heat for 1 minute. Gradually stir in the stock and wine and stir until the mixture boils. Add the herb mixture and turkey slices. Cover and simmer for 30 minutes. Season to taste with salt and pepper. Remove the bay leaf before serving.

If liked, cold cooked duck, chicken or game may be used instead of turkey. **Serves 6**

Chicken in Cider with Apples

4 chicken portions
3 large cooking apples, peeled and chopped
1 pint (600 ml) **Bulmers** Dry Cider
2 bay leaves
salt and pepper
2 oz (50 g) butter
lemon slices to garnish

Put the chicken portions into a saucepan that will just hold them comfortably. Pack the apples around the chicken to fill the pan almost completely. Pour over the cider and add the bay leaves, salt,

pepper and butter. Cover and bring to the boil and simmer for one hour. Transfer the chicken to a dish and remove the bay leaves. Sieve or liquidise the remaining liquid, adjust the seasoning and pour over the chicken. Garnish with lemon slices. **Serves 4**

Rabbit and Cider Casserole

2 oz (50 g) streaky bacon
1 medium onion, peeled and finely chopped
1 oz (25 g) butter
1 rabbit, jointed
8 oz (225 g) small whole carrots, scraped *or* peeled
8 oz (225 g) small pickling onions, peeled and left whole
1 bottle **Bulmers** No 7 Cider (approx ½ pint (300 ml))
½ pint (300 ml) stock
2 bay leaves
salt and pepper
1 oz (25 g) cornflour
2–4 tablespoons (30–60 ml) single cream *or* top of the milk

Remove the rind from the bacon, cut into pieces and fry in the butter along with the chopped onion. Put the bacon and onion in a casserole dish and fry the rabbit joints in the same fat until browned. Add to the casserole with the carrots, whole onions, stock, bay leaves, salt and pepper. Cover and put into a moderate oven (350°F, 180°C, Gas Mark 5) for about 1½ hours or until the rabbit is tender. Just before serving blend the cornflour and cream together, add to the casserole and re-heat.

Serve with jacket potatoes.
Serves 4–5

Chicken and Asparagus Flan

8 in (20 cm) cooked pastry flan case
2 eggs, beaten

10½ oz (297 g) can **Campbell's** Condensed Asparagus Soup, undiluted
3 tablespoons (45 ml) milk
salt and pepper
8 oz (225 g) cooked chicken, chopped
3 oz (75 g) cheese, grated
1 tablespoon (15 ml) fresh parsley, chopped

Place the flan case on a baking tray. Combine all the other ingredients together, mixing well. Pour into the flan case, spreading the mixture so that the chicken is evenly distributed. Bake at 350°F, 180°C, Gas Mark 4, for 25–35 minutes until the filling has set.

Serve hot or cold. **Serves 6**

Chicken Vol-au-Vents

10½ oz (297 g) can **Campbell's** Condensed Cream of Chicken Soup
6 oz (175 g) cooked chicken, minced
salt and pepper
1 tablespoon (15 ml) parsley, chopped
8 medium *or* 4 large vol-au-vent cases

Mix the undiluted soup with the chicken, season well and stir in the chopped parsley. Bake the vol-au-vent cases and fill with the chicken mixture.

These may be served either hot or cold. If serving hot, heat the filling mixture thoroughly in a saucepan, stirring occasionally, while the vol-au-vent cases are cooking. **Serves 4**

Monday Pie

6 oz (175 g) cooked chicken
2 oz (50 g) peas
2 oz (50 g) carrots, sliced
2 oz (50 g) mushrooms, sliced
1 can **Chef** Chunky Soup, Chicken Flavour

1 teaspoon (5 ml) parsley,
  chopped
salt and pepper
1 oz (25 g) butter
4 oz (100 g) cheese, grated
12 oz (350 g) mashed potato

Layer the chicken pieces,
vegetables, soup and parsley in a
2 pint (1.2 litre) ovenproof dish.
Add the seasonings, butter and
2 oz (50 g) of the cheese to the
potato. Fork over the chicken.
Sprinkle the rest of the cheese on
top and bake for 20–25 minutes at
400°F, 200°C, Gas Mark 6, until
golden brown.   **Serves 4**

Poacher's Pot

12 oz (350 g) boneless rabbit
4 rashers streaky bacon
2 medium onions, peeled and
  cut into rings
1 tablespoon (15 ml) parsley,
  chopped
salt and pepper
1 can **Chef** Chunky Soup,
  Chicken Flavour

Cut the rabbit into small pieces.
Remove the rind from the bacon
and cut into ½ in (1 cm) pieces.
Place a layer of onion rings in the
bottom of an ovenproof dish,
reserving enough for the top layer.
Mix the rabbit, bacon, parsley, salt
and pepper and place on top of the
onion. Pour over the soup and
arrange the remaining onion rings
on top. Cook in the oven at 350°F,
180°C, Gas Mark 4, for 1½ hours.
  Serve with jacket potatoes.
Serves 4–5

Chesswood

Coq à la Champignon

1 medium onion, peeled and
  chopped
2 tablespoons (30 ml) oil
4 chicken portions
1 can **Chesswood** Sliced
  Mushrooms in Creamed
  Sauce
generous pinch dried mixed
  herbs

salt and freshly ground black
  pepper

Fry the onion until soft but not
browned and remove to a
casserole. Fry the chicken pieces in
the same oil until golden on both
sides. Put the chicken in the
casserole. Cover the chicken with
the Sliced Mushrooms in Creamed
Sauce and sprinkle over the dried
herbs. Season to taste. Cook with
the lid on for 1 hour in an oven
pre-heated to 350°F, 180°C,
Gas Mark 4.
  Serve with buttered noodles or
creamed potatoes. This dish may
be cooked in a large saucepan on
the hob if preferred, for
approximately 30–40 minutes.
Serves 4

Curry Puff

8 oz (200 g) prepared flaky
  pastry
1 can **Chesswood** Curry with
  Chicken and Mushrooms
a little beaten egg to glaze

Divide the pastry in half. Roll out
each half into an oblong shape
about 6 × 10 in (15 × 25 cm).
Spread the curry over the surface of
one oblong to within 1 in (2.5 cm)
of the edge and brush the pastry
edges with water. Fold the remaining pastry in half lengthways. Snip at 1 in (2.5 cm)
intervals along the folded side to
within 1 in (2.5 cm) of the edges.
Unfold and place on top of the
other piece of pastry and press the
edges firmly together. Brush with
beaten egg and place in the centre
of an oven pre-heated to 450°F,
230°C, Gas Mark 8, for 10–15
minutes.
  Serve hot with salad or other
vegetables.   **Serves 4**

CHIVERS

Sparkling Chicken Slice

1 **Chivers** Lemon Jelly, made up
  to ¾ pint (375 ml) only
¼ pint (125 ml) white wine
  vinegar

8 oz (200 g) cooked chicken
sliced tomatoes to garnish

Add the vinegar to the made-up
jelly and leave in a cold place or the
refrigerator until beginning to
thicken and almost set. Stir in the
neatly cut chicken and pour into a
1½ pint (900 ml) dish or mould,
previously rinsed with cold water.
Leave to set in the refrigerator. To
serve, quickly dip the container in
hot water to loosen the sides before
turning out on to a serving dish.
  Garnish with sliced tomatoes to
serve.   **Serves 4**

Colman's

Casseroled Chicken Pieces

1 chicken, quartered
2 oz (50 g) butter
1 head celery, chopped
1 green pepper, de-seeded and
  diced
½ pint (300 ml) chicken stock
1 packet **Colman's** Onion Sauce
  Mix
½ pint (300 ml) milk
2 tomatoes, peeled, de-seeded
  and chopped

Fry the chicken in the butter until
browned on all sides. Add the
celery and green pepper and fry
until softened but not browned.
Add the stock, cover and simmer
for 25 minutes. Make up the sauce
mix as directed, add to the casserole and cook for a further 25
minutes. Put into a serving dish
and garnish with the chopped
tomato.
  Serve with pasta shells or
rice.   **Serves 4**

Chicken with Mushroom and Celery

4 chicken pieces
1 oz (25 g) flour
salt and pepper
1 oz (25 g) butter
1 tablespoon (15 ml) cooking oil
½ head celery, cleaned and sliced
1 packet **Colman's** Mushroom Sauce Mix
½ pint (300 ml) milk
1 tablespoon (15 ml) parsley, chopped
toast triangles to serve
chopped parsley to garnish

Toss the chicken in a bag with the flour, salt and pepper. Melt the butter in a frying pan with the cooking oil and brown the chicken on all sides. Add the celery and quickly soften it in the fat. Meanwhile, make up the mushroom sauce as directed, using a large saucepan with a lid, add the chicken, celery and any juices from the frying pan. Cook, covered, over a low heat for 45 minutes.

Serve surrounded by toasted triangles of bread and sprinkled with parsley.   **Serves 4**

Chicken Picnic Pie

12 oz (350 g) shortcrust pastry
1 large chicken, uncooked
1 lb (450 g) sausagemeat
1 packet **Colman's** Seasoning Mix for Chicken
3 rashers streaky bacon, with rinds removed, diced
beaten egg to glaze

Line an 8 in (20 cm) diameter, deep cake tin with two-thirds of the pastry. Remove the chicken meat from the bone and cut into strips. Put a layer of chicken in the pie crust. Sprinkle with seasoning mix. Cover with a layer of sausagemeat then more seasoning mix, and another layer of chicken and mix. Finish with the bacon. Roll out the remaining third of pastry to form a lid. Dampen the edge and cover the pie, seal well and trim. Make the trimmings into pastry

decoration. Brush with beaten egg and prick the lid with a fork. Bake in a pre-heated oven at 400°F, 200°C, Gas Mark 6, for 40 minutes or until golden. Reduce the heat and bake for a further 1 hour at 325°F, 160°C, Gas Mark 3. Remove from the oven and cool. Chill before cutting.   **Serves 6–8**

Chicken Wine Pie

1 cooked chicken
1½ oz (35 g) butter
6 oz (150 g) mushrooms
3 oz (75 g) streaky bacon, cut into 1 in (2.5 cm) pieces
1 packet **Colman's** Coq au Vin Casserole Mix
7 oz (198 g) packet frozen puff pastry, thawed
egg *or* milk to glaze

Remove the chicken from the carcass and cut into 1–1½ in (2.5–4 cm) cubes. Melt the butter and fry the mushrooms and streaky bacon. Add the chicken, Coq au Vin Casserole Mix and ½ pint (300 ml) water. Bring to the boil and stir until thickened. Pour into a 1½ pint (900 ml) pie dish. Roll out the pastry 1 in (2.5 cm) larger than the rim of the pie dish. Trim off ¾ in (2 cm) of the pastry, dampen the edge of the dish, put the strip of pastry on the edge, brush with water and cover with the lid. Press to seal and decorate with any pastry trimmings. Prick with a fork, brush with the beaten egg or milk and bake at 375°F, 190°C, Gas Mark 5, for 35 minutes or until golden.   **Serves 6**

Rabbit Pie

4 lb (2 kg) rabbit, cut into serving pieces
2 tablespoons (30 ml) seasoned flour
2 oz (50 g) butter
8 oz (225 g) button mushrooms, washed
2 oz (50 g) streaky bacon, diced
1 packet **Colman's** Savoury White Sauce Mix
½ pint (300 ml) milk
8 oz (227 g) packet frozen puff pastry, thawed
milk *or* beaten egg to glaze

Toss the rabbit pieces with the seasoned flour. heat the butter in a heavy saucepan, add the rabbit pieces and fry until brown on all sides. Add the mushrooms and bacon and cook for a minute or two. Pour into a pie dish. Make up the sauce mix as directed and pour over the rabbit in the dish. Roll out the pastry to fit the dish. Dampen the edge, place on the dish, seal and trim. Use the trimmings to make pastry leaves. Brush with milk or beaten egg. Cook in the oven at 375°F, 190°C, Gas Mark 5, for 25 minutes. Reduce the heat to 300°F, 150°C, Gas Mark 2, cover the pie with a sheet of greaseproof paper and cook for 1 hour more or until the rabbit is cooked.
Serves 6

FRANK COOPER®

Chicken Fricassée

1 level teaspoon (5 ml) cornflour
1 can **Frank Cooper's** New England Chicken Soup with Sweetcorn
12 oz (300 g) cooked chicken, cubed
1 red *or* green pepper, deseeded and coarsely chopped
1 teaspoon (5 ml) soy sauce

Blend the cornflour with a little of the cold soup. Heat the remaining soup and stir in the cornflour, chicken, pepper and soy sauce. Bring to the boil, stirring, and simmer for a few minutes until heated through.

Serve with boiled rice or noodles.   **Serves 2–3**

Festive Turkey

2 tablespoons (30 ml) corn oil
1 small can pimentos, chopped
1 onion, finely chopped
½ oz (15 g) cornflour
½ pint (250 ml) chicken stock
6 tablespoons (90 ml) **Frank Cooper's** Cranberry Sauce
1 dessertspoon (10 ml) soy sauce

1 dessertspoon (10 ml) lemon
juice
12 oz (300 g) cooked turkey,
chopped
5 oz (125 g) water chestnuts,
sliced
6 oz (150 g) long grain rice,
cooked

Heat the corn oil and sauté the
pimentos and onion for 2–3
minutes. Stir in the cornflour,
stock, cranberry sauce, soy sauce
and lemon juice, bring to the boil
and simmer for 1 minute. Add the
turkey and water chestnuts and
continue to cook for a further 5
minutes.   Serve on a bed of rice.
Serves 3–4

Game Pie

12 oz (300 g) braising steak,
cubed
12 oz (300 g) piece gammon,
cubed
2 tablespoons (30 ml) cornflour
pepper
2 tablespoons (30 ml) corn oil
1 can **Frank Cooper's** Game
Soup
13 oz (370 g) packet puff pastry,
thawed *or* puff pastry made
with 6 oz (150 g) flour
beaten egg to glaze

Coat the steak and gammon with
the cornflour, seasoned with the
pepper. Heat the corn oil, brown
the meat, add the soup and bring
to the boil. Cover and simmer
gently for 1½ hours. Pour into a
pie dish and allow to cool. Cover
with the pastry, brush with the
beaten egg and cook at 425°F,
220°C, Gas Mark 7 for 25–30
minutes until golden brown.
Serves 4–6

Pigeon and Red Wine Sauce

2 young pigeons
2 level tablespoons (30 ml)
seasoned cornflour
2 tablespoons (30 ml) corn oil
1 onion, peeled and chopped
1 can **Frank Coopers'** Game
Soup
4 tablespoons (60 ml) red wine

Clean the pigeons and coat with
the cornflour. Heat the corn oil and
fry the pigeons until lightly
browned. Remove to a casserole
dish. Fry the onion until soft, add
any remaining cornflour, the soup
and red wine. Pour the sauce on to
the pigeons, cover and cook at
325°F, 170°C, Gas Mark 3 for
1 hour. Serve with boiled rice.
Serves 2

Turkey Pie

12 oz (300 g) cooked turkey *or*
chicken, cubed
1 can **Frank Cooper's** Turkey
Soup with Chestnut and
Cranberry
2 tablespoons (30 ml) stuffing
mix
12 oz (368 g) packet puff pastry,
thawed
egg for glazing

Mix together the turkey, soup and
stuffing mix and place in the base
of a 2 pint (1 litre) pie dish. Cover
with the pastry, brush with beaten
egg and cook at 425°F, 220°C, Gas
Mark 7, for 35–40 minutes until
golden brown.   **Serves 4–6**

Chicken Chasseur

2 oz (50 g) butter
2 tablespoons (30 ml) oil
4 chicken breasts
1 onion, finely chopped
1 clove garlic, crushed
4 oz (100 g) mushrooms, finely
sliced
4 tomatoes, skinned, with
seeds removed, diced
1 can **Crosse & Blackwell** Red
Wine Pour over Sauce
chopped parsley to garnish

Melt the butter and heat the oil in a
frying pan. Gently fry the chicken
breasts until tender. Remove and
keep hot. Leaving a little fat in
the pan, fry the onion and garlic
until soft. Add the mushrooms and
tomatoes and stir in the sauce.
Simmer gently for 2 minutes.
Arrange the chicken breasts on a

plate and pour over the sauce.
Sprinkle with parsley.   **Serves 4**

Chicken and Pasta Hot Pot

4 chicken joints
2 oz (50 g) butter *or* margarine
1 sachet **Maggi** French Onion
Soup
1 level tablespoon (15 ml)
cornflour
¾ pint (450 ml) water
15 oz (425 g) can **Crosse & Blackwell** Spaghetti Spirals

Fry the chicken joints in the butter
until golden brown. Meanwhile,
blend the soup powder with the
flour in a bowl and gradually add
the water. Pour over the chicken
joints and bring to the boil,
stirring continuously. Cover with
a tightly-fitting lid and simmer for
1 hour or until the chicken is
tender. Add the Spaghetti Spirals
to the pan, stir and reheat for 4
minutes before serving. **Serves 4**

Duck in Oriental Orange Sauce

4–5 lb (2–2.5 kg) duck, jointed
seasoned flour
butter for frying
2 medium onions, peeled and
chopped
4 oz (100 g) mushrooms,
washed and sliced
¼ pint (150 ml) stock
1 jar **Elsenham** Oriental Orange
Cooking Sauce

Coat the duck in the seasoned
flour. Fry in the butter until well
browned and then transfer to a
casserole dish. Fry the onions and
mushrooms for 3 minutes, add
them to the duck and pour on the
stock and Cooking Sauce. Cover
and cook at 325°F, 160°C, Gas Mark
3, for about 1½ hours or until
tender.

   Serve with boiled rice. To vary
the recipe, with equally delicious
results, use pork or chicken.
Serves 4–5

GALE'S

Roast Duck with Apple Stuffing

4½–5 lb (2–2.25 kg) duck
6 slices granary bread
1 lb (450 g) cooking apples,
    peeled and finely chopped
1 medium onion, peeled and
    finely chopped
1 teaspoon (5 ml) mixed herbs
2 tablespoons (30 ml) **Gale's**
    Honey
1 tablespoon (15 ml) sherry
1 oz (25 g) walnuts, chopped
    (optional)
salt and pepper

Remove the crusts from the bread
and crumble into large pieces.
Combine the apples and onion
with the bread. Add the other
ingredients and mix well together.
Stuff the duck with the mixture.
Prick the skin all over, rub the
outside of the duck with salt and
pepper and roast on a rack at 425°F,
220°C, Gas Mark 7, for 15 minutes
and then at 375°F, 190°C, Gas
Mark 5, allowing 15 minutes to the
pound plus 15 minutes over.
Serves 4

Roast Chicken with Walnut and Bacon Stuffing

4 oz (100 g) fresh breadcrumbs
4 oz (100 g) **Haywards** Pickled
    Walnuts, drained and
    chopped
4 oz (100 g) bacon, chopped
1 egg, beaten
3½ lb (1.5 kg) roasting chicken

Mix the breadcrumbs, walnuts,
bacon and egg together until well
blended. Place in the neck end of
the chicken and fold over the flap
of skin to hold the stuffing secure.
Cover the bird with foil and cook at
400°F, 200°C, Gas Mark 6, for 1½

hours. Open the foil and return the
chicken to the oven for a further
15 minutes to brown the skin.
Serves 4

Homepride

Chicken with Bacon and Bananas

4 chicken joints, about 8 oz
    (225 g) each (no larger)
1 sachet **Homepride** Coat &
    Cook, Southern Fried Flavour
2 large bananas
½ oz (15 g) butter, melted
4 rashers lean back bacon
12 oz (350 g) can sweetcorn

Wash the chicken and dry carefully.
Apply the Homepride Coat &
Cook according to the packet instructions. Place the coated chicken
in a grill pan and grill gently for
10 minutes under a pre-heated
grill. Turn over and cook for a
further 10 minutes.

Meanwhile, skin the bananas
and cut in half. Brush with the
melted butter. Cut the rinds off the
bacon and cut each rasher into
3 pieces. Stretch and roll up each
piece of bacon and thread on to 2
skewers. Add the bacon rolls and
bananas to the grill pan for the last
10 minutes. Heat the sweetcorn.
Lift the chicken, bacon rolls and
bananas on to a warm serving
dish.

Serve with the sweetcorn.
Serves 4

Chicken Marengo

4 chicken joints, skinned
2 oz (50 g) streaky bacon, with
    rinds removed, cut into 1 in
    (2.5 cm) pieces
1 can **Homepride** Tomato and
    Onion Cook-in-Sauce
2 oz (50 g) butter, softened
2 tablespoons (30 ml) parsley,
    chopped
1 small French loaf

Place the chicken portions in a
casserole dish, and place the bacon
pieces on top. Add the sauce, cover

and cook in the oven at 375°F,
190°C, Gas Mark 5 for 1½ hours.

Slice the loaf, mix the butter
with the parsley and spread the
mixture over both sides of each
slice and toast. Arrange the bread
around the edge of a shallow
serving dish and place the chicken
mixture in the centre.

Serve with green beans.
Serves 4

Crispy Pineapple Ginger Chicken

4 chicken portions
1 tablespoon (15 ml) lemon
    juice
1 tablespoon (15 ml) oil
1 sachet **Homepride** Coat &
    Cook, Southern Fried Flavour
15 oz (425 g) can pineapple
    rings, drained
½ teaspoon (2.5 ml) ground
    ginger
2 tablespoons (30 ml) soft light
    brown sugar

Wipe the chicken portions with
kitchen paper and place them in a
bowl with the lemon juice and oil.
Cover and leave for 30 minutes
then drain and dry the chicken.
Coat the chicken portions evenly
with the contents of the Coat &
Cook sachet. Place on a lightly
greased baking sheet and bake at
400°F, 200°C, Gas Mark 6, for
30 minutes. Add the pineapple
rings to the baking sheet, with the
ginger and sugar sprinkled on top.
Cook for a further 15 minutes until
the chicken portions are crisp and
golden brown and the pineapple is
sticky and glazed.

Serve immediately with
buttered pasta shells and a mixed
green salad.   **Serves 4**

Boxing Day Pie

13 oz (370 g) packet **Jus-rol**
    Shortcrust Pastry, thawed
13 oz (370 g) cooked Christmas
    meats (chicken, ham, turkey)
1 tablespoon (15 ml) parsley,
    chopped
1 tablespoon (15 ml) chicken
    stock
salt and pepper
beaten egg to glaze

Roll out two-thirds of the pastry
and use to line a 7 in (18 cm)
sandwich tin. Add the sliced meat
and chopped parsley in layers and
season well with salt and black
pepper. Moisten with the chicken
stock and cover with the remaining pastry, rolled out fairly thinly.
Use the pastry trimmings to
decorate the top of the pie and
glaze with beaten egg. Bake at
400°F, 200°C, Gas Mark 6, for 30–35
minutes until golden brown. Cool
for 10 minutes before removing
from the tin.   **Serves 6–8**

Chicken with Cream and Lemon

3–3½ lb (1½ kg) roasting
    chicken with giblets
¾ oz (18 g) butter
1 small lemon
dried thyme
1 medium onion, peeled and
    finely chopped
1 tablespoon (15 ml) flour
4 oz (100 g) **Kerrygold** Frozen
    Cream, thawed

Make a stock using ½ pint
(300 ml) water, the giblets, root
vegetables and seasoning. Put the
pared rind of ½ lemon, a good
pinch of dried thyme and
seasoning inside the chicken. Melt
the butter in a flameproof casserole

over a moderate heat and brown
the chicken slowly and thoroughly
all over. This may take 15–20
minutes. Remove from the pan
and keep warm. Cook the onion
slowly in the casserole. Replace the
chicken, add the juice of the lemon
and ¼ pint (125 ml) stock. Cover
the pan tightly, bring to the boil on
top of the stove and then put in a
very moderate oven, 325°F, 160°C,
Gas Mark 3, for 50–60 minutes or
until tender. Baste and turn from
time to time.

When the chicken is cooked,
remove from the pan and set on
one side. Skim the fat from the
liquid and mix with the flour. Add
the cream to the casserole, bring to
the boil, mix some of the hot liquid
with the flour paste and return to
the pan. Re-boil and reduce to
thicken if necessary.

Cut the chicken into joints, place
in a casserole, pour the sauce over
and return to the oven for a few
minutes to warm through. Serve
with rice or pasta and a green
vegetable or salad.   **Serves 4–5**

Turkey Breasts in Cider Cream Sauce

2 tablespoons (30 ml) oil
2 small onions, peeled and
    sliced
2 (8 oz, 225 g) turkey breasts
2 tablespoons (30 ml) plain
    flour
14 fl oz (400 ml) dry cider
salt and pepper
3 large red peppers, de-seeded
    and sliced
¼ pint (125 ml) **Kerrygold**
    Double Cream, thawed

Heat the oil in a frying pan. Add
the onions and fry until soft but
not brown. Cut the turkey breasts
into 8 pieces and coat in the flour.
Add to the pan and fry on all sides
until golden brown. Remove the
turkey from the pan. Stir in any
remaining flour and cook for
1 minute. Gradually add the cider,
stirring constantly. Season to taste
with salt and pepper and bring to
the boil. Return the turkey and
peppers to the pan. Reduce the
heat and simmer for 15–20

minutes, or until the turkey is
cooked. Remove from the heat and
stir in the cream.

Serve with buttered noodles.
Serves 4

Knorr

Chicken Pot Roast

2–3 tablespoons (30–45 ml) oil
3½ lb (1.5 kg) chicken
1 large onion, sliced
4 carrots, peeled and quartered
4 sticks celery, cut in 1 in
    (2.5 cm) pieces
4 rashers streaky bacon, cut in
    half
chicken giblets
3 tablespoons (45 ml)
    Worcestershire sauce
¼ pint (125 ml) **Knorr** chicken
    stock
salt and pepper
1 lb (400 g) potatoes, peeled
    and cut in 2 in (5 cm) chunks

Heat the oil in a large saucepan,
big enough to hold the chicken and
vegetables. Brown the chicken
lightly on all sides. Remove the
chicken from the pan and drain off
the oil. Arrange the onion, carrots,
celery, bacon, chicken and chicken
giblets in the pan, pour over the
sauce and stock. Season, cover the
pan and bring to the boil. Turn
down the heat and simmer for
1¼ hours. Add the potatoes and
simmer for a further hour. Remove
the giblets and serve.
Serves 4–6

Chicken with Sweetcorn and Bacon Stuffing

4 lb (1.8 kg) roasting chicken
4 rashers streaky bacon, chopped
6 oz (150 g) packet frozen sweetcorn
6 tablespoons (90 ml) parsley and thyme stuffing mix
6 tablespoons (90 ml) boiling water
6 tablespoons (90 ml) Madeira wine
grated rind of 1 lemon
2 oz (50 g) butter
salt and pepper
6 medium potatoes, peeled and quartered
6 carrots, peeled and quartered
6 parsnips, peeled and quartered
1 level tablespoon (15 ml) plain flour
½ pint (250 ml) **Knorr** chicken stock
watercress and bacon rolls to garnish

Wash and dry the chicken. Fry the bacon gently in a frying pan, add the sweetcorn and stir until thawed out, then add the stuffing mix, boiling water and Madeira wine. Cover and leave to absorb the liquid for 5 minutes. Use to stuff the chicken, then truss it. Place in a double roaster, spread with butter and season well. Cover and roast at 350°F, 180°C, Gas Mark 4 for 30 minutes. Remove the lid, baste and add the vegetables. Cook for 1 hour longer, turning the vegetables over once. Remove the chicken to a serving dish. Arrange the vegetables around and keep hot. Pour off most of the fat. Put the roasting pan on a medium heat, stir in the flour and cook, stirring until browned. Stir in the stock and bring to the boil to make the gravy.

Serve at once, garnished with the watercress and bacon rolls.
Serves 4

Country Chicken

2 tablespoons (30 ml) oil

4 chicken joints
2 carrots, peeled and sliced
2 leeks, washed and sliced
1 small cauliflower, cut into florets
½ pint (250 ml) **Knorr** chicken stock
salt and pepper

Heat the oil in a frying pan and brown the chicken until golden brown all over. Place in an ovenproof casserole dish with the carrots, leeks and cauliflower. Pour over the stock and season well. Cook at 350°F, 180°C, Gas Mark 4 for 1 hour.   **Serves 4**

Savoury Chicken

3 tablespoons (45 ml) oil
4 chicken joints, skinned
8 oz (200 g) chipolata sausages
1½ lb (600 g) white cabbage, shredded
1 cooking apple, sliced
1 tablespoon (15 ml) cornflour
½ pint (250 ml) **Knorr** chicken stock
½ pint (250 ml) cider

Heat the oil in a frying pan and brown the chicken and sausages all over. Place the cabbage, apple, chicken and sausages in an ovenproof casserole. Add the cornflour to the frying pan with the stock and cider, stirring all the time. Bring to the boil and pour over the chicken. Cover and cook at 350°F, 180°C, Gas Mark 4 for about 1 hour.

Serve with carrots and roast potatoes.   **Serves 4**

LEA & PERRINS

Chicken Fiesta

4 tablespoons (60 ml) thick mayonnaise
¼ pint (150 ml) double cream, whisked until thick
2 level teaspoons (10 ml) **Lea & Perrins** Concentrated Curry Sauce

1 level tablespoon (15 ml) apricot jam
12 oz (350 g) cooked chicken, coarsely chopped
4 oz (100 g) grapes, halved and de-seeded
salt and pepper
watercress sprigs to garnish

Fold the mayonnaise into the whisked cream and fold in the concentrated curry sauce and apricot jam. Stir in the chicken and grapes and season to taste. Serve chilled, garnished with the watercress sprigs.   **Serves 4**

Poacher's Stew with Oatmeal Dumplings

1 oz (25 g) lard
1 large onion, chopped
2 lb (1 kg) rabbit, cut into 8 pieces
1 oz (25 g) flour
½ pint (250 ml) chicken stock
2 tablespoons (30 ml) **Lea & Perrins** Worcestershire Sauce
salt and pepper
Dumplings
3 oz (75 g) self-raising flour
large pinch salt
1 oz (25 g) fine oatmeal
1½ oz (40 g) shredded suet
3–4 tablespoons (50–60 ml) cold water

Heat the lard in a large pan and fry the onions gently for 5 minutes. Coat the rabbit in flour and add to the pan. Fry for 5 minutes, turning the meat frequently. Add the stock and Worcestershire Sauce and bring to the boil, stirring occasionally. Season, reduce the heat, cover and simmer gently for 1 hour.

For the dumplings, sift together the flour and salt and stir in the oatmeal. Add the suet and mix to a soft dough with water. Shape into 8 balls, approximately 1½ in (4 cm) in diameter. Add these to the stew and continue to simmer for 20–25 minutes until the dumplings are risen and cooked.
Serves 4

Poussin with Country Stuffing

Stuffing
½ oz (15 g) butter
1 large onion, finely chopped
3 oz (75 g) fresh white
  breadcrumbs
4 oz (100 g) button mushrooms,
  finely chopped
¼ teaspoon (1.25 ml) dried
  thyme
2 teaspoons (10 ml) **Lea &
  Perrins** Worcestershire Sauce
3 tablespoons (45 ml) fresh
  parsley, chopped
salt and pepper

4 poussins (baby chickens each
  weighing 12 oz–1 lb (350–
  450 g) or 2 slightly larger ones
  split in half before serving
1 oz (25 g) softened butter
¾ pint (400 ml) chicken stock
salt and pepper
Sauce
1 teaspoon (5 ml) tomato purée
2 teaspoons (10 ml) **Lea &
  Perrins** Worcestershire Sauce
salt and pepper
watercress sprigs to garnish

For the stuffing, heat the butter in
a pan, add the onion and fry gently
until soft, about 5 minutes.
Remove from the heat and mix
together with all the remaining
stuffing ingredients. Use to stuff
the poussins. Place the poussins in
a roasting pan and spread the
breasts with the softened butter.
Pour the chicken stock into the
roasting pan and season the
poussins. Roast at 375°F, 190°C,
Gas Mark 5, for 1 hour. Remove
from the pan and keep warm.
  For the sauce, pour the cooking
liquid from the pan into a
saucepan, add the tomato purée
and Worcestershire Sauce. Bring to
the boil and reduce to give about
¼ pint (150 ml). Check the
seasoning.
  To serve, garnish the poussins
with the watercress sprigs and
hand the sauce separately.
Serves 4

Spicy Creamed Chicken

1 lb (500 g) cooked chicken
½ pint (250 ml) mayonnaise
2 tablespoons (30 ml) **Lea &
  Perrins** Worcestershire Sauce
1 tablespoon (15 ml) single
  cream (optional)
½ oz (15 g) onion, finely grated
  or chopped
½ oz (15 g) stuffed green
  olives, sliced
salt and pepper
½ green pepper, sliced into
  rings

Cut the chicken into bite sized
cubes. Blend together the
mayonnaise, Worcestershire
Sauce and cream, if used. Stir in
the chicken, onion, olives and
seasoning. Transfer to a serving
dish and garnish with the green
pepper rings.   **Serves 6**

Wiltshire Rabbit & Bacon Pie

1 lb (500 g) rabbit, jointed
¾ pint (400 ml) chicken stock
2 tablespoons (30 ml) oil
1 large onion, peeled and sliced
1 oz (25 g) flour
1 tablespoon (15 ml) **Lea &
  Perrins** Worcestershire Sauce
1 lb (500 g) cooked bacon joint,
  cubed
7½ oz (212 g) can butter beans,
  drained
salt and pepper
7½ oz (212 g) pack frozen puff
  pastry, thawed
beaten egg *or* milk to glaze

Place the jointed rabbit and stock
in a pan. Cover and simmer for
30 minutes until the rabbit is
tender. Reserve the stock and
remove meat from the bones. Heat
the oil in a large pan, add the onion
and fry gently until soft, about
5 minutes. Stir in the flour and
cook for 1 minute. Remove from
the heat and gradually add the
reserved stock and Worcestershire
Sauce, stirring well between each
addition. Add the cooked rabbit
meat and cooked bacon. Stir in the
butter beans and season to taste.
Transfer the mixture to a 3 pint
(1.8 litre) pie dish and leave to
cool.
  Roll out the pastry on a floured
surface to just over 1 in (2 cm)
larger than the top of the pie dish
and cut a ½ in (1 cm) strip from
the edge. Dampen the pie dish
edge and place the strip around it.
Brush the pastry strip with water
and cover the pie with pastry lid.
Seal the edge and flute. Decorate
the top of the pie with pastry
'leaves' made from trimmings.
Glaze with beaten egg or milk and
bake at 400°F, 200°C, Gas Mark 6
for 30 minutes, until pastry is
golden brown and well risen.
Serves 6

Mazola

Cheddar Fried Chicken

4 small chicken portions,
  (boned breasts are ideal)
1 egg, beaten
6 tablespoons (90 ml) fresh
  breadcrumbs
1 oz (50 g) Cheddar cheese,
  finely grated
½ level teaspoon (2.5 ml) dry
  mustard
Mazola pure corn oil for frying

Skin the chicken portions and trim
off any excess fat. Dip the portions
into the beaten egg and then coat
in a mixture of the breadcrumbs,
cheese and mustard. Heat the corn
oil in a deep fryer to 375°F, 190°C
and fry the chicken for 7–8 minutes
until crisp and golden brown.
Drain on kitchen paper and serve
hot or cold.   **Serves 4**

Nestlé

Blanquette of Chicken

1½ lb (600 g) boneless chicken
2 onions, sliced
1 bouquet garni
1 pint (500 ml) chicken stock
2½ oz (62 g) butter
2 oz (50 g) flour
1 small can **Nestlés** Ideal Milk
2 egg yolks, beaten
juice of 1 lemon
crisp bacon rolls, watercress
    and lemon slices to garnish

Put the chicken, onions, bouquet garni and stock in a saucepan, bring to the boil, cover and simmer gently for about 1½ hours or until tender. Strain off the liquid and make up to 1 pint (500 ml) with water. Cut the meat into bite size pieces and keep hot. Blend together the butter, flour and the stock, bring to the boil, stirring continuously, and simmer for 2 minutes. Add the Ideal Milk and the egg yolks and reheat but do not boil. Pour over the meat and garnish with bacon rolls, watercress and lemon slices cut into 'butterflies'.

Serve with savoury rice. This dish can also be made using diced leftover turkey and stock made from the turkey carcass.
Serves 4–6

Chicken in Cream Sauce

1 clove garlic (optional)
2 oz (50 g) butter
4 chicken joints
6 tablespoons (90 ml) wine
    vinegar *or* malt vinegar
4 tablespoons (60 ml) tomato
    purée
1 teaspoon (5 ml) sugar
6 teaspoons (30 ml) French
    mustard
1 teaspoon (5 ml)
    Worcestershire sauce
4 oz (100 g) can **Nestlé's** Cream

Peel the garlic if used and place in a large flameproof casserole with the butter. Melt the butter over a moderate heat and fry the pieces of chicken until well browned. Reduce the heat and fry for a further 10 minutes. Add the vinegar, cover and cook gently for 10 minutes. Remove the chicken pieces from the casserole and keep hot. Discard the garlic. Mix the tomato purée, sugar, French mustard and Worcestershire sauce together, stir the mixture into the juices remaining in the casserole and simmer until reduced by about a quarter. Stir in the cream and simmer, without boiling, for 2–3 minutes. Pour the sauce over the chicken pieces and serve immediately. **Serves 4**

Anniversary Turkey

1 small onion, peeled and
    chopped
a little butter for frying
½ clove garlic, crushed
1 tablespoon (15 ml) tomato
    purée
½ level teaspoon (2.5 ml) curry
    powder
2 tablespoons (30 ml) lemon
    juice
2 tablespoons (30 ml) apricot
    jam
1 Chicken **Oxo** Cube, crumbled
¼–½ pint (150–300 ml)
    mayonnaise
12 oz–1 lb (350–450 g) cooked
    turkey, chopped
8 oz (225 g) grapes, green and
    black mixed, halved and
    de-seeded
salt and pepper to taste
1½ oz (40 g) flaked almonds,
    toasted
sprigs watercress *or* parsley to
    garnish

Sauté the onion gently in the butter with the garlic for 5 minutes or until soft, then add the tomato purée, curry powder, 1 tablespoon (15 ml) of the lemon juice, the apricot jam and the crumbled Oxo cube. Heat gently until the jam has melted, then sieve or liquidise. Leave to cool then stir into the mayonnaise and fold in the turkey. Cover and chill in the refrigerator overnight.

When ready to serve, toss the grapes in the remaining lemon juice and stir into the turkey mayonnaise, taste and check the seasoning. Pile into a serving dish and sprinkle with the almonds. Garnish with the watercress or parsley sprigs. **Serves 6**

Canadian Chicken Supreme

1 level teaspoon (5 ml) ground
    nutmeg
3 lb (1.3 kg) chicken, cut into
    4 pieces
2 oz (50 g) butter
½ level teaspoon (2.5 ml) dried
    tarragon
salt and pepper
4 tablespoons (60 ml) dry white
    wine
4 tablespoons (60 ml) single
    cream *or* top of the milk
4 rounded tablespoons (80 ml)
    fresh chives, chopped
8 oz (225 g) long grain rice
3 medium carrots, peeled and
    grated
2 Red **Oxo** Cubes, crumbled
    and dissolved in 1 pint
    (600 ml) hot water

Rub the nutmeg into the chicken joints, melt 1½ oz (40 g) of the butter in a large pan and brown the chicken. Sprinkle the tarragon and seasoning on top. Add the white wine and cream or top of the milk. Bring to the boil, cover and simmer gently for 20 minutes. Add the chives and simmer gently for a further 30 minutes, or until the chicken is tender. Cook rice and carrots in the Oxo stock for about 20 minutes, until all the liquid has been absorbed. Stir the remaining butter into the rice mixture. Arrange the rice on a serving dish with the chicken joints and pour the sauce on top. **Serves 4**

Chicken Pie Romanoff

1½ oz (40 g) margarine
4 oz (100 g) mushrooms,
    washed and quartered
1 oz (25 g) flour
2 Chicken **Oxo** Cubes,
    crumbled and dissolved in
    ½ pint (275 ml) hot water
¼ pint (150 ml) single cream
3 lb (1.3 kg) roasting chicken,
    cooked and boned
2 green peppers, de-seeded and
    sliced, blanched for
    2 minutes in boiling water
salt and pepper
lemon juice
6 oz (175 g) flaky *or* rough puff
    pastry, well chilled
beaten egg *or* milk to glaze

Melt ½ oz (15 g) margarine and
sauté the mushrooms. Remove
from the pan and keep warm. Place
the remaining 1 oz (25 g)
margarine, the flour and Chicken
Oxo in a saucepan over a moderate
heat. Bring to the boil, whisking
continuously. Cook for 2–3
minutes, still whisking, until
thickened, smooth and glossy.
Add the cream, cubed chicken,
mushrooms and green peppers.
Season to taste and add the lemon
juice. Pour into a 2 pint (1.2 litre)
pie dish and leave to cool.

   Roll out the chilled pastry to 1 in
(2.5 cm) larger than the pie dish.
Cut off narrow strips round the
edge of the pastry. Damp the rim of
the dish and edge with the pastry
strips. Damp the strips and cover
the filling with the remaining
pastry, pressing down gently to
seal the edges. Flute the edges,
make a hole in the centre of the pie
and decorate the top of the pie with
pastry leaves made from the
trimmings. Glaze with the beaten
egg or milk and bake on the second
shelf from the top of the oven at
425°F, 220°C, Gas Mark 7, for
30–40 minutes, until risen, crisp
and browned.   **Serves 4**

Roast Garlic Chicken

1 onion, peeled and finely
    chopped
salt and pepper

2 oz (50 g) fresh white
    breadcrumbs
2 tablespoons (30 ml) fresh
    parsley, chopped
½ teaspoon (2.5 ml) dried
    thyme
grated rind of ½ lemon
2 oz (50 g) garlic sausage, finely
    chopped
1 egg, beaten
3 lb (1.3 kg) oven-ready
    chicken
1½ oz (40 g) margarine
2 tablespoons (30 ml) flour
2 Chicken **Oxo** Cubes,
    crumbled and dissolved in
    ⅔ pint (400 ml) hot water
2 tablespoons (30 ml) lemon
    juice
parsley sprigs and rolls of garlic
    sausage to garnish

Combine the onion, seasoning,
breadcrumbs, parsley, thyme,
lemon rind and garlic sausage and
bind together with the egg. Use to
stuff the neck end of the chicken.
Secure and truss the bird then
weigh it. Place in a roasting tin,
season lightly and dot the
margarine all over the skin. Roast
in the middle of a fairly hot oven
(400°F, 200°C, Gas Mark 6) for
about 1¼ hours (allowing 15–20
minutes per lb (450 g) , plus 20
minutes over) until tender, basting
several times. Remove the bird to a
serving dish and keep warm. Stir
the flour into 2 tablespoons (30 ml)
of the pan juices then slowly add
the Chicken Oxo and the lemon
juice. Bring to the boil, season to
taste and simmer for 2–3 minutes
before serving with the chicken.
Garnish with the parsley and rolls
of garlic sausage.   **Serves 4**

Two Fruit Duck

3 oz (75 g) packet **Paxo** Sage and
    Onion Stuffing Mix
½ grapefruit
grated rind of 1 orange
oven ready duck, approx. 4 lb
    (2 kg) in weight

salt
orange slices to garnish

Make up the stuffing as directed on
the packet. Remove the pith and
membranes from the grapefruit,
chop the flesh and add to the
stuffing mix with the orange rind.
Mix well. Stuff the duck, weigh
and calculate the cooking time
allowing 30 minutes per lb (450 g).
Prick the skin deeply all over with
a fork, sprinkle the breast with salt
and roast at 375°F, 190°C, Gas
Mark 5.   **Serves 4**

SCHWARTZ

Hot Mexicano Turkey

1 tablespoon (15 ml) cooking
    oil
8 oz (227 g) onions, peeled and
    sliced
12 oz (340 g) cold cooked
    turkey, cut into chunks
1 packet **Schwartz** Spice'n'Easy
    Mix for Chili con Carne
14 oz (396 g) can tomatoes
14 oz (396 g) can baked beans in
    tomato sauce
¼ pint (142 ml) stock
¼ pint (142 ml) natural yoghurt
    (optional)

Using a large saucepan, fry the
onions in the oil until soft and just
beginning to colour. Stir in all the
remaining ingredients except the
yoghurt. Cover and simmer gently
for 20 minutes. If a less hot chili
flavour is required, stir in the
yoghurt in swirls at the end of the
cooking time.

   Serve with jacket potatoes or
crusty bread. Do not reheat this
dish. Not suitable for freezing.
Serves 4

Stir Fry Turkey

4 oz (113 g) butter
15 oz (425 g) can pineapple
  pieces
14 oz (396 g) can bean shoots *or*
  use 8 oz (225 g) fresh if
  available
1 each red and green pepper,
  de-seeded and very thinly
  sliced
4 oz (113 g) mushrooms, wiped
  and thinly sliced
4 oz (113 g) celery, thinly sliced
12 oz (340 g) cooked turkey, cut
  into thin strips
1 tablespoon (15 ml) **Schwartz**
  Minced Onion
1 oz (28 g) cornflour
2 tablespoons (30 ml) soy sauce
2 tablespoons (30 ml) clear
  honey
½ teaspoon (2.5 ml) **Schwartz**
  Ground Ginger
¼ teaspoon **Schwartz** Garlic
  Granules
½ teaspoon (2.5 ml) **Schwartz**
  Ground Black Pepper
salt to taste
toasted almond flakes to
  garnish

Melt the butter over a low heat in a
large frying pan or wok. Drain the
pineapple pieces and reserve the
juice. If using tinned bean shoots
drain and discard the liquid. Add
the pineapple pieces, bean shoots,
peppers, mushrooms, celery,
turkey and minced onion to the
frying pan. Fry very quickly,
stirring, for just long enough to
heat the turkey. Blend the cornflour with the pineapple juice, soy
sauce, clear honey, ginger, garlic
and black pepper. Pour over the
frying pan mixture and bring to
the boil, stirring. Add salt to taste.
Serve immediately while the vegetables are still crisp and crunchy,
garnished with the toasted almond
flakes. Serve with boiled rice. This
dish should not be reheated and is
not suitable for freezing.
Serves 4

Stuffed Duck with Orange and Cranberry Sauce

4 lb (1.8 kg) duck
8 oz (227 g) fresh white
  breadcrumbs
2 oz (57 g) shredded suet
1 tablespoon (15 ml) **Schwartz**
  Ground Coriander
2 teaspoons (10 ml) **Schwartz**
  Marjoram
1 teaspoon (5 ml) **Schwartz**
  Onion Salt
¼ teaspoon **Schwartz** Ground
  Black Pepper
1 orange
1 egg (size 3), beaten
½ oz (14 g) cornflour
½ pint (285 ml) fresh,
  unsweetened orange juice
9 oz (255 g) **Ocean Spray**
  Cranberry Sauce
sugar to taste (optional)
watercress and 2 cutlet frills to
  garnish

To make the stuffing, combine the
breadcrumbs, suet, coriander,
marjoram, onion salt and pepper.
Remove the rind and juice from
half the orange and add to the stuffing. Mix in the egg until all
ingredients are thoroughly combined. Use to stuff the duck at the
tail end. Sprinkle the breast with
salt and pepper. Weigh, place in a
roasting tin with a little oil, cover
with foil and cook for 30 minutes
per lb (450 g) in the oven, pre-
heated to 375°F, 190°C, Gas
Mark 5. If necessary, remove the
foil half an hour before the end of
the cooking time so that the skin
becomes crisp and golden. Meanwhile, to make the sauce, place the
cornflour in a small saucepan.
Blend in the orange juice, cranberry sauce and sugar if used.
Bring to the boil, stirring.

  Place the duck on a carving dish,
spoon over a little of the sauce and
serve the remainder separately.
Garnish by arranging orange
slices, cut from the remaining half
orange, on top of the duck. Place
the cutlet frills on the leg ends and
watercress around the sides. The
cooked duck may be stored for up

to 2 days in a refrigerator, and the
meat, off the bone, for up to
1 month in a freezer.   **Serves 4**

Sweet and Sour Fritters

4 oz (125 g) plain flour
salt
1 tablespoon (15 ml) oil
¼ pint (150 ml) water
½ teaspoon (2.5 ml) baking
  powder
12 oz (340 g) can pineapple
  chunks
1 tablespoon (15 ml) soya sauce
¼ pint (150 ml) **Schweppes**
  Ginger Cordial
5 tablespoons (100 ml) wine
  vinegar
1 tablespoon (20 ml) sugar
1½ tablespoons (300 ml)
  cornflour
1 green pepper, de-seeded and
  cut into chunks
12 oz (350 g) uncooked chicken,
  cut into bite sized pieces
deep fat *or* oil for frying

Sieve the flour with a good pinch
of salt into a bowl and gradually
blend in the oil and water until
smooth, then beat hard. Leave the
batter to stand while preparing the
rest of the recipe. Place the
pineapple and juice from the can,
the soya sauce, cordial, vinegar
and sugar into a pan and bring to
the boil. Blend the cornflour with a
little water then stir into the
pineapple mixture and bring to the
boil, stirring until thick and
smooth. Add the green pepper to
the sauce and keep warm. Stir the
baking powder into the batter then
dip the chicken pieces in it and fry
in deep fat or oil until golden
brown and cooked through. Drain
thoroughly on kitchen paper.

  Serve, with the sauce poured
over, on a bed of rice.   **Serves 4**

Sharwood's

Clementine Duck

5–6 lb (2.5–3 kg) duck
Stuffing
1 onion, peeled and diced
2 cloves garlic, crushed
3 tomatoes, chopped
6 oz (150 g) **Sharwood's**
 Basmati Rice, cooked
1 heaped teaspoon (15 g)
 Sharwood's Mild *or* Medium
 Curry Powder
4 oz (100 g) duck *or* chicken
 livers, chopped
grated rind and juice of
 1 orange
grated rind and juice of 1 lime
1 teaspoon (5 ml) salt
slices of orange and lime to
 garnish

Using a sharp knife, slice the meat away from the bones, starting at the central backbone and working down each side. When the knuckle joints are reached, break the bone away. Cut the rib bones with scissors and pull the rib cage away. Mix the stuffing and place in the cavity. Reshape the duck, securing top and bottom with wooden cocktail sticks. Prick the skin thoroughly. Roast for 1½–2 hours at 400°F, 200°C, Gas Mark 6. Garnish with the orange and lime slices to serve.
Serves 6 as a main dish

Devilled Chicken

Dry devil mixture
3 teaspoons (15 ml)
 Sharwood's Vencat Curry
 Powder
1 teaspoon (5 ml) dry mustard
1 teaspoon (5 ml) ground
 ginger
1 teaspoon (5 ml) salt

2 teaspoons (10 ml) sugar
good pinch black pepper
4 chicken quarters, skinned
Devilled sauce
1 tablespoon (15 ml)
 Sharwood's Green Label
 Mango Chutney
1 tablespoon (15 ml) tomato
 ketchup
1 tablespoon (15 ml) brown
 sauce
1 tablespoon (15 ml)
 Worcestershire sauce
1 tablespoon (15 ml)
 Sharwood's Soy Sauce
dash of Tabasco sauce
1 can **Sharwood's** Sweetcorn
 and watercress to serve

Mix together the ingredients for the dry devil mixture, sprinkle over the chicken quarters and allow to stand for 1 hour. Sprinkle with a little oil, cover and bake for 15 minutes at 400°F, 200°C, Gas Mark 6. Reduce the oven heat to 350°F, 180°C, Gas Mark 4. Make up the devilled sauce and spoon over the chicken quarters. Cover and bake for a further 30 minutes, basting occasionally.

 Serve on a bed of sweetcorn and garnish with watercress.
Serves 4

Sweet and Sour Chicken

oil for frying
1 teaspoon (5 ml) salt
3 chicken portions
10½ oz (297 g) can **Sharwood's**
 Sweet and Sour Sauce
1 lb 3 oz (539 g) can
 Sharwood's Whole Apricots,
 drained, halved and stoned
few toasted flaked almonds to
 garnish

Heat the oil in a frying pan, sprinkle the oil with the salt, then add the chicken portions and cook for 15–20 minutes. Drain the chicken well, then remove all the flesh. Heat the sweet and sour sauce, add the apricots and pieces of chicken and simmer for 5–10 minutes. Sprinkle with almonds to serve. **Serves 3**

SHIPPAMS

Chunky Chicken Surprise

approx 8 oz (225 g) cooked
 potato, mashed with butter,
 salt and pepper and the yolk
 of an egg
14½ oz (418 g) can **Shippams**
 Chunky Chicken in Savoury
 White Sauce
2 dessertspoons (20 ml)
 Parmesan cheese, grated
2 dessertspoons (20 ml) crisp
 breadcrumbs
1 oz (25 g) butter

Pipe or fork the mashed potato round the edges of 4 individual ovenproof dishes, or one large dish. Heat the Chunky Chicken in a saucepan and, when hot, pour into the centre of the mashed potato. Mix together the cheese and breadcrumbs and sprinkle over the chicken, dot with the butter and put under a hot grill until lightly browned. Serve immediately. **Serves 4**

Savoury Pancakes

4 large *or* 8 small pancakes
4 oz (100 g) cooked mixed
 vegetables
2 (7¼ oz, 205 g) cans **Shippams**
 Chunky Chicken in Barbecue
 Sauce
slices of grilled tomato to
 garnish

Prepare the pancakes in the usual way and keep hot on a plate over a saucepan of hot water. Heat the vegetables and Chicken in Barbecue Sauce gently together in a saucepan. When hot, divide the mixture equally between the pancakes and roll up. Place in a hot serving dish and garnish with slices of grilled tomato.
Serves 4

Crispy Topped Pie

1 onion, peeled and chopped
2 oz (50 g) mushrooms, wiped
 and sliced
2 oz (50 g) margarine
2 oz (50 g) **Marvel**, made up to
 1 pint (500 ml) with water
8 oz (200 g) cooked chicken
1 teaspoon (5 ml) lemon juice
salt and pepper
1 large packet **Smash** Potato
 Pieces
3 oz (75 g) cheese, grated
a little butter

Gently fry the onions and the
mushrooms in the margarine until
soft. Stir in the flour and then the
liquid Marvel, to make a sauce. Stir
in the chicken, lemon juice and
seasoning to taste. Empty the
mixture into a greased ovenproof
dish. Make up the Smash, mix in
the cheese and a little butter. Fork
or pipe the potato over the chicken
mixture, making it nice and
knobbly. Bake in a fairly hot oven,
400°F, 200°C, Gas Mark 6 for 25–30
minutes until crisp and golden
brown.

 Serve hot. Leftover cooked
vegetables can be added to this
recipe for variety.   **Serves 4**

Savoury Envelopes

1 medium packet **Smash** Potato
 Pieces
10½ oz (297 g) can condensed
 celery soup
1 level teaspoon (5 ml) curry
 paste
6 oz (150 g) cooked chicken, cut
 into fairly big pieces
8 cooked pancakes, made from
 ½ pint (250 ml) batter
2 eggs, beaten
dried breadcrumbs to coat
fat or oil for frying

Make up the Smash, following the
directions on the packet. Mix in
the undiluted soup, curry paste
and the chicken. Divide the mix-

ture evenly between the pancakes
and fold into a square or triangular
shape. Coat in the beaten egg and
breadcrumbs, pressing the crumbs
on firmly. Fry the envelopes for
about 5 minutes in deep or shallow
fat or oil until they are golden
brown all over, turning as
necessary. Drain well on kitchen
paper before serving hot.
Serves 4

Stork

Chicken with Herbs

4 chicken portions
2 tablespoons (30 ml) seasoned
 flour
2 teaspoons (10 ml) fresh sage,
 chopped
2 oz (50 g) **Stork** Margarine
2 oz (50 g) bacon, derinded and
 chopped
¼ pint (150 ml) dry white wine
½ pint (275 ml) chicken stock
2 tomatoes, skinned and
 chopped
2 teaspoons (10 ml) tomato
 purée
12 sage leaves, roughly
 chopped
salt and pepper
1 tablespoon (15 ml) cornflour

Remove the skin from the chicken
portions. Coat each portion with
seasoned flour. Melt the Stork and
fry the chicken and bacon until
golden brown. Add the remaining
ingredients except the cornflour.
Bring to the boil and transer to an
ovenproof dish. Place in the centre
of a preheated oven (350°F, 180°C,
Gas Mark 4) for ¾ to 1 hour until

the chicken is cooked. Blend the
cornflour with a little water and
add to the chicken. Bring just to
boiling point, stirring until
thickened.   **Serves 4**

Chicken with Mandarin Sauce

3 lb (1.3 kg) chicken
2 oz (50 g) butter
10½ oz (297 g) can **John West**
 Mandarin Oranges
1 level tablespoon (15 ml)
 cornflour
juice and rind of 1 lemon
4 tablespoons (60 ml)
 blackcurrant jelly
4 oz (100 g) cranberries (fresh
 or frozen)

Rub the chicken with the butter
and roast at 325°F, 160°C,
Gas Mark 3 for 1¼ hours. Strain
the juice from the mandarin
oranges and blend 2 tablespoons
(30 ml) of the juice with the
cornflour. Make up the remaining
juice to ½ pint (300 ml) with water
and bring to the boil, pour on to
the cornflour mixture and return to
the heat, stirring all the time, until
thick, then cook for 2–3 minutes
on low heat. Add the rind and juice
of the lemon, the blackcurrant
jelly, cranberries and mandarin
oranges. Serve hot or cold with the
chicken.   **Serves 4**

whitworths

Crunchy Chicken Drumsticks

8 chicken drumsticks
1 egg, beaten
3 oz (75 g) sachet **Whitworths**
 Country Stuffing Mix
oil for deep frying

Dip the drumsticks in the beaten egg, then into the dry stuffing mix, ensuring an even coating. Heat the oil and fry the coated drumsticks until golden brown and cooked through. Serve hot.   **Serves 4**

Rabbit Casserole with Savoury Dumplings

1 tablespoon (15 ml) oil
1 lb (450 g) rabbit, cubed
1 medium onion, peeled and sliced
2 carrots, peeled and sliced
2 rashers streaky bacon, with rinds removed, chopped
1 tablespoon (15 ml) flour
1 pint (600 ml) stock
bouquet garni
salt and pepper
Dumplings
3 oz (75 g) sachet **Whitworths** Country Stuffing Mix
2 oz (50 g) plain flour
1 oz (25 g) butter *or* margarine
1 egg, beaten
2–3 tablespoons (30–45 ml) milk

Heat the oil in a saucepan. Add the rabbit, onion, carrots and bacon

and cook gently, stirring occasionally, for 4–5 minutes. Stir in the flour and gradually add the stock. Add the bouquet garni and seasoning, bring to the boil, partially cover and simmer for 45–50 minutes or until tender.

Meanwhile prepare the dumplings. Combine the stuffing mix and flour, rub in the butter or margarine and stir in the beaten egg and sufficient milk to give a soft, but not sticky dough. Divide the dough into 8 dumplings. Remove the bouquet garni and pour the rabbit mixture into a casserole dish. Top with the dumplings and cover the dish with a lid or foil. Bake in a pre-heated oven at 400°F, 200°C, Gas Mark 6 for 30–40 minutes.   **Serves 4**

Chicken Waldorf

1 medium chicken
3 red skinned apples
juice of ½ a lemon
4–6 sticks celery, finely chopped
3 oz (75 g) walnuts, roughly chopped
¼ pint (150 ml) **Young's** Dairy Cream
2 heaped tablespoons (40 ml) mayonnaise
salt and black pepper
1 oz (25 g) walnut halves to garnish
1 bunch watercress to garnish

Roast or poach the chicken in the usual way and leave to cool. Remove all flesh (discarding the skin and bones which can be used to make soup) and cut into bite sized pieces. Dice the unpeeled apples and pour the lemon juice over to stop discolouration. Mix together the chicken, celery, apple and chopped walnuts. Whip the cream until nearly stiff and fold in the mayonnaise and seasoning. Toss the chicken mixture in the dressing and pile on to a serving dish with the walnut halves and watercress to garnish.
Serves 6–8

BEEF

Corned Beef Crusty Pie

8 oz (225 g) white *or* hearty
  green cabbage, chopped
8 oz (225 g) carrot, peeled and
  coarsely grated
4 oz (125 g) swede, peeled and
  coarsely grated
½ pint (275 ml) beef stock
1 teaspoon (5 ml) mixed herbs
salt and pepper
12 oz (340 g) can **Armour**
  Corned Beef
4 oz (125 g) self-raising flour
2 oz (50 g) porridge oats
2 oz (50 g) butter *or* margarine
approx 2 tablespoons (30 ml)
  cold water
beaten egg *or* milk to glaze

Put the vegetables, herbs and stock
into a pan and boil together for 2–3
minutes. Take the pan off the heat,
strain about half the liquid and
reserve to use later as gravy. Slice
the corned beef and halve the
slices. Fill a 2 pint (1 litre) pie dish
with layers of vegetables in their
remaining liquid and the corned
beef, seasoning each layer. To
make the pastry, mix the flour with
salt, pepper and the oats in a bowl.
Melt the butter or margarine in a
pan and mix it into the dry ingredients. Add enough cold water to
make a fairly firm dough. Roll out
the pastry, allowing extra for a
border, and cover the dish. Pierce
through the centre, brush with egg
or milk and decorate with pastry
leaves. Bake in the middle of the
oven at 375°F, 190°C, Gas Mark 5,
for 35–40 minutes until browned
on top. Heat the remaining stock
for gravy.

Serve the pie hot with jacket
baked potatoes, cauliflower and
leeks.   **Serves 4–6**

Corned Beef Dipper

12 oz (340 g) can **Armour**
  Corned Beef
1 small onion
2 oz (50 g) fresh bread
1 teaspoon (5 ml) mixed herbs
1 medium egg, beaten
salt and pepper
Coating
plain *or* self-raising flour
1 medium egg, beaten with
  2 teaspoons (10 ml) cold
  water
2 oz (50 g) fresh *or* dried
  breadcrumbs
deep *or* shallow oil for frying

Mince or liquidise the corned beef,
onion and bread and mix with the
herbs, egg, salt and pepper. Shape
into small cakes or balls, or large
burgers. Toss them in the flour
then coat with egg and breadcrumbs. Fry in the heated oil 2–3
minutes each side until browned
and crisp. Drain on kitchen paper.

Serve hot with a tangy sauce (see
below) for parties or the large size
with shaphetti in tomato sauce and
courgettes or peas for a meal.

Tangy Sauce
8 oz (226 g) can tomatoes
½ (8 oz, 226 g) can apricots,
  drained and chopped
salt and pepper

Put the tomatoes into a pan and
boil until thick. Add the apricots
and salt and pepper to taste.
Makes 28 small or 6 large

Corned Beef and Lentil Pot

4 oz (125 g) lentils
1 large onion, peeled and
  chopped
4 oz (125 g) carrot, coarsely
  grated
½ teaspoon (2.5 ml) thyme
¾ pint (375 ml) beef stock

8 oz (226 g) can tomatoes
salt and pepper
12 oz (340 g) can **Armour**
  Corned Beef
1 lb (500 g) potatoes, boiled and
  thinly sliced
½ oz (15 g) butter, melted

Butter a 2 pint (1 litre) oven dish.
Put the lentils, onion, carrot,
thyme, stock, tomatoes, salt and
pepper into a pan. Bring to the
boil, cover and simmer for 10–15
minutes, stirring several times,
until the lentils are just tender. Cut
the corned beef into thin slices. Fill
the pie dish with layers of lentil
mixture and corned beef. Arrange
the sliced potatoes on top and
drizzle the melted butter over
them. Bake near the top of the
oven, pre-heated to 375°F, 190°C,
Gas Mark 5, for 30–35 minutes
until browned on top.

Serve hot with cauliflower in
white sauce and crusty brown
bread.   **Serves 4–6**

Corned Beef Vienna Bakes

6 Vienna crisp rolls *or* 1 small
  French stick loaf
2 oz (50 g) butter *or* margarine
1 small red pepper, de-seeded
  and chopped
1 clove garlic, chopped
  (optional)
12 oz (340 g) can **Armour**
  Corned Beef, chopped
few drops Tabasco *or* other
  sauce
salt and pepper
1½ oz (40 g) butter *or*
  margarine

Split along the middle of the rolls
or the loaf and scoop out some
crumbs from inside. Melt the
butter or margarine in a pan and
cook the pepper and garlic in it for
about 5 minutes to soften. Mix in
the scooped-out crumbs with the

corned beef, sauce, salt and pepper to taste. Remove the pan from the heat. Spread inside the bread with butter or margarine and fill with the corned beef mixture. Replace the tops and wrap completely in foil. Bake towards the top of the oven, pre-heated to 400°F, 200°C, Gas Mark 6, for 15–20 minutes. Cut in 1 in (2 cm) wide slices and serve hot with green salad.
Serves 4–6

Devilled Corned Beef and Parsnip Hash

2 oz (50 g) butter *or* margarine
1 lb (500 g) parsnips, peeled and cut in small wedges
6 oz (175 g) onion, peeled and thinly sliced
½ oz (15 g) plain *or* self-raising flour
½ pint (275 ml) beef stock
1 tablespoon (15 ml) made mustard
1 tablespoon (15 ml) sweet chutney
salt and pepper
12 oz (340 g) can **Armour** Corned Beef, cubed
2 tablespoons (30 ml) fresh parsley, chopped

Melt the butter or margarine in a large frying pan and mix in the parsnips and onion. Cover and cook gently for 10–15 minutes, stirring several times, until the vegetables are soft and lightly browned. Whisk the flour into the stock with the mustard, chutney, salt and pepper, pour into the pan and stir until the mixture thickens. Mix in the corned beef carefully so as not to break up the cubes. Sprinkle the parsley on top and serve with fried potato croquettes and spinach or Brussels sprouts.
Serves 4

Superman Supper

12 oz (340 g) can **Armour** Corned Beef
15½ oz (439 g) can baked beans in tomato sauce
4 wholewheat long baps, split
1½–2 tablespoons (20–30 ml)

chunky brown pickle
1 oz (25 g) cheese, grated
small packet potato crisps, lightly crushed
chopped parsley to garnish

Cut the corned beef into 8 slices and each into 3 widthways. Heat the baked beans gently. Toast the baps on both sides and put them on a fireproof platter. Spoon the hot baked beans on top and cover with the corned beef pieces. Grill for 1–2 minutes to heat the corned beef then top with the pickle, cheese and crisps. Grill briefly to melt the cheese slightly.

Serve hot, garnished with parsley.   **Serves 4–6**

ATORA

Chilli Beef Roll

1 medium onion, peeled and chopped
1 clove garlic, crushed
2 tablespoons (30 ml) vegetable oil
8 oz (250 g) minced beef
1 red pimento (pepper) canned *or* fresh, chopped
2 teaspoons (10 ml) mild chilli powder
salt and ground black pepper
6 oz (150 g) self-raising flour, sifted
3 oz (75 g) **Atora** Shredded Suet
water to mix
a little milk to glaze

Fry the onion and garlic in the oil until softened. Add the mince and brown, then add the pimento and chilli powder. Season, cover and cook very gently for about 20 minutes. Make the pastry by mixing the flour and suet together and forming a firm dough by adding water. Roll out to a large rectangle ¼ in (5 mm) thick. Spread the mince mixture on it, roll up and trim the edges. Place on a baking sheet, glaze with a little milk if liked, and bake at 375°F, 190°C, Gas Mark 5, for about 30 minutes.

Serve with a tomato sauce.
Serves 4

Quick Steak and Kidney Pan Pudding

4 oz (100 g) self-raising flour
2 oz (50 g) **Atora** Shredded Suet
pinch salt
pinch dried herbs
water to mix
15 oz (425 g) can steak and kidney pie filling
4 oz (100 g) mushrooms, washed and quartered
½ teaspoon (2.5 ml) dried thyme (optional)
Worcestershire sauce

Mix the flour, suet, salt and herbs to a firm dough with the water, then roll out on a lightly floured surface to a round to fit the size of the saucepan you intend using. Mix the pie filling with the mushrooms, thyme and a few dashes of Worcestershire sauce. Place the dough on top of the meat, cover and cook gently for about 25 minutes. Serve hot from the pan.   **Serves 4**

Chili con Carne

1 tablespoon (15 ml) oil
1 large onion, peeled and sliced
1 green pepper, de-seeded and sliced (optional)
1 lb (450 g) minced beef
15 oz (425 g) can **Batchelors** Red Kidney Beans
3 teaspoons (45 ml) chilli powder (medium hot)
1 teaspoon (5 ml) salt
1 tablespoon (15 ml) tomato purée
black pepper to taste

Heat the oil in a pan and cook the onions and green pepper until soft. Add the meat and stir well. Drain the beans, reserving 2 tablespoons (30 ml) of the liquid. Stir the beans, liquid and remaining ingredients into the pan. Cover and cook gently for 1 hour or until the meat is tender.
Serves 4

Beef and Celery Horseshoe

½ can **Baxters** Minced Beef
1 stalk celery with leaves, chopped
1 tablespoon (15 ml) **Baxters** Tomato Pickle
12 oz (350 g) frozen puff pastry, thawed
salt and pepper
beaten egg to glaze

Mix together the minced beef, chopped celery and tomato pickle. Add a pinch of salt and pepper. Roll out the pastry to a rectangle about 10 in (25 cm) long. Spread the meat mixture over the pastry, leaving a small margin all round. Roll up the pastry as for a swiss roll and seal the ends with the join on the underside. Shape into a horseshoe and make cuts in the pastry 2 in (5 cm) apart. Place on a baking sheet and brush the top with beaten egg. Put into a moderate oven at 400°F, 200°C, Gas Mark 6, for 20–25 minutes until well risen and golden brown. Serve hot.   **Serves 2**

Boeuf à la Bourgogne

1½ lb (675 g) topside *or* shoulder steak, diced
8 oz (225 g) bacon, diced
1 can **Baxters** Burgundy Wine Sauce
8 oz (225 g) button mushrooms
12 button onions

Put the beef and bacon into a large saucepan and pour over the Burgundy Wine Sauce. Simmer for 2 hours. Lightly fry the mushrooms and onions, add to the meat and continue simmering for a further hour.

Serve with boiled rice or mashed potatoes and fresh green vegetables.   **Serves 4**

Beef Popovers

2 oz (50 g) **Be-Ro** Plain Flour
salt and pepper
1 egg
¼ pint (125 ml) milk
Filling
4 oz (100 g) minced beef
1 tablespoon (15 ml) tomato ketchup
salt and pepper
3 tablespoons (45 ml) **Be-Ro** Plain Flour

Mix together the flour, salt and pepper in a bowl, make a well in the centre and add the egg and a little of the milk. Stir well, blending in the flour and beat until smooth. Add half the milk gradually, beating thoroughly. Stir in the remaining milk and leave to stand for 30 minutes. Mix together the filling ingredients and shape into 12 balls. Put a little lard in 12 patty tins and place in the oven at 425°F, 220°C, Gas Mark 7, until the lard is melted and hot. Place a meat ball in each patty tin and pour over the batter to nearly fill each tin. Bake for 20 minutes on the second shelf from the top until puffy and golden. Serve hot.
Serves 4–5

Carbonnade of Beef

2 oz (50 g) butter *or* margarine
2 medium onions, peeled and chopped
2 level teaspoons (10 ml) **Bisto**
1 oz (25 g) plain flour
salt and pepper
1 lb (450 g) blade bone steak, cut into 1 in (2.5 cm) cubes
1 teaspoon (5 ml) malt vinegar
1 level teaspoon (5 ml) demerara sugar
1 teaspoon (5 ml) Worcestershire sauce
½ pint (300 ml) brown ale
4 slices of French bread, 1 in (2.5 cm) thick
French mustard
sprigs of parsley to garnish

Melt the fat in a frying pan, add the onions and fry until tender, then place in a 3 pint (1.8 litre) shallow casserole dish. Mix together the Bisto, flour and salt and pepper in a bowl. Add the meat and toss to coat evenly. Add the meat to the frying pan and fry quickly to brown on all sides. Place the meat in the casserole dish. Stir the vinegar, sugar, Worcestershire sauce and brown ale into the frying pan, bring to the boil and pour into the casserole. Cover with a lid or foil and place in the middle of the oven pre-heated to 325°F, 160°C, Gas Mark 3 for 2 hours or until the meat is cooked.

Spread each slice of French bread with mustard, arrange the bread on top of the meat and press down lightly. Return the casserole to the oven, uncovered, for a further 20–30 minutes until the bread is crisp and brown.

Garnish the Carbonnade of Beef with a few sprigs of parsley and serve with jacket potatoes and green beans.   **Serves 4**

Minced Beef Loaf

4 oz (100 g) streaky bacon
12 oz (350 g) cooked beef
1 medium onion, peeled
2 oz (50 g) fresh white bread
1 level tablespoon (15 ml) parsley, chopped
1 standard egg
5½ oz (156 g) can condensed mushroom soup, undiluted
salt and pepper
2 level teaspoons (10 ml) **Bisto**
cucumber slices, tomato wedges and sprigs of watercress to garnish

Remove the rinds and bones from the bacon. Mince the bacon, beef, onion and bread finely into a bowl. Add the parsley, egg, soup, salt and pepper and Bisto and mix together until well blended. Grease a 1 lb (450 g) loaf tin with melted fat or oil, place the mixture into the tin and smooth the top with the back of a metal spoon. Cover the top with foil, place on a baking sheet and cook in the middle of the oven, pre-heated to 350°F, 180°C, Gas Mark 4, for 1 hour. Turn out of the tin immediately if to be served hot, otherwise leave to cool in the tin. Loosen the edges of the loaf with a knife and turn out on to a serving dish. Garnish with the cucumber, tomato and sprigs of watercress.   **Serves 4–6**

Blue Band

Beef Cobbler

1 oz (25 g) flour
½ teaspoon (2.5 ml) basil
pinch of mace
salt and black pepper
1 lb (450 g) stewing steak
1 oz (25 g) **Blue Band** Margarine
2 leeks, washed and finely sliced
8 oz (225 g) carrots, peeled and sliced
½ pint (275 ml) beef stock
bay leaf
Topping
6 oz (175 g) self-raising flour sieved with ½ teaspoon (2.5 ml) salt
4 oz (125 g) **Blue Band** Margarine
3 tablespoons (45 ml) water
dash Worcestershire sauce

Mix the flour with the basil, mace and seasoning and toss the meat in this until well coated. Sauté the meat in the melted margarine until browned. Add the leeks, carrots, stock and bay leaf. Bring to the boil. Place in an ovenproof dish and bake in a moderate oven at 350°F, 180°C, Gas Mark 4, for 1–1½ hours until tender. Remove the bay leaf.

To make the topping, rub the margarine into the flour until the mixture resembles fine bread-crumbs. Add the water and a dash

of Worcestershire sauce and mix to form a soft dough. Roll out on a lightly floured surface to ½ in (1 cm) thickness. Cut into 2 in (5 cm) rounds and place over-lapping on top of the meat. Bake in a hot oven at 425°F, 220°C, Gas Mark 7, for 20–25 minutes, until the topping is browned.

Can be frozen or reheated.
Serves 4

Lattice Pie

shortcrust pastry made with 8 oz (225 g) flour
1 large onion, peeled and finely chopped
1 oz (25 g) butter
1 lb (450 g) minced beef
1 Red Cube from **Bovril**
8 oz (225 g) mushrooms, sliced
6 tablespoons (90 ml) tomato ketchup
¼ pint (150 ml) water
1½ tablespoons (20 ml) cornflour
8 oz (225 g) fresh tomatoes, skinned and thickly sliced
a little beaten egg

Line an 8 in (20 cm) pie dish with the pastry, retaining the trimmings. Fry the onion in the butter until it is soft and golden. Add the meat and cook gently, stirring well, until browned. Add the crumbled Bovril cube and mushrooms and continue cooking for 5 minutes. Take off the heat and stir in the tomato ketchup, water and cornflour until well mixed.

When the meat mixture has cooled completely, put into the pastry case and cover with sliced tomatoes. Cut the pastry trim-mings into strips and arrange in a lattice over the tomatoes. Brush with a little beaten egg to glaze. Bake at 425°F, 220°C, Gas Mark 7, for 45 minutes.

Serve hot or cold.   **Serves 4**

Oxtail and Tomato Casserole

1 large oxtail
a little oil for frying
1 large onion, peeled and sliced
½ oz (15 g) plain flour
sprig each of thyme and parsley
1 bay leaf
1 Red Cube from **Bovril** dissolved in 1½ pints (900 ml) water
1 tablespoon (15 ml) tomato purée
4 tomatoes, skinned
¼ bottle red wine
salt and pepper

Cut the oxtail into sections. Brown in a little oil, then add the onion and fry until it is soft and golden. Drain off the surplus fat and work the flour into the onions. Mix well and add the herbs, stock, tomato purée, tomatoes, wine and seasoning. Bring to the boil, then cover and simmer for 5 hours. Adjust the seasoning before serving.   **Serves 4**

Savoury Meat Roll

4 oz (100 g) bacon
8 oz (225 g) minced beef
3 oz (75 g) fresh brown breadcrumbs
salt and pepper
1 egg, beaten
1 Red Cube from **Bovril**
2 tablespoons (30 ml) water

Take an empty soup can and remove both ends. Mince the bacon and mix with the beef, breadcrumbs, salt, pepper and egg. Add the crumbled Bovril cube and water and mix well. Stand the can on a large piece of kitchen foil and fill with the meat mixture. Bring the foil up over the sides and close firmly on top. Steam for 2 hours and then leave to cool for 15 minutes. Remove the foil and unmould the meat roll on to a serving dish. Leave until com-pletely cold.

Cut into rounds to serve with salad.   **Serves 4**

Steak and Mushroom Pie

1¼ lb (575 g) chuck steak, trimmed and cubed
1 oz (25 g) seasoned flour
1 large onion, peeled and sliced
1 Red Cube from **Bovril**, crumbled
8 oz (225 g) tomatoes
1 teaspoon (5 ml) thyme
4 oz (100 g) button mushrooms, washed and sliced
8 oz (225 g) frozen puff pastry, thawed
beaten egg *or* milk to glaze

Toss the steak in the seasoned flour. Put the meat, onion, Bovril cube, tomatoes and thyme in a saucepan, cover with water and bring to the boil. Cover and simmer gently for 1½ hours. Add the mushrooms. Empty the meat and vegetables into a 2¼–2½ pint (1.3–1.5 litre) pie dish, place a pie funnel in the middle of the dish, and pour over sufficient gravy to half fill the dish.

Roll out the pastry to 1 in (2.5 cm) larger than the dish, cut a ½ in (1 cm) strip off the pastry and place on the dampened edge of the dish. Dampen the edge of the remaining pastry and place over the filling, trim and seal firmly. Decorate the top with pastry 'leaves', brush with beaten egg or milk and bake at 425°F, 220°C, Gas Mark 7 for 20 minutes. Reduce the heat to 350°F, 180°C, Gas Mark 4 for a further 10 minutes.

Serve with the remaining gravy.   **Serves 5**

Topside with Herbs and Ale

1½ lb (750 g) topside of beef
2 tablespoons (30 ml) oil
2 large onions, peeled and thinly sliced
salt and pepper
pinch each dried thyme, rosemary, sage and mustard powder
¼ pint (150 ml) brown ale
½ Red Cube from **Bovril**

dissolved in ¼ pint (150 ml) water
1 bay leaf

Cut the beef into 6 slices and brown lightly in the oil. Put the meat into an ovenproof dish. Fry the onions gently until soft and golden. Season with salt, pepper, herbs and mustard and arrange the onions on the beef. Pour in the ale and stock and add the bay leaf. Cover and cook at 325°F, 170°C, Gas Mark 3, for 2 hours. Serve at once.   **Serves 6**

Baked Veal Chops with Ratatouille

4 veal chops
2 tablespoons (30 ml) **Trex** Pure Vegetable Oil
1 can **Buitoni** Ratatouille
salt and freshly ground black pepper
8 oz (227 g) **Buitoni** Pasta Shells
½ oz (15 g) butter

Heat the oil, brown the chops on both sides and transfer to a casserole dish. Pour on the contents of the can of ratatouille and season with the salt and black pepper. Cover and cook in the centre of the oven at 350°F, 180°C, Gas Mark 4, for 1 hour.

Cook the pasta in boiling, salted water for 9 minutes, drain, return to the pan and toss in the butter. Transfer to a serving dish and serve as an accompaniment to the veal chops.   **Serves 4**

Italian Veal with Peppers

2 lb (1 kg) stewing veal
3 tablespoons (45 ml) **Trex** Pure Vegetable Oil
2 large onions, sliced
2 green peppers, de-seeded and sliced
2 (10 oz, 283 g) cans **Buitoni** Napolitan Sauce
salt and ground black pepper

2 teaspoons (10 ml) mixed herbs
12 oz (340 g) **Buitoni** Tagliatelle Verdi

Cut the meat into 1 in (2 cm) cubes and fry in the heated oil until brown on all sides. Transfer to a casserole dish. Cook the onions until golden and place on top of the meat. Add the peppers to the casserole, pour in the Napolitan Sauce and season with salt, ground black pepper and mixed herbs. Cover and cook in the oven at 350°F, 180°C, Gas Mark 4, for 1½–2 hours.

Serve with the cooked tagliatelle.   **Serves 4–6**

Beef Casserole

1 lb (450 g) braising steak, trimmed and cut into cubes
2 tablespoons (30 ml) oil
1 rasher rindless streaky bacon, diced
2 small onions, peeled and sliced
2 tomatoes, sliced
4 oz (100 g) mushrooms, washed and sliced
2 large carrots, peeled and chopped
salt and pepper
1 teaspoon (5 ml) paprika pepper
¾ pint (450 ml) **Bulmers** Strongbow
cornflour to thicken (optional)

Heat the oil in a frying pan and fry the meat until brown. Remove and place in a casserole dish. Fry the bacon and the vegetables. Add to the casserole. Season well with the salt, pepper and paprika and pour over the cider. Put into a moderate oven (350°F, 180°C, Gas Mark 4) for about 1½ hours. Thicken the gravy with the cornflour dissolved in a little cold water if desired.

Serve in bowls with chunks of crusty bread.   **Serves 4**

Campbell's

Autumn Beef Casserole

1¼–1½ lb (575–675 g) stewing beef, trimmed and cut into 1 in (2.5 cm) cubes
10½ oz (297 g) can **Campbell's** Condensed Cream of Tomato Soup, undiluted
1 oz (25 g) dripping *or* lard
1 large onion, peeled and sliced
2–3 carrots, peeled and thickly sliced
2 leeks, washed thoroughly and cut into 1 in (2.5 cm) pieces
2 stalks of celery, washed and cut into 1 in (2.5 cm) pieces
¼ pint (150 ml) beer *or* stock
sprig of thyme

Melt the fat in a pan, add the beef and brown quickly. When evenly coloured, remove to a 3–4 pint (1–2 litre) casserole dish. Brown the onion in the fat and add to the casserole, with the carrots, leeks and celery. Mix the soup with a fork and pour into the casserole, add the beer or stock and the thyme. Stir the mixture well and put the lid on the casserole. Bake on the centre shelf of a moderate oven, 350°F, 180°C, Gas Mark 4, for 1½–1¾ hours or until the meat is tender.　**Serves 4**

Beef Strogonoff

1 tablespoon (15 ml) oil
1 lb (450 g) stewing beef, cut into strips
1 onion, peeled and sliced
10½ oz (297 g) can **Campbell's** Condensed Consommé, undiluted
4 oz (100 g) mushrooms, washed and sliced
5 oz (142 g) carton soured cream

Heat the oil in a saucepan and fry the beef until browned. Add the onion and continue frying until the onion is soft. Add the consommé and simmer for 45 minutes. Add the mushrooms and

simmer for a further 15 minutes, pour in the soured cream and reheat gently, but do not allow to boil.　**Serves 4**

Mince and Dumpling Casserole

1 oz (25 g) dripping
1 lb (450 g) minced beef
10½ oz (297 g) can **Campbell's** Condensed Stock Pot, undiluted
1 tablespoon (15 ml) tomato purée
1½ soup cans water
4 oz (100 g) self-raising flour
2 oz (50 g) shredded suet
1 teaspoon (5 ml) dried herbs
salt and pepper

Heat the dripping in a saucepan, add the mince and cook, stirring, until brown. Mix in the soup, tomato purée and water. Simmer slowly for 35–40 minutes.

　To make the dumplings, sift the flour into a bowl, stir in the suet, herbs, salt and pepper. Add enough water to form a soft dough. Roll the dough in floured hands to form 8 small balls. Place on the mince mixture, put a lid on the pan and simmer for 20 minutes, until the dumplings are cooked. Serve immediately.　**Serves 4**

Spiced Beef

1 lb (450 g) stewing steak, cubed
1 tablespoon (15 ml) oil
1 level teaspoon (5 ml) mixed spice
1 level tablespoon (15 ml) flour
10½ oz (297 g) can **Campbell's** Condensed Onion Soup (French Style), undiluted
8 oz (227 g) can tomatoes
1 dessertspoon (10 ml) vinegar

Brown the steak in the oil in a saucepan. Add the mixed spice and flour and mix well. Add the remainder of the ingredients and bring to the boil, stirring. Simmer slowly for 1½ hours until the meat is tender.　**Serves 4**

Carnation.

Meat Loaf

1 small can **Carnation** Evaporated Milk
1 lb (450 g) fresh minced beef
2 oz (50 g) fresh breadcrumbs
1 small onion, peeled and grated
2 tablespoons (30 ml) green pepper, de-seeded and chopped
1 tablespoon (15 ml) prepared mustard
½ teaspoon (2.5 ml) salt
pepper

Lightly mix all the ingredients together and put into a small loaf tin (approximately 7 × 3 × 2 in (18 × 8 × 5 cm)). Bake in a fairly hot oven at 375°F, 190°C, Gas Mark 5, for about 45 minutes. Allow to stand for about 10 minutes before serving.
　Serve hot or cold.　**Serves 4**

Somerset Stewed Steak

1 lb (450 g) braising steak, cubed
salt and pepper
1 tablespoon (15 ml) oil
1 medium onion, peeled and sliced
1 teaspoon (5 ml) mixed herbs
¼ pint (150 ml) cider
1 can **Chef** Chunky Soup, Beef Flavour
triangles of fried bread to garnish

Season the meat with salt and pepper. Heat the oil in a saucepan and fry the meat until brown. Add the onion and mixed herbs and fry for another 2 minutes. Stir in the cider and the Chef soup. Bring to the boil, cover and simmer for about 1½ hours until the meat is tender.
　Serve, garnished with triangles of fried bread, with a green vegetable.　**Serves 4**

Beef with Beer and Mushrooms

1–1½ lb (500–750 g) stewing steak, cut into 1 in (2.5 cm) cubes
2 tablespoons (30 ml) oil
1½ oz (40 g) flour
½ pint (250 ml) brown ale
½ pint (250 ml) brown stock
1 carrot, peeled and diced
1 small turnip, peeled and diced (optional)
1 can **Chesswood** Small Whole Mushrooms, drained
salt and pepper

Heat the oil in a pan, add the meat and cook until browned on all sides. Add the flour and cook for a few minutes over a low heat. Gradually add the stock and ale and bring to the boil. Add the carrot and turnip, if used, and simmer for 1 hour. Add the Small Whole Mushrooms and cook for 30 minutes more then season to taste. **Serves 4–6**

Corned Beef Pie

shortcrust pastry made with 4 oz (100 g) flour
1 oz (25 g) butter
2 medium onions, peeled and chopped
12 oz (340 g) can corned beef, mashed
1 can **Chesswood** Small Whole Mushrooms, drained and chopped
2 teaspoons (10 ml) Worcestershire sauce
2 tablespoons (30 ml) parsley, chopped
2 egg whites, stiffly beaten
4 oz (100 g) Cheddar cheese, grated

Use the pastry to line a 7 in (18 cm) flan ring. Bake 'blind' for 15 minutes at 400°F, 200°C, Gas Mark 6. Remove the baking beans and return to the oven for a few minutes more. Melt the butter in a

pan and fry the onion until soft. Mix with the corned beef, mushrooms, Worcestershire sauce and parsley and empty the mixture into the baked flan case, packing it down well. Fold the cheese into the beaten egg whites and pile evenly on top of the corned beef mixture. Bake for approximately 10 minutes at 450°F, 230°C, Gas Mark 8, or until the topping is golden.
Serves 4

Beef and Tomato Soufflé

1 oz (25 g) butter
½ tablespoon flour
8 oz (227 g) can **Cirio** Tomatoes
4 oz (100 g) mushrooms, chopped
salt and pepper
8 oz (225 g) lean roast beef, finely minced
3 eggs, separated, plus 1 extra egg white
1 shallot, chopped (optional)

Melt the butter, add the flour and cook for a minute or two, stir in the tomatoes and juice, mushrooms, salt and pepper and boil until the sauce thickens. Blend in the minced beef and add extra salt and pepper if necessary. Add the egg yolks and pass the mixture through a sieve. Mix in the shallot, if used, beat the egg whites until stiff and lightly fold these into the mixture. Pour into a greased 1 pint (600 ml) soufflé dish, cover with greaseproof paper and bake for 20 minutes at 400°F, 200°C, Gas Mark 6.
Serve immediately. **Serves 2**

Surprise Veal Rolls in Rich Tomato Sauce

2 rounded tablespoons (40 ml) thyme and parsley stuffing mix
2 rounded tablespoons (40 ml) sage and onion stuffing mix
8 tablespoons (120 ml) hot water *or* chicken stock

4 veal escalopes (each weighing about 4–5 oz (100–150 g))
4 slices lean ham
seasoned flour
2 tablespoons (30 ml) cooking oil
Sauce
4 oz (100 g) mushrooms, washed and thinly sliced
3 tablespoons (45 ml) cooking oil
1 small onion, peeled and finely chopped
2 tablespoons (30 ml) **Cirio** Tomato Purée
14 oz (396 g) can **Cirio** Tomatoes
salt and pepper
chopped parsley to garnish

Stir the two stuffing mixes together and add the hot water or stock. Leave to stand for 10 minutes. Beat the escalopes between 2 sheets of greaseproof paper until they are thin, remove the paper and lay 1 slice of ham on each escalope. Divide the stuffing into 4 equal portions and spread one portion on each slice of ham. Roll up each portion tightly and secure with thin string or thread. Dust lightly with seasoned flour. Heat the oil in a frying pan, add the veal rolls and brown lightly all over. Remove to a shallow casserole dish.

To make the sauce, heat the oil and fry the mushrooms gently, remove and keep warm. Fry the onion for about 4 minutes, add the tomato purée and cook for 1 minute, then stir in the chopped tomatoes and juice, salt and pepper. Simmer gently until the sauce thickens. Return the mushrooms to the pan, stirring carefully.

Pour the tomato sauce over the veal rolls in the casserole dish, cover and cook for 1 hour at 325°F, 160°C, Gas Mark 3.

To serve, garnish with chopped parsley. **Serves 4**

Colman's

Beef Olives Provencale

8 slices lean beef, beaten out
thinly to 4 in (10 cm) squares
1½ oz (35 g) butter
1 slice bacon, chopped
1 onion, peeled and chopped
1 oz (25 g) fresh white
breadcrumbs
8 oz (225 g) sausagemeat
1 tablespoon (15 ml) mixed
herbs
1 packet **Colman's** Beef
Provencale Casserole Mix
½ pint (275 ml) water

To make the stuffing, melt ½ oz
(15 g) butter in a saucepan. Add
the bacon and onion and fry until
soft. Add the breadcrumbs,
sausagemeat and herbs. Remove
from the heat and mix well. Spread
the stuffing mix on the meat and
roll up. Secure with string. Melt
the rest of the butter in a casserole
dish or heavy pan. Fry the meat
rolls on all sides. Mix the Beef
Provencale Casserole Mix with
½ pint (275 ml) water and pour
over the beef olives. Cover and
simmer gently for 1½ hours or
until tender. Remove the string
and serve at once.   **Serves 4**

Beef Steak Pudding

12 oz (350 g) suet crust pastry
1½ lb (700 g) lean stewing
steak
1 onion, peeled and finely
chopped
1 packet **Colman's** Beef
Bourguignon Casserole Mix
cold water

Roll out the pastry dough to a 10 in
(26 cm) diameter circle. Cut a
right-angled segment out of the
circle and set aside. Moisten the
cut edges of the dough circle and
put into a 2 pint (1 litre) pudding
basin. Press down and trim with a
sharp knife. Toss the beef and
onion with the Casserole Mix and
put into the basin. Pour over
enough water to come half way up

the sides. Knead the remaining
dough and roll out to a circle large
enough to cover the basin. Dampen the edges and seal. Grease a
large piece of foil. Make a 1 in
(2.5 cm) pleat in the centre and tie
over the pudding basin. Stand the
pudding in a pan of boiling water,
with the water coming half way up
the side of the basin. Cook,
covered, on top of the stove for
4 hours. Add more boiling water
to the pan as it evaporates. Remove
the basin from the pan, remove the
foil and serve at once with a clean
napkin tied around the basin.
Serves 4–6

Mexican Stuffed Peppers

4 large, even-sized green
peppers
1 lb (450 g) lean minced beef
1 small onion, peeled and
chopped
1 packet **Colman's** Chilli Con
Carne Mix
¼ pint (150 ml) water
salt
4 oz (100 g) Cheddar cheese,
grated

Cut a slice off the base of each
pepper so that they will stand up,
then cut a lid off the top of each one
and remove the seeds. Cook the
peppers in boiling, salted water for
5 minutes. Drain well and stand
them in a greased, ovenproof dish.
Remove the stalks from the pepper
lids and chop the lids finely. Put
the minced beef, chopped pepper
lids and onion in a saucepan and
cook over a medium heat,
breaking up the minced beef with
a fork, until well browned. Stir in

the Chilli Con Carne Mix and
water and bring to the boil,
stirring. Add salt to taste. Spoon
the chilli mixture into the green
pepper shells. Cover and bake in
the oven at 350°F, 180°C, Gas
Mark 4, for 25 minutes. Sprinkle
with the grated cheese and return
to the oven for a further 5 minutes.
Serve at once.   **Serves 4**

Spicy Hamburgers with Sauce Chasseur

1½ lb (700 g) minced beef
2 teaspoons (10 ml) **Colman's**
English Mustard, made up
2 teaspoons (10 ml) salt
½ teaspoon (2.5 ml) ground
pepper
4 baps *or* hamburger rolls
Sauce
2 oz (50 g) butter
1 onion, peeled and finely
chopped
2 tablespoons (30 ml) vinegar
⅓ pint (200 ml) water
1 oz (25 g) sugar
1 tablespoon (15 ml) dry
Colman's English Mustard,
made up
1 tablespoon (15 ml) lemon
juice
6 tablespoons (90 ml) tomato
ketchup
2 tablespoons (30 ml) tomato
purée
dash cayenne pepper
salt and pepper

Mix all the hamburger ingredients
together in a bowl then shape into
4 hamburgers about ¾ in (2 cm)
thick. Place on grill pan. To make
the sauce, melt the butter in a
saucepan and fry the onion for
2 minutes over a low heat. Stir in
the rest of the ingredients and
bring to the boil. Simmer for about
20 minutes. Use either hot or cold.
To cook the hamburgers, place
under a pre-heated grill or over
charcoal and cook for about
5–6 minutes on each side. Place
each on a toasted bun and serve
with the sauce.   **Serves 4**

Steak Stroganoff

1½ lb (700 g) rump steak
2 oz (50 g) butter
4 oz (100 g) mushrooms, washed and sliced
4 tomatoes, sliced
1 packet **Colman's** Beef Stroganoff Casserole Mix
¼ pint (150 ml) milk
5 oz (142 ml) carton soured cream
2 tablespoons (30 ml) parsley, chopped

Cut the steak into thin strips. Melt the butter in a frying pan and quickly fry the steak. Add the mushrooms and tomatoes and cook for 1 minute. Remove the steak and vegetables. Mix the Stroganoff Mix with the milk, add to the pan and cook, stirring until thickened. Return the meat and vegetables to the pan and cook for 5 minutes. Stir in the soured cream, sprinkle with the parsley and serve at once. **Serves 4**

Tamale Pie

1 tablespoon (15 ml) oil
1 large onion, peeled and chopped
4 oz (100 g) mushrooms, wiped and quartered
1 lb (450 g) lean minced beef
1 packet **Colman's** Chilli Con Carne Mix
½ pint (300 ml) water
salt

Topping
6 oz (150 g) self-raising flour
½ teaspoon (2.5 ml) salt
2 oz (50 g) margarine
2 oz (50 g) stoned green olives, chopped
1 egg
¼ pint (150 ml) milk

Heat the oil and sauté the onion until transparent, add the mushrooms and continue to cook for a further 2 minutes. Stir in the minced beef, breaking it down with a fork, and cook until well browned. Stir in the Chilli Con Carne Mix and then the water and bring to the boil, stirring. Add salt to taste, then transfer the mixture to a 3 pint (1.8 litre) ovenproof dish.

To make the topping, sift the flour and salt into a mixing bowl, rub in the margarine until the mixture resembles fine crumbs and stir in the olives. Beat the egg and milk together and stir into the dry ingredients. Starting at the outside edge, spread the topping over the meat, until completely covered. Bake in the oven at 350°F, 180°C, Gas Mark 4, for about 40 minutes, until well browned and a skewer inserted into the centre of the topping comes out clean.

Serve at once with a green salad or vegetables. **Serves 4**

FRANK COOPER®

Beef Loaf Espagnol

12 oz (340 g) can corned beef, mashed
1 clove garlic, chopped
1 small onion, peeled and finely chopped
pepper
2 teaspoons **Frank Cooper's** Horseradish Relish
1 egg, beaten
8 oz (227 g) can peeled tomatoes, drained

Mix together the corned beef, garlic, onion, pepper and horseradish. Bind together with the egg. Press into a 1 lb (450 g) loaf tin, place the tomatoes on top and cover with foil. Bake at 350°F, 180°C, Gas Mark 4, for 40–50 minutes. **Serves 4**

Beef Olives with Horseradish

8 thin slices topside of beef
3 oz (75 g) fresh breadcrumbs
1½ oz (40 g) shredded suet
1 tablespoon (15 ml) parsley, chopped
2 level tablespoons (30 ml) **Frank Cooper** Horseradish Relish
salt and pepper

1 egg, lightly beaten
1 onion, peeled and chopped
¾ pint (375 ml) beef stock

Lay the pieces of meat out flat and trim off any excess fat. Mix together the breadcrumbs, suet, parsley, horseradish and seasoning. Bind with the egg. Divide the stuffing between the pieces of meat, roll up and place in an ovenproof dish. Sprinkle over the onion and add the stock, cover and cook at 325°F, 160°C, Gas Mark 3, for 1½ hours. **Serves 4**

Veal Hot Pot

1¼ lb (575 g) stewing veal
1 oz (25 g) seasoned flour
2 oz (50 g) dripping *or* cooking fat
8–12 button onions, peeled
4 oz (100 g) button mushroms, washed
1 can **Crosse & Blackwell** Tomato and Ham Pour over Sauce
½ can water
1 tablespoon (15 ml) parsley, chopped

Cut the veal into 1 in (2.5 cm) cubes and toss in the seasoned flour. Heat the dripping in a flame-proof casserole or large saucepan and gently fry the onions for 4–5 minutes until lightly browned. Remove from the casserole and reserve. Add the meat to the fat remaining in the casserole and fry over a high heat, stirring frequently until browned. Add the can of Tomato and Ham Sauce and the half can of water, cover tightly and simmer for 1 hour. Add the mushrooms and reserved button onions and simmer for a further 25–30 minutes. Sprinkle with the parsley just before serving.

Serve with rice, noodles or baked potatoes. **Serves 4–5**

Veal Escalopes with Mushroom Sauce

4 veal escalopes
2 oz (50 g) plain flour sifted with a little salt and freshly ground pepper
2 egg whites, lightly beaten
4 oz (125 g) fresh breadcrumbs
2 oz (50 g) Edam cheese, grated
1 teaspoon (5 ml) dry mustard
4 tablespoons (60 ml) **Flora** Oil

Sauce

2 oz (50 g) **Flora** Margarine
1 medium onion, peeled and finely chopped
1 clove garlic, crushed
4 oz (125 g) button mushrooms, washed and sliced
2 tablespoons (30 ml) dry white wine
salt and freshly ground black pepper
½ pint (275 ml) natural low-fat yoghurt
parsley and tomato wedges

Remove any visible fat from the meat, then beat with a meat mallet or rolling pin until thin. Mix together the breadcrumbs, cheese and mustard. Coat the veal in the seasoned flour, dip into the egg white then toss in the breadcrumb mixture until well coated on both sides. Heat the oil in a large frying pan over a medium heat and cook the veal escalopes for about 5 minutes on each side until they are crisp and golden. Keep warm.

To make the sauce, melt the margarine in a pan over a medium heat and sauté the onion and garlic until tender but not brown. Add the mushrooms and sauté for 1 minute. Add the wine and seasoning and simmer for 1 minute. Stir in the yoghurt and heat through carefully without boiling. Place the veal escalopes on a dish and pour the sauce down the middle, garnish with the parsley and tomato wedges.

Serve immediately. The sauce should not be reheated or it will curdle. **Serves 4**

Californian Meat Cakes

1 small onion, peeled and chopped
1 oz (25 g) dripping *or* bacon fat
7 oz (198 g) can **Fray Bentos** Lean Cut Corned Beef
8 oz (225 g) potatoes, cooked and sieved
salt and pepper
1 egg yolk
6 rashers streaky bacon, with rinds removed

Fry the onion in the dripping until tender. Mash the corned beef and mix with the potatoes and onion, season well and mix in the egg yolk. Shape the mixture into six patties about 1 in (2.5 cm) in depth, wrap a rasher of bacon around each and secure with a wooden cocktail stick. Put on to an ovenproof dish and bake in a fairly hot oven (400°F, 200°C, Gas Mark 6) for 20–25 minutes until the bacon is brown and crisp. **Serves 3**

Edinburgh Beef Scone

7 oz (198 g) can **Fray Bentos** Lean Cut Corned Beef
1 small can condensed tomato soup, undiluted
1 tablespoon (15 ml) piquant chutney
8 oz (225 g) self-raising flour
2 oz (50 g) margarine
salt and pepper
milk

Mash the Corned Beef with half the can of soup and the chutney. Put the flour into a bowl and rub in the margarine, add the seasoning and mix to a soft dough with milk; put on to a floured board and roll into a rectangle 6 × 9 in (15 × 23 cm). Brush the edges with milk, spread the corned beef mixture over the dough, then roll up. Put on to a baking tin, with the cut edge underneath, slash either side of the roll with a sharp knife, brush with milk and bake in a hot oven (425°F, 220°C, Gas Mark 7) for

25–30 minutes, until brown. Serve sliced, with the rest of the heated soup as a sauce. **Serves 4**

Flanagan

shortcrust pastry made with 8 oz (225 g) flour
1 oz (25 g) butter
1 onion, peeled and chopped
2 sticks celery, chopped
2 oz (50 g) mushrooms, washed and sliced
12 oz (340 g) can **Fray Bentos** Lean Cut Corned Beef
1½ oz (40 g) flour
½ pint (300 ml) stock
½ teaspoon (2.5 ml) dry mustard
salt and pepper
¼ teaspoon marjoram
beaten egg *or* milk to glaze

Roll out the pastry and use to line an 8 in (20 cm) flan ring or sandwich tin. From the trimmings, cut strips for lattice. Melt the butter in a pan. Lightly fry the onion, add the celery and mushrooms, then the corned beef cut into chunks. Stir in the flour and cook for a minute. Gradually stir in the stock and seasonings. Bring to the boil and pour into the flan case. Arrange the lattice strips on top. Brush with egg or milk. Bake in a fairly hot oven (400°F, 200°C, Gas Mark 6) for about 40 minutes. **Serves 4–6**

Texas Hash

2 oz (50 g) dripping *or* lard
2 medium onion, peeled and chopped
2 cloves garlic, finely chopped
1 lb (450 g) potatoes, peeled, diced and cooked
12 oz (340 g) can **Fray Bentos** Lean Cut Corned Beef, cut into small dice
salt and pepper

Heat the dripping in a frying pan and fry the chopped onions and garlic until soft but not brown. Add the potatoes, cook gently for a few minutes, then add the corned beef. Season, and mix well together. Allow to brown on the underside, then turn to brown on top. Serve hot. **Serves 4**

Simple Simon Pie

3 baby marrow *or* courgettes, washed and cut into ¼ in (0.5 cm) slices
2 medium onion, peeled and sliced
3 tablespoons (45 ml) cooking oil
12 oz (340 g) can **Fray Bentos** Lean Cut Corned Beef
3 tomatoes, skinned and sliced
salt and pepper
2 tablespoons (30 ml) tomato purée
¼ pint (150 ml) stock *or* water
2 eggs
¼ pint (150 ml) milk
2 oz (50 g) cheese, finely grated

Fry the marrow slices and onions in oil until just tender. Chop the corned beef into small pieces. Put a layer of the fried vegetables into the casserole, a layer of corned beef, and then a layer of sliced tomatoes. Season well and repeat this again until all the vegetables and beef have been used up. Mix the tomato purée and water together, pour over the top and cover. Bake in a moderate oven (350°F, 180°C, Gas Mark 4) for 30 minutes. Meanwhile, beat the eggs and add the milk, cheese and a little seasoning. Remove the lid, pour this mixture into the casserole and continue to cook for a further 30 minutes.   **Serves 4**

Beef and Walnut Pie

8 oz (225 g) stewing beef, cut into cubes
½ oz (12.5 g) margarine
1 oz (25 g) flour
½ pint (250 ml) Red **Oxo** stock
1 tablespoon (15 ml) tomato purée
¼ pint (125 ml) vinegar from a jar of **Haywards** Pickled Walnuts
6 **Haywards** Pickled Walnuts, chopped

7½ oz (212 g) packet frozen puff pastry, thawed
beaten egg to glaze

Fry the meat in the margarine until browned on all sides. Stir in the flour, stock, tomato purée and vinegar. Bring to the boil, cover, reduce the heat and simmer for 1 hour, until the meat is tender. Add the chopped walnuts. Pour into a pie dish and leave to cool. Roll out the pastry on a floured surface, dampen the edge of the pie dish with egg and cover the meat with the pastry. Glaze with the beaten egg and bake at 425°F, 220°C, Gas Mark 8, for 30 minutes, until the pastry is risen and golden brown.

The pickled walnuts, which have a distinctive taste, give a rich, dark, spicy gravy which is most appetising.   **Serves 4**

Pickled Beef

8 oz–1 lb (225–325 g) stewing beef, cut into cubes
½ oz (12.5 g) margarine
1 red pepper, de-seeded and diced
2 oz (50 g) flour
1 small can peeled tomatoes
½ pint (250 ml) Red **Oxo** stock
½ pint (250 ml) beer
9½ oz (262.5 g) jar **Haywards** Clear Mixed Pickles
bouquet garni

Fry the meat in the margarine until browned on all sides. Add the red pepper and fry gently for 5 minutes. Stir in the flour, tomatoes, stock, beer and pickles. Bring to the boil and add the bouquet garni. Pour into a casserole dish, cover and cook at 350°F, 180°C, Gas Mark 4, for 2 hours or until the meat is tender.   **Serves 4**

Beef Scramble

½ oz (15 g) dripping
1 onion, peeled and finely chopped
1 lb (450 g) minced beef
1 level tablespoon (15 ml) **Heinz** Sweet Pickle
salt and pepper
15¼ oz (432 g) can **Heinz** Thick Vegetable and Beef Broth
creamed potato to serve

Melt the dripping in a frying pan, add the onion and cook until golden. Stir in the minced beef and cook for 10 minutes, stirring frequently. Add the sweet pickle, salt and pepper and soup. Heat through thoroughly. Pipe or fork the creamed potato around the edge of a flameproof serving dish and brown under the grill, pour the beef mixture into the middle and serve immediately.
Serves 4

Homepride

Bachelor's Beefburger Supper

8 fresh *or* frozen beefburgers
1 tablespoon (15 ml) oil
10 oz (283 g) can new potatoes, drained
15 oz (425 g) can whole baby carrots, drained
13¼ oz (376 g) can **Homepride** Tomato and Onion Cook-in-Sauce
1 lb 2 oz (510 g) can green beans, drained
½ oz (15 g) butter *or* margarine

Fry the beefburgers in oil for 3–4 minutes on each side. Drain and place, overlapping, down one side of a shallow, ovenproof dish and add rows of potatoes and carrots. Pour over the can of Cook-in-Sauce, cover and bake at 350°F, 180°C, Gas Mark 4, for 40 minutes. Uncover, add a row of beans and dot with the butter or margarine. Cover and cook for a further 10–15 minutes.

Serve immediately with crisp wholewheat rolls.   **Serves 4**

Beef and Potato Hotpot

1 lb (450 g) minced beef
a little fat *or* oil for frying
1 can **Homepride** Chilli Cook-
 in-Sauce
12 oz (350 g) potatoes, peeled
 and thinly sliced
salt and pepper
butter
3 oz (75 g) cheese, grated

Fry the minced beef in the fat or oil
until well browned. Drain and add
the Cook-in-Sauce to the meat.
Spread a quarter of the mince
mixture in the base of a greased
2 pint (1.2 litre) casserole dish.
Cover with a layer of potatoes and
continue layering mince and
potato slices, finishing with
potatoes. Season with the salt and
pepper and dot with knobs of
butter. Sprinkle with the grated
cheese and bake at 375°F, 190°C,
Gas Mark 5 for 1–1¼ hours.
 Serve with a green vegetable.
Serves 4

Stuffed Cabbage

1 lb (450 g) minced beef
a little fat to fry
1 can **Homepride** Chilli Cook-
 in-Sauce
8 cabbage leaves, blanched for
 5 minutes in boiling salted
 water, then drained
1 pint (500 ml) cheese sauce
1 oz (25 g) cheese, grated

Fry the minced beef in a little fat
until well browned and drain well.
Add the sauce, stir well and bring
to the boil. Cover and simmer
gently for 5 minutes, stirring
occasionally. Divide the meat mixture evenly between the cabbage
leaves, roll up and place in a
shallow, ovenproof dish. Pour the
cheese sauce over the cabbage rolls
and sprinkle with the grated
cheese. Bake in the oven at 375°F,
190°C, Gas Mark 5, for 30–35
minutes, until golden brown.
 Serve with carrots.   **Serves 4**

Mince and Vegetable Pie

1 tablespoon (15 ml) oil
4 oz (125 g) onion, peeled and
 chopped
4 oz (125 g) carrot, peeled and
 grated
4 oz (125 g) turnip, peeled and
 grated
12 oz (350 g) minced beef
4 oz (125 g) sausagemeat
1 tablespoon (15 ml) flour
¼ pint (150 ml) stock
1 tablespoon (15 ml) chutney
salt and freshly ground black
 pepper
13 oz (370 g) packet **Jus-rol**
 Shortcrust Pastry, thawed
beaten egg to glaze

Heat the oil in a frying pan and
cook the onion, carrot and turnip
gently for 5 minutes. Add the
mince and sausagemeat and cook
for a further few minutes until they
begin to turn brown. Stir well to
break up the meat. Remove from
the heat and stir in the flour. Add
the stock and bring to the boil,
stirring all the time. Add the
chutney and salt and pepper to
taste. Leave the mixture to get
cold. Roll out half the pastry to line
a 10 in (25 cm) pie plate. Press the
pastry gently into the base of the
plate. Roll out the remaining
pastry to a circle slightly larger
than the plate to cover the pie.
Spoon the cold filling into the
pastry-lined plate and dome it in
the centre. Moisten the edge of the
pastry with a little water and then
lift the pastry cover over the filling.
Press the edges firmly together.
Trim the edge and make the scraps
into pastry 'leaves' to decorate the
top. Flute the edge of the pie.
Brush over the pastry top with
beaten egg. Make a hole in the
centre of the pastry. Bake in a pre-
heated oven at 400°F, 200°C, Gas
Mark 6, for about 40 minutes, or
until the pastry is crisp and golden
brown.   **Serves 6–8**

Puff Topped Beef and Wine Pie

1½ lb (700 g) chuck steak,
 cubed
1 oz (25 g) seasoned flour
3 tablespoons (45 ml) oil
1 onion, peeled and chopped
8 oz (225 g) mushrooms, wiped
 and sliced
¼ pint (150 ml) red wine
¼ pint (150 ml) beef stock
salt and freshly ground pepper
1 teaspoon (5 ml) dried basil
13 oz (370 g) packet **Jus-rol** Puff
 Pastry, thawed
beaten egg to glaze

Toss the meat in the seasoned
flour. Heat the oil in a pan and fry
the meat until sealed. Remove the
meat. Fry the onion and mushrooms until soft. Tip in any
remaining flour and cook for
2 minutes. Remove from the heat
and add the wine and stock.
Return to the heat and bring to the
boil, stirring all the time. Season
and add the herbs, then return the
meat to the sauce. Cover and allow
to simmer for 2–2½ hours. Transfer the beef in sauce to a 2 pint
(1.2 litre) pie dish and allow to
cool.
 Roll out the pastry and using a
2½ in (6.5 cm) cutter cut out
18–20 circles. Cut out the centres
of these with a 1 in (2.5 cm) cutter.
Top the pie with the pastry rings
and glaze with beaten egg. Bake in
a pre-heated oven at 425°F, 220°C,
Gas Mark 7 for 15 minutes. Reduce
the oven heat to 350°F, 180°C,
Gas Mark 4, for a further 15
minutes. Serve hot.   **Serves 4**

Gaelic Steaks

4 T-bone steaks
2 oz (50 g) **Kerrygold** Butter
8 oz (225 g) mushrooms, washed and sliced
¼ pint (125 ml) **Kerrygold** Double Cream
2 tablespoons (30 ml) Irish whiskey

Fry the steaks in 1 oz (25 g) of the butter until cooked. Place on a hot dish. Place the remaining butter in the pan and cook the mushrooms. Add the whiskey and cream. Heat gently but do not boil, stirring all the time. Pour over the steaks and serve. **Serves 4**

Braised Beef with Pasta

1 tablespoon (15 ml) oil
1½ lb (600 g) braising steak, cubed
3 oz (75 g) pasta shells
2 carrots, peeled and sliced
2 sticks celery, sliced
1 pint (500 ml) **Knorr** beef stock
1 tablespoon (15 ml) tomato purée
1 small packet frozen peas
salt and pepper

Heat the oil and brown the meat all over for about 3–4 minutes. Place the pasta, carrots and celery in the base of a deep, ovenproof casserole. Cover with the meat, stock, tomato purée and season well. Cover and cook at 350°F, 180°C, Gas Mark 4, for about 1½ hours, or until the meat is tender. Add the peas 10 minutes before the cooking time is finished.
Serves 4

Crispy Beef

1 tablespoon (15 ml) oil
1 lb (400 g) minced beef
1 onion, peeled and chopped

½ pint (250 ml) **Knorr** beef stock
1 small packet mixed vegetables
seasoning
Topping
1½ oz (40 g) butter
3 oz (75 g) plain flour
2 oz (50 g) Cheddar cheese, grated

Heat the oil and sauté the meat and onion for 3–5 minutes. Add the stock and simmer for 10 minutes. Stir in the vegetables and seasoning and pour into an oven-proof pie dish. Rub the butter into the flour, stir in the cheese and sprinkle over the meat. Cook at 375°F, 190°C, Gas Mark 5, for 30 minutes.
Serve with fresh vegetables and mashed potatoes. **Serves 4**

Curried Beef Pie

1 tablespoon (15 ml) oil
1 lb (400 g) minced beef
1 onion, peeled and chopped
2 level tablespoons (30 ml) curry powder
1 oz (25 g) cornflour
1 pint (500 ml) **Knorr** beef stock
1½ lb (600 g) potatoes, cooked and mashed
beaten egg

Heat the oil in a large, deep frying pan and sauté the minced beef and onion for 4–5 minutes. Add the curry powder, cornflour and stock and simmer gently for 20 minutes, stirring occasionally. Turn on to a serving dish, bordered with the mashed potato, which has been brushed with egg and placed under a pre-heated grill for 3–4 minutes.
Serve with carrots and cabbage or cauliflower. **Serves 4**

Leek and Beef Braise

2 lb (800 g) chuck steak in one piece
2 teaspoons (10 ml) mustard, made up
4 oz (100 g) fresh breadcrumbs

1 onion, peeled and chopped
3 tomatoes, skinned and chopped
2 tablespoons (30 ml) salad cream
2 tablespoons (30 ml) parsley, chopped
salt and pepper
1 oz (25 g) dripping
½ pint (250 ml) **Knorr** beef stock
1 lb (400 g) carrots, peeled and thinly sliced
1 lb (400 g) leeks, washed and sliced

Beat the meat with a rolling pin to flatten. Season well and spread with the mustard. In a basin combine the breadcrumbs, onion, tomatoes, parsley, seasoning and salad cream. Once well mixed spread on the meat. Roll up and secure with string but not too tightly. Melt the dripping in a large, fireproof dish and brown the meat all over. Roast for 10 minutes at 375°F, 190°C, Gas Mark 5. Place the leeks, carrots and stock round the meat, cover and bake for 2½ hours at 325°F, 170°C, Gas Mark 3.
To serve, place the meat on a serving dish. Serve the vegetables and juice separately, with jacket potatoes. **Serves 4–6**

Pot Roast

2 tablespoons (30 ml) oil
1 large onion, peeled and chopped
8 oz (200 g) carrots, peeled and diced
4 sticks celery, chopped
2 lb (800 g) piece brisket of beef
1 parsnip, peeled and diced
½ pint (250 ml) **Knorr** beef stock
salt and pepper

Heat the oil in a frying pan and sauté the vegetables for 3–4 minutes. Put them into a deep, ovenproof casserole. Put the meat into the oil and brown well all over to seal in the juices. Place on top of the vegetables, add the stock and seasoning. Cover and cook at 325°F, 160°C, Gas Mark 3, for

2½–3 hours.

When cooked serve the meat and vegetables on a hot dish and the liquor separately. Jacket potatoes go very well with this dish.
Serves 4–6

Spiced Topside

4 lb (1.8 kg) topside of beef
seasoned flour
1 tablespoon (15 ml) dripping *or* oil
1 wineglass red wine
1 bay leaf
3 cloves
1 onion, peeled and sliced
¼ pint (125 ml) **Knorr** beef stock

Heat the dripping or oil in a large saucepan, deep enough to hold the joint. Toss the meat in seasoned flour and brown all over in the hot fat. Pour off any surplus fat and add the remaining ingredients. Cover the pan tightly and simmer gently, allowing 35–45 minutes to the lb (450 g). When cooked, dish up the meat, remove any fat from the gravy and serve with carrots, onions and potatoes.

Suet Medley

1 lb (400 g) stewing steak, cubed
2 onions, peeled and sliced
1 large cooking apple, peeled and diced
1 parsnip, peeled and diced
½ small swede, peeled and diced
salt and pepper
1 teaspoon (5 ml) mixed herbs
6 oz (150 g) suet pastry
1 oz (25 g) seasoned flour
⅛ pint (75 ml) **Knorr** beef stock

Line a 1½ pint (900 ml) greased pudding basin with three-quarters of the pastry. Toss the meat in the seasoned flour and place in basin alternating with the remaining ingredients. Season well. Pour over the stock, cover with the remaining pastry, sealing the edges well, cover the basin with greaseproof paper and a pudding cloth or foil. Steam for 2½–3 hours.

To serve, make extra gravy and serve with boiled potatoes and brussels sprouts. **Serves 4**

Corned Beef and Apple Sandwich

8 slices bread
butter for spreading
12 oz (340 g) can **Libby's** Corned Beef, chilled
French mustard
1 eating apple, thinly sliced

Spread both sides of the bread with the butter. Slice the corned beef thinly, place on 4 slices of the bread, spread with French mustard, top with the apple slices and cover with the remaining bread slices. Toast in an infra red grill or, on both sides, under an ordinary grill, until golden brown and crisp. **Serves 4**

Libby's Lattice Flan

1 tablespoon (15 ml) oil
6 oz (150 g) onion, chopped
1 small green pepper, de-seeded and chopped
pinch rosemary
8 oz (200 g) shortcrust pastry
12 oz (340 g) can **Libby's** Corned Beef

Sauce
½ oz (12.5 g) butter
½ oz (12.5 g) flour
¼ pint (125 ml) milk
salt and pepper

beaten egg to glaze

Heat the oil in a frying pan and fry the onion and pepper until soft. Mix the rosemary and fried mixture with the corned beef. Line an 8 in (20 cm) fluted flan ring with the pastry, reserving the trimmings. Place the butter, flour and milk in a saucepan. Bring to the boil, whisking continuously and season to taste. Place the corned beef mixture in the flan case and cover with the sauce. Roll

out the remaining pastry and cut into narrow strips, twist and lay over the flan to make a lattice. Seal well to the edge of the flan. Brush with beaten egg, place in an oven pre-heated to 400°F, 200°C, Gas Mark 6, for 20–25 minutes.
Serves 4–6

Beef Stew with Herb Dumplings

1½ lb (675 g) stewing steak, cubed
1 oz (25 g) seasoned plain flour
1 oz (25 g) dripping
1 large onion, peeled and thinly sliced
1 medium carrot, peeled and diced
1 medium turnip, peeled and diced
1 stick celery, diced
1 teaspoon **Marmite**
½ pint (300 ml) hot water
Dumplings
4 oz (100 g) self-raising flour
2 oz (50 g) shredded suet
pinch salt
2 teaspoons (10 ml) fresh herbs, chopped *or* 1 teaspoon (5 ml) dried mixed herbs
cold water to mix

Coat the steak with the seasoned flour, fry in the dripping until brown, remove and keep warm. Fry the vegetables until golden, stir in the remaining flour and gradually add the Marmite dissolved in the hot water. Bring to the boil, stirring well. Add the meat, mix well and adjust seasoning to taste. Cover, lower the heat and simmer very gently for 2 hours until the beef is tender.

Half an hour before serving time, mix the flour, suet, salt and herbs and add about 4 tablespoons (60 ml) cold water, sufficient to make a soft dough. Shape into 8 balls, drop into the casserole, cover and cook for the last 20 minutes' cooking time.
Serves 4

Mazola

Raised Veal and Ham Pie

Pastry
¼ pint (125 ml) **Mazola** Pure Corn Oil
¼ pint (125 ml) water
12 oz (300 g) plain flour
¼ level teaspoon salt

Filling
1 lb (400 g) pie veal, trimmed and cubed
8 oz (200 g) uncooked ham, trimmed and cubed
1 level teaspoon (5 ml) salt
pinch each parsley and thyme
juice and grated rind 1 small lemon
½ pint (250 ml) jellied stock, well seasoned *or* ½ pint (250 ml) stock made with a chicken stock cube plus ½ oz (15 g) dissolved gelatine
beaten egg *or* milk to glaze

Bring the corn oil and water to the boil in a saucepan and remove from the heat. Stir in the sieved flour and salt and beat to form a smooth dough, using a wooden spoon. Line a deep 6 in (15 cm) cake tin, preferably loose-bottomed, with approximately three-quarters of the pastry. Mix together the veal, ham, salt, herbs and lemon and place in the pastry case. Warm the stock and pour 3 tablespoons (45 ml) over the meat. Cover with the remaining pastry, using the trimmings for 'leaves' to decorate the top. Make a hole in the centre of the pie to allow the steam to escape and glaze with the beaten egg or milk. Cook at 425°F, 220°C, Gas Mark 7, for 20 minutes, then at 300°F, 150°C, Gas Mark 2, for a further 2–2½ hours. If necessary, cover with foil or greaseproof paper to prevent over-browning. Allow the pie to cool in the tin. Using a small funnel, slowly pour the cooled stock into the pie until full.
Serves 6–8

Minced Beef Sandwich

1 medium onion, peeled and finely chopped
8–12 oz (225–350 g) raw minced beef
cooking oil *or* fat for frying
3 teaspoons (15 ml) cornflour
1 Red **Oxo** Cube, crumbled and dissolved in 3 tablespoons (45 ml) hot water
2 tablespoons (30 ml) peas, cooked
salt and pepper
5 oz (150 g) flour
4 oz (100 g) rolled oats
½ level teaspoon (2.5 ml) salt
4 oz (100 g) margarine
1 tomato, sliced
Oxo gravy to serve

Gently fry the onion and mince in a little oil or fat until the mince is browned. Sprinkle the cornflour over the meat, stir the mixture well and add the Oxo stock, peas and seasoning. Stir over a low heat until the liquid is absorbed. Put the flour, rolled oats and salt into a bowl and rub in the margarine. Press half the mixture into a 7½ in (19 cm) square tin, spread the meat mixture on top, then cover with the remaining flour mixture. Press well down. Bake at 375°F, 190°C, Gas Mark 5, for about 40 minutes. Turn out on to a heatproof dish, top with the sliced tomato and put under a hot grill to cook the tomato.
Serve with the Oxo gravy.
Serves 4

Steak in Peppered Sauce

2 oz (50 g) margarine
4 rump steaks (each about 6–8 oz (175–225 g))
1 small onion, peeled and finely chopped
1 oz (25 g) plain flour
4 tomatoes, skinned and de-seeded
1 green pepper, de-seeded and sliced
2 tablespoons (30 ml) capers
pinch mixed herbs
1 tablespoon (15 ml) tomato purée
2 tablespoons (30 ml) sherry (optional)
2 tablespoons (30 ml) fresh parsley, chopped
1 Red **Oxo** Cube, crumbled and dissolved in ¼ pint (150 ml) hot water
salt and pepper

Melt the margarine in a frying pan and fry the steaks and onion. Turn the steaks once and fry to personal taste. Remove the meat and keep hot. Stir the flour into the remaining fat in the frying pan and cook, stirring all the time, for 1 minute. Chop the tomatoes and add, with the green pepper, to the pan. Add the remaining ingredients and bring to the boil, stirring all the time, then reduce the heat and simmer for 5 minutes. Return the steaks to the pan and reheat in the sauce. Serve immediately.
Serve with sauté potatoes and a green salad containing plenty of chopped fresh herbs. **Serves 4**

Veal Estrella

4 pieces pie veal (each about 5 oz (150 g))
salt and pepper
1 oz (25 g) margarine
1 large onion, peeled and sliced
2 tablespoons (30 ml) flour
15 oz (425 g) can peeled tomatoes
1 Chicken **Oxo** Cube, crumbled and dissolved in ⅓ pint (200 ml) hot water
1 tablespoon (15 ml) tomato purée
1 tablespoon (15 ml) capers
1 tablespoon (15 ml) caper liquid
chopped parsley to garnish

Season the veal with salt and pepper. Melt the margarine in a pan and brown the pieces of veal all over. Transfer to a casserole dish. Brown the onion in the same pan then stir in the flour and cook for 1 minute. Add the tomatoes, Chicken Oxo, tomato purée, salt and pepper, capers and liquid and bring to the boil. Pour over the veal, cover and cook in a moderate oven (350°F, 180°C, Gas Mark 4) for about 1¼ hours, or until tender. Garnish with the chopped parsley.

Serve with new potatoes and a mixture of spring vegetables.
Serves 4

RY·KING

Meatballs in Tomato Sauce

8 oz (200 g) minced beef
8 oz (200 g) sausagemeat
6 slices **Ry-King** Light, crushed
salt and pepper
beaten egg to mix
1 small onion, peeled and chopped
1 oz (25 g) margarine
1 oz (25 g) flour
14 oz (396 g) can tomatoes
1 tablespoon (15 ml) tomato purée
½ pint (250 ml) stock
1 teaspoon (5 ml) marjoram
2 slices **Ry-King** Light, crumbled, and chopped parsley to garnish

Mix together the minced beef, sausagemeat and crushed Ry-King, season and add sufficient beaten egg to bind. Form into small balls. Melt the margarine in a large pan, fry the onion, stir in the flour then add the tomatoes plus juice, purée, marjoram and seasoning. Bring to the boil, add the meatballs and a little stock if necessary to ensure the liquid covers the meatballs, then simmer gently for 45 minutes.

Serve topped with the crumbled Ry-King and chopped parsley.
Serves 4

SCHWARTZ

Schwartz Carbonnade of Beef

2 tablespoons (30 ml) cooking oil
1½ lb (681 g) stewing steak, trimmed and cubed
8 oz (227 g) onions, peeled and sliced
4 oz (113 g) celery, sliced
1 packet **Schwartz** Spice'n'Easy Mix for Beef Casserole
½ pint (285 ml) stout beer
¼ pint (142 ml) boiling water
Topping (optional)
4 slices French bread each approx 3 in (8 cm) thick
2 oz (57 g) Red Leicester cheese, grated and tossed in **Schwartz** Paprika

Fry the stewing steak and prepared vegetables in the oil in a pan until the meat is browned and the vegetables are beginning to soften. Transfer to a casserole dish. Stir in the contents of the Schwartz Spice'n'Easy packet, the beer and water until all ingredients are thoroughly combined. Cover and cook for 2 hours in the oven at 350°F, 180°C, Gas Mark 4 or until the meat is tender.

Meanwhile, cover the slices of French bread with cheese and paprika. Float the bread slices on top of the casserole at the end of the cooking time. Return the dish to the oven for approximately 5–10 minutes until the cheese is melted and bubbling over the bread.

Serve immediately with green vegetables and creamed potatoes. The casserole may be stored, without the bread topping, for up to 2 days in a refrigerator or up to 2 months in a freezer. **Serves 4**

Spice Islands

12 oz (340 g) corned beef
1 medium onion, peeled and chopped
1 tablespoon (15 ml) oil

½ teaspoon (2.5 ml) **Schwartz** Marjoram
½ teaspoon (2.5 ml) **Schwartz** Thyme
½ teaspoon (2.5 ml) **Schwartz** Paprika
salt
1 lb (454 g) mashed potatoes
selection **Bick's** Relishes

Cut the corned beef into small cubes. Heat the oil in a frying pan and sauté the onions until soft. Add the corned beef, herbs, paprika and salt. Cook for about 5 minutes, turning regularly until all the ingredients are cooked. Form the mashed potato into 4 rings, dot with butter and brown under a hot grill. Pile the mixture into the hot potato rings and serve with vegetables and variety of Relishes. **Serves 4**

The Great American Success

1 lb (450 g) minced beef
1 small onion, peeled and finely chopped
1 teaspoon (5 ml) **Schwartz** Mixed Herbs
salt and pepper
1 egg, beaten
oil for coating
6 bread baps
Bick's Chili Sauce Relish

Mix the minced beef and onion together, add the herbs and a generous amount of salt and pepper. Bind ingredients with the egg. Divide into 6, shape into flat cakes, brush with oil and cook under a hot grill for 4–6 minutes, turning once. Place each hamburger into a roll and cover with the Chili Sauce Relish.

Serve hot with chips and salad or baked beans, mushrooms and onion rings. **Serves 6**

Winter Minced Beef and Vegetable Pie

2 tablespoons (30 ml) cooking oil
10 oz (284 g) minced beef
4 oz (113 g) swede, peeled and finely chopped
4 oz (113 g) onion, peeled and sliced
1½ oz (42 g) plain flour
14 oz (397 g) can tomatoes
2 teaspoon (10 ml) **Schwartz** Italian Seasoning
½ teaspoon (2.5 ml) **Schwartz** Garlic Granules
¼ teaspoon **Schwartz** Ground Black Pepper
1 teaspoon (5 ml) salt
1 beef stock cube
12 oz (340 g) prepared shortcrust pastry
beaten egg
Schwartz Sesame Seeds to garnish
tomato slices (optional)

Fry the minced beef, swede and onions in the oil until the meat is brown and the vegetables are beginning to soften. Drain off the excess oil, stir in the flour, tomatoes and juice, Italian seasoning, garlic granules, black pepper, salt and the crumbled stock cube. Bring to the boil and simmer for 5 minutes. Meanwhile, roll out half the pastry and use to line an 8 in (20 cm) pie dish. Roll out the remaining pastry to form a lid. Pour in the prepared meat filling, brush the edges with beaten egg and cover with the pastry lid. Seal the edges and decorate as desired. Brush the pie surface with beaten egg and sprinkle liberally with sesame seeds. Cook in the oven pre-heated to 400°F, 200°C, Gas Mark 6 for 30 minutes. Garnish with slices of tomato to serve. **Serves 4–6**

Sharwood's

Escalopes Cordon Bleu

4 veal escalopes
black pepper
5 oz (150 g) ham, cut into 4 slices
7 oz (200 g) Gruyère cheese, cut into 4 thin slices
10 oz (283 g) can **Sharwood's** White Wine Sauce
watercress to garnish

Place the escalopes in an oven-proof dish and season with freshly ground black pepper. Lay a slice of ham, then a slice of cheese, on top of each escalope. Pour over the white wine sauce, cover and bake for 1¼ hours at 350°F, 180°C, Gas Mark 4, or until tender. To serve, garnish with watercress. **Serves 4**

Steak, Kidney and Butter Bean Pudding

8 oz (225 g) self raising flour
½ level teaspoon (2.5 ml) salt
4 oz (100 g) shredded suet
¼ pint (150 ml) cold water
14¾ oz (417 g) can **Tyne Brand** Steak with Kidney Pie Filling
7¾ oz (219 g) can butter beans, drained

Grease a 1½ pint (900 ml) pudding basin. Mix the flour, salt and suet. Stir in the water with a knife to form a soft dough and knead with the fingertips until smooth. Remove a quarter of the dough; roll out the remainder on a lightly floured surface and use to line the pudding basin. Roll out the remaining dough to fit the top of the basin. In a separate bowl, combine the pie filling with the butter beans. Spoon the mixture into the pastry-lined basin. Brush the edge with water and place the circle of dough on top. Press the

edges firmly together, cover with foil or greaseproof paper and steam for 1¼–1½ hours. Serve piping hot. **Serves 3**

Uncle Ben's

Stir-fried Steak and Vegetables

1 lb (450 g) fillet *or* rump steak, cut into thin strips
2 tablespoons (30 ml) soy sauce
2 tablespoons (30 ml) sherry
1 clove garlic, crushed
1 medium carrot, scrubbed and grated
1 green pepper, with seeds removed, finely chopped
1 stick celery, finely chopped
2–3 slices fresh green *or* stem ginger
2 tablespoons (30 ml) oil
8 oz (225 g) **Uncle Ben's** American Long Grain Rice

Marinate the steak in a mixture of the soy sauce, sherry and garlic for 30 minutes, turning occasionally. Mix the green pepper with the celery and ginger. Heat the oil in a large frying pan or wok, add the steak, vegetables and ginger and fry over a fairly high heat, stirring regularly for about 3–4 minutes, until the steak is brown and the vegetables are cooked but still crisp. Serve with the rice, either boiled or fried. **Serves 4**

Veal Goulash

1 lb (450 g) onions, peeled and finely sliced
2 tablespoons (30 ml) oil *or* lard for frying
1½ lb (675 g) shoulder *or* leg of veal, cubed
¼ pint (150 ml) stock
salt and pepper
2 tablespoons (30 ml) paprika pepper
1 tablespoon (15 ml) tomato purée
2 teaspoons (10 ml) cornflour

¼ pint (150 ml) soured cream
8 oz (225 g) **Uncle Ben's**
American Long Grain Rice

Fry the onions in the oil or lard until soft but not brown. Rub through a sieve into a casserole dish. Add the veal and cover with the stock. Season with the salt, pepper and paprika. Cover and cook at 325°F, 160°C, Gas Mark 3 for about 1 hour, until the meat is tender. Add the tomato purée. Mix the cornflour gradually with the soured cream to form a thin paste, add to the casserole and reheat gently for a further 15 minutes, but do not allow to boil. Serve with boiled rice.   **Serves 4**

Cheesy Chilli Pie

½ oz (15 g) **White Cap** Pure
Blended White Fat
1 lb (450 g) minced beef
1 small onion, peeled and
chopped
1 oz (25 g) flour
1 level teaspoon (5 ml) chilli
powder
¼ pint (150 ml) stock
15½ oz (440 g) can red kidney
beans
2 tablespoons (30 ml) tomato
purée
salt and pepper
Cheese Pastry
4 oz (100 g) **White Cap** Pure
Blended White Fat
8 oz (200 g) plain flour
½ level teaspoon (2.5 ml) salt
pinch mustard
pinch cayenne pepper
3 oz (75 g) cheese, grated
3 tablespoons (45 ml) water
milk to glaze

For the filling, heat the White Cap in a medium-sized saucepan. Fry the minced beef until brown. Add the onion and cook for 2–3 minutes. Stir in the flour and chilli powder and mix well. Add the stock gradually, stirring con-

tinuously and bring to the boil. Cook 1–2 minutes, until thickened. Add the remaining ingredients and leave to cool. To make the cheese pastry, rub the White Cap into the sieved dry ingredients until the mixture resembles fine breadcrumbs. Stir in the cheese. Add water and mix to a firm dough. Knead lightly. Place the filling in a 2 pint (1 litre) pie dish, roll out the pastry and cover the top. Trim, flake and flute the edge. Glaze with milk. Bake in a pre-heated oven at 400°F, 200°C, Gas Mark 6, for 25–30 minutes until the pastry is golden brown. Serve hot.   **Serves 4**

whitworths

Meatballs in Tomato Sauce

1 lb (450 g) minced beef
1 clove garlic, crushed
3 oz (75 g) sachet **Whitworths**
Country Stuffing Mix
1 egg, made up to just over
¼ pint (150 ml) with water
salt and pepper
3 tablespoons (45 ml) oil
Sauce
1 medium onion, peeled and
chopped
1 stick celery, chopped
3 tablespoons (45 ml) dried
mushrooms, sliced
15 oz (425 g) can tomatoes
pinch sugar
salt and pepper
1 teaspoon (5 ml) mixed herbs

Mix all the ingredients for the meatballs except the oil. Turn on to a lightly floured board and divide into 18 small balls. Heat the oil in a large frying pan, add the meatballs and cook gently, stirring occasionally, until lightly browned. Remove from the pan with a slotted spoon and drain. Add the sauce ingredients and stir well to break up the tomatoes. Add the meatballs, cover and simmer gently for about 30 minutes.
Serves 4–6

Veal Imperial

3 oz (75 g) butter
4 veal escalopes *or* boneless
chops
¼ pint (150 ml) veal *or* chicken
stock
1 oz (25 g) flour
¼ pint (150 ml) **Young's** Dairy
Cream
3 tablespoons (45 ml) medium
sherry
salt and black pepper
2 oz (50 g) button mushrooms,
washed
1 tin asparagus spears
2 tablespoons (30 ml) Parmesan
cheese, grated

Melt 2 oz (50 g) of the butter in a large frying pan and fry the escalopes until they are brown on both sides, remove them from the pan and keep warm. Add the stock to the pan, bring to the boil to collect all the meat juices, stir and strain off. Melt the remaining butter in the pan and blend in the flour, cook for 1 minute then add the strained stock, cream, sherry and seasoning. Bring to the boil, stirring continuously and place the meat in the sauce. Add the whole mushrooms and simmer gently until the meat is tender. Drain the asparagus spears.

When cooked, arrange the meat on a heatproof serving dish, coat with the sauce and garnish with the asparagus. Sprinkle the Parmesan cheese over the top and brown in a hot oven (425°F, 220°C, Gas Mark 7) or under the grill.
Serves 4

LAMB

Mrs Leech's Lamb Hot Pot with Crunchy Dumplings

1–1½ lb (500–750 g) boned stewing lamb (lean breast *or* shoulder)
3 tablespoons (45 ml) vegetable oil
1 onion, peeled and sliced
2 carrots, peeled and sliced
2 tablespoons (30 ml) flour
¾ pint (375 ml) stock
2 bay leaves
salt and ground black pepper
8 oz (225 g) can butter beans, drained
Dumplings
6 oz (150 g) self-raising flour
3 oz (75 g) **Atora** Shredded Suet
grated rind of 1 lemon
1 teaspoon (5 ml) mixed dried herbs
salt and ground black pepper
water to mix

Cut the meat into cubes and fry quickly in the oil to brown. Remove to a plate. Add the onion and carrots to the pan and fry gently until softened, about 10 minutes. Stir in the flour, then add the stock and bring to the boil, stirring until thickened. Add the bay leaves and seasoning and return the meat to the pan. Transfer to an ovenproof casserole dish, cover and cook for about 1 hour at 350°F, 180°C, Gas Mark 4.

Stir in the butter beans. Make up the dumplings by mixing the dry ingredients together and mixing to a stiff dough with the water. Divide into eight small balls. Drop into the casserole, cover again and return to the oven for about another 30 minutes, uncovering after 15 minutes to let the dumplings go crunchy and browned on top.

Serve hot with green leafy vegetables or leeks.   **Serves 4**

Braised Leg of Lamb with Rosemary

1 leg *or* ½ leg of lamb
garlic slivers
1 can **Baxters** Sauce Provençale
rosemary leaves
fresh rosemary *or* parsley to garnish

Spike the lamb well with the slivers of garlic, put in a casserole and cover with the Sauce Provençale. Scatter liberally with the rosemary leaves. Cover with a lid and cook for 1½ hours in the oven at 350°F, 180°C, Gas Mark 4, then turn the meat, baste with the sauce and cook with the lid off for a further 20 minutes.

To serve, slice the meat on a large plate, spoon the sauce over the slices and garnish with fresh rosemary or parsley.
Serves 4–6

Lamb and Potato Bake

1 rounded tablespoon (20 g) plain flour
¼ teaspoon crushed rosemary
1 level teaspoon (5 ml) salt
shake of pepper
1½ lb (675 g) potatoes, peeled and thinly sliced
1 medium onion, peeled and thinly sliced
2 level teaspoons (10 ml) **Bisto**
4 lamb chump chops
sprigs of parsley to garnish

Mix the flour, rosemary, salt and pepper together. Arrange layers of potato and onion in a 3 pint (1.8 litre) casserole, finishing with a layer of potatoes and sprinkling seasoned flour between the layers. Blend the Bisto with a little water in a measuring jug and make up to ½ pint (300 ml) with water. Pour over the potatoes. Place the chops on top and cook, uncovered, in the middle of the oven pre-heated to 375°F, 190°C, Gas Mark 5, for about 1 hour, until the chops and potatoes are cooked.

Garnish with parsley and serve with a green vegetable or salad.
Serves 4

BON

Fricassé of Lamb

1½ lb (675 g) breast of lamb, boned
2 onions, peeled and sliced
1 red *or* green pepper, de-seeded and sliced
1 tablespoon (15 ml) cornflour
1 Chicken **Oxo** Cube, dissolved in ½ pint (300 ml) water
4 tablespoons (60 ml) **Bon** White Cooking Wine
1 bay leaf
1 clove
pinch nutmeg
3 peppercorns
1 teaspoon (5 ml) salt
2 tablespoons (30 ml) soured cream
sprigs of parsley and lemon wedges to garnish

Trim the lamb and cut into 1 in (2.5 cm) pieces. Place in a casserole dish with the onions and peppers. Mix the cornflour with a little water and stir into the Oxo stock in a saucepan. Bring to the boil and stir until thickened. Add the Bon, bay leaf, clove, nutmeg, peppercorns and salt. Pour into the casserole, cover and cook in a preheated oven at 350°F, 180°C, Gas Mark 4, for 1½ hours or until the meat is tender. Remove the bay leaf, clove and peppercorns. Stir in the soured cream just before serving, taking care that the mixture does not boil afterwards.

Serve on a bed of boiled rice, garnished with the sprigs of parsley and lemon wedges.

Serves 4

Devilled Lamb Chops

4 lamb chump chops
1 large onion, peeled and finely chopped
1 oz (25 g) butter
4 tablespoons (60 ml) redcurrant jelly
2 Red Cubes from **Bovril**
3 tablespoons (45 ml) vinegar

Grill the chops crisply. Meanwhile, fry the onion in the butter until soft and golden. Add the redcurrant jelly, crumbled Bovril cubes and vinegar, and stir over a low heat until the jelly has melted. Bring to the boil, cover and simmer over a low heat for 5 minutes. Pour the sauce over the chops and serve at once.

If liked, a little mustard and a pinch of ground mixed spice may be added to the sauce before cooking.   **Serves 4**

Devon Lamb Stew

1½ oz (40 g) butter
5 lamb chops
1¼–1½ lb (575–675 g) small potatoes, peeled and halved
8 oz (225 g) small whole onions, peeled
½ red pepper, de-seeded and cut into strips
½ green pepper, de-seeded and cut into strips

8 oz (225 g) button mushrooms, washed and sliced
1 tablespoon (15 ml) flour
1 Chicken Cube from **Bovril**, dissolved in ¼ pint (150 ml) water
½ pint (300 ml) white wine
¼ pint (150 ml) cream
salt and pepper
2 tablespoons (30 ml) chopped mint to garnish

Melt the butter in a large pan. Fry the chops for 5 minutes, then transfer to an ovenproof dish. Add the potatoes, onions and peppers to the fat, and fry for 3–4 minutes. Stir in the mushrooms and flour and fry another 1–2 minutes. Stir in the stock, wine and cream, add salt and pepper and bring to the boil, stirring all the time. Pour the vegetable mixture over the chops, cover and bake at 350°F, 180°C, Gas Mark 4, for 35–40 minutes, until the meat is tender.

Serve garnished with chopped mint.   **Serves 5**

Shoulder of Lamb in Cider

1 large lemon
salt and pepper
1 teaspoon (5 ml) dried rosemary
1 shoulder of lamb
½ pint (300 ml) **Bulmers** Dry Woodpecker Cider
2 large cooking apples
2 teaspoons (10 ml) cornflour (optional)
a little cider to mix (optional)

Grate the lemon peel and squeeze out the juice. Put the salt, pepper, lemon peel and rosemary into the lamb. Place the lamb in a roasting tin, add the cider and juice of the lemon. Cook for about 1½–2 hours at 350°F, 180°C, Gas Mark 5. Peel and core the apples, slice thickly and place on the lamb 20 minutes before the end of the cooking time.

When serving, hand the juices separately as a sauce, thickened, if liked, by mixing the cornflour with a little cider, adding it to the sauce and bringing to the boil.

Delicious served with roast potatoes and fresh green peas.
Serves 4

Family Croquettes

12 oz (350 g) cold cooked lamb, minced
5½ oz (156 g) **Campbell's** Condensed Chicken Soup
8 oz (225 g) potatoes, peeled, cooked and creamed
pinch dried rosemary
salt and pepper
2 oz (50 g) flour, seasoned with salt and pepper
1 large egg, well beaten
dried breadcrumbs for coating
deep fat for frying

Put the lamb into a mixing bowl and stir in the undiluted soup, creamed potatoes, rosemary and seasoning. Divide the mixture into 6 equal portions and shape them into flat, round croquettes. Coat each croquette first in the flour, then in the beaten egg and finally in the breadcrumbs so that they are evenly and completely coated. Heat the deep fat to 360°F, 185°C (when a piece of bread dropped into the hot fat browns in 1 minute). Cook the croquettes in 2 batches, frying them for about 5 minutes, until they are golden brown. Drain well on kitchen paper.

Serve with shredded, cooked cabbage and sauté potatoes.
Serves 6

Hot Spiced Lamb

1 tablespoon (15 ml) oil
8 small lamb chump chops
1 onion, peeled and sliced
1 clove garlic, crushed
1 teaspoon (5 ml) chilli powder
1 tablespoon (15 ml) curry powder
10½ oz (297 g) can **Campbell's** Condensed Lentil Soup, undiluted
½ pint (300 ml) water
3 tablespoons (45 ml) natural yoghurt
2 oz (50 g) salted peanuts

Heat the oil in a saucepan and fry the chops until browned. Add the onion and garlic, and cook for a further 3–4 minutes. Sprinkle the chilli and curry powders into the pan, cook for 1–2 minutes then add the soup and water, mix well and simmer slowly for 45–50 minutes. Stir in the yoghurt and peanuts just before serving. **Serves 4**

Lucky Day Lamb

4 oz (100 g) haricot beans, soaked overnight in water to cover
1 oz (25 g) dripping
3½–4 lb (1.5–1.75 kg) shoulder of lamb joint
1 medium onion, peeled and sliced
4 oz (100 g) mushrooms, washed and thinly sliced
½ teaspoon (2.5 ml) dried rosemary
10½ oz (297 g) can **Campbell's** Condensed Lentil Soup
½ soup can water
small bunch of watercress to garnish

Drain the soaked beans, put them in a saucepan, cover with fresh, cold water, bring to the boil and boil steadily for about 10 minutes. Meanwhile, melt the dripping in a roasting tin and brown the lamb on all sides. Transfer the joint to a plate, add the onions to the fat in the tin and cook them slowly until tender. Add the mushrooms, rosemary and undiluted soup.

Drain the beans and stir them into the other ingredients with half a soup can of water. Bring to the boil and then reduce the heat, put the lamb into the tin and cover completely with foil. Cook on the centre shelf of a moderately hot oven, 375°F, 190°C, Gas Mark 5, for 2½ hours or until the joint and the beans are tender.

Serve the lamb on a large dish, surrounded by the sauce and garnished with the watercress. **Serves 6**

Mushroom and Lamb Bake

1 tablespoon (15 ml) oil
4 lamb chops
1 onion, peeled and chopped
1 can **Chesswood** Sliced Mushrooms in Creamed Sauce
4 oz (113 g) packet frozen peas
2 teaspoons (10 ml) mixed herbs
¼ pint (125 ml) milk
salt and pepper

Fry the chops on both sides in the oil to seal. Place in an ovenproof dish. Gently fry the onion to soften. Mix the Sliced Mushrooms in Creamed Sauce with the onion, peas and herbs. Add the milk to the sauce and season to taste. Pour the sauce over the chops, cover and bake for 1 hour at 350°F, 180°C, Gas Mark 4. **Serves 4**

Loin of Lamb with Tomato and Anchovy Stuffing and Sauce

2–3 lb (1–1.5 kg) loin of lamb, boned
4–5 tablespoons (60–75 g) fresh white breadcrumbs
2 tablespoons (30 ml) herbs, chopped (a mixture of parsley, chives, thyme and marjoram)
salt and pepper
6 anchovy fillets
14 oz (396 g) can **Cirio** Peeled Tomatoes
2 tablespoons (30 ml) onion, peeled and finely chopped
1 oz (25 g) butter
2 eggs, beaten
seasoned flour
browned breadcrumbs for coating
a little dripping
Sauce
3 shallots, peeled and finely chopped
½ oz (15 g) butter
1 tablespoon (15 ml) flour
2 anchovy fillets
remainder of can of tomatoes with seeds removed (see above)
1 teaspoon (5 ml) parsley, chopped
½ chicken stock cube

Put the breadcrumbs into a bowl with the herbs and seasoning. Cut the anchovy fillets into small pieces. Take 3 tomatoes from the can, remove the seeds and chop the tomatoes finely. Soften the onion in the butter, add the tomatoes and cook for 1 minute. Add to the breadcrumb mixture with the anchovies and 1 beaten egg. Mix well together. Spread the mixture over the inside of the lamb, roll up and tie securely. Roll the lamb in seasoned flour, brush with the remaining egg and roll in the browned crumbs. Heat the dripping in a roasting tin and, when smoking hot, put in the meat, baste and leave to roast for about 1 hour at 450°F, 230°C, Gas Mark 8 for the first 10 minutes then at 400°F, 200°C, Gas Mark 6 for the remainder of the cooking time.

To make the sauce, brown the shallots lightly in the butter, add the remainder of the can of tomatoes, chopped and with seeds removed, plus the juice, stir in the flour and add the finely chopped anchovy fillets and ½ stock cube. Bring to the boil and simmer for 4–5 minutes, then add the juices from the lamb. Stir well and season if necessary—the sauce should be quite spicy.

Serve the lamb hot with vegetables and hand the sauce separately. **Serves 6**

Colman's

Breast of Lamb with Mint

1 packet **Colman's** Bread Sauce Mix
⅓ pint (180 ml) cold milk
2 teaspoons (10 ml) **Colman's** Fresh Garden Mint
8 oz (225 g) dried apricots, soaked overnight, drained and chopped
1–2 breasts of lamb, about 2 lb (1 kg) in weight, boned
salt and pepper

Make up the bread sauce mix using the milk. Remove from the heat and stir in the mint and the apricots. Spread on the inside of the breast of lamb, roll up and secure with string. Season with the salt and pepper. Wrap loosely in foil and place in a roasting tin. Cook at 350°F, 180°C, Gas Mark 4, for 1¼ hours. Uncover and cook for a further 15 minutes to brown.

Serve with new potatoes, boiled in their skins, and peas.
Serves 4

Lamb Pot Roast

2–3 lb (1–1.5 kg) rolled breast *or* shoulder of lamb
1 onion, peeled and chopped
¾ pint (450 ml) water
1 packet **Colman's** Navarin of Lamb Casserole Mix
4 oz (100 g) long grain rice
2 oz (50 g) raisins
1 teaspoon (5 ml) dried mint
4 oz (113 g) packet frozen peas

Put the meat and onion into a casserole dish and cover with the water. Cover and cook in a slow oven at 325°F, 160°C, Gas Mark 3, for 60 minutes. Stir in the Navarin of Lamb Casserole Mix, rice,

raisins and mint. Cover and cook for another 20 minutes. Add the frozen peas, stir, and cook for a further 5 minutes. Serve at once.
Serves 6

Moussaka

1½ lb (700 g) aubergines, thinly sliced
1 oz (25 g) butter
1 oz (25 g) oil
1 onion, peeled and finely chopped
2 cloves garlic, crushed
1½ lb (700 g) lean lamb, minced
14 oz (396 g) can tomatoes
2 tablespoons (30 ml) tomato purée
1 teaspoon (5 ml) dried thyme
1 teaspoon (5 ml) dried rosemary
1 packet **Colman's** Savoury White Sauce Mix
½ pint (300 ml) milk
2 tablespoons (30 ml) Parmesan cheese, grated

Sprinkle the aubergines with salt and leave for 10 minutes, then rinse and dry. Heat the butter and oil in a large frying pan. When hot, cover the base with aubergine slices and fry quickly on both sides. Set the fried slices aside and do the rest, adding more oil if necessary. Fry the onion and garlic, add the lamb and cook until browned. Add the tomatoes, purée and herbs. Make up the sauce mix with the milk as directed. Place layers of aubergine and meat sauce in a casserole, spoon the savoury sauce on top and sprinkle with the cheese. Bake for 1 hour at 375°F, 190°C, Gas Mark 5. **Serves 4–6**

Navarin of Lamb Pot au Feu

8 best end of neck lamb chops
2 onions, peeled and finely sliced
1 small turnip, peeled and diced
2 carrots, peeled and sliced
1 packet **Colman's** Navarin of Lamb Casserole Mix

½ pint (275 ml) cold water
8 oz (225 g) potatoes, peeled and sliced
1½ oz (35 g) butter
1 tablespoon (15 ml) parsley, chopped

Put the chops, onions, turnip, parsnips and carrots in a casserole dish. Stir the Navarin of Lamb Casserole Mix into the water, pour over the meat and vegetables and place the potatoes on the top, dot with butter and cover. Cook in a slow oven at 325°F, 160°C, Gas Mark 3, for 45 minutes. Remove the lid, turn the heat up to 375°F, 190°C, Gas Mark 5, and cook for a further 15 minutes, or until browned on top.

Serve sprinkled with the chopped parsley. **Serves 4**

FRANK COOPER®

Lamb Kebabs with Mint Dip

Dip
4 oz (100 g) cream cheese
3 tablespoons (45 ml) real mayonnaise
2 teaspoons (10 ml) **Frank Cooper** Concentrated Mint Sauce
black pepper
Kebabs
small cubes lean lamb
small tomatoes
shallots *or* pieces of onion
bacon rolls
small button mushrooms
green pepper, sliced
corn oil

Blend together the cream cheese, mayonnaise and mint sauce. Add black pepper to taste and chill.

Alternate the kebab ingredients on skewers and brush evenly with the corn oil. Grill for 6–7 minutes, turning the skewers regularly. Serve the kebabs on a bed of rice with individual bowls of mint dip. **Serves 4**

Lamb and Leek Casserole

2 tablespoons (30 ml) corn oil
4 lamb cutlets, trimmed
1 can **Frank Cooper's** Venison Soup
2 medium leeks, cleaned and thickly sliced

Heat the corn oil in a flameproof casserole and brown the cutlets on each side. Pour over the soup, add the leeks, cover and bake at 350°F, 180°C, Gas Mark 4, for 1 hour or until the lamb is tender.
Serves 4

Lamb Pilau

3 tablespoons (45 ml) corn oil
5 oz (125 g) long grain rice
1¼ lb (500 g) cooked lamb, trimmed and cubed
1 medium onion, peeled and thinly sliced
1 can **Frank Cooper's** Consomme
1 level teaspoon (5 ml) **Frank Cooper's** Concentrated Mint Sauce
4 oz (100 g) mushrooms, washed and sliced
4 oz (100 g) frozen French beans
salt and pepper
sliced hard-boiled egg to garnish

Heat the corn oil and brown the rice, meat and onion. Stir in the soup and mint sauce, bring slowly to the boil, cover and simmer for 20 minutes. Add the mushrooms, beans and seasoning and continue to simmer for 5–10 minutes until the liquid is absorbed. Garnish with the sliced hard-boiled egg.
Serves 4

Mint Stuffed Shoulder of Lamb

2 tablespoons (30 ml) corn oil
2 level tablespoons (30 ml) onion, peeled and chopped
2 oz (50 g) breadcrumbs
2 tablespoons (30 ml) **Frank Cooper's** Concentrated Mint Sauce

1 level teaspoon (5 ml) parsley, chopped
salt and pepper
1 level tablespoon (15 ml) sugar

1 shoulder of lamb, boned

Heat the corn oil and sauté the onion for 3–4 minutes. Add the remaining stuffing ingredients and mix well. Fill the lamb with the stuffing, roll up tightly and secure with string. Place the meat in a roasting tin and cook at 375°F, 190°C, Gas Mark 5, allowing 35 minutes per lb (450 g).
Serves 4–5

Lamb Noisette Parcels

8 noisettes of lamb *or* 8 cutlets, boned, rolled and tied
salt and black pepper
4 oz (100 g) liver paté
1½ lb (680 g) puff pastry
beaten egg for glazing
1 can **Crosse & Blackwell** Red Wine Pour over Sauce

Season the noisettes with salt and pepper and spread a little paté on the top of each. Roll out the pastry thinly and cut into 16 (4 in, 10 cm) circles. Place each noisette on a round of pastry, dampen the edges and cover with another circle. Seal well. Brush with egg and decorate with any pastry trimmings. Place on a baking sheet and bake in the oven, pre-heated to 400°F, 200°C, Gas Mark 6 for 10 minutes, then at 350°F, 180°C, Gas Mark 4 for 15 minutes. Heat the sauce in a small saucepan.

Serve the noisette parcels with the sauce, pommes parisienne (small fried potato balls) and French beans in garlic butter.
Serves 4

Marinaded Lamb Cutlets

8 best end lamb cutlets
3 tablespoons (45 ml) **Crosse & Blackwell** Olive Oil mixed

with 2 tablespoons (30 ml) wine vinegar *or* lemon juice
2 rounded teaspoons (15 ml) **Crosse & Blackwell** Mixed Herbs
2–3 oz (50–75 g) fresh breadcrumbs, finely crumbled
Crosse & Blackwell Redcurrant Jelly for serving

Place the cutlets in a large, shallow dish and pour the oil mixture over. Sprinkle with 1 teaspoon (5 ml) of the herbs, turn the cutlets over and sprinkle with the remaining herbs. Set aside to marinate for at least 2 hours, turning the cutlets occasionally. Press both sides of the cutlets into the breadcrumbs until well coated. Cook under a very hot grill for about 5 minutes on each side, basting with the remaining marinade. The breadcrumbs should become very dark brown and crisp and the meat remain moist. If the cutlets are very thick, extend the cooking time accordingly.

Serve with Crosse & Blackwell Redcurrant Jelly.　　**Serves 4**

Homepride

Lamb and Red Wine Cobbler

1 lb (450 g) boned shoulder of lamb, cut into 1 in (2.5 cm) cubes
1 can **Homepride** Red Wine Cook-in-Sauce
6 oz (150 g) **Homepride** Self-raising Flour, sifted with a pinch of salt
1½ oz (40 g) margarine
6 tablespoons (90 ml) milk
a little milk to glaze

Place the lamb in a casserole dish and add the sauce. Cook at 325°F, 160°C, Gas Mark 3 for 1½ hours, stirring occasionally.

Rub the margarine into the flour, add the milk and mix to a soft dough. Knead on a lightly floured surface until smooth, roll out to 1 in (2.5 cm) thickness and cut into five (2 in, 5 cm) circles. Increase the oven temperature to 400°F, 200°C, Gas Mark 6. Uncover the casserole, place the scone rounds on top, brush with milk and return to the oven for a further 25 minutes until golden brown.

Serve with peas and carrots.
Serves 4

Old English Fidget Pie

1½ lb (750 g) shoulder of lamb, cut into 1 in (2.5 cm) cubes
1 large potato, peeled and sliced
1 cooking apple, cored and chopped
1 onion, peeled and sliced
13¼ oz (376 g) can **Homepride** White Wine with Cream Cook-in-Sauce
3 oz (75 g) butter *or* margarine
3 oz (75 g) lard
8 oz (200 g) **Homepride** Plain Flour
pinch of salt
¼ pint (150 ml) iced water
1 teaspoon (5 ml) lemon juice
beaten egg to glaze

Place the lamb, potato, apple, onion and the Cook-in-Sauce in a 2 pint (1 litre) pie dish. Cover and bake at 350°F, 180°C, Gas Mark 4, for 45 minutes. Meanwhile, prepare the rough puff pastry. Cut the fat into small cubes. In a bowl, combine the flour and salt and then add the fat. Add sufficient water and lemon juice to mix to a firm dough with a round-bladed knife. Turn on to a lightly floured surface and roll out to a 5 × 12 in (12 × 30 cm) rectangle. Fold into 3 by bringing the bottom third upwards and the top third of the pastry downwards over it. Press the edges with a rolling pin and give the pastry a quarter turn. Repeat the rolling out and folding process. Place in a polythene bag and chill for 15 minutes. Repeat the rolling, folding and resting process twice more. Roll out the pastry 2 in (5 cm) larger than the pie dish. Remove the pie filling from the oven, uncover and increase the temperature to 425°F, 220°C, Gas Mark 7. Cut a 1 in (2.5 cm) strip of pastry, place on the dampened rim of the dish and

brush with water. Place the rest of the pastry on top. Press the edges together, seal well and flute. Decorate with shapes cut from the pastry trimmings. Brush with the beaten egg and bake for 30 minutes or until the pastry is well risen and golden brown. Serve hot.
Serves 4–6

Orange-Barbecue Lamb Chops

4 loin lamb chops
grated rind and juice of 1 orange
1 oz (25 g) butter *or* margarine, softened
1 clove garlic, crushed
3–4 sprigs watercress, chopped
1 sachet **Homepride** Coat & Cook, Barbecue Flavour
watercress to garnish

Marinate the chops in the orange juice for 30 minutes. Combine the orange rind, butter, garlic and watercress together in a bowl. Spread on kitchen foil about ½ in (1 cm) thick. Chill until firm then cut into 4 portions with a small, fluted biscuit cutter. Drain the chops and dry on kitchen paper. Coat the chops evenly with the contents of the Coat & Cook sachet. Place under a pre-heated grill and cook for 5–8 minutes on each side.

Garnish with watercress and serve the orange butter separately.
Serves 4

Cutlets en Croute

8 lamb cutlets
salt and pepper
1 oz (25 g) butter
1 tablespoon (15 ml) mint jelly
13 oz (370 g) packet **Jus-rol** Puff Pastry, thawed
beaten egg to glaze

Trim the cutlets to expose 1 in (2.5 cm) tail bone. Season with salt and pepper. Melt the butter in a frying pan and brown the cutlets on both sides. Leave to cool. When

cool, spread the mint jelly over the top of the cutlets. Roll the pastry into a rectangle 18 × 20 in (45 × 50 cm). Cut into 8 long strips and brush with the beaten egg. Wrap a strip of pastry round each cutlet, egg side outside, overlapping each turn slightly over the previous one to enclose the cutlet. Start winding from the bone and leaving a little bone exposed. Bake in a pre-heated oven at 425°F, 220°C, Gas Mark 7, for 15 minutes, then reduce the heat to 350°F, 180°C, Gas Mark 4, and cook for a further 20 minutes. Place on absorbent paper for a few minutes before serving.
Makes 8

Lamb Plait

8 oz (225 g) lean minced lamb
¼ teaspoon dried mint
4 oz (100 g) onion, peeled and chopped
2 oz (50 g) red pepper, de-seeded and chopped
1 oz (25 g) fresh white breadcrumbs
1 tablespoon (15 ml) Worcestershire sauce
1 egg
salt and pepper
7½ oz (215 g) packet **Jus-rol** Puff Pastry, thawed
beaten egg to glaze

Mix together the lamb, mint, onion, pepper, breadcrumbs and Worcestershire sauce. Beat the egg, stir into the mixture and season well. Roll out the pastry to a rectangle 9 × 12 in (23 × 30 cm) and place on a baking sheet. Put the lamb mixture down the centre. Cut strips diagonally on the pastry from the edge to near the filling, about 1 in (2.5 cm) apart, on both sides. Dampen the edges of the pastry with water. Fold the pastry at one end over the filling and then plait the strips across the filling. Turn in the other end piece of pastry to enclose the filling. Brush with the beaten egg and bake in a pre-heated oven at 425°F, 220°C, Gas Mark 7, for 15 minutes, then reduce to 350°F, 180°C, Gas Mark 4, for a further 30 minutes.
Serves 4

Cider and Lamb Casserole

salt and pepper
2½ lb (1 kg) middle neck of lamb
2 oz (50 g) dripping
8 oz (200 g) onions, peeled and sliced
1 medium celeriac, peeled and cubed
8 oz (200 g) carrots, peeled and thinly sliced
1 oz (25 g) plain flour
¼ pint (125 ml) **Knorr** chicken stock
½ lemon, cut in wedges
½ pint (250 ml) cider
1 teaspoon (5 ml) mixed herbs

Season the cut sides of the meat well and brown in the melted dripping in a frying pan. Place in an ovenproof casserole. Brown the onions and celeriac in the fat and add to the dish with the carrots. Season well. Stir the flour into the frying pan and gradually add the stock, lemon, cider and herbs. Bring to the boil, pour over the meat and cover. Cook at 350°F, 180°C, Gas Mark 4 for 2–2½ hours.

Serve with baked potatoes and cauliflower.   **Serves 4–6**

Country Lamb Casserole

8 lamb cutlets
1½ oz (40 g) seasoned cornflour
2 tablespoons (30 ml) oil
1 lb (400 g) shallots, peeled
14 oz (397 g) can peeled tomatoes
4 oz (100 g) small button mushrooms, washed
¾ pint (375 ml) **Knorr** beef stock
salt and pepper

Coat the cutlets in the seasoned cornflour, shaking off any excess. Heat the oil in a frying pan, add the cutlets and brown on both sides.

Put them into an ovenproof casserole. Add the shallots, tomatoes, mushrooms, stock and seasoning. Cover and cook at 350°F, 180°C, Gas Mark 4 for 1 hour. Serve with savoury rice. **Serves 4**

Lancashire Hot Pot

2 lb (800 g) potatoes, peeled and sliced
2 lb (800 g) best end of neck of mutton, divided into cutlets
3 sheeps kidneys, sliced
1 large onion, peeled and sliced
½ pint (250 ml) **Knorr** beef stock
a little oil

Place a layer of potatoes in the base of a greased, deep ovenproof casserole. Layer the cutlets, kidneys and onion on top, then cover with the remaining potato slices overlapping each other. Pour over the stock, cover and cook at 350°F, 180°C, Gas Mark 4, for about 2 hours. About 20 minutes before the end of the cooking time, remove the lid, brush the potatoes with oil, leave the cover off and continue cooking to brown the potatoes.

Serve with braised vegetables cooked in the oven at the same time.   **Serves 4**

Savoury Lamb

½ leg lamb, cubed
1 clove garlic, crushed
2 medium onions, peeled and thinly sliced
1 oz (25 g) butter
1 tablespoon (15 ml) oil
salt and pepper
1 tablespoon (15 ml) tomato purée
½–1 teaspoon (2.5–5 ml) Tabasco sauce
¼ pint (125 ml) **Knorr** chicken stock
½ oz (15 g) plain flour

Heat the butter and oil together in a saucepan and fry the lamb on all sides until brown. Remove the pan from the heat. Fry the onion and garlic for a few minutes until soft.

Add the tomato purée, flour, stock, seasoning and Tabasco sauce. Stir until thickened. Stir in the lamb, cover and simmer for 45 minutes to 1 hour until the meat is tender.

Serve with plain boiled rice to which has been added a blanched and chopped green pepper. **Serves 4**

Somerset Lamb Casserole

1 tablespoon (15 ml) oil
1½ lb (600 g) middle neck of lamb, cut into chops
1 large onion, peeled and sliced
1 lb (400 g) potatoes, peeled and sliced
12 oz (300 g) cooking apples, cored, peeled and sliced
1 pint (500 ml) **Knorr** beef *or* chicken stock

Heat the oil in a frying pan and sauté the lamb until brown all over and the onion soft and transparent—about 3–4 minutes. Layer half of the potato in the base of an ovenproof casserole and cover with the lamb, onion, apples and stock. Top with the remaining potatoes, overlapping the slices. Cook at 375°F, 190°C, Gas Mark 5 for 1–1½ hours or until the meat is tender.

Serve with carrots and green vegetables if desired.   **Serves 4**

LEA & PERRINS

Turkish Lamb

2¼ lb (1 kg) shoulder of lamb, boned
salt and pepper
Stuffing
4 oz (100 g) cooked long grain rice
1 clove garlic, crushed
¼ teaspoon ground allspice
grated rind ½ a lemon
2 oz (50 g) sultanas
1 oz (25 g) blanched almonds, chopped
1 tablespoon (15 ml) natural yoghurt
2 teaspoons (10 ml) **Lea & Perrins** Worcestershire Sauce

1 egg yolk
salt and pepper
Baste
2 tablespoons (30 ml) natural
   yoghurt
1 tablespoon (15 ml) **Lea &
Perrins** Worcestershire Sauce
1 tablespoon (15 ml) oil
salt and pepper

Open the shoulder of lamb and
season well. For the stuffing, mix
all the ingredients together,
seasoning well. Use to stuff the
meat along the cavity from where
the bone has been removed. Tie
the joint securely in 4 or 5 places,
being careful to push the stuffing
firmly inside, and place in a
roasting tin. For the baste, mix all
the ingredients together and use to
brush all over the joint. Repeat two
or three times during cooking.
Cook the lamb in the oven at 375°F,
190°C, Gas Mark 5, allowing
30 minutes per lb (450 g) plus
30 minutes—approximately
1¾ hours. Cover with foil when it
is golden brown to prevent
excessive browning.   **Serves 4**

Glazed Stuffed Breast of Lamb

14½ oz (411 g) can **Libby's**
   Apricot Halves
6 oz (150 g) long grain rice,
   cooked
1 small onion, peeled and
   chopped
1 clove garlic, crushed
1 egg, beaten
salt and pepper
2 breasts of lamb, boned *or* 3 lb
   (1.25 kg) leg of lamb, boned
2 sprigs fresh rosemary

Drain the apricots, reserving the
syrup. Chop 10 apricot halves and
mix with the rice, onion, garlic,
egg and seasoning. Lay the breasts
of lamb end to end, and spread
with the stuffing mixture. Roll up
diagonally and secure. For leg of
lamb, fill the bone cavity with
stuffing. Wrap tightly in foil. Roast

for about 1 hour for breast or
1½ hours for leg in an oven pre-
heated to 375°F, 190°C, Gas
Mark 5. Boil the reserved syrup to
reduce by half. Increase the oven
temperature to 425°F, 220°C, Gas
Mark 7. Unwrap the foil and brush
the lamb with the syrup. Return to
the oven for 10 minutes to glaze.
Brush the lamb with the remaining
syrup and place on a serving dish.
Arrange the remaining apricots
around the joint and garnish with
rosemary. Serve hot or cold.
Serves 4–6

Libby Lamb Kebabs

1 lb (450 g) top leg of lamb,
   cubed
14½ oz (411 g) can **Libby's**
   Apricot Halves
1 small red pepper, cut into
   large dice
1 small green pepper, cut into
   large dice
4 oz (100 g) button mushrooms
4 oz (100 g) button onions
salt and black pepper
½ teaspoon (2.5 ml) powdered
   garlic

Arrange the ingredients on 8–12
skewers. Mix the syrup with the
seasonings and brush the kebabs.
Place under a moderate grill for 10
minutes, turning once and frequently brushing with syrup.
Serve on a bed of cooked rice.
Serves 4–6

Braised Lamb in Cider

8 best end of neck lamb cutlets
1 oz (25 g) dripping
1 medium onion, peeled and
   thinly sliced
4 medium carrots, peeled and
   thinly sliced
4 oz (100 g) button mushrooms,
   washed
2 teaspoons (10 ml) fresh
   parsley, chopped
1 oz (25 g) plain flour
½ pint (300 ml) dry cider
1 teaspoon (5 ml) **Marmite**

Trim any excess fat from the cutlets
and fry them in the dripping until
brown on both sides. Remove
from the pan and keep warm. Fry
the onion, carrots and mushrooms
in the pan for 5 minutes, add the
parsley and continue cooking for
1 minute. Stir in the flour and cook
for a further 2 minutes. Gradually
blend in the cider and stir in the
Marmite. Cook gently, stirring
well, until the mixture comes to the
boil and thickens. Put the chops in
a casserole, cover with the
vegetables and sauce and put on
the lid. Cook at 350°F, 180°C, Gas
Mark 4, for 1 hour.   **Serves 4**

Stuffed Lamb Cushion

3 lb (1.5 kg) shoulder of lamb
4 oz (100 g) fresh white
   breadcrumbs
2 oz (50 g) walnut halves,
   chopped
1 small onion, peeled and finely
   chopped
½ teaspoon (2.5 ml) dried
   mixed herbs
1 teaspoon (5 ml) **Marmite**
1 tablespoon (15 ml) hot water
1 tablespoon (15 ml) milk
salt and pepper

Ask the butcher to 'tunnel' bone
the meat, to leave a cavity for the
stuffing, but give him one or two
days' notice.
   Put the breadcrumbs into a bowl
and add the walnuts and onion.
Add the herbs and mix the
ingredients thoroughly. Stir the
Marmite into the hot water and
add the milk. Mix in the breadcrumbs and season with salt and
pepper (do not squeeze the breadcrumbs together, just mix them
lightly with a fork). Pack into the
cavity in the lamb and hold the
edges of the meat together with
metal skewers or by stitching with
firm thread, not forgetting the
smaller, knuckle end. Put the joint
into a roasting tin and roast at
350°F, 180°C, Gas Mark 4, for
2¼ hours. Remove the skewers or
thread before serving.   **Serves 6**

Lamb Cutlets in Pastry

4 lamb cutlets
4 slices tomato
garlic salt
pepper
8 oz (225 g) **McDougall's** Flaky
   Pastry Mix
beaten egg to glaze
tomato wedges to garnish

Trim cutlets and place a slice of tomato on each. Season with a little garlic salt and pepper. Make up pastry as directed on the bag. Roll out the pastry on a floured board to an oblong, 14 × 8 in (35 × 20 cm) and cut into eight 14 × 1 in (35 × 2.5 cm) strips. Brush strips with beaten egg and wrap 2 strips around each cutlet, overlapping slightly and keeping glazed side uppermost. Place on a baking sheet in the middle of an oven pre-heated to 425°F, 220°C, Gas Mark 7, and bake for 10 minutes. Reduce temperature to 350°F, 180°C, Gas Mark 4 and bake for a further 20–25 minutes until the pastry is golden brown.

   Place on a warmed serving dish and garnish with tomato wedges. Serve with carrots and potatoes.
Serves 4

Devilish Lamb

4 lamb chump chops
1 level teaspoon (5 ml) dry
   mustard
¼ level teaspoon (1.25 ml)
   ground ginger
1 level teaspoon (5 ml) brown
   sugar
2 teaspoons (10 ml) oil
1 tablespoon (15 ml)
   Worcestershire sauce
2 level tablespoons (30 ml)
   tomato purée
1 tablespoon (15 ml) vinegar

2 Red **Oxo** Cubes, crumbled
a little grated orange rind
salt and pepper

Place a large piece of foil in a roasting tin. Put the chops on top of the foil. Combine all the remaining ingredients in a basin. Spread the devilled mixture over the lamb and fold the foil over the chops, enclosing them in a parcel. Cook in the oven at 375°F, 190°C, Gas Mark 5, for about 45 minutes.
   Serve with creamed potatoes, peas and carrots.   **Serves 4**

Melting Meat Pasties

8 oz (200 g) self-raising flour
pinch salt
4 oz (100 g) lard
water to mix
6–8 oz (175–225 g) lamb,
   cooked and minced
8 oz (225 g) leftover mashed
   potato
1 level tablespoon (15 ml)
   tomato purée
pinch mixed herbs
salt and pepper
1 Red **Oxo** Cube, crumbled and
   dissolved in 2 tablespoons
   (30 ml) hot water
oil for frying
Oxo gravy to serve

Put the flour and salt into a basin and rub in the lard. Add enough water to mix to a firm dough, roll out thinly and cut into 4 pieces, each about 5–6 in (13–15 cm) square. Mix together the lamb, potato, tomato purée, mixed herbs, salt and pepper with the Oxo stock. Divide the mixture into 4 and place a portion on each pastry square. Moisten the edge of the pastry with water, fold over the filling into a triangular shape and pinch the edges together. Fry in hot oil about ½ in (1 cm) deep for about 8 minutes, or until golden brown. Serve with the Oxo gravy.
Serves 4

Piquant Lamb

3–3½ lb (1.5–1.75 kg) shoulder
   of lamb
¼ teaspoon dried rosemary
   (optional)

1 level tablespoon (15 ml)
   brown sugar
½ level teaspoon (5 ml) ground
   ginger
1 tablespoon (15 ml) vinegar
1 level tablespoon (15 ml) flour
1½ level tablespoons (22 ml)
   tomato ketchup
1 level teaspoon (5 ml) brown
   pickle
2 Red **Oxo** Cubes, crumbled
1 level teaspoon (5 ml) salt
2 oz (50 g) butter, melted
a little lard to roast
Oxo gravy to serve

Make shallow cuts in the surface of the lamb and sprinkle with the rosemary. Mix all the remaining ingredients together and spread completely over the lamb. Place in a roasting tin with the lard and cook at 325°F, 170°C, Gas Mark 3 for 2¼–2¾ hours, basting occasionally.
   Serve with Oxo gravy.
Serves 6

Potato Moussaka

1½ oz (40 g) margarine
1 large onion, peeled and finely
   chopped
1 lb (450 g) minced lamb
1 clove garlic, crushed
1 Chicken **Oxo** Cube, crumbled
   and dissolved in ⅓ pint
   (200 ml) hot water
2 tablespoons (30 ml) tomato
   purée
salt and pepper
1½ lb (675 g) potatoes, peeled
   and sliced
1 oz (25 g) flour
½ pint (275 ml) milk
pinch nutmeg
2 oz (50 g) Cheddar cheese,
   grated

tomato slices and a sprig of parsley to garnish

Melt 1 oz (25 g) of the margarine in a pan and fry the onion gently until golden. Add the lamb and garlic and stir in the Chicken Oxo stock, tomato purée and seasoning and cook for 5 minutes. Cook the potatoes in boiling water for 5–10 minutes then drain well. Place the remaining margarine, the flour, milk and nutmeg in a saucepan over moderate heat and bring to the boil, whisking continuously. Cook for 2–3 minutes then add 1 oz (25 g) of the grated cheese.

Lightly grease a casserole dish and line the base with a layer of potatoes. Next add half the meat mixture, followed by half the remaining potatoes. Spread a little of the sauce on top and repeat the layers, finishing with the sauce. Sprinkle the remaining cheese on top. Bake in the middle of a moderately hot oven (375°F, 190°C, Gas Mark 5) for 40–45 minutes. Garnish with the tomato slices and sprig of parsley to serve.
Serves 4

Thatched Pie

1 tablespoon (15 ml) oil
1 large onion, peeled and chopped
2 carrots, peeled and sliced
2 sticks celery, chopped
1 tablespoon (15 ml) flour
1 Red **Oxo** Cube, crumbled
¼ pint (150 ml) water
12 oz (350 g) lamb, cooked and diced
1 level tablespoon (15 ml) tomato purée
1 lb (450 g) potatoes, peeled, cooked and diced
1 oz (25 g) butter, melted
1 oz (25 g) fresh breadrumbs

Heat the oil in a pan and fry the onion, carrot and celery slowly for 5 minutes. Stir in the flour, crumbled Oxo cube and water. Bring to the boil, stirring, and add the lamb and the tomato purée. Simmer for 2 minutes then transfer to a 1½ pint (900 ml) pie dish. Put the potatoes on top, pour

over the melted butter and sprinkle with the breadcrumbs. Bake at 400°F, 200°C, Gas Mark 6 for about 25 minutes.   **Serves 4**

Lamb with a Tang

2 lb (1 kg) lean breast of lamb, boned
3 oz (85 g) packet **Paxo** Parsley and Thyme Stuffing Mix
grated rind and juice of 1 orange
oil
salt

Empty the contents of the packet of stuffing into a bowl and stir in the orange rind. Make the orange juice up to ½ pint (300 ml) of liquid with boiling water and add to the stuffing. Leave to stand for 15 minutes. Spread the stuffing over the boned surface of the meat, roll up and tie securely. Weigh the joint and calculate the cooking time, allowing 40 minutes per lb (450 g) plus 20 minutes extra. Place in a roasting tin, brush with the oil and sprinkle with salt. Roast at 350°F, 180°C, Gas Mark 4, until cooked. Slice and serve.
Serves 4

Stuffing for Lamb

To bring out the flavour of lamb you can use either **Paxo** Sage and Onion or Parsley and Thyme. If you feel like experimenting, you can add 2 oz (50 g) of dried fruit, 2 oz (50 g) of sweetcorn or 1 oz (25 g) chopped apricots to one full pack of Paxo. If you add any other liquid to a Paxo stuffing—orange juice, lemon juice, stock or white wine—always use the same total of mixed liquid as recommended on the pack.

Lamb Exotica with Ratatouille

5 large, lean lamb chops
1 small onion, peeled and chopped
1 clove garlic, crushed with a little salt
¼ pint (150 ml) **Rose's** Lime Juice Cordial
2 tablespoons (30 ml) oil
1 teaspoon (5 ml) chilli powder
1 teaspoon (5 ml) ground ginger
1 teaspoon (5 ml) curry powder
1 teaspoon (5 ml) turmeric
1 green pepper, de-seeded
Ratatouille
3 medium courgettes, sliced, sprinkled lightly with salt and left to stand for about ½ hour in a colander
2 onions, peeled and sliced
remainder of green pepper
2 (14 oz, 396 g) cans tomatoes, chopped
remainder of marinade from lamb

Prick the chops all over and lay them in a dish. Mix the onion, garlic, lime juice, oil and spices to make a marinade. Pour over the chops and leave for at least 2 hours, turning the chops occasionally. Line a grill pan with foil and grill the chops for about 10 minutes on each side, basting frequently with the juices and a little of the marinade.

For the ratatouille, rinse and drain the courgettes, reserve 5 thin slices of the green pepper and chop the remainder. Heat the remaining marinade in a saucepan with the courgettes, onions, chopped pepper and tomatoes and simmer, covered, for up to 30 minutes, until the vegetables are cooked. They should still be slightly crunchy.

Garnish each chop with a slice of green pepper and serve with the ratatouille.   **Serves 5**

SCHWARTZ

Minty Lamb and Redcurrant Chops

8 lamb cutlets *or* 4 lamb chump chops
a little cooking oil
8 oz (227 g) onions, peeled and sliced
1 oz (28 g) plain flour
¾ pint (327 ml) stock
2 teaspoons (10 ml) **Schwartz** Seasoning Salt
2 teaspoons (10 ml) **Schwartz** Mint
¼ teaspoon **Schwartz** Ground Black Pepper
3 oz (85 g) redcurrant jelly
8 oz (227 g) button mushrooms, wiped

Fry the lamb chops in a little cooking oil until brown on all sides. Transfer to a casserole dish. Fry the onions in 2 tablespoons (30 ml) cooking oil until soft and just beginning to colour. Stir in the flour. Blend in the stock followed by all the remaining ingredients except the mushrooms. Bring to the boil and pour over the chops. Cover and cook in the oven pre-heated to 350°F, 180°C, Gas Mark 4 for approximately 1½ hours or until the meat is tender. Add the mushrooms 30 minutes before the end of the cooking time.

The cooked dish may be stored in a refrigerator for up to 2 days, or for up to 1 month in a freezer.
Serves 4

Sharwood's

Colonel Skinner's Fancy

12 oz (350 g) shortcrust pastry
1 lb (500 g) mutton, cubed
4 tablespoons (60 ml) **Sharwood's** Mango Chutney
1 tablespoon (15 ml) cornflour
1 tablespoon (15 ml) parsley, chopped

2 teaspoons (10 ml) salt
freshly ground black pepper
egg to glaze

Line an 8 in (21 cm) pie dish with part of the pastry. Mix the mutton, chutney, cornflour, parsley and seasoning and spoon into the pastry case. Roll out the remaining pastry to cover the pie. Seal well and use any trimmings to decorate. Glaze with the beaten egg. Bake for 1–1½ hours at 350°F, 180°C, Gas Mark 4. Serve hot or cold.   **Serves 6**

Greek Spiced Lamb

Marinade
2 tablespoons (30 ml) olive oil
1 tablespoon (15 ml) **Sharwood's** Lemon Juice
1 tablespoon (15 ml) parsley, chopped
finely grated rind of 1 lemon
1 heaped teaspoon (15 ml) **Sharwood's** Garam Masala Curry Spices
1 small onion, finely chopped
2 cloves garlic, crushed

1 lb (450 g) lamb fillet, thinly sliced
4 pitta breads
salad ingredients, for example, lettuce, green pepper, black olives
2 tablespoons (30 ml) lemon juice

Mix together the marinade ingredients. Toss the lamb in the marinade and leave for 1 hour. Meanwhile prepare the salad and toss in the lemon juice. Warm the pitta breads. Grill the lamb for 10–15 minutes, turning frequently and brushing with the marinade. Slit the pitta breads open and pile some lamb and salad in each.

If preferred, the lamb may be served with rice, allowing 8–10 oz (225–275 g) for 4 servings.
Serves 4

Lamb Stuffed Chilli Marrow

1 large marrow, cut into 6 rings
1 oz (25 g) butter
1 onion, peeled and chopped
2 cloves garlic, crushed
3 teaspoons (15 ml) **Sharwood's** Medium *or* Hot Curry Powder
1 tablespoon (15 ml) flour
12 oz (350 g) cooked lamb, finely chopped
¼ pint (125 ml) stock
1 small can **Sharwood's** Pimientos, chopped
2 oz (50 g) butter

Scoop the seeds out of the centre of the marrow rings and place the rings on a greased baking dish. Sauté the onion in the butter and stir in the garlic, curry powder and flour. Add the meat and cook quickly. Stir in the stock and pimientos and season well. Spoon into the marrow rings. Dot each one with butter. Cover with foil. Bake for 1 hour at 350°F, 180°C, Gas Mark 4.   **Serves 4**

whitworths

Lamb and Potato Hotpot

2 lb (800 g) middle neck of lamb
1 large onion, peeled and sliced
2 large carrots, peeled and sliced
4 oz (100 g) **Whitworths** Soup and Broth Mixture, soaked overnight
salt and pepper
1 pint (500 ml) chicken stock
2 lb (800 g) potatoes, peeled and thinly sliced

Trim excess fat from the lamb and discard. Place the meat in a large, ovenproof casserole, cover with onions and carrots. Drain the soup and broth mixture and place in casserole. Season well and pour over the stock. Arrange potato slices on top, then cover with a lid or foil and cook for 2 hours at 350°F, 180°C, Gas Mark 4. Remove lid or foil and bake for a further 30 minutes to crisp potatoes.
Serves 4

PORK

Pork Fillet with Mushrooms

2 lb (900 g) pork fillet, cut into
    ½–¾ in (2 cm) slices
butter for frying
½ lb (225 g) button
    mushrooms, washed
juice of 2 lemons
1 dessertspoon (10 ml) fresh
    thyme
1 can **Baxters** White Wine Sauce
chopped parsley or asparagus
    tips to garnish

Fry the pork slices in butter in a
large frying pan, browning on
both sides, and add the mushrooms. Continue frying lightly,
add the juice of the lemons and the
fresh thyme. Pour in the can of
Wine Sauce, reduce the heat and
simmer for 20 minutes, stirring
occasionally. Garnish with
chopped parsley or asparagus
tips.   **Serves 4**

Spicy Spare Ribs à l'Indochine

6 spare rib chops *or* 3 lb (1.3 kg)
    spare ribs, chopped and
    trimmed
1 can **Baxters** Sweet and Sour
    Sauce
2 teaspoons (10 ml) thick soy
    sauce
3 cloves garlic, crushed
1 red pepper, de-seeded and
    sliced
2 bay leaves
chopped parsley and spring
    onions to garnish

Arrange the chops or spare ribs in
a shallow baking pan or cast iron
casserole. Pour the Sweet and Sour
sauce into a bowl and blend in the
soy sauce, garlic, red pepper and

bay leaves. Pour the mixture over
the chops and leave overnight to
marinate. One hour before
required, turn the chops or ribs
and place in a pre-heated oven
(350°F, 180°C, Gas Mark 4) and
bake for 45 minutes.
    Serve on a bed of boiled rice
with a parsley and spring onion
garnish.   **Serves 6**

Pork and Apple Hot Pot

1 oz (25 g) lard
1½ lb (675 g) lean pork slices
2 onions, peeled and sliced
1 clove garlic, crushed
8 oz (225 g) carrots, peeled and
    thinly sliced
1 large cooking apple, peeled,
    cored and sliced
½ oz (15 g) cornflour
1 Chicken **Oxo** Cube, dissolved
    in ½ pint (300 ml) water
4 tablespoons (60 ml) **Bon**
    White Cooking Wine
1 teaspoon (5 ml) mixed herbs
salt and pepper
1 lb (450 g) potatoes, peeled
    and sliced

Melt the lard in a frying pan and fry
the pork until lightly browned on
each side. Place in a deep casserole
dish. Fry the onions and garlic for
5 minutes and add to the pork.
Place a layer of carrots and a layer
of apple on top of the mixture in
the casserole dish. Drain off any
excess fat from the frying pan, mix
the cornflour with a little water and
add this to the pan along with the
Oxo stock, Bon and mixed herbs.
Bring to the boil, stirring until
thickened. Season and add to the
casserole. Arrange the potato slices
on top, cover and cook for 2 hours
at 350°F, 180°C, Gas Mark 4.
    Serve with a green vegetable.
Serves 4

Pork and Apple Bake

1½ oz (40 g) plain flour
pinch ground nutmeg
salt and pepper
2 lb (1 kg) lean pork, cubed
2 oz (50 g) butter
1 large onion, peeled and
    chopped
6 oz (150 g) button mushrooms,
    washed and sliced
1 Red Cube from **Bovril**,
    dissolved in ¾ pint (450 ml)
    water
2 eating apples, peeled, cored
    and sliced
1 tablespoon (15 ml) redcurrant
    jelly
¼ pint (150 ml) fresh soured
    cream

Mix the flour, nutmeg, salt and
pepper together in a bowl and toss
the pork in this mixture. Melt the
butter and fry the onion for
5 minutes until soft and golden.
Add the pork and fry until the meat
is brown all over. Remove from the
heat and add the mushrooms and
any remaining seasoned flour.
Gradually pour on the stock,
return to the heat and stir until the
sauce thickens. Cover and cook at
350°F, 180°C, Gas Mark 4, for
1½ hours. Stir the apples and
redcurrant jelly into the meat,
cover and cook for a further 20
minutes.
    Stir in the soured cream just
before serving.   **Serves 4**

Porker's Pudding

3 oz (75 g) self-raising flour
3 oz (75 g) fresh white
  breadcrumbs
2 oz (50 g) shredded suet
pinch salt
1½ lb (675 g) lean pork, diced
2 lean bacon rashers, finely
  chopped
2 medium onions, finely
  chopped
¾ lb (350 g) eating apples,
  peeled, cored and sliced
1 teaspoon (5 ml) soft light
  brown sugar
½ teaspoon (2.5 ml) dried sage
4 tablespoons (60 ml) dry cider
4 tablespoons (60 ml) water
1 Chicken Cube from **Bovril**
salt and pepper

Mix together the flour,
breadcrumbs, suet and salt and
mix with enough cold water to
make a firm, soft pastry. Roll into a
circle and cut out one quarter for
the lid. Use the larger piece to line
a greased 2 pint (1.2 litre) pudding
basin. Mix together the pork,
bacon, onions, sugar and sage and
arrange alternate layers of meat
mixture and apples in the basin.
Mix the cider, water and crumbled
Bovril cube, season well with salt
and pepper and pour over the meat
and apple. Put on the pastry lid,
sealing the edges firmly, and cover
with greased greaseproof paper
and kitchen foil, tying well. Boil
for 3 hours in a large, covered
saucepan, taking care not to let the
saucepan boil dry—top up if
necessary with boiling water from
time to time. Remove the pudding
and leave to stand for 5 minutes
before turning out on to a hot
serving dish.   **Serves 4**

Somerset Pork Chops

2 tablespoons (30 ml) oil
4 pork loin *or* spare rib chops
1 oz (25 g) butter
1 oz (25 g) plain flour
1 Red Cube from **Bovril**
½ pint (300 ml) dry cider
salt and pepper
6 oz (150 g) Cheddar cheese,
  grated

2 tablespoons (30 ml) single
  cream
2 eating apples, peeled, cored
  and diced

Heat the oil and fry the chops for
about 20 minutes until cooked
through. Meanwhile, prepare the
sauce by melting the butter and
working in the flour. Cook for
1 minute and then add the
crumbled Red Cube, cider, salt
and pepper. Bring to the boil,
stirring well, then cook for 2
minutes. Remove from the heat
and add 5 oz (125 g) of the cheese.
Stir until the cheese has melted,
then stir in the cream, followed by
the apples. Arrange the chops in a
shallow, ovenproof dish and cover
with the sauce. Sprinkle on the
remaining cheese, brown under a
hot grill and serve at once.
Serves 4

Quick Fry Pork and Peppers

1–1¼ lb (400–500 g) pork
  steak, trimmed and cut into
  strips
Brown and Polson Cornflour
2 tablespoons (30 ml) corn oil
1 large carrot, peeled and cut
  into matchsticks
1 green pepper, de-seeded and
  sliced
2 tablespoons (30 ml) soy sauce
1 tablespoon (15 ml) demerara
  sugar
2 tablespoons (30 ml) sherry
6 radishes, sliced
7 oz (198 g) can apricots,
  drained and sliced

Coat the meat in the cornflour.
Heat the corn oil in a heavy-based
frying pan and fry the meat for
3–4 minutes, stirring all the time.
Add the carrot, green pepper, soy
sauce, sugar and sherry and fry for
a further 2–3 minutes, stirring
continuously. Add the radishes
and apricots and stir for a further
minute.

Best served immediately on a
bed of boiled rice.   **Serves 4**

Pork Goulash

1 tablespoon (15 ml) oil
4 pork spare rib chops
2 onions, peeled and sliced
1 level tablespoon (15 ml)
  paprika pepper
10½ oz (297 g) can **Campbell's**
  Condensed Cream of Tomato
  Soup
½ soup can water

Heat the oil in a saucepan and fry
the chops until browned. Remove
from the pan and keep hot. Fry the
onion until soft then sprinkle the
paprika pepper into the pan and
mix well. Add the soup and water,
stir well and bring to the boil. Place
the chops back in the pan and cook
slowly for 1¼ hours.   **Serves 4**

Savoury Pork Chops

4 pork loin *or* spare rib chops
1 packet sage and onion
  stuffing mix
10½ oz (297 g) can **Campbell's**
  Condensed Lentil Soup

Dip the chops in water, shake
them and toss into the dry sage and
onion mix. Fry them in lard for
12–15 minutes until tender and
brown. Make up the remainder of
the stuffing into small balls and fry
these also. Place on a hot serving
dish and pour over the can of
undiluted soup, which has been
heated following the directions on
the can.
  Serve with the stuffing balls.
Serves 4

Pork & Pickle Plait

1 lb (400 g) pork sausagemeat
2 tablespoons (30 ml) **Crosse &
  Blackwell** Branston Pickle

2 tablespoons (30 ml) **Chef**
  Tomato Ketchup
salt and pepper
13 oz (325 g) packet puff pastry
egg to glaze

Heat the oven to 400°F, 200°C,
Gas Mark 6. Mix the sausagemeat,
Branston Pickle, tomato ketchup
together and season with salt and
pepper. Roll out the pastry to an
oblong 10 × 12 in (25 × 37 cm)
and place on a baking sheet.

Spread the sausage mixture
down the centre of the pastry
leaving ¼ in (0.5 cm) border at the
top and bottom and 3–4 in (7.5–
10 cm) border on each side. Cut
the pastry borders at an angle at
1 in (2.5 cm) intervals within ½ in
(1.25 cm) of the sausage filling.
Fold in the end pieces, dampen the
pastry edges and fold the pastry
strips over the filling from
alternate sides. Brush the plait well
with the beaten egg. Bake in the
oven for 40 minutes until golden
brown. Serve hot or cold.
Serves 4–6

![Chesswood]

Chinese Pork with Vegetables

6 tablespoons (90 ml) oil
1 lb (500 g) lean pork, cut into
  strips
8 oz (200 g) cabbage, shredded
1 green pepper, de-seeded and
  sliced
1 large onion, peeled and
  chopped
2 oz (50 g) courgettes, sliced
1 can **Chesswood** Sliced Large
  Mushrooms, drained
1 teaspoon (5 ml) ground
  ginger
salt and pepper
3 tablespoons (45 ml) soy sauce
½ oz (15 g) sugar
¼ pint (125 ml) water
1 tablespoon (15 ml) cornflour
2 tablespoons (30 ml) water

Heat the oil in a large frying pan
and fry the pork, stirring to ensure
even cooking. Add all the vegetables and the ginger, salt and
pepper. Cook for 5 minutes,
stirring continuously. Add the soy
sauce, sugar and water, blend the
cornflour and water and add to the
mixture. Cook until the sauce has
thickened.　　**Serves 4**

CHIVERS

Spicy Pork

1 lb (400 g) lean pork, cut into
  1 in (2.5 cm) cubes
2 level tablespoons (30 ml)
  cornflour, seasoned with salt
  and pepper
1 clove garlic, crushed
2 tablespoons (30 ml) cooking
  oil
8 oz (226 g) can pineapple
  chunks
1 medium green pepper, de-
  seeded and sliced
4 oz (100 g) mushrooms,
  washed and sliced
4 tomatoes, skinned and
  quartered
1 chicken stock cube dissolved
  in ¼ pint (125 ml) boiling
  water
3 tablespoons (45 ml) **Chivers**
  Olde English Marmalade
1 tablespoon (15 ml) soy sauce

Toss the pork cubes in half the
cornflour, add the garlic and fry in
the oil until browned. Drain the
pineapple and reserve the juice.
Add the green pepper to the pork
and cook gently for 15 minutes,
adding the mushrooms after
5 minutes and the tomatoes after
10 minutes. Mix the chicken stock
with ¼ pint (150 ml) of pineapple
juice from the can, the marmalade
and soy sauce. Blend the remaining cornflour with a little cold
water, add to the marmalade
mixture, bring to the boil and cook
briefly, stirring continuously.
Pour the sauce over the pork and
heat through.

Serve on a bed of boiled white or
brown rice.　　**Serves 4**

Sweet Sour Pork Chops

4 large pork chops
2 oz (50 g) butter
2 medium onions, peeled and
  chopped
1 cooking apple, chopped
15 oz (425 g) can **Cirio** Cherries
2 tablespoons (30 ml) **Cirio**
  Wine Vinegar
2 tablespoons (30 ml) brown
  sugar
salt and pepper

Trim the chops, melt the butter in a
pan and fry the chops until brown
on both sides. Put into a casserole
dish. Lightly fry the onion, add the
apple, stoned cherries and juice,
vinegar, brown sugar and
seasoning. Mix well and pour this
mixture over the chops. Cover and
cook in a moderately hot oven
(375°F, 190°C, Gas Mark 5) for
1 hour.

Serve with new potatoes and
French beans.　　**Serves 4**

Colman's

Piquant Pancakes

8 (7 in, 18 cm) pancakes
1 lb (500 g) minced pork
8 oz (225 g) cooking apples,
  peeled and chopped
8 oz (225 g) onions, peeled and
  chopped
1 packet **Colman's** Pork
  Piquant Casserole Mix
½ pint (275 ml) cold water
2 oz (50 g) butter *or* margarine

Put the pork, apples, onions and
Pork Piquant Casserole Mix in a
saucepan with the water. Mix well
and cook over a low heat for
35 minutes, stirring frequently.
Divide the mixture between the
pancakes, roll up and place in an
ovenproof dish. Dot with the
butter, cover with a lid of foil and
heat in the oven at 400°F, 200°C,
Gas Mark 6 for 20–25 minutes.
Serve at once.　　**Serves 4**

Pork Piquant with Pineapple

2–3 lb (1–1.5 kg) pork for roasting
3 medium onions, peeled and chopped
1 packet **Colman's** Pork Piquant Casserole Mix
½ pint (275 ml) cold water
14 oz (396 g) can pineapple chunks

Put the pork into a casserole dish with the onions, Pork Piquant Mix and water. Cover and cook for 2 hours at 325°F, 160°C, Gas Mark 3. Remove from the oven and stir in half the pineapple juice from the can and the pineapple chunks. Cook for a further 10 minutes and serve at once.   **Serves 6–8**

FRANK COOPER®

Pork Chops with Sweet and Sour Sauce

4 pork chops
1 egg, beaten
breadcrumbs
corn oil
Sauce
2 tablespoons (30 ml) **Frank Cooper's** Fine Cut 'Oxford' Marmalade
¼ pint (125 ml) water
1 dessertspoon (10 ml) cornflour
2 tablespoons (30 ml) sherry

Coat the chops with egg and then breadcrumbs. Heat the corn oil and fry the chops for 3 to 4 minutes on each side. Drain and keep warm. Place the marmalade, vinegar and soy sauce in the pan and heat gently. Blend the cornflour with the sherry and gradually stir into the pan. Bring to the boil and simmer for 1 minute. Serve the sauce with the chops.
Serves 4

Pork and Cranberry Casserole

2 tablespoons (30 ml) corn oil
1 lb (400 g) stewing pork, cubed
1 onion, peeled and sliced
3 sticks celery, sliced
4 oz (100 g) mushrooms, washed and sliced
½ pint (250 ml) chicken stock
6½ oz (185 g) jar **Frank Cooper's** Cranberry Sauce
1 tablespoon (15 ml) cornflour

Heat the corn oil in a flameproof casserole, add the meat and sauté for 2–3 minutes. Add the onion, celery and mushrooms and cook for a further 3–4 minutes. Add the stock and cranberry sauce, bring to the boil, cover and cook at 350°F, 180°C, Gas Mark 4, for 1 hour.

Blend the cornflour with a little cold water and stir into the casserole 5 minutes before the end of the cooking time.   **Serves 4**

Homepride

Porky Bean Pot

3 oz (75 g) dried haricot beans
12 oz (350 g) belly pork, with rind and bone removed, cut into 2 in (5 cm) pieces
a little oil *or* fat for frying
4 oz (100 g) cooked ham
4 frankfurter sausages
1 can **Homepride** White Wine with Cream Cook-in-Sauce
freshly chopped parsley to garnish

Cover the beans with boiling water and leave to soak for 2 hours. Fry the belly pork in the oil or fat until well browned, and drain. Chop the ham and frankfurters into 1 in (2 cm) pieces. Place the beans, pork, ham and frankfurters in a large casserole dish, add the Cook-in-Sauce and stir. Cover and place in the oven at 350°F, 180°C, Gas Mark 4 for 2 hours, stirring occasionally. Sprinkle with parsley to serve.   **Serves 4**

Honeyed Kebabs with Apple

2 tablespoons (30 ml) soy sauce
5 tablespoons (75 ml) clear honey
1 level teaspoon (5 ml) ground ginger
2 tablespoons (30 ml) **Jif** Lemon Juice
1 lb (450 g) boned shoulder of pork, cubed
1 large green *or* red pepper, de-seeded and cut into squares
4 small onions, peeled and halved
2 apples, quartered, cored and tossed in **Jif** Lemon Juice
8 medium sized mushrooms, washed

Combine the soy sauce, honey, ground ginger and lemon juice in a large non-metallic bowl. (Metallic containers affect the flavour of marinading meat). Add the pork pieces to the marinade and leave for 3–4 hours, turning occasionally. Thread the meat on to 4 skewers, alternating with pieces of green pepper, onion, apple and mushrooms. Put the kebabs under a hot grill for about 15–20 minutes, turning frequently and basting with the remaining marinade, until cooked.

Serve hot, on a bed of rice.
Serves 4

Kellogg's

Pork Chops with Tangy Orange Sauce

4 pork loin chops
1–2 cloves garlic, crushed
salt and freshly ground black pepper
Sauce
½ pint (300 ml) **Kellogg's** Rise & Shine Orange (made up)

1 onion, peeled and finely
    sliced
salt and pepper
1 tablespoon (15 ml) cornflour
2 tablespoons (30 ml) vinegar
flaked, toasted almonds, orange
    slices and sprigs of
    watercress to garnish

Place the chops in a roasting tin. Sprinkle with the garlic and seasoning and bake in a moderately hot oven (400°F, 200°C, Gas Mark 6) for about 30 minutes.

Pour the Rise & Shine into a saucepan, add the onion and seasoning and bring to the boil. Cover and simmer over a low heat for 20 minutes. Blend the cornflour with the vinegar and stir into the pan. Bring back to the boil, stirring, and simmer for a further 5 minutes.

To serve, spoon a little of the sauce over the chops on a serving dish and garnish with the almonds, orange slices and watercress. Serve the remaining sauce separately.   **Serves 4**

Pork and Apple Casserole

4 rashers streaky bacon,
    chopped
1 onion, peeled and sliced
1½ lb (600 g) stewing pork,
    cubed
½ pint (250 ml) **Knorr** chicken
    stock
¼ pint (125 ml) cider
1 tablespoon (15 ml) cornflour
1 large cooking apple, cored
    and thickly sliced
4–6 small tomatoes, skinned

Fry the bacon in a large frying pan, add the onion and pork and brown well all over. Put into an ovenproof casserole. Add the stock and cider, cover and cook at 325°F, 170°C, Gas Mark 3, for about 2 hours. Blend the cornflour with a little water and add to the casserole with the apple and tomatoes 15 minutes

before the end of the cooking time.

Serve with mashed potatoes mixed with a little cooked and mashed swede.   **Serves 4–6**

Pork in Soured Cream Sauce

4 tablespoons (60 ml) corn oil
2 slices white bread, cubed
2 tablespoons (30 ml) chopped
    parsley
1 lb (400 g) lean pork, cubed
1 onion, finely chopped
1 packet **Knorr** Country
    Mushroom Soup
1 pint (500 ml) water
5 oz (142 ml) carton soured
    cream

Heat half the corn oil in a pan, add the bread and fry until golden brown. Drain and mix with parsley and leave on one side. Heat remaining corn oil and sauté the pork and onion for 3–5 minutes. Add the soup mix and water and bring to the boil, stirring. Cover and simmer for 1–1¼ hours, stirring occasionally. Remove from the heat, stir in the soured cream and serve garnished with the croutons and parsley.   **Serves 4**

Wheatmeal Pork Savoury

1 lb (450 g) hand *or* belly of
    pork, minced
1 large onion, peeled and
    chopped
salt
freshly ground black pepper
2 cooking apples, peeled, cored
    and sliced
6 **McVitie's** Digestive Biscuits

Well butter a 2½ pint (1.5 litre) pie dish. Put the minced pork in a frying pan with the onion and fry quickly to lightly brown and let any fat run out. Drain off excess fat and put the meat in the pie dish. Season well and arrange the apples neatly over the meat. Crumble the

McVitie's digestive biscuits over the apples and bake in the oven pre-heated to 350°F, 180°C, Gas Mark 4, for about 1 hour. If it gets too brown on top, cover with a piece of foil.   **Serves 4**

American Spare Ribs

2 tablespoons (30 ml) oil
12 oz (350 g) onions, peeled
    and chopped
2 cloves garlic, crushed
4 tablespoons (60 ml) vinegar
2½ oz (62 g) can tomato purée
¼ teaspoon chilli powder
6 tablespoons (90 ml) clear
    honey
2 Red **Oxo** Cubes, crumbled
½ pint (300 ml) water
2½ lb (1.5 kg) pork ribs
salt and freshly ground black
    pepper

Heat the oil in a saucepan, add the onion and fry gently until pale golden brown and soft. Add the remaining ingredients except the pork ribs and seasoning and bring to the boil, stirring, then simmer without a lid for 10 minutes. Arrange the ribs in a single layer in a shallow, ovenproof dish, season with pepper and salt and pour over half the sauce. Roast in the oven at 375°F, 190°C, Gas Mark 5, for 45 minutes. Remove from the oven and drain off the surplus fat or blot with kitchen paper. Coat with the remaining sauce and roast for a further 15–30 minutes until golden brown and tender.

Serve with a crisp green salad and warm bread rolls.   **Serves 4**

Pork and Tarragon Pie

1 tablespoon (15 ml) margarine
1 onion, peeled and chopped
3 oz (75 g) bacon, with rinds
 removed, chopped
1 lb (450 g) minced pork
1 Chicken **Oxo** Cube, crumbled
 and dissolved in ⅓ pint
 (200 ml) hot water
salt and pepper
1 teaspoon (5 ml) dried
 tarragon
shortcrust pastry made with
 6 oz (175 g) flour
beaten egg *or* milk for glazing
tomato wedges and a sprig of
 parsley to garnish

Melt the margarine and fry the
onion and bacon gently for
5 minutes until soft. Add the pork
and cook gently for a further
5 minutes, stirring occasionally.
Stir in the Chicken Oxo, bring to
the boil, cover and simmer for
10 minutes. Season well, add the
tarragon and mix thoroughly.
Leave to cool. Roll out two-thirds
of the pastry and use to line an 8 in
(21 cm) shallow, fluted flan tin or
pie plate with a removable base.
Fill with the pork mixture. Roll out
the remaining pastry to make a lid.
Damp the edges of the pie and
cover with the lid. Press the edges
well together and trim. Cut a slit in
the centre and decorate the top
with pastry leaves cut from the
trimmings. Glaze with the egg or
milk and bake in a hot oven (425°F,
220°C, Gas Mark 7) for 15 minutes.
Reduce the heat to 350°F, 180°C,
Gas Mark 4 and continue to cook
for 30–40 minutes until golden
brown. Remove from the tin.

Serve hot with baked jacket
potatoes and a green vegetable or
cold with a mixed salad, garnished
with the tomato wedges and sprig
of parsley.   **Serves 4**

Mustard Roast Pork

3 oz (85 g) packet **Paxo** Sage and
 Onion Stuffing Mix
2 tablespoons (30 ml) French
 mustard
3 lb (1.5 kg) boned belly pork
 (approx)

Make up the stuffing as directed on
the packet. Stir in the French
mustard. Spread the stuffing over
the meat, roll up and tie securely
with fine string. Weigh the joint
and calculate cooking time allowing 35 minutes per 1 lb (450 g) plus
35 minutes. Put the joint into a
roasting tin and roast at 375°F,
190°C, Gas Mark 5. If desired mix
together 1 tablespoon (15 ml)
French mustard with 2 tablespoons (30 ml) vinegar and after
1 hour of roasting brush the joint
with the mixture. Repeat every 20
minutes. Cut into thick slices and
serve.   **Serves 4–6**

Pork Bretonne

½ pint (250 ml) dry cider
3 oz (85 g) packet **Paxo** Sage and
 Onion Stuffing Mix
2–3 lb (1.5 kg) loin pork
oil
salt

Heat the cider and add to the
stuffing. Spread the stuffing over
the meat, roll up and tie securely.
Weigh the joint and calculate the
cooking time, allowing 35 minutes
per lb (450 g) plus 35 minutes
extra. Rub the scored rind with the
oil and sprinkle with salt to give
crisp crackling. Put the joint into a
roasting tin and roast at 375°F,
190°C, Gas Mark 5. Slice and
serve.   **Serves 4–6**

Pancake Rolls

3 tablespoons (45 ml) **Spry**
 Crisp 'n Dry

8 oz (225 g) boneless pork,
 finely shredded
1 large onion, peeled and diced
2 oz (50 g) mushrooms, washed
 and diced
½ level teaspoon (2.5 ml) salt
1 level teaspoon (5 ml) sugar
freshly ground pepper
2 tablespoons (30 ml) soy sauce
8 oz (227 g) can bean sprouts
Batter
1 egg, beaten
4 oz (100 g) plain flour, sieved
 with 2 oz (50 g) cornflour
pinch salt
⅓ pint (450 ml) water
Spry Crisp 'n Dry for shallow
 frying
Spry Crisp 'n Dry for deep
 frying

Heat the 3 tablespoons (45 ml) of
Crisp 'n Dry in a large frying pan
and add the pork, onions and
mushrooms. Fry for 2–3 minutes,
stirring all the time. Add the
remaining filling ingredients and
mix well. Leave to cool.

To make the batter, stir the egg
into the dry ingredients and add
the water, a little at a time, to form
a thin batter. Heat a little Crisp 'n
Dry in a frying pan, pour in
sufficient batter to cover the base
and cook the pancakes on one side
only until dry, but not golden.
Drain on kitchen paper. Repeat,
using most of the remaining
batter, to make 6–8 pancakes.
Spread 2 tablespoons (30 ml) of
the filling on each pancake. Fold
the ends over and roll up the
pancakes, sealing the edges with
the remaining batter. Heat the
Crisp 'n Dry for deep frying in a
medium sized saucepan to 360°F
(185°C) and gently fry the pancake
rolls for 5–6 minutes, until golden
brown.

Serve immediately.
Makes 6–8

Sweet and Sour Pork with Vegetables

Batter
1 egg
1 oz (25 g) plain flour sieved
 with salt and pepper
¼ pint (150 ml) water

Sauce
¾ pint (450 ml) brown stock
1 oz (25 g) cornflour, blended
  with a little stock
1 tablespoon (15 ml) vinegar
1 tablespoon (15 ml) soy sauce
1 level tablespoon (15 ml)
  brown sugar
3 tablespoons (45 ml) mango
  chutney
2 teaspoons (10 ml) tomato
  purée
1 small cauliflower, washed
  and sprigged
1 small onion, diced
1 small green pepper, diced
2 oz (50 g) mushrooms, sliced
  thinly

1 lb (450 g) belly pork, cubed
Spry Crisp 'n Dry for deep
  frying

First make the batter. Stir the egg
into the sieved ingredients. Add
the water, a little at a time, and
beat to a smooth batter. Leave to
stand.

Place the sauce ingredients in a
large pan, bring to the boil and
simmer gently until thickened,
stirring occasionally. Cook the
vegetables in boiling, salted water
for 10 minutes. Drain and add to
the sauce and simmer gently for
5–10 minutes.

Heat the Crisp 'n Dry in a large
pan to 360°F, 185°C. Coat the pork
in the prepared batter and fry in
the hot oil for 4–5 minutes, until
the batter is crisp and golden
brown. Drain and place in a hot
serving dish. Pour over the sauce
and serve immediately.

Serve with rice or noodles.
Serves 4–6

whitworths

Orange Pork Chops

2 medium onions, peeled and
  sliced
4 pork chops
salt and pepper
grated rind and juice of 1 small
  orange

3 oz (75 g) sachet **Whitworths**
  Country Stuffing Mix
1 oz (25 g) butter

Preheat the oven to 375°F, 190°C,
Gas Mark 5. Place the onion rings
in a large shallow serving dish.
Arrange the chops on top and
season. Make the orange juice up
to 7 fl oz (200 ml) with hot water.
Add the rind and stuffing mix. Stir
well and allow to stand for a few
minutes. Place spoonfuls of the
stuffing in the centre of each chop.
Dot with butter and bake for 45–55
minutes.   **Serves 4**

Pork and Apple Loaf

1 lb (450 g) lean pork, minced
3 oz (75 g) sachet **Whitworths**
  Country Stuffing Mix
2 eating apples, peeled, cored
  and grated
approx ⅓ pint (200 ml) hot
  water
salt and black pepper

Place all the ingredients in a bowl
and mix thoroughly. Turn the
mixture into a lightly greased 1 lb
(450 g) loaf tin and press down
well. Cover with foil and bake in
the centre of a pre-heated oven
(350°F, 180°C, Gas Mark 4) for
1 hour. Remove the foil and cook
for a further 20–30 minutes, then
drain off any excess liquid and
turn out on to a serving dish. Serve
hot or chilled.   **Serves 4**

Pork and Lentil Casserole

1½ lb (600 g) belly pork
1 tablespoon (15 ml) oil
2 medium onions, peeled and
  sliced
6 oz (175 g) **Whitworths** Red
  Split Lentils
2 carrots, peeled and sliced
1½ pints (900 ml) chicken stock
¼ teaspoon mixed herbs
1 bay leaf
salt and pepper

Trim the skin, bones and excess fat
from the pork. Cut the meat into
1 in (2.5 cm) cubes. Heat the oil
and fry the onions and pork for

5 minutes, then remove from the
pan and place in a large ovenproof
casserole. Add the remaining
ingredients and stir well. Cover
the casserole and cook for about
2 hours, or until the lentils are very
soft, at 350°F, 180°C, Gas Mark 4.
Serves 4

Young's
SEAFOODS LTD

Pork in Sour Cream Sauce

1 lb (450 g) pork fillet *or* lean,
  boneless pork chops
rind and juice of 2 small lemons
1 medium onion, peeled and
  finely chopped
1 clove garlic, crushed
2 oz (50 g) butter
1 tablespoon (15 ml) flour
¼ pint (150 ml) dry white wine
½ pint (300 ml) **Young's** Dairy
  Cream, soured overnight
  with 2 teaspoons (10 ml)
  lemon juice from the recipe
salt and pepper
1 tablespoon (15 ml) fresh
  parsley, chopped

Cut the meat into bite sized pieces
and leave to marinate in the lemon
juice and rind for at least 8 hours.
Drain and dry the meat and reserve
the marinade. Fry the onion and
garlic in the butter for 2–3 minutes
until turning golden, then remove
from the pan. Add the meat and fry
until sealed on all sides then
remove. Sprinkle the flour on the
residue in the pan and stir well.
Add the wine, marinade, soured
cream and seasoning to taste and
stir until smooth. Return the meat
and onion to the pan with the
chopped parsley and simmer
gently until tender, about 5–10
minutes.

Serve with rice or potatoes and a
crisp salad. Try using this recipe
with Young's peeled prawns in
place of the pork for a really special
dish.   **Serves 4**

HAM and BACON

Ham Dango

8 oz (250 g) leeks, cleaned and
   sliced
1 large onion, peeled and sliced
1 large cooking apple, peeled,
   cored and chopped
2 oz (50 g) butter
2 level teaspoons (10 ml) sugar
14 oz (396 g) can tomatoes
1 teaspoon (5 ml) mixed herbs
¼ pint (125 ml) stock
¼ pint (125 ml) sweet cider *or*
   light ale
1 lb (454 g) **Armour** Ham,
   chopped
salt and pepper
1 tablespoon (15 ml) mashed
   potato powder

Cook the leeks, onion and apple in
the butter for about 20 minutes,
without browning, until soft. Mix
in the sugar, tomatoes and herbs.
Stir well and add the stock and
cider or ale. Simmer for 15
minutes. Add the ham, seasoning
and mashed potato powder to
taste. Serve hot.   **Serves 6–8**

ATORA

Leek and Bacon Pie

4 oz (100 g) self-raising flour,
   sifted
4 oz (100 g) wholemeal flour,
   sifted
4 oz (100 g) **Atora** Shredded
   Suet
1 teaspoon (5 ml) baking
   powder
pinch of salt
1 egg (size 3), beaten
water to mix

Filling
8 oz (250 g) bacon, chopped
1 oz (25 g) butter
1 lb (500 g) leeks, washed and
   sliced
4 oz (100 g) mushrooms,
   washed and sliced
2 eggs (size 3), beaten
½ teaspoon (2.5 ml) dried
   thyme
salt and ground black pepper
milk *or* a little beaten egg to
   glaze

Mix the flours, suet, baking
powder and salt to a firm dough
with the egg and water. Divide the
pastry in two and roll out both
pieces to fit the top and base of an
8 in (20 cm) pie dish. Line the base
with pastry. Meanwhile, fry the
bacon gently in the butter, then
add the prepared leeks. Cover the
pan and cook very gently for
10 minutes, then add the mushrooms and cook for a few minutes
more. Remove from the heat and
stir in the eggs, thyme and
seasoning. Spoon into the pastry
base. Damp the edges, top with
the remaining pastry, seal and
crimp the edges. Make a cross or
slits in the top of the pastry, glaze
with milk or a little more beaten
egg and decorate with pastry
trimmings, if liked. Stand the pie
on a baking sheet and bake at
375°F, 190°C, Gas Mark 5 for
30 minutes or until browned and
crisp.   **Serves 4–6**

Bean and Ham Supper

1 oz (25 g) butter
1 oz (25 g) floùr
¾ pint (450 ml) milk
1 heaped teaspoon (10 ml)
   Dijon mustard *or* 1 flat
   teaspoon (5 ml) English
   mustard

salt and pepper
6 oz (170 g) packet frozen
   sweetcorn
15 oz (425 g) **Batchelors** Butter
   Beans, drained
3 thick slices of ham, cooked
2 tablespoons (30 ml) double
   cream
2 oz (50 g) strong Cheddar
   cheese

Melt the butter, stir in the flour and
cook for 1 minute. Add the milk,
bring to the boil and cook for 2
minutes, stirring, until thickened
and smooth. Add the mustard,
seasoning, sweetcorn and beans.
Place 2 slices of the ham in a
casserole dish and pour over half
the sauce mixture. Add the rest of
the ham and sauce. Top with the
cream and sprinkle with cheese.
Bake for 25 minutes in a pre-heated
oven at 375°F, 190°C, Gas Mark 5.
Serves 4

Cassoulet

8 oz (225 g) salt pork *or* sliced
   bacon, diced
dripping *or* butter for frying
15 oz (425 g) can **Batchelors**
   Cannellini Beans, drained
1 bouquet garni of mixed herbs
salt and pepper
2 cloves garlic, crushed
8 oz (225 g) smoked pork
   sausages, sliced 1 in (2.5 cm)
   thick
stock
15 oz (425 g) can peeled
   tomatoes
1 dessertspoon (10 ml) tomato
   purée
a pinch of sugar
browned breadcrumbs

Lightly fry the meat and place in a
casserole dish. Add the beans,
bouquet garni, seasoning, garlic
and sliced sausages. Cover with
stock and place in the oven pre-
heated to 350°F, 180°C, Gas Mark 4

for 30 minutes. Cook the tomatoes to a pulp and add the purée with salt, pepper and sugar. Spoon this over the casserole and mix in. Cover the top with breadcrumbs and return to the oven, covered, for a further 30 minutes.
Serves 4–6

Sweet and Sour Gammon

2 lb (900 g) gammon, cut into 1 in (2.5 cm) cubes
1 can **Baxters** Sweet and Sour Sauce
1 onion, peeled and sliced in strips
1 bulb stem ginger, grated pineapple rings

Spread the gammon cubes evenly in an open pan. Pour the Sweet and Sour Sauce into a bowl and add the onion and ginger. Pour this mixture over the gammon and simmer for 45 minutes, stirring gently. To serve, place one or two pineapple rings per person on a bed of boiled rice and ladle a generous portion of the gammon and sauce over each serving. Serve with mixed or steamed vegetables.
Serves 4–6

Bacon and Egg Pie

shortcrust pastry made with 8 oz (200 g) **Be-Ro** Flour
8 oz (200 g) streaky bacon
3 eggs, lightly beaten
salt and pepper
pinch mixed herbs (optional)
beaten egg or milk to glaze

Divide the pastry in two, roll out and line an 8 in (20 cm) ovenproof plate or foil baking dish. Remove the rinds and cut the bacon into small pieces and add to the beaten eggs with the seasoning and herbs, if used. Pour the mixture on

to the pastry, damp the edge and cover with the second round of pastry. Seal the edges and decorate with pastry 'leaves'. Make a hole in the centre and brush with beaten egg or milk. Bake in a moderately hot oven at 375°F, 190°C, Gas Mark 5, for about 35–40 minutes.
Serve hot or cold.   **Serves 4–6**

Savoury Bacon Roll

suet pastry made with 8 oz (200 g) **Be-Ro** Self-raising Flour
8 oz (200 g) streaky bacon, chopped
1 small onion, peeled and chopped
1 teaspoon (5 ml) parsley, chopped

Fry the bacon and onion gently for 2–3 minutes then add the parsley. Make the pastry, roll into an oblong and spread the bacon mixture to within 1 in (2 cm) of the edges. Damp the edges with water and roll up tightly. Place on a greased baking tray and bake in a moderately hot oven at 400°F, 200°C, Gas Mark 6, for about 45 minutes.   **Serves 4**

Celery and Ham Mornay

8 oz (227 g) **Birds Eye** Potato Waffles
2 sticks celery, each cut into 4 pieces
1/2 pint (250 ml) cheese sauce
4 slices ham
chopped parsley to garnish

Simmer the celery pieces for 10–15 minutes until tender. Cook the waffles according to pack instructions. Cut each slice of ham in half and wrap around a piece of celery. Place on top of the waffles and pour over the cheese sauce.
Serves 4

Huntingdon Fidget Pie

8 oz (200 g) thick lean back bacon *or* gammon
4 oz (100 g) onions, peeled and chopped

8 oz (200 g) cooking apples, peeled, cored and chopped
salt and freshly ground black pepper
1/8 pint (40 ml) dry cider
1 sheet **Birds Eye** Puff Pastry, thawed
beaten egg to glaze

Remove any rind from the bacon or gammon and dice. Mix well with the onions and apples and season. Put in a 1–1½ pint (600–900 ml) pie dish and pour over the cider. Roll out the pastry sheet on a floured surface and cover the pie. Roll out any pastry trimmings and make leaves to decorate. Make a small hole in the centre of the pie to allow the steam to escape. Brush with beaten egg and bake in the centre of an oven pre-heated to 425°F, 220°C, Gas Mark 7, for approximately 20 minutes. Lower the temperature to 350°F, 180°C, Gas Mark 4, for a further 30 minutes or until the pastry is crisp and brown. If the pastry begins to brown too quickly, cover with foil.   **Serves 2–3**

Hereford Cider and Honey Gammon

3–4 lb (1.5–2 kg) gammon ham
4 oz (100 g) dried breadcrumbs
2 tablespoons (30 ml) brown sugar
cider to bind
2 tablespoons (30 ml) honey
1/2 pint (300 ml) **Bulmers** Special Reserve Medium Sweet Cider

Cover the gammon with water, bring to the boil and simmer for 1 hour. Remove from the water and peel away the skin. Mix together breadcrumbs, sugar, and cider to bind and firmly press the mixture on to the sides of the gammon. Place the gammon in a casserole or shallow, ovenproof dish, pour in the cider and honey and bake for about 1¼ hours at 375°F, 190°C, Gas Mark 5, basting from time to time.   **Serves 6**

Campbell's

Ham and Celery Rolls

1 medium can celery hearts
6 slices cooked ham *or* bacon
salt and pepper
10½ oz (297 g) can **Campbell's**
Cream of Celery Soup

Drain the celery hearts, reserving the liquid. Using one to each slice of ham, roll the celery hearts in the ham slices and place in an oven-proof dish. Season and cover with the soup, diluted with the liquid from the celery hearts. Bake in a moderate oven (350°F, 180°C, Gas Mark 4) or grill until heated through.   **Serves 4**

Chesswood

Baked Ham Rolls

1 can **Chesswood** Sliced
Mushrooms in Creamed
Sauce
2 tomatoes, skinned and
chopped
8 thin slices cooked ham
2 oz (50 g) cheese, grated
2 oz (50 g) fresh breadcrumbs

Heat the Sliced Mushrooms in Creamed Sauce with the chopped tomatoes. Spread each slice of ham with the mixture. Roll up the slices of ham and place in an ovenproof dish. Sprinkle with the cheese and breadcrumbs and brown under the grill or in the oven.   **Serves 4**

Colman's

Stuffed Baked Potatoes

4 baking potatoes
1 packet **Colman's** Savoury
White Sauce Mix
½ pint (300 ml) milk
4–6 oz (100–175 g) cooked ham,
chopped
2 tablespoons (30 ml) freshly
chopped chives and parsley,
mixed
1 tablespoon (15 ml) **Colman's**
French Mustard
4 oz (100 g) cheese, grated

Wash the potatoes, prick with a fork and put into the oven at 350°F, 180°C, Gas Mark 4, for 45 minutes to 1 hour, until soft. Make up the white sauce mix as directed. Cut the potatoes in half lengthwise, scoop out the insides and mix with the savoury white sauce. Add the ham, herbs and mustard, and pile back into the potato skins. Place in an ovenproof dish, sprinkle with the cheese and place under a hot grill until golden.   **Serves 4**

Cranberry Cidered Ham

2 lb (800 g) collar of bacon
1 onion, peeled and sliced
1 carrot, peeled and sliced
1 leek, cleaned and chopped
pepper
½ pint (250 ml) dry cider
Sauce
rind of 1 orange
rind and juice of ½ lemon
6½ oz (185 g) jar **Frank Cooper**
   Cranberry Sauce
seasoning
½ oz (15 g) cornflour

Soak the bacon in cold water for 2 hours. Drain, place in a large pan, cover with water and bring to the boil. Discard the water. Place the bacon in an ovenproof dish. Add the vegetables and cider, cover and cook at 325°F, 170°C, Gas Mark 3, for 2 hours. Remove the bacon and keep warm.

   Strain the liquor into a pan and reserve the vegetables. Add the orange rind, lemon rind and juice, cranberry sauce and seasoning. Blend the cornflour with a little cold water and stir into the sauce, bring to the boil and boil for 1 minute.

   Place the bacon on a serving dish with the vegetables and serve the sauce separately.   **Serves 4–6**

Ham and Pineapple Plate Pie

8 oz (200 g) shortcrust pastry
2 level tablespoons (30 ml)
   cornflour
1 can **Frank Cooper's** New
   England Chicken Soup with
   Sweetcorn
8 oz (200 g) cooked ham, diced
8 oz (227 g) tin pineapple
   pieces, drained

Roll out half the pastry and use to line a 9 in (23 cm) pie plate. Blend the cornflour with a little of the cold soup. Heat the remaining soup and stir in the cornflour, ham and pineapple. Bring to the boil, stirring. Pour into the pastry case and cover with the remaining pastry. Bake at 400°F, 200°C, Gas Mark 6, for 30 minutes.
Serves 4–6

ELSENHAM

Vintage Orange Gammon

1 gammon ham
¼ bottle cider per lb (450 g) of
   ham
2–3 bay leaves
cloves to decorate
sufficient **Elsenham** Vintage
   Orange Marmalade to glaze
   (approximately 1 jar for every
   4–5 lb (1.8–2 kg))

Soak the ham for 24 hours in cold water. Remove and wipe dry. Place in a large saucepan with the cider and sufficient cold water to cover the ham. Add the bay leaves. Bring slowly to the boil and simmer until cooked, allowing 20 minutes to the lb (450 g). When cooked, allow the ham to cool in its own stock. When cold, peel off the skin, and stick in the cloves in a diamond pattern. Coat the ham with the marmalade and finish off under a hot grill, allowing the marmalade peel to burn slightly.
**4–5 lb (1.8–2 kg) ham serves
approximately 8**

Gammon Chops en Croute

1 level tablespoon (15 ml) plain
  flour
1 level teaspoon (5 ml) soft
  brown sugar
1 level teaspoon (5 ml) mustard
  powder
freshly ground black pepper
4 bacon chops
few drops Tabasco sauce
8 oz (227 g) can pineapple
  rings, drained
4 thin slices Gouda cheese
13 oz (370 g) packet **Jus-rol** Puff
  Pastry, thawed
beaten egg to glaze

Mix the flour, sugar, mustard and
pepper together in a small
polythene bag and toss the bacon
chops in this mixture, one at a
time. Place the chops on a board,
sprinkle each with a little Tabasco
sauce, place a pineapple ring in the
centre of each and top with a slice
of cheese. Roll the pastry out
thinly. Cut into 4 squares, large
enough to wrap around the chops.
Place a chop in the centre of each
piece of pastry. Moisten the edges
of the pastry and fold over to cover
the meat completely and press
together to seal. Place the chops on
a dampened baking tray, brush
with beaten egg and bake in the
oven pre-heated to 425°F, 220°C,
Gas Mark 7 for about 40 minutes.
  Serve with a mixed salad or
green vegetables. **Serves 4**

Ham and Pepper Flan

7½ oz (215 g) packet **Jus-rol**
  Shortcrust Pastry, thawed
8 oz (225 g) cooked ham, diced
3 tablespoons (45 ml) green
  pepper, de-seeded and finely
  chopped
½ (10½ oz, 298 g) tin
  condensed cream of chicken
  soup, undiluted
2 eggs

¼ pint (150 ml) milk
ground black pepper

Roll out the pastry and use to line
an 8 in (20 cm) flan tin or china flan
dish. Mix together the diced ham,
chopped pepper and chicken
soup. Whisk the eggs with the
milk and add to the mixture.
Season with black pepper and
pour into the flan case. Place on a
hot baking sheet and bake in a
pre-heated oven at 400°F, 200°C,
Gas Mark 6, for about 35–40
minutes until set and brown on
top. **Serves 4**

Ham and Rhubarb Casserole

8 oz (200 g) ham ends, diced
1 oz (25 g) seasoned flour
1 onion, peeled and cut into
  rings
1 teaspoon (5 ml) mixed herbs
4 oz (100 g) rhubarb, cut in
  ½ in (1 cm) pieces
¾ pint (375 ml) **Knorr** chicken
  stock
Dumplings
1½ oz (40 g) plain flour
½ oz (15 g) suet, finely
  chopped
½ teaspoon (2.5 ml) baking
  powder
salt and pepper
water for mixing

Toss the ham in the seasoned flour
and put into an ovenproof
casserole. Add the onions, herbs,
rhubarb and ¼ pint (150 ml) of the
stock. Cover and cook at 350°F,
180°C, Gas Mark 4, for 30 minutes,
then add the remaining stock. In
the meantime mix the flour, suet,
baking powder and seasoning
with cold water into a light dough.
Form into balls and put them into
the stew when the liquid is
boiling. Cover and cook for a
further 30 minutes.
  Serve with baked potatoes.
Serves 2

Onion and Ham Savoury

4 oz (100 g) macaroni
1 packet **Knorr** Onion Sauce
  Mix
½ pint (250 ml) milk
10½ oz (298 g) can chopped
  ham, diced

Cook the macaroni in boiling
salted water until tender and
drain. Make up the packet of sauce
mix as directed using the milk. Stir
in the macaroni and simmer gently
for 5 minutes. **Serves 3–4**

LEA & PERRINS

Bacon Pot Roast

3 lb (1.4 kg) green hock bacon
  joint, boned and rolled
4 carrots, peeled and quartered
2 onions, peeled and quartered
½ pint (250 ml) water
2 tablespoons (30 ml) **Lea &
  Perrins** Worcestershire Sauce
1½ lb (700 g) potatoes, peeled
  and quartered

Soak the bacon hock for at least
8 hours, or overnight if possible.
Place in a 6 pint (3.5 litre) casserole
dish with the carrots and onions.
Pour over the water and
Worcestershire Sauce. Cover the
casserole and cook at 350°F, 180°C,
Gas Mark 4, for 1 hour. Add the
potatoes, return to the oven and
cook for a further 40–45 minutes.
Place the bacon on a deep serving
plate, surround with the
vegetables and spoon over the
cooking liquor. **Serves 6–8**

Bacon and Bean Cauliflower Cheese

1 cauliflower, cut into florets
1 oz (25 g) butter
1 onion, peeled and chopped
4 rashers back bacon, with
   rinds removed, chopped
1 oz (25 g) flour
½ pint (300 ml) milk
16 oz (454 g) can baked beans
1 Red **Oxo** Cube, crumbled
4–6 oz (100–175 g) Cheddar
   cheese, grated

Cook the cauliflower in boiling, salted water. Melt the butter and lightly fry the onion and bacon. Stir in the flour and cook for a minute. Remove from the heat and gradually stir in the milk. Return to the heat and bring to the boil, stirring. Add the baked beans and Oxo cube and simmer for about 5 minutes. Remove from the heat, add the cheese and stir until the cheese has melted. Drain the cauliflower and pour the sauce over.   **Serves 4**

Bacon, Onion and Apple Loaf

1 lb (450 g) collar bacon *or*
   gammon, minced
¼ pint (150 ml) cider
½ oz (15 g) margarine
2 onion, peeled and finely
   chopped
2 cooking apples, peeled, cored
   and finely chopped
1 Chicken **Oxo** Cube, crumbled
2 egg yolks
1 tablespoon (15 ml) fresh
   parsley, chopped
salt and pepper
12 oz (350 g) shortcrust pastry
8 oz (225 g) streaky bacon, with
   rinds removed
beaten egg *or* milk to glaze

Soak the bacon in the cider overnight. Melt the margarine and gently fry the onion, apple and Chicken Oxo for a few minutes until soft, then remove from the heat. Add the bacon and cider mixture and mix well. Stir in the egg yolks and parsley and season to taste. Line a 7 in (18 cm) square or 8 in (20 cm) round cake tin with a removable base with three-quarters of the pastry, pressing it firmly into the corners. Stretch the bacon rashers with the back of a knife and use 6 oz (175 g) of the bacon to line the pastry base and sides. Spoon half the bacon and cider mixture into the tin. Make a layer of the remaining bacon rashers over the mixture and spoon in the remaining bacon mixture. Press down gently and smooth the surface. Fold in any bacon rasher ends. Roll out the remaining pastry to make a lid, damp the pastry edges and place over the filling. Pinch the edges well together and mark with a fork. Make a slit in the centre and decorate the top with leaves made from the trimmings of pastry. Glaze with the beaten egg or milk. Bake in a moderate oven (350°F, 180°C, Gas Mark 4) for 1 hour. Push the loaf carefully out of the tin and, leaving the base intact, brush the sides and top of the loaf with the beaten egg. Turn up the oven to 400°F, 200°C, Gas Mark 6, and cook for a further 15 minutes until crisp and browned.

Serve hot with potatoes and carrots or sprouts, or serve cold in slices with chutney or salad. Good for picnics, too.   **Serves 4**

Beany Bombs

4 crisp bread rolls
4 oz (100 g) streaky bacon, with
   rinds removed, cooked and
   chopped
8 oz (227 g) can baked beans
1 Red **Oxo** Cube
1 tablespoon (15 ml) pickle
½ oz (15 g) butter *or*
   margarine, melted

Cut the tops off the bread rolls, hollow out the bread from the centre and make into bread-crumbs. Mix the breadcrumbs, bacon and beans, then crumble in the Oxo cube and add the pickle. Stuff the filling into the hollowed-out rolls, replace the lids and brush with the melted butter or margarine. Cook in the oven at 350°F, 180°C, Gas Mark 4, for 15 minutes, until hot and crisp. **Serves 4**

Cornish Bacon Pudding

12 oz (350 g) collar bacon,
   without rind or fat
8 oz (225 g) self-raising flour
½ level teaspoon (2.5 ml) salt
4 oz (120 g) shredded suet
approx ¼ pint (150 ml) cold
   water to mix
1 large onion, peeled and
   chopped
1½ oz (40 g) fresh white
   breadcrumbs
1 Red **Oxo** Cube, crumbled
1 level tablespoon (15 ml)
   parsley, chopped
2 level tablespoons (30 ml)
   tomato ketchup
2 level tablespoons (30 ml)
   water
a little pepper
Oxo gravy to serve

Put the bacon into a basin, cover with water and leave overnight, then drain and mince. Sieve the flour and salt into a bowl and stir in the suet. Add water to mix to a soft dough. Knead lightly until smooth. Roll out two-thirds of the pastry and use to line a well-greased 1½ pint (900 ml) pudding basin. Mix together the remaining ingredients and place in the pastry-lined basin. Moisten the edges of the pastry with water, roll the remaining pastry out into a cricle and use to cover the filling, pressing the edges well together. Cover with a double thickness of buttered greaseproof paper or a single layer of buttered aluminium foil. Steam steadily for about 2 hours.

Serve with the Oxo gravy.
Serves 4–6

Bacon Bonus

4 oz (100 g) butter beans
¾ pint (450 ml) apple juice
3 sticks celery, trimmed and
  chopped
2 leeks, cleaned and sliced
6 oz (175 g) swede, peeled and
  cut into ½ in (1 cm) pieces
6 oz (175 g) parsnip, peeled and
  cut into ½ in (1 cm) pieces
6 oz (175 g) turnip, peeled and
  cut into ½ in (1 cm) pieces
2 carrots, peeled and sliced
1 **Wall's** Bacon Joint
1 teaspoon (5 ml) dried basil
pepper and salt

Put the butter beans into a 4 pint,
(2.5 litre) casserole dish, pour over
the apple juice and leave them
overnight to soak. Next day, add
the prepared celery, leeks, swede,
parsnip, turnip and carrots. Nestle
the bacon joint in the centre and
sprinkle over the basil. Cover the
dish and cook the meal at 325°F,
160°C, Gas Mark 3 for 3 hours, or
until all the ingredients are tender.
Check the seasoning.

  Serve with Brussels sprouts and
creamed potatoes.   **Serves 4**

Bacon and Lentil Pot Roast

2 onions, peeled and chopped
2 carrots, peeled and sliced
6 oz (175 g) red lentils
1 **Wall's** Bacon Joint
½ pint (300 ml) orange juice,
  from a carton
¼ pint (150 ml) water
pepper

Put the onions, carrots and lentils
into a 3 pint (1.8 litre) casserole
dish and nestle the joint in the
centre. Pour over the orange juice
and water and season with pepper
only. Cover the dish and cook at
325°F, 160°C, Gas Mark 3, for
1½–1¾ hours or until the lentils
are soft.

  A few potatoes can be placed on
the oven shelves beside the
casserole to bake in their jackets at
the same time and the meal
completed with freshly cooked
cabbage.   **Serves 4**

Bacon Steaks with Jamaican Topping

4 **Wall's** Bacon Steaks
3 oz (75 g) fresh breadcrumbs
1 oz (25 g) walnuts, finely
  chopped
13½ oz (382 g) can crushed
  pineapple, drained
1 dessertspoon (10 ml) honey
watercress and sliced tomatoes
  to garnish

Grill the steaks on one side for
5 minutes and then turn them over
and grill the other side for just
2 minutes. Mix the breadcrumbs
with the walnuts, pineapple and
honey and divide the topping
between the steaks. Return the pan
to the grill and cook the steaks for a
further 5 minutes or until they are
golden brown.

  Serve garnished with the watercress and tomato.   **Serves 4**

Layered Bacon and Potato Fry

4 oz (100 g) **Wall's** Streaky
  Bacon Rashers, with rinds
  removed, cut into 1 in
  (2.5 cm) pieces
1 tablespoon (15 ml) oil
1 lb (450 g) potatoes, peeled
  and thinly sliced
salt and pepper
1 large onion, peeled and thinly
  sliced
4 oz (100 g) Cheddar cheese,
  grated
½ oz (15 g) butter

Fry the bacon in a frying pan until
it is crisp then remove from the
pan with a slotted spoon. Add the
oil to the bacon fat in the pan and
swirl it around. Cover the bottom
of the pan with about one-third of
the potato slices. Season them and
spread over half the onion, bacon
and cheese. Repeat the layers and
finish with the rest of the potatoes.
Cover with a lid and fry gently for
35 minutes. Add a little more oil to
the pan during cooking if the
potatoes seem to be sticking.
Remove the pan lid and dot the top
layer of potatoes with the butter.
Brown quickly under a hot grill.
Slide on to a heated plate or serve
from the pan. Serve hot.
Serves 4

Tomato Bacon Casserole

1 **Wall's** Bacon Joint
8 oz (227 g) packet **Wall's** Pork
  Chipolata Sausages
1 tablespoon (15 ml) oil
1 oz (25 g) butter
8 oz (225 g) leeks, trimmed and
  sliced
2 sticks celery, chopped
8 oz (225 g) cooking apples,
  peeled, cored and thickly
  sliced
2 tablespoons (30 ml) plain
  flour
14 oz (396 g) can tomatoes
½ pint (300 ml) dry cider
pepper

Cut the bacon joint into 1 in
(2.5 cm) pieces and twist each
sausage in half. Heat the oil and
butter, add the leeks and celery
and cook them gently for
5 minutes until starting to soften.
Add the bacon and sausages and
when the pieces are sealed stir in
the apples. Mix in the flour and
then stir in the tomatoes and cider.
Bring the casserole to the boil, add
plenty of pepper—no salt should
be required—and transfer the
mixture to a casserole dish. Cook at
350°F, 180°C, Gas Mark 4 for
1¼ hours.   **Serves 4**

SAUSAGES

Sausage Savoury

1 lb (450 g) pork *or* beef
    sausages
8 medium potatoes, peeled and
    thinly sliced
1 lb (450 g) can tomatoes
2 large onions, thinly sliced
salt and pepper
½ pint (300 ml) stock made
    with a Red Cube from **Bovril**

Grill the sausages until lightly
browned. Put on to kitchen paper
to absorb surplus fat. Fill a
saucepan with alternate layers of
potatoes, roughly chopped
tomatoes (reserving the juice),
onions and sausages, seasoning
the layers with salt and pepper,
and finishing with a layer of
potatoes. Pour in the tomato liquid
and the stock. Cover and simmer
for 45 minutes, and serve hot.
Serves 4

Simple Cassoulet

1 lb (450 g) chipolata sausages
4 oz (100 g) bacon with rind
    removed, chopped
1 tablespoon (15 ml) oil
1 large onion, sliced
1 tablespoon (15 ml) flour
1 Red Cube from **Bovril**
    dissolved in ¼ pint (150 ml)
    water
15 oz (425 g) can kidney beans,
    drained
salt and pepper
½ teaspoon (2.5 ml) mixed
    herbs
thin slices French bread
2 oz (50 g) Cheddar cheese,
    grated

Gently fry the sausages and bacon,
without additional fat, for 5
minutes. Remove from the pan.

Add the oil and fry the onion for
3–4 minutes. Sprinkle the flour
over the onion and cook for a
further minute, stirring to prevent
sticking. Stir the Red Cube from
Bovril stock into the onion, add the
kidney beans and seasoning.
Bring to the boil. Place the
sausages and bacon, onion, stock
and kidney beans in an ovenproof
dish. Cover and bake at 350°F,
180°C, Gas Mark 4 for 30 minutes.
Remove the lid and place the
French bread over the filling,
sprinkle with cheese and place in
the oven at 400°F, 200°C, Gas Mark
6 for about 15 minutes until golden
brown.   **Serves 4**

Canadian Pasties

8 oz (225 g) plain flour
pinch salt
2 oz (50 g) lard
2 oz (50 g) margarine
cold water to mix
Filling
1 egg, hard-boiled and
    chopped
8 oz (225 g) pork sausagemeat
5½ oz (142 g) can **Campbell's**
    Condensed Cream of
    Mushroom Soup, undiluted
2 oz (50 g) cheese, grated
a little made English mustard
salt and pepper
a little beaten egg or milk

Sift the flour and salt into a bowl,
add the fats cut into small pieces
and rub them in gently until the
mixture resembles fine bread-

crumbs. Stir in sufficient cold
water to make a fairly stiff dough,
turn on to a floured work surface
and knead gently until smooth.
Wrap the pastry in greaseproof
paper and leave in a cool place
while preparing the filling. Mix
the egg and sausagemeat with the
undiluted soup, cheese, made
mustard and seasoning.

Divide the pastry into four. Roll
each piece into a 7 in (18 cm) round
and trim the edges. Divide the
filling between the rounds, then
dampen the pastry edges and draw
up the sides, enclosing the contents completely. Crimp the top to
seal the edges well together and
brush the pasties with the beaten
egg or milk to glaze. Leave the
pasties to rest in a cool place for 15
minutes then bake them on the
centre shelf of a moderately hot
oven, 400°F, 200°C, Gas Mark 6, for
50 minutes or until the pastry is
golden brown.   **Serves 4**

Savoury Envelope

8 oz (225 g) pork sausagemeat
10½ oz (297 g) can **Campbell's**
    Condensed Vegetable Soup
pinch mixed herbs
garlic salt
8 oz (225 g) puff pastry
beaten egg to glaze

Mix the sausagemeat and
undiluted soup together with a
fork until well blended and add the
herbs and garlic salt. Roll out the
pastry into a 10 in (25 cm) square.
Brush the edges with beaten egg
and place the sausagemeat mixture
in the centre. Lift the corners of the
pastry to the middle and seal to
resemble an envelope. Crimp the
sealed edges and brush all over
with beaten egg. Bake at 425°F,
220°C, Gas Mark 7, for
approximately 25 minutes.
Serves 4

Casseroled Sausages

1 box **Chef** Tomato Soup
4 rashers streaky bacon,
 chopped
1 onion, peeled and sliced
1–2 oz (25–30 g) lard *or* cooking
 fat
4 thick pork sausages, skinned
1 small egg, beaten
3 level tablespoons (45 ml) sage
 and onion stuffing mix
7 oz (200 g) can sweetcorn,
 drained

Prepare the tomato soup as
instructed on the label. Fry the
bacon and onion in a casserole for
4–5 minutes until the onion is soft
but not browned. Remove from
the casserole and reserve. Cut the
sausages in half lengthways and
coat with the beaten egg and
stuffing mix. Fry the sausages in
the fat remaining in the casserole
until lightly browned. Add the
fried onion and bacon, the
sweetcorn and the prepared soup,
cover with a tight fitting lid and
simmer for 35–40 minutes.
 Serve with mashed potato, rice,
pasta or crusty bread.
Serves 3–4

FRANK COOPER®

Picnic Plait

1 lb (400 g) sausagemeat
1 small onion, finely chopped
1 level teaspoon (5 ml) dried
 sage, crumbled
salt and pepper
2 tablespoons (30 ml) **Frank
 Cooper's** Apple Sauce
13 oz (368 g) packet puff pastry
milk to glaze

Mix together the sausagemeat,
onion, sage and seasoning. Roll
out the puff pastry to an oblong
approximately 14 × 11 in

(36 × 28 cm), place the filling
along the centre and spread the
apple sauce on top. Cut diagonal
slits along each side of the pastry
and use to criss-cross over the
filling, damping the edges to seal
carefully. Brush with milk, lift on
to a baking sheet and bake at 400°F,
200°C, Gas Mark 6, for 35–40
minutes until well risen and
golden brown.　**Serves 4**

Sausage Bonanza

1 large onion, peeled and
 chopped
fat for frying
1 lb (400 g) pork sausages
13¼ oz (376 g) can **Del Monte**
 Crushed Pineapple
1 medium sized can baked
 beans
salt and pepper

Fry the onion in the fat for a few
minutes. Add the sausages and
continue to fry until beginning to
go brown. Drain the pineapple
and stir the fruit into the sausage
and onion mixture. Add the baked
beans to the pan. Transfer to an
ovenproof dish and cook in the
oven at 375°F, 190°C, Gas Mark 5
for 45 minutes without a lid. Serve
with jacket potatoes.　**Serves 4**

Skewered Sausages

1 lb (400 g) pork chipolata
 sausages
1 lb 3 oz (538 g) can
 Hartleys New Potatoes,
 drained
8 oz (200 g) tomatoes, halved
2 tablespoons (30 ml) **Chivers**
 Olde English Marmalade
¼ pint (125 ml) chicken stock
1 teaspoon (5 ml) tomato purée
1 teaspoon (5 ml)
 Worcestershire sauce

3 level teaspoons (15 ml)
 cornflour

Thread the sausages, potatoes and
tomatoes alternately on to 4 long
skewers. Mix the marmalade with
the stock, tomato purée and
Worcestershire sauce in a small
saucepan and simmer for about 5
minutes. Blend the cornflour with
a little cold water, add to the pan,
stirring, and bring gently to the
boil, stirring all the time, until
thick. Brush the sausages and
vegetables on the skewers with the
sauce and cook under a medium
hot grill.
 Serve hot.　**Serves 4**

Haywards

Sausage and Pickle Flan

6 oz (150 g) shortcrust pastry
4 skinless sausages
2 tablespoons (30 ml)
 Hayward's Sweet Brown
 Pickle
2 eggs
½ pint (250 ml) milk
salt and pepper
2 oz (50 g) cheese, grated

Line a 7 in (18 cm) flan ring or
sandwich tin with the pastry. Cut
the sausages in half lengthways
and arrange in the flan case.
Spread the pickle over the sausages. Beat together the eggs, milk
and seasonings. Pour into the flan
case and sprinkle on the cheese.
Bake at 425°F, 220°C, Gas Mark 7
for 35–40 minutes.　**Serves 4**

Sausage Wheel

7½ oz (212 g) packet frozen
    puff pastry, thawed
1 lb (500 g) pork sausagemeat
2 tablespoons (30 ml)
    Haywards Sweet Brown
    Pickle
4 **Haywards** Pickled Walnuts,
    finely chopped
2 **Haywards** Gherkins, finely
    chopped

Roll out the pastry very thinly on a
floured board and leave in a cool
place while preparing the rest of
the ingredients. Combine the
sausagemeat with the pickle,
walnuts and gherkins. Roll out the
sausagemeat to the same size as
the pastry, place on top of the
pastry and roll up like a swiss roll.
Cut into slices, place on a baking
sheet with space between each
slice and bake at 400°F, 200°C,
Gas Mark 6, for 30 minutes.
Serves 4

Homepride

Barbecued Sausages

1 lb (450 g) pork sausages
streaky bacon rashers
1 can **Homepride** Barbecue
    Cook-in-Sauce

Wrap one rasher of bacon round
each sausage. Place in a shallow
casserole dish and bake in the oven
at 400°F, 200°C, Gas Mark 6 for
30 minutes. Remove from the oven
and drain off the fat. Add the
Cook-in-Sauce, cover and return
to the oven for a further 25–30
minutes, basting occasionally.

Serve with creamed potatoes
and sweetcorn.   **Serves 4**

Sweet-Sour
Frankfurters with Herb
Dumplings

8–12 frankfurters
1 small cauliflower, broken into
    florets
¼ cabbage, shredded
4 sticks celery, sliced

½ medium cucumber, diced
    but not skinned
1 red pepper, de-seeded and
    diced
2 turnips, peeled, quartered
    and thinly sliced
1 (13¼, 376 g) can **Homepride**
    Sweet and Sour Cook-in-
    Sauce
4 oz (100 g) **Homepride** Self-
    raising Flour
2 oz (50 g) shredded suet
salt and pepper
1 teaspoon (5 ml) dried
    tarragon
approx 3 tablespoons (45 ml)
    water to mix

Place the frankfurters, vegetables
and can of Homepride Sweet and
Sour Cook-in-Sauce in a saucepan.
Cover and cook over a moderate
heat for 20 minutes. Mix together
dry ingredients with sufficient
water to make a stiff dough. Divide
into 8 pieces and shape into balls.
Add to the stew and cook, covered,
for a further 13 minutes. Serve
hot.   **Serves 4**

Knorr

Sausage Supper

1 tablespoon (15 ml) oil
1 lb (400 g) beef sausages
1 onion, peeled and sliced
1 oz (25 g) cornflour
¾ pint (375 ml) **Knorr** beef
    stock
2 tablespoons (30 ml) tomato
    purée

Heat the oil and sauté the sausages
until lightly browned all over and
the onions until soft and transparent. Remove the sausages and
onions from the pan and gradually
stir in the cornflour and stock.
Cook for 1 minute, stirring all the
time. Return the sausages and
onions to the pan with the tomato
purée and simmer gently for 15
minutes.

Serve hot with savoury rice.
Serves 4

Sausage Supper Dish

2 tomatoes
1 lb (450 g) pork or beef
    sausages
1 can sweetcorn
2 lb (900 g) mashed potatoes
1 packet **Knorr** Onion Sauce
    Mix
½ pint (300 ml) milk
2 oz (50 g) grated cheese

Slice the tomatoes and arrange in
the bottom of an ovenproof dish.
Fry the sausages until browned on
all sides and arrange over the
tomatoes with the sweetcorn.
Spread the mashed potatoes on
top. Make up the Onion Sauce as
directed, pour over the potato and
sprinkle with the grated cheese.
Bake in a moderate oven (350°F,
180°C, Gas Mark 4) for 30 minutes.
Serves 4

LEA & PERRINS

Cidered Sausages

12 large pork sausages
2 tablespoons (30 ml) oil
1 large onion, peeled and sliced
2 tablespoons (30 ml) **Lea &
    Perrins** Worcestershire Sauce
2 oz (50 g) flour
1 pint (500 ml) sweet cider
½ pint (250 ml) chicken stock
1 teaspoon (5 ml) salt
black pepper

Cook the sausages until browned
on both sides. Heat the oil in a
large saucepan. Add the onions
and Worcestershire sauce and fry
until soft. Remove from the heat
and stir in the flour. Gradually stir
in the cider and stock. Return to
the heat and stir the sauce until it
thickens. Season to taste. Place the
sausages in a 3 pint (1.7 litre)
shallow ovenproof dish. Pour the
sauce over the sausages and cover
with foil. Bake in the oven at 375°F,
190°C, Gas Mark 5, for 30 minutes.
Serve with mashed potato.
Serves 6

Sausage and Bacon Crunch

1 lb (450 g) sausages
4 rashers streaky bacon
1 onion, peeled and chopped
1 cauliflower
½ pint (300 ml) cheese sauce
4 oz (100 g) **McVitie's** Digestive Biscuits, crushed

Fry the sausages and bacon until brown, then lift out and put in a casserole dish. Add the onion to the fat remaining in the pan and fry gently for 5 minutes, lift out with a slotted spoon and add to the sausages.

Meanwhile, cook the cauliflower in small sprigs in plenty of boiling, salted water until tender, then drain well and place on top of the sausages.

Cover with the cheese sauce, sprinkle with the crushed biscuits and bake in the oven pre-heated to 350°F, 180°C, Gas Mark 4, for 30 minutes.

Serve with rolls or French bread.   **Serves 4**

Poor Man's Goose

8 oz (225 g) onions, peeled and sliced into rings
2½ oz (65 g) butter
1½ lb (675 g) potatoes, peeled, cooked and drained
1 Red **Oxo** Cube
8 oz (225 g) pork sausagemeat

Lightly fry the onions in ½ oz (15 g) of the butter until tender. Drain. Cream the potatoes with the remaining butter and spread half the potato in the base of an ovenproof casserole dish. Place half the fried onion on top of the potato. Crumble the Oxo cube over the sausagemeat and mix well together. Spread the sausagement

in the casserole dish, place the remaining onion rings on top and spread or pipe the remaining potato over. Bake at 375°F, 190°C, Gas Mark 5, for about 45 minutes, until the potato is golden brown.
Serves 4

SCHWARTZ

Crispy Topped Sage and Sausage Bake

8 oz (227 g) onions, peeled and sliced
6 oz (170 g) carrots, peeled and sliced
1 large cooking apple, peeled, cored and finely chopped
1 oz (28 g) plain flour
1 tablespoon (15 ml) **Schwartz** Paprika
1 tablespoon (15 ml) **Schwartz** Seasoning Salt
1 lb (454 g) pork sausagemeat (non-herby)
2 teaspoons (10 ml) **Schwartz** Sage
¼ teaspoon **Schwartz** Garlic Granules
¼ teaspoon **Schwartz** Ground Black Pepper
1 lb (454 g) potatoes, peeled and thinly sliced
a little oil for brushing and **Schwartz** Seasoning Salt for sprinkling

Place the onions, carrots and apple in a 3 pint (1.8 litre) casserole dish. Mix the flour, paprika and seasoning salt together. Add to the casserole and stir so that the vegetables are well coated. Combine the sausagemeat with the sage, garlic granules and black pepper and spread to form a layer covering the vegetables. Arrange the sliced potatoes on top to completely cover the sausagemeat. Brush with oil and sprinkle liberally with seasoning salt. Cook, uncovered, in the oven pre-heated to 400°F, 200°C, Gas Mark 6, for 1½ hours until the potatoes are cooked, crisp and golden brown.

This dish may be stored in a refrigerator for up to 2 days or frozen for up to 2 months.
Serves 4

Sausage Marengo

2 tablespoons (30 ml) cooking oil
8 oz (227 g) onions, peeled and sliced
1 lb (454 g) thick pork sausages
½ oz (15 g) cornflour
14 oz (396 g) can tomatoes
4 oz (113 g) can sweetcorn, drained
2 tablespoons (30 ml) sweet sherry
3 teaspoons (15 ml) **Schwartz** Seasoning Salt
1 teaspoon (5 ml) **Schwartz** Marjoram
½ teaspoon (2.5 ml) **Schwartz** Thyme
¼ teaspoon **Schwartz** Ground Black Pepper
cooked, shredded cabbage for garnish

Heat the oil in a large frying pan and fry the onions until soft and just beginning to colour. Drain and transfer to a plate. If necessary, add a little more oil to the pan and quickly fry the sausages until brown on all sides. Drain off any excess oil. Return the onions to the pan. Blend the cornflour with 2 tablespoons (30 ml) of the juice from the can of tomatoes and add to the pan with the remaining juice and tomatoes. Stir in all remaining ingredients except the cabbage. Bring to the boil, stirring, and simmer for 30 minutes, uncovered. Place the sausages on a serving dish with a little of the sauce spooned over. Garnish the edge of the plate with the cabbage and serve the remaining sauce separately.

Serve with boiled potatoes. This dish may be stored in a refrigerator for up to 2 days or in a freezer for up to 1 month.   **Serves 4**

Barbecue Bangers

1 lb (450 g) sausages
1 medium onion, peeled and sliced
4 fl oz (114 ml) bottle **Schweppes** Tomato Juice Cocktail
2 teaspoons (10 ml) made mustard
1 teaspoon (5 ml) Worcestershire sauce
salt and black pepper

Sauce
1 small onion, peeled and chopped
4 fl oz (114 ml) bottle **Schweppes** Tomato Juice Cocktail
2 teaspoons (10 ml) sugar
2 tablespoons (30 ml) tomato purée
2 dessertspoons (20 ml) Worcestershire sauce
½ pint (250 ml) water
2 dessertspoons (20 ml) cornflour blended with a little cold water

Prick the sausages and place in a roasting tin with the onions on top. Mix together the tomato juice, mustard and Worcestershire sauce with black pepper and a pinch of salt then pour over the sausages. Cook in a fairly hot oven, 400°F, 200°C, Gas Mark 6, for about 50 minutes, turning once or twice until the sausages are cooked. Lift the sausages and onions on to a warm serving dish and keep hot.

For the sauce, fry the onion in the residue in the roasting tin and stir in the remaining ingredients, including the blended cornflour. Bring to the boil, stirring continuously until thickened. Serve with the sausages. **Serves 4**

Glazed Sausages

Chilli Sausages
1 teaspoon (5 ml) chilli powder
1 tablespoon (15 ml) tomato ketchup
½ teaspoon (2.5 ml) paprika pepper
1 small onion, peeled and finely grated
1 lb (454 g) packet **Wall's** Pork Thick Sausages

Mix the chilli powder, tomato ketchup, paprika pepper and onion together. Separate the sausages and place them into the grill pan, removing the rack. Brush the glaze mixture over the sausages and then grill them for 10–15 minutes, or until golden brown and cooked. Turn the sausages frequently as they cook, basting them each time with more of the glaze, so that the flavour really penetrates. Serve hot or cold.

Curried Sausages
2 teaspoons (10 ml) curry paste
2 teaspoons (10 ml) apricot jam
1 teaspoon (5 ml) lemon juice
¼ teaspoon ground coriander
1 lb (454 g) packet **Walls** Pork and Beef Thick Sausages

Mix the curry paste, apricot jam, lemon juice and coriander together then glaze and cook as for Chilli Sausages above. **Serves 4–6**

Sausage and Bacon Pan Fry

2 tablespoons (30 ml) oil
1 lb (454 g) packet **Wall's** Pork Thick Sausages
2 large onions, peeled and sliced
7.05 oz (200 g) packet **Wall's** Streaky Bacon Rashers
1 lb (450 g) potatoes, peeled and parboiled
grated rind and juice of ½ lemon

salt and black pepper
chopped parsley to garnish

Fry the sausage in 1 tablespoon (15 ml) of oil until golden brown and cooked. Transfer to a plate and keep warm. Wipe out the frying pan, heat the rest of the oil and fry the onions gently until almost cooked. Cut the rashers into fours, add to the onion and cook for a few minutes; then slice the potatoes and add them to the pan. Very carefully, turning the mixture occasionally, cook these ingredients together until the potato is brown (about 10 minutes). Cut each sausage diagonally into three, add to the pan with the lemon rind and juice, season well and when the flavours are well distributed sprinkle the dish with parsley and serve with a tomato and chive salad. **Serves 4**

Sausage Hot Pot

1 lb (454 g) packet **Wall's** Pork with Herb Thick Sausages
1 tablespoon (15 ml) oil
12 oz (350 g) onions, peeled and sliced
2 sticks celery, wiped and chopped
1 lb (450 g) carrots, peeled and sliced
salt and pepper
½ pint (300 ml) beef stock
2 teaspoons (10 ml) Worcestershire sauce
1 teaspoon (5 ml) mixed herbs
pinch of garlic salt (optional)
1 oz (25 g) butter
1 lb (450 g) potatoes, peeled and thinly sliced

Quickly and lightly brown the sausages in the oil and transfer them to a plate. Add the onions to the pan and when they are soft, but not brown, mix in the celery and carrots and cook the vegetables together for a few minutes. Sprinkle the mixture with salt and pepper and turn half of it into a 4 pint (2.5 litre) casserole dish. Add the sausages and then the rest of the vegetable mixture to the casserole.

Mix the stock with the

Worcestershire sauce, herbs and garlic salt and pour it into the dish. Overlap the sliced potatoes on top, dot with butter and bake at 400°F, 200°C, Gas Mark 6 for 1¼ hours.
Serves 4

Spicy Sausage Pilaf

1 lb (454 g) packet **Wall's** Pork Family Size Sausages, cooked
2 tablespoons (30 ml) oil
8 oz (225 g) onion, peeled and chopped
8 oz (225 g) long grain rice
1 tablespoon (15 ml) curry powder
1 teaspoon (5 ml) ground ginger
½ teaspoon (2.5 ml) chilli seasoning
½ teaspoon (2.5 ml) ground cloves
pinch of garlic salt
2 tablespoons (30 ml) tomato purée
2 tablespoons (30 ml) Worcestershire sauce
1½ pint (900 ml) stock
1 oz (25 g) salted peanuts

Chop each sausage into four and leave on one side.

Heat the oil in a covered frying pan; add the onions and fry them for 5 minutes or until starting to soften but not brown. Stir in the rice, curry powder, ginger, chilli, cloves, garlic salt, tomato purée, vinegar and Worcestershire sauce and when they are well blended mix in the stock. Slowly bring the liquid to the boil and then add the sausage pieces. Cover the pan and simmer the mixture for 25–30 minutes, or until the rice is soft to the centre and has absorbed all the liquid. Adjust the seasoning, scatter with peanuts and serve accompanied by tomato and green salads.   **Serves 4–6**

Sweet and Sour Sausages

2 carrots, peeled and sliced
2 sticks celery, wiped and chopped
1 green pepper, de-seeded and chopped
1 onion, peeled and chopped
salt
2 tablespoons (30 ml) tomato ketchup
¼ pint (150 ml) malt vinegar
2 tablespoons (30 ml) soy sauce
2 tablespoons (30 ml) clear honey
2 tablespoons (30 ml) cornflour
8 oz (227 g) can pineapple slices
½ pint (300 ml) water
1 lb (454 g) packet **Wall's** Pork and Beef Family Size Sausages, cooked

Put the carrots, celery, pepper and onion into a pan, cover with water, add salt and bring to the boil. Boil for 5 minutes and drain. In a pan mix the tomato ketchup with the vinegar, soy sauce and honey. Blend the cornflour to a smooth paste with the juice from the pineapple. Cut the pineapple slices into pieces and add them to the pan with the water. Bring this mixture slowly to the boil and stir a little of the hot liquid into the cornflour paste, then mix the paste into the main bulk of the liquid and, stirring all the time, bring the sauce to the boil. Add the vegetables and sausages and simmer the mixture for 10–15 minutes, or until the ingredients are well blended and heated through.

Serve with boiled rice and perhaps a salad.   **Serves 4**

whitworths

Sausage and Bacon Cobbler

4 oz (125 g) streaky bacon, with rinds removed
8 oz (225 g) chipolata sausages
1 dessertspoon (10 ml) oil
1 medium onion, peeled and sliced
8 oz (225 g) tomatoes, skinned and sliced
1 green pepper, de-seeded and sliced
3 tablespoons (45 ml) stock
salt and pepper
Topping
5 oz (150 g) plain flour
3 oz (75 g) sachet **Whitworths** Country Stuffing Mix
1 dessertspoon (10 ml) baking powder
1 oz (25 g) butter or margarine
5 fl oz (150 ml) milk
milk *or* beaten egg for brushing

Roll the bacon rashers and hold in place with wooden cocktail sticks. Cut each sausage in half. Heat the oil, add the bacon and sausages and cook until lightly browned. Remove the cocktail sticks and place the bacon and sausages in a casserole dish. Arrange layers of the onion, tomatoes and peppers on top of the meat. Pour over the stock and season. Cover and bake in a pre-heated oven at 400°F, 200°C, Gas Mark 6 for 30–40 minutes.

Meanwhile prepare the scone topping. Mix the flour, stuffing mix and baking powder and rub in the butter. Gradually add sufficient milk to give a fairly soft dough. Knead lightly on a floured board. Roll out to 1 in (2.5 cm) thick and cut into 8 (2 in, 5 cm) rounds. Remove the cover from the casserole, place scone rounds on top and brush with milk or egg. Increase the oven temperature to 450°F, 230°C, Gas Mark 8 and bake for 8–10 minutes until golden brown.   **Serves 4**

OFFAL

ATORA

Wheaty Liver Loaf

8 oz (250 g) lamb's liver *or*
    chicken livers, chopped
4 oz (100 g) streaky bacon,
    chopped
1 small onion, peeled and
    chopped
1 garlic clove, crushed
    (optional)
2 tablespoons (30 ml) vegetable
    oil
1 tablespoon (15 ml) flour
½ pint (250 ml) stock
1 teaspoon (5 ml) marjoram
1 tablespoon (15 ml) tomato
    purée
salt and ground black pepper
Pastry
4 oz (100 g) self-raising flour
4 oz (100 g) wholemeal flour
4 oz (100 g) **Atora** Shredded
    Suet
2 teaspoons (10 ml) baking
    powder
2 tablespoons (30 ml) fresh
    parsley, chopped
water to mix

Fry the liver, bacon, onion and
garlic, if used, in the oil, until
browned and softened, about
5 minutes. Stir in the flour, then
gradually add the stock, stirring
continuously. Bring to the boil,
add the marjoram and tomato
purée, season to taste and simmer
for about 10 minutes, uncovered,
so that the liquid becomes
reduced. Allow to cool while
preparing the dough.

Grease a 2 lb (1 kg) loaf tin and
line the base with greased greaseproof paper. Mix the flours, suet,
baking powder and parsley
together, then add enough water
to mix to a firm dough. Divide the
dough into four and roll out into
rectangles to fit the loaf tin. The
base rectangle may have to be
slightly smaller than that at the
top. Place a layer of dough in the
base of the prepared tin, trimming
to fit if necessary, or moulding
gently with the fingers. Top with
one-third of the liver mixture.
Continue with dough and liver
layers, finishing with dough.
Cover with greased greaseproof
paper and foil and bake at 350°F,
180°C, Gas Mark 4, for about
1 hour. Turn out on to a warm
serving plate and serve hot with a
good rich gravy or tomato sauce.
Serves 4

BON

Kidney Stroganoff

1¼ lb (575 g) lamb's kidneys,
    skinned, cored and halved
½ oz (15 g) plain flour
1 oz (25 g) lard
2 onions, peeled and sliced
1 green pepper, de-seeded and
    sliced
4 oz (100 g) mushrooms,
    washed and sliced
4 tablespoons (60 ml) **Bon** Red
    Cooking Wine
½ teaspoon (2.5 ml) dried
    thyme
salt and pepper
2 tablespoons (30 ml) soured
    cream

Cut each kidney half into 3 pieces
and toss in the flour. Melt the lard
in a saucepan and fry the onions
until tender. Add the green
peppers and mushrooms and fry
lightly. Add the kidneys and sauté
for 10 minutes, then stir in the
Bon. Sprinkle the thyme into the
mixture and season to taste.
Simmer for 20 minutes, covered.
Just before serving, stir in the
soured cream, taking care that the
mixture does not boil afterwards.

Serve on a bed of buttered
noodles. **Serves 4**

Bovril

Crispy Liver Bake

12 oz (350 g) lamb's *or* pig's
    liver
6 rashers streaky bacon,
    chopped and with rinds
    removed
2 leeks, carefully washed and
    sliced into rings
1 Red Cube from **Bovril**,
    dissolved in ½ pint (300 ml)
    water
6 oz (150 g) plain flour
3 oz (75 g) butter
3 oz (75 g) Cheddar cheese,
    grated
salt and pepper
a little cornflour blended with
    cold water
chopped parsley to garnish

Cut the liver into thin slices. Put
the bacon rashers into a dry frying
pan, heat gently until the fat runs
and then lift out and keep warm.
Fry the liver in the fat until just
coloured and place in a greased,
shallow, ovenproof dish. Fry the
leeks until golden and spread on
top of the liver, cover with the
bacon rashers and pour in enough
stock to come halfway up the
mixture in the dish.

Sift the flour into a basin and rub
in the butter until the mixture

looks like fine breadcrumbs. Mix in the cheese and season with salt and pepper. Sprinkle the mixture over the contents of the dish, but do not press down. Bake at 400°F, 200°C, Gas Mark 6, for 35 minutes, until golden brown, and serve hot. Thicken the remaining stock with the blended cornflour and serve separately.

Garnish with the chopped parsley to serve. **Serves 4**

Kidney and Bacon Pie

1 tablespoon (15 ml) oil
1 lb (450 g) ox kidney
4 oz (100 g) bacon, chopped
1 onion, peeled and sliced
10½ oz (297 g) can **Campbell's** Condensed Ox Tail Soup
½ can water
7½ oz (212 g) packet flaky pastry

Heat the oil in a frying pan. Cut the kidney into 1 in (2.5 cm) squares, fry for 4–5 minutes until browned. Remove from the pan and put in a 1½ pint (900 ml) pie dish. Fry bacon and onion for 3–4 minutes. Add soup and water to the frying pan and mix well. Pour the mixture over the kidney and (if mixture is hot) leave until cold. Cover with pastry and bake in the oven at 400°F, 200°C, Gas Mark 6 for 30–35 minutes. **Serves 4**

Liver and Mushroom Casserole

1 tablespoon (15 ml) oil
1 lb (450 g) lamb's *or* pig's liver, sliced
2 onions, peeled and sliced
4 oz (100 g) mushrooms, washed and sliced
10½ oz (297 g) can **Campbell's** Condensed Ox Tail Soup
1 soup can water

Heat the oil in a saucepan and fry

the liver for 5 minutes on each side then remove from the pan and keep warm. Fry the onions until tender, and then the mushrooms for a minute or two. Add the soup and water and mix together. Place the liver back in the pan and simmer slowly for 25 minutes. **Serves 4**

Chunky Liver Stew and Herby Dumplings

1 large onion, peeled and sliced
1½ oz (40 g) dripping *or* cooking fat
1 lb (450 g) lamb's liver
1½ oz (40 g) seasoned flour
15 oz (425 g) can **Chef** Chunky Tomato and Vegetable Soup
¼ pint (150 ml) stock *or* water
Dumplings
8 oz (225 g) self-raising flour
1 level teaspoon (5 ml) salt
3 oz (75 g) lard *or* cooking fat
2 teaspoons (10 ml) **Crosse & Blackwell** Mixed Herbs
4 tablespoons (60 ml) water

Fry the onion in the dripping for 3–4 minutes. Trim the liver, cut into 1 in (2.5 cm) cubes and toss in the seasoned flour. Fry the liver with the onions for 8–10 minutes then stir in the soup and stock and bring to the boil. Lower the heat then cover with a tight-fitting lid and simmer for 10 minutes.

To make the dumplings, sieve the flour and salt into a bowl. Rub in the lard until the mixture

resembles fine breadcrumbs. Stir in the mixed herbs. Mix to a soft dough with the water. Divide into 8 even-sized pieces and shape into balls. Place on top of the liver stew, replace the lid and simmer for a further 20 minutes.

Serve hot, with extra vegetables, if desired. **Serves 4–5**

Kidney and Mushroom Pudding

6 oz (150 g) self-raising flour
3 oz (75 g) shredded suet
salt and pepper
water to mix
12 oz (300 g) lamb's kidneys, cored and diced
1 tablespoon (15 ml) seasoned flour
1 can **Chesswood** Small Whole Mushrooms, drained, reserving the brine

Mix the flour, suet and seasoning with sufficient water to make a firm dough. Roll out two-thirds of the pastry and line a greased 1½ pint (750 ml) pudding basin. Toss the kidneys in the seasoned flour and pack with the drained mushrooms into the pastry case. Pour in sufficient reserved mushroom brine to come three-quarters of the way up the pudding. Roll out the remaining pastry to form a lid, moisten the edges of the pastry and seal well together. Cover securely with foil or greaseproof paper and steam or boil for 2–2½ hours. **Serves 4**

Liver in Yoghurt Sauce

1 lb (500 g) lamb's liver
¼ pint (125 ml) beef stock
1 can **Chesswood** Sliced Large
   Mushrooms, drained
1 tablespoon (15 ml) tomato
   ketchup
2 teaspoons (10 ml) prepared
   English mustard
5 fl oz (142 g) carton natural
   yoghurt
salt and pepper
1 tablespoon (15 ml) parsley,
   chopped

Pour boiling water on to the liver
and allow to soak for 30 minutes.
Drain the liver and cut into ½ in
(1 cm) thick slices. Place the liver
in a saucepan with the stock,
mushrooms and tomato ketchup,
bring to the boil, cover and simmer
gently for 20 minutes or until
tender. Stir in the mustard and
yoghurt. Season to taste and
reheat. Sprinkle with the parsley
just before serving.   **Serves 4**

FRANK COOPER®

Liver and Pheasant Casserole

4 rashers streaky bacon,
   chopped
1 lb (400 g) lamb's liver, sliced
1 level tablespoon (15 ml)
   cornflour
1 can **Frank Cooper's** Cream of
   Pheasant Soup
chopped parsley to garnish

Fry the bacon until crisp and
transfer to a casserole dish. Coat
the liver in the cornflour and
brown in the hot bacon fat. Place
the liver and soup in the casserole
dish, cover and bake at 325°F,
170°C, Gas Mark 3, for 1 hour.
Garnish with the chopped parsley.
Serves 4

Kidneys à la Maison

2 tablespoons (30 ml) oil
1 onion, peeled and sliced
1 green pepper, de-seeded and
   sliced
8 lamb's kidneys, halved and
   cored
4 rashers streaky bacon,
   chopped
1 can **Crosse & Blackwell** Red
   Wine Pour over Sauce

Heat the oil in a frying pan and fry
the onion and pepper for 2
minutes. Add the kidneys and
bacon and cook until the kidneys
are tender. Stir in the sauce and
continue cooking for 5 minutes.
   Serve with rice and mixed
salad.   **Serves 4**

Liver and Bacon Kebabs

8–12 oz (225–350 g) lamb's liver
4–6 oz (100–175 g) smoked
   bacon
4 oz (100 g) mushrooms
1 tablespoon (15 ml) **Crosse &
   Blackwell** Olive Oil
1 can **Crosse & Blackwell** Sweet
   & Sour Pour over Sauce
cooked rice to serve

Cut the liver into 8–12 small
pieces. Remove the rind from the
bacon, cut each slice in half
crosswise and make into rolls.
Thread the liver, bacon rolls and
mushrooms alternately on to four
skewers. Brush with oil. Grill the
kebabs quickly for about 8–10
minutes, turning them frequently.
   Meanwhile heat the Sweet &
Sour Sauce in a small saucepan
over a gentle heat. Arrange the
kebabs on a bed of rice and pour
over the Sweet & Sour Sauce. Serve
immediately. If preferred, the
sauce may be served separately.
Serves 4

Pan Style Liver and Bacon

4 rashers bacon, with rinds
   removed, chopped
1 oz (25 g) butter
12 oz (350 g) lamb's liver, cut
   into small pieces
10½ oz (297 g) can **Heinz**
   Vegetable Soup
chopped parsley to garnish

Fry the bacon in the butter for
1 minute, add the liver and fry
quickly until browned all over. Stir
in the soup and heat through.
Serve garnished with the chopped
parsley.   **Serves 4**

Tongue Slices in Wine Sauce

1 oz (25 g) butter
1 oz (25 g) plain flour
½ level teaspoon (2.5 ml) dry
   mustard
15 oz (425 g) **Heinz** Beef Soup
2 tablespoons (30 ml) red wine
salt and pepper
4–6 slices tongue, cooked
parsley sprigs to garnish

Melt the butter in a saucepan and
stir in the flour and mustard
powder. Gradually stir in the soup
and red wine. Continue stirring
until the sauce is thickened and
smooth. Season to taste then add
the slices of tongue to the sauce
and heat through. Arrange the
tongue and sauce on a serving dish
and garnish with sprigs of
parsley.   **Serves 4**

Homepride

Liver and Kidney Kebabs

8 lamb's kidneys
12 oz (350 g) lamb's, ox *or* pig's
   liver
1 sachet **Homepride** Coat &
   Cook, Sage and Onion
   Flavour

1 red pepper, de-seeded and
   cut into squares
1 green pepper, de-seeded and
   cut into squares
8 prunes, with stones removed

Using a sharp knife, cut from the curved sides almost through each kidney and open out, cut sides uppermost. Cut away the central membranes and fat with kitchen scissors. Pull away the outer skin from underneath. Trim any tough skin and membranes from the liver and cut into cubes. Coat the meat evenly with the contents of the Coat & Cook sachet. Thread the pepper squares, kidney halves, liver and prunes alternately on to 4 long skewers. Cover a grill pan with kitchen foil. Position the kebabs on the grill pan so they will each receive even heat. Cook under a pre-heated grill for 5–7 minutes, turning frequently.

Serve on a bed of boiled rice with a tomato and cucumber salad. **Serves 4**

Knorr

Country Paté

1 **Knorr** Beef Stock Cube
2 tablespoons (30 ml) boiling
   water
2 tablespoons (30 ml) sherry
8 oz (200 g) pig's liver, minced
8 oz (200 g) belly of pork,
   minced
1 clove garlic, crushed
1 level teaspoon (5 ml)
   rosemary
4 oz (100 g) streaky bacon

Dissolve the stock cube in the water and sherry. In a basin mix together the liver, pork, garlic, rosemary and stock. Line a small loaf tin with the streaky bacon and add the meat mixture, being careful not to move the bacon. Level the top. Cover tightly with foil and stand the loaf tin in a dish with water to come half way up the tin. Bake at 325°F, 170°C, Gas Mark 3 for 1½ hours. Remove the tin from the water and allow the paté to cool slightly before turning out. **Serves 4–8**

Liver and Kidney Crumble

½ lb (200 g) lamb's liver, cut in
   thin slices
½ lb (200 g) lamb's kidneys,
   cut in thin slices
½ lb (200 g) bacon, de-rinded
   and sliced
2 onions, peeled and sliced
2 oz (50 g) dripping
2 oz (50 g) seasoned flour
2 tablespoons (30 ml) tomato
   ketchup
½ pint (250 ml) **Knorr** beef stock
1 teaspoon (5 ml) herbs
4 oz (100 g) fresh breadcrumbs
3 oz (75 g) Cheddar cheese,
   grated

Toss the liver and kidney in the seasoned flour. Heat the dripping in a frying pan and brown the liver and kidney for 3–4 minutes with the onion and bacon. Place in an ovenproof dish. Stir the remaining flour into the frying pan, add the stock, herbs and ketchup, bring to the boil and pour over the meat. Mix the breadcrumbs and cheese together and spoon over the meat. Bake at 350°F, 180°C, Gas Mark 4, for 25–30 minutes or until tender and the top is golden brown.

Serve with parsnips, spinach and boiled potatoes. **Serves 4**

LEA & PERRINS

Kidneys Provencal

1½ tablespoons (22 ml) oil
1 onion, peeled and sliced
1 small red and 1 small green
   pepper, cored, de-seeded and
   cut into strips
1½ tablespoons (22 ml) **Lea &
   Perrins** Worcestershire Sauce
1½ lb (65 g) lamb's kidneys,
   halved, cored and tossed in
   1 oz (25 g) plain flour
2½ oz (73 g) can tomato purée
14 oz (397 g) can tomatoes
1 bay leaf
salt
freshly ground black pepper
pasta twists to serve

Heat the oil in a large pan. Add the onions and pepper strips. Stir in the Worcestershire sauce and fry for 5 minutes. Add the kidneys coated in flour and fry until they are brown (about 5 minutes). Stir in the tomato purée, tomatoes and bay leaf. Bring the mixture to the boil and transfer to a 2½ pint (1.4 litre) casserole. Cook in an oven at 375°F, 190°C, Gas Mark 5, for 30–40 minutes. Season to taste. Serve with pasta twists. **Serves 6**

Savoury Ducks (Faggots)

1 lb (500 g) pig's liver, roughly
   chopped
2 large onions, peeled and
   roughly chopped
6 oz (150 g) fresh white
   breadcrumbs
2 oz (50 g) shredded suet
1 tablespoon (15 ml) **Lea &
   Perrins** Worcestershire Sauce
½ level teaspoon (2.5 ml) dried
   sage
salt and pepper
Gravy
1 oz (25 g) lard
1 onion, peeled and sliced
2 carrots, peeled and grated
1 oz (25 g) flour
¾ pint (400 ml) beef stock
2 teaspoons (10 ml) **Lea &
   Perrins** Worcestershire Sauce
salt and pepper

Mince the liver and onions and mix with the breadcrumbs, suet, sage, Worcestershire Sauce and seasoning. Divide the mixture into 8 pieces and shape roughly into balls. Place in a greased 2 pint (1 litre) shallow, ovenproof dish and bake, uncovered, at 350°F, 180°C, Gas Mark 4 for 30 minutes. Turn each Savoury Duck over.

Meanwhile, for the gravy, heat the lard in a pan and add the onion and carrot. Fry gently for 5 minutes. Stir in the flour and cook for 1 minute. Remove from the heat and blend in the stock and Worcestershire Sauce. Return to the heat and bring to the boil, stirring. Simmer for 10 minutes then strain, season, pour over the Savoury Ducks and return the dish to the oven. Cook for a further 20 minutes. **Serves 4**

Chicken Liver Risotto

2 oz (50 g) margarine
1 lb (450 g) chicken livers, trimmed
2 rashers streaky bacon, with rinds removed, cut into strips
1 onion, peeled and chopped
4 oz (100 g) long grain rice
1 Chicken **Oxo** Cube, crumbled
10¼ oz (290 g) can vegetable juice *or* ½ pint (300 ml) seasoned tomato juice
1 teaspoon (5 ml) tarragon, chopped
2 bay leaves
salt and pepper
4 oz (113 g) packet frozen peas
6½ oz (184 g) can pimentos (optional)
chopped parsley to garnish

Melt the margarine and sauté the chicken livers, bacon, onion and rice for 5–8 minutes. Stir in the Chicken Oxo, vegetable or tomato juice, herbs and seasoning. Bring to the boil and simmer gently for 20 minutes. Add the peas and sliced pimentos if used, and cook for a further 5 minutes.

Serve, garnished with the chopped parsley, with a green salad. **Serves 4**

Kidneys in Wine Sauce

1 oz (25 g) margarine
1 onion, peeled and sliced
1 clove garlic, crushed
8 lamb's kidneys, halved, skinned and cored
1½ tablespoons (22 ml) flour
4 tablespoons (60 ml) dry white wine
1 Red **Oxo** Cube, crumbled and dissolved in ⅓ pint (200 ml) hot water
salt and pepper
4 oz (100 g) mushrooms, halved
4 tablespoons (60 ml) soured cream
chopped parsley to garnish

Melt the margarine in a pan and sauté the onion and garlic gently for 5 minutes until soft. Add the kidneys and fry until well sealed all over. Stir in the flour and cook for 1 minute, then gradually add the wine, Red Oxo and seasoning. Bring to the boil, cover and simmer for 10 minutes. Add the mushrooms and continue cooking for 5–10 minutes until tender. Stir in the soured cream, adjust the seasoning and reheat without boiling. Sprinkle with parsley to serve. **Serves 4**

Liver Corn Cakes

8 oz (225 g) liver
1 large onion, peeled and roughly chopped
2 Red **Oxo** Cubes, crumbled and dissolved in ¾ pint (450 ml) hot water
8 oz (225 g) leftover mashed potato
1 small packet frozen sweetcorn, thawed
salt and pepper
1 egg, beaten
browned breadcrumbs
fat *or* oil for frying
Oxo gravy to serve

Simmer the liver and onion in the Oxo stock for about 15 minutes, then strain, reserving the stock to make the gravy. Mince the liver and onions and mix with the potato, sweetcorn and seasoning. With floured hands, shape into flat cakes. Brush with beaten egg and coat in breadcrumbs. Fry for about 15 minutes in shallow fat or oil, turning occasionally.

Serve with Oxo gravy made with the reserved stock. **Serves 4**

Savoury Liver Pasties

8 oz (225 g) plain flour
salt
3 oz (75 g) lard
8 oz (225 g) cooked, mashed potato
Filling
1 oz (25 g) margarine
8 oz (225 g) liver (chicken, lamb's *or* pig's), cut into pieces
4 oz (100 g) bacon scraps, cut into small pieces
1 onion, peeled and coarsely chopped
¾ oz (20 g) plain flour
8 oz (227 g) can peeled tomatoes
1–2 Red **Oxo** Cubes, crumbled
salt and pepper
Oxo gravy to serve

To make the pastry, sieve the flour and salt into a basin and rub in the lard. Add the mashed potato and work together until a manageable dough. It should not be necessary to add water, but if it does not 'bind' then add a very little water. Divide the dough into 4 pieces and roll out into circles.

To make the filling, melt the margarine and fry the liver for about 10 minutes or until tender. Remove from the pan and cut or mince coarsely. Add the bacon and onion to the pan and cook for a few minutes. Stir in the flour and cook for a minute. Add the tomatoes, crumbed Oxo cube and seasoning and bring to the boil. Add the liver and mix well together. Allow to cool slightly, then place a little of the filling on each pastry circle. Moisten the edge with cold water, fold over and seal well together. Carefully place the pasties on a baking tray and cook at 400°F, 200°C, Gas Mark 6, for 35–40 minutes.

Serve with Oxo gravy. **Serves 4**

Stuffed Potatoes with Liver and Oxo

4 large potatoes, washed and scored around the middles
1 oz (25 g) margarine
8 oz (225 g) liver, cut into small pieces
1 large onion, peeled and chopped
salt and pepper
a little butter and milk
1–2 Red **Oxo** Cubes, crumbled
1 carrot, peeled, sliced and boiled
Oxo gravy to serve

Bake the potatoes at 400°F, 200°C,

Gas Mark 6, for 1–1½ hours. Melt the margarine and fry the liver and onion for about 15 minutes, or until tender. Season with salt and pepper. Remove the potatoes from the oven and cut in halves. Take a spoonful of potato from each half and put into a basin. Add a little butter and milk to the potato and mix well together. Place a little of the liver and onion mixture into each potato half, sprinkle the crumbled Oxo Cube(s) over the liver, spread the creamed potato over the top and garnish with the sliced carrot. Reheat in the oven for about 10 minutes.

Serve with the Oxo gravy.

Serves 4

RYVITA

Kidney Scrambles

½ oz (15 g) butter
6 oz (175 g) lamb's kidneys, skinned, cored and chopped
4 eggs
4 tablespoons (60 ml) milk
salt and pepper
4 **Ryvita**
chopped parsley to garnish

Melt the butter in a pan and fry the kidneys gently for 3–4 minutes until well sealed and lightly browned. Whisk the eggs with the milk and seasonings and pour over the kidneys. Continue to cook slowly, stirring all the time, until the eggs are thick and creamy. Spoon on to the Ryvita, sprinkle with the chopped parsley to serve.
Serves 4

Mustard-topped Liver and Bacon

7.05 oz (200 g) packet **Wall's** Streaky Bacon Rashers
1 tablespoon (15 ml) cooking oil
8 oz (225 g) onions, peeled and sliced

1 lb (450 g) lamb's liver, cut into strips
10½ oz (297 g) can condensed oxtail soup, undiluted
Topping
6 slices French bread
1 oz (25 g) butter
1 dessertspoon (10 ml) English mustard, made up

Cut the rind and any small bones from the bacon and cut each rasher into four. Fry the bacon in the oil for a few minutes, then stir in the onions and continue cooking the mixture until the onions start to soften. Add the pieces of liver and fry them until sealed, finally stirring in the soup, plus a can of water. Bring the mixture to the boil, cover and simmer for 20–25 minutes until cooked.

Spread the slices of bread with an even layer of butter and mustard. When the liver is ready, empty it into a 2–2½ pint (1.5 litre) casserole dish, arrange the bread slices on top and put the dish under a pre-heated grill to brown the bread. **Serves 4**

Sausage and Kidney Turbigo

4 lamb's kidneys
2 tablespoons (30 ml) oil
1 oz (25 g) margarine
4 oz (100 g) **Wall's** Streaky Bacon Rashers
8 oz (227 g) packet **Wall's** Pork Chipolatas
1 large onion, peeled and chopped
4 oz (100 g) button mushrooms, washed and trimmed
1 tablespoon (15 ml) plain flour
1 tablespoon (15 ml) tomato ketchup
½ pint (300 ml) stock
1 bay leaf
salt and pepper
toast triangles and chopped parsley to garnish

Remove the skin and cores from the kidneys, halve them and cut each half into two. Heat the oil and margarine, fry the kidneys until sealed and transfer to a plate. Cut

the rind and any small bones from the bacon rashers and cut each into four; fry the pieces with the chipolatas until both are brown. Transfer to the plate with the kidneys. Fry the onions and mushrooms in the remaining fat and when they start to brown stir in the flour then, off the heat, mix in the tomato ketchup and gradually blend in the stock. Return the pan to the heat and, stirring all the time, bring the sauce to the boil. Add the bay leaf and check the seasoning. Return the kidneys, bacon and chipolatas to the pan, cover and simmer for 20–25 minutes until all the ingredients are tender. Garnish with toast triangles and chopped parsley before serving. **Serves 4**

whitworths

Liver and Bacon Braise

1 lb (450 g) lamb's liver (8 slices)
1 onion, peeled and chopped
3 oz (75 g) sachet **Whitworths** Country Stuffing Mix, made up according to pack instructions
8 rashers streaky bacon, with rinds removed
¼ pint (150 ml) beef stock
1 teaspoon (5 ml) cornflour
salt and pepper

Pre-heat the oven to 350°F, 180°C, Gas Mark 4. Place the liver slices in the base of a shallow, ovenproof dish. Mix the onion and prepared stuffing mix together and spread the mixture evenly over the top of the liver. Cover the top of each liver slice with a rasher of bacon. Pour the stock around the liver, cover with a lid or foil and cook for about 40 minutes at 350°F, 180°C, Gas Mark 4 until the liver is tender. Carefully drain off the liquid. Blend the cornflour with a little cold water and gradually add the stock. Bring to the boil and, stirring continuously, cook until thickened. Season and pour round the liver or serve separately if preferred. **Serves 4**

CURRIES

Oriental Curry Sauce

1 large onion, peeled and
  chopped
1 tablespoon (15 ml) vegetable
  oil
1 oz (25 g) **Allinson** 100%
  Wholewheat Flour
2 teaspoons (10 ml) Madras
  curry powder
½ pint (300 ml) stock or water
1 medium apple, chopped
1 tomato, chopped
2 teaspoons (10 ml) coconut,
  grated or desiccated
1 teaspoon (5 ml) lemon juice
6 almonds, chopped
½ oz (15 g) seedless raisins
2 teaspoons (10 ml) greengage
  jam or marmalade
2 teaspoons (10 ml) chutney

Fry the onion lightly in the oil, add
the flour and curry powder and fry
for a further few minutes.
Gradually blend in the stock or
water, followed by the other ingredients. Cook gently for 10 minutes,
stirring frequently. Simmer until
the apple is soft and the sauce has
thickened.

Add the sauce to pre-cooked
meat, fish, chicken, mixed vegetables or hard-boiled eggs. Serve
with boiled rice. **Serves 4**

Curried Chicken 'Taj Mahal'

6 chicken joints
1 can **Baxters** Madras Hot Curry
  Sauce
2 tablespoons (30 ml) **Baxters**
  Mango Chutney

2 apples, finely chopped

Put the chicken joints into a
casserole. Pour the curry sauce into
a bowl and add the chutney and
apples. Pour this mixture over the
chicken pieces. Cover the dish and
cook for 1¼ hours at 350°F, 180°C,
Gas Mark 4.

Serve with boiled rice and
poppadums. **Serves 6**

Curried Vegetables 'Kashmir Style'

6 potatoes, peeled and sliced
6 large carrots, peeled and
  sliced
6 small turnips, peeled and
  sliced
1 can **Baxters** Madras Hot Curry
  Sauce
1 small can peeled tomatoes
4 medium onions, peeled and
  sliced
2 cloves garlic, finely chopped
1 tablespoon (15 ml) stem
  ginger, chopped
8 oz (227 g) packet frozen peas
5 oz (142 ml) natural yoghurt
handful of chopped mint

Put the potatoes, carrots and
turnips in a saucepan and add the
curry sauce and tomatoes. Cook
over a low heat bringing slowly to
the boil and simmer gently. Add
the onions, pepper and garlic to
the simmering vegetables,
followed by the ginger and peas.
Continue simmering for about
8 minutes more and then stir in the
yoghurt and mint.

Serve with poppadums, boiled
rice and chutneys. **Serves 6**

Fruity Chicken Curry

1 large cooked chicken
4 bananas, sliced
1 small can pineapple chunks
1 can **Baxters** Medium Curry
  Sauce

5 oz (142 ml) natural yoghurt
juice of 2 lemons
2 tablespoons (30 ml) **Baxters**
  Apricot Jam
paprika pepper

Take the meat from the carcass and
cut into strips. Pour the can of
curry sauce into a bowl and stir in
the yoghurt, lemon juice and jam.
Gently stir in the bananas and
pineapple, then the chicken, and
garnish with the paprika.

Serve with cucumber or seedless
grapes and rice salad. **Serves 5**

Carnation.

Curried Lamb

1 lb (450 g) cooked leg or
  shoulder of lamb
1 clove garlic, peeled and finely
  chopped
2 medium onions, peeled and
  finely chopped
1 small apple, peeled and finely
  chopped
2 oz (50 g) dripping
2 dessertspoons (20 ml) curry
  powder
1 teaspoon (5 ml) curry paste
½ oz (15 g) flour
stock or water
1 small can **Carnation**
  Evaporated Milk
grated rind and juice ½ lemon
1 dessertspoon (10 ml) chutney
1 oz (25 g) blanched almonds,
  chopped
1 oz (25 g) sultanas
salt and pepper
2 dessertspoons (20 ml) tomato
  purée
gherkins, pimento and lemon
  to garnish

Remove the excess fat and dice the
meat. Melt the dripping in a saucepan and fry the vegetables lightly.
Stir in the curry powder, paste and
flour and continue cooking for a

few minutes. Gradually stir in the Carnation milk made up to 1 pint (600 ml) with the stock or water. Add the lemon rind and juice. Bring to the boil then add the chutney, almonds, sultanas, seasoning and tomato purée. Simmer for about 30 minutes. Add the meat and adjust the seasoning. Simmer for 10 minutes.

Serve with boiled rice and garnish with the gherkins, pimento and lemon. **Serves 4**

FRANK COOPER®

Chicken Curry

2 tablespoons (30 ml) corn oil
1 onion, peeled and chopped
1 level tablespoon (15 ml) curry powder
1 level teaspoon (5 ml) curry paste
1 oz (25 g) cornflour
¾ pint (375 ml) chicken stock
1 dessertspoon (10 ml) **Frank Cooper's** Cranberry Sauce
juice of 1 small lemon
1 oz (25 g) sultanas
2 level tablespoons (30 ml) desiccated coconut, infused in 6 tablespoons (90 ml) boiling water
12 oz (300 g) cooked chicken, shredded
4 oz (100 g) mushrooms, washed and sliced

Heat the corn oil and lightly fry the onion. Stir in the curry powder, curry paste and cornflour and cook for 1 minute. Add the stock, bring to the boil, stirring, then add the apple, cranberry sauce, lemon juice, sultanas, coconut liquid, chicken and mushrooms. Simmer for 15 minutes. **Serves 3–4**

Chicken Kashmir

1 tablespoon (15 ml) corn oil
1 onion, peeled and chopped
12 oz (300 g) cooked chicken, cubed
1 can **Frank Cooper's** Kashmir Chicken Soup

14½ oz (410 g) can apricots, drained

Heat the corn oil and fry the onions until golden brown. Add the chicken, soup and apricots, and simmer gently for 10–12 minutes. **Serves 3–4**

Creamy Chicken Curry

13¼ oz (375 g) can **Del Monte** Crushed Pineapple
1 medium onion, peeled and chopped
1 tablespoon (15 ml) oil
knob of butter
1 can condensed chicken soup
5 oz (142 g) carton sour cream
1 tablespoon (15 ml) curry paste
12 oz (300 g) cooked chicken pieces

Drain the pineapple, reserving the syrup. Fry the onion in the oil and butter together until transparent but not brown. Add the pineapple. Stir in the chicken soup, sour cream and curry paste. Add the cooked chicken and reserved syrup. Heat through over a low heat. **Serves 4**

Channa Dhal (Curried Chick Peas)

12 oz (350 g) **Granose** Chick Peas
2½ pint (1.5 litres) water
1 teaspoon (5 ml) salt
3 tablespoons (45 ml) melted butter *or* margarine
1 teaspoon (5 ml) cumin seed
1 medium onion, peeled and finely chopped
1 in (2.5 cm) piece fresh root ginger, peeled and finely chopped
1 teaspoon (5 ml) turmeric
½ teaspoon (2.5 ml) ground cumin

1 teaspoon (5 ml) ground coriander
1 teaspoon (5 ml) garam masala
½ teaspoon (2.5 ml) chilli powder
1 tablespoon (15 ml) fresh coriander leaves, chopped

Soak the chick peas overnight. Cook them in a large saucepan with the water and the salt for 1 hour, until tender. In a second large pan heat the butter or margarine and cook with the cumin seed for 1 minute. Add the onion and cook for a further 5 minutes. Stir in the ginger and cook gently until the onion becomes golden brown. Combine the turmeric, ground cumin, coriander, garam masala and chilli powder in a small mixing bowl with 2 tablespoons (30 ml) of water to make a paste. Add the paste to the onion mixture in the pan and fry for 3–4 minutes, stirring constantly, or until the mixture is well blended. Add the chick peas and the cooking liquid to the pan and bring to the boil. Cover and simmer for 30 minutes, keeping the peas whole.

Serve in a warmed dish and garnish with coriander leaves. **Serves 4**

Homepride

Beef Madras

1 lb (450 g) stewing beef, cut into cubes
pinch ground cinnamon
¼ green pepper, de-seeded and chopped
13¼ oz (375 g) can **Homepride** Madras Classic Curry Sauce
5 oz (142 ml) carton natural yoghurt (optional)
sprig of watercress to garnish

Place the beef in a casserole, sprinkle with cinnamon, add the green pepper and pour over the can of curry sauce. Cook, covered, in a pre-heated oven at 350°F, 180°C, Gas Mark 4 for about 2 hours, until the meat is tender. Ten minutes before serving stir in the yoghurt, if liked. **Serves 4**

Curried Indian Vegetables

1 medium-sized aubergine, peeled and sliced
1 onion, peeled and cut into rings
2 carrots, peeled and cut into 2 in (5 cm) thin sticks
13¼ (375 g) can **Homepride** Madras Classic Curry Sauce
2 courgettes, washed and sliced
8 oz (225 g) cauliflower florets
1 oz (25 g) mushrooms, washed and sliced
4 oz (100 g) whole green beans, halved crosswise

Sprinkle the aubergine slices with salt and leave for 30 minutes. Rinse and dry thoroughly. Place the onion and carrots in a large, heavy saucepan and add the can of curry sauce. Stir well, bring to the boil, cover and simmer very gently for 25 minutes. Add the remaining vegetables and continue to simmer gently, stirring occasionally, until cooked but still crisp—about 1 hour. Serve immediately.

This is a hot curry.   **Serves 4**

Dansak Style Drumsticks

8 chicken drumsticks
a little lemon juice
13¼ oz (375 g) can **Homepride** Dansak Classic Curry Sauce
1 oz (25 g) raisins
few lettuce leaves and ½ onion, cut into rings, to garnish

Score the surface of each drumstick with three slashes, using a sharp knife. Sprinkle the surface of each one with a little lemon juice. Place in a bowl and pour over the can of curry sauce. Cover and leave to marinate for 1–2 hours. Place the chicken mixture in a casserole with the raisins and cook, covered, in an oven pre-heated to 350°F, 180°C, Gas Mark 4, for about 1½ hours, until the chicken is tender.

Serve hot, garnished with the lettuce and onion rings. This is a medium hot curry.   **Serves 4**

Lamb Cassoulet in Dansak

2 oz (50 g) dried haricot *or* butter beans
1 lb (450 g) mutton *or* lamb, trimmed and cut into cubes
4 oz (100 g) chipolata sausages, sliced
1 clove garlic, crushed (optional)
freshly ground black pepper
13¼ oz (376 g) can **Homepride** Dansak Classic Curry Sauce
sprig of parsley to garnish

Soak the beans overnight in a bowl of cold water. Place the mutton or lamb in a casserole and add the sausages, garlic and black pepper. Stir in the can of curry sauce and the well drained beans. Cover and cook in the oven, pre-heated to 350°F, 180°C, Gas Mark 4, for about 2 hours, until the meat is tender.

Serve hot, garnished with the parsley sprig. This is a medium hot curry.   **Serves 4**

Piquant Almond Cream Lamb in Korma

1 lb (450 g) stewing lamb, cut into cubes
2 oz (50 g) whole blanched almonds
13¼ oz (376 g) can **Homepride** Korma Classic Curry Sauce
juice of 1 lime (optional)
2 tablespoons (30 ml) double cream
1 tablespoon (15 ml) freshly chopped chives to garnish
4 lime wedges to garnish

Place the lamb in a casserole dish. Add the almonds and the can of curry sauce. Mix thoroughly and cover with a lid. Cook in a pre-heated oven at 350°F, 180°C, Gas Mark 4, for about 2 hours, until the lamb is tender. Ten minutes before the end of the cooking time, stir in the lime juice and cream.

Serve hot, sprinkled with the chives and garnished with the wedges of lime. This is a mild curry.   **Serves 4**

Pork Braised with Honey and Korma

1 oz (25 g) butter
2 tablespoons (30 ml) clear honey
1 lb (450 g) pork, cut into cubes
1 clove garlic, crushed (optional)
coarsely grated rind ½ lemon
coarsely grated rind ½ orange
13¼ oz (376 g) can **Homepride** Korma Classic Curry Sauce
2 tablespoons (30 ml) plain yoghurt (optional)
lemon and orange slices to serve

Melt the butter in a heavy, flame-proof casserole and add the honey and pork. Stir constantly over a medium heat until the meat is lightly browned. Add the garlic, lemon and orange rind. Stir in the can of curry sauce. Remove from the heat, cover and cook in a pre-heated oven at 350°F, 180°C, Gas Mark 4 for about 2 hours, until the pork is tender.

This is a mild curry. Serve hot with lemon and orange slices and the yoghurt if liked.   **Serves 4**

LEA & PERRINS

Beef Curry

1 oz (25 g) lard
2 large onions, peeled and chopped
1 oz (25 g) desiccated coconut
1½ lb (680 g) stewing steak, cut into cubes
14 oz (396 g) can tomatoes
4 level teaspoons (20 ml) **Lea & Perrins** Concentrated Curry Sauce
salt and pepper

Heat the lard in a pan and fry the onions and coconut for 2 minutes. Add the beef and fry for 5 minutes, stirring occasionally. Stir in the tomatoes, cover and simmer gently for 2½–3 hours until the meat is tender. Stir in the concentrated curry sauce and season to taste.
Serves 4

Meat Balls with Sweet Curry Sauce

1 large onion, peeled and grated *or* finely chopped
1 lb (450 g) raw minced beef
2 oz (50 g) fresh white breadcrumbs
salt and pepper
Sauce
1½ oz (40 g) butter
1 small onion, peeled and chopped
8 oz (227 g) can apple purée
8 oz (227 g) can pineapple rings
2 level teaspoons (10 ml) **Lea & Perrins** Concentrated Curry Sauce
1 level teaspoon (5 ml) tomato purée
1 canned red pepper, chopped

Combine the onion, beef and breadcrumbs and season. Form into 16 balls each approximately the size of a walnut. Heat the butter in a shallow pan and fry the onion and meatballs for 5 minutes, turning occasionally. Add the apple purée and the juice from the pineapple rings. Bring to the boil. Stir in the coarsely chopped pineapple, concentrated curry sauce and tomato purée. Return to the boil and simmer gently for 15 minutes. Adjust the seasoning and stir in the red pepper.
Serves 4

Prawn and Egg Curry

1 oz (25 g) butter
1 onion, peeled and chopped
1 level teaspoon (5 ml) tomato purée
2 level teaspoons (10 ml) **Lea & Perrins** Concentrated Curry Sauce
8 oz (225 g) cooked, peeled prawns
6 eggs, hard boiled

Heat the butter in a pan and fry the onion gently for 6 minutes. Stir in the tomato purée, curry sauce and prawns. Simmer gently for 3 minutes. Coarsely chop 4 of the eggs and add to the pan. Reheat and serve garnished with the remaining 2 eggs, halved.
Serves 4

Coconut Curry

1 chicken
2 oz (50 g) fat *or* oil for frying
2 onions, peeled and chopped
1 tablespoon (15 ml) curry powder
½ pint (300 ml) stock
2 oz (50 g) **Mapletons** Creamed Coconut
3 tablespoons (45 ml) desiccated coconut

Joint and skin the chicken and fry in the fat or oil until golden. Add the onions and curry powder and continue to fry until the onions are brown. Put the chicken and onions in a saucepan, add the stock, creamed coconut and desiccated coconut and simmer for about 45 minutes.   **Serves 4**

Fruity Curried Lamb

1 tablespoon (15 ml) oil
2 large onions, peeled and chopped
1 level tablespoon (15 ml) curry powder
1½ lb (675 g) lamb fillet, cut into 1 in (2.5 cm) cubes
½ oz (15 g) seasoned flour
1 Red **Oxo** Cube, crumbled
¼ pint (150 ml) water
8 oz (227 g) can pineapple rings
2 oz (50 g) sultanas
salt and pepper
boiled rice to serve

Heat the oil in a large pan and fry the onions and curry powder for 3 minutes. Toss the lamb cubes in the seasoned flour and fry for a further 3 minutes. Add the Oxo cube, water and pineapple juice from the can. Bring to the boil, stirring, and season to taste. Cover and simmer for 1 hour. Add the pineapple rings, cut into quarters, with the sultanas, and cook for a further 15 minutes.
    Serve with the boiled rice.
Serves 4

Chicken Curry

2 large onions, peeled and finely chopped
1 clove garlic, chopped
butter, cooking fat *or* ghee for frying
2 whole tomatoes *or* 1 dessertspoon (10 ml) tomato purée
1 small stick cinnamon
2–3 cloves
2–3 green cardamoms
2 oz (50 g) cooking fat
1 dessertspoon (10 ml) **Rajah** Ground Dhaniya (ground coriander)
1 teaspoon (5 ml) **Rajah** Chilli Powder
½ teaspoon (2.5 ml) **Rajah** Ground Ginger
¼ teaspoon **Rajah** Garlic Powder
1 teaspoon (5 ml) **Rajah** Paprika
1 teaspoon (5 ml) **Rajah** Haldi (turmeric)
1 teaspoon (5 ml) **Rajah** Ground Jeera (ground cumin)
1 jointed chicken, approx 3 lb (1.3 kg)
salt
desiccated coconut to garnish (optional)

Using a saucepan, fry the onions and garlic in the butter, cooking fat or ghee until golden brown. Then add the tomatoes and spices and cook on a low heat for 5 minutes. Add sufficient water or stock to form a fairly thick gravy, then cover the pan and simmer for approximately 1¼ hours or until the chicken is tender.
    Serve garnished with desiccated coconut.   **Serves 3–4**

Chicken Tandoori

1 tablespoon (15 ml) **Rajah** Tandoori Masala
1 tablespoon (15 ml) lemon juice
2 (5 oz, 142 ml) cartons natural yoghurt
1 chicken, skinned and cut into 6 or 8 pieces
onion rings, lemon quarters and sliced tomatoes to garnish

Mix the Tandoori Masala thoroughly with the lemon juice and the yoghurt. Make long, deep cuts in the chicken pieces with a sharp knife and soak in the yoghurt mixture overnight or longer (minimum 12 hours). Remove the chicken pieces from the mixture and drain off any excess. Heat the oven to 350°F, 180°C, Gas Mark 4. Wrap the chicken in a piece of foil and bake for 1 hour 10 minutes. Remove from the foil and drain. Place under a hot grill, turning the chicken pieces over until both sides are reddish brown.

Serve on a bed of boiled rice, garnished with onion rings, lemon quarters, sliced tomatoes and accompanied by French bread.
Serves 3–4

Keema (Minced meat) Curry

1 large onion, peeled and very finely chopped
¼ teaspoon **Rajah** Garlic Powder
2 oz (50 g) butter, cooking fat or ghee for frying
1 tablespoon (15 ml) **Rajah** Madras Curry Powder
1 teaspoon (5 ml) tomato purée or 2 tomatoes, sliced
1 lb (450 g) minced beef
1 small carton yoghurt
salt

Fry the onion and garlic powder in the butter, cooking fat or ghee until golden brown. Add the curry powder and tomato purée, mixing thoroughly and cook on a high heat for 2 minutes. Then add the minced beef, yoghurt and salt to taste. Mix well and cook slowly for about 1 hour or until the meat is cooked.

This curry whould be slightly moist and peas can be added before serving if liked.   **Serves 4**

Raita (Yoghurt with Salad Pieces)

5 oz (142 ml) carton natural yoghurt
2 tablespoons (30 ml) cucumber, peeled
1 medium onion, peeled
Rajah Chilli Powder

Mix the yoghurt with very small strips of peeled cucumber, and finely chopped onion. Sprinkle lightly with chilli powder to serve.

Spiced Onion or Aubergine Bhajias

2 tablespoons (30 ml) baison (gram flour)
1 teaspoon (5 ml) salt
24 **Rajah** Dhaniya (coriander seeds)
water to mix
butter, cooking fat or ghee for deep frying
1 large onion, peeled and sliced (not in rings) or 2 medium aubergines, sliced ⅛ in (0.25 cm) thick but not peeled
¼ teaspoon **Rajah** Haldi (turmeric)

Mix the baison flour, salt and spices with water to form a thick batter of a consistency similar to porridge. Heat the butter, cooking fat or ghee until blue smoke appears. Cover the onions or aubergines generously on both sides with the batter and drop as many slices as the pan will hold into the deep, boiling fat. Fry until golden brown.   **Serves**

Spinach Rajah

1 lb (450 g) spinach, carefully washed and chopped
2 large onions, peeled and finely chopped

Rajah Chilli Powder to taste
butter, cooking fat or ghee for frying
salt

Fry the onions in the butter, cooking fat or ghee until golden brown. Add the chilli powder and spinach. Cover the pan with a close fitting lid and cook until dry. Add salt and stir.   **Serves 3–4**

Traditional Curry with Dhaniya

2 teaspoons (10 ml) **Rajah** Dhaniya (coriander)
1 teaspoon (5 ml) **Rajah** Haldi (ground turmeric)
1 teaspoon (5 ml) **Rajah** Jeera (ground cumin)
½ teaspoon (2.5 ml) **Rajah** Chilli Powder
water
2 onion, peeled and thinly sliced
2 oz (50 g) oil or butter
2 tablespoons (30 ml) tomato purée or 3 tomatoes, peeled and chopped
1 lb (450 g) meat, chicken or fish, cut in pieces

Mix the spices into a paste with water (approximately ½ a cup). Using a saucepan fry the onions in the oil or butter until light brown. Add the paste to the onions and fry for 3 minutes. Then add the tomato purée or peeled tomatoes and the meat and continue to fry for a further 5 minutes, stirring briskly. Then add 1½–2 cups of water and salt to taste and simmer until the meat is tender.
Serves 4

Fresh Cucumber Chutney

Cut cucumber into thin strips, wash and sprinkle with 2 teaspoons (10 ml) of water, a few drops of lemon juice and **Rajah** Chilli Powder, vinegar and salt to taste.

SCHWARTZ

Turkey Curry with Mangoes

2 tablespoons (30 ml) cooking oil

8 oz (227 g) onions, peeled and sliced

2 tablespoons (30 ml) **Schwartz** Curry Powder, Mild, Medium, Hot *or* Extra Hot

1 oz (28 g) plain flour

14 oz (397 g) tin mangoes

chicken stock

4 oz (113 g) raisins

½ oz (14 g) desiccated coconut

½ teaspoon (2.5 ml) salt

1 lb (454 g) cooked turkey, roughly chopped

Heat the cooking oil in a large saucepan. Add the onions and fry until soft and just beginning to colour. Stir in the curry powder and flour and fry gently for 1 minute. Drain the mangoes and make the juice up to 1¼ pints (750 ml) with stock. Stir into the saucepan followed by the raisins, coconut and salt. Bring to the boil, stirring. Stir in the turkey meat, taking care to keep it in whole pieces. Cover and simmer for 30 minutes, adding the mango pieces 5 minutes before the end of the cooking time.

Serve with boiled rice and accompaniments as desired, for instance, poppadums, chappatis, relishes, peppers, bananas, gherkins and melon. Do not reheat this dish. Not suitable for freezing.
Serves 4

Sharwood's

Beef Curry with Tomatoes

2 tablespoons (30 ml) oil

3 heaped teaspoons (45 ml) **Sharwood's** Vencat Curry Powder

1 medium onion, peeled and sliced

2 cloves garlic, crushed

1 lb (500 g) lean beef, cubed

14 oz (396 g) can plum tomatoes

1 tablespoon (15 ml) **Sharwood's** Peach Chutney

1 cinnamon stick (optional)

5 oz (142 ml) carton natural yoghurt

Heat the oil and cook the onions and garlic until soft. Add the curry powder and cook for a further few minutes. Add the meat to the pan and cook quickly until evenly browned. Add the entire contents of the can of tomatoes, the chutney and cinnamon stick (if used). Cook for 2 hours or until the meat is tender. Stir in the yoghurt just before serving and heat through.
Serves 4

Bengal Pork Hot Pot

2 onions, peeled and sliced

2 oz (50 g) butter

1 sachet **Sharwood's** Bengal Hot Curry Sauce Mix

½ pint (250 ml) water

3 tablespoons (45 ml) **Sharwood's** Green Label Mango Chutney

1 lb (500 g) lean cooked pork, sliced

1½ lb (750 g) potatoes, peeled and par-boiled

Sauté the onions for 2–3 minutes. Stir in the Bengal Sauce Mix, water and chutney, to make a sauce. Add the meat. Lay a covering of potatoes in the base of a buttered casserole dish, add the meat and top with a layer of potatoes. Dot with the remaining butter and bake for ¾–1 hour at 350°F, 180°C, Gas Mark 4.   **Serves 4**

Carrot Braise

2 onions, peeled and sliced

2 oz (50 g) butter

1 heaped teaspoon (15 ml) **Sharwood's** Mild *or* Hot Curry Paste

1 lb (500 g) carrots, quartered

3 tablespoons (45 ml) water

Sauté the onions in the butter, stir in the curry paste and cook for

3 minutes. Add the carrots and coat in the sauce, stir in the water and simmer for 20 minutes.
Serves 6 as an accompaniment

Chicken Kashmir

1 sachet **Sharwood's** Kashmir Mild Curry Sauce Mix

2 tablespoons (30 ml) natural yoghurt

juice of 1 lime *or* lemon

6 chicken drumsticks, skinned

1 onion, peeled and sliced in rings

1 oz (25 g) butter

4 tablespoons (60 ml) soured cream

½ packet **Sharwood's** Basmati Rice

1 lime, sliced, to garnish

Blend the Kashmir Sauce Mix, yoghurt and lime juice. Add the chicken and coat evenly. Chill for 2 hours. Sauté the onion, add the chicken and the marinade. Cover and simmer gently for approximately 1 hour until tender. Place the chicken on a serving dish. Blend the cooking liquid with the soured cream and heat through. Pour the sauce over the chicken.

Serve with the Basmati rice and garnish with the slices of lime.
Serves 6

Cucumber and Tomato Raita

¼ cucumber, diced

1 tablespoon (15 ml) onion, peeled and chopped

1 teaspoon (5 ml) salt

2 firm tomatoes, diced

5 oz (142 ml) carton natural yoghurt

½ teaspoon (2.5 ml) **Sharwood's** Garam Masala Curry Spices (optional)

Place the cucumber and onion in a bowl, sprinkle with the salt and leave for 1 hour. Gently press off any excess liquid from the cucumber. Add the tomatoes to the cucumber. Stir the yoghurt and cumin (if used), together, and pour over the cucumber and tomato, turning them over with a spoon to coat evenly. Chill before serving.
Serves 4–6 as a side salad

Lamb Tikka Kebabs with Mint Chutney

Marinade
1 tablespoon (15 ml)
   Sharwood's Curry Paste
5 oz (142 ml) carton natural
   yoghurt
2 pieces **Sharwood's** Stem
   Ginger, finely chopped
1 tablespoon (15 ml)
   Sharwood's Lemon Juice
1 lb (500 g) lean lamb, cubed
Mint chutney
3 tablespoons (45 ml)
   Sharwood's Garden Mint
   Sauce
2 teaspoons (10 ml) chilli
   powder *or* chilli sauce
1 small onion, peeled and
   chopped
1 teaspoon (5 ml) salt
onion rings and lemon wedges
   to garnish

Mix together the marinade
ingredients. Toss the lamb in the
marinade, ensuring that all the
meat is coated and leave in the
refrigerator overnight. Thread the
lamb on to 4 skewers and grill for
15 minutes, turning frequently,
until all the meat is well cooked.
   For the mint chutney simply
blend together all the ingredients.
Garnish the kebabs with the onion
rings and lemon wedges.
   Serve with chapatis and the mint
chutney.   **Serves 4**

Maharanee's Biryani

2 lb (1 kg) lean lamb, diced
Marinade
10 oz (300 g) natural yoghurt
6 heaped teaspoons (approx
   45 ml) **Sharwood's** Mild or
   Medium Curry Powder
2 teaspoons (10 ml) salt
2 tablespoons (30 ml) lime *or*
   lemon juice
2 onions, peeled and sliced
4 oz (100 g) butter
1 packet **Sharwood's** Pilau Rice
1 teaspoon (5 ml) salt
1 pint (500 ml) stock, boiling
2 oz (50 g) raisins
2 oz (50 g) flaked almonds

Marinate the lamb, preferably
overnight. Sauté the onions, drain
and place in a casserole dish. Drain
and fry the lamb for 4 minutes
stirring frequently, and add to the
onions. Rinse the whole sachet of
rice, drain, mix with the salt and
the enclosed sachet of spices. Pile
on top of the lamb. Add the boiling
stock, cover tightly and bake at
350°F, 180°C, Gas Mark 4 for
1 hour. Garnish with raisins and
almonds.
Serves 12 as part of a buffet

Palak Aloo

2 onions, peeled and finely
   chopped
2 oz (50 g) butter
1 teaspoon (5 ml) salt
2 heaped teaspoons (20 ml)
   Sharwood's Garam Masala
   Curry Spices
1½ lb (750 g) potatoes, peeled,
   par-boiled and cut into
   quarters
8 oz (250 g) frozen spinach,
   thawed

Sauté the onions in the butter. Stir
in the salt and garam masala. Add
the potatoes and spinach, cover
and cook for approximately 15
minutes or until the potato is
tender.
Serves 6 as an accompaniment

Pig Stick Ribs

2 lb (900 g) Chinese spare ribs
   of pork
2 oz (50 g) butter
1 can **Sharwood's** Vindaloo
   Extra Hot Curry Sauce

Sauté the ribs in the butter. Stir in
the sauce and simmer for 1 hour
until the sauce has reduced and the
flesh is tender.
Serves 12 as part of a buffet

Prawn Curry

2 tablespoons (30 ml) oil
1 large onion, peeled and sliced
2 cloves garlic, crushed
3 heaped teaspoons (45 ml)
   Sharwood's Vencat Curry
   Powder

2 oz (50 g) **Sharwood's**
   Creamed Coconut
¼ pint (150 ml) milk, warmed
pinch paprika pepper
2 tablespoons (30 ml)
   Sharwood's Tomato Purée
8 oz (250 g) peeled prawns
1 lb (500 g) spinach, cooked,
   drained and chopped
   (optional)

Heat the oil in a pan and lightly
cook the onion and garlic until
soft. Add the curry powder and
cook for 2–3 minutes. Dissolve the
coconut in the warmed milk then
add to the onion mixture together
with the paprika and tomato
purée. Stir in the prawns and
spinach, if liked, cover the pan and
cook gently for 10 minutes.
Serves 4

Shish Kebabs

12 oz (350 g) minced lamb *or*
   beef
1 onion, peeled and chopped
2 teaspoons (10 ml) lemon juice
2 heaped teaspoons (20 ml)
   Sharwood's Medium *or* Hot
   Curry Powder
1 tablespoon (15 ml) natural
   yoghurt
1 egg, beaten
2 tablespoons (30 ml) gram or
   plain flour
2 tablespoons (30 ml) chopped
   coriander leaves
1½ teaspoons (7.5 ml) salt

Knead all the ingredients together
to make a smooth mixture: Divide
into 6. Shape round 2 skewers, 3 to
a skewer. Place on a tray and
refrigerate for 2 hours. Barbecue or
grill for 15–20 minutes. Serve hot
or cold.
Serves 6 as an accompaniment

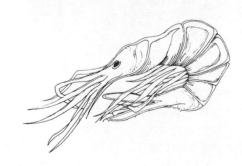

Vegetable Curry

1 tablespoon (15 ml) oil
1 large onion, peeled and sliced
3 heaped teaspoons (30 ml)
   Sharwood's Vencat Curry
   Powder
¼ pint (150 ml) stock
2 tablespoons (30 ml)
   Sharwood's Tomato Purée
   (optional)
fresh vegetables, e.g.
1 small cauliflower,
   broken into sprigs and par-
   boiled
6 oz (150 g) carrots, peeled,
   sliced and par-boiled
2 oz (50 g) green beans,
   topped and tailed and par-
   boiled
4 oz (100 g) mushrooms,
   sliced
15 oz (425 g) can **Sharwood's**
   Red Kidney Beans, drained,
   or any other canned
   vegetable
salt and pepper

Heat the oil and cook the onion
until soft. Stir in the curry powder
and cook for a further few minutes.
Gradually add the stock and
tomato purée and bring to the boil.
Add all the vegetables, cover and
simmer gently for 15 minutes.
Season to taste.   **Serves 4**

Ring-a-Curry-Rice

8 oz (225 g) long grain rice
1 pint (568 ml) water
salt
2 oz (50 g) butter
14½ oz (418 g) can **Shippams**
   Chunky Chicken in Curry
   Sauce
twists of cucumber to garnish

Simmer the rice in 1 pint (600 ml)
salted water until the liquid is
absorbed and the rice tender. Pack
firmly into a 7 in (18 cm) buttered
ring mould. Melt the butter in a
saucepan and spoon evenly over

the rice, cover loosely with foil and
bake for 30–35 minutes in the
centre of the oven at 400°F, 200°C,
Gas Mark 6. Heat the Chunky
Chicken gently in a saucepan.
Turn out the ring of rice on to a hot
serving dish, carefully pile the
chicken in the centre and garnish
with the cucumber twists.
Serves 4

Stuffed Curried Peppers

4 equal-sized green *or* red
   peppers
4 oz (100 g) long grain rice
¾ pint (426 ml) water
salt
14½ oz (418 g) can **Shippams**
   Chunky Chicken in Curry
   Sauce
2 tablespoons (30 ml) water

Cut the tops off the peppers and
reserve. Remove the cores and
seeds then put the peppers in a pan
of boiling, salted water and
simmer for 5 minutes. Remove
and drain. Cook the rice in ¾ pint
(450 ml) of salted water until
tender and the water is absorbed.
Stir the cooked rice into the
Chunky Chicken. Stand the
peppers upright in an ovenproof
dish, fill each with the chicken and
rice mixture and replace the tops.
Put 2 tablespoons (30 ml) of water
in the dish around the peppers to
prevent drying and cover loosely
with foil. Bake for 30–40 minutes
in the centre of the oven at 375°F,
190°C, Gas Mark 5, until
tender.   **Serves 4**

Curried Patties

2 tablespoons (30 ml) **Spry**
   Crisp 'n Dry
8 oz (225 g) minced beef
1 small onion, peeled and finely
   diced
½ oz (15 g) plain flour
1 clove garlic, skinned and
   crushed
2 level teaspoons (10 ml) curry
   powder

½ level teaspoon (2.5 ml) chilli
   powder
¼ level teaspoon (1.25 ml)
   turmeric
2 level teaspoons (10 ml)
   tomato purée
½ oz (15 g) sultanas
1 apple, diced
¼ pint (150 ml) beef stock
Pastry
6 tablespoons (90 ml) **Spry**
   Crisp 'n Dry beaten with
   3 tablespoons (45 ml) water
8 oz (225 g) plain flour sieved
   with ½ level teaspoon
   (2.5 ml) salt
small carton natural yoghurt

In a large frying pan heat the Crisp
'n Dry. Add the minced beef and
onion and fry gently for 3–4
minutes, stirring well. Add the
remaining ingredients and simmer gently for 15–20 minutes.
Leave to cool.

To make the pastry, pour the
liquid into the dry ingredients in a
steady stream and mix to form a
soft dough. Knead lightly on a
floured surface, roll out very thinly
and cut into 4 in (10 cm) squares.
Place 1 tablespoon (15 ml) of the
filling on each square, damp the
edges and fold over to form
triangles. Place on a baking sheet
and bake in the middle of the oven
pre-heated to 400°F, 200°C, Gas
Mark 6, for 20–25 minutes. Place
the patties on a serving dish and
pour over the yoghurt. Serve hot.
Makes 9–10 patties

PASTA and RICE

Golden Savoury Rice with Bacon

8 oz (200 g) bacon
4 oz (100 g) mushrooms, washed and sliced
4 hard-boiled eggs
1 packet **Batchelors** Golden Savoury Rice

Chop the bacon and halve the mushrooms. Cook the Savoury Rice as directed. Fry the bacon until crisp, then gently fry the mushrooms. Cut the hard-boiled eggs into quarters and combine all ingredients together.   **Serves 4**

Quick Spaghetti Milanese

6 oz (175 g) spaghetti
4 rashers streaky bacon
margarine for frying
1 onion, peeled and finely chopped
1 clove garlic, crushed
1 teaspoon (5 ml) mixed herbs
1 packet **Batchelors** Barbeque Beef and Tomato Soup
1 pint (575 ml) water
4 oz (100 g) mushrooms, washed and sliced

Cook the spaghetti in a pan of boiling, salted water for 10 minutes. De-rind the bacon, cut into small pieces and fry in the margarine for 5 minutes. Add the onion and garlic to the pan and cook for 2–3 minutes. Add the herbs and soup, mix well and stir in the water. Bring to the boil, stirring until thick. Cook for 5 minutes. Add the mushrooms to the pan and heat through. Drain the spaghetti and pile on to a hot serving dish. Pour the sauce over and serve immediately.
Serves 2

Risotto Provencale

1 lb (450 g) salt pork or bacon, cut into ½ in (1 cm) strips
1 red or green pepper, de-seeded and sliced
olive oil for frying
12 oz (350 g) long grain rice
1 can **Baxters** Sauce Provencale
1½ pints (900 ml) water
1 heaped teaspoon (10 ml) oregano *or* mixed herbs
parsley, roughly chopped

Fry the pork or bacon and pepper in the oil until the meat browns. Turn down the heat, add the rice and continue to fry for a further minute. Mix the can of sauce with the water and herbs and stir into the pork whilst continuing to fry. Simmer gently until the liquid is absorbed, then scatter with the roughly chopped parsley and serve at once with a mixed green salad.
Serves 6

Spaghetti with Stir Fry

8 oz (200 g) spaghetti
1 teaspoon (5 ml) oregano
freshly ground black pepper
10 oz (283 g) packet **Birds Eye** Country Stir Fry
4 oz (100 g) cooked meat— ham, beef *or* chicken
5 fl oz (142 ml) carton soured cream
watercress to garnish

Cook the spaghetti in a large saucepan of boiling, salted water for about 12 minutes, until tender. Drain, toss in black pepper and oregano and keep hot. Cook the Stir Fry according to packet

instructions. Cut the cooked meat into strips and add to the pan with the soured cream. Heat gently, without boiling, for 2–3 minutes, adjusting seasoning if necessary. Spoon the spaghetti into a serving dish and add the sauce. Garnish with watercress.   **Serves 4**

Stir Fry Fish Risotto

4 oz (100 g) long grain rice
7 oz (198 g) packet **Birds Eye** Buttered Smoked Haddock
1 oz (25 g) butter
2 teaspoons (10 ml) oil
10 oz (283 g) packet **Birds Eye** Mediterranean Stir Fry
1 oz (25 g) flaked almonds, toasted

Cook the rice in boiling, salted water for about 11 minutes, until tender. Cook the smoked haddock according to pack instructions, remove the fish from the bag and flake. Heat the butter and the oil in a large frying pan. Add the Stir Fry vegetables, flaked haddock and rice. Stir-fry over a medium to high heat for 4–6 minutes.

Serve in a shallow dish, sprinkled with toasted almonds.
Serves 4

Grilled Pork with Risotto

1 tablespoon (15 ml) oil
2 medium onions, peeled and sliced
8 oz (225 g) long grain rice
1 level tablespoon (15 ml) **Bisto**
salt and pepper
4 oz (100 g) mushrooms, washed and sliced
7 oz (198 g) can sweetcorn with red and green peppers
8 thick pork rashers

1 level tablespoon (15 ml) chopped parsley

Heat the oil in a large frying pan, add the onions and fry for 3–4 minutes, until soft. Stir in the rice and cook for 1 minute. Blend the Bisto with a little water in a measuring jug; make up to 1½ pints (900 ml) with water. Stir into the rice, with salt and pepper. Bring to the boil and cook gently for 15 minutes. Stir in the mushrooms and drained sweetcorn. Cook for a further 5–10 minutes, until the rice is cooked. Add more boiling water, if necessary.

Meanwhile, heat the grill. Place pork rashers on the grill rack and cook for 10–15 minutes, turning once, until crisp and golden brown. Stir the chopped parsley into the risotto, place it on a warmed serving dish and arrange the rashers on top.   **Serves 4**

Pasta Shells Salad

4 oz (100 g) **Buitoni** pasta shells
4 oz (100 g) button mushrooms, washed and chopped
10 oz (283 g) can **Buitoni** Peperonata

Cook the pasta according to the directions on the packet. Drain and rinse thoroughly under the cold tap. Combine the mushrooms with the peperonata and pasta. Serve chilled.   **Serves 4**

Spaghetti Carbonara

1 lb (450 g) **Buitoni** Spaghetti
4 oz (100 g) smoked bacon, cut into thin strips
2 tablespoons (30 ml) oil
4 eggs
2 tablespoons (30 ml) cream *or* top of the milk
2 oz (50 g) **Buitoni** Parmesan Cheese, grated
salt and black pepper

Cook the spaghetti according to the directions on the packet. Heat the oil in a large pan and fry the bacon gently until it is just cooked. Meanwhile beat the eggs in a bowl, add the cream, half the cheese, the salt and plenty of freshly ground black pepper. Stir the spaghetti into the pan with the bacon. Remove from the heat and immediately add the egg mixture which will cook by the heat of the spaghetti. Serve at once, sprinkled with the remaining cheese.
Serves 4–6

Tagliatelle with Cheese and Ham

8 oz (225 g) **Buitoni** Tagliatelle
salt
5 fl oz (142 ml) carton soured cream
3 tablespoons (45 ml) milk
2 oz (50 g) butter
2 oz (50 g) **Buitoni** Parmesan Cheese
½ teaspoon (2.5 ml) dried basil
a little grated nutmeg
freshly ground black pepper
6 oz (175 g) cooked ham, cubed

Cook the tagliatelle as directed on the packet and drain well. Place the remaining ingredients in a saucepan and heat gently, stirring occasionally. Add the cooked tagliatelle and mix well. Serve immediately, with the Parmesan cheese.   **Serves 4**

Cannelloni au Gratin

8 oz (200 g) cannelloni
3 oz (75 g) breadcrumbs
1 hard-boiled egg, finely chopped
1 tablespoon (15 ml) parsley, chopped
2 cans **Chesswood** Sliced Mushrooms in Creamed Sauce
2 teaspoons (10 ml) Parmesan cheese, grated

Cook the cannelloni as directed on the packet. Meanwhile, make the stuffing. Mix together the egg, the breadcrumbs (reserving 2 tablespoons (30 ml)) and 1 can Sliced Mushrooms in Creamed Sauce. Season to taste. Carefully cut the cannelloni lengthways, lay some stuffing along the centre of each and fold into their original form. Lay them in a well-greased, oven-proof dish and coat with the second can of Sliced Mushrooms in Creamed Sauce. Sprinkle with the reserved breadcrumbs and the grated cheese and bake towards the top of the oven for 15 minutes at 425°F, 220°C, Gas Mark 7.
Serves 4–6

Mushroom Pasta Bake

6 oz (150 g) onions, peeled and sliced
1 can **Chesswood** Sliced Large Mushrooms, drained
2 oz (50 g) margarine
6 oz (150 g) short cut macaroni, cooked
2 tablespoons (30 ml) parsley, chopped
3 eggs, beaten
½ pint (250 ml) milk
5 fl oz (142 ml) carton soured cream
2 teaspoons (10 ml) salt
black pepper
8 oz (200 g) tomatoes, skinned and sliced
chopped parsley to garnish

Lightly fry the onions and mushrooms in the margarine. Place half the macaroni in the base of a shallow 3 pint (1.5 litre) lightly greased, ovenproof dish. Spoon the mushroom mixture and the parsley on top and finish with the remaining macaroni. Mix the eggs with the milk, soured cream and seasoning and pour into the dish. Top with the sliced tomatoes and bake for 35–40 minutes at 375°F, 190°C, Gas Mark 5.

Sprinkle with chopped parsley to serve.   **Serves 4**

Spaghetti with Anchovy Sauce

6 oz (175 g) **Cirio** Thin Spaghetti
1 clove garlic, minced
2 tablespoons (30 ml) parsley, chopped
1 tablespoon (15 ml) oil
4 anchovies
2 level tablespoons (30 ml) **Cirio** Tomato Purée
4 tablespoons (60 ml) boiling water
Parmesan cheese, grated

Cook the spaghetti in boiling, salted water for 9 minutes. Drain well. Fry the garlic and parsley in the hot oil until brown, wash and mash the anchovies and add to the garlic. Simmer gently for a few minutes. Stir in the tomato purée diluted with the boiling water and simmer for a further minute. Place the spaghetti in a serving dish and pour over the sauce.

Serve topped with the grated Parmesan cheese. **Serves 4**

Tomato Macaroni Cheese

8 oz (225 g) **Cirio** Short Macaroni
½ oz (15 g) butter
½ oz (15 g) flour
¼ pint (150 ml) milk
14 oz (396 g) can **Cirio** Peeled Tomatoes
1 level teaspoon (5 ml) dry mustard
8 oz (225 g) cheese, grated
salt and pepper

Cook the macaroni in boiling, salted water for 12 minutes. Drain well. Melt the butter in a pan, add the flour and, stirring, cook for 1 minute. Add the milk gradually, stirring constantly. Drain the liquid from the tomatoes and make up to ¼ pint (150 ml) with water, add to the sauce gradually and cook gently, stirring, for 1 minute. Stir in the salt, pepper, mustard and 6 oz (175 g) of the cheese. Add the macaroni.

Arrange a layer of tomatoes in the base of a lightly buttered, ovenproof dish, cover with a layer of the macaroni cheese, then a layer of tomatoes and end with the remaining macaroni. Top with the remaining 2 oz (50 g) of cheese and brown in a very hot oven (475°F, 240°C, Gas Mark 9) or under a hot grill. **Serves 4**

Colman's

Lasagne

1 packet **Colman's** Cheese Sauce Mix
½ pint (300 ml) milk
1 packet **Colman's** Spaghetti Sauce Mix
½ pint (300 ml) water
1 oz (25 g) butter
2 onions, peeled and chopped
1 lb (450 g) lean minced beef
1 teaspoon (5 ml) dried rosemary
1 teaspoon (5 ml) oregano
12 oz (350 g) lasagne sheets, cooked and drained
2 tablespoons (30 ml) Parmesan cheese, grated
parsley sprigs to garnish

Make up the cheese sauce mix and the spaghetti sauce mix. Fry the onions gently in the butter until soft, add the beef and cook for a further 8 minutes, then add the herbs and the spaghetti sauce. Place a layer of lasagne in a square or oblong dish. Cover with half the meat mixture and then the cheese sauce. Repeat the layers, ending with cheese sauce. Sprinkle with the Parmesan cheese. Bake at 400°F, 200°C, Gas Mark 6, for 40 minutes, or until the top is well browned.

Garnish with parsley sprigs to serve. **Serves 4**

Pasta Bake

8 oz (225 g) pasta shells
1 lb (450 g) minced beef
2 onions, peeled and chopped
1 clove garlic, crushed
1 packet **Colman's** Spaghetti Sauce Mix
½ pint (300 ml) water
2 oz (50 g) Parmesan cheese, grated

Cook the pasta shells in lots of boiling, salted water for 12–14 minutes and drain. Fry the beef, onion and garlic together in a saucepan. When browned, pour off the excess fat. Mix the spaghetti sauce mix with the water and add to the meat. Cook, stirring, until thickened. Place a layer of pasta in the bottom of an ovenproof dish, pour over half the meat and spaghetti sauce, cover with the rest of the pasta shells and finish with a layer of meat and sauce. Sprinkle with the Parmesan cheese and put into the oven for 15 minutes at 375°F, 190°C, Gas Mark 5. Serve at once. **Serves 4**

FRANK COOPER®

Savoury Macaroni Supper

2 tablespoons (30 ml) corn oil
1 lb (400 g) minced beef
2 medium onions, peeled and sliced
1 can **Frank Cooper's** Venison Soup
salt and black pepper
6 oz (150 g) cut macaroni
1 oz (25 g) Parmesan cheese, grated
1 tablespoon (15 ml) parsley, chopped
1 tomato, sliced

Heat the corn oil, brown the meat and sauté the onions for 3–4 minutes. Stir in the soup and seasoning and simmer gently for 20 minutes. Cook the macaroni in boiling, salted water for 10 minutes until tender, and drain. Stir the macaroni into the meat, heat through and pour into a serving dish. Mix together the cheese and parsley, sprinkle over the dish and place the sliced tomato on top. **Serves 4**

Harlequin Risotto

1 oz (25 g) butter
6 oz (150 g) long grain rice
1 small onion, peeled and
  chopped
2 oz (50 g) sweetcorn
1 small red pepper, de-seeded
  and chopped
2 oz (50 g) mushrooms, sliced
1 pint (500 ml) chicken stock
5 oz (142 g) can **Crosse &
  Blackwell** Ham and Tongue
  Roll, cubed
salt and pepper

In a saucepan over a low heat, melt
the butter and stir-fry the rice and
vegetables for about 4 minutes.
Stir in the stock and the meat roll.
Cook for 20 minutes or until the
rice has absorbed the stock. Season
to taste before serving.
Serves 3–4

Paella

1 tablespoon (15 ml) oil
4 oz (100 g) raw chicken
1 packet **Crosse & Blackwell**
  Rice & Things, Savoury Rice
  & Peppers Flavour
4 oz (100 g) peas, cooked
4 oz (100 g) prawns, cooked
4 oz (100 g) mussels, cooked

Heat the oil in a large frying pan.
Add the chicken and fry until
sealed. Stir in the Rice & Things
and cook as directed. Just before
the end of the cooking time, stir in
the peas, prawns and mussels.

This is particularly tasty served
with an endive and pepper salad.
Serves 4

Savoury Rice

8 oz (200 g) long grain rice
1 chicken stock cube

12 oz (300 g) cold, cooked
  chicken, turkey, ham *or*
  prawns
1 red pepper, de-seeded and
  chopped
1 small onion, peeled and
  chopped
8 oz (200 g) can sweetcorn
13¼ oz (375 g) **Del Monte**
  Crushed Pineapple
1 small can garden peas
4 tablespoons (60 ml) French
  dressing

Boil the rice in water containing
the stock cube. Cool. Chop the
meat into small pieces. Combine
with all the remaining ingredients
except the French dressing. Just
before serving toss in the dressing.
Serve with green salad.
Serves 4

Macaroni Brunch Bake

8 oz (100 g) quick cook
  macaroni
6 oz (150 g) packet **Findus**
  Haddock Fillets
1 can condensed tomato soup,
  undiluted
4 oz (100 g) mature Cheddar
  cheese, grated
salt and black pepper
1 tomato, sliced
parsley sprigs to garnish

Cook the macaroni as directed.
Cook the fish according to pack
directions. In a bowl place the
drained macaroni, skinned and
flaked fish, condensed soup and
2 oz (50 g) of the cheese. Mix well
and season. Place the mixture in an
ovenproof dish, cover with the
remaining cheese and cook under
a moderate grill until golden
brown.

To serve, garnish with the
tomato slices and parsley.
Serves 4

Spicy Kedgeree

1 packet **Findus** Smoked
  Haddock Fillets

3 eggs
2 oz (50 g) butter
1 medium onion, peeled and
  chopped
8 oz (225 g) long grain rice
1 teaspoon (5 ml) curry paste
1 pint (500 ml) water
1 tablespoon (15 ml) parsley,
  chopped
2 tablespoons (30 ml) single
  cream
lemon wedges to garnish

Cook the fish as directed, and soft-
boil the eggs for 5 minutes. Melt
1 oz (25 g) of the butter in a large
frying pan, add the onion and fry
until golden brown. Stir in the rice
and cook for a few minutes until
transparent, add the curry paste
and mix well. Carefully add the
water and the juices from the fish,
bring to the boil and simmer for 15
minutes or until the rice is cooked,
adding more water if necessary.
Meanwhile, skin and flake the
fish, shell the eggs—chopping 2
and slicing the remaining egg.
When the rice is cooked, stir in the
parsley, fish, chopped eggs, cream
and remaining butter. Season
well.

Serve garnished with the sliced
egg and lemon wedges.
Serves 4

Smoked Pork Sausage
with Tagliatelle

8 oz (225 g) tagliatelle
8 oz (225 g) firm white
  mushrooms
8 oz (225 g) smoked pork
  sausages, thickly sliced
2 oz (50 g) black olives, stoned
Dressing
2 tablespoons (30 ml) red wine
  vinegar
freshly ground black pepper
6 tablespoons (90 ml) **Flora** Oil
4 tablespoons (60 ml) tomato
  chutney

Cook the pasta in boiling, salted
water for about 8–10 minutes until

cooked. Drain, rinse under cold water and drain again. Add the mushrooms, sausages and olives to the tagliatelle.

For the dressing, mix together the vinegar and seasoning, then whisk in the oil and tomato chutney. Pour the dressing over the tagliatelle and mix carefully. Place in a serving dish.
Serves 2

Roman Risotto

1 small onion, peeled and chopped
1 clove garlic, chopped
2 tablespoons (30 ml) oil
6 oz (175 g) long grain rice
1 pint (600 ml) stock
12 oz (340 g) can **Fray Bentos** Lean Cut Corned Beef
2–3 red peppers, canned
2 oz (50 g) frozen peas
salt and pepper
grated cheese to serve

Fry the onion and garlic in the oil until tender. Add the rice and fry for a few minutes. Add the stock, bring to the boil and simmer for 20 minutes until the rice has absorbed the stock. Dice the corned beef and add to the rice mixture with the sliced peppers, cooked peas and seasoning. Cook for another 10 minutes. Serve with grated cheese.   **Serves 4**

HELLMANN'S

Prawn and Pasta Salad

4 oz (100 g) pasta shells
1 pint (500 ml) fresh prawns, shelled *or* 6 oz (175 g) frozen prawns, thawed
juice and grated rind of 1 lemon
1 teaspoon (5 ml) parsley, chopped
2 level tablespoons (30 ml) tomato purée

6 fl oz (150 ml) **Hellmann's** Real Mayonnaise
salt and black pepper
lemon twist and parsley sprig to garnish

Cook the pasta shells in boiling, salted water for 12–14 minutes until tender, drain and rinse in cold water. Mix together the prawns, lemon rind and juice and the parsley. Stir in the pasta shells. Blend together the tomato purée and mayonnaise and stir into the pasta. Season and chill before serving.

Garnish with the lemon twist and parsley sprig.
Serves 4 as a main course

Kellogg's

Chinese Style Noodles

3½ oz (100 g) packet **Kellogg's** Super Noodles Chicken Flavour
2 tablespoons (30 ml) oil
3 large spring onions, chopped
1 oz (25 g) flaked almonds
4 oz (100 g) cooked chicken, diced
1 carrot, peeled and coarsely grated
1 oz (25 g) button mushrooms, sliced
salt and pepper
few drops soy sauce
2 spring onions to garnish

Make up the noodles according to packet instructions. Meanwhile, heat the oil in a frying pan. Add the spring onions, almonds, chicken, carrot and mushrooms, and cook over a high heat for about 3–4 minutes, stirring constantly. Reduce the heat and add the cooked noodles and seasoning. Heat through for a further 3–4 minutes. Add the soy sauce and mix well together.

Serve at once, garnishing each portion with a spring onion.
Serves 2

Prawn Ring

2 (8 oz, 227 g) bags **Kellogg's** Boil-in-the-bag Rice

4 oz (100 g) frozen peas
6 oz (175 g) frozen sweetcorn
1½ oz (40 g) butter
1½ oz (40 g) plain flour
1 pint (600 ml) milk
salt and pepper
8 oz (225 g) peeled prawns
2 tablespoons (30 ml) tomato purée
1 teaspoon (5 ml) lemon juice
3 lemon slices and 6 whole prawns to garnish

Cook the rice according to packet instructions. Cook the peas and sweetcorn in boiling water for 5 minutes and drain well.

Meanwhile, make the sauce. Melt the butter in a saucepan, stir in the flour and cook for 1 minute. Remove from the heat and add the milk gradually, stirring constantly. Return to the heat and bring to the boil, stirring until smooth and thickened. Add the seasoning, prawns, tomato purée and lemon juice, and simmer gently for 2–3 minutes.

Mix together the cooked rice, peas and sweetcorn. Butter a 2½ pint (1.5 litre) ring mould and pack the rice firmly into it. Allow the rice to settle, then unmould the ring carefully on to a heated serving plate. Fill the centre with the prawn sauce and serve any extra sauce separately. Garnish with halved lemon slices and whole prawns.   **Serves 6–8**

KERRYGOLD

Tuna or Salmon Macaroni

2 oz (50 g) macaroni
3½ oz (99 g) can tuna *or* salmon
½ (15 oz, 425 g) can ready-to-serve cream of mushroom soup
2 tablespoons (30 ml) dry **Kerrygold** Plenty (instant milk)
4 oz (100 g) packet frozen peas
salt and pepper
1½–2 oz (40–50 g) Cheddar cheese, grated

Cook the macaroni in boiling,

salted water until it is tender. Meanwhile, drain the oil from the tuna or salmon. Flake the fish into a small baking dish and stir in the soup, milk powder, peas and seasoning to taste. Drain the macaroni and rinse it in cold water. Add the macaroni to the tuna mixture and fold together well. Sprinkle the cheese over the top and bake in the oven at 350°F, 180°C, Gas Mark 4, for 30 minutes.   **Serves 2**

Knorr

Ham and Mushroom Risotto

2 tablespoons (30 ml) oil
2 onions, peeled and chopped
8 oz (200 g) long grain rice
1½ pint (750 ml) **Knorr** chicken stock
2 oz (50 g) mushrooms, sliced
4 oz (100 g) ham, cubed
4 oz (100 g) frozen peas

Heat the oil in a saucepan and fry the rice until golden brown and the onion until soft and transparent. Add the mushrooms, ham, peas and stock and bring to the boil. Cover and simmer for 20 minutes, or until all the liquid has been absorbed.   **Serves 4**

Noodle Savoury

1½ pint (750 ml) **Knorr** beef *or* chicken stock
8 oz (200 g) ribbon noodles
3 oz (75 g) streaky bacon, chopped
2 oz (50 g) mushrooms, washed and sliced
7 oz (198 g) can sweetcorn, drained
2 tablespoons (30 ml) single cream
3 oz (75 g) cheese, grated

Simmer the stock and noodles in a pan until all the liquid has been absorbed. Fry the bacon and mushrooms without any fat in a

frying pan for 2–3 minutes. Stir into the noodles, add the sweetcorn and stir in the cream. Place in an ovenproof dish, sprinkle with cheese and brown under a hot grill. Serve immediately.
Serves 3–4

Savoury Fried Rice

2 tablespoons (30 ml) oil
4 oz (100 g) long grain rice
¾ pint (375 ml) **Knorr** chicken stock
4 oz (100 g) bacon, grilled and chopped
1 small red pepper, de-seeded and chopped

Heat the oil in a large frying pan. Fry the rice until golden brown, about 5–10 minutes. Add the stock, bacon and red pepper and simmer gently for 25–30 minutes until the liquid is absorbed and the rice is tender. Delicious served with chicken casserole.
Serves 2

LEA & PERRINS

Oriental Rice Salad

6 oz (175 g) long grain rice, cooked and cooled
1 small onion, peeled and finely chopped
2 in (5 cm) cucumber, diced
2 oz (50 g) roasted peanuts
1 oz (25 g) sultanas
8 oz (227 g) can pineapple rings, coarsely chopped
Dressing
4 tablespoons (60 ml) oil
2 level teaspoons (10 ml) **Lea & Perrins** Concentrated Curry Sauce
juice of ½ a lemon
salt and pepper

Mix together the rice, onion, cucumber, peanuts and sultanas and fold in the pineapple. For the dressing, whisk all the ingredients together until well blended. Add sufficient dressing to the rice mixture to moisten.   **Serves 4–6**

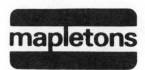

Coconut Rice for Curries

½ pint (300 ml) milk
2 tablespoons (30 ml) **Mapletons** Creamed Coconut
5 oz (150 g) long grain rice
½ pint (300 ml) water

Heat the milk with the creamed coconut until it has melted. Leave to cool. Cook the rice in the mixed water and coconut milk for 20 minutes or until all the liquid is absorbed.   **Serves 1–2**

Italian Macaroni

12 oz (350 g) macaroni
1½ oz (40 g) butter
1½ oz (40 g) plain flour
1 Red **Oxo** Cube, crumbled and dissolved in ½ pint (300 ml) hot water
½ pint (275 ml) milk
8 oz (225 g) cheese, grated
2 level tablespoons (30 ml) tomato purée
salt and pepper
4 oz (100 g) cooked ham, diced

Cook the macaroni, following packet instructions, and drain. Melt the butter in a saucepan, add the flour and cook for a minute. Remove from the heat and stir in the Oxo stock and milk gradually. Return to the heat and bring to the boil, stirring. Cook for a minute, then remove from the heat and add 6 oz (175 g) of the cheese, with the tomato purée and seasoning. Stir in the macaroni and ham. Place in an ovenproof dish, sprinkle the remaining cheese over and bake at 400°F, 200°C, Gas Mark 6, for about 15 minutes.   **Serves 4–6**

Pillau Rice

2 cups **Rajah** Basmatti Rice
1 onion, peeled and sliced
3 oz (75 g) butter, margarine *or* ghee
1 teaspoon (5 ml) salt
4 cardamoms
1 large piece cinnamon stick
5–6 cloves
3–4 bay leaves
½ teaspoon (2.5 ml) **Rajah** Haldi (turmeric)
4 cups water

Wash the rice and soak in cold water for about 1 hour. Fry the onion in the butter until golden brown. Add the spices and fry for 2 minutes, then add the drained rice and fry for a further 2 minutes. Add the water and bring to the boil. Simmer on a low flame until the rice is tender (approximately 20 minutes). **Serves 4**

Savoury Rice

8 oz (225 g) long grain white *or* brown rice
1 onion, peeled and sliced
1 clove garlic, crushed
2 sticks celery, washed and chopped
2 small peppers, red and green, de-seeded and chopped
knob of margarine
blade of mace (optional)
½ teaspoon (2.5 ml) turmeric
1 oz (25 g) sultanas
1 tablespoon (15 ml) tomato purée
salt and pepper
2 chicken stock cubes
1¼ pints (700 ml) hot water
¼ pint (150 ml) **Rose's** Lime Juice Cordial
1 oz (25 g) salted peanuts

Wash the rice. Fry the vegetables gently in the margarine until softened. Stir in the rice, spices, sultanas, tomato purée and seasoning to taste. Dissolve the stock cubes in the water and add the cordial. Pour the liquid on to the rice. Simmer, covered, for about 25 minutes (about 40 minutes for brown rice) until all the liquid is absorbed. Stir in the peanuts just before serving

A delicious accompaniment to meat or fish, Savoury Rice makes a satisfying light meal on its own. **Serves 4**

Sharwood's

Masala Chicken Risotto

½ packet **Sharwood's** Basmati Rice
2 onions, peeled and diced
2 oz (50 g) butter
2 heaped teaspoons (30 ml) **Sharwood's** Garam Masala
4 tomatoes, peeled and diced
1 teaspoon (5 ml) salt
¾ pint (435 ml) stock
8 oz (250 g) chicken, cooked and sliced
1 can **Sharwood's** Okra, drained
½ red pepper, de-seeded and diced
coriander leaves for garnish

Rinse the rice thoroughly until the water runs clear. Sauté the onion until soft, add the rice and fry until transparent. Add the garam masala, tomatoes, salt and stock. Simmer for 10 minutes. Arrange the chicken, okra and peppers on top. Cook slowly for 15 minutes so that the chicken is heated through. **Serves 4 as a supper dish**

Rice with Chick Peas

6 oz (150 g) **Sharwood's** Basmati Rice
1 teaspoon (5 ml) salt
2 tablespoons (30 ml) oil
1 heaped teaspoon (15 ml) **Sharwood's** Mild *or* Medium Curry Powder
4 onions, peeled and sliced
1 teaspoon (5 ml) **Sharwood's** Garam Masala
6 oz (150 g) chick peas, canned
3 oz (75 g) butter

Cook the rice in boiling, salted water for 5 minutes. Drain. In a flameproof casserole dish heat the oil, add the spices and cook for 10–20 seconds. Stir in the onions, rice and chick peas and fry for 2–3 minutes. Place the butter in small knobs on top of the rice, cover with a sheet of foil and then the lid. Bake in the oven for 45 minutes at 350°F, 180°C, Gas Mark 4. **Serves 6 as an accompaniment**

Saffron Rice

pinch saffron threads (alternatively, a large pinch of turmeric may be used)
3 tablespoons (45 ml) oil
1 large onion, peeled and finely sliced
8 oz (250 g) **Sharwood's** Basmati Rice
4–6 cloves

Place the saffron in a small bowl and pour 2 tablespoons (30 ml) boiling water over it. Leave to soak for approximately 10 minutes. (Not necessary if using turmeric). Heat the oil in a large pan and cook the onions until soft. Add the rice and cook gently for a few minutes. Add 1 pint (600 ml) of boiling, salted water to the pan, together with the cloves and turmeric, if used. Bring to the boil, add the soaked saffron and turn the heat down to simmering temperature. Cover and cook for 20–25 minutes, or until the rice has absorbed all the liquid. **Serves 4**

Indonesian Fried Rice

7 tablespoons (100 ml) **Spry** Crisp 'n Dry
1 large onion, peeled and sliced

1 clove garlic, skinned and
crushed
1 level teaspoon (5 ml) curry
powder
½ level teaspoon (2.5 ml)
coriander
½ level teaspoon (2.5 ml) chilli
powder
½ teaspoon (2.5 ml)
Worcestershire sauce
4 oz (100 g) cooked chicken,
diced
4 oz (100 g) cooked ham, diced
2 oz (50 g) peeled prawns
(optional)
4 oz (100 g) frozen peas
6 oz (175 g) cooked rice
salt and pepper
Omelette
1 egg, beaten
2 tablespoons (30 ml) water
salt and pepper
1 tablespoon (15 ml) **Spry** Crisp
'n Dry

Heat the Crisp 'n Dry in a large
frying pan. Fry the onion and
garlic until soft, add the spices and
Worcestershire sauce and cook for
1–2 minutes. Stir in the meat,
prawns (if used) and peas and cook
for a further 3–4 minutes. Add the
rice and seasoning and fry very
gently for 7–10 minutes. Meanwhile, make the omelette. Add the
water to the beaten egg and
season. Heat the Crisp 'n Dry in a
frying pan and pour in the mixture. When set, cut into strips.
Turn the fried rice on to a serving
dish and decorate with a lattice of
omelette strips.
Serve hot.   **Serves 6**

Stork

Canelloni with Cheese Sauce

6 canelloni
1 large onion, peeled and
chopped
4 oz (100 g) mushrooms,
chopped
2 cloves garlic, crushed
2 oz (50 g) **Stork** Margarine

7 oz (198 g) can tuna, drained
and flaked
14 oz (396 g) pimentos, drained
and diced, reserving a little
for garnish
2 oz (50 g) fresh breadcrumbs
Sauce
2 oz (50 g) **Stork** Margarine
2 oz (50 g) flour
1 pint (575 ml) milk
salt and pepper
4 oz (100 g) cheese, grated

Cook the canelloni as directed on
the packet. Sauté the onion, mushrooms and garlic in the margarine
until softened. Add the tuna,
pimentos and breadcrumbs and
cook over a low heat for 5 minutes,
stirring continuously. Stuff the
canelloni with the filling and place
in an ovenproof dish. Place all
sauce ingredients except the
cheese in a saucepan and bring to
the boil over moderate heat,
stirring continuously. Boil for 2–3
minutes. Remove from the heat
and add 3 oz (75 g) of the cheese.
Pour the sauce over the canelloni.
Garnish with the rest of the
pimentos and scatter over the
remaining cheese. Bake in the
centre of the oven at 400°F, 200°C,
Gas Mark 6, for 30 minutes until
bubbly and golden brown.
   Serve with a salad.   **Serves 4**

Lentil Lasagne

1 oz (25 g) **Stork** Margarine
2 medium-sized onions, peeled
and chopped
2 oz (50 g) bacon, chopped
1 clove garlic, crushed
1 lb (450 g) minced beef
4 oz (100 g) mushrooms,
washed and sliced
½ pint (300 ml) beef stock
15 oz (425 g) can tomatoes
1 teaspoon (5 ml) mixed herbs
salt and pepper
2 oz (50 g) lentils, cooked for
30 minutes in boiling water
Lasagne and Sauce
8 oz (225 g) wholewheat
lasagne
2 oz (50 g) **Stork** Margarine
2 oz (50 g) wholewheat flour

1 pint (575 ml) milk
salt and pepper
2 oz (50 g) All-Bran
2 oz (50 g) Parmesan cheese,
grated

To make the meat mixture, melt
the margarine, add the onion and
cook gently until soft. Add the
bacon and cook for 2 minutes. Stir
in the garlic and mince and cook
until the mince has browned,
stirring frequently. Pour off any
excess fat and add the remaining
ingredients. Cover and cook
gently for 30 minutes. Season to
taste. Cook the lasagne in boiling,
salted water for about 30 minutes
or until just tender.
   To make the sauce, melt the
margarine, stir in the flour, return
to the heat and cook for 1 minute,
stirring continuously. Remove
from the heat and gradually stir in
the milk. Return to the heat and
bring to the boil, stirring all the
time, then cook for 2–3 minutes.
Using a large, oblong, ovenproof
dish, layer the ingredients starting
with the mince, then the lasagne,
followed by the sauce. There will
be two layers of each. Sprinkle
with the cheese and bake in the
oven at 400°F, 200°C, Gas Mark 6,
for 20 minutes.   **Serves 4**

Luxury Pasta

12 oz (350 g) ribbon noodles
2 oz (50 g) **Stork** Margarine
3 fl oz (75 ml) double cream
4 oz (100 g) ham, chopped
4 oz (100 g) Cheddar cheese,
finely grated
1 teaspoon (5 ml) basil
salt and black pepper

Cook the noodles in plenty of
boiling, salted water for about
12 minutes until cooked. Drain in
a colander, return to the pan and
stir in the remaining ingredients
until every strand is thoroughly
coated. Season well. Turn out on to
a hot dish and serve at once.
Serves 3–4

Spaghetti Alabama

8 oz (225 g) wholewheat
  spaghetti
1 lb (450 g) scampi, fresh *or*
  frozen
seasoned flour
1½ oz (40 g) **Stork** Margarine
1 onion, peeled and chopped
1–2 cloves garlic, peeled and
  crushed
2 sticks celery, chopped
1 red pepper, de-seeded and
  chopped
½ oz (15 g) flour
½ pint (275 ml) chicken stock
1 glass white wine (optional) *or*
  extra stock
2 tablespoons (30 ml) tomato
  relish
1 teaspoon (5 ml) horseradish
  sauce
1 teaspoon (5 ml) lemon juice
3 oz (75 g) button mushrooms,
  washed
chopped parsley to garnish

Cook the spaghetti according to
instructions on the packet. Coat
the scampi in seasoned flour and
fry in 1 oz (25 g) of the margarine
for 6–8 minutes. Keep warm. Melt
the remaining margarine and
sauté the onion, garlic, celery and
red pepper for 5 minutes. Add the
flour, stir well, and cook for 1–2
minutes longer. Add the stock
slowly, stirring all the time over a
medium heat until the sauce comes
to the boil. Cook for 2–3 minutes.
Add the remaining ingredients
and continue to cook for a further
5–10 minutes.
  Serve the scampi sauce on a bed
of spaghetti, sprinkled with the
chopped parsley.   **Serves 4**

Macaroni Medley

4 oz (100 g) macaroni
2 oz (50 g) margarine
4 oz (100 g) mushrooms,
  washed and quartered
1½ oz (40 g) plain flour
¾ pint (450 ml) milk
3 tomatoes, peeled and cut into
  wedges
4 oz (100 g) cooked peas
10 oz (283 g) can **Tyne Brand**
  Stuffed Pork Roll, cut into
  small chunks
4 oz (100 g) cheese, grated
1 level teaspoon (5 ml) salt
pepper

Cook the macaroni in boiling,
salted water until tender, then
drain. Heat the margarine in a
saucepan and fry the mushrooms
for 2 minutes. Remove from the
pan and keep hot. Stir in the flour
and cook for 2 minutes. Remove
from the heat and gradually stir in
the milk. Return to the heat, bring
to the boil, stirring continuously,
and cook for 1 minute. Add the
macaroni, tomatoes, peas, Stuffed
Pork Roll, mushrooms and half the
cheese. Heat, stirring well. Add
the seasoning and turn the mixture
into a 1¼ pint (750 ml) ovenproof
dish, sprinkle with the remaining
cheese and place under a hot grill
until golden brown. Serve hot.
Serves 4

Uncle Ben's

Beef and Rice Ragout

1 can **Uncle Ben's** Ready
  Cooked Rice
1 small onion, chopped
2 sticks celery, chopped
4 oz (100 g) butter
12 oz (350 g) minced beef
2 tablespoons (30 ml) tomato
  purée
¾ pint (450 ml) stock

Prepare the rice and keep hot. Fry
the onion and celery in 2 oz (50 g)
of the butter, until tender. Place
the rice in a casserole dish and top
with the onion/celery mixture. Fry
the minced beef in the remaining
butter until brown and mix in the
tomato purée. Heat the stock and
add to the casserole with the
minced beef. Cover and cook in
the oven at 350°F, 180°C, Gas
Mark 4, for about 1 hour.
Serves 2

Lamb and Saffron Rice

2 large onions, peeled and
  chopped
2 cloves garlic, crushed
½ oz (15 g) fresh green *or* stem
  ginger
2 oz (50 g) clarified butter
1½ lb (675 g) lean shoulder *or*
  leg of lamb, cubed
½ teaspoon (2.5 ml) chilli
  powder
1 teaspoon (5 ml) turmeric
2 oz (50 g) cashew nuts,
  chopped
8 oz (225 g) **Uncle Ben's**
  American Long Grain Rice
¼ teaspoon saffron powder
1 medium green pepper, de-
  seeded and chopped
2 tablespoons (30 ml) fresh
  mint, chopped
2 tablespoons (30 ml) fresh
  parsley, chopped
juice of 1 lemon
¼ pint (150 ml) yoghurt
2–3 tablespoons (30–45 ml)
  milk
½ teaspoon (2.5 ml) ground
  coriander
salt
1 teaspoon (5 ml) garam masala
  or ¼ teaspoon each cloves,
  cinnamon, cardamom

Fry the onion in 1 oz (25 g) of the
butter until soft and fry the garlic
and ginger for a moment or two.
Fry the lamb in the rest of the
butter until well browned,
sprinkle in the chilli powder,
turmeric and nuts and fry gently
for a further 5–6 minutes, stirring
well. Stir in the onions. Boil the
rice with the saffron, but remove
from the heat after 10–12 minutes
and drain. Add the green pepper,
herbs, lemon juice, yoghurt, milk
and coriander. Season with salt
and the garam masala or spices.
  Place a thin layer of the rice
mixture in a casserole dish, then a
layer of the lamb mixture and
repeat, finishing with a layer of
rice. Cover and bake in the oven at
350°F, 180°C, Gas Mark 4, for
about 1 hour.   **Serves 4**

Bacon and Haddock Kedgeree

7.05 oz (200 g) packet **Wall's** Streaky Bacon Rashers
2 oz (50 g) butter
4 oz (100 g) long grain rice, cooked
2 eggs, hard-boiled, shelled and chopped
8 oz (225 g) smoked cod *or* haddock, poached and flaked
1 tablespoon (15 ml) fresh parsley, chopped
freshly ground black pepper
lemon wedges to garnish

Cut the rinds from the bacon rashers and fry the rashers over a medium heat until brown. Keeping four rashers to one side, chop the rest into 1 in (2.5 cm) pieces and return them to the pan. Add the butter and when it has melted stir in the rice, eggs and fish (removing any skin and bones), together with the parsley and black pepper. Stirring all the time, heat the ingredients thoroughly. Turn the kedgeree into a warm serving dish and garnish with the reserved bacon rashers and lemon wedges before serving.   **Serves 4**

Spaghetti Alla Carbonara

12 oz (300 g) spaghetti
1 oz (25 g) butter
8 oz (200 g) **Wall's** Middle Bacon Rashers, diced
1 tablespoon (15 ml) parsley, chopped
salt and pepper
1 tablespoon (15 ml) Parmesan cheese, grated
2 large eggs, beaten

Cook the spaghetti in a large saucepan of boiling water until it is tender but still firm.

Meanwhile, melt the butter in a frying pan, add the bacon and fry until crisp. Stir in the parsley and plenty of seasoning. Keep hot.

Drain the spaghetti and empty into a large, heated bowl. Add the bacon mixture (including the fat in the pan), the cheese and eggs and toss together thoroughly for about 1 minute. Serve immediately.
Serves 4

Tuna Lasagne

4 oz (100 g) lasagne, cooked in boiling, salted water
1 oz (25 g) butter
1 oz (25 g) flour
½ pint (250 ml) milk
7 oz (198 g) can **John West** Skipjack Tuna
salt and pepper
1 teaspoon (5 ml) fennel
1 teaspoon (5 ml) parsley, chopped
4 tomatoes, skinned and roughly chopped
2 oz (50 g) cheese, grated
sprig of parsley to garnish

Cook the lasagne. Meanwhile, melt the butter in a pan and blend in the flour and milk. Flake the tuna into the sauce and add the seasoning, herbs and tomatoes.

Layer this mixture with the lasagne, sprinkle the grated cheese on top and place under a hot grill for a few minutes to brown. Garnish with the sprig of parsley.
Serves 4

Prawn Risotto

2 oz (50 g) butter
4 oz (100 g) onion, peeled and chopped
6 oz (175 g) courgettes, washed and sliced
4 oz (100 g) button mushrooms, washed and sliced
10 oz (275 g) long grain rice
1¾ pints (1 litre) hot chicken stock
1 teaspoon (5 ml) turmeric
1 heaped tablespoon (20 ml) Parmesan cheese, grated
8 oz (225 g) **Young's** North Atlantic Prawns
salt and pepper
grated Parmesan cheese to serve

Heat half the butter in a saucepan and fry the onion, courgettes and mushrooms gently until soft. Add the rice and stir until translucent. Add the hot stock gradually, with the turmeric, adding more as the previous addition becomes absorbed. Cook over a medium heat, uncovered, stirring from time to time. When the liquid is almost absorbed, add the prawns, the remaining butter, Parmesan cheese and salt and pepper to taste.

Serve with more Parmesan cheese handed separately.
Serves 4

EGGS and CHEESE

Cheesy Bread and Butter Pudding

8 slices stale **Allinson** Wholewheat Bread
vegetable margarine
Cheddar cheese, thinly sliced
1 egg
½ pint (300 ml) milk
sea salt

Spread the bread with the margarine and cut into triangles. Line the base of a medium-sized casserole dish with half the bread, cover with slices of cheese and top with the remaining bread, spread side uppermost. Beat the egg and milk lightly together, season with sea salt and pour the mixture over the bread in the casserole dish. Bake for 45 minutes at 350°F, 180°C, Gas Mark 4 until crisp and golden brown.   **Serves 2–3**

Cheese and Onion Tart

shortcrust pastry made with 8 oz (200 g) **Be-Ro** Flour
2 large onions, peeled and chopped
4 oz (100 g) cheese, grated
2 tablespoons (30 ml) milk
salt and pepper
milk to glaze

Divide the pastry in two and roll out and line an 8 in (20 cm) ovenproof plate with one piece. Cook the onions in boiling, salted water for 5 minutes then drain. Spread the onions over the pastry, top with the grated cheese and

milk and season with salt and pepper. Cover with the other round of pastry and seal the edges well. Decorate, if liked, with the pastry trimmings and brush with milk. Bake in a moderately hot oven at 400°F, 200°C, Gas Mark 6, for about 30 minutes.
Serves 4–6

Blue Cheese Flan

1 oz (25 g) margarine
1 oz (25 g) lard
4 oz (100 g) plain flour, sifted
1 Red Cube from **Bovril**, dissolved in 4 teaspoons (20 ml) water
½ oz (12 g) butter
1 small onion, chopped
2 oz (50 g) celery, chopped
4 oz (100 g) blue cheese
2 oz (50 g) cream cheese
2 eggs, beaten
¼ pint (142 ml) single cream
salt and pepper
1 tomato, sliced

Rub the margarine and lard into the flour, until it resembles breadcrumbs. Add the Red Cube from Bovril stock and mix to form a stiff dough. Roll out and line a 7–8 in (18–20 cm) flan ring. Fry onion and celery in butter for 5 minutes. Mash the blue and cream cheeses, add the onion and celery. Gradually mix in the eggs and cream. Season with salt and pepper. Transfer the mixture to the pastry case. Bake at 400°F, 200°C, Gas Mark 6 for 20 minutes. Place the tomato rings on top of the flan and return to the oven for a further 10 minutes until golden.
Serves 6–8

Cheese and Apple Fondue

1 clove garlic
1 level tablespoon (15 ml) cornflour
¼ level teaspoon dry mustard
¼ level teaspoon paprika pepper
¾ pint (450 ml) **Bulmers** Apple Juice
1½ lb (675 g) English Cheddar cheese, coarsely grated

Rub the inside of a heavy casserole or pan with the cut clove of garlic. Blend the cornflour, mustard and paprika with a little apple juice. Warm the rest of the apple juice in the casserole, add the grated cheese and stir until melted. Stir in the blended cornflour. Bring to the boil and simmer gently for 10–15 minutes, until creamy, stirring continuously.

Serve with chunks of crisp French bread or hot toast.
Serves 6

Cheese and Onion Delight

1 lb (450 g) small whole onions, peeled
Bulmers Woodpecker Cider
1 teaspoon (5 ml) salt
knob of butter

Sauce
2 oz (50 g) plain flour
2 oz (50 g) butter
1 pint (600 ml) milk
4 oz (100 g) English Cheddar cheese, grated
chopped parsley to garnish

Place the onions in a fairly large saucepan. Pour enough Woodpecker cider over the onions to come half way up them. Add the salt and butter. Simmer gently until the onions are soft but still whole.

Meanwhile, prepare the cheese sauce. Mix the flour into the melted butter and gradually add the milk, stirring well. Season and bring to the boil. Remove from the heat and add the grated cheese. Arrange onions in a dish, pour the sauce over and sprinkle with the chopped parsley.

Delicious served with roast lamb or beef. **Serves 4–5**

Celery Soufflé

1½ oz (40 g) butter
1 oz (25 g) flour
10½ oz (297 g) can **Campbell's** Condensed Cream of Celery Soup, undiluted
3 eggs, separated
salt and pepper

Melt the butter in a saucepan and add the flour. Blend well together then add the undiluted soup. Bring to the boil and remove from the heat. Stiffly whisk the egg whites. Add the yolks to the soup mixture, add the seasoning and beat well. Fold in the egg whites and pour into a greased 1½ pint (900 ml) soufflé dish. Bake in a pre-heated oven at 350°F, 180°C, Gas Mark 4, for 30 minutes. Serve immediately. **Serves 3–4**

Poached Eggs with Cheese Sauce

10½ oz (297 g) can **Campbell's** Condensed Cream of Mushroom Soup, undiluted
¼ soup can milk
4 eggs
4 slices toast
4 oz (100 g) cheese, grated
salt and pepper

Put the undiluted soup and the milk in a frying pan and mix well. Heat until the soup comes just to the boil. Slide the eggs into the pan, one at a time, and poach in

the usual way. Lift the cooked eggs on to the toast and keep warm. Add the cheese to the soup mixture and heat until the cheese melts. Season to taste. Spoon the sauce over the eggs and serve immediately. **Serves 4**

Eggs Florentine

8 oz (225 g) frozen chopped spinach, thawed
2 oz (50 g) butter
white pepper
salt
4 eggs
1 box **Chef** Cheese Sauce Mix
½ pint (300 ml) milk
2 oz (50 g) grated cheese
1 teaspoon (5 ml) paprika

Gradually heat the spinach with the butter until hot and well blended, season with the pepper and salt. Divide into 4 individual dishes. Poach the eggs very lightly and place one egg in each dish on the spinach. Make up the Cheese Sauce as instructed on the box and pour over the eggs. Sprinkle each one with a little of the grated cheese and sprinkle lightly with paprika. Bake on the top shelf of an oven pre-heated to 400°F, 200°C, Gas Mark 6, for 10 minutes or until golden brown.

Alternatively assemble all the ingredients while hot and grill until golden brown. Serve immediately. **Serves 4**

Cheese and Mushroom Souffle

1 oz (25 g) butter
1 onion, peeled and finely chopped
1 can **Chesswood** Small Whole Mushrooms, finely chopped and drained, reserving brine
½ oz (15 g) flour
3 eggs, separated

3 oz (75 g) cheese, finely grated
pinch of cayenne pepper

Melt the butter and fry the onion gently until transparent. Add the mushrooms and flour and cook for a few minutes over a gentle heat. Gradually beat in the brine from the mushrooms and bring to the boil, stirring all the time. Allow to cool slightly then beat in the egg yolks, cheese and seasoning. Beat egg whites stiffly and fold lightly into the mixture. Place in a soufflé dish on the middle shelf of the oven, pre-heated to 375°F, 190°C, Gas Mark 5, for 35–40 minutes. Serve immediately. **Serves 4**

Creamy Mushroom Omelette

1 can **Chesswood** Sliced Large Mushrooms, drained
1½ oz (40 g) butter
5 fl oz (142 ml) carton soured cream
¼ teaspoon dried tarragon
4 eggs, separated

Sauté the mushrooms gently in ½ oz (15 g) of the butter, stir in the soured cream, tarragon and seasoning and simmer gently for 2 minutes. Keep hot. Beat the egg yolks with 4 tablespoons (60 ml) water, salt and pepper. Whisk the egg whites stiffly and fold into the yolks. Melt the remaining butter in a large omelette pan and pour in the egg mixture. Cook over a moderate heat until golden brown on the underside—about 2 minutes. Place under a moderately hot grill until brown and risen. Spoon the mushroom filling into the middle, fold over, place on a warmed plate and serve immediately. **Serves 2**

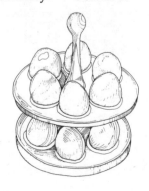

Colman's

Bread and Cheese Puff

2 packets **Colman's** Bread
  Sauce Mix
1 pint (575 ml) milk
2 eggs, separated
4 oz (100 g) Cheddar cheese,
  grated

Grease a 1½ pint (900 ml) soufflé
or casserole dish. Make up the
bread sauce with the milk as
directed and when thickened beat
in the 2 egg yolks and the cheese.
Mix until the cheese has melted.
Leave to cool, then fold in the
stiffly beaten egg whites. Bake in a
pre-heated oven at 375°F, 190°C,
Gas Mark 5, for 30 minutes or
until golden and set.

Serve at once with a mixed
salad.　　**Serves 4**

Curried Eggs

6–8 eggs
1 packet **Colman's** Curry Sauce
  Mix
½ pint (300 ml) water
2 tablespoons (30 ml) mango
  chutney
1 tablespoon (15 ml) sultanas
6 cocktail gherkins, cut into fan
  shapes, to garnish

Hard-boil the eggs and remove the
shells. Keep whole. Make up the
sauce mix as directed and stir in
the chutney and sultanas. Put the
eggs into a serving dish, pour over
the hot sauce and garnish with the
gherkins.

Serve with rice, poppadoms and
cucumber mixed with yoghurt.
Serves 4

Spanish Omelette

2 medium potatoes, peeled and
  chopped into ½ in (1 cm)
  cubes
1 tablespoon (15 ml) olive oil

1 oz (25 g) butter
8 oz (227 g) packet **Findus**
  Summer Harvest Mix
1 medium onion, peeled and
  chopped
salt and black pepper
6 eggs, beaten

Heat the oil and butter together in
a large, non-stick frying pan, add
the potatoes and cook over a
moderate heat for 15 minutes,
stirring occasionally, until golden
brown. Cook the Summer Harvest
Mix as directed and drain. Add the
onion to the potato and fry until
transparent. Stir in the Summer
Harvest Mix and season well. Pour
in the eggs and cook over a
moderate heat until firm. To set the
top, place under a hot grill. Serve
by loosening the base from the pan
with a palette knife and slide
carefully on to a hot serving plate.
Serve immediately.　　**Serves 6**

Cheese Soufflé Flan

7½ oz (215 g) packet **Jus-rol**
  Shortcrust Pastry, thawed
1 oz (25 g) butter
1 oz (25 g) plain flour
¼ pint (150 ml) milk
6 oz (175 g) Cheddar cheese,
  grated
3 large eggs, separated
pinch cayenne pepper

Roll out the pastry and use to line
an 11 in (28 cm) flan tin. Leave in a
cool place. Melt the butter in a
saucepan. Remove from the heat
and stir in the flour. Add all the
milk and whisk the sauce until it
thickens and comes to the boil.
Simmer for a few seconds and then
remove from the heat and beat in
all but one tablespoon (15 ml) of
the cheese. Beat the egg yolks into
the mixture gradually. Stir in the
cayenne pepper. Whisk the egg
whites until they are light and
frothy but not dry and stir lightly
into the mixture, using a metal
spoon. Pour the mixture into the
prepared flan case and sprinkle

over the remaining cheese. Bake in
a pre-heated oven at 400°F, 200°C,
Gas Mark 6, for 35–40 minutes.
Serve hot immediately it is taken
out of the oven.　　**Serves 6–8**

Kellogg's

Crunchy Baked Eggs

½ oz (15 g) low-calorie spread
4 oz (100 g) mushrooms, sliced
6 oz (175 g) tomatoes, skinned
  and chopped
salt and pepper
4 eggs
Topping
¾ oz (20 g) **Kellogg's** Special K
1 oz (25 g) Cheddar cheese,
  finely grated
1 tablespoon (15 ml) chopped
  parsley

Gently melt the low-calorie spread
in a small saucepan. Add the
mushrooms and tomatoes and
cook gently, covered, for 5
minutes. Season with salt and
pepper and spread the mixture in a
shallow, ovenproof dish. Break the
eggs on top of the vegetables and
bake in a moderately hot oven
(375°F, 190°C, GasMark 5) for 10
minutes.

Meanwhile, mix together the
topping ingredients. Sprinkle over
the eggs and return to the oven for
a further 5–10 minutes, until the
cheese has melted and the topping
is golden brown.　　**Serves 4**

Creamed Spinach Supper

1 egg
8 oz (225 g) packet frozen
  chopped spinach
2 streaky bacon rashers, with
  rinds removed, chopped
¼ onion, peeled and chopped
1 tablespoon (15 ml) butter
1 tablespoon (15 ml) flour
4 tablespoons (60 ml) milk *or*
  single cream

dash of Worcestershire sauce
salt and pepper
1 tomato, sliced
2 processed **Kerrygold** Cheese
Slices

Hard-boil the egg for 10 minutes. At the same time, cook the spinach according to the directions on the packet. Drain the spinach well, pressing out all the excess moisture. Fry the chopped bacon and onion until the onion is tender and add the butter. When it has melted, stir in the flour and cook for 1 minute. Stir in the milk or cream and bring to the boil, stirring until thickened. Add the spinach, Worcestershire sauce and seasoning to taste and mix well. Empty into a heated, ovenproof flan dish and keep hot.

Shell the egg and slice it. Arrange with the tomato slices on the spinach mixture. Cut the cheese slices into strips and arrange them in a lattice fashion over the top. Bake in the oven pre-heated to 350°F, 180°C, Gas Mark 4, for 10–15 minutes or until the cheese has melted and is lightly browned. Alternatively, brown under the grill.   **Serves 1**

Crackerbarrel Wafers

5 oz (125 g) **Kraft** Crackerbarrel
Mature Cheddar Cheese
1½ oz (40 g) **Kraft** Superfine
Soft Margarine
few drops Worcestershire sauce
4 oz (100 g) plain flour
salt and pepper

Finely grate the cheese into a bowl, add the margarine and mix well. Add the Worcestershire sauce, flour and seasonings and mix to a stiff dough, using the fingers. Divide the mixture in half and form each half into a roll 1½ in (3.5 cm) in diameter. This is easily done using cling film to wrap the dough in. Place the dough in a refrigerator for 2–3 hours to chill thoroughly. Pre-heat the oven to

375°F, 190°C, Gas Mark 5. Cut the rolls into ¼ in (0.5 cm) slices and bake on a greased baking sheet for 10–12 minutes until lightly golden.

Dairylea Fondue

1 clove garlic
¼ pint (125 ml) dry cider
7 oz (198 g) tub **Kraft** Dairylea
Cheese Spread
1 dessertspoon (10 ml)
cornflour, mixed to a smooth
cream with 2 tablespoons
(30 ml) cider
nutmeg *or* paprika pepper

Rub the cut clove of garlic round the inside of a heavy saucepan or fondue dish. Place ¼ pint (125 ml) cider in the pan and pring to the boil. When at boiling point gradually add the cheese spread, stirring all the time and allowing the cheese to melt slowly. When all the cheese has melted, add the cornflour mixture to thicken the fondue. Season with a little nutmeg or paprika.

Serve with cubes of brown or white toasted bread, or chunks of French bread.

Dairylea Tartlets

6 oz (150 g) shortcrust pastry
4 oz (100 g) **Kraft** Dairylea
Cheese Spread
1 egg, beaten
½ small onion, peeled and
finely chopped
1 slice ham, chopped
1 teaspoon (5 ml) mixed herbs
salt and pepper

Preheat oven to 375°F, 190°C, Gas Mark 5. Roll out the pastry to ⅛ in (0.25 cm) thick and cut into 2½ in (7 cm) circles to line twelve tartlet tins. Cream the cheese spread until softened and gradually beat in the egg. Mix in the remaining ingredients and divide the mixture between the pastry cases. Bake in a.pre-heated oven at 375°F, 190°C, Gas Mark 5 for 20 minutes, until golden brown.
Makes 12

Cheesy McVitie's Digestive Savoury

4 oz (100 g) butter
8 oz (225 g) onions, peeled and
sliced
1 lb (450 g) courgettes, sliced
2 green peppers, de-seeded and
sliced
1 lb (450 g) tomatoes
1 tablespoon (15 ml) cornflour
½ pint (300 ml) milk
salt and pepper
4 oz (100 g) Cheddar cheese,
grated
4 oz (100 g) **McVitie's** Digestive
Biscuits, crushed

Melt 1 oz (25 g) of the butter in a large frying pan and add the onion, courgettes and peppers and fry gently, stirring continuously. Reserve one tomato for garnish, then cover the remainder with boiling water for 10 seconds, drain and then skin and chop. Stir into the vegetables and cook for a further 10 minutes.

Meanwhile make the sauce. Melt 1 oz (25 g) of the remaining butter in a saucepan, stir in the cornflour, add the milk and bring to the boil, stirring until thickened. Season well and add the cheese to the sauce. Season the vegetable mixture and empty into a large dish. Spoon over the cheese sauce. Place in a moderate oven pre-heated to 350°F, 180°C, Gas Mark 4, for 20 minutes. Melt the remaining butter and mix with the crushed biscuits. Spread over the sauce and return to the oven for a further 10 minutes. Serve with a salad.
Serves 4–6

Savoury Cheesecake

6 oz (175 g) **McVitie's** Digestive
   Biscuits, crushed
3 oz (75 g) butter, melted
pinch of salt
8 oz (225 g) Cheshire cheese,
   finely grated
8 oz (225 g) cottage cheese
2 oz (50 g) salted peanuts
½ small onion, peeled
2 oz (50 g) ham *or* salami
2 in (5 cm) piece of cucumber,
   peeled

Mix the crushed biscuits with the
butter and salt and press into a 7 in
(18 cm) round cake tin, lined with
foil. Place the cottage cheese, 1 oz
(25 g) of the peanuts, onion, ham
or salami and cucumber in a
liquidiser and blend until smooth.
Put the Cheshire cheese in a bowl,
stir in the mixture from the
liquidiser and mix well. Spread
over the biscuit mixture and chill
in the refrigerator. Lift out of the
cake tin, remove the foil, place on a
dish and decorate the top with the
remaining peanuts.

   Serve with a green salad.
Serves 4–6

Cauliflower Cheese Pots

1 medium cauliflower, divided
   into florets
1 oz (25 g) butter
1 oz (25 g) plain flour
½ teaspoon (2.5 ml) mustard
   powder
¼ pint (150 ml) milk
4 oz (100 g) Cheddar cheese,
   grated
1 teaspoon (5 ml) **Marmite**
2 sticks celery, thinly sliced
salt and pepper
2 rashers streaky bacon, grilled
   until crisp, then crumbled

Cook the cauliflower in boiling
water until just tender. Drain and
reserve ¼ pint (150 ml) of the
cooking liquid. Divide the cauliflower between 4 large individual

ovenproof dishes. Melt the butter
and work in the flour, cook for 1
minute and then gradually work in
the reserved cooking liquid and
the milk. Stir over medium heat
until the mixture boils and
thickens and then simmer for 2
minutes. Take off the heat and add
3 oz (75 g) of the cheese and the
Marmite and celery. Stir well to
melt the cheese and then season to
taste. Spoon the sauce over the
cauliflower and sprinkle with the
remaining cheese. Grill until
golden and bubbling.

   Serve at once, sprinkled with the
crumbled bacon.   **Serves 4**

Cheese, Egg and Potato Balls

1 packet (5–6 servings) instant
   mashed potato
2 Red **Oxo** Cubes, crumbled
   and dissolved in 1 pint
   (600 ml) hot water
½ oz (15 g) butter *or* margarine
4 oz (100 g) Cheddar cheese,
   grated
1 small onion, peeled and
   grated
4 eggs, hard-boiled and
   chopped
salt and pepper
1 egg, beaten
golden breadcrumbs to coat
deep fat *or* oil for frying

Make up the potato as directed on
the packet, using the Oxo stock
instead of water. Add the butter,
cheese, onion, hard-boiled eggs
and seasoning, and mix well.
Using floured hands, shape into
8 balls. Dip into the beaten egg,
then coat completely in the breadcrumbs. Deep fry in hot fat or oil
until golden brown and crisp.
Drain well.   **Makes 8 balls**

Egg Croustades

½ stale large white loaf
deep fat or oil for frying

8 eggs
a little milk
1 Red **Oxo** Cube, crumbled
2 oz (50 g) butter
bacon rolls to garnish (optional)

Cut four 1 in (2.5 cm) thick slices
of white bread into 3 × 3½ in
(8 × 9 cm) oblongs and hollow out
the centres using a 2½ in (7 cm)
plain cutter. Fry these croustades
in deep fat or oil until crisp and
lightly browned. Keep warm. Beat
together the eggs, milk and Oxo
cube. Melt the butter in a saucepan
and scramble the egg mixture in
the usual way.

   To serve, spoon the scrambled
eggs into the croustades and garnish with bacon rolls, if liked.
Serves 4

Stuffed Chinese Omelette

2 tablespoons (30 ml) cooking
   oil
1 oz (25 g) button mushrooms,
   washed and sliced
1 medium onion, peeled and
   finely sliced
1 spring onion, topped, tailed
   and sliced
3 oz (75 g) prawns
2 oz (50 g) beansprouts
2 eggs
1 Red **Oxo** Cube, crumbled
salt and pepper

Heat the oil and lightly fry the
mushrooms, onion, spring onion,
prawns and bean shoots together.
Turn the mixture into a basin and
keep warm. Lightly beat the eggs
with the Oxo cube and seasoning,
pour into the pan and make an
omelette. Turn the omelette out on
to a warm plate, tip the filling into
the omelette and roll up tightly.
Serve immediately.

Serves 1–2

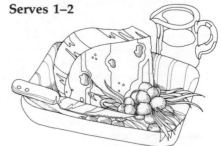

French Omelette (Omelette Savoyarde)

1 medium potato, peeled and
 finely diced
butter *or* margarine for frying
Primula Cheese Spread
2–3 eggs, beaten
salt and pepper

Fry the diced potato in a frying pan
in a little butter or margarine until
cooked through and beginning to
brown. Cut the cheese spread into
very small cubes and mix with the
beaten eggs. Season to taste. Pour
the eggs over the potatoes in the
pan and turn the pan, tipping it
slightly so that the liquid runs to
the edges and cooks. Serve when
the underside is beginning to
brown and the top is just set. Turn
out on to a hot plate to serve, but
do not fold over. **Serves 1**

Swiss Fondue

a little butter
1 clove garlic, peeled (optional)
¼ pint (150 ml) dry white wine
6 oz (175 g) **Primula** Cheese
 Spread
1 teaspoon (5 ml) potato flour *or*
 arrowroot, mixed with a little
 paprika pepper
1 liqueur glass kirsch
cubes of bread *or* toast to serve

Butter the sides and base of a
fireproof casserole dish and rub
with the cut clove of garlic, if liked.
Put in the wine and melt the cheese
in this, stirring over a low heat
until the cheese and wine are completely blended. Mix the potato
flour or arrowroot mixture with the
kirsch, stir into the cheese and
continue stirring until the mixture
thickens. Keep hot over a methyl-
ated spirit stove or similar heater at
the table.

 Serve with the cubes of bread or
toast, each person spearing a cube
of bread on their fork then dipping
it into the fondue to eat.

 An alternative version of fondue
may be made by substituting dry
cider for the wine, and brandy or
Calvados for the kirsch.

Salmon Soufflé Omelette

1 jar **Princes** Salmon and
 Shrimp Spread
1 stick celery
2 eggs, separated
pinch of salt
2 tablespoons (30 ml) milk
½ oz (15 g) butter
1 tablespoon (15 ml) soured
 cream
chopped chives and sliced
 tomato to garnish

Mix the spread with the chopped
celery. Add the salt and milk to the
egg yolks and mix well. Whisk the
whites until stiff and fold into the
egg yolk mixture. Melt the butter
in a 6 in (15 cm) omelette pan,
pour in the egg mixture and cook
gently until golden brown and set
underneath. Cook the top surface
under a hot grill for 2 minutes until
golden brown. Place the salmon
and shrimp mixture on half of the
omelette, fold over and pour
soured cream and chopped chives
on the top.
 Serve immediately, garnished
with parsley and tomato.
Serves 1

RY·KING

Savoury Crunch Slice

14 slices **Ry-King** Wheat, finely
 crushed
2 eggs
2 tablespoons (30 ml) oil
2 tablespoons (30 ml) water
2 oz (50 g) margarine
1 large onion, peeled and
 chopped
5 large tomatoes, each cut into
 8 pieces
3 rashers bacon, with rinds
 removed, chopped

1 small green pepper, de-
 seeded and chopped
4 oz (100 g) mushrooms,
 washed and quartered
salt and pepper
6–8 oz (150–200 g) Cheddar
 cheese, grated

Mix together the crushed Ry-King,
eggs, oil and water and press into
the base of a swiss roll tin approximately 9½ × 14 in (24 × 36 cm).
Melt the margarine, gently fry the
onion then add all the other
vegetables and fry for 5 minutes,
season to taste and spread over the
base. Top with grated cheese and
bake for 15–20 minutes at 400°F,
200°C, Gas Mark 6.

SCHWARTZ

Cheesey Basil Soufflé

2 oz (57 g) butter
2 oz (57 g) plain flour
⅓ pint (190 ml) milk
6 eggs (size 3), separated
2 teaspoons (10 ml) **Schwartz**
 Basil
2 tablespoons (30 ml) **Schwartz**
 Onion Powder
½ teaspoon (2.5 ml) **Schwartz**
 Garlic Salt
4 oz (113 g) Cheddar cheese,
 grated
8 oz (227 g) cooked ham, very
 finely chopped

Pre-heat the oven to 375°F, 190°C,
Gas Mark 5. Melt the butter in a
saucepan, stir in the flour and
blend in the milk. Allow to cool
slightly before adding the egg
yolks, basil, onion powder, garlic
salt, cheese and ham. Mix well.
Grease a 2 pint (1.2 litre) soufflé
dish. Whisk the egg whites until
stiff and carefully fold into the
saucepan mixture. Pour into the
soufflé dish and cook in the oven
for 45 minutes to 1 hour or until
well risen, golden and firm.
 Serve immediately with sauté
potatoes and vegetables as desired. Not suitable for freezing.
Serves 4–6

Nest Egg Pie

2 oz (57 g) butter
8 oz (227 g) onion, peeled and
  sliced
2 lb (910 g) mashed potatoes
8 oz (227 g) Red Leicester
  cheese, grated
2 teaspoons (10 ml) **Schwartz**
  Dill Weed
2 teaspoons (10 ml) **Schwartz**
  Grill Seasoning
4 tomatoes, sliced
4 eggs (size 3)
4 rashers bacon, de-rinded,
  halved and rolled

Melt the butter and fry the onions
until soft and just beginning to
colour. Stir into the potatoes. Add
6 oz (175 g) of the cheese, the dill
weed and Grill Seasoning. Mix
well. Grease a large, fairly shallow
ovenproof dish and place a layer of
sliced tomatoes to cover the
bottom, reserving a few slices for
garnishing the top. Cover with the
potato mixture and spread evenly.
Make 4 fairly deep, evenly spaced
hollows. Break the eggs into the
hollows. Arrange the reserved
tomato slices around the eggs and
sprinkle with the remaining
cheese, taking care not to drop any
on the eggs. Cook in a pre-heated
oven at 400°F, 200°C, Gas Mark 6
for 35–40 minutes or until the eggs
are set and the cheese is golden.
Cook the bacon rolls in the oven for
15 minutes and use to garnish the
finished dish. Not suitable for
reheating or freezing. **Serves 4**

Cheese Aigrettes

3 tablespoons (45 ml) **Spry**
  Crisp 'n Dry
¼ pint (150 ml) water
3 oz (75 g) plain flour, sieved
2 eggs, beaten
2 oz (50 g) Cheddar cheese,
  finely grated
pinch of salt
pinch of mustard
Spry Crisp 'n Dry for deep
  frying

Place the oil and water in a saucepan and bring to the boil. Remove
from the heat and add all the flour.
Beat well with a wooden spoon
until the mixture is smooth and
falls away from the side of the pan.
Allow to cool slightly. Add the
beaten eggs gradually and mix
well. Stir in the cheese and the
seasoning.

Heat the Spry Crisp 'n Dry to
360°F, 185°C. Fry teaspoons of the
mixture until puffed up, golden
and crisp—about 10 minutes.
Drain well and serve hot sprinkled
with salt. **Makes 20–24**

Bacon Baked Omelette

3 oz (75 g) butter
4 oz (100 g) **Wall's** Half
  Gammon, chopped
1 onion, peeled and thinly
  sliced
1 potato, cooked, peeled and
  sliced
2 tomatoes, skinned and
  chopped
1 green pepper, cored, de-
  seeded and chopped
3 large eggs
2 teaspoons (10 ml) cold water
pinch dried mixed herbs
salt and pepper

Melt 1 oz (25 g) of the butter in a
frying pan and fry the gammon
until it is crisp. Remove the pan
from the heat and stir in the onion,
potato, tomatoes, and green
pepper. Beat together the eggs,
water, herbs and seasoning to
taste. Add the gammon and
vegetable mixture and combine
well. Put the remaining butter in a
straight-sided 1 pint (500 ml)
ovenproof dish and melt in the
oven at 350°F, 180°C, Gas Mark 4.
Pour in the egg mixture and bake
for 25 minutes or until set and
brown. Serve hot with a crisp
green salad. **Serves 4**

Stuffed Eggs

4 eggs
3¾ oz (106 g) can **John West**
  Skippers
2 tablespoons (30 ml)
  mayonnaise
a few chives to garnish

Hard-boil the eggs. Leave to cool
and cut in half lengthwise. Scoop
out the yolks and put in a basin.
Drain the Skippers and add to the
yolks with the mayonnaise. Mash
with a fork. Fill the eggs with the
prepared filling and garnish with
chives.

Serve on a bed of lettuce.

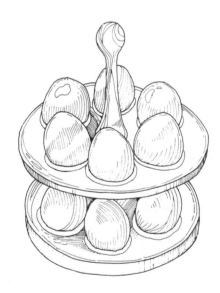

QUICHES and PIZZAS

Quiche Lorraine

Pastry

8 oz (225 g) **Allinson** 100% Wholewheat Flour
4 oz (100 g) vegetable margarine
1 teaspoon (5 ml) sea salt
approximately 8 teaspoons (40 ml) cold water

Filling

2 eggs (size 2), beaten
½ pint (300 ml) milk
2 oz (50 g) hard cheese, grated
2 oz (50 g) of one of the following, or a mixture: cooked, chopped bacon; chopped green pepper; cooked sweetcorn; chopped mushrooms; chopped onions; sliced tomatoes; cooked spinach
sea salt and pepper

Make the pastry, using the method described in the Harvest Pie recipe on p.143. Roll out thinly and use to line an 8 in (20 cm) flan tin.

Mix the eggs, milk, cheese, choice of filling and seasoning. Pour into the prepared pastry case and bake in a pre-heated oven (350°F, 180°C, Gas Mark 4) for 30–40 minutes. Serve hot or cold.
Serves 6

Salmon Flan

shortcrust pastry
7½ oz (213 g) **Armour** Red *or* Pink Salmon
2 eggs, beaten

¼ pint (142 ml) single cream
salt and pepper
grated cheese

Line a 7 in (18 cm) flan tin with shortcrust pastry and fill with a mixture made of the salmon, beaten eggs, single cream and seasoning to taste. Top with the grated cheese and bake for 35–40 minutes at 350°F, 175°C, Gas Mark 5.

Serve hot or cold.　　**Serves 4**

Prawn Quiche 'Rajah'

8 oz (225 g) shortcrust pastry
1 lb (450 g) prawns, peeled
1 can **Baxters** Medium Curry Sauce
4 tablespoons (60 ml) single cream
3 eggs
1 egg yolk
1 oz (25 g) Cheddar cheese, grated

Line a 9 in (23 cm) flan tin with the pastry and spread the prawns evenly over the base. Pour the curry sauce into a bowl and add the cream, eggs, and egg yolk. Beat together. Pour this mixture over the prawns and scatter with the cheese. Bake for 30–40 minutes in a pre-heated oven at 400°F, 200°C, Gas Mark 6 until golden brown and well set. Serve hot or cold with a well dressed green salad.
Serves 6

Chesswood Quiche

Shortcrust pastry made with
　4 oz (100 g) plain flour
2 cans **Chesswood** Sliced Mushrooms in Creamed Sauce

4 oz (100 g) cooked ham, chopped
½ oz (15 g) grated cheese
1 tomato, sliced

Preheat oven to 400°F, 200°C, Gas Mark 6. Line a 7 in (18 cm) flan ring with pastry. Bake 'blind' for 15–20 minutes. Remove the greaseproof paper, etc, and return the pastry case to the oven for 3–5 minutes. Empty the Sliced Mushrooms in Creamed Sauce in a saucepan with the cooked ham, heat through and pour into the baked flan case. Sprinkle grated cheese round the edge and place 3 slices of tomato in the centre. Return to the oven for a further 5 minutes.　**Serves 4**

Mushroom and Cheese Pizza

6 oz (150 g) self-raising flour
pinch of salt
1 oz (25 g) margarine
4 fl oz (100 ml) milk

Topping

1 can **Chesswood** Sliced Mushrooms in Creamed Sauce
8 oz (250 g) tomatoes, skinned and roughly chopped
1 small onion, peeled, chopped and lightly fried
2 teaspoons (10 ml) mixed herbs
3 oz (75 g) Cheddar cheese, grated

Sieve the flour and salt into a bowl, rub in the margarine and bind with the milk to make a soft dough. Heat the Sliced Mushrooms in Creamed Sauce, tomatoes, onion and mixed herbs together in a saucepan. Roll out the dough to a 10 in (26 cm) round, spread with the topping to within ½ in (1 cm) of the edge and sprinkle the grated cheese on top. Bake for 30 minutes at 400°F, 200°C, Gas Mark 6.
Serves 4

Pizza Napoli

½ oz (15 g) fresh yeast
a little lukewarm water
8 oz (225 g) plain flour
Topping
1 small jar **Cirio** Condi Cirio
8 oz (225 g) can **Cirio** Peeled
  Tomatoes, drained and
  chopped
a little garlic, finely sliced
4–5 anchovy fillets
a little marjoram
salt

Dissolve the yeast in the water and pour on to the flour. Knead well until firm and not too moist, cover with a cloth and leave to rise for approximately 2 hours in a dry, warm place. When the dough is well risen, roll out lightly into a round approximately ¼ in (0.5 cm) thick and press with the palm of the hand on to a greased tin.

Pour the Condi Cirio on to the dough and spread evenly with a spoon. Arrange the tomatoes and anchovy fillets on top with the garlic. Sprinkle with a little marjoram and a pinch of salt. Bake in a very hot oven (475°F, 240°C, Gas Mark 9) for about 10 minutes. Serve immediately.

Cheddar or similar cheese may be substituted for the anchovy and garlic, if preferred.   **Makes one 10–12 in (25–30 cm) pizza**

Colman's

Spinach and Mushroom Quiche

8 oz (225 g) shortcrust pastry
12 oz (350 g) packet frozen
  spinach
2 oz (50 g) butter
8 oz (225 g) mushrooms,
  washed and sliced
1 packet **Colman's** Onion Sauce
  Mix

½ pint (300 ml) cold milk
4 oz (100 g) cream cheese
chopped parsley to garnish

Roll out the pastry to line a 9 in (23 cm) flan dish. Fill with foil and beans and bake blind for 20 minutes in a pre-heated oven at 425°F, 220°C, Gas Mark 7. Remove the foil and beans and set aside. Cook the spinach, drain well and chop. Melt the butter and cook the mushrooms quickly. Make up the sauce mix as directed and beat in the cream cheese. Put the spinach and mushrooms in the flan case, pour over the sauce and bake for 15 minutes at 400°F, 200°C, Gas Mark 6, or until firm.

Sprinkle with the chopped parsley to serve.   **Serves 4**

Frying Pan Pizza

6 oz (175 g) self-raising flour
½ level teaspoon (2.5 ml) salt
½ oz (15 g) lard *or* cooking fat
1 large egg, beaten and made
  up to ¼ pint (150 ml) with
  milk
2 tablespoons (30 ml) **Crosse &
  Blackwell** Olive Oil
Topping
3 tomatoes, roughly chopped
1 small onion, peeled and
  chopped
1 rounded teaspoon (7.5 ml)
  Crosse & Blackwell Mixed
  Herbs
3 tablespoons (45 ml) **Chef**
  Tomato Ketchup
3 **Swiss Knight** Cheese
  Portions, sliced
4 black olives
4 anchovies

Sieve the flour and salt into a bowl and rub in the lard. Mix to a soft dough with the egg and milk mixture. Knead lightly on a floured board until smooth then roll out to a 7–8 in (18–20 cm) round. Heat 1 tablespoon (15 ml) of the oil in a frying pan and place the dough in the pan. Cover with a tight-fitting

lid and cook over a medium heat for 5 minutes until well risen and firm. Meanwhile, in a separate pan, fry the tomatoes and onion in the remaining oil for 3–4 minutes, stir in the herbs and tomato ketchup. Spread on top of the pizza base and cover with the sliced cheese. Remove from the heat and place under a hot grill until the cheese just melts. Decorate with the olives and anchovies and serve immediately.   **Serves 4–6**

Homepride

Tuna and Tomato Quiche

8 oz (200 g) shortcrust pastry
1 can **Homepride** Tomato &
  Onion Cook-in-Sauce
2 eggs, beaten
7 oz (198 g) can tuna, drained
parsley sprig to garnish

Line an 8 in (20 cm) flan ring or dish with the pastry. Pour the Cook-in-Sauce into a bowl and add the eggs and tuna. Mix well and pour into the flan case. Bake in a pre-heated oven for 45 minutes at 400°F, 200°C, Gas Mark 6. Garnish with the parsley sprig.

Serve with a mixed salad.
Serves 4

Cream and Leek Quiche

7½ oz (215 g) packet **Jus-rol**
  Shortcrust Pastry, thawed
2 lb (900 g) leeks
2 oz (50 g) butter
2 oz (50 g) lean cooked ham,
  diced
2 egg yolks
½ pint (300 ml) single cream
salt and pepper

Roll out the pastry and use to line an 8 in (20 cm) pie dish or tin. Chop the white part of the leeks and simmer in the butter for 5 minutes. Add the ham. Spread this mixture on the pastry. Beat together the egg yolks and cream

and season with salt and pepper.
Pour over the leeks. Bake in a pre-heated oven at 400°F, 200°C,
Gas Mark 6, for 20 minutes.
Lower the heat to 375°F, 190°C,
Gas Mark 5, for a further
20 minutes until the quiche is well
risen and golden brown.
Serves 4–6

Kellogg's

Smoked Fish Flan

1 oz (25 g) **Kellogg's** 30% Bran
  Flakes, finely crushed
5 oz (150 g) plain flour
1½ oz (40 g) butter *or*
  margarine
1½ oz (40 g) lard
water to mix
Filling
8 oz (225 g) smoked whiting *or*
  cod
5.3 oz (150 g) carton natural
  yoghurt
4 tablespoons (60 ml) milk
4 oz (113 g) carton cottage
  cheese
2 eggs, beaten
1 tablespoon (15 ml) chopped
  parsley
1 teaspoon (5 ml) lemon rind,
  finely grated
salt and pepper

Mix the 30% Bran Flakes with the
flour. Rub in the butter and lard
until the mixture resembles fine
crumbs and add enough water to
mix to a firm dough. Roll out the
pastry to line an 8 in (20 cm) flan
ring or dish and chill while pre-paring the filling.

Poach the fish in a little water for
about 10 minutes, then drain and
flake. Mix together the remaining
ingredients. Arrange the fish in
the base of the flan case and pour
the egg mixture over. Bake in a
moderately hot oven (375°F, 190°C,
Gas Mark 5) for 35–45 minutes,
until the filling has set.

Serve warm or cold, cut into
slices, and accompany with a
mixed salad.   **Serves 6**

Sharwoods'

Curried Quiche

shortcrust pastry made with
  6 oz (175 g) plain flour
½ oz (15 g) margarine
1 small onion, sliced
4 oz (100 g) streaky bacon,
  diced
4 oz (100 g) mushrooms, sliced
1 heaped teaspoon (15 ml)
  Sharwood's Vencat Curry
  Powder
3 eggs, beaten
5 oz (142 ml) carton natural
  yoghurt
1 tablespoon (15 ml)
  Sharwood's Tomato Purée
parsley sprig to garnish

Make up the pastry, use to line an
8 in (20 cm) flan ring, then bake
'blind'. Melt the margarine and
lightly fry the onion, bacon and
mushrooms. Add the curry
powder and cook for a further few
minutes. Place the mixture in the
baked flan case. Beat together the
eggs, yoghurt and tomato purée
and pour over the bacon mixture.
Bake for 25 minutes at 375°F,
190°C, Gas Mark 5, or until set.
Garnish with a sprig of parsley.
Serves 4

Beef and Bacon Pizza

Pastry
8 oz (225 g) self-raising flour
½ level teaspoon (2.5 ml) salt
2 oz (50 g) margarine
¼ pint (150 ml) milk
Topping
10 oz (283 g) can **Tyne Brand**
  Minced Beef with Onion
2 medium-sized tomatoes, cut
  into wedges
2 rashers streaky bacon, with
  rinds and bone removed
2 level tablespoons (30 ml)

thyme and parsley stuffing
  mix, dry

Combine the flour and salt in bowl
and rub in the margarine with the
fingertips. Stir in the milk and mix
to a dough. Roll out on a lightly
floured surface to a circle the size of
a dinner plate, about 10 in (25 cm).
Lift carefully on to a greased
baking sheet. Brush the edge with
water and fold over ½ in (1 cm) all
around the circumference. Pinch
together to raise the edge. Spread
the Minced Beef with Onion
evenly inside the circle and
arrange the tomatoes around the
edge. Roughly chop the bacon and
sprinkle with the stuffing mix over
the meat. Bake in an oven pre-heated to 400°F, 200°C, Gas Mark 6,
for 25 minutes. Serve hot.
Serves 4

Wall's

Cumberland Flan

7.05 oz (200 g) packet
  shortcrust pastry, thawed
2 eggs (size 3)
¼ pint (150 ml) single cream *or*
  milk
salt and pepper
7 oz (198 g) can sweetcorn
  kernels, drained
4 spring onions, trimmed and
  chopped
1 lb (454 g) packet **Richmond**
  Pork Cumberland Sausage *or*
1 lb (454 g) packet **Wall's**
  Pork Thick Sausages

Line an 8 in (20 cm) flan ring with
the pastry and leave it in a cool
place (overnight if liked) to rest.
Beat the eggs and cream or milk
together and add plenty of season-ing. Mix the sweetcorn and onions
together and place them in the
bottom of the flan case. Arrange
the Cumberland sausage on top in
a spiral or the thick pork sausages
as spokes of a wheel and very
carefully pour in the egg liquid.
Bake the flan at 375°F, 190°C, Gas
Mark 5, for 35 minutes or until well
risen and golden brown.

Serve hot with vegetables or cold
with salad.   **Serves 4**

Pan Pizza

6 oz (175 g) self-raising flour
pinch of mixed herbs
salt and pepper
4 tablespoons (60 ml) oil
cold water to mix

Topping
2 tomatoes, sliced
7½ oz (215 g) can sliced
　mushrooms in cream sauce
3 oz (85 g) packet **Wall's**
　German Style Sausage
3 oz (75 g) cheese, grated

Sift the flour and salt into a bowl, add the mixed herbs and then bind the ingredients together with 2 tablespoons (30 ml) of the oil and enough cold water to make a fairly soft mixture. Knead it lightly and roll the dough into an 8 in (20 cm) round. Heat 1 tablespoon (15 ml) of the oil in an 8 in (20 cm) frying pan, add the dough and cook it slowly until brown underneath. Carefully turn out the dough on to a plate. Heat the remaining oil and slip the pizza base back into the pan, cooked side uppermost. Arrange the tomatoes on the cooked side with the mushrooms in cream sauce over them; overlap the sausage slices on top so that the mushroom mixture is covered and scatter over the cheese. Cook the underside of the pizza for about 5 minutes more, or until brown, and then slip the frying pan under the grill to brown the cheese.
　Serve with a green salad.
Serves 3–4

Luxury Seafood Quiche

Pastry
5 oz (150 g) plain flour
pinch salt
pinch paprika
4 oz (100 g) cream cheese
2 oz (50 g) butter, softened
1 egg yolk beaten with
　2 teaspoons (10 ml) water

Filling
1 oz (25 g) butter
1 medium green pepper, de-
　seeded and sliced
2 oz (50 g) button mushrooms,
　wiped and sliced
3 eggs
¼ pint (150 ml) milk
5 oz (142 ml) carton single
　cream
salt and pepper
1 clove garlic, crushed
4.41 oz (125 g) can **John West**
　Mackerel Fillets in oil,
　drained
3.7 oz (105 g) can **John West**
　Smoked Mussels, drained
3¼ oz (92 g) can **John West**
　Prawns, rinsed and dried

To make the pastry, sift together the flour, salt and paprika, then work in the remaining ingredients to give a soft, manageable dough. Roll out on a lightly floured surface and use to line an 11 in (27 cm) oval flan dish. Prick the base and bake 'blind' for 10 minutes at 400°F, 200°C, Gas Mark 6. Mean-while, melt the butter and sauté the sliced pepper and mushrooms. Beat together the eggs, milk and cream and season to taste. Arrange the vegetables, garlic and fish in the base of the flan. Pour the egg mixture over and bake for a further 25 minutes until set.　**Serves 6**

Pissaladiere

Pastry
6 oz (150 g) plain flour
pinch of salt
1 teaspoon (5 ml) dried thyme
3 oz (75 g) mixed margarine
　and lard
approx 6 teaspoons (30 ml)
　water

Filling
2 tablespoons (30 ml) olive oil
1 lb (450 g) onions, peeled and
　sliced
14 oz (397 g) can **John West**
　Tomatoes
1 clove garlic, crushed
1 bay leaf
salt and pepper

1¾ oz (50 g) can **John West**
　Anchovy Fillets
black olives

Sift the flour and salt together, add the thyme and rub in the fats until the mixture resembles fine crumbs. Add sufficient water to mix to a soft, manageable dough then roll out on a lightly floured surface and use to line a 14 – 4½ in (35 × 11 cm) tranche flan tin. Prick the base with a fork and bake 'blind' for 20 minutes at 400°F, 200°C, Gas Mark 6. Meanwhile heat the olive oil and sauté the onions without browning. Add the tomatoes, garlic and bay leaf, then season generously with salt and pepper. Simmer until the onions are soft and no free liquid remains. Remove the bay leaf then spread the mixture over the base of the pastry case. Cut the anchovies in half lengthwise and arrange in a lattice over the filling. Cut the olives in half, removing the stones, and use to garnish the flan. Brush the surface with olive oil and return to the oven for 15 minutes. Serve hot or cold.　**Serves 4–6**

VEGETARIAN MAIN MEALS

Cheesy Courgette Bake

1 lb (450 g) courgettes, washed
  and sliced
a little vegetable oil for frying
1 tablespoon (15 ml) **Allinson**
  100% Wholewheat Flour
1 oz (25 g) vegetable margarine
1/8 pint (75 ml) milk
2 eggs, separated
4 oz (100 g) cheese, grated
1–2 tablespoons (15–30 ml)
  wholewheat breadcrumbs

Fry the courgettes gently in the
vegetable oil until tender. Make a
thick sauce by gently heating the
flour and margarine together and
then, off the heat to prevent lumps
forming, stirring in the milk
gradually. Return to the heat and
bring to the boil, stirring, until the
sauce thickens.

Whip the egg whites until stiff.
Stir the egg yolks, cheese and half
the breadcrumbs into the sauce
then fold in the stiffly whisked egg
whites. Arrange the courgettes in
the base of a 1½ pint (750 ml) ovenproof dish, pour on the sauce and
sprinkle with the remaining
breadcrumbs. Bake at 375°F,
190°C, Gas Mark 5 for 20 minutes.
Serves 4

Harvest Pie

6 oz (175 g) **Allinson** 100%
  Wholewheat Flour
3 oz (75 g) vegetable margarine
½ teaspoon (2.5 ml) sea salt
approximately 6 teaspoons
  (30 ml) cold water
1 large carrot, peeled and finely
  chopped
1 small swede, peeled and
  finely chopped
1 cooking apple, peeled and
  finely chopped

2 sticks celery, finely chopped
3 medium onions, peeled and
  finely chopped
4 oz (100 g) fresh or canned
  chestnuts, chopped

To make the pastry, mix the flour
and salt and rub in the margarine
until the mixture resembles fine
breadcrumbs. Add the water a
little at a time, mixing well, until a
stiff dough is formed. Rest the
pastry for about 15 minutes, in a
cool place or a refrigerator, before
rolling out, to make it easier to
handle.

Mix the chopped vegetables
with the apple, season well, add
the chestnuts and place the
mixture in a 1½ pint (900 ml) pie
dish.

Roll out the pastry thinly to
cover the pie dish and bake the pie
in the oven, pre-heated to 350°F,
180°C, Gas Mark 4, for 45 minutes.
Serves 4

Appleford

Boston Baked Beans

8 oz (225 g) dried haricot beans
1 onion, peeled and chopped
2 tablespoons (30 ml) oil
8 oz (227 g) can tomatoes
1 teaspoon (5 ml) salt
1 teaspoon (5 ml) dry mustard
2 teaspoons (10 ml)
  Appleford's Crude Black
  Strap Molasses
1 teaspoon (5 ml) **Appleford's**
  Muscovado Raw Brown
  Sugar
pepper

Cover the beans with plenty of
cold water and leave to soak for
several hours or overnight. Drain
and rinse the beans, put into a pan,
cover with water and simmer until
tender—about 1 hour. Drain,
reserving the liquid.

Fry the onion in the oil without
browning for 10 minutes, then add
the beans. Measure the tomatoes
and make up to ½ pint (300 ml)
with the reserved bean liquid if
necessary. Add to the beans,
together with the remaining ingredients. Bring to the boil and transfer to an ovenproof casserole, cover
and bake in a pre-heated oven
(300°F, 150°C, Gas Mark 2) for 3–4
hours, stirring from time to time. It
won't hurt the beans to be in the
oven for longer than this, but add a
little extra bean liquid if they
appear to be drying out.

Delicious served straight from
the casserole with hot garlic bread
or crusty rolls, or with jacket
potatoes and a salad. Makes a
nourishing snack served on
wholewheat toast.   **Serves 3–4**

BEANFEAST

Beanfeast Lasagne

4 oz (100 g) lasagne
salt
1 packet **Beanfeast** Bolognese
1 oz (25 g) plain flour
pinch mustard powder
½ pint (275 ml) milk
4 oz (100 g) cheese, grated

Cook the lasagne in boiling, salted
water for 10–15 minutes. Make up
the Beanfeast as directed. Place the
margarine, flour, mustard and
milk in a saucepan over a moderate
heat. Bring to the boil, whisking
continuously. Cook for 2–3
minutes then add half the cheese
and remove from the heat. Place
alternate layers of Beanfeast,
lasagne and cheese sauce in a
serving dish, ending with a layer
of sauce. Sprinkle with the
remaining cheese. Bake in a
moderately hot oven (375°F, 190°C,
Gas Mark 5) for about 25 minutes.
Serves 4

Chinese Beanfeast

1 packet **Beanfeast** Supreme
8 oz (226 g) can pineapple,
   drained
2 oz (50 g) butter
4 oz (100 g) bamboo shoots
4 oz (100 g) beansprouts
salt and pepper
1 packet crispy noodles
1 tablespoon (15 ml) soy sauce

Make up the Beanfeast as directed.
Chop the pineapple into small
pieces. Melt half the butter in a
frying pan and lightly fry the
bamboo shoots, beansprouts and
pineapple. Add to the Beanfeast
and season. Fry the crispy noodles
in the remaining butter.

Serve the Beanfeast mixture
surrounded by the noodles and
sprinkled with the soy sauce.
Serves 4

Country Cobbler

1 packet **Beanfeast** Soya Mince
   with Onion
2 tablespoons (30 ml) cooking
   oil
4 oz (125 g) button mushrooms,
   washed and halved
8 oz (225 g) self-raising flour
pinch of salt
2 oz (50 g) butter
¼ pint (150 ml) milk
a little milk to glaze

Make up the Beanfeast as directed.
Heat the oil and fry the mushrooms until tender. Add to the
cooked Beanfeast and pour into an
ovenproof dish. Sieve the flour
and salt into a bowl, rub in the
butter and mix to a soft dough with
the milk. Roll out thickly and cut
into twelve 2 in (5 cm) rounds.
Arrange the scone rounds on top of
the cooked Beanfeast, overlapping
one another slightly, brush with
milk and bake in a fairly hot oven
(375°F, 190°C, Gas Mark 5) for
about 25 minutes.   **Serves 4**

Savoury Chilli Pancakes

1 packet **Beanfeast** Mexican
   Chilli
1 large egg, separated
pinch of salt
4 oz (125 g) plain flour
½ pint (275 ml) milk
1 oz (25 g) margarine, melted
Parmesan cheese or cheese
   sauce to serve

Make up the Beanfeast as directed.
Beat the egg yolk and salt together.
Sieve the flour into a mixing bowl,
then gradually add the milk and
beat to a smooth consistency. Beat
in the egg yolk mixture and add the
melted margarine. Beat the egg
white stiffly and fold in. Fry the
pancakes and keep warm. When
all the pancakes are made, fill them
with the Beanfeast, roll up and
serve with a sprinkle of Parmesan
cheese on top, or with cheese sauce
poured over.   **Serves 4**

Stuffed Green Peppers

1 packet **Beanfeast** Paella Style
4 small green peppers
1 chicken stock cube
⅓ pint (200 ml) boiling water
2 tablespoons (30 ml) tomato
   purée

Make up the Beanfeast as directed.
Remove the tops of the peppers
and reserve. Scoop out the pith
and seeds and blanch the peppers
in boiling water for 5 minutes,
then drain. Fill the peppers with
the Beanfeast and replace the tops.
Place in an ovenproof serving
dish. Mix the stock cube with the
boiling water and the tomato
purée, pour over the peppers and
cook in a moderate oven (350°F,
180°C, Gas Mark 4) for about
45 minutes, until tender, basting
occasionally.   **Serves 4**

Mediterranean Stir Fry Flan

10 oz (283 g) packet **Birds Eye**
   Mediterranean Stir Fry
8 oz (227 g) packet **Birds Eye**
   Shortcrust Pastry, thawed
4 oz (100 g) Cheddar cheese,
   grated
2 eggs
¼ pint (125 ml) milk
2 tablespoons (30 ml) single
   cream or top of the milk
1 tablespoon (15 ml) fresh
   parsley, chopped
salt and pepper

Roll out the pastry and line an 8 in
(20 cm) flan ring. Bake blind by
lining the pastry case with foil.
Remove the foil when pastry case
is cooked. Cook the Stir Fry
according to pack instructions,
arrange in the pre-baked flan case
and cover with the cheese. Lightly
whisk the eggs with the milk and
cream, add the chopped parsley
and season to taste. Spoon the
mixture over the flan filling and
bake in the centre of a pre-heated
oven at 400°F, 200°C, Gas Mark 4
and bake for a further 10 minutes,
until the filling is set and the pastry
crisp and golden brown.
Serves 4–6

Special Continental Pancakes

4 oz (100 g) plain flour
pinch salt
1 egg
½ pint (250 ml) milk
1 tablespoon (15 ml) melted
   butter
mixed herbs
10 oz (283 g) packet **Birds Eye**
   Continental Stir Fry
2 oz (50 g) cheese, grated
chopped parsley to garnish

To make the pancakes, sift the
flour and salt together and beat to a
smooth batter with the egg, half
the milk and the melted butter. Stir
in the remaining milk. Add a
pinch of mixed herbs. Use to make
about 8 pancakes. Cook the Stir
Fry according to the pack instructions. Spoon the Stir Fry vegetables over half the pancake and
fold. Place in an ovenproof dish·
and sprinkle with cheese. Place
under a hot grill and cook until
golden brown and bubbling.
Garnish with chopped parsley.
Serves 4

Cheese and Yoghurt Moussaka

1 lb (500 g) aubergines, sliced, sprinkled with salt and left for 30 minutes
¼ pint (125 ml) oil
1 large onion, peeled and sliced
1 clove garlic, crushed
1 green pepper, de-seeded and sliced
1 lb (500 g) tomatoes, skinned and chopped
1 can **Chesswood** Button Mushrooms, drained
8 oz (200 g) Mozzarella cheese, sliced
2 tablespoons (30 ml) flour
4 eggs, beaten
5 fl oz (142 g) carton natural yoghurt
3 oz (75 g) Cheddar cheese, grated

Wash the aubergines in cold water and pat dry with kitchen paper. Heat 2 tablespoons (30 ml) oil in a frying pan and fry the aubergine slices on both sides, adding more oil as necessary. Fry the onion, garlic and green pepper until soft. Mix together the flour, eggs, yoghurt and Cheddar cheese. Put half the aubergines in the bottom of a large, greased ovenproof dish then add half the onion and pepper mixture, half the tomatoes and half the mushrooms. Cover with the Mozzarella cheese then repeat the layers in reverse order, ending with the aubergines. Pour the yoghurt mixture over the top and bake for 30 minutes until golden brown at 400°F, 200°C, Gas Mark 6.
Serves 4

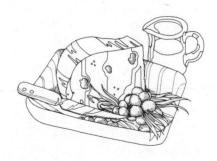

Vegetable Pie

1 can **Chesswood** Small Whole Mushrooms, drained
1 lb (500 g) tomatoes, skinned, quartered and diced
1 leek, cleaned and sliced
1 onion, peeled and finely chopped
salt and pepper
1 tablespoon (15 ml) Worcestershire sauce
pinch mixed dried herbs
6 oz (150 g) shortcrust pastry
beaten egg to glaze

Arrange the vegetables in layers in a pie dish and cover with the pastry. Make vents to allow steam to escape and decorate with pastry 'leaves'. Glaze with the beaten egg. Bake for 30–35 minutes at 375°F, 190°C, Gas Mark 5.
Serves 4

Cirio Vegetables au Gratin

1½ lb (675 g) leeks, well washed and cut into rings
1 head of celery, chopped
1 cauliflower, separated into florets
14 oz (396 g) **Cirio** Peeled Tomatoes
4 oz (100 g) cheese, grated: any stale cheese will do, but the addition of a little Parmesan will give more flavour
1 oz (25 g) fresh breadcrumbs

Poach the leeks and celery in the minimum of salted water for 10 minutes. The celery should remain crisp to add to the interest of the dish. Drain and place in a shallow, ovenproof dish. Cook the cauliflower in salted water until tender, drain and spread over the leeks and celery. Top with the contents of the can of tomatoes and cover with the grated cheese and breadcrumbs. Bake in a hot oven (400°F, 200°C, Gas Mark 6) for 15 minutes or place the dish under a

medium hot grill until the cheese bubbles and browns slightly.
Serve for supper with toast or hot rolls. The recipe may be varied by laying rashers of streaky bacon on top before grilling or baking.
Serves 4–6

Soufflé Piperade

2 tablespoons (30 ml) pure vegetable *or* olive oil
1 large onion, peeled and finely sliced
2 green peppers, de-seeded and cut into thin strips
1 clove garlic, minced
14 oz (396 g) **Cirio** Tomatoes, drained
1 teaspoon (5 ml) salt
pepper
5 eggs, separated
¼ teaspoon cream of tartar
a little marjoram *or* oregano

Heat the oil in a large, non-stick frying pan over medium heat, add the onion and green peppers and cook for 5 minutes, stirring occasionally. Add the garlic, tomatoes, salt and pepper. Continue to cook for about 15 minutes, until the vegetables are tender. Well butter an ovenproof platter or casserole dish and arrange the cooked vegetables around the edge. Heat the oven to 350°F, 180°C, Gas Mark 4. Whip the egg whites until foamy, add the cream of tartar and continue beating until the mixture is stiff but not dry. Beat the egg yolks with salt until mixed smooth, fold gently into the beaten whites and spoon the egg mixture into the centre of the dish. Smooth the surface and sprinkle with a little marjoram or oregano. Bake in the centre of the oven for 20 minutes and serve immediately.
Serves 4

Tomato Slice

8 oz (225 g) flaky pastry
6 oz (175 g) Cheddar cheese, grated
2 eggs, beaten
3 oz (75 g) fine white breadcrumbs
2 teaspoons (10 ml) mixed herbs
salt and black pepper
14 oz (396 g) can **Cirio** Peeled Tomatoes
1 medium onion, peeled and sliced into rings
a little oil for frying
1 medium red pepper, de-seeded and sliced into rings about ¼ in (0.5 cm) thick
2 teaspoons (10 ml) Parmesan cheese, grated
a little cornflour
Worcestershire sauce (optional)

Roll out half the pastry into an oblong approximately 4 × 10 in (10 × 25 cm). Place on a greased baking tray. Mix the Cheddar cheese with the beaten eggs, breadcrumbs, herbs and salt and pepper. Spread the mixture on to the pastry, leaving a border of ½ in (1 cm) all round. Drain the tomatoes, reserving the juice, and roughly chop. Place on top of the cheese mixture and sprinkle lightly with salt. Fry the onion gently in a little oil until softened but not brown, drain and place on top of the tomatoes. Roll out the remaining pastry, dampen the edges and place on top of the pastry on the tray. Bake in a pre-heated oven for 10 minutes at 450°F, 230°C, Gas Mark 8, then reduce the heat to 400°F, 200°C, Gas Mark 6 for a further 15 minutes, or until the pastry is a light golden brown. Place the pepper rings on top of the cooked pastry slice, sprinkle with the Parmesan cheese and put under the grill until just brown.

Thicken the tomato juice with the cornflour and season to taste, adding Worcestershire sauce if liked. Hand the sauce separately to serve. **Serves 4**

Colman's

Vegetable Flan

8 oz (225 g) shortcrust pastry
1 packet **Colman's** Parsley Sauce Mix
½ pint (300 ml) milk
12 oz (350 g) packet frozen spinach
4 leeks, cut into ¼ in (0.5 cm) rounds
2 oz (50 g) butter
4 tomatoes, sliced

Roll out the pastry to fit a 9 in (23 cm) flan dish. Fill with foil and beans and bake blind for 20 minutes in a pre-heated oven at 425°F, 220°C, Gas Mark 7, then remove foil and beans. Make up the sauce mix as directed. Cook the spinach, drain well and chop. Soften the leeks in the butter. Arrange the spinach in the base of the baked flan case, cover with the leeks and pour over the sauce. Top with the tomatoes and bake at 350°F, 180°C, Gas Mark 4, for 25 minutes. **Serves 4**

Aubergine and Chick Pea Bake

6 oz (175 g) **Granose** Chick Peas
cooking oil
1 lb (450 g) aubergines, peeled and cut into 1 in (2.5 cm) cubes
1 lb (450 g) onions, peeled and cut into thick slices
1 lb (450 g) tomatoes, skinned and chopped
salt and pepper to taste

Soak the chick peas overnight. Cook until tender in plenty of boiling water then drain. Heat the oil in a heavy frying pan and fry the aubergines until they are golden brown on all sides, then drain. Fry the onions until just turning brown. Place the auber-gines, chick peas and onions in a large casserole, add the tomatoes and heat through in a moderate oven.

Lentil Patties

1 cup **Granose** Brown Lentils, cooked and mashed
⅓ cup walnuts, finely ground
½ cup dry breadcrumbs
3 eggs, beaten
3 tablespoons (45 ml) celery, finely chopped
3 tablespoons (45 ml) onion, peeled and grated
oil for frying

Mix the ingredients thoroughly, drop by tablespoonfuls into an oiled frying pan and brown on both sides. Serve with any gravy.

Note: a breakfast cup or mug is a suitable measure for this recipe. **Makes 6–8 patties**

Spring Savoury Cakes

cooked, mashed potato to serve 4
a little chopped spring onion
2 eggs, hard-boiled and chopped
2 oz (50 g) cheese, grated
salt and pepper
beaten egg
dried parsley and thyme stuffing mix
10½ oz (297 g) can **Heinz** Cream of Tomato Soup
Worcestershire sauce to taste

Mix the mashed potato with the spring onion, eggs, cheese and seasoning. Shape into flat cakes, dip in the beaten egg and coat in the parsley and thyme stuffing mix. Fry on both sides until golden. Meanwhile, sharpen the soup with a dash of Worcestershire sauce to taste and heat. Serve the potato cakes with the soup as a sauce. **Serves 4**

ITONA

Cottage Pie

2 onions, peeled and chopped
2 tablespoons (30 ml) cooking oil
4 oz (100 g) dry weight **Itona** TVP Beef Flavoured Mince, reconstituted as directed on packet
3 tablespoons (45 ml) flour
1 tablespoon (15 ml) tomato paste
¾ pint (450 ml) water
salt and pepper to taste
1½ lb (675 g) potatoes, peeled, cooked and mashed
1 oz (25 g) cheese, grated

Fry the onions gently in the oil until transparent. Add the reconstituted TVP mixed with the flour and tomato paste and gently mix in the water. Season and bring slowly to the boil, stirring. Allow to simmer for 3 minutes. Pour the mixture into a warmed ovenproof dish, cover with the prepared mashed potato, sprinkle the grated cheese on top and bake or grill until lightly browned.

This recipe may be varied by adding sliced, cooked carrots to the TVP, with 2 teaspoons (10 ml) Yeasty or Marmite, or Worcestershire sauce. **Serves 4**

Kellogg's

Baked Onion Parcels

4 large onions, peeled and left whole
8 oz (227 g) packet frozen chopped spinach, thawed
1 oz (25 g) **Kellogg's** All-Bran or Bran Buds
2 eggs, hard-boiled and chopped
salt
8 oz (227 g) packet shortcrust pastry mix
milk to glaze

Cook the onions in boiling water for 10 minutes. Drain and cool. Scoop out the centres with a small spoon and save for another recipe. To make the stuffing, mix the spinach, All-Bran, eggs and salt together. Use to fill the onions.

Make up the pastry mix according to packet instructions and roll out into four 6 in (15 cm) squares. Place an onion in the centre of each pastry square, moisten the edges and bring the four corners to the top of the onion, sealing all edges well. Place on a baking tray. Brush the onion parcels with a little milk and bake in a moderate oven at 350°F, 180°C, Gas Mark 4 for 45 minutes. Serve hot. **Serves 4**

Cheese and Vegetable Medley

4 oz (100 g) bag **Kellogg's** Boil-in-the-bag Rice
8 oz (227 g) packet frozen mixed vegetables
3 eggs, hard-boiled
4 oz (100 g) Cheddar cheese, grated
2 tomatoes, sliced

Cook the rice according to packet instructions. Drain well. Cook the vegetables according to packet instructions then drain and mix with the rice. Turn half the rice mixture into a well-buttered 2 pint (1 litre) flameproof dish. Slice the eggs and arrange over the rice, then cover with the remaining rice. Sprinkle over the cheese and top with the sliced tomatoes. Place under a pre-heated grill until the cheese has melted and the tomatoes are cooked. **Serves 4**

Lentil Rissoles with Tomato Sauce

4 oz (100 g) lentils, soaked overnight
1 onion, peeled and finely chopped
1 oz (25 g) **Kellogg's** All-Bran or Bran Buds
2 oz (50 g) fresh white breadcrumbs
1 tablespoon (15 ml) tomato purée
salt and pepper
1 teaspoon (5 ml) dried sage
1 egg, beaten
beaten egg to coat
dried breadcrumbs to coat
oil to deep fry

Sauce
1 onion, peeled and finely chopped
2 tablespoons (30 ml) oil
½ oz (15 g) plain flour
½ pint (300 ml) stock
8 oz (227 g) can peeled tomatoes
1 tablespoon (15 ml) tomato ketchup
salt and pepper

Cook the lentils in water to cover for about 30–40 minutes, or until tender. Drain, Mix the lentils, onion, All-Bran, breadcrumbs, tomato purée, seasoning, sage and egg together. Leave to stand for 30 minutes. Shape the mixture into 8 balls, dip each in beaten egg and coat in breadcrumbs.

To make the sauce, lightly fry the onion in the oil until tender. Stir in the flour and cook for 1 minute. Remove from the heat and blend in the stock and tomatoes. Return to the heat and bring to the boil, stirring. Add the tomato ketchup and seasoning to taste. Place the sauce in a liquidiser and blend until smooth. Return to the pan and reheat.

Fry the rissoles in deep, hot oil for 5 minutes. Drain on kitchen paper and serve with tomato sauce. **Serves 4**

LEA & PERRINS

Savoury Stuffed Onions with Cheese Sauce

4 large onions, carefully peeled and left whole

Stuffing

2 large tomatoes, skinned, de-seeded and chopped
2 oz (50 g) Cheddar cheese, finely grated
2½ oz (65 g) fresh brown breadcrumbs
1 oz (25 g) walnuts, chopped
2 teaspoons (10 ml) **Lea & Perrins** Worcestershire Sauce

Sauce

½ oz (15 g) butter
1 teaspoon (5 ml) **Lea & Perrins** Worcestershire Sauce
½ oz (15 g) flour
½ pint (250 ml) milk
3 oz (75 g) Cheddar cheese, finely grated
salt and pepper

Place the onions in boiling, salted water and cook for 30 minutes. Cut off tops and bottoms of the onions and push out the centres, leaving a large cavity in each for the stuffing. Stand the onions on a greased ovenproof plate or shallow dish. Chop the onion centres and divide in two.

For the stuffing, mix all the ingredients together including half the chopped onion. Season well. Fill the centres of the onions with the stuffing. Bake at 375°F, 190°C, Gas Mark 5, for 30 minutes.

For the sauce, heat the butter in a pan, add the Worcestershire sauce and the remaining chopped onion. Fry gently for 5 minutes. Stir in the flour and cook for a further minute. Remove from the heat and gradually add the milk, stirring continuously. Return to the heat and stir until the sauce thickens. Add the cheese, stirring until the cheese melts. Season to taste. Serve the sauce with the stuffed onions.   **Serves 4**

McVitie's Digestive Nut Rissoles

2 oz (50 g) margarine
2 oz (50 g) plain flour
½ pint (300 ml) water
1 teaspoon (5 ml) salt
freshly ground black pepper
1 tablespoon (15 ml) fresh chives, chopped
½ tablespoon (7.5 ml) fresh marjoram
1 teaspoon (5 ml) yeast extract
2 oz (50 g) brazil nuts, chopped
6 oz (175 g) **McVitie's** Digestive Biscuits, crushed
1 egg, beaten
oil for frying

Melt the margarine in a saucepan, stir in the flour and cook for a few minutes. Blend in the water, continue cooking until the mixture begins to thicken, remove from the heat and stir in the salt, pepper, chives, marjoram, yeast extract, nuts and 3 oz (75 g) of the biscuits. Cool and then thoroughly chill the mixture. When chilled, shape the mixture into 8 rissoles. Dip the rissoles into the beaten egg and then into the remaining biscuit crumbs. Heat a little oil in a frying pan and fry the rissoles gently until golden brown on both sides. Serve immediately.   **Makes 8**

Lentil and Savormix Rissoles

4 oz (100 g) split red lentils, washed and soaked overnight in 1½ pint (900 ml) water
3 onions, peeled and chopped
a little oil for frying
4 oz (100 g) **Savormix**
4 oz (100 g) fresh breadcrumbs
2 eggs
salt

pinch each marjoram and thyme
¼ pint (150 ml) water
2 tablespoons (30 ml) milk
deep *or* shallow oil for frying

Cook the lentils in the water in which they soaked overnight, until quite soft. Fry the onions gently in oil until soft and mix with the lentils, Savormix, 3 oz (75 g) of the breadcrumbs, 1 egg, beaten, salt, herbs and water. Leave to stand for 30 minutes. Beat the remaining egg with the milk, dip the rissoles into this and coat with the rest of the breadcrumbs. Fry in plenty of oil in a frying pan or deep fry.   **Serves 4**

Quick Cheese Pudding

3 tablespoons (45 ml) flour
6 oz (175 g) cheese, grated
2 oz (50 g) **Savormix**
⅛ pint (75 ml) water
½ pint (300 ml) milk
3 eggs
salt and pepper

Mix the flour with the cheese. Mix the Savormix with the water and add to the flour and cheese. Add the milk slowly then add the eggs one at a time, and season. Pour into a greased pie dish and cook for 30–40 minutes at 400°F, 200°C, Gas Mark 6.   **Serves 4**

Swiss Savoury Loaf

4 oz (100 g) nuts
4 oz (100 g) **Savormix**, mixed with ¼ pint (150 ml) water
2 oz (50 g) cheese, grated
1 cooking apple, peeled and chopped
4 oz (100 g) mushrooms, washed and chopped (optional)
2 eggs, beaten

Roast the nuts at 300°F, 150°C, Gas Mark 2, for about 30 minutes, then grate and add to the Savormix with the grated cheese, apple and mushrooms if used. Bind with the beaten eggs, pour into a well greased 1 lb (500 g) loaf tin and bake at 350°F, 180°C, Gas Mark 4, for about 1 hour.   **Serves 4**

Baked Marmite Potatoes

4 medium potatoes, scrubbed
   and scored round to prevent
   splitting
1 teaspoon (5 ml) **Marmite**
salt and pepper
2 oz (50 g) butter
2 oz (50 g) cheese, grated
chopped parsley to garnish

Bake the potatoes in the oven for
about 2½–3 hours at 350°F, 180°C,
Gas Mark 4. When cooked, cut the
potatoes in half, scoop out the
centres and put into a basin. Mix
with the Marmite, seasoning,
butter and about 1½ oz (40 g) of
the cheese. Replace the mixture in
the skins, sprinkle with the
remaining cheese and put under a
hot grill until the cheese melts and
bubbles.

   Garnish with the chopped
parsley.   **Serves 2–4**

Cadbury's Marvel

Brazilian Ring

8 oz (200 g) Brazil nuts, finely
   chopped
6 medium tomatoes, peeled
   and roughly chopped
2 oz (50 g) dry **Marvel**
   dissolved in 3 tablespoons
   (45 ml) water
4 oz (125 g) brown bread-
   crumbs
2 tablespoons (30 ml)
   wholewheat flour
2 tablespoons (30 ml) rolled
   oats
2 teaspoons (10 ml) dried sweet
   basil
1 teaspoon (5 ml) dried thyme
1 teaspoon (5 ml) salt
¼ pint (125 ml) tomato juice
dried breadcrumbs
Sauce
2 oz (50 g) margarine
2 oz (50 g) plain flour

1½ pint (800 ml) liquid **Marvel**
6 oz (150 g) cheese, grated
salt and pepper
a few whole Brazil nuts to
   garnish

Combine all the ingredients for the
nut ring together in a large bowl
and mix well together. Taste and
adjust the seasoning then pack the
mixture into a 2 pint (1 litre) ring
mould, greased and coated with
the dried breadcrumbs. Bake at
375°F, 190°C, Gas Mark 5, for about
50 minutes. Test with a skewer: it
should be firm and coming slightly
away from the edge when cooked.

   Meanwhile, make the sauce by
whisking all the ingredients,
except the cheese and Brazil nuts,
over a gently heat until boiling and
thickened. Add the cheese (off the
heat) and season well. Turn the nut
ring on to a hot plate and pour the
sauce over, garnishing with the
whole nuts.

   This nut ring is delicious served
with cooked broccoli and carrots
filling the centre, and covered with
the sauce. Extra vegetables and the
remaining sauce are served
separately.   **Serves 8–10**

Country Flan

Pastry
8 oz (250 g) wholewheat flour
1 teaspoon (5 ml) dried mixed
   herbs
pinch salt
4 oz (125 g) hard margarine
Filling
1 onion, peeled and chopped
1 green pepper, de-seeded and
   chopped
8 oz (225 g) courgettes, washed
   and sliced
4 oz (100 g) mushrooms, wiped
   and sliced
1 oz (25 g) margarine
1 oz (25 g) flour
½ pint (275 ml) liquid **Marvel**
salt and pepper
4 oz (100 g) Red Leicester
   cheese, grated

Sift the flour, salt and herbs into a
bowl and rub in the margarine.
Add just enough water to make a

firm dough. Wrap the dough in
cling-film or foil and chill for
30 minutes. When chilled, roll out
and use to line a 9 in (23 cm) flan
dish or tin. Bake blind, lined with
greaseproof paper and dried
beans, at 375°F, 190°C, Gas Mark 5,
for 15 minutes then remove the
beans and paper and continue
cooking for a further 15 minutes.
While the pastry case is cooking,
soften the prepared vegetables in
the margarine over a gentle heat,
blend in the flour then the Marvel
and stir until the mixture thickens;
season to taste. Remove from the
heat, add half the cheese and pour
the filling into the flan case.
Sprinkle the remaining cheese
over the top. Bake for a further 15
minutes at the same temperature.
Serve hot or cold.   **Serves 6–8**

RY·KING

Baked Savoury Tomatoes

6 good sized ripe tomatoes
3 slices **Ry-King** Brown Rye,
   crushed
3 oz (75 g) cheese, grated
½ teaspoon (2.5 ml) basil *or*
   marjoram
salt and pepper

Cut the tops off the tomatoes and
carefully scoop out the pulp. Mix
the crushed Brown Rye with the
tomato pulp and grated cheese,
add herbs and season to taste. Pile
the cheese mixture back into the
tomatoes, allowing it to stand
'proud' of the top, replace the
tomato lids at an angle and stand
the tomatoes in a shallow, ovenproof dish. Bake for 15–20 minutes
in a pre-heated oven at 350°F,
180°C, Gas Mark 4.

   These are ideal for high tea or
supper or as a side vegetable.
Serves 6

SCHWARTZ

Savoury Leek and Rosemary Flan

1 oz (28 g) margarine
2 oz (57 g) lard
6 oz (170 g) plain flour
1 teaspoon (5 ml) **Schwartz** Seasoning Salt
1½ teaspoons (7.5 ml) **Schwartz** Rosemary
cold water for mixing
Filling
8 oz (227 g) leeks, trimmed, washed and cut into approx 2 in (5 cm) pieces
1 oz (28 g) margarine
1 oz (28 g) plain flour
½ pint (285 ml) milk
4 oz (113 g) mushrooms, wiped and sliced
½ teaspoon (2.5 ml) **Schwartz** Rosemary
1 teaspoon (5 ml) **Schwartz** Seasoning Salt
¼ teaspoon **Schwartz** Ground White Pepper
4 oz (113 g) Cheddar cheese, grated
3 hard-boiled eggs (size 3)
1 large tomato, sliced, to garnish

Rub the margarine and lard into the flour, stir in the seasoning salt, rosemary and enough cold water to form a soft dough. Roll the pastry out on a floured surface and use to line a greased 8 in (20 cm) flan dish. Place a round of greased greaseproof paper slightly larger then the pastry case inside the pastry, greased side down. Half fill with uncooked dried beans or rice. Place in the oven pre-heated to 400°F, 200°C, Gas Mark 6, and cook for 15 minutes or until the pastry is set. Remove the baking beans and paper, return to the oven and cook for a further 10 minutes until the pastry is crisp.

Meanwhile, to make the filling, cook the leeks in boiling, salted water for 10 minutes and drain carefully, keeping the pieces intact. Pat dry with a paper kitchen towel. Meanwhile, melt the margarine in a saucepan and stir in the flour followed by the milk, mushrooms, rosemary, seasoning salt and pepper. Bring to the boil, stirring, add the cheese and cook over a low heat until melted. Do not overcook or the cheese will become stringy and tough. Reserve 6 pieces of leek for garnish and gently stir the remainder into the sauce. Slice the hard-boiled eggs and arrange them in the base of the pastry case. Pour over the sauce and decorate, using the remaining leeks and the tomato slices. Serve hot or cold.

Not suitable for freezing, but may be stored in a refrigerator for up to 2 days.   **Serves 4–6**

Sharwood's

Ratatouille with Eggs

14 oz (400 g) can **Sharwood's** Ratatouille
3 eggs
oil for frying
chopped parsley to garnish

Heat the ratatouille in a saucepan. Shallow fry the eggs in the hot oil. Serve the eggs on top of the ratatouille, sprinkle with the parsley.

Alternatively, place the ratatouille in an ovenproof dish, make 3 dips and break an egg into each. Bake in the oven for 15–20 minutes at 350°F, 180°C, Gas Mark 4, or until the egg whites have set.

Serve with bread croûtons.
Serves 3

Stuffed Aubergines

2 aubergines
1 tablespoon (15 ml) oil
1 medium onion, peeled and sliced
2 cloves garlic, crushed
1 heaped teaspoon (15 ml) **Sharwood's** Vencat Curry Powder
1 teaspoon (5 ml) **Sharwood's** Garam Masala Curry Spices
1 large potato, peeled, diced and par-boiled
1 large carrot, peeled, diced and par-boiled
2 tomatoes, skinned and chopped
4 oz (125 g) frozen peas
salt and freshly ground black pepper
¼ pint (100 ml) stock

Cut the aubergines in half lengthwise. Slash the flesh, lightly sprinkle the cut side with salt and put aside. Heat the oil in a pan and cook the onion and garlic gently until soft. Add the curry powder and garam masala and continue cooking for a few minutes. Add the par-boiled vegetables to the onion mixture together with the tomatoes and peas. Remove the flesh carefully from the aubergines and chop the flesh roughly. Add to the other vegetables in the pan. Add the stock and cook gently for 10 minutes. Cook the aubergine skins in boiling, salted water for 5 minutes. Drain well. Fill them with the vegetable mixture and bake for 20 minutes at 350°F, 180°C, Gas Mark 4.   **Serves 4**

Aubergine and Tomato Pie

Sauce
14 oz (396 g) can tomatoes
1 small onion, peeled and finely chopped
1 carrot, peeled and finely chopped
1 stick celery, finely chopped
salt and pepper
½ level teaspoon (2.5 ml) sugar
pinch oregano
pinch basil
approximately ¼ pint (150 ml) **Spry** Crisp 'n Dry
1 lb (450 g) aubergines, thinly sliced and tossed in seasoned flour

8 oz (225 g) Bel Paese *or* Edam
cheese, thinly sliced
1 oz (25 g) Parmesan cheese,
grated
Spry Crisp 'n Dry for shallow
frying

Place all the sauce ingredients in a
saucepan and simmer gently for
15–20 minutes. Cool and purée or
sieve.

In a large frying pan heat sufficient oil to cover the base of the
pan. Gently fry the aubergines,
adding more oil if required. When
the aubergines are golden brown
drain well on kitchen paper. Pour
2 tablespoons (30 ml) Crisp 'n Dry
into a deep, ovenproof dish and
layer the aubergines, sliced cheese
and tomato sauce, finishing with
the sauce. Sprinkle with the
Parmesan cheese and bake in the
middle of a pre-heated oven at
375°F, 190°C, Gas Mark 5, for 25–30
minutes. **Serves 4–6**

Stork

Irish Potato Bake

1½ lb (675 g) potatoes, peeled
and sliced
8 oz (225 g) onions, peeled and
sliced
4 oz (100 g) Irish Cheddar
cheese, grated
2 oz (50 g) **Stork** Margarine,
melted
salt and black pepper

Arrange the vegetables and cheese
in layers in a casserole dish,
reserving a little cheese for the top.
Begin and finish with potato.
Season each layer and pour over
the melted margarine. Cover and
bake in a moderate oven at 350°F,
180°C, Gas Mark 4, for 45–50
minutes, or until the vegetables
are tender. Sprinkle the remaining
cheese over the top and brown
under a hot grill for a few minutes.
Serves 4

TREX

Onion and Cheese Potato Cakes

8 tablespoons (120 ml) **Trex**
Pure Vegetable Oil for
shallow frying
8 oz (225 g) onions, finely
chopped
1½ lb (680 g) potatoes, boiled
and mashed
2 oz (50 g) cheese, grated
salt and pepper

Heat 2 tablespoons (30 ml) of the
Trex and fry the onions without
browning for 3 minutes. Add the
onions to the mashed potato with
the grated cheese and salt and
pepper. Form into round cakes.
Heat the remaining Trex and fry
the cakes until golden brown on
both sides. **Serves 4**

whitworths

Country Nut Rissoles

4 oz (125 g) split red lentils
1 large onion, peeled and
chopped
1 tablespoon (15 ml) oil for
frying
4 oz (125 g) blanched almonds,
chopped
1 egg
2 (3 oz, 75 g) sachets
Whitworths Country Stuffing
Mix
salt and pepper
beaten egg

Pre-heat oven to 400°F, 200°C,
Gas Mark 6. Place the lentils in a
medium saucepan and add
1¾ pint (1 litre) water. Bring to
the boil, cover and simmer for
20–25 minutes or until tender.
Drain. Heat the oil in a frying pan.
Add the onion and cook gently
until transparent. Mix the lentils,
onion, almonds, egg, 1 sachet of
the stuffing mix and the seasoning
together to form a firm dough.

Shape into rissoles on a lightly
floured board. Dip the rissoles in
the beaten egg and finally in the
remaining stuffing mix. Place in a
heat-proof dish and bake for 25–30
minutes until lightly brown.
Serve hot with a home-made
tomato sauce. **Serves 4**

Stuffed Peppers

½ oz (15 g) butter
1 small onion, peeled and
chopped
4 oz (125 g) **Whitworths** Brown
Rice
½ teaspoon (2.5 ml) dried
mixed herbs
½ pint (300 ml) chicken stock
3 oz (75 g) Gouda cheese,
grated
2 oz (50 g) sweetcorn
2 large tomatoes, chopped
2 oz (50 g) salted peanuts,
roughly chopped
salt and freshly ground black
pepper
4 green peppers
4 oz (125 g) Gouda cheese,
grated and 2 tomatoes,
sliced, to garnish

Melt the butter over a moderate
heat and fry the onion, stirring
occasionally, for 3–4 minutes until
soft and transparent. Stir in the
rice and cook for a further 5
minutes. Add the herbs and stock
and bring to the boil. Cover tightly
and cook until tender. Stir in the
cheese, sweetcorn, tomatoes, peanuts and seasoning.

With the point of a sharp knife,
cut the tops off the peppers.
Remove the seeds and discard.
Blanch the shells in boiling water
for 5 minutes. Drain well then
place in an ovenproof dish. Heat
the grill.

Divide the rice mixture between
the pepper shells. Sprinkle on half
the cheese, cover with the tomato
slices and sprinkle with the
remaining cheese. Place under the
grill and cook until the cheese has
melted and browned. Serve
immediately. **Serves 4**

VEGETABLES

Lyonnaise Beans

2 oz (50 g) butter
1 large onion, peeled and finely chopped
1 tablespoon (15 ml) parsley, finely chopped
salt and pepper
15 oz (425 g) can **Batchelors** Butter Beans

Melt the butter in a saucepan, add the onion and parsley and season to taste. Cook gently until the onions are soft but not browned. Heat the Butter Beans in the normal way, drain, toss in the onion mixture and serve.

Blue Band

Cauliflower Polonais

1 cauliflower
2 oz (50 g) **Blue Band** Margarine
2 oz (50 g) breadcrumbs
2 eggs, hard-boiled
1 tablespoon (15 ml) parsley, chopped
2 tablespoons (30 ml) Worcestershire sauce

Cook the cauliflower in boiling, salted water until just tender, and drain. Melt the margarine in a small pan and fry the breadcrumbs until golden. Sieve the hard-boiled eggs and mix with the breadcrumbs and parsley. Place the cauliflower in an ovenproof dish, scatter the egg and breadcrumb mixture over the top and pour over the Worcestershire sauce. Bake near the top of the oven at 350°F, 180°C, Gas Mark 4, for 10 minutes.
 Serve on its own or with meat dishes. **Serves 4**

 **BULMER**

Potato Casserole

2 lb (900 g) potatoes, peeled and cut into thin slices
1 medium onion, peeled and chopped
4 oz (100 g) cheese, grated
salt and pepper
½ pint (300 ml) **Bulmers** Strongbow cider

Arrange alternate layers of potato, onion and cheese in a casserole dish (saving a little cheese to sprinkle on top). Season each layer, ending with the potatoes on the top. Pour in the cider, cover and cook for 45 minutes at 400°F, 200°C, Gas Mark 6, or until the potatoes are cooked. Remove the lid, sprinkle with the reserved cheese and replace in the oven until golden brown on top.
 Serve with hot or cold meats, or on its own as a nourishing light meal. **Serves 4**

Campbelled Cabbage

4 oz (100 g) streaky bacon rashers
½ oz (15 g) butter
4 oz (100 g) leeks, thoroughly cleaned and sliced into rings
 or 4 oz (100 g) onions, peeled and sliced
1½ lb (675 g) cabbage, cleaned and shredded
10½ oz (297 g) can **Campbell's** Condensed Stock Pot Soup, undiluted
5 oz (142 g) carton soured cream
salt and pepper

Cut the rinds and any small bones from the bacon and chop into pieces. Melt the butter in a large pan, add the leeks or onions with the bacon and cook over a low heat until tender but not coloured. Stir in the cabbage with the undiluted soup plus ⅓ soup canful of water and the soured cream, bring to the boil, then reduce the heat and simmer uncovered for about 10 minutes, or until the cabbage is tender. Check the seasoning.
Serves 4

Chesswood

Cauliflower Crisp

1 cauliflower, broken into sprigs
4 oz (100 g) bacon, chopped
½ oz (15 g) butter
1 can **Chesswood** Sliced Mushrooms in Creamed Sauce
¼ pint (125 ml) milk
2 oz (50 g) cheese, grated
2 tablespoons (30 ml) browned breadcrumbs
parsley sprigs to garnish

Cook the cauliflower until just tender. Meanwhile, fry the bacon in the butter in a saucepan, add the Sliced Mushrooms in Creamed Sauce with the milk and heat through. Place the cauliflower in an ovenproof dish, pour over the mushroom and bacon mixture, sprinkle with the cheese and breadcrumbs and brown under a hot grill. Garnish with parsley sprigs. **Serves 2–3**

Mushroom and Potato Bake

4 medium potatoes, peeled and sliced
1 can **Chesswood** Button Mushrooms, drained
salt and pepper

3 tablespoons (45 ml) flour
1 oz (25 g) butter
5 fl oz (150 ml) milk

Place a layer of potato in a buttered, ovenproof dish and sprinkle with salt and pepper. Dredge with the flour and dot with the butter. Add half the mushrooms. Repeat the layers of potato and mushrooms, finishing with a layer of potato, and pour the milk over. Bake for 1¼ hours at 375°F, 190°C, Gas Mark 5, until the potato is soft and the top is browned.   **Serves 4**

Ratatouille

1 medium aubergine
salt
2 tablespoons (30 ml) **Crosse & Blackwell** Olive Oil
1 clove garlic, peeled and finely chopped
1 medium onion, peeled and sliced
1 green pepper, de-seeded and sliced
2 courgettes, sliced
3 tomatoes, peeled and sliced
½ level teaspoon (2.5 ml) **Crosse & Blackwell** Dried Thyme
½ level teaspoon (2.5 ml) **Crosse & Blackwell** Dried Parsley
pepper

Thinly slice the aubergine and place in a colander. Sprinkle liberally with salt and set aside for about 30 minutes. Rinse and dry thoroughly. Heat the oil in a large, heavy-based saucepan and fry the onion gently until transparent but not browned. Add the remaining ingredients and simmer very gently for 35–40 minutes or until the vegetables are soft. Take care not to cook too quickly as this will cause the vegetables to break up. Season to taste.

Serve hot or cold with French bread as a starter, or hot as a vegetable with main meal dishes.   **Serves 4–6**

Broccoli with Lemon Sauce

1 oz (25 g) butter
1 oz (25 g) flour
½ pint (250 ml) chicken stock
2 egg yolks
2 tablespoons (30 ml) lemon juice
salt and pepper
1 packet **Findus** Broccoli Spears

Melt the butter in a small saucepan, add the flour and cook gently for 2–3 minutes. Gradually add the stock and bring to the boil, stirring occasionally. Allow to cool slightly before stirring in the egg yolks and lemon juice. Season to taste. Serve poured over the broccoli, cooked according to directions.
Serves 4

Cauliflower Niçoise

10½ oz (300 g) packet **Findus** Cauliflower Fleurettes
1 small onion, peeled and finely sliced
7 oz (200 g) firm tomatoes, skinned, halved and de-seeded
1 oz (25 g) butter
1 small clove garlic, crushed (optional)
salt and pepper
1 tablespoon (15 ml) parsley, chopped

Cook the cauliflower as directed on the packet and drain well. Melt the butter and fry the onion and garlic, if used, until soft. Lightly stir in the roughly chopped tomato. Heat through and season to taste. Arrange the cauliflower in a serving dish and top with the tomato mixture and the parsley.
Serves 3–4

Crispy Green Beans

1 packet **Findus** Haricots Verts, cooked as directed
1 small onion, peeled and chopped

1 oz (25 g) butter
1 oz (25 g) flaked almonds
1 tablespoon (15 ml) water
1 tablespoon (15 ml) lemon juice
salt and pepper

Cut the beans into 2 in (5 cm) pieces. Fry the onion and almonds in the butter. Add the water, lemon juice, seasoning and beans and heat very gently for 2–3 minutes.   **Serves 3–4**

Italian Style Beans

8 oz (227 g) packet **Findus** Haricots Verts
2 oz (50 g) streaky bacon, chopped
2 large tomatoes, skinned and chopped
½ oz (15 g) butter
salt and pepper

Cook the beans according to the pack directions. Meanwhile, fry the bacon and tomatoes in the butter for a few minutes. Drain the beans, add the bacon and tomatoes and toss lightly together. Season to taste before serving.
Serves 2–3

Creamed Green Beans

1 lb (450 g) French *or* runner beans
2 oz (50 g) mushrooms, washed and sliced
1 oz (25 g) **Kerrygold** Butter
¼ pint (125 ml) **Kerrygold** Double Cream, frozen *or* thawed

Top and tail the beans, removing any stringy sides. Slice diagonally into thin strips. Cook in boiling, salted water for about 8–10 minutes. Meanwhile fry the mushrooms in the butter and keep warm. Drain the beans and return to the pan with the mushrooms and pan juices. Add the cream and reheat gently. Mix well and serve at once.   **Serves 4**

Murphy's Potatoes

2 lb (1 kg) potatoes, peeled and
    finely diced
1 large onion, peeled and finely
    diced
1 oz (25 g) flour
3 tablespoons (45 ml) parsley,
    chopped
salt and freshly ground black
    pepper
¼ pint (125 ml) **Kerrygold**
    Double Cream
¼ pint (125 ml) hot milk
1 oz (25 g) **Kerrygold** Cheddar
    Cheese, grated

Place the potatoes and onion in a
bowl and mix thoroughly with the
flour, parsley, salt and pepper.
Pour the hot milk on to the double
cream and mix well to blend.
Spread the potato mixture in a
large, ovenproof dish and pour
over the milk and cream. Sprinkle
with the cheese and bake in a hot
oven (400°F, 200°C, Gas Mark 6),
for about 1 hour or until the
potatoes are cooked.

The cream can be used either
thawed or frozen. If still frozen,
warm it gently with the not milk
until thawed.

Serves 4–6

Knorr

Curried Potato Casserole

2 tablespoons (30 ml) oil
1 onion, peeled and chopped
2 teaspoons (10 ml) curry
    powder
1 oz (25 g) cornflour
2 tablespoons (30 ml) tomato
    purée
¾ pint (375 ml) **Knorr** chicken
    stock
1 lb (400 g) potatoes, peeled,
    parboiled and sliced

Heat the oil in a frying pan and
lightly fry the onion for 2–3
minutes until soft and transparent.
Add the curry powder, cornflour,
tomato purée and stock and bring
to the boil, stirring from time to
time. Place the potatoes in a

casserole, cover with the sauce and
bake at 350°F, 180°C, Gas Mark 4,
for 30 minutes.

Serve with hot or cold meat and
fresh vegetables.   **Serves 4**

Mixed Vegetable Casserole

8 oz (200 g) courgettes, washed
    and thickly sliced
8 oz (200 g) tomatoes, skinned
    and sliced
3 oz (75 g) onion, peeled and
    thinly sliced
3 oz (75 g) carrots, peeled and
    thinly sliced
2 oz (50 g) button mushrooms,
    washed and sliced
2 teaspoons (10 ml) fresh
    parsley, chopped
¼ pint (125 ml) **Knorr** chicken
    or beef stock
1 clove garlic, crushed
    (optional)
salt and pepper
2 oz (50 g) Cheddar cheese,
    grated (optional)

Layer all the ingredients except the
cheese in an ovenproof casserole
dish. Season well and pour over
the stock. Cover and cook at 400°F,
200°C, Gas Mark 6, for about
1 hour, depending on the thickness of the vegetables.

Serve with hot or cold meat.
Alternatively, uncover the dish
when cooked, sprinkle with the
grated cheese and brown under
the grill.   **Serves 4**

LEA & PERRINS

Spicy Red Cabbage

2 oz (50 g) butter
4 oz (100 g) onions, peeled and
    sliced
1 lb (450 g) red cabbage,
    shredded
8 oz (225 g) cooking apples,
    peeled and sliced
2 oz (50 g) brown sugar
⅛ pint (75 ml) vinegar

2 tablespoons (30 ml) **Lea &
Perrins** Worcestershire Sauce

Melt the butter and fry the onions,
then add the red cabbage and
apples. Cover and cook gently for
20 minutes. Sprinkle in the sugar,
add the vinegar and Worcestershire sauce. Cover and cook slowly
for a further 10 minutes.
Serves 6

Stir-Fried Cabbage

1 oz (25 g) butter
2 tablespoons (30 ml) oil
1 lb (450 g) white cabbage,
    finely shredded
2 teaspoons (10 ml) **Lea &
Perrins** Worcestershire Sauce
1 teaspoon (5 ml) lemon juice
salt and freshly ground black
    pepper

Heat the butter and oil in a large
saucepan. Add the cabbage and
gently fry, stirring, for about
5 minutes until the cabbage has
softened. Add the remaining
ingredients and fry over a high
heat, stirring, until the cabbage
begins to turn crisp and brown
around the edges. Serve immediately.   **Serves 4**

Worcestershire Glazed Vegetables

1 lb (500 g) carrots, parsnips *or*
    new potatoes
1½ oz (40 g) butter
1 tablespoon (15 ml) demerara
    sugar
2 teaspoons (10 ml) **Lea &
Perrins** Worcestershire Sauce
salt and pepper

Cook the vegetables in boiling
water until just tender. Drain and
return to the pan with the remaining ingredients. Continue to
cook, carefully turning the vegetables, until the sugar has melted
and the vegetables are evenly
coated, about 3–4 minutes.
Serves 4

Savoury Stuffed Tomatoes

4 large tomatoes
2 oz (50 g) fresh white breadcrumbs
1 small onion, peeled and finely grated
2 teaspoons (10 ml) parsley, chopped
1 teaspoon (5 ml) **Marmite**
1 tablespoon (15 ml) hot water
salt and pepper
½ oz (15 g) butter

Cut the tops from the tomatoes and keep on one side. Scoop out the flesh and roughly chop. Turn the tomatoes upside down on kitchen paper to drain. Mix together the tomato pulp, breadcrumbs, onion, parsley, Marmite, hot water, salt and pepper. Stuff the tomatoes with the mixture and top with flakes of butter. Replace the tomato 'lids'. Put into a shallow, ovenproof dish and grill under medium heat for 10 minutes.

Serve with cheese or cold meat. **Serves 4**

Outline

Carrot and Cucumber Vichy

1 large cucumber
8 oz (225 g) new carrots
½ oz (15 g) **Outline** Low Fat Spread
pinch of sugar
large pinch of salt
1 dessertspoon (10 ml) chopped parsley
pepper

Peel the cucumber, cut in half lengthwise, then cut across in ½ in (1.25 cm) slices. Blanch in boiling salted water for 1 minute, drain, refresh and set aside. Peel and quarter the carrots and put in a

pan with Outline, sugar, salt and enough water to cover. Cook until tender (about 10 minutes) with the lid on. Take the lid off the pan, continue cooking until the water has evaporated; add the prepared cucumber and parsley. Season with pepper. Toss the vegetables carefully until coated with the glaze. **Serves 4**

Gratin de Crecy

2 lb (1 kg) potatoes
1 lb (450 g) carrots
2 onions, peeled and sliced
2 oz (50 g) **Outline** Low Fat Spread
salt and pepper
1 pint (600 ml) natural low fat yoghurt

Peel, slice and parboil the potatoes for 10 minutes. Slice the carrots and cook with the onions in a little salted water for about 20 minutes, until the carrots are tender. Grease the gratin dish with Outline and in it put a layer of potatoes. Place some of the carrot and onion mixture on top and dot this with Outline. Season and continue the layers until the vegetables are used up. Finish with a layer of potatoes. Pour the yoghurt over the top. Bake at 325°F, 160°C, Gas Mark 3 for 2 hours. **Serves 6**

PRIMULA®

Spinach and Cheese

1 can spinach purée
a little butter
Primula Cheese Spread to taste

Stir the butter into the spinach purée and add cheese spread to taste, stirring over a low heat until well mixed and the mixture is creamy.

Spinach prepared this way makes an excellent base for poached eggs or white fish as a substantial supper or light lunch dish.

Sharwoods

Vegetable Chow-Mein

3 tablespoons (45 ml) oil
2–3 cloves garlic, crushed
8 oz (200 g) carrots, cut into julienne strips
1 green pepper, de-seeded and cut into julienne strips
8 oz (200 g) button mushrooms, sliced
¼ cucumber, cut into julienne strips
1 teaspoon (5 ml) salt
3 tablespoons (45 ml) **Sharwood's** Green Label Mango Chutney
2 pieces **Sharwood's** Stem Ginger, sliced
8 oz (200 g) folded vermicelli

Heat the oil in a large frying pan or wok and gently cook the garlic, carrots, pepper, mushrooms, cucumber and salt for 5–10 minutes, tossing continuously. Stir in the chutney and ginger. Cook the vermicelli in rapidly boiling, salted water for 4–5 minutes. Drain and add to the vegetables. Serve immediately. **Serves 4 as a side dish**

Sweet Potatoes

1½ lb (675 g) potatoes, peeled, cooked and mashed
2 oz (50 g) butter
1 level teaspoon (5 ml) nutmeg
salt and pepper to taste
10½ oz (297 g) can **John West** Mandarin Oranges

Mix all the ingredients together. Divide the mixture into small balls and flatten with a fork. Bake on a well-greased baking tray at 325°F, 160°C, Gas Mark 3, for 15 minutes, then turn the potato cakes over and continue cooking until they are golden brown. **Serves 4**

SALADS

Corned Beef and Salad Platter

12 oz (340 g) can **Armour** Corned Beef, cut into 16 slices
lettuce leaves
watercress sprigs to garnish

Vegetable Herb Salad
8 oz (227 g) frozen *or* 15½ oz (439 g) can mixed vegetables, drained
1 tablespoon (15 ml) vinaigrette dressing
¼ teaspoon (1.25 ml) mixed herbs
salt and pepper

Cook the frozen vegetables and drain well. Mix the vegetables with the vinaigrette and herbs and season to taste.

Butter Bean Salad
15½ oz (439 g) can butter beans, well drained
2 tablespoons (30 ml) vinaigrette dressing
good pinch dry mustard
4 spring onions, chopped
1 oz (25 g) Caerphilly cheese, chopped
salt and pepper

Mix the mustard into the vinaigrette and add the other ingredients, with seasoning to taste.

Rice Salad
4 oz (100 g) long grain rice, cooked
2 sticks celery, chopped
½ oz (15 g) raisins
1 oz (25 g) salted peanuts, roughly chopped

2 tablespoons (30 ml) vinaigrette dressing
salt and pepper

Mix all the ingredients together, with seasoning to taste.

Red Cabbage Pickle
about 8 oz (225 g) pickled red cabbage
8 small pickled onions

Mix both together.

Tossed Tomatoes
4 large tomatoes, skinned and halved
2 tablespoons (30 ml) vinaigrette dressing
2 tablespoons (30 ml) parsley, freshly chopped

Put the tomatoes in a dish and spoon the vinaigrette over them several times during a 30 minutes period. Serve sprinkled with the parsley.

To serve the salads, lay the lettuce leaves half way round a large platter and arrange the corned beef slices on them. Put the tomatoes, flat side down, around the corned beef, with the other salads in front. Garnish with the watercress. **Serves 8**

Bean and Onion Salad

1 medium onion, peeled and sliced
2 ripe tomatoes, peeled
15 oz (425 g) can **Batchelors** Red Kidney Beans, drained
1 stick celery, chopped
1 dessertspoon (10 ml) parsley, chopped
salt and pepper
French dressing, made with 2 tablespoons (30 ml) olive

oil, 4 tablespoons (60 ml) vinegar and seasoning

Simmer the onion in salted water until just tender. Cut the tomatoes in half, remove the seeds and slice each half into four. Put the beans into a bowl with the onion, tomatoes, celery, parsley and seasoning. Moisten well with the French dressing and mix well.

Serve with cold meat or as a starter. **Serves 4**

Chicken and Tuna Salad Veronique

6 oz (170 g) **Buitoni** Pasta Shells
6 oz (170 g) cold cooked chicken, shredded
7 oz (198 g) can tuna, drained and flaked
8 oz (225 g) green grapes, halved and de-seeded
3–4 tablespoons (45–60 ml) thick mayonnaise
2 tablespoons (30 ml) soured cream (optional)
salt and pepper
6 tablespoons (90 ml) French dressing
shredded lettuce and sliced tomato to garnish

Cook the pasta shells as directed on the packet. Combine the chicken, tuna and nearly all the grapes in a basin with the mayonnaise and soured cream. Season to taste with salt and pepper. Drain the pasta and toss in the French dressing. Arrange the pasta around the edge of the dish alternating with the lettuce. Pile the chicken and tuna mixture in the centre and scatter over the remaining grapes. Garnish with the sliced tomato. **Serves 4–6**

BURGESS

Continental Salad

½ medium cucumber, diced
1 lb (450 g) potatoes, peeled, cooked and diced
2 green peppers, de-seeded and thinly sliced
8 rounded tablespoons (160 ml) **Burgess** Sauce Tartare
1 clove garlic
lettuce
watercress
chopped chives *or* parsley to garnish

Mix the cucumber, potatoes and green pepper with the Sauce Tartare. Cut the clove of garlic and rub around the serving bowl, line with lettuce and watercress, pile the salad in the centre and sprinkle with the chives or parsley.

Potato Salad

1 lb (450 g) potatoes, peeled and cooked
5 rounded tablespoons (100 ml) mayonnaise *or* salad cream
2 rounded teaspoons (15 ml) **Burgess** Creamed Horseradish
salt
lettuce
finely chopped parsley to garnish

Dice the potatoes or cut into slices. Thoroughly mix together the mayonnaise and Creamed Horseradish, add salt to taste, then lightly fold in the potatoes. Serve on a bed of lettuce and sprinkle with finely chopped parsley.

For cold potato salad, chill well before serving; but for a change try hot potato salad which is popular on the Continent, simply by using hot potatoes with this recipe.
Serves 4

Egg and Mushroom Italienne

6 oz (150 g) pasta wheels
1 green pepper, de-seeded and thinly sliced
3 eggs, hard-boiled and quartered
1 can **Chesswood** Small Whole Mushrooms, drained
1 can red kidney beans, drained
3–4 tablespoons (45–60 ml) mayonnaise
paprika pepper and chopped parsley to garnish

Cook the pasta according to instructions on the packet and refresh with cold water. Combine all the ingredients together. Sprinkle with a little paprika and garnish with chopped parsley.

Serve as a starter or a salad accompaniment for cold meats.
Serves 6

Colman's

Cold Curried Chicken with Pineapple

1 packet **Colman's** Curry Sauce Mix
½ pint (300 ml) water
12 oz (350 g) cold cooked chicken
8 oz (227 g) can pineapple cubes, drained
4 oz (110 g) green, seedless grapes
1 green apple, chopped
4 tablespoons (60 ml) thick mayonnaise
1 teaspoon (5 ml) lemon juice
1 lettuce
2 oz (50 g) flaked almonds, toasted
lemon wedges to garnish

Make up the sauce mix as directed and allow to cool. Cut the chicken into bite-sized pieces and place in a mixing bowl. Add the pineapple cubes, grapes and apple tossed with the lemon juice and fold in the sauce and mayonnaise.

Place on a bed of lettuce and sprinkle with the toasted almonds. Garnish with lemon wedges.
Serves 4

FRANK COOPER

Fish Salad

7 oz (200 g) can mackerel, drained and flaked
1 dessert apple, cored and diced
1 medium potato, boiled, peeled and diced
4 oz (100 g) frozen peas, cooked
2 sticks celery, chopped
4 tablespoons (60 ml) **Frank Cooper's** Tartare Sauce
lettuce

Mix together all the ingredients. Chill before serving on a bed of lettuce. Canned salmon or tuna may be used in place of the mackerel.   **Serves 4**

Devilled Cauliflower Salad

1 small cauliflower
1 tablespoon (15 ml) **Crosse & Blackwell** Mango Chutney
juice of ½ lemon
2 teaspoons (10 ml) **Crosse & Blackwell** Olive Oil
1 level teaspoon (5 ml) curry powder

Break the cauliflower into sprigs and boil in salted water until just tender. Drain well. Sieve or finely chop the Mango Chutney and mix with the lemon juice, oil and curry powder to make a thick dressing. Toss the cauliflower sprigs in the dressing just before serving.
Serves 3–4

Mandarin Salad

1 packet **Crosse & Blackwell** Rice & Things, Savoury Rice & Vegetables Flavour
2 tablespoons (30 ml) French dressing
11 oz (312 g) can mandarin oranges, drained

Cook the Rice & Things according to the packet directions. Empty into a bowl, cover and chill. When cold, mix in the French dressing and add the mandarin oranges, carefully mixing them into the rice.
    Serve with cold meats.
Serves 4

Maryland Salad

4 oz (100 g) long grain rice
1 tablespoon (15 ml) oil
3 rashers streaky bacon, finely chopped
6 oz (175 g) cooked chicken, diced
7 oz (198 g) can sweetcorn, drained
3 tablespoons (45 ml) **Crosse & Blackwell** Salad Cream
1 tablespoon (15 ml) parsley, chopped
1 banana (optional)
a little lemon juice

Wash the rice and cook in salted water for the time recommended on the packet. Rinse in cold water and drain thoroughly. Heat the oil and fry the bacon until crisp. Drain well. Mix together the cold rice, bacon, chicken, sweetcorn, salad cream and parsley. Stir thoroughly to coat all the ingredients.
    Serve garnished with slices of banana dipped in a little lemon juice to prevent browning.
Serves 4

Pasta Salad

3 oz (75 g) pasta shells
5 oz (142 g) can **Crosse & Blackwell** Ham and Beef Meat Roll
8–10 **Crosse & Blackwell** Stuffed Manzanilla olives
1 piece canned red pimento

3 tablespoons (45 ml) **Crosse & Blackwell** Waistline Seafood Sauce

Cook the pasta shells following the instructions on the packet. Drain well. Cut the Ham and Beef Roll and the canned pimento into matchstick strips. Carefully mix together all the ingredients just before serving.   **Serves 3–4**

Salad Niçoise

3 tablespoons (45 ml) **Crosse & Blackwell** Waistline Low Calorie Dressing
8 oz (225 g) sliced green beans, cooked
2 tomatoes, sliced
¼ cucumber, sliced
7 oz (198 g) can tuna, drained and flaked
lettuce
1 hard-boiled egg, sliced
6–8 anchovies

Mix the dressing with the green beans, tomatoes, cucumber and tuna and arrange on a serving dish. Garnish with the lettuce, slices of hard-boiled egg and anchovies.   **Serves 3–4**

Evergreen Salad

2 grapefruit
6 leaves fresh mint
2 teaspoons (10 ml) lemon juice
2 tablespoons (30 ml) Dry **Dubonnet**
2 tablespoons (30 ml) salad oil
1 lettuce

Peel the grapefruit, removing all the white pith, then cut into segments. Collect any juice and put it into a screw-topped jar with the chopped mint, lemon juice, Dubonnet, oil, salt and ground pepper. Shake hard until it becomes cloudy. Wash and shred the lettuce. Mix with the grapefruit and toss in the dressing.
Serves 4

Sunshine Salad

6 oz (150 g) packet **Findus** Sweetcorn, cooked
4 oz (100 g) mushrooms, washed and sliced
2 teaspoons (10 ml) chives *or* spring onions, chopped
1 dessertspoon (10 ml) vinaigrette dressing (¼ vinegar, ¾ oil with salt, pepper and herbs to taste)

Combine all ingredients in a bowl and chill.   **Serves 4–6**

Bean Salad

8 oz (225 g) **Granose** Red Kidney Beans
8 oz (225 g) **Granose** White Beans (Small Lima *or* Haricot)
4 oz (100 g) **Granose** Chick Peas
1 red pepper, de-seeded and chopped
1 small onion, peeled and chopped *or* 3 spring onions
1 clove garlic (optional)
2 tablespoons (30 ml) fresh chives, chopped
2 tablespoons (30 ml) white vinegar
1 tablespoon (15 ml) lemon juice
6 tablespoons (90 ml) olive oil
½ teaspoon (2.5 ml) salt

Soak the beans overnight, place in a large saucepan and bring to the boil over a moderately high heat. Boil steadily for 10 minutes then cover the pan and simmer for 30–40 minutes, or until the beans are tender. Drain and allow to cool. In a large salad bowl combine the beans, red pepper, onion, garlic and chives. In a small bowl combine the vinegar, lemon juice, oil and salt and mix well. Add to the bean mixture and stir well. Chill in the refrigerator for 30 minutes before serving.

Curried Potatoes

10 oz (283 g) can **Hartleys** New
  Potatoes
1 red-skinned eating apple
2 oz (50 g) sultanas
3 tablespoons (45 ml)
  mayonnaise
1 dessertspoon (10 ml) curry
  powder
1 dessertspoon (10 ml) lemon
  juice
1 dessertspoon (10 ml) mango
  or tomato chutney

Drain the liquid from the potatoes.
Slice the potatoes and cut the apple
into small chunks. Mix the potatoes, apple and sultanas together.
Combine all the remaining ingredients and stir into the potato
mixture.

Chicken Rice Salad

8 oz (225 g) cooked chicken or
  turkey
4 oz (100 g) cooked rice
4 **Haywards** Pickled Walnuts,
  chopped
8 **Haywards** Silverskin Onions
2 large tomatoes, with seeds
  removed, diced
4 **Haywards** Gherkins, sliced
2 oz (50 g) sultanas
2 oz (50 g) button mushrooms,
  wiped and sliced
2 tablespoons (30 ml) French
  dressing

Dice the chicken or turkey and mix
with the other ingredients in a
large bowl. Toss in the French
dressing and chill before serving.
Serves 4

Caravan Salad

15¼ oz (432 g) can **Heinz**
  Potato Salad
Cheshire or Wensleydale
  cheese, diced
hard-boiled eggs, chopped
celery, chopped
tomatoes, chopped
nuts, chopped
lemon juice
salt and pepper
shredded lettuce to serve

Mix together the potato salad with
the cheese, hard-boiled eggs,
vegetables and nuts. Season with
the lemon juice, salt and pepper.
Arrange the lettuce around the
edge of a serving dish and place
the salad in the centre.   **Serves 4**

HELLMANN'S

American Rice Salad

8 oz (200 g) brown rice
4 oz (100 g) peanuts
2 oz (50 g) raisins
1 apple, cored and diced
3 sticks celery, chopped
6 fl oz (150 ml) **Hellmann's**
  Real Mayonnaise

Cook the rice in boiling, salted
water for 30 minutes until tender,
drain and leave to cool. Mix
together the rice, peanuts, raisins,
apple and celery. Stir in the
mayonnaise and chill before
serving.
Serves 4 as a main course salad

Chicken and Almond Salad

6 oz (150 g) long grain rice
6 oz (150 g) cooked chicken,
  diced
2 oz (50 g) almonds, flaked
2 oranges, peeled and chopped
1 teaspoon (5 ml) lemon juice
6 fl oz (150 ml) **Hellmann's**
  Real Mayonnaise

black pepper

Cook the rice in boiling, salted
water for 20 minutes until tender,
drain and rinse in cold water. Mix
together the rice, chicken,
almonds, oranges and lemon juice.
Stir in the mayonnaise. Season to
taste and chill before serving.
Serves 4 as a main course salad

Chicory and Clementine Salad

1 head chicory
1 small carrot, peeled and
  grated
2 clementines or satsumas,
  peeled and segmented
1 tablespoon (15 ml)
  Hellmann's Real Mayonnaise

Arrange the chicory leaves in the
base of a serving dish. Mix
together the carrot and clementines or satsumas and stir in the
mayonnaise. Place the mixture on
top of the chicory leaves and chill
before serving.
Serves 4 as a side salad

Indian Salad

6 oz (150 g) long grain rice
1–2 level tablespoons (15–
  30 ml) curry powder
1 apple, cored and diced
6 oz (150 g) cooked chicken,
  cubed
2 teaspoons (10 ml) lemon juice
2 oz (50 g) sultanas
1 tablespoon (15 ml) mango
  chutney
5 fl oz (125 ml) **Hellmann's**
  Real Mayonnaise
1 fresh peach or a few fresh
  apricots, chopped (optional)
salt and pepper

Cook the rice in boiling, salted
water, to which the curry powder
has been added, until tender.
Drain and rinse in cold water. Mix
together the apple, cooked
chicken, lemon juice, sultanas and
chutney. Stir in the rice, mayonnaise and fresh peach or apricots.
Season to taste, and chill before
serving.
Serves 4 as a main course salad

Leicester Salad

4 oz (100 g) white grapes
4 oz (100 g) Red Leicester
  cheese, cubed
2 oz (50 g) walnuts, roughly
  chopped
12 oz (375 g) white cabbage,
  shredded
4 small tomatoes, quartered
5 fl oz (125 ml) **Hellmann's**
  Real Mayonnaise

Wash the grapes, cut in half and
remove the pips. Mix together the
grapes, Red Leicester, walnuts,
white cabbage and tomatoes. Stir
in the mayonnaise and chill before
serving.
Serves 4 as a main course salad

Pepper Potato Salad

1 lb (400 g) new potatoes,
  peeled
1 small red pepper, de-seeded
  and finely chopped
½ teaspoon (2.5 ml) chilli
  powder
¼ teaspoon paprika pepper
3 tablespoons (45 ml)
  Hellmann's Real Mayonnaise

Cook the potatoes in boiling,
salted water until just tender,
drain and when cool cut into dice.
Add the pepper, chilli powder and
paprika and stir in the
mayonnaise. Chill before serving.
Serves 4 as a side salad

Pork and Mushroom Salad

6 oz (150 g) pasta hoops
4 oz (100 g) small button
  mushrooms, lightly fried
6 oz (150 g) cooked pork, cubed
1 apple, cored and diced
10 black olives, stoned
6 fl oz (150 ml) **Hellmann's**
  Real Mayonnaise
salt and pepper

Cook the pasta hoops in boiling,
salted water for 12–14 minutes
until tender, drain and rinse in
cold water. Mix together the
mushrooms, pork, apple and

olives. Stir in the pasta hoops and
mayonnaise, and season to taste.
Chill before serving.
Serves 4 as a main course salad

Special Chinese Prawns

6 oz (175 g) beansprouts
8 oz (200 g) can water
  chestnuts, drained and sliced
½ pint (250 ml) fresh prawns,
  shelled *or* 4 oz (100 g) frozen
  prawns, thawed
2 oz (50 g) button mushrooms,
  washed and sliced
2 tablespoons (30 ml)
  Hellmann's Real Mayonnaise
salt and pepper

Mix together the beansprouts,
water chestnuts, prawns and
mushrooms. Stir in the mayonnaise and season to taste. Chill
before serving.   **Serves 4**

Waldorf Salad

1 medium eating apple, cored
  and chopped
2 sticks celery, chopped
2 oz (50 g) walnuts, roughly
  chopped
3 tablespoons (45 ml)
  Hellmann's Real Mayonnaise
lettuce

Mix together the apple, celery and
walnuts. Stir in the mayonnaise
and chill before serving on a bed of
lettuce.
Serves 4 as a side salad

Kellogg's

Tuna and Prawn Salad

4 oz (100 g) bag **Kellogg's** Boil-
  in-the-bag Rice
7 oz (198 g) can tuna, drained
4 oz (100 g) peeled prawns
½ small cucumber
4 tablespoons (60 ml)
  mayonnaise
¼ teaspoon Tabasco sauce
juice of ½ lemon

2 oz (50 g) seedless raisins
2 oz (50 g) shelled walnuts,
  chopped
1 red pepper, de-seeded and
  chopped
salt and pepper
2 tomatoes, cut into wedges

Cook the rice according to packet
instructions. Drain and rinse in
cold water, then allow to drain
thoroughly. Leave until cold. Flake
the tuna roughly with a fork and
mix in half the prawns. Cut 8 thin
slices of cucumber and reserve for
garnish. Dice the remaining
cucumber and add to the fish with
the rice, mayonnaise, Tabasco
sauce, lemon juice, raisins,
walnuts and red pepper. Mix well
and season to taste. Place in a salad
bowl or serving dish and garnish
with the remaining prawns, sliced
cucumber and tomato wedges.
Chill before serving.   **Serves 4**

Carrot, Pineapple and Cheese Salad

1 large carrot, peeled and grated
⅓ (13¼ oz, 376 g) can crushed
  pineapple
2 tablespoons (30 ml)
  Kerrygold Grated Cheddar
  Cheese
2 tablespoons (30 ml) salad
  cream
2–3 lettuce leaves
watercress sprigs to garnish
  (optional)

Drain the pineapple in a sieve,
reserving the syrup, and add the
pineapple to the grated carrot with
the cheese. Mix 1 tablespoon
(15 ml) of the reserved pineapple
syrup with the salad cream then
fold this dressing into the carrot
mixture. Line a plate with lettuce
leaves and pile the salad on top.
Add a few watercress sprigs, if
liked.   **Serves 1**

Mediterranean Salad

7 oz (198 g) can tuna in oil
freshly ground pepper
½ lemon
4 oz (100 g) **Kerrygold** Frozen
 Double Cream
 (6 tablespoons (90 ml)
 thawed)
6 hard-boiled eggs
Salad
½ small head celery
12 oz (300 g) tomatoes
juice of ½ lemon
Dressing
8 oz (200 g) ripe tomatoes
½ clove garlic
½ bayleaf
salt and pepper
½ teaspoon (2.5 ml) sugar
3 tablespoons (45 ml) salad oil
½ teaspoon (2.5 ml) tomato
 purée

First prepare the dressing: wipe
the tomatoes, cut out the small core
at the stalk end, squeeze gently to
remove the seeds and slice
roughly. Place the tomatoes and
garlic, uncrushed, in a small pan,
add the bayleaf, seasoning, sugar,
oil and tomato purée; bruise the
tomatoes with a wooden spoon,
cover and simmer gently until the
tomatoes are soft and pulpy.
Remove the piece of garlic then rub
the dressing through a strainer and
allow to cool.

 Empty the tuna into a bowl and
using a wooden spoon, pound
down well with freshly ground
pepper and a little grated lemon
rind. Slowly add the cream and
lemon juice, working the mixture
well between each addition.
Spoon the tuna fish cream into
6 individual serving dishes.

 Scald and skin the tomatoes for
the salad. Cut into quarters and
remove the seeds. Cut the sticks of
celery in slices about ¼ in (0.5 cm)
thick. Add the juice of half the
lemon to the tomato dressing,
check the seasoning and use this to
dress the tomato and celery. Put a
large spoonful of the salad on top
of the tuna fish cream. Quarter the
hard-boiled eggs and arrange
around the salad. Cover with clear
film and chill lightly.

Serve with brown bread and
butter.   **Serves 6**

LEA & PERRINS

Carnival Salad with Walnut Dressing

Dressing
1 oz (25 g) walnut halves,
 ground or very finely
 chopped
3 tablespoons (45 ml) salad oil
1 tablespoon (15 ml) lemon
 juice
2 teaspoons (10 ml) **Lea &
Perrins** Worcestershire Sauce
salt and pepper

6 tomatoes, peeled and thinly
 sliced
1 medium avocado, peeled and
 thinly sliced
6 spring onions, chopped

Blend all the dressing ingredients
together and season well. Just
before serving arrange the sliced
tomatoes and avocado on
individual serving plates and
sprinkle with the spring onions.
Spoon the dressing over the
salad.   **Serves 4**

Spiced Grapefruit Salad

1 head chicory
1 small crisp lettuce, shredded
2 in (5 cm) piece cucumber,
 diced
1 grapefruit, peeled and cut
 into segments
Dressing
4 tablespoons (60 ml) soured
 cream
1 tablespoon (15 ml) salad oil
1 tablespoon (15 ml) **Lea &
Perrins** Worcestershire Sauce
salt and pepper

Arrange a few chicory leaves
around the edge of the serving
plate. Chop the remainder and
place in a bowl with the shredded
lettuce, diced cucumber and
grapefruit segments, reserving a
few for garnish. Blend all the

dressing ingredients together and
season well. Add to the salad, toss
the ingredients together and pile
on to the serving plate. Garnish
with the reserved grapefruit
segments.   **Serves 4**

Peach Sunrise

lettuce leaves
14½ oz (411 g) can **Libby's**
 Sliced Peaches, drained
8 oz (200 g) cottage cheese
2 oz (50 g) salted cashew nuts
cayenne pepper

Arrange the lettuce on a serving
plate, place the peach slices in a
semi-circle to one side and pile the
cottage cheese in the centre.
Sprinkle the cashew nuts round
the cottage cheese and garnish
with cayenne pepper.

 Serve as a light lunch or supper
snack.   **Serves 2–4**

Cadbury's Marvel

Chilly Tang

3 tablespoons (45 ml) **Marvel**
¼ pint (125 ml) water
2 (5 oz, 142 ml) cartons natural
 yoghurt
½ cucumber, sliced *or* chopped
2 oz (50 g) pickled gherkins,
 chopped
1 or 2 sticks celery, washed and
 chopped
4 oz (100 g) cooked chicken
1 tablespoon (15 ml) parsley,
 chopped
lettuce to serve
chopped chives to garnish

Blend the Marvel with the water
and mix in the yoghurt. Mix the
chopped vegetables and chicken,
with the parsley, into the yoghurt
mixture and chill for about
2 hours.

 To serve, line a dish with lettuce
leaves, spoon the chicken mixture
into the centre and sprinkle the
chives on top.   **Serves 4**

Cheese and Apple Salad

2 dessert apples, cored and
 diced
2 medium potatoes, peeled,
 cooked and diced
Primula Cheese Spread
Kavli Mayonnaise
a little cream (optional)

Mix the diced apples and potatoes
with the cheese spread cut into
tiny dice. Dress the salad with the
mayonnaise, diluted with a little
cream if liked.

Chilli Cucumber

2 cucumbers
1 teaspoon (5 ml) salt
1 large clove garlic, crushed
 with a little salt
1 green chilli, finely chopped
 and with seeds removed
4 tablespoons (60 ml) **Rose's**
 Lime Juice Cordial
freshly ground black pepper
chopped fresh parsley to
 garnish (optional)

Peel the cucumbers, cut in half
lengthwise and scoop out the
seeds with a spoon. Cut the flesh
diagonally into slices, put into a
bowl and sprinkle with the salt.
Leave for about 30 minutes, then
drain off the liquid and pat the
cucumber dry with kitchen paper.
Transfer to a serving dish. Mix
1½ teaspoons (7.5 ml) of the
chopped chilli with the garlic into
the lime juice and pour this over
the cucumber. Sprinkle liberally
with the pepper and chill for an
hour before serving.

 Serve with meat or as a salad on
its own, sprinkled with chopped
parsley, if liked.   **Serves 4–8**

Colourful Cabbage

1 red and 1 green pepper
1 small onion, peeled and
 thinly sliced
½ cucumber, chopped
2 tomatoes, sliced
½ small, firm cabbage, finely
 sliced
1 teaspoon (5 ml) capers
a good pinch caraway seeds
 (optional)
Dressing
4 tablespoons (80 ml) **Rose's**
 Lime Juice Cordial
4 tablespoons (80 ml) salad oil
2 tablespoons (40 ml) clear
 honey
½ teaspoon (2.5 ml) paprika
 pepper
½ teaspoon (2.5 ml) salt

Cut the peppers across the centres,
remove the pith and seeds then cut
thinly into rings. Mix all the vegetables and the capers together.
Add the caraway seeds if liked.
Blend all the dressing ingredients
together and toss the vegetables in
the dressing.   **Serves 6–8**

Europa Salad

1 small fennel, finely sliced
2 oranges, peeled and divided
 into segments, reserving any
 juice
4 oz (100 g) garlic sausage, cut
 into strips
½ a red pepper, de-seeded and
 finely chopped
1 tablespoon (20 ml) fresh
 mixed herbs, chopped
Dressing
3 tablespoons (60 ml) **Rose's**
 Lime Juice Cordial
3 tablespoons (60 ml) salad oil
1 teaspoon (5 ml) French
 mustard
salt and pepper

Remove any pips from the orange
segments and mix all the salad
ingredients in a salad bowl.
Measure all the dressing ingredients into a screw-topped jar,
adding any reserved orange juice.
Shake well and pour over the salad
ingredients.

The dressing can be made up in
large amounts and stored in a jar in
the refrigerator, ready for
immediate use with any salad.
Serves 4–6

Insalata Pastini

4 oz (100 g) pasta shells
1 tablespoon (15 ml) oil
3 tomatoes, cut into eighths
2 eggs, hard-boiled and
 quartered
1 small onion, peeled and
 grated
2 (1¾ oz, 50 g) cans anchovies,
 drained thoroughly
1 oz (25 g) black olives
½ cucumber, thinly sliced
Dressing
2 tablespoons (40 ml) olive oil
4 tablespoons (80 ml) **Rose's**
 Lime Juice Cordial
2 tablespoons (40 ml) wine
 vinegar
salt and freshly ground black
 pepper

Cook the pasta in boiling, salted
water with 1 tablespoon (15 ml) oil
added, until still slightly firm.
Drain and run under cold water to
cool. Mix the tomatoes, eggs,
onion, anchovies and olives with
the cooled pasta shells. Blend all
the dressing ingredients together,
adding the seasoning. Mix into the
pasta and other ingredients and
pile in the centre of a large, flat
serving dish. Arrange the
cucumber slices around the edge
and sprinkle more freshly ground
pepper over the top of the salad.

 A selection of thinly sliced
continental cold meats would
make this into a complete meal.
Serves 6

Uncle Ben's

Tropical Rice Salad

1 can **Uncle Ben's** Ready
 Cooked Rice
2 tablespoons (30 ml) oil
2 tablespoons (30 ml) vinegar
a little garlic salt

salt and pepper
6 oz (175 g) peeled prawns
1 small can pineapple pieces, drained
2 sticks celery, chopped
4 oz (100 g) grapes, halved and with seeds removed (preferably a mixture of green and black)
lettuce leaves to serve
strips of green and red pepper and wedges of tomato to garnish

Prepare the rice according to the instructions on the can. Toss the cooked rice in the oil and vinegar mixed with the seasonings whilst still warm. Add the prawns, celery, pineapple pieces and grapes. Mix well. Spoon on to a bed of lettuce and garnish with the strips of pepper and tomatoes.
Serves 4

Bean Sprout Salad

10 oz (275 g) fresh bean sprouts
4 oz (100 g) button mushrooms, washed, trimmed and quartered
8 oz (225 g) frozen sweetcorn, cooked
12 sprigs fresh parsley
¼ pint (150 ml) soured cream
1 tablespoon (15 ml) malt vinegar
1 tablespoon (15 ml) soy sauce
1 teaspoon (5 ml) sugar
salt and pepper
4 rashers **Wall's** Streaky Bacon, fried *or* grilled

Mix the bean sprouts with the mushrooms, sweetcorn and parsley. Put the soured cream into a jar, add the vinegar, sugar and seasoning and shake them all together. Pour the dressing over the salad and toss the ingredients so that they are completely coated. Put the salad into a serving bowl, cut the cooked bacon rashers into pieces and scatter them over the surface of the salad before serving.
Serves 4

Italian Salad

7 oz (198 g) **John West** Tuna Steak in Oil
1 tablespoon (15 ml) salad oil
2 tablespoons (30 ml) vinegar
¼ teaspoon mustard powder
salt and pepper
15¼ oz (432 g) can kidney beans, drained
3 large sticks celery, trimmed and chopped
1 small onion, skinned and cut into fine rings

Drain the oil from the tuna and mix with the salad oil, vinegar and mustard powder. Season generously and whisk with a fork until smooth. Place the tuna, in large pieces, the kidney beans, celery and onion in a salad bowl, pour the dressing over and toss well. Chill until required. Serve in individual bowls.   **Serves 4**

Salad Niçoise

1 small round lettuce, washed and gently dried
8 oz (225 g) cold cooked potatoes, diced
4 oz (100 g) cold, cooked green beans, sliced
7 oz (198 g) can **John West** Skipjack Tuna, drained and divided into small chunks
1¾ oz (42 g) can anchovies, drained of oil
12 black olives
2 large hard-boiled eggs, cut into wedges
4 medium tomatoes, skinned and cut into quarters

Dressing
4 tablespoons (60 ml) salad oil
½ level teaspoon (2.5 ml) salt
¼ level teaspoon caster sugar
¼ level teaspoon dry mustard
shake of pepper
2 tablespoons (30 ml) vinegar *or* lemon juice

Line a shallow serving bowl with the lettuce. Fill with potatoes and scatter the beans over the top. Stud with pieces of the tuna. Decorate attractively with the rest of the ingredients, criss-crossing with the anchovies.

For the dressing, beat the oil with the salt, sugar, mustard and pepper. Add the vinegar or lemon juice and whisk until thick. Pour gently over the salad and serve immediately.   **Serves 4**

SAUCES, RELISHES, MARINADES and STUFFINGS

ATORA

Apple and Prune Stuffing

8 oz (250 g) dried prunes, soaked overnight
2 large cooking apples, peeled and grated
rind and juice of 1 lemon
2 sticks of celery, finely chopped
1 onion, finely chopped
1 goose or duck liver, chopped
a little oil for frying
4 oz (100 g) fresh white breadcrumbs
3 oz (75 g) **Atora** Shredded Suet
1 teaspoon (5 ml) dried rubbed sage
1 egg, size 3, beaten
salt
black pepper, ground

Cook the soaked prunes gently in the soaking water for 15 minutes. Drain, reserving the juice. Stone and chop the prunes. Prepare the apples and mix with the lemon rind and juice. Fry the celery, onion and chopped liver in a little oil until just cooked. Mix all the ingredients together, adding a little of the prune juice if needed to make a firm but soft mixture. Spoon into the chosen end of the bird.

Sufficient for a small goose or large duck.

Chestnut and Mushroom Stuffing

8 oz (250 g) fresh white breadcrumbs
4 oz (125 g) **Atora** Shredded Suet

1 onion, finely chopped
1–2 cloves garlic, crushed
4 oz (100 g) bacon or ham, chopped
8 oz (250 g) fresh roasted chestnuts, shelled or canned and drained, chopped
4 oz (100 g) mushrooms, chopped
2 eggs, size 3, beaten
2 teaspoons (10 ml) dried marjoram or oregano
salt
black pepper, ground

Mix up all the ingredients and spoon into the chosen end of the bird.

Sufficient for a medium turkey or large chicken.

BURGESS

Horseradish Butter

4 oz (100 g) butter
4 dessertspoons (40 ml) **Burgess** Creamed Horseradish
salt and freshly ground black pepper

Beat the butter to a soft cream, then beat in the Creamed Horseradish and season with salt and pepper. Work the butter into a roll, wrap in waxed paper and put in a cool place until firm. Slice for serving.

This keeps well in the refrigerator and is excellent on grilled chops or steak, gammon rashers and sausages or with grilled liver.
Makes 10 portions

Carnation®

Cheese Sauce

½ large can **Carnation** Evaporated Milk

¾ teaspoon (3.75 ml) salt
½ teaspoon (2.5 ml) dry mustard
6 oz (175 g) Cheddar cheese, grated
¾ teaspoon (3.75 ml) Worcestershire sauce

Put the Carnation milk, salt, mustard and cheese into a small saucepan. Heat gently and stir until the cheese dissolves and the sauce thickens. Add the Worcestershire sauce. Adjust seasoning and serve immediately with fish, vegetables or pasta.
Makes ½ pint (300 ml)

Cucumber Sauce

½ oz (15 g) butter
1 tablespoon (15 ml) chopped onion
½ oz (15 g) flour
1 small can **Carnation** Evaporated Milk
½ teaspoon (2.5 ml) salt
1 tablespoon (15 ml) lemon juice
3 in (8 cm) piece cucumber

Melt the butter in a saucepan, add the onion, fry lightly then add the flour. Cook for a few minutes then remove from the heat and gradually stir in the Carnation milk made up to ½ pint (300 ml) with water. Bring to the boil and add the salt, lemon juice and grated cucumber. Simmer for about 5 minutes. Serve with meat or fish.
Makes ½ pint (300 ml)

Mustard Sauce

¾ oz (3.75 ml) butter
¾ oz (3.75 ml) flour
2 tablespoons (30 ml) dry mustard
1 small can **Carnation** Evaporated Milk

1 tablespoon (15 ml) lemon
  juice
1 teaspoon (5 ml) vinegar
½ teaspoon (2.5 ml) salt
¼ teaspoon pepper

Melt the butter in a saucepan, add
the flour and mustard and cook
gently for a few minutes. Remove
from the heat and gradually stir in
the Carnation milk made up to
¾ pint (450 ml) with water. Bring
to the boil then add the lemon
juice, vinegar and seasoning.
Simmer for about 5 minutes. Serve
with herrings, ham or pork.
Makes ¾ pint (450 ml)

Shrimp Sauce

1 oz (25 g) butter
1 tablespoon (15 ml) chopped
  onion
1 oz (25 g) flour
1 teaspoon (5 ml) tomato purée
1 small can **Carnation**
  Evaporated Milk
2 oz (50 g) frozen, canned *or*
  fresh shrimps
½ teaspoon (2.5 ml) salt
pepper
1–2 tablespoons (15–30 ml)
  lemon juice

Melt the butter in a saucepan,
lightly fry the onion and add the
flour and tomato purée. Cook for a
few minutes, remove from the heat
and gradually stir in the Carnation
milk made up to ½ pint (300 ml)
with water. Bring to the boil,
stirring continuously and add the
shrimps, seasoning and lemon
juice. Simmer for about 5 minutes.
Serve with fish, rice or pasta.
Makes ½ pint (300 ml)

certo

Pepper Relish

6–8 medium sized peppers
  (green and red mixed)
½ pint (300 ml) vinegar
2¾ lb (1.25 kg) sugar
1 bottle **Certo**

For best colour use equal amounts
of green and red sweet peppers. To
prepare the peppers, cut open and

discard seeds and finely chop the
pepper flesh. Measure the sugar
and vinegar into a large preserving
pan, and add 14 oz (400 g) of the
prepared peppers. Mix well and
bring to a full rolling boil over high
heat, stirring constantly. Boil
rapidly for 2 minutes, stirring.
Remove from the heat, stir in the
Certo. Leave to cool for 5 minutes.
Skim if necessary, pot and cover in
the usual way.

Rosemary Jelly

large bunch rosemary (approx
  1 oz, 25 g)
½ pint (300 ml) white vinegar
1 lb (450 g) sugar
1 bottle **Certo**
green colouring

Wash the rosemary thoroughly.
Snip off the tender leaves and
reserve them. Put the vinegar and
sugar into a saucepan with the rest
of the rosemary tied in a bunch and
stir over a low heat until the sugar
has dissolved. Remove the bunch
of rosemary. Bring to the boil and
boil for 1 minute. Strain the syrup
through muslin and return to the
saucepan. Stir in the Certo, bring
to the boil and boil for 2 minutes.
Add the reserved rosemary and
çolouring. Allow to cool slightly to
prevent the rosemary floating.
Skim if necessary. Pot and cover in
the usual way.

CHAMBOURCY

Creamy Horseradish Sauce

1½ tablespoons (45 ml)
  horseradish sauce
1 small carton **Chambourcy**
  Natural Yoghurt
2 oz (50 g) gherkins, chopped
1 teaspoon (5 ml) lemon juice
salt and pepper to taste

Mix all the ingredients together.
  Serve as an accompaniment to
roast beef.

Barbecue Sauce

1 large onion, peeled and finely
  chopped
3 oz (75 g) butter
1 dessertspoon (10 ml) **Cirio**
  Tomato Purée
2 tablespoons (30 ml) **Cirio**
  Wine Vinegar
2 tablespoons (30 ml) demerara
  sugar
¼ pint (150 ml) water
2 teaspoons (10 ml) made
  mustard
2 tablespoons (30 ml)
  Worcestershire sauce

Fry the onion in the melted butter
for 5 minutes until soft and
golden. Stir in the tomato purée
and cook for a further 3–4 minutes.
Blend together the remaining
ingredients and add gradually to
the tomato mixture. Simmer for
10 minutes, stirring frequently.
  Serve with roast, grilled or
baked meats.

Magele Chilli Sauce

1 large onion, peeled and
  chopped
1 large knob butter
14 oz (396 g) can **Cirio** Peeled
  Tomatoes
2 apples, chopped into small
  dice
2 oz (50 g) sultanas, washed
2 oz (50 g) desiccated coconut
2 oz (50 g) sliced almonds
salt
1 dessertspoon (10 ml) chilli
  powder (or less if a milder
  sauce is required)

Fry the onion gently in the butter
until soft and transparent. Add the
contents of the can of tomatoes
together with the apples, sultanas,
coconut, almonds, salt and chilli
powder. Simmer for about 30
minutes.
  Serve hot or cold. The sauce is
delicious hot, poured over kebabs
and served with plain boiled rice,
or served cold with buffet dishes.

Quick Tomato Sauce

4 tablespoons (60 ml) **Cirio** Tomato Purée
1²/₃ teacups water
2 level tablespoons (30 ml) flour

Mix the tomato purée with most of the water. Mix the flour with the remaining water and stir until smooth. Add to the tomato mixture. Bring to the boil and simmer gently for 2 minutes, stirring constantly.

Serve with cold meats.

Apple and Mint Chutney

1½ lb (600 g) cooking apples, cored, peeled and chopped
½ lb (200 g) onions, peeled and finely chopped
¼ pint (125 ml) vinegar
¼ pint (125 ml) water
1 teaspoon (5 ml) salt
1 tablespoon (15 ml) **Frank Cooper's** Concentrated Mint Sauce
8 oz (200 g) sugar
rind and juice of 1 lemon

Place all the ingredients into a large pan. Bring to the boil and simmer for 45 minutes. Pour into warm jars, seal and label.

Cream of Tomato and Cheese Sauce

8 oz (200 g) cream cheese
1 can **Frank Cooper's** Tomato Soup with Prawns
1 small green pepper, de-seeded and finely chopped
2 small sticks celery, finely chopped
½ level teaspoon (2.5 ml) garlic salt
black pepper

Place the cream cheese in a bowl and gradually whisk in the soup until evenly blended. Stir in the green pepper, celery, garlic salt and black pepper. Chill before serving.

Serve with grilled or fried meats or kebabs   **Serves 6–8**

Mint and Onion Sauce

2 teaspoons (10 ml) **Frank Cooper's** Ready to Serve Mint Sauce
1 small onion, peeled and finely chopped
few leaves watercress, chopped
1 teaspoon (5 ml) caster sugar
salt and pepper
1 tablespoon (15 ml) hot water
2 tablespoons (30 ml) vinegar

Mix together all the ingredients. Chill before serving.

A good sauce to serve with lamb.

Scampi Sauce

1 can **Frank Cooper's** Cream of Scampi Soup
5 oz (142 ml) carton soured cream
8 oz (227 g) can water chestnuts, drained and thinly sliced

Mix the soup and soured cream together in a saucepan and stir in the water chestnuts. Bring slowly to the boil, stirring all the time.

Serve hot with grilled halibut, sole or plaice.   **Serves 4–6**

Viennese Sauce

½ oz (15 g) butter
1 level tablespoon (15 ml) cornflour
5 oz (142 ml) carton soured cream
2 teaspoons (10 ml) **Frank Cooper's** Horseradish Relish
1 dessertspoon (10 ml) capers, chopped
1 tablespoon (15 ml) parsley, chopped
salt and pepper

Melt the butter, stir in the cornflour and cook gently for 1 minute. Remove from the heat and stir in the soured cream. Return to the heat, bring to the boil, stirring, and simmer for 1 minute. Add the horseradish, capers, parsley and seasoning.

Serve hot with fish.
Serves 2–4

Cumberland Sauce

1 orange
1 lemon
4–5 tablespoons (60–75 ml) **Crosse & Blackwell** Redcurrant Jelly
¼ level teaspoon dry mustard
pinch ground ginger
pinch black pepper

Pare about half of the rind from the orange and lemon and cut into very thin slivers. Place in a bowl and cover with boiling water and soak for 5 minutes. Drain well. Heat the redcurrant jelly in a small saucepan together with the drained orange and lemon peel, the juice of the orange and lemon, mustard, ginger and pepper. Add more spices to taste if required.

Serve with roast lamb, baked gammon, or game.
Makes about ⅓ pint (190 ml)

Sauce Verte

4 oz (100 g) packet **Findus** Chopped Spinach
3 tablespoons (45 ml) mayonnaise
1 clove garlic, crushed
1 tablespoon (15 ml) wine vinegar
salt and black pepper

Cook the spinach as directed, drain off any excess liquid and cool. Pass through a fine sieve or liquidise, add the remaining ingredients and mix well.

Serve chilled as an accompaniment to fried plaice.

HELLMANN'S

Cold Curry Sauce

4 tablespoons (60 ml)
    Hellmann's Real Mayonnaise
1 tablespoon (15 ml) milk
1 teaspoon (5 ml) lemon juice
2 tablespoons (30 ml) mango
    chutney
1 dessertspoon (10 ml) curry
    paste
½ level teaspoon (2.5 ml)
    paprika

Blend all the ingredients well
together and chill.
    Serve with cold chicken or
turkey.   **Serves 4**

Minted Mushroom Sauce

1 tablespoon (15 ml) pure corn
    oil
4 oz (100 g) mushrooms,
    washed and sliced
1 teaspoon (5 ml) fresh mint,
    chopped
salt and pepper
¼ pint (125 ml) beef stock
¼ pint (125 ml) milk
1 tablespoon (15 ml)
    Hellmann's Real Mayonnaise

Heat the corn oil and sauté the
mushrooms for 3–4 minutes. Add
the mint, seasoning, beef stock
and milk, bring to the boil,
stirring, and simmer for 5 minutes.
Gently stir in the mayonnaise just
before serving.
    Serve hot with spring lamb.
Serves 4

Prawn Cocktail Sauce

6 fl oz (150 g) **Hellmann's** Real
    Mayonnaise
2 level tablespoons (30 ml)
    tomato purée
1 teaspoon (5 ml) lemon juice
1 level teaspoon (5 ml) caster
    sugar
4–5 drops Tabasco sauce
paprika pepper

Blend the mayonnaise with the

tomato purée, stir in the lemon
juice, caster sugar and Tabasco
sauce and add paprika to taste.
Chill.
    Serve with seafood.
Serves 4–6

Spicy Sauce

2 oz (50 g) button mushrooms,
    washed and finely sliced
1 tablespoon (15 ml) tarragon
    vinegar
3 tablespoons (45 ml)
    Hellmann's Real Mayonnaise
4 drops Tabasco sauce
1 teaspoon (5 ml)
    Worcestershire sauce
½ level teaspoon (2.5 ml)
    paprika pepper
black pepper

Toss the mushrooms in the vinegar
and marinate for 30 minutes. Mix
together the mayonnaise, Tabasco
sauce, Worcestershire sauce,
paprika and black pepper to taste.
Add the mushrooms and any
remaining vinegar.
    Serve with hot chicken or
turkey.   **Serves 4**

Thousand Island Dressing

4 tablespoons (60 ml)
    Hellmann's Real Mayonnaise
2 tablespoons (30 ml) milk
1 dessertspoon (10 ml) chilli
    sauce
1 level tablespoon (15 ml)
    tomato purée
1 level tablespoon (15 ml) sweet
    pickle
1 level teaspoon (5 ml) sugar
1 hard-boiled egg, finely
    chopped

Blend the mayonnaise smoothly
with the milk. Stir in the chilli
sauce, tomato purée, pickle, sugar
and chopped egg. Chill.
    Serve with cold meats and
salads.   **Serves 4**

> Quick Tip: To add extra richness
> and creaminess to all savoury
> sauces, both hot and cold, stir in a
> tablespoon or two of **Hellmann's**
> Real Mayonnaise just before ser-
> ving. Do not boil once the mayon-
> naise has been added.

Orange Sauce

2½ oz (65 g) sugar
5 tablespoons (75 ml) water
¼ pint (150 ml) meat stock
4 tablespoons (60 ml) wine
    vinegar
3 rounded tablespoons (60 ml)
    Keiller Little Chip Orange
    Jelly Marmalade
2 level teaspoons (10 ml)
    cornflour

Place the sugar and water in a
small, heavy-based saucepan and
heat gently until the sugar
dissolves. Increase the heat and
boil rapidly until the mixture
becomes a deep golden brown
caramel. Remove from the heat
immediately and carefully add the
wine vinegar, stock and
marmalade. Simmer gently until
the caramel and marmalade melt.
Blend the cornflour with a little
water and stir into the sauce. Bring
to the boil, stirring continuously,
until the sauce thickens.
    Serve with roast duck.
Makes about ½ pint (300 ml)

Knorr

Quick Tomato Sauce

¾ oz (20 g) cornflour
½ level teaspoon (2.5 ml) dry
    mustard
1 level tablespoon (15 ml) soft
    brown sugar
3 level tablespoons (45 ml)
    tomato purée
¾ pint (375 ml) **Knorr** chicken
    stock

In a basin blend together the
cornflour, mustard, sugar and
tomato purée. Gradually add the
stock to the blended ingredients.
Pour the sauce into a saucepan,
bring to the boil and simmer for
1 minute. Serve hot.

167

LEA & PERRINS

Curry Relish

1 level teaspoon (5 ml) **Lea & Perrins** Concentrated Curry Sauce
1 level teaspoon (5 ml) tomato purée
2 tablespoons (30 ml) apricot jam
1 banana, chopped
1 apple, cored and finely chopped
1 oz (25 g) walnuts, chopped

Blend together the concentrated curry sauce, tomato purée and jam. Mix in the remaining ingredients. If possible, leave for 2 hours before serving.

Serve with cold meats or bread and cheese. **Serves 6–8**

Devilled Butter

2 tablespoons (30 ml) dry English mustard
2 tablespoons (30 ml) **Lea & Perrins** Worcestershire Sauce
4 oz (100 g) softened butter

Cream together the mustard and Worcestershire Sauce and work into the butter until smooth.

Spread over meat or fish before grilling to give a spicy flavour or chill in the refrigerator and place pieces on top of grilled food before serving. Keeps in the refrigerator for 1 month.
Makes 6–8 portions

Leamington Sauce

1 oz (25 g) butter
1 small onion, peeled and finely chopped
grated rind ½ an orange
juice 2 oranges
1 teaspoon (5 ml) **Lea & Perrins** Worcestershire Sauce
¼ pint (150 ml) chicken stock
1 tablespoon (15 ml) redcurrant jelly
salt and pepper
2 teaspoons (10 ml) cornflour
1 tablespoon (15 ml) water

Melt the butter in a pan, add the onion and fry gently until soft but not coloured. Add the remaining ingredients, except the cornflour, and simmer gently until smooth, about 5 minutes. Blend the cornflour with water and add to the sauce. Continue cooking, stirring all the time, until thickened and smooth.

Serve with roast duck and pheasant, baked or boiled ham, grilled or fried gammon rashers, pork and lamb chops. **Serves 4**

Mushroom Sherry Sauce

1 onion, peeled and finely chopped
½ oz (15 g) butter
6 oz (150 g) mushrooms, washed and finely chopped
½ oz (15 g) flour
½ pint (250 ml) beef stock
1 tablespoon (15 ml) **Lea & Perrins** Worcestershire Sauce
1 tablespoon (15 ml) sherry
salt and pepper

Fry the onion gently in the butter for 5 minutes. Add the mushrooms and fry for 2 minutes. Remove from the heat, stir in the flour, return to the heat and cook for 1 minute. Remove from the heat and blend in the stock. Bring to the boil, stirring. Add the remaining ingredients and simmer for 5 minutes. Check the seasoning and serve hot. **Serves 6**

Worcestershire Marinade

4 tablespoons (60 ml) **Lea & Perrins** Worcestershire Sauce
2 tablespoons (30 ml) cooking oil
4 tablespoons (60 ml) water
juice of ½ a lemon
4 strips lemon peel
salt

Mix together all the ingredients and pour over meat. Leave to marinate in the refrigerator for at least 12 hours, turning the meat occasionally.

Use for the cheaper cuts of meat to tenderise them and add flavour. Use also as a marinade for cut up meats before stewing or casseroling, for kebabs and fish before grilling.
Enough to marinate 1–1½ lb (450–675 g) meat.

Peach Relish

14½ oz (411 g) can **Libby's** Peach Slices, drained, with syrup reserved
3 tablespoons (45 ml) green pepper, finely chopped
1 level tablespoon (15 ml) cornflour
1 tablespoon (15 ml) vinegar
¼ teaspoon cayenne pepper
good shake freshly ground black pepper

Chop the peaches and mix with the green pepper. Place the remaining ingredients in a saucepan with ¼ pint (150 ml) syrup. Bring to the boil, whisking continuously until thickened. Stir in the peach mixture and spoon into a bowl. Chill completely.

Serve with homemade beefburgers in baps. Any remaining relish can be stored in the refrigerator for a few days.
Makes about 1 lb (450 g)

McVitie's Digestive Stuffing

2 oz (50 g) streaky bacon, with rinds removed, chopped
1 oz (25 g) butter
1 small onion, peeled and finely chopped
4 oz (100 g) **McVitie's** Digestive Biscuits, crushed
1 tablespoon (15 ml) parsley, chopped
grated rind of 1 small *or* ½ a large lemon

salt and pepper
1 egg, beaten

Melt the butter in a saucepan and fry the bacon and onion until soft. Remove the pan from the heat, add all the remaining ingredients and mix thoroughly.

This is a good stuffing for meat, especially pork or poultry. McVitie's Digestives used in place of breadcrumbs give a pleasing crunchy texture to the stuffing.

Mazola

Mazola Marinades

Chinese Marinade
4 tablespoons (60 ml) **Mazola** Pure Corn Oil
2 tablespoons (30 ml) dry sherry
1 tablespoon (15 ml) soy sauce
1 tablespoon (15 ml) stem ginger sauce
salt and pepper

Herb Marinade
4 tablespoons (60 ml) **Mazola** Pure Corn Oil
2 tablespoons (30 ml) lemon juice
2 cloves garlic, crushed
2 tablespoons (30 ml) onion, peeled and finely chopped
1 level teaspoon (5 ml) dried marjoram

Spiced Marinade
4 tablespoons (60 ml) **Mazola** Pure Corn Oil
½ level teaspoon (2.5 ml) each ground coriander, cumin and turmeric
2 tablespoons (30 ml) onion, peeled and finely chopped
salt and pepper

Select one of the recipes and blend together all the marinade ingredients given. Place meat or poultry in a shallow dish and brush over with the marinade to coat evenly. Marinate the food for at least 2–3

hours, preferably overnight, turning and basting several times.

Savoury White Sauce

2 tablespoons (60 ml) **Mazola** Pure Corn Oil
1½ level tablespoons (22.5 ml) flour *or* cornflour
½ pint (250 ml) milk
salt and pepper

Blend together the corn oil and flour in a saucepan. Gradually stir in the milk and bring to the boil, stirring. Simmer gently for 1–2 minutes. Add seasoning to taste.

To vary, add chopped parsley, cheese or chopped capers to the cooked sauce.
Makes about ½ pint (300 ml)

Nestlé

Cheese Sauce

6 oz (175 g) can **Nestlé's** Cream
3 oz (75 g) Cheddar cheese, grated
4–5 tablespoons (60–75 ml) milk *or* water
salt and pepper to taste

Slowly heat the cream in a small saucepan until it reaches boiling point. Add the grated cheese and stir until the sauce is smooth. Stir in enough milk or water to make the required thickness. Season to taste and serve immediately.

This sauce becomes firm on cooling and makes a delicious cheese spread.
Makes about ½ pint (300 ml)

Savoury Cream Sauce

6 oz (175 g) can **Nestlé's** Cream
1 rounded tablespoon (20 ml) capers
1 oz (25 g) butter
2 teaspoons (10 ml) lemon juice
3 tablespoons (45 ml) white wine vinegar
salt and pepper to taste

Slowly heat the cream in a small saucepan until it reaches boiling point. Stir in the capers, butter, lemon juice and wine vinegar. Bring back to the boil, season to taste and serve immediately.

Serve with chicken, pork, veal and fish.
Makes about ½ pint (300 ml)

whitworths

Fig and Apricot Chutney

9 oz (250 g) **Whitworth** Figs, with stalks removed, chopped
9 oz (250 g) dried apricots, chopped
12 oz (350 g) onions, peeled and chopped
1 clove garlic, crushed
8 oz (225 g) granulated sugar
1 teaspoon (5 ml) made mustard
½ teaspoon (2.5 ml) mixed spice
1 teaspoon (5 ml) salt
¾ pint (450 ml) white wine vinegar

Place all the ingredients in a large saucepan. Bring slowly to the boil, stirring occasionally to ensure that the sugar dissolves. Simmer uncovered, stirring occasionally, for about 1 hour or until the mixture is the consistency of thick jam. Allow to cool slightly. Put into warm jars, cover and label in the usual way.

HOT PUDDINGS

Apricot Pudding

8 oz (225 g) apricots, cooked
    and sweetened
1 oz (25 g) vegetable margarine
1 oz (25 g) **Allinson** 100%
    Wholewheat Flour
⅓ pint (200 ml) milk
1 egg, separated
2 oz (50 g) brown sugar

Place the apricots in a 1½ pint
(1 litre) pie dish. Melt the margarine in a pan, stir in the flour,
remove from the heat and gradually blend in all the milk. Return
the pan to the heat and cook gently
until the sauce thickens, stirring
constantly. Whisk the egg white
until very stiff. Add the egg yolk,
sugar and egg white to the sauce,
mix well and then pour over the
apricots. Bake for 25 minutes in a
pre-heated oven (375°F, 190°C,
Gas Mark 5). Serve immediately.
Serves 4

Baked Almond Pudding

4 oz (125 g) vegetable
    margarine
4 oz (125 g) soft brown sugar
2 eggs, beaten
6 oz (175 g) **Allinson** 100%
    Wholewheat Flour
1 teaspoon (5 ml) baking
    powder
½ teaspoon (2.5 ml) sea salt
2 tablespoons (30 ml) milk
few drops almond essence
2 oz (50 g) almonds, chopped
jam

Cream the margarine and sugar
until they are light and fluffy. Beat
in the eggs a little at a time. Fold in
the flour, sieved with the baking
powder, then stir in the milk,
almond essence and nuts. The

mixture should be soft enough to
drop easily from a spoon.

Spread the jam in the base of a
greased 1 pint (600 ml) ovenproof
dish, pour the pudding mixture on
top and bake at 350°F, 180°C, Gas
Mark 4 for about 45 minutes until
well risen and firm.

This mixture can also be made
into a steamed pudding. Steam for
1½ hours.   **Serves 4–6**

Bran and Honey Pudding

8 oz (225 g) **Allinson** Bran Plus
12 oz (350 g) breadcrumbs
    made from **Allinson**
    Wholewheat Bread
2 teaspoons (10 ml) ground
    cinnamon (optional)
4 oz (125 g) honey
5 fl oz (150 ml) hot water
2 teaspoons (10 ml) vegetable
    margarine
1 lb (450 g) cooking apples,
    peeled and chopped

Mix together the bran, breadcrumbs, cinnamon, honey, water
and margarine. Layer alternately
with the apples in a greased 2 pint
(1.2 litre) pie dish, finishing with a
layer of the bran mixture. Cover
and bake for 45 minutes at 375°F,
190°C, Gas Mark 5.   **Serves 4**

Ambrosia

Chocolate Rice

15½ oz (439 g) **Ambrosia**
    Creamed Rice
3 oz (75 g) plain chocolate,
    grated
1 oz (25 g) caster sugar
1 egg
¼ pint (150 ml) single cream
1 oz (25 g) demerara sugar

Put the creamed rice into an
ovenproof dish and stir in the
chocolate and sugar. Beat the egg
and cream together and mix into
the rice. Bake at 325°F, 170°C,
Gas Mark 3 for 45 minutes. Just
before serving, sprinkle with the
demerara sugar.   **Serves 4**

Toffee Rice Pudding

2 oz (50 g) caster sugar
15½ oz (439 g) **Ambrosia**
    Creamed Rice
2 oz (50 g) mixed candied peel,
    chopped
1½ oz (40 g) soft dark brown
    sugar

Put the caster sugar into a small,
thick-bottomed pan and heat
gently until the sugar turns golden
and then forms a pale golden
syrup. Stir in the rice and add the
peel. Mix well and put into a
1¼ pint (750 ml) ovenproof dish.
Sprinkle the brown sugar on top.
Bake at 350°F, 180°C, Gas Mark 4,
for 25 minutes.

Serve hot.   **Serves 4**

ATORA

Chocolate and Black Cherry Loaf

3 oz (75 g) self-raising flour,
    sifted
1 oz (25 g) cocoa
3 oz (75 g) fresh white
    breadcrumbs
3 oz (75 g) **Atora** Shredded Suet
2 oz (50 g) soft brown sugar
2 tablespoons (30 ml) golden
    syrup, slightly warmed
2 eggs (size 3), beaten
a little milk to mix
15 oz (425 g) can black cherries,
    stoned and drained
cream to serve

Grease a 1 lb (450 g) loaf tin and line the base with greased grease-proof paper. Sift the flour and cocoa together, then mix in the rest of the ingredients, using half the cherries and adding enough milk to make a soft dropping consistency. Turn into the prepared loaf tin and bake at 350°F, 180°C, Gas Mark 4 for about 1 hour until cooked and risen. Allow to stand for a few minutes, then turn out onto a warmed serving dish and serve with the remaining cherries and cream.   **Serves 4–6**

Figgy Pudding

8 oz (225 g) dried figs, de-stalked and chopped
6 oz (150 g) fresh breadcrumbs
2 oz (50 g) self-raising flour
4 oz (100 g) **Atora** Shredded Suet
6 oz (150 g) soft dark brown sugar
3 oz (75 g) sultanas
2 oz (50 g) candied *or* mixed peel, chopped
2 oz (50 g) almond flakes, lightly toasted
½ teaspoon (2.5 ml) ground nutmeg
pinch of salt
3 eggs (size 3), beaten
5 tablespoons (75 ml) milk
5 tablespoons (75 ml) sherry *or* brandy
cream, soured cream *or* custard sauce to serve

Mix all the dry ingredients together. Beat the eggs with the milk and sherry or brandy. Add the liquid to the dry ingredients and mix thoroughly. Turn into a greased 2 pint (1.2 litre) basin, with the base lined with a circle of greased greaseproof paper. Cover with pleated, greased greaseproof paper and a double thickness of foil and steam or boil for 5–6 hours.

Turn out on to a warm serving dish and serve hot with cream, soured cream or real custard sauce.

Apple and Cinnamon Layer Pudding

suet pastry made with 8 oz (200 g) **Be-Ro** Self-raising Flour
1 lb (500 g) apples
2 oz (50 g) sultanas
1 teaspoon (5 ml) ground cinnamon
sugar to sweeten

Divide the pastry into four pieces and roll out into circles, each one a little larger then the last. Peel and slice the apples and mix with the sultanas, cinnamon and sugar. Grease a 1¾ pint (1 litre) basin, place the smallest circle of pastry in the bottom, add a layer of fruit mixture and continue the layers, ending with a layer of pastry. Cover and steam for 2 hours then turn out and dredge with caster sugar.

Any other fuit or jam may be used in place of the apple and cinnamon mixture in this pudding.   **Serves 4–6**

Chocolate Pear Meringue

14½ oz (410 g) can pear halves
1 sachet **Bird's** Chocolate Flavoured Whisk & Serve
1 egg, separated
2 oz (50 g) caster sugar

Heat the oven to 375°F, 190°C, Gas Mark 5. Drain the pears and arrange them in the bottom of a 1½ pint (900 ml) ovenproof dish. Make up the Whisk & Serve as directed. Add the egg yolk and mix well. Pour over the pears. Whisk the egg white until stiff and gradually whisk in the sugar. Swirl over the custard and bake for 10 minutes until lightly browned. Serve hot.   **Serves 4**

Lemon Semolina Crunch

1 oz (25 g) butter
1 tablespoon (15 ml) golden syrup
8 digestive biscuits
1 packet **Bird's** Whisk and Serve Semolina
2 tablespoons (30 ml) lemon curd

Crush the digestive biscuits. Melt the butter and syrup together in a saucepan until golden and bubbling and stir in the biscuit crumbs until well coated. Make up the semolina as directed on the sachet and stir in the lemon curd. Pour the lemon semolina into a serving dish, sprinkle generously with the crunchy biscuit mixture and serve.

Crispy Raspberry Pudding

3 oz (75 g) demerara sugar
4 oz (125 g) fresh white breadcrumbs
2 oz (50 g) butter, melted
1 packet **Brown & Polson** Raspberry Blancmange Powder
1 tablespoon (30 ml) sugar
½ pint (275 ml) milk
7½ oz (212 g) can raspberries *or* loganberries

Stir the demerara sugar and breadcrumbs into the melted butter. Make up the blancmange as directed using only 1 tablespoon (30 ml) sugar, ½ pint (300 ml) milk and the juice from the can of fruit. Whisk in the fruit and pour into a shallow, ovenproof dish. Sprinkle with the breadcrumb mixture and cook at 375°F, 190°C, Gas Mark 5, for 15 minutes until crisp.

Serve hot with custard.
Serves 4

Baked Sweet Vermicelli

4 oz (100 g) **Buitoni** Vermicelli
1 pint (600 ml) creamy milk
½ pint (300 ml) double cream
1 teaspoon (5 ml) powdered
  cinnamon
4 oz (100 g) butter
4 oz (100 g) caster sugar
4 egg yolks

Cook the vermicelli in the milk for
10 minutes, stirring occasionally.
Add the cream, cinnamon, butter,
sugar and beaten egg yolks and
mix well. Pour into an ovenproof
dish and cook in an oven pre-
heated to 350°F, 180°C, Gas Mark 4,
for 30 minutes.   **Serves 4**

Cadbury's

Tangy Apple Charlotte

1½ lb (650 g) cooking apples,
  peeled, cored and sliced
grated rind and juice of 2 small
  oranges
2 oz (50 g) sugar
1 teaspoon (5 ml) ground
  cinnamon
3 oz (75 g) butter
2 oz (50 g) demerára sugar
4 oz (100 g) fresh breadcrumbs
3 large **Cadbury's** Flakes
¼ pint (150 ml) natural yoghurt
single cream *or* chocolate sauce
  to serve

Stew the apples with the sugar,
juice, cinnamon and half the butter
until soft. Mix the orange rind,
demerara sugar and breadcrumbs
together then crumble in 2 of the
Flakes. Put half the apple into a
lightly buttered, 1½ pint (800 ml)
ovenproof dish, then half the
breadcrumbs. Spread half the
yoghurt on top before repeating
the layers, omitting the yoghurt.
Melt the remaining butter and
pour over the top. Bake at 375°F,
190°C, Gas Mark 5, for about

25 minutes until crisp and a rich,
golden colour. Spread the
remaining yoghurt in the centre
and sprinkle with the remaining
Flake, crumbled.

  Serve with single cream or
chocolate sauce.   **Serves 4–6**

Chocolate Cap Pudding

4 oz (125 g) margarine
4 oz (125 g) caster sugar
6 oz (175 g) self-raising flour,
  sifted with a pinch of salt
1 tablespoon (15 ml) **Camp**
  Coffee and Chicory Essence
2 eggs
1 tablespoon (15 ml) cooking
  chocolate drops
4 oz (125 g) slab cooking
  chocolate

Cream the fat and sugar until light
and gradually add the eggs. Fold in
the flour, Camp Essence and
chocolate drops. Carefully turn the
mixture into a greased 2 pint
(1.2 litre) pudding basin, securely
cover with greased paper and
steam for about 2 hours.

  To serve, turn out on to a
warmed serving dish and pour
melted chocolate over the top to
give a thick chocolate cap to the
pudding. Accompany with a sweet
white sauce.   **Serves 6–8**

Carnation.

Apple Soufflé

1 small can **Carnation**
  Evaporated Milk
1 oz (25 g) butter
1 oz (25 g) flour
2 eggs, separated
2 oz (50 g) caster sugar
2 tablespoons (30 ml) apple
  purée

Make the Carnation milk up to
½ pint (300 ml) with water. Melt
the butter in a saucepan and stir in

the flour. Blend well and cook for
1 minute. Remove from the heat
and gradually stir in the milk until
well blended. Return to the heat,
stir until mixture comes to the boil
and cook for 2–3 minutes. Remove
from the heat, add the sugar and
beat in the egg yolks one at a
time, beating hard between each
addition. Beat in the apple purée.
Whisk the egg whites until stiff,
fold into the mixture and pour into
a greased 6 in (15 cm) soufflé dish.
Cook in a fairly hot oven (375°F,
190°C, Gas Mark 5) for 40 minutes.
Serve immediately.   **Serves 4**

Lemon Custard Sponge

2 oz (50 g) margarine
5 oz (150 g) caster sugar
2 eggs, separated
2 oz (50 g) self-raising flour
grated rind and juice of
  2 lemons (approx
  5 tablespoons (75 ml) of
  juice)
1 small can **Carnation**
  Evaporated Milk

Cream the margarine, add the
sugar and beat well until light and
fluffy. Add the egg yolks and
continue beating. Fold in the flour,
a little at a time, adding lemon rind
and juice between each addition.
Add the Carnation milk, made up
to ½ pint (300 ml) with water.
Whisk the egg whites until stiff
and fold in very carefully. Pour the
mixture into a buttered 2½ pint
(1.8 litre) pie dish and place in a
baking tin half full of warm water.
Bake in a moderate oven (350°F,
180°C, Gas Mark 4) for 50 minutes
until golden brown.   **Serves 4**

Queen of Puddings

3 oz (75 g) fresh breadcrumbs
¼ oz (7 g) butter
1 dessertspoon (10 ml) caster
  sugar
grated rind ½ lemon
1 small can **Carnation**
  Evaporated Milk
2 eggs, separated
1 tablespoon (15 ml) raspberry
  jam

3 oz (75 g) caster sugar
glacé cherries and angelica to
    decorate

Put the breadcrumbs, butter,
1 dessertspoon (10 ml) sugar and
the lemon rind into a basin. Make
the Carnation milk up to ¾ pint
(450 ml) with hot water. Pour on to
the crumbs and allow to stand for
10 minutes. Beat the egg yolks into
the mixture. Turn into a buttered
1 pint (600 ml) pie dish and bake in
a moderate oven (350°F, 180°C, Gas
Mark 4) for about 30 minutes until
set. Spread the top with jam.
Whisk the egg whites stiffly and
whisk in 1 oz (25 g) of the caster
sugar. Fold in the remainder.
Pile the meringue on top of the
pudding and bake in a cool oven
(300°F, 150°C, Gas Mark 2)
for about 40 minutes, until the
meringue is firm and lightly
browned. Decorate with the
cherries and angelica.   **Serves 4**

Toffee Apple Pudding

2 oz (50 g) butter
6 oz (175 g) demerara sugar
8 oz (225 g) self-raising flour
½ teaspoon (2.5 ml) salt
4 oz (100 g) finely shredded
    suet
1 small can **Carnation**
    Evaporated Milk
1 lb (450 g) cooking apples,
    peeled, cored and sliced

Soften the butter and spread over
the base and sides of a 2 pint
(1.2 litre) pudding basin. Sprinkle
evenly with 2 oz (50 g) of the
sugar. Sieve the flour and salt into
a mixing bowl, add the suet and
mix well. Make the Carnation milk
up to ¼ pint (150 ml) with water,
add to the dry ingredients and mix
to a soft dough. Fill the basin with
alternate layers of pastry, apples
and sugar, finishing with pastry.
Cover with buttered greaseproof
paper or aluminium foil and steam
for 2½ hours.   **Serves 4–6**

CHIVERS

Farmhouse Apple Cobbler

1 lb (400 g) cooking apples,
    peeled, cored and sliced
1 oz (25 g) butter
4 tablespoons (60 ml) sugar
juice and grated rind of
    1 orange
4 oz (100 g) self-raising flour
2 oz (50 g) margarine
2 tablespoons (30 ml) milk
3 tablespoons (45 ml) **Chivers**
    Olde English Marmalade

Cook the apples for 5 minutes in a
saucepan with the butter, 3 tablespoons (45 ml) of the sugar, and
the juice and grated orange rind
and pour into a 1½ pint (750 ml)
ovenproof dish. Sieve the flour,
stir in the remaining sugar and rub
in the margarine, then mix to a soft
dough with the milk. On a floured
surface roll out to a rectangle
measuring 6 × 12 in (15 × 30 cm).
Spread with the marmalade and
roll up from the long side, like a
swiss roll. Cut into about 10 slices
and lay them, cut side down, on
top of the apple. Bake in the oven,
set at 425°F, 220°C, Gas Mark 7, for
20–25 minutes until golden brown.
    Serve hot with custard or cream.
Serves 4–5

Old Fashioned Upside-Down Pudding

6 oz (150 g) fresh white
    breadcrumbs
3 tablespoons (45 ml) **Chivers**
    Olde English Marmalade
15½ oz (439 g) can pear halves
6 oz (150 g) margarine
6 oz (150 g) caster sugar
2 eggs
¼ pint (125 ml) milk
good pinch ground mixed spice
2 level teaspoons (10 ml)
    arrowroot

Spread the marmalade in the base
of a greased 7½ in (18.7 cm) round,
deep cake tin with 3 sliced pear
halves arranged on top. Cream the

margarine and sugar and gradually
beat in the eggs, milk, breadcrumbs and spice. The mixture
may look curdled at this stage.
Spoon into the tin and bake in a
pre-heated oven at 350°F, 180°C,
Gas Mark 4, for about 1 hour.
    Blend the arrowroot with a little
of the pear juice, add the remainder and bring slowly to the boil
until thickened and transparent.
Carefully turn out the pudding on
to a hot plate and arrange the
remaining pears on top.
    Serve with the thickened juice
and single cream or custard.
Serves 4–6

Victorian Coconut Pudding

2 oz (50 g) butter
4 tablespoons (60 ml) **Chivers**
    Olde English Marmalade
2 oz (50 g) desiccated coconut
6 oz (150 g) self-raising flour
4 oz (100 g) sugar
4 oz (100 g) soft margarine
5 tablespoons (75 ml) milk
2 eggs

Melt the butter in a saucepan with
3 tablespoons (45 ml) of the
marmalade, add the coconut and
spoon the mixture into a buttered
2 pint (1.2 litre) basin. Beat the
remaining ingredients together,
including the rest of the marmalade, and pour into the basin.
Cover with greased foil or paper
and steam for 1½ hours. Turn out
and serve with custard or cream.
Serves 5–6

FRANK COOPER®

Bread and Marmalade Pudding

6 oz (150 g) fresh white
  breadcrumbs
3 oz (75 g) raisins
3 oz (75 g) currants
2 oz (50 g) brown sugar
¾ level teaspoon (4 ml) mixed
  spice
3 tablespoons (45 ml) **Frank
  Cooper's** Fine Cut 'Oxford'
  Marmalade
1 oz (25 g) butter, melted
1 egg, beaten
milk to mix

Mix together all the ingredients,
using sufficient milk to give a soft,
dropping consistency. Place in an
ovenproof dish and bake at 350°F,
180°C, Gas Mark 4, for 1¼ hours.
Serves 6

Steamed Apple and Lemon Pudding

3 tablespoons (45 ml) **Frank
  Cooper's** Apple Sauce
4 oz (100 g) margarine
4 oz (100 g) caster sugar
2 eggs
grated rind and juice of 1 lemon
4 oz (100 g) plain flour
1 level teaspoon (5 ml) baking
  powder

Grease a 2 pint (1 litre) pudding
basin and place the apple sauce in
the bottom. Cream together the
butter and sugar until light and
fluffy and gradually beat in the
eggs. Stir in the lemon rind and
juice and fold in the sieved flour
and baking powder. Place the
mixture on top of the apple, cover
with a cloth or kitchen foil and
secure tightly, allowing room for
the pudding to rise. Steam for
1½ hours.   **Serves 6**

Hot Ginger Sponge

13¼ oz (376 g) can **Del Monte**
  Crushed Pineapple
4 oz (100 g) self-raising flour
4 oz (100 g) soft margarine
4 oz (100 g) castor sugar
2 eggs
2 tablespoons (30 ml) milk
2 level teaspoons (10 ml)
  ground ginger

Drain the pineapple, reserving the
juice. Beat together all the ingredients, except the pineapple, until
smooth. Put the pineapple and
some of the pineapple syrup into
an ovenproof dish. Spoon over the
ginger mixture and bake for about
45 minutes in the oven, pre-heated
to 375°F, 190°C, Gas Mark 5, until
cooked.

Serve hot with cream or custard,
made with some of the pineapple
syrup instead of milk.
Serves 4–6

Sweet and Saucy

14½ oz (411 g) can **Del Monte**
  Pear Halves, drained
Sauce
2 oz (50 g) soft brown sugar
½ packet **Brown & Polson**
  Chocolate Blancmange
  Powder
½ pint (275 ml) milk
Sponge
4 oz (125 g) butter
4 oz (125 g) sugar
2 eggs, beaten
½ teaspoon (2.5 ml) vanilla
  essence
½ packet **Brown & Polson**
  Chocolate Blancmange
  Powder
3 oz (75 g) self-raising flour
pinch salt
1–2 tablespoons (15–30 ml)
  milk
icing sugar

Place the pears in the base of a
buttered 2 pint (1.2 litre) deep,

ovenproof dish. For the sauce, mix
the sugar and blancmange powder
to a paste with a little of the milk.
Heat the remaining milk, stir into
the paste and pour over the pears.
For the sponge, cream together the
butter and sugar until light and
creamy and gradually add the eggs
and vanilla essence. Carefully fold
in the sieved blancmange powder,
flour and salt. Add sufficient milk
to give a soft, dropping consistency. Spoon the mixture over the
sauce. Bake at 375°F, 190°C, Gas
Mark 5, for 30–35 minutes until
well risen. Dust with icing sugar
before serving.   **Serves 4–6**

Dietade

Lemon Cheese Soufflé

8 oz (225 g) cottage cheese
3 eggs, separated
juice 1 lemon
grated rind 2 lemons
1 oz (25 g) **Dietade** Fruit Sugar

Sieve the cottage cheese and mix
with the egg yolks, lemon juice
and grated lemon rind. Mix in the
fruit sugar. Whisk the egg whites
stiffly and fold carefully into the
mixture until it is well blended.
Butter a 1½ pint (1 litre) soufflé
dish and tie greaseproof paper to
come to 2 in (5 cm) above the rim.
Fill with the cheese mixture and
stand the soufflé dish on a baking
tray. Bake in a pre-heated oven
(400°F, 200°C, Gas Mark 6) for
about 25 minutes, until well risen
and set. Serve immediately.
Serves 4

GALE'S

Baked Banana Boats

4 bananas
1 oz (25 g) butter
1 tablespoon (15 ml) **Gale's**
  Honey
squeeze of lemon juice
1 orange, thinly sliced

Place the peeled bananas in a
greased baking dish. Melt the
butter and honey in a small pan

and pour over the bananas. Add a squeeze of lemon juice. Bake for 20 minutes at 350°F, 180°C, Gas Mark 4.

Use the orange slices for sails and cocktail sticks for masts.
Serves 4

Peach Layer Pudding

1 lb 13 oz (822 g) can sliced peaches
3 oz (75 g) shredded suet
4 oz (100 g) fresh breadcrumbs
2 oz (50 g) **Grape Nuts**
3 oz (75 g) demerara sugar
4 oz (100 g) lemon curd
Sauce
syrup from the peaches
1 level tablespoon (15 ml) cornflour
2 rounded teaspoons (20 ml) lemon curd

Drain the syrup from the peaches and reserve for the sauce. Mix together all the dry ingredients and layer into a greased, oven-proof 2 pint (1 litre) dish with the lemon curd and peaches, ending with the crumb mixture. Spoon about 2 tablespoons (30 ml) of the peach syrup over the surface and bake in an oven pre-heated to 400°F, 200°C, Gas Mark 6, for 30–35 minutes until nicely browned. Thicken the rest of the syrup from the peaches with the cornflour and stir in the lemon curd.

Serve the sauce hot with the pudding. **Serves 4**

Homepride

Apple, Fig and Orange Roly-Poly Pudding

4 oz (100 g) **Homepride** Self-raising Flour
large pinch of salt
2 oz (50 g) shredded suet
4 tablespoons (60 ml) milk
2 cooking apples, peeled, cored and sliced
3 oz (75 g) dried figs, chopped
2 tablespoons (30 ml) caster sugar
grated rind of ½ orange
2 tablespoons (30 ml) golden syrup
4 tablespoons (60 ml) orange juice
6 tablespoons (90 ml) water

Mix the flour, salt and suet in a bowl. Make a well in the centre and add the milk. Mix to a soft dough, knead gently and roll out on a lightly floured surface to a rectangle 8 × 12 in (20 × 30 cm). Leaving a ½ in (1 cm) border all round, cover the dough with the apples, figs, sugar and orange rind. Roll up from a narrow side and pinch the ends to seal. Lift the suet roll carefully on to a well greased, shallow, ovenproof dish with the seam side down. Heat the golden syrup, orange juice and water and pour over the roll. Bake at 350°F, 180°C, Gas Mark 4, for 45 minutes, or until golden brown, basting once.

Serve hot with the remaining syrup. **Serves 6–8**

Keiller Bread Pudding

8 oz (225 g) stale bread
½ pint (300 ml) milk
2 oz (50 g) butter
6 oz (175 g) mixed dried fruit, washed
2 tablespoons (30 ml) **Keiller** Dundee Orange Marmalade
2 oz (50 g) demerara sugar
2 level teaspoons (10 ml) mixed spice
1 large egg, lightly beaten
caster sugar for sprinkling

Heat the oven to 350°F, 180°C, Gas Mark 4. Break the bread into small pieces and place in a medium sized bowl. Heat the milk and butter in a saucepan until the butter has melted, then pour over the bread. Leave to soak for 15 minutes. Beat the soaked bread with a fork until smooth. Add the dried fruit, marmalade, sugar, mixed spice and egg, beat well together. Spoon the mixture into a greased 1½ pint (1 litre) pie dish and bake in the centre of the pre-heated oven for 1½ hours. Sprinkle with caster sugar. Serve hot with Fulcreem Co. Custard. Alternatively, cool and serve cut into slices.
Serves 6–8

Baked Apples

4 medium cooking apples
2 oz (50 g) soft brown sugar
3 oz (85 g) packet **Kraft** Philadelphia Soft Cheese
2 teaspoons (10 ml) honey
2 oz (50 g) chopped mixed nuts

Core the apples and cut a slit around the centre of each. Place the apples in a baking tin with a little water around the base of each. Fill the centres with 2 teaspoons (10 ml) brown sugar. Bake in a pre-heated oven at 350°F, 180°C, Gas Mark 4, for 40 minutes, until apples are soft. Blend together the cheese and honey and add the nuts.

Serve the apples hot with the nut and honey topping. **Serves 4**

Banana and Orange Crumble

2 oz (50 g) margarine
4 oz (100 g) plain flour
2 oz (50 g) granulated sugar
½ packet **Lyons** Polka Dots
grated rind and juice of
 2 oranges
4 small bananas
1 teaspoon (5 ml) lemon juice

Rub the margarine into the flour until the mixture resembles fine breadcrumbs. Stir in the sugar, Polka Dots and orange rind. Peel and slice the bananas and place in the base of a shallow, ovenproof dish. Pour over the orange and lemon juices and cover with the crumble mixture. Bake near the top of the oven, pre-heated to 400°F, 200°C, Gas Mark 6, for 30–40 minutes.

Serve warm with cream, custard or an orange sauce. **Serves 4**

December Pudding

1 packet **Lyons** Suet Dumpling
 Mix
½ teaspoon (2.5 ml) mixed
 spice
2 oz (50 g) soft brown sugar
4 oz (100 g) fresh white
 breadcrumbs
1 packet **Lyons** Polka Dots
2 oranges
1 carrot, peeled and grated
1 egg (size 3)
3 tablespoons (45 ml) pale ale
1 dessertspoon (10 ml) black
 treacle

Orange Butter
3 oz (75 g) unsalted butter
4 oz (100 g) icing sugar, sieved
1 orange
1 teaspoon (5 ml) Cointreau *or*
 Grand Marnier

Lightly grease a 2 pint (1.2 litre) pudding basin. Mix together the suet dumpling mix, mixed spice, sugar, breadcrumbs, Polka Dots, finely grated orange rind and

carrot. Stir in the lightly beaten egg, juice of 1½ oranges, pale ale and black treacle. Turn into a lightly greased 2 pint (1.2 litre) pudding basin. Cover with a double layer of greaseproof paper or foil and secure with string. Place in a steamer over a pan of hot water or into a large saucepan half-filled with hot water. Cover and steam for 4 hours.

To make the Orange Butter, cream the butter until pale and soft, beat in the sugar and the finely grated orange rind. Gradually add the juice of half an orange and the Cointreau or Grand Marnier, taking care that the mixture does not curdle. Pile into a small dish and leave in the refrigerator until required.

To serve, turn out the pudding on to a warmed plate and serve with the Orange Butter. December Pudding can be made up to 2 weeks in advance and served as a lighter alternative to Christmas Pudding. After steaming, cover with foil and store in the refrigerator. Steam for a further 1 hour to re-heat before serving. **Serves 6**

Steamed Mocha Nut Pudding

2 oz (50 g) butter
5 oz (125 g) plain flour
2 level teaspoons (10 ml)
 baking powder
2 oz (50 g) soft brown sugar
1 oz (25 g) **Lyons** Polka Dots
1 oz (25 g) walnuts, chopped
1 egg (size 3)
3½ tablespoons (50 ml) strong
 black coffee

Chocolate and Coffee Sauce
3 oz (75 g) **Lyons** Polka Dots
1 tablespoon (15 ml) granulated
 sugar
3 tablespoons (45 ml) strong
 black coffee
knob of butter

Rub the butter into the sifted flour and baking powder until the mixture resembles fine breadcrumbs. Stir in the sugar, Polka Dots and nuts. Beat the egg and

black coffee together and mix into the dry ingredients. Place in a lightly greased 1 pint (600 ml) pudding basin. Cover with a double layer of foil or greaseproof paper and steam over a saucepan of boiling water for 1½ hours.

To make the sauce, place all the ingredients in a basin over a saucepan of hot (not boiling) water and stir until smooth. Beat vigorously until glossy. Turn the pudding out on to a warmed plate and serve with the hot sauce. **Serves 4**

Topsy Turvy Dessert

2 tablespoons (30 ml) orange
 marmalade
2 large oranges
4 oz (100 g) butter *or* margarine
4 oz (100 g) caster sugar
2 eggs (size 3)
6 oz (150 g) self-raising flour
½ packet **Lyons** Polka Dots
milk to mix

Spread the marmalade over the base of a greased 1½ pint (850 ml) ovenproof dish. Peel and thinly slice the oranges and arrange on top of the marmalade. Cream the fat and sugar together until light and fluffy. Gradually beat in the eggs, one at a time, adding a little of the flour with the second egg to prevent curdling. Fold in the remaining flour, Polka Dots and sufficient milk to give a soft, dropping consistency. Spread evenly over the oranges. Bake in the centre of the oven, pre-heated to 350°F, 180°C, Gas Mark 4, for 1 hour. Allow to stand for 10 minutes before turning out on to a warmed plate. **Serves 4**

Almond-Stuffed Peaches

6 peaches, skinned, stoned and
 halved *or* 16 oz (454 g) can
 peach halves, drained
½ **McVitie's** Dark Orange Cake

1 oz (25 g) blanched almonds,
  chopped
1 oz (25 g) crystallised orange *or*
  lemon peel, coarsely chopped
¼ pint (150 ml) concentrated
  frozen orange juice, thawed
cream to serve (optional)

Place the peach halves in a
shallow, ovenproof dish, with
hollow sides uppermost. Coarsely
grate the Dark Orange Cake and
mix with the almonds, crystallised
orange or lemon and 2 tablespoons
(30 ml) of the orange juice. Divide
the mixture between the peach
halves, pressing into the hollows.
Spoon the remaining orange juice
over and around the peaches. Bake
in a moderately hot oven pre-
heated to 375°F, 190°C, Gas Mark 5,
for 15–20 minutes. Serve hot, with
cream if liked.
  McVitie's Jamaica Ginger or
Lemon Spice Cake may be used to
vary this recipe.   **Serves 6**

Golden Fruit Slices

1 **McVitie's** Golden Syrup Cake
1 oz (25 g) butter
1 lb (450 g) fresh fruit, sliced
  (apricots, cherries, plums,
  peaches)
4 fl oz (100 ml) orange juice
2 tablespoons (30 ml) Grand
  Marnier *or* Cointreau
  (optional)
ice cream to serve

Slice the Golden Syrup Cake into
8 pieces and place 2 pieces on each
of 4 serving plates. Melt the butter
in a frying pan and when sizzling
add the prepared fruit. Cook over a
high heat for 2–3 minutes. Add the
orange juice and cook for a further
3 minutes. Stir in the liqueur if
used. Spoon the fruit mixture over
the Golden Syrup Cake slices and
top each with a scoop of ice cream.
Serve at once.
  McVitie's Jamaica Ginger, Dark
Orange or Lemon Spice Cake may
be used to vary this recipe.
Serves 4

Cadbury's Marvel

Plum Puffle

1½ lb (600 g) plums *or* damsons
4 oz (125 g) sugar
2 oz (50 g) sultanas
8 oz (225 g) cottage cheese
3 eggs, separated
3 oz (75 g) self-raising flour
½ teaspoon (2.5 ml) ground
  nutmeg
¾ pint (400 ml) liquid **Marvel**

Stew the fruit with 1 oz (25 g)
sugar and a very little water if
necessary, then sieve to remove
stones. Add the sultanas to the
fruit purée, adjust the sweetness
then put just over half into a
greased, 2½ pint (1.25 litre)
ovenproof dish. Simmer the
remaining fruit purée for about
10 minutes to serve as a sauce.
  Beat the cottage cheese, egg
yolks and remaining sugar
together. Sieve the flour and
nutmeg and fold into the cheese,
alternately with the Marvel.
Finally, fold in the whisked egg
whites, pour on top of the purée in
the dish and bake at 350°F, 180°C,
Gas Mark 4, for about 1 hour,
until well risen and a good colour.
If browning too much, lay a piece
of paper on top.
  Serve with the plum sauce.
Serves 6

Spiced Fruit Custard

1 lb (450 g) rhubarb
3 oz (75 g) soft brown sugar
grated rind and juice of 1 large
  orange
2 large slices brown toast
2 teaspoons (10 ml) ground
  cinnamon
3 eggs, lightly beaten
1 pint (550 ml) liquid **Marvel**
knob of butter
¾ oz (20 g) bran
2 tablespoons (40 ml) demerara
  sugar

Cut the rhubarb into even lengths
then stew with the sugar, grated
rind and orange juice for 5–10

minutes. Pour into an ovenproof
dish. Cut the crusts off the toast
then cut into smallish cubes and
put on top of the rhubarb with the
cinnamon. Bring the Marvel and
butter almost to the boil then beat
in the eggs and strain the custard
over the rhubarb. Sprinkle the
bran and demerara sugar mixed
together on top. Bake at 350°F,
180°C, Gas Mark 4, for about 50
minutes until set.
  Serve with single cream if liked.
Other fruit such as gooseberries or
apples may be substituted when in
season.   **Serves 5**

NESCAFÉ.

Coffee Fudge Pudding

8 oz (227 g) can pineapple
  slices, drained
4 oz (100 g) vanilla fudge, cut
  into slices
4 oz (100 g) margarine
4 oz (100 g) caster sugar
2 large eggs
4 oz (100 g) self-raising flour,
  sifted
1 level dessertspoon (10 ml)
  Nescafé dissolved in
  1 tablespoon (15 ml) boiling
  water
milk to mix

Butter a 2 pint (1.2 litre) ovenproof
dish, place the pineapple in the
bottom and cover with the fudge.
Using a wooden spoon or electric
mixer, cream the margarine and
sugar together until light and
fluffy. Beat the eggs in thoroughly,
one at a time. Using a metal spoon,
fold in half the flour and the
dissolved Nescafé, then fold in the
remaining flour. Add a little milk
if necessary to mix to a soft,
dropping consistency. Spread the
mixture over the fudge. Place on
the middle shelf of an oven pre-
heated to 350°F, 180°C, Gas Mark 4,
and bake for about 45–50 minutes,
until well risen, golden brown and
firm. Invert on to a plate and serve
immediately.
  Serve with Fulcreem Co.
Custard or Nestlé's Cream.
Serves 4–6

Baked Egg Custard

2–4 eggs *or* egg yolks
1–2 oz (25–50 g) sugar
2 tablespoons (30 ml) **Ovaltine**
1 pint (600 ml) milk

Beat the eggs and sugar together. Heat the milk and whisk in the Ovaltine. Pour the hot, but not boiling, milk mixture over the eggs and blend well. Pour into a casserole or pie dish. Stand the dish in another half filled with cold water and bake for approximately 1¼–1½ hours in a very slow oven, 275°F, 140°C, Gas Mark 1, until quite firm. **Serves 4**

Feather Sponge Pudding

3 oz (75 g) **Ovaltine** Drinking Chocolate
2 tablespoons (30 ml) water
3 oz (75 g) margarine
2 oz (50 g) sugar
2 eggs
4 oz (100 g) sieved flour (with plain flour add 1 teaspoon (5 ml) baking powder)

Mix the drinking chocolate with the water, stirring well until smooth. Cream the margarine and sugar and add the eggs gradually, beating well. Then stir in the drinking chocolate and sieved flour. Put into a greased and floured basin, allowing room to rise. Cover with greased paper or foil and steam for 1½ hours. Turn out and serve with chocolate sauce. **Serves 4–5**

Variations
Chocolate Raisin Pudding. As above but add 3 oz (75 g) seedless raisins.
Chocolate Orange Sponge. As above but add the finely grated rind of 2 oranges. Serve with orange or chocolate and orange sauce.

RY·KING

Baked Apples

3 slices **Ry-King** Brown Rye, crumbled
2 oz (50 g) sultanas *or* raisins
2–3 tablespoons (30–45 ml) clear honey
4 good sized cooking apples

Combine the crumbled Brown Rye with the raisins and honey and mix well. Core the apples and score round the middle of each one. Fill the cavity of each apple with the Brown Rye mixture, pressing well down. Place in a shallow, oven-proof dish and place approximately 4 tablespoons of water in the dish. Cook for 25–30 minutes at 350°F, 180°C, Gas Mark 4, until the apples are tender.
    Serve hot with cream or custard. **Serves 4**

Wholemeal Pancakes

6 slices **Ry-King** Brown Rye, finely crushed
2 eggs
2 oz (50 g) flour
½ pint (250 ml) milk
¼ pint (125 ml) water
lard *or* oil to fry

Place the Ry-King crumbs in a bowl and beat in the eggs, flour, milk and water. Allow to stand for 15–20 minutes. When ready to make the pancakes it may be necessary to add a little more water. Using a small frying pan melt a little lard or oil then proceed in the normal way for pancakes. You will not be able to toss these pancakes.

Suggested Fillings
Stewed apples with sultanas. Cream cheese mixed with a little natural yoghourt and some sliced canned apricots.
Makes 6 pancakes

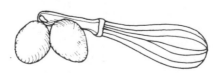

SCHWARTZ

Sherry and Mincemeat Pudding

2 tablespoons (30 ml) clear honey
approx 8 oz (225 g) mincemeat
4 oz (113 g) caster sugar
4 oz (113 g) soft margarine
6 oz (170 g) self-raising flour
1 teaspoon (5 ml) **Schwartz** Ground Cinnamon
1 teaspoon (5 ml) **Schwartz** Ground Nutmeg
2 eggs (size 3)
2 tablespoons (30 ml) sweet sherry

Sauce
2 oz (57 g) butter
1 oz (28 g) cornflour
1 oz (28 g) caster sugar
¾ pint (427 ml) milk
sweet sherry to taste

Place the honey in a 2½ pint (1.5 litre) basin and spread over the inside of basin with a knife. Press a thin coating of mincemeat over the honey to line the basin. Place all the remaining pudding ingredients in a large bowl. Mix well until thoroughly combined. Spoon the mixture into the prepared basin. Cover with greaseproof paper and a pudding cloth tied securely with string. Steam over a low heat for 2 hours in a covered saucepan half-filled with boiling water. Top up with boiling water occasionally as necessary.

    To make the sauce, melt the butter in a saucepan and stir in the cornflour, followed by the sugar and milk. Bring to the boil, stirring. Add the sherry to taste and cook for 1–2 minutes.

    Turn the cooked pudding on to a warm plate and serve with the sauce. This pudding may be made in advance, stored in a refrigerator for up to 3 days and reheated by resteaming, or frozen for up to 6 months. **Serves 4–6**

Sharwood's

Ginger and Banana Pancakes

Pancake batter
4 oz (100 g) flour sifted with a
  pinch of salt
1 egg
½ pint (250 ml) milk
Filling
3 bananas
1 tablespoon (15 ml) double
  cream
3 pieces **Sharwood's** Stem
  Ginger, chopped
icing sugar
2 tablespoons (30 ml) brandy
  (optional)

Prepare the pancake batter and use
it to make a batch of pancakes.
Mash the bananas with the cream
and stir in the stem ginger. Divide
this mixture between the pancakes
and roll up each one. Dredge the
pancakes with icing sugar. Set
alight the brandy and pour it over
the pancakes, if liked.
**Makes 6–8 pancakes, depending
on size**

Orange Bran Pudding

4 oz (125 g) **Stork** Margarine
4 oz (125 g) caster sugar
2 eggs (size 3)
5 oz (150 g) self-raising flour
1 teaspoon (5 ml) baking
  powder
1 oz (25 g) bran
rind and juice of 1 orange
2–3 tablespoons (30–45 ml)
  orange marmalade

Place all the ingredients except the
marmalade in a mixing bowl and
beat together for 2–3 minutes until
well mixed. Spoon the marmalade
into the base of a greased 2 pint
(900 ml) **pudding basin**. Place the
sponge mixture over the marmalade and level with a palette knife.
Cover with greaseproof paper or
foil and steam for 1½ hours. Turn
out on to a serving dish and serve
with custard or an orange sauce.
Serves 4–6

Chocolate and Pear Upside Down Cake

2 oz (50 g) butter
2 oz (50 g) demerara sugar
14½ oz (410 g) can **John West**
  Pear Halves
1 oz (25 g) walnuts, chopped
1 packet chocolate sponge mix

Melt the butter and sugar over a
low heat and pour into an 8 in
(20 cm) lined sandwich tin. Slice
the pears and arrange in the base of
the tin. Place the chopped nuts in
the centre. Make up the sponge
mix according to the packet
directions and spread on top of the
fruit. Bake at 375°F, 190°C, Gas
Mark 5, for 30 minutes. Turn out
and serve hot or cold.

whitworths

Prune Popovers

8 oz (200 g) **Whitworths** Prunes
½ pint (250 ml) water
2 tablespoons (30 ml) lemon
  juice
1 tablespoon (15 ml)
  Whitworths Dark Brown
  Sugar
2 oz (50 g) butter
4 oz (100 g) **Whitworths** Caster
  Sugar
2 eggs, separated
4 oz (100 g) **Whitworths** Self-
  raising Flour
2 tablespoons (30 ml) milk
cream *or* custard to serve

Grease 6 small pudding basins or
cups. Put the prunes, water and
lemon juice into a pan and bring to
the boil. Lower the heat and
simmer for 10 minutes. Strain the
prunes and mix the juice with the
brown sugar. Stone the prunes and
add to the syrup. Divide the fruit
mixture between the 6 small
containers.

Cream together the butter and
sugar, beat in the egg yolks and
fold in the sifted flour. Stir in the
milk to give a soft, dropping
consistency. Whisk the egg whites
until stiff and fold into the sponge
mixture. Divide the mixture
between the 6 containers. Cover
each with foil and steam gently for
45 minutes. Turn out and serve hot
with cream or custard.   **Serves 6**

Spicy Fig Pudding

13 oz (375 g) **Whitworth** Figs,
  chopped
4 oz (125 g) raisins
2 oz (50 g) stem ginger,
  chopped
6 oz (175 g) fresh white
  breadcrumbs
4 oz (125 g) shredded suet
4 oz (125 g) self-raising flour
2 tablespoons (30 ml) brandy *or*
  rum
2 eggs
grated rind and juice of
  1 orange
1 teaspoon (5 ml) mixed spice

Grease a 1½ pint (900 ml) pudding
basin. Combine all the dry ingredients. Beat the brandy, eggs and
orange juice together. Add this to
the dry ingredients and mix well.
Cover with pleated, buttered foil.
Steam for 4 hours.   **Serves 4–6**

COLD DESSERTS

Brown Bread Ice Cream

2 oz (50 g) butter
3 oz (75 g) stale breadcrumbs, made from **Allinson** Wholewheat Bread
6 oz (175 g) granulated sugar
4 egg yolks
½ pint (300 ml) milk *or* single cream
2 tablespoons (30 ml) sweet sherry
½ pint (300 ml) double cream, lightly whipped

Melt the butter, add the bread-crumbs and fry until crisp. Sprinkle on half the sugar and continue to fry until the sugar has caramelised, stirring constantly. Pour on to a wooden board, leave to cool, then crush into fine crumbs with a rolling pin.

Beat the egg yolks with the re-maining sugar until light and fluffy. Scald the milk or single cream and pour slowly on to the egg mixture, beating constantly. Return to the pan and heat gently without boiling, stirring con-stantly until the mixture has thickened enough to coat the back of the spoon. Remove from the heat and leave to cool. When cool, stir in the breadcrumbs and sherry, then fold in the double cream.

Pour into a rigid container and freeze rapidly, either in the ice-making compartment of the refrigerator, or in the freezer. After 1 hour, or when the mixture begins to set, stir well with a fork to distribute the crumbs evenly. Transfer to a storage container, and return to the freezer.
Serves 6

Alpen

Strawberry Fool Layers

8 oz (225 g) strawberries, fresh *or* frozen, thawed
¼ pint (150 ml) double cream, whipped
sugar to taste
4 oz (100 g) butter
8 oz (225 g) **Alpen**
4 whole strawberries to decorate

Purée the strawberries and mix into the whipped cream. Add sugar to taste. Melt the butter and stir in the Alpen. Spoon alternate layers of strawberry fool and Alpen into tall glasses. Top each with a whole strawberry to decorate.
Serves 4

Ambrosia

Butterscotch Creams

2 oz (50 g) butter
3 oz (75 g) demerara sugar
15½ oz (439 g) **Ambrosia** Creamed Semolina
1 oz (25 g) plain chocolate, grated
1 oz (25 g) walnut halves, finely chopped
¼ pint (150 ml) double cream

Melt the butter and stir in the sugar. Continue stirring over a low heat for 3 minutes and then stir into the creamed semolina until well mixed. Put into 4 individual dishes and chill. Mix the chocolate and walnuts together and sprinkle evenly on top of the semolina. Whip the cream and pipe a large rosette on top of each portion.
Serves 4

Lemon Snow

15½ oz (439 g) **Ambrosia** Creamed Semolina
juice and finely grated rind of 2 lemons
2 egg whites
3 oz (75 g) caster sugar
crystallised lemon slices for decoration

Put the semolina into a bowl and fold in the lemon juice and rind until well mixed. Whisk the egg whites to stiff peaks and gradually whisk in the sugar until the mixture is thick and shiny. Fold into the semolina mixture until completely blended. Pile into individual glasses and chill for 1 hour.

Decorate with crystallised lemon slices. **Serves 6**

Tipsy Laird (Raspberry Trifle)

6 slightly stale sponge cakes *or* 1 swiss roll
6–8 heaped dessertspoons (90 ml) **Baxters** Raspberry Jam
rind of 1 lemon, finely grated
¼ pint (150 ml) sherry
2 tablespoons (30 ml) brandy
1 can **Baxters** Raspberries
1 pint (600 ml) thick, rich custard
½ pint (300 ml) double cream
castor sugar to taste
1 or 2 drops vanilla essence
glacé cherries, angelica and chopped nuts to decorate

Split the sponge cakes, spread each half with jam and arrange in a glass serving dish. If using a swiss roll, cut into slices, spread with jam and arrange on the base and sides of

the dish. Sprinkle with the grated lemon rind. Mix together the sherry and brandy and pour over the sponge, allowing it to soak thoroughly. Drain the juice from the raspberries and arrange the fruit over the sponge. Make up the custard and allow to cool slightly before pouring over the fruit. Allow to become cold and firm. Whip the cream until it just holds its shape, add castor sugar to taste and the vanilla essence. Spread the cream over the custard and decorate with the glacé cherries, angelica and chopped nuts.
Serves 6–8

Chocolate Mint Ripple

¼ pint (150 ml) double cream
 or 1 sachet Bird's Dream Topping plus ¼ pint (150 ml) cold milk
½ pint (300 ml) cold milk
1 sachet **Bird's** Mint Chocolate Angel Delight
chocolate curls *or* grated chocolate to decorate

Whisk the cream steadily until it starts to thicken, or make up the Dream Topping as directed on the sachet. Put the milk into a basin, sprinkle in the Mint Chocolate Angel Delight and whisk until creamy. Serve in small sundae glasses, layering the cream or Dream Topping with the chocolate dessert. Decorate with chocolate curls or grated chocolate to serve.   **Serves 4**

Loganberry Bombe

2 sachets **Bird's** Dream Topping
½ pint (300 ml) milk
¼ oz (7 g) butter, softened
8 oz (225 g) loganberries
sugar to taste

Make up 1 sachet of Dream Topping as directed, whisk through the softened butter and use to coat the inside of a 1½ pint (900 ml) pudding basin. Put to freeze.

Make up the second sachet of Dream Topping as usual, whisk through the loganberries and add sugar to taste. Put into the prepared basin and put to freeze.

If deep frozen, leave at room temperature for about 1 hour before serving.

Brown & Polson

Caramel Whips

1 packet **Brown & Polson** Caramel Blancmange Powder
2–3 tablespoons (30–45 ml) sugar
¾ pint (425 ml) milk
6 oz (170 g) can evaporated milk, well chilled
chocolate vermicelli to decorate

Make up the blancmange as directed using only ¾ pint (450 ml) of milk. Leave to cool, stirring occasionally. Whisk the evaporated milk until thick and creamy then whisk in the blancmange. Pour into 4 individual glass dishes and leave to set in the refrigerator or a cool place for 1–2 hours. Decorate with the chocolate vermicelli.   **Serves 4**

Dutch Milk Tart

6 oz (175 g) digestive biscuits, crushed
3 oz (75 g) butter, melted
1 packet **Brown & Polson** Vanilla Blancmange Powder
¾ pint (425 ml) milk
2–3 tablespoons (30–45 ml) sugar
2 eggs, separated
ground cinnamon

Stir the biscuits into the melted butter, press into an 8 in (20 cm) flan dish and chill. Blend the blancmange powder with a little of the milk and stir in the sugar and egg yolks. Heat the remaining milk and add to the blancmange mixture. Return to the heat, bring to the boil, stirring, and simmer for 1 minute. Remove from the heat. Whisk the egg whites until

stiff, fold into the blancmange mixture and pour into the biscuit case. Sprinkle with ground cinnamon and chill for 2 hours before serving.   **Serves 4–6**

Rhubarb and Ginger Layered Fool

1 lb (450 g) rhubarb, wiped, trimmed and cut into pieces
a little water
sugar to taste
1 packet **Brown & Polson** Vanilla Blancmange Powder
½–1 level teaspoon (2.5–5 ml) ground ginger
2–3 tablespoons (30–45 ml) sugar
1 pint (568 ml) milk
3 tablespoons (45 ml) fresh single cream
ground ginger to decorate

Cook the rhubarb in the minimum of water, adding sugar to taste, until just tender. Make up the blancmange as directed, adding the ground ginger to the blancmange powder before mixing. Allow to cool slightly and stir in the cream. Layer the blancmange with the rhubarb in 4 individual glass dishes. Sprinkle with a little ground ginger and chill beofre serving.   **Serves 4**

Sherry Cups

1 packet **Brown & Polson** Caramel Blancmange Powder
2–3 tablespoons (30–45 ml) sugar
1 pint (568 ml) milk
4 tablespoons (60 ml) sherry
¼ pint (142 ml) carton fresh single cream
fresh whipped cream to decorate

Make up the blancmange as directed. Stir in the sherry and cream and pour into 4 individual glass dishes. Leave to set in a refrigerator or cool place for 1–2 hours. Decorate with the cream.
 Serve with macaroons or sponge fingers.   **Serves 4**

Cadbury's

Dreamy Chocolate Mousse

1 packet **Pascall** Marshmallows
6 tablespoons (100 ml) milk
finely grated rind and juice of
   2 oranges
orange squash
3 tablespoons (60 ml)
   Cadbury's Drinking
   Chocolate
½ pint (284 ml) whipping
   cream

Reserve 4 marshmallows. Melt the remainder gently in the milk. Add the finely grated rind of the oranges. Remove any pips from the orange juice and make up to ¼ pint (150 ml) with the squash. Stir the juice and drinking chocolate into the milk and leave to cool. When cold, whip most of the cream and fold into the liquid, pour into glasses and leave to set. Decorate with whirls of whipped cream and the marshmallows.
Serves 4

Mocha Magic

4 oz (100 g) fresh brown
   breadcrumbs
5 oz (125 g) demerara sugar
1 teaspoon (5 ml) instant coffee
   powder
2 oz (50 g) **Cadbury's** Drinking
   Chocolate
¼ pint (142 ml) double cream
¼ pint (142 ml) single cream
1 oz (25 g) **Bournville** Plain
   Chocolate, grated

Mix the breadcrumbs, sugar, coffee and drinking chocolate together. Whip the creams together, not too stiffly. Place layers of cream and the bread-crumb mixture in a glass bowl, ending with cream on top. Cover with grated chocolate and chill for as long as possible.

This dessert should ideally be made at least 24 hours in advance.
Serves 6–8

Yoghurt Jelly

1 **Chivers** Strawberry
   Flavoured Jelly
10 oz (284 g) can **Hartleys**
   Strawberries
1 small carton strawberry
   yoghurt
1 large **Cadbury's** Flake
¼ pint (150 ml) whipping
   cream

Dissolve the jelly in ½ pint (250 ml) boiling water. Whisk the straw-berries and juice into the jelly, squashing the fruit, then whisk in the yoghurt. It should make up to 1 pint (568 ml); if not, add a little fruit juice or water. Pour into a glass bowl and set in the ref-rigerator, stirring occasionally before it sets to disperse the fruit. Crumble the Flake in the centre and pipe whipped cream round the edge.   **Serves 4**

Carnation.

Carnation Yoghurt

14½ oz (410 g) can **Carnation**
   Evaporated Milk
warm boiled water
2 level tablespoons (30 ml)
   dried skimmed milk powder
2 level tablespoons (30 ml)
   bought natural yoghurt

Pour the Carnation milk into a 2 pint (1 litre) measuring jug and make up to 1½ pint (900 ml) with warm boiled water. Whisk in the dried milk and the yoghurt and pour into one of the following: an electric yoghurt maker, a large warmed thermos flask or a slow cooker. These methods will take about 3 hours. You can also use a large, empty, clean coffee jar which has been warmed. Fill with yoghurt and cover tightly, placing the coffee jar in an airing cupboard or similar warm place overnight. The yoghurt may not be as thick as when made by other methods— add extra dried milk to subsequent batches to make the thickness you prefer. When made store in the

refrigerator. The yoghurt thickens slightly on storage.
Makes 1½ pints (900 ml)

Caribbean Brulée

13½ oz (385 g) can sweetened
   apple slices
3 large bananas, peeled and
   sliced
2 tablespoons (30 ml) brandy
6 fl oz (170 ml) double cream
8 fl oz (225 ml) **Carnation**
   yoghurt (see recipe above)
8 oz (225 g) soft brown sugar

In an ovenproof dish combine the apple slices and bananas and sprinkle the brandy over. Beat the cream until stiff. Lightly beat in the yoghurt and spoon evenly over the fruit. Sift the sugar over to give an even layer and place under a preheated grill to caramelise the sugar. Chill.

To serve, tap the caramel to break.   **Serves 6–8**

Luxury Ginger Ice Cream

2 eggs, separated
3 oz (75 g) caster sugar
pinch salt
1 large can **Carnation**
   Evaporated Milk
2 tablespoons (30 ml) stem
   ginger, chopped with syrup

One hour before making the ice cream set the refrigerator at the coldest point.

Beat the egg yolks, sugar and salt in a bowl until creamy. Heat the Carnation milk gently but do not boil and pour on to the egg yolk mixture. Cook in a double boiler or a basin over a pan of hot water, stirring, until the custard thickens enough to coat the back of the spoon. Sieve, add the stem ginger and allow to cool. Whip the egg whites until stiff and fold into the custard. Pour into ice trays and place in the ice making compart-ment of the refrigerator until frozen.   **Serves 4**

Rich Vanilla Ice Cream

14½ oz (410 g) can **Carnation** Evaporated Milk
2 eggs, beaten
4 level tablespoons (60 ml) caster sugar
½ teaspoon (2.5 ml) vanilla essence
2 egg whites

In a heavy saucepan combine half the Carnation Milk with the beaten whole eggs and sugar. Cook, stirring continuously, over a low heat until it forms a thick custard. Strain into a bowl and stir in the vanilla. Cover and refrigerate until well chilled. Also refrigerate the rest of the Carnation Milk. Beat the egg whites until stiff, whip the chilled Carnation Milk until stiff and fold both into the chilled custard. Pour into a freezer container or mould and freeze.

Allow to soften in the refrigerator for 1 hour before serving. **Makes 2 pints (1.1 litre)**

CHIVERS

Summer Haze

1 **Chivers** Lime Flavour Jelly
¼ pint (125 ml) water
¼ pint (125 ml) concentrated **Kia-Ora** Lemon and Lime Drink
3 eggs, separated
3 oz (75 g) caster sugar
¼ pint (125 ml) whipping cream and green glacé cherries to decorate (optional)

Dissolve the jelly in ¼ pint (125 ml) water in a saucepan, add the lemon and lime drink then make up to ¾ pint (375 ml) with cold water. Leave until almost setting but not lumpy. Whisk the egg yolks with the sugar until they become pale in colour, stir in the jelly then leave in a cool place until beginning to set. Fold in the stiffly whisked egg whites, pour into a 2½ pint (1.5 litre) serving dish and leave to set. Decorate with the whipped cream and green glacé cherries if liked. **Serves 4–6**

Caribbean Custard

1 pint (600 ml) cold custard
3 tablespoons (45 ml) cream *or* top of milk
13¼ oz (375 g) can **Del Monte** Crushed Pineapple
1 banana, sliced
2 oz (50 g) desiccated coconut
1 oz (25 g) sugar

Stir the cream into the custard. Drain the pineapple and stir into the custard with the sliced banana. Spoon into individual glass dishes or a serving bowl. Mix the coconut and sugar and brown under the grill. Allow to cool then sprinkle on top of the custard and fruit. **Serves 6**

Pineapple Alaska

13¼ oz (375 g) can **Del Monte** Crushed Pineapple
5 oz (125 g) sugar
¼ pint (150 ml) whipping cream
4 trifle sponges
apricot jam
2 egg whites

Drain the pineapple. Slice the trifle sponges. Sandwich the slices together with the jam, cream and pineapple and press into a 1 lb (450 g) loaf tin. Put to freeze. When frozen, just before serving, ease out of the tin and place on an ovenproof dish or plate. Heat the oven to 400°F, 200°C, Gas Mark 6. Whisk the egg whites until stiff, whisk in half the remaining sugar then stir in the other half. Cover the frozen loaf with the meringue and place in the oven for 10–15 minutes until browned. Serve immediately. **Serves 4**

Dietade

Coffee Whip

1 pint (600 ml) strong coffee, unsweetened

1 oz (25 g) gelatine
1 oz (25 g) **Dietade** Fruit Sugar
2 egg whites

Put the gelatine in half a cup of heated but not boiling coffee and stir until dissolved. Strain the remaining coffee, add the fruit sugar and leave in a cool place until the mixture starts to set. Whisk the egg whites stiffly and fold into the mixture.

Serve chilled, in individual glasses. **Serves 4**

Fruit in Caramel

1 lb (450 g) **Dietade** Fruit Sugar
8 fl oz (240 ml) water
3 bananas
2 eating apples
2 oranges
1 pear
2 oz (50 g) grapes
4 oz (100 g) plain cake *or* trifle sponge
whipped cream, yoghurt *or* custard to serve

Put the sugar and water into a heavy saucepan and heat gently until the sugar has dissolved. When completely dissolved, increase the heat and cook the syrup until it is a rich caramel colour. Watch it carefully, so that it does not burn. Peel the fruit, cut the bananas into ¼ in (0.5 cm) slices and the rest of the fruit into quarters. Cut the cake into 1 in (2.5 cm) cubes. Put the cake into the bottom of a serving dish or bowl. Once the syrup is thick enough to coat the back of a spoon, add the fruit, off the heat, and stir gently until the fruit is well coated. Spoon the caramelised fruit over the cubed cake and serve cold with whipped cream or yoghurt.

This recipe can also be served hot, with custard. **Serves 4–6**

Ginger Up Ice Cream

juice of ½ a lemon
water
2 pots **Elsenham** Ginger Up
1 large can evaporated milk
1 oz (25 g) gelatine

Add sufficient water to the lemon juice to make up 2 fl oz (60 ml) of liquid. Bring to the boil and add to the gelatine, which has been previously soaked in water, and set aside to cool. In a large bowl, beat the evaporated milk until thickened. Fold in the Ginger Up and then add the cooled gelatine mixture. Pour into individual dishes or one large dish and freeze.   **Serves 6–8**

Caramelised Bananas

2 large bananas
½ can **Findus** Concentrated
    Orange Juice
2 tablespoons (30 ml)
    Cointreau
¼ pint (125 ml) double cream,
    whipped
jellied orange slices and halved
    walnuts to decorate

Skin the bananas and split lengthwise. Place in an ovenproof dish and pour over the orange juice and Cointreau. Place the dish on a baking tray and cook in a pre-heated oven (400°F, 200°C, Gas Mark 6) for 25 minutes. Spoon the sauce over the bananas half-way through the cooking time. Allow to cool, lift on to individual serving dishes, pipe with cream and decorate with the orange slices and walnuts.   **Serves 2**

Chocolate Mousse Alaska

1 chocolate swiss roll cut into
    8 slices
4 tubs **Findus** Chocolate
    Mousse
2 egg whites, whisked until
    stiff
4 oz (100 g) castor sugar

Pre-heat the oven to 475°F, 240°C, Gas Mark 9. Divide the swiss roll equally between 4 individual ovenproof plates. Turn out the frozen mousse from the tubs and place centrally on the swiss roll slices. Whisk half the sugar into the egg whites and fold in the remaining sugar. Pile the meringue mixture on top of the mousse and swiss roll, covering them completely. Bake for 4 minutes, and serve immediately.
Serves 4

Orange Sorbet Baskets

2 oz (50 g) sugar
½ pint (300 ml) water
1 can **Findus** Concentrated
    Orange Juice, thawed
6 large oranges
2 egg whites
angelica leaves to decorate

Dissolve the sugar in the water and boil for 5 minutes. Stir in the orange juice. Pour into a shallow dish and allow to cool then freeze. When half set, tip into a chilled bowl and mix well to obtain an even texture. Whisk the egg whites until stiff and stir into the orange mixture. Return to the freezer until completely firm.

Meanwhile, prepare the orange baskets. With a sharp knife remove nearly a whole quarter segment from each orange, leaving a strip wide enough for the handle. Remove the other quarter segment in the same way. Remove the flesh of the orange and chop finely.

To serve, divide the chopped oranges between the baskets and scoop spoonfuls of sorbet over the top. Decorate with the angelica 'leaves'. Serve immediately or freeze on a suitable plate until required.   **Serves 6**

Kellogg's

Lime Delight

5 oz (150 g) plain flour
½ teaspoon (2.5 ml) salt
1 tablespoon (15 ml) caster
    sugar
2 oz (50 g) **Kellogg's** Corn
    Flakes, finely crushed
4 tablespoons (60 ml) vegetable
    oil
2 tablespoons (30 ml) cold
    water
Filling
½ pint (300 ml) double cream
14 oz (396 g) can sweetened
    condensed milk
6 tablespoons (90 ml) fresh lime
    juice
few drops green food colouring
    (optional)
¾ teaspoon (4 ml) finely grated
    lime rind (optional)
lime slices to decorate

Put the flour, salt, sugar and crushed Corn Flakes into a mixing bowl. Add the oil and water, stirring with a fork until well mixed. Turn into a deep 8–9 in (20–23 cm) pie plate and, using the back of a spoon, press evenly and firmly over the base and sides. Prick all over with a fork. Bake in a hot oven (450°F, 230°C, Gas Mark 8) for 10 minutes, or until lightly browned. Cool completely before filling.

Whip the cream until it stands in stiff peaks. Put the sweetened condensed milk into a mixing bowl and gradually add the lime juice, stirring constantly. Stir in the food colouring and lime rind, then fold in three-quarters of the whipped cream. Pour into the prepared case, swirl the surface and chill for about 2 hours, until firm.

Decorate with the remaining whipped cream and lime slices.
Serves 6–8

Festive Chestnut Cream

1 pint (568 ml) packet
Kerrygold Double Cream,
thawed
15½ oz (440 g) can chestnut
purée, sweetened
1 tablespoon (15 ml) icing
sugar, sifted
½ teaspoon (2.5 ml) vanilla
essence
4 oz (125 g) packet meringue
stars
1 oz (25 g) plain chocolate,
grated

Whisk the cream until just thick.
Beat the chestnut purée with the
icing sugar and vanilla essence
until smooth and creamy. Gradually add the cream to the chestnut
purée mixture and blend well. Pile
the mixture into a peak in the
centre of a serving dish. Press the
meringue stars all over the mixture
and sprinkle with grated chocolate. Chill until required. Serve
with extra Kerrygold cream,
thawed, if liked.

To prevent the meringues from
softening, arrange on top of the
mixture no more than 2 hours
before serving.   **Serves 8–10**

Strawberry Cream Cordon Bleu

1 lb (400 g) strawberries, fresh
    or frozen
6 oz (150 g) caster sugar
finely grated rind and juice of
    ½ orange *or* 2–3 table-
    spoons (30–45 ml) brandy
1 small box ratafia biscuits *or*
    3–4 macaroons
3 teaspoons (15 ml) powdered
    gelatine
juice of ½ lemon made up to
    2½ oz (75 ml) with water
8 oz (200 g) **Kerrygold** Frozen
    Whipping Cream, thawed
2 egg whites
pinch of salt

4 oz (100 g) **Kerrygold** Frozen
Whipping Cream, thawed
and whipped, and small
whole strawberries to
decorate

Hull and slice the strawberries into
a large bowl. Pour over the sugar,
add the grated orange rind, crush
the fruit a little with a stainless
steel fork and leave to stand for 30
minutes. Stir occasionally. Break
the ratafias in half or the
macaroons into pieces about the
size of a 10p piece. Sprinkle over
the orange juice or brandy. Soak
the powdered gelatine in the water
and lemon juice, melt and add to
the strawberries. Leave to stand in
a cool place until just beginning to
set, stirring occasionally. Lightly
whip the cream and fold into the
strawberry mixture. Whip the egg
whites with a pinch of salt until the
mixture stands in soft peaks. Fold
into the strawberry cream. Place a
spoonful of the soaked ratafias or
macaroons in the bottom of individual coupe glasses and spoon the
lightly setting mixture on top.
Cover and leave in a cool place for
2–3 hours until ready to serve.
Decorate with whipped cream and
small whole strawberries.

If you wish to make this recipe
the day before use only 2 teaspoons (10 ml) gelatine, cover and
store as above. If the strawberry
cream has been stored in a refrigerator it may be necessary to
take it out and leave it at room
temperature for 30 minutes so that
the mixture becomes a little softer
before serving.   **Serves 6–8**

Burnt Raspberry Creams

8 oz (200 g) raspberries
3 oz (85 g) packet **Kraft**
    Philadelphia Soft Cheese
5 fl oz (142 ml) carton sour
    cream
½ oz (15 g) icing sugar
4 oz (100 g) caster sugar

Divide the raspberries between
four ramekins or individual, heat-

proof dishes. Cream the cheese,
gradually beat in the sour cream
until smooth and creamy, and add
the icing sugar. Spoon the mixture
into the four dishes and level with
a knife. Sprinkle 1 oz (25 g) caster
sugar evenly over the surface of
each dish and place under a hot
grill until the sugar has caramelised. Cool. Chill thoroughly before
serving.

This recipe is delicious with any
soft fruit.   **Serves 4**

Chocolate Cream Ice

1 egg (size 3)
1 egg yolk
1 oz (25 g) caster sugar
1 packet **Lyons** Polka Dots
½ pint (275 ml) milk
¼ pint (150 ml) double cream,
    lightly whipped

Whisk the whole egg, egg yolk and
sugar together until light and
fluffy. Dissolve the Polka Dots in
the milk over a low heat, stirring all
the time. Bring to boiling point
and pour over the egg mixture,
stirring vigorously. Return to the
saucepan and cook over a low heat,
stirring all the time, until the
custard thickens. Do not allow to
boil. Remove from the heat, cover
with a sheet of greaseproof paper
and allow to cool. When the
custard is cold fold in the lightly
whipped cream. Pour into a rigid
freezer container or ice tray and
freeze for approximately 3–4
hours, until solid.

To serve, remove the Chocolate
Cream Ice from the freezer
30 minutes before serving and
leave in the refrigerator. Serve
with wafers if liked. Freezer life is
2 months.   **Serves 4**

Chocolate Marnier

¾ pint (425 ml) milk
finely grated rind and juice of
   2 oranges
1 tablespoon (15 ml) caster
   sugar
3 eggs (size 3), separated
¾ packet **Lyons** Polka Dots
1 tablespoon (15 ml) Grand
   Marnier
½ oz (15 g) gelatine
½ pint (275 ml) double cream,
   whipped
a few **Lyons** Polka Dots to
   decorate

Heat the milk and orange rind
until hot but not boiling. Whisk
the sugar and egg yolks together
until pale and thick. Pour the hot
milk on to the eggs, return to the
saucepan and stir continuously
over a low heat until slightly
thickened. Remove from the heat
and stir in the Polka Dots and
Grand Marnier until the chocolate
is dissolved. Dissolve the gelatine
in the juice of one orange in a basin
over a saucepan of hot (not boiling)
water. Stir into the custard and
allow to cool. To speed the cooling
process, stand the basin in a bowl
of ice cubes. When the mixture
begins to thicken, whisk the egg
whites until stiff and fold carefully
into the custard. Pour quickly into
an oiled, 1½ pint (900 ml) mould.
Chill for 1 hour or until set.

   To serve, carefully turn out on to
a serving dish and cover completely with the whipped cream,
smoothing evenly with a palette-
knife. Pipe a border of cream
around the top and bottom edges
and decorate with the Polka Dots.
Serves 6

Coffee Mallow Ice Cream

15 oz (425 g) packet
   marshmallows
¾ pint (450 ml) very strong
   Lyons Coffee
½ pint (300 ml) double cream

Put the marshmallows into a large
bowl and pour the hot coffee over
them. Stir well until they have
melted to the size of hazelnuts. (If

the coffee gets cold too quickly, set
the bowl over a pan of simmering
water for a minute or two.) Cool.
Whip the cream lightly and fold in
the mixture. Freeze until it starts to
set. Stir carefully with a fork, place
mixture in an ice tray and return to
the freezer. One hour before
serving remove from the freezer
and leave in the refrigerator.
Serves 4

Apricot and Almond Crunch

6 **McVitie's** Digestive Biscuits,
   roughly crushed with 1 oz
   (25 g) melted butter
1 medium carton double cream
2 teaspoons (10 ml) caster sugar
3 drops vanilla essence
1 medium can apricots
2 oz (50 g) flaked almonds
few roasted almonds to
   decorate

Whip the cream until stiff and fold
in the sugar and vanilla essence.
Roughly chop the apricots and add
with the almonds to the cream and
sugar mixture. Place half the mixture into a serving dish and
sprinkle the biscuit crumbs over
this. Spread the remaining mixture over the crumbs. Decorate
with the toasted almonds.

   Place in the freezing compartment overnight and serve frozen.
Serves 6

Apricot Yoghurt Wedge

1 oz (25 g) desiccated coconut
4 oz (100 g) **McVitie's** Digestive
   Biscuits, crushed
2 oz (50 g) butter *or* margarine,
   melted
4 oz (100 g) dried apricots
scant ¼ pint (150 ml) boiling
   water
½ pint (300 ml) natural yoghurt
3 tablespoons (45 ml) honey
2 eggs

apricots and whipped cream to
   decorate

Place the coconut in a heavy saucepan and stir over a moderate heat
until a light golden brown.
Remove from the pan at once. Mix
with the biscuits and melted butter
and press into a round foil dish
about 9 in (23 cm) in diameter.
Cover the apricots with boiling
water and leave to stand for 30
minutes. Blend in a liquidiser or
processor until smooth then add
the remaining ingredients and mix
well. Pour into the foil dish and
bake in a moderate oven at 350°F,
180°C, Gas Mark 4, for 30–35
minutes or until set. Remove and
leave to cool, then refrigerate for
several hours before serving.
Decorate with the apricots and
whipped cream.   **Serves 8**

Banana and Apricot Jelly

2 (4¾ oz, 135 g) packets orange
   jelly
4 medium sized ripe bananas
1 lb 13 oz (822 g) can apricot
   halves
1 **McVitie's** Lemon Spice Cake

Rinse a 2 pint (1.2 litre) ring
mould with cold water and leave
wet. Make up the jellies according
to the manufacturer's instructions
using ¾ pint (450 ml) boiling
water and ¾ pint (450 ml) cold
water. Peel and slice one banana
and drain the can of apricots. Place
a slice of banana in the hollow of
each apricot half. Pour a small
amount of jelly in the base of the
mould. Chill to set. When set place
a layer of banana-filled apricots on
top, cut side down, and again set
in jelly. Repeat until all the apricots
and bananas have been used,
setting each layer before adding
the next and peeling the bananas
as needed.

   Slice the cake thickly and place
on top of the jelly. Slowly pour the
remaining jelly over the cake.
Allow to set before turning out to
serve.   **Serves 6**

Dolce Torinese

2 oz (50 g) hazelnuts
4 oz (100 g) butter
5 oz (150 g) caster sugar
7 oz (200 g) **McVitie's** Digestive
 Biscuits, crushed
1 egg, lightly beaten
2 oz (50 g) cocoa powder
3 tablespoons (45 ml) brandy

Spread the hazelnuts on a baking sheet and toast under a hot grill for a few minutes, turning over to stop them burning. Remove from the heat, rub off the skins and then chop roughly. Cream the butter and sugar together until light and fluffy. Mix the biscuits with the nuts and stir into the creamed mixture. Blend the egg, cocoa and brandy, add to the mixture and mix well. Form into a sausage shape, wrap in foil and leave in the refrigerator for at least 6 hours, or overnight.

Slice finely and serve after dinner with black coffee. This is a chocolate dessert for which Turin in Italy is famous. Drinking chocolate may be used in place of the cocoa.

Sherry Tortoni

6 oz (175 g) **McVitie's** Digestive
 Biscuits, crushed
3 eggs
4 oz (100 g) butter
3 oz (75 g) sugar
2 tablespoons (30 ml) medium
 sherry
1 teaspoon (5 ml) almond
 essence

Lightly grease a 1½ pint (900 ml) soufflé dish and spread a thick layer of crumbs over the base. Separate the eggs and beat the whites with a rotary or electric whisk until they form soft peaks. In a bowl cream the butter, sugar and egg yolks until light and fluffy, add the sherry and almond essence and mix well. Carefully fold in the egg whites until evenly distributed. Pour layers of this egg mixture separated by the crushed biscuits into the soufflé dish. This should make about 6 layers. Serve cold, with cream if liked.
Serves 6

Tropical Ginger and Orange Trifle

1 **McVitie's** Jamaica Ginger
 Cake
4 oranges, peeled and cut into
 segments
8 tablespoons (120 ml) Curacao
 or orange juice
4 egg yolks
2 oz (50 g) caster sugar
3 tablespoons (45 ml) cornflour
few drops vanilla essence
1 pint (600 ml) milk
3 tablespoons (45 ml) ginger
 wine *or* syrup
¾ pint (450 ml) double cream
orange slices, toasted almonds
 and stem ginger to decorate

Thinly slice the ginger cake and place in the base of a trifle dish. Top with the orange segments and sprinkle over the Curacao or orange juice.

In a saucepan combine the egg yolks, caster sugar, cornflour and vanilla essence. Gradually add the milk and ginger wine or syrup and bring to the boil. Cook for 2–3 minutes, cool and pour over the trifle base. Chill until lightly set.

Whip the cream until it stands in soft peaks and swirl it over the top of the trifle. Decorate with the orange slices, toasted almonds and stem ginger.

McVitie's Dark Orange, Lemon Spice or Golden Syrup Cake may be used instead of Jamaica Ginger Cake to vary the recipe.
Serves 8

Maxwell House

Iced Mocha Mousses

3 eggs, separated
3 oz (75 g) caster sugar
2 oz (50 g) plain chocolate
1 tablespoon (15 ml) **Maxwell
 House** Instant Coffee
2 tablespoons (30 ml) water
1 sachet **Bird's** Dream Topping
¼ pint (150 ml) cold milk
Bird's Chocolate Flavoured Ice
 Magic

Whisk the egg yolks with the sugar until thick and creamy. Place the chocolate, coffee and water in a bowl over a pan of hot water and heat gently until melted then whisk into the egg mixture. Make up the Dream Topping as directed on the sachet and fold two-thirds into the mousse, keeping the remaining third for decoration. Whisk the egg whites until stiff and carefully fold into the mousse. Spoon into individual freezerproof ramekin dishes. Put to freeze for 2–3 hours.

Just before serving remove from the freezer and top with a generous layer of Ice Magic and a swirl of Dream Topping.
Serves 4–5

Nestlé

Banana Chocolate Pudding

7–8 in (18–20 cm) plain
 chocolate sponge cake *or* trifle
 sponges
juice of 1 orange mixed with
 2–3 tablespoons (30–45 ml)
 sweet sherry
1 lb (450 g) bananas, sliced and
 mixed with 6 oz (170 g) can
 Nestlé's Cream
1 oz (25 g) icing sugar, sieved

Cut the cake into quarters then cut each quarter crossways into 2 or 3 thin slices. Very lightly butter a 1½ pint (900 ml) bowl and line with the slices of chocolate cake, reserving some to make a cover for the top. Carefully spoon the sherry mixture over the cake to moisten it, reserving some for the top. Fill the bowl with the cream and banana mixture. Cover with the remaining sponge cake and spoon over the remaining sherry mixture. Press the top firmly, cover with a plate and weigh down evenly. Chill for several hours.

To serve, turn the pudding out on to a serving dish, sprinkle with the icing sugar and serve immediately. **Serves 5–6**

Strawberry Cream Pie

4 oz (100 g) digestive biscuits, crushed
1 tablespoon (15 ml) sugar
2 oz (50 g) butter, melted
Filling
1 small can *or* ½ large can **Nestlé's** Milk
4 oz (113 g) can **Nestle's** Cream
2 tablespoons (30 ml) Strawberry **Nesquick**
grated rind and juice of 1 lemon
grated chocolate and halved strawberries to decorate

Mix together the crushed biscuits, sugar and melted butter. Press the biscuit mixture into the bottom and sides of a 7 in (18 cm) pie dish or flan case and chill until firm.

To make the filling mix together the Nestlé's Milk, Nestlé's Cream and Nesquik. Add the lemon juice and rind and stir until the mixture thickens. Pour into the prepared case and refrigerate until set. Decorate with the grated chocolate and strawberries. **Serves 4–6**

Cold Chocolate Soufflé

3 eggs, separated
3 oz (75 g) **Ovaltine** Drinking Chocolate
1½ oz (40 g) sugar
1 teaspoon (5 ml) vanilla essence
½ pint (300 ml) milk
1½ level dessertspoons (15 ml) powdered gelatine
3 tablespoons (45 ml) water
¾ pint (450 ml) whipped cream *or* whipped evaporated milk

Cook the egg yolks, drinking chocolate, sugar, vanilla essence and milk gently until they form a smooth custard. Dissolve the gelatine in the hot water and stir into the custard. When cool, fold in the stiffly beaten cream. Allow to thicken slightly, then fold in the stiffly beaten egg whites. Pour into a soufflé dish tied with a band of greased paper outside (standing several inches above the top of dish). When quite firm decorate with cream and nuts and remove the paper. **Serves 6**

Pineapple Caramel Sweet

a little corn oil *or* melted lard
4 oz (100 g) granulated sugar
4 tablespoons (60 ml) cold water
11 oz (312 g) can mandarin oranges
1 large banana
2 tablespoons (30 ml) **Rayner's Crusha** Pineapple Milk Shake Syrup
arrowroot to thicken

Oil or lightly grease a baking sheet. Put the granulated sugar in a pan with the cold water. Heat gently until all the sugar is dissolved then bring to the boil and boil gently until golden, not dark brown. Pour thinly on to the baking sheet. Leave to become hard. Drain the juice from the oranges, mix with the Crusha and thicken with arrowroot, following instructions on the packet. Allow to cool. Stir in the oranges and the peeled and sliced banana. Take the caramel off the baking sheet and break up with a rolling pin or a large weight. Put the fruit in glasses and top with the caramel pieces. **Serves 3**

Strawberry Mousse

½ oz (15 g) powdered gelatine
5 tablespoons (75 ml) water
4 large eggs, separated
4 oz (100 g) castor sugar
7 tablespoons (105 ml) undiluted evaporated milk
2 tablespoons (30 ml) **Rayner's Crusha** Strawberry Milk Shake Syrup
1 large punnet ripe strawberries
2 tablespoons (30 ml) sherry
¼ pint (150 ml) double cream, whipped, for decoration

Put the gelatine into a cup with the water and place the cup in a pan of gently simmering water until the gelatine is dissolved. Meanwhile, whisk the egg yolks and castor sugar until very thick and mousse-like, with an electric mixer if possible. Whisk in the evaporated milk and Crusha. Reserve a few strawberries for decoration, finely chop or liquidise the rest, and stir into the mixture. Add the sherry. Whisk the egg whites until very stiff. Whisk the gelatine into the mixture and then fold in the egg whites, using a metal spoon. Pour into a bowl and leave to set in a cold place (not a refrigerator) until set. Place the reserved strawberries round the edge and decorate with cream. **Serves 6**

Dreamy Delight

6 trifle sponges *or* 5 oz (125 g) plain cake
¼ pint (150 ml) **Rose's** Lime Juice Cordial
14 oz (397 g) can condensed milk
finely grated rind and juice of ½ lemon
2 teaspoons (10 ml) gelatine
¼ pint (142 ml) whipping cream
green food colouring
2 **Cadbury's** Flakes

Split the sponges in half or cut up the cake and use to line the base of an 8 in (20 cm) loose-based cake tin, leaving no holes. Soak the cake with half the lime juice. Empty the condensed milk into a bowl and stir in the remaining lime juice, the lemon rind and the strained juice. Dissolve the gelatine in 2 tablespoons (30 ml) water and, when quite clear, trickle into the mixture, stirring well. Fold in the lightly whipped cream and a little colouring, pour on to the sponge base and leave overnight to set.

To serve, push the base out of the tin, then slide the dessert on to a serving plate. Decorate with pieces of Flake around the edge. **Serves 6–8**

Lime Mousse

1 **Chivers** Lime Flavour Jelly
6 oz (175 g) cream cheese
4 tablespoons (80 ml) **Rose's** Lime Juice Cordial
2 egg whites
2 oz (50 g) caster sugar
chocolate curls or a **Cadbury's** Flake to decorate

Dissolve the jelly then make up to 1 pint (568 ml) with water or any complementary-flavoured fruit juice. Soften the cream cheese— when bought loose, this is often softer than the packet varieties. Whisk the lime juice then the jelly into the cheese, making the mixture quite smooth. Leave in a cool place until beginning to set. Whisk the egg whites stiffly then whisk in the sugar until as stiff again. Fold this into the thickening cheese mixture, divide between 6 individual dishes and leave for several hours to set. Decorate with the curls of chocolate or the crushed Flake.   **Serves 6**

ROWNTREE'S

Blackcurrant Brulée

1 **Rowntree's** Blackcurrant Jelly
8 oz (225 g) blackcurrants, fresh or frozen
2 tablespoons (30 ml) water
3 eggs, separated
4 oz (100 g) castor sugar
½ pint (300 ml) double cream
soft brown sugar

Make up the jelly using only ½ pint (300 ml) of water, and allow to cool. Simmer the blackcurrants with the water until they are tender, then rub through a sieve to obtain a purée. Whisk the egg

yolks and castor sugar in a basin, stand it over a pan of hot water and whisk until the contents are smooth and creamy. Add the fruit purée. Remove from the heat and continue to whisk until the mixture is cold. Whisk in the cold jelly and half the cream, lightly whipped. Lastly, fold in the stiffly whisked egg whites and leave to set in the refrigerator, in a fire-proof dish which it fills to within ½ in (1 cm) of the top. Whip the remaining cream and spread it evenly over the set soufflé mixture. Cover this with an ⅛ in (0.3 cm) layer of soft brown sugar and place immediately under a very hot grill until the sugar caramelises. Remove from the heat at once and chill again before serving. **Serves 4**

Gaelic Coffee Mousse with Walnuts

6 tablespoons (90 ml) whisky
1 **Rowntree's** Orange or Lemon Jelly
½ pint (300 ml) good quality strong coffee
¼ pint (150 ml) water
small tub double cream
2 tablespoons (30 ml) icing sugar
4 oz (100 g) walnuts, chopped into quarters
3 tablespoons (45 ml) single cream

Put a tablespoon (15 ml) of whisky into each of six burgundy glasses. Melt the jelly in the hot coffee and add water to make up to 1 pint (600 ml). Pour half of this evenly into the six glasses, stir, and chill until set. Chill the remaining jelly until syrupy, then whip until light. Whip the double cream, not too stiffly, and fold half into the whipped jelly. Fold in the icing sugar and walnuts. Pour on top of the six set jellies. Mix the rest of the whipped cream with the single cream, chill and pour carefully on top. Serve each with a slender cocktail spoon as the finishing touch. This recipe is also delicious made with rum, grated orange rind and a dash of cinnamon. **Serves 6**

Praline Tropicana

2 oz (50 g) granulated sugar
2 tablespoons (30 ml) water
2 oz (50 g) unblanched almonds
4 egg yolks
5 oz (150 g) caster sugar
pinch arrowroot
½ pint (300 ml) milk
1 **Rowntree's** Tangerine Jelly dissolved in 3 tablespoons (45 ml) hot water
2–3 tablespoons (30–45 ml) Cointreau
½ pint (300 ml) double cream
6 sponge finger biscuits
Decoration
¼ pint (150 ml) double cream
¼ pint (150 ml) single cream
1–2 tablespoons (15–30 ml) apricot jam, sieved

Stir the sugar and water in a small pan over low heat until dissolved. Stir in the almonds and bring to the boil. Boil without stirring until the syrup turns a rich golden brown. Pour the praline on to an oiled tray and leave to cool.

Mix the egg yolks, sugar and arrowroot well in a bowl. Heat the milk and gradually stir into the yolks. Place the bowl over a pan of gently boiling water and cook, stirring, until the mixture thickens and coats the back of the spoon. Add the tangerine jelly and transfer to a large mixing bowl.

Crush the praline between paper with a rolling pin and add to the jelly mixture with 1 tablespoon (15 ml) of the Cointreau. Cool until just beginning to set, stirring occasionally then fold in the lightly whipped cream. Pour half the mixture into a 6 in (15 cm) cake tin. Dip the sponge fingers in the remaining liqueur, arrange in the tin and cover with the rest of the mixture. Chill until set. Turn out on to a serving dish.

To decorate, cover with fairly thickly whipped double and single cream mixed together, reserving 2–3 tablespoons (30–45 ml) of the cream. Using an icing bag, pipe lines of sieved apricot jam across the top and draw a knife across to 'feather' the jam. Pipe round with cream.   **Serves 6**

St Clement's Delight

juice and rind of ½ lemon
1 tablespoon (15 ml) sugar
¼ pint (150 ml) water
½ **Rowntree's** Lemon Jelly
1 egg yolk
juice of 1 orange
3 tablespoons (45 ml) lemon juice

Topping
½ pint (300 ml) water
3 tablespoons (45 ml) sugar
1 **Rowntree's** Orange Jelly
2 egg whites
grated orange and lemon peel *or* crystallised fruit to decorate

Put the lemon juice, sugar and water into a pan. Bring to the boil then add the jelly to dissolve. Leave until cool but not set and then beat in the egg yolk. Pour a little into the bottom of 4 large individual glasses and leave to set in the refrigerator.

To make the topping, put the orange and lemon juice into a pan with the water and sugar. Bring to the boil and add the jelly to the liquid. Leave until cool but not set. Whisk the egg whites until stiff and fold into the jelly mixture when cool. Pour on top of the lemon base in the glasses and leave to set.

Decorate with a little grated lemon and orange rind or crystallised orange and lemon slices.
Serves 4

Ice Cream

4 eggs, separated
4 oz (100 g) soft brown sugar *or* caster sugar
10 fl oz (284 ml) **St Ivel** Whipping Cream

Beat together the egg yolks and sugar. Whisk the egg whites until very stiff. Fold the egg yolks, sugar and egg whites together. Whip the cream until thick. Fold the mixtures together. Pour into a container and freeze.

Any fruit or syrup may be added to the ice cream for variation of flavour.

Crushed Strawberry Ice

8 oz (225 g) fresh strawberries
1 oz (25 g) icing sugar
8.5 fl oz (241 ml) bottle **Schweppes** Lemonade
2 egg whites

Wash, hull and slice the strawberries. Mash or liquidise them to make a purée. Stir in the icing sugar and lemonade, pour into a shallow container and place in the freezing compartment of a refrigerator or in a freezer. When beginning to thicken and freeze, take it out and break up the ice crystals. Whisk the egg whites stiffly and fold into the strawberry mixture. Return to the freezer and leave until frozen.   **Serves 4**

Lime Sorbet

6 oz (175 g) sugar
1 pint (550 ml) water
½ pint (275 ml) **Schweppes** Lime Flavour Cordial
1 egg white
ice cream wafers to serve

Carefully dissolve the sugar in the water and, when quite clear, boil for 5 minutes. Cool. Add the Lime Flavour Cordial then pour into a metal or plastic container to freeze. When half frozen, turn into a bowl and whisk to break up the crystals. Fold in the stiffly beaten egg white then return to the freezer until firm.

Serve in scoops with wafers.
Serves 6

Peppermint Sorbet

1½ pints (800 ml) milk
6 tablespoons (120 ml) **Schweppes** Peppermint Cordial
4 oz (100 g) granulated sugar
4 egg whites

2 oz (50 g) **Bournville** plain chocolate, grated
sprigs of fresh mint to decorate (optional)

Gently heat the milk, peppermint cordial and sugar in a pan until the sugar has dissolved. Bring to the boil then cool. Pour the liquid into a metal container and put into the freezer, or ice making compartment of the refrigerator and leave until semi-frozen. Mash up the half-frozen mixture with a fork then fold in the stiffly beaten egg whites. Return to the freezer. Stir occasionally until the mixture freezes completely. Divide the sorbet between about 8 glasses, sprinkle thickly with the grated chocolate and decorate with sprigs of fresh mint when available.
Serves 6–8

Sharwood's

Chaat (Spiced Fresh Fruit Salad)

Fresh fruit suggestions:
apples, cored and chopped
bananas, skinned and thickly sliced
tangerines, peeled and segmented
pears, cored and chopped
Sharwood's Canned Fruits suggestions:
black cherries, drained and stoned
whole apricots, drained, halved and stoned
white grapes, drained
melon cubes, drained
golden figs, drained
lychees, drained
2 tablespoons (30 ml) **Sharwood's** Lemon Juice
1 teaspoon (5 ml) sugar
1 heaped teaspoon (15 ml) **Sharwood's** Garam Masala Curry Spices

Select both some fresh fruits and some canned fruits, depending on availability. Mix together the lemon juice, sugar and garam masala and sprinkle over the fruit. Refrigerate overnight. Stir the fruit salad before serving.

Coconut Pudding

1½ pints (850 ml) creamy milk
3 oz (75 g) caster sugar
4 oz (100 g) **Sharwood's** Creamed Coconut
2 oz (50 g) unsalted butter, melted
2 oz (50 g) sultanas
2 tablespoons (30 ml) rose water
2 oz (50 g) flaked almonds, toasted, to decorate

Bring the milk and sugar to the boil. Set aside. Blend the creamed coconut with the melted butter in a pan and heat for 5 minutes. Add the milk and leave to thicken over a low heat, stirring all the time. When the milk has been reduced by half add the dry fruits and rose water. Leave to cool before serving. Decorate with the toasted almonds.   **Serves 6**

Maraschino Ice-cream

4 eggs, separated
5 oz (150 g) caster sugar
2 (5 oz, 142 ml) cartons natural yoghurt
2 (5 oz, 142 ml) cartons soured cream
12 **Sharwood's** Cocktail Cherries, chopped
1 tablespoon (15 ml) cherry juice from jar
few drops cochineal
1 tablespoon (15 ml) kirsch (optional)
6–8 **Sharwood's** Cocktail Cherries to decorate

Whisk together the egg yolks and sugar until thick and pale in colour. Fold in the yoghurt, soured cream, cherries, cherry juice, cochineal and kirsch, if used. Turn the mixture into a plastic container and leave in the freezer compartment of the refrigerator until just set around the edges. Remove and whisk the mixture to break up the crystals. Stiffly whisk the egg whites and fold into the mixture.

Return the mixture to the container and leave in the freezer until frozen.

Serve in individual glasses, each decorated with a cherry.
Serves 6–8

Stork
Elizabethan Flan

2 oz (50 g) **Stork** Margarine, melted
4 oz (100 g) ginger biscuits, crushed
2 lemons
2–3 tablespoons (30–45 ml) sherry *or* white wine
2–3 oz (50–75 g) caster sugar
¾ pint (425 ml) double cream
mimosa balls and angelica to decorate

Mix the margarine with the ginger biscuits and press into an 8 in (20 cm) flan ring. Cut the rind of 1 lemon into strips and place in boiling water for a few seconds then drain. Grate the rind of the remaining lemon and place in a mixing bowl with the juice of both lemons, the sherry or wine and sugar. Slowly add ½ pint (300 ml) of the cream and whisk the mixture until thick and creamy. Pour over the biscuit base. Whisk the remaining cream and pipe on top of the flan. Decorate with the mimosa balls and angelica. Use the strips of lemon rind to sprinkle over the centre of the flan.
Serves 6

Baked Alaska

3 trifle sponges *or* a piece of sponge cake a little larger than a family sized block of ice cream
2 tablespoons (30 ml) orange juice
8 oz (225 g) fresh fruit (strawberries, bananas, oranges, peaches) *or* 15 oz (425 g) can of fruit

3 egg whites (size 2)
6 oz (175 g) caster sugar
1 Family Block **Wall's** Raspberry Ripple Ice Cream

Put the sponge on an ovenproof plate and soak it with the orange juice. (If canned fruit is used, use the syrup to soak the sponge and omit the orange juice.) Prepare the fruit, if using fresh fruit, and place it on top of the sponge. Set aside in a cool place until needed. Whisk the egg whites until stiff and standing in straight peaks. Add 3 tablespoons (45 ml) of the sugar and re-whisk until the meringue regains the original stiffness, then carefully fold in the remaining sugar. Place the ice cream on top of the fruit-covered sponge and cover it *completely* with the meringue (if any ice cream shows through the meringue it will be exposed to the heat and melt). Bake the Alaska immediately in the oven, pre-heated to 450°F, 230°C, Gas Mark 8, for 3–5 minutes or until tinged golden brown.   **Serves 6**

Cherry Ring

1 litre **Wall's** Italiano Black Cherry Ice Cream
6 well-baked meringue shells
15 oz (425 g) can pitted black cherries
1 teaspoon (5 ml) arrowroot powder

Put the ice cream into a bowl. Break up the meringues, stir them into the ice cream and spoon the mixture into a 1¾ pint (1 litre) ring mould. Place in the freezer for a minimum of 30 minutes. Strain the black cherries, and mix a little of the syrup with the arrowroot in a pan to make a smooth paste. Stir in the rest of the syrup and, stirring all the time, bring the sauce to the boil to clear and thicken. Stir in the cherries and leave the sauce on one side to cool.

To serve the dessert, dip the ring mould in hot water for a quick count of 5 and invert it on to a serving dish. Spoon the cherries into the centre, allowing some of the sauce to trickle over the edge of the ring and serve immediately.
Serves 6

Ice Cream Brûlée

12 oz (350 g) raspberries, fresh
 or frozen and thawed
1 litre **Wall's** Italiano Choc 'n'
 Hazelnut Ice Cream
¼ pint (150 ml) double cream,
 whipped
3 tablespoons (45 ml) demerara
 sugar

Place the raspberries in the bottom of a deep, 2 pint (1.2 litre) soufflé dish. Spoon the ice cream on top and spread the cream over the surface evenly. Sprinkle the top thickly with demerara sugar and put into the freezer or ice compartment of the refrigerator. When required, place the dish under a hot, pre-heated grill and cook until the sugar has caramelised. Serve immediately. **Serves 4–6**

Pineapple and Orange Fluff

15½ oz (440 g) can **John West**
 Pineapple Rings in Natural
 Juice, drained and with juice
 reserved
rind and juice of 1 medium
 orange
½ oz (15 g) gelatine
2 egg whites
2 oz (50 g) caster sugar
whipped cream to decorate
 (optional)

Roughly chop the pineapple and place in a liquidiser with the pineapple juice and half the orange rind. Blend to give a thick purée. Dissolve the gelatine in the orange juice and stir into the pineapple purée. Chill until just on the point of setting. Meanwhile, whisk the egg whites to soft peaks. Add the sugar and continue whisking until it is incorporated. Fold the egg whites into the pineapple mixture and spoon into individual glass dishes. Chill until set. Decorate with whipped cream if desired, and the remaining grated orange rind. **Serves 4**

Spiced Fruit Compôte

10 oz (283 g) can **John West**
 Pear Quarters in Fruit Juice
15½ oz (440 g) can **John West**
 Pineapple Rings in Natural
 Juice
10 oz (283 g) can **John West**
 Apricot Halves in Fruit Juice
10½ oz (298 g) can **John West**
 Mandarin Orange Segments
 in Natural Juice
6 cloves
1 cinnamon stick, broken into
 4 pieces
¼ pint (150 ml) sweet white
 wine
4 oz (100 g) fresh *or* frozen
 raspberries

Drain all the fruit, reserving the juices, and cut the pears and pineapple rings into halves. Arrange the fruit in a glass serving dish. Place the fruit juices, cloves and cinnamon stick in a saucepan, bring to the boil and continue boiling rapidly for 5 minutes. Add the wine and boil rapidly for a further 5 minutes. Pour over the fruit and leave to go cold. Just before serving, stir in the raspberries. **Serves 6–8**

Boodles Orange Fool

4 trifle sponges
½ pint (300 ml) **Young's** Dairy
 Cream
1 oz (25 g) icing sugar
2 oranges
1 lemon
8 tablespoons (120 ml) **Young's**
 Dairy Cream to decorate

Cut each sponge in half and place in the bottom of a serving dish. Whip the cream and icing sugar together until soft and fluffy. Grate the rind from the fruit and reserve half of it for decoration. Squeeze the orange and lemon juice and add it, together with half of the rind, to the cream. Pour over the sponge cakes and weigh down

with a saucer. Refrigerate overnight, remove the saucer, and decorate with the remaining cream (whipped) and the fruit rind. **Serves 4**

Devon Delight

1 lb (450 g) fruit: strawberries,
 raspberries, blackberries etc.
5 oz (125 g) castor sugar
7½ fl oz (250 ml) **Young's**
 Dairy Cream
pinch of salt
1 sachet gelatine dissolved in
 2 tablespoons (30 ml) boiling
 water
7½ fl oz (250 ml) **Young's**
 Dairy Cream, soured
 overnight with 3 teaspoons
 (15 ml) lemon juice

Liquidise the fruit with 2 oz (50 g) of the sugar and sieve if necessary to remove the pips. Heat the unsoured cream with the remaining sugar and the salt, gently, without boiling, to dissolve the sugar. Leave to cool. When the cream is cool, add the dissolved gelatine, ¼ pint (150 ml) of the fruit purée and the soured cream. Pour into a wetted 1–1½ pint (600–900 ml) mould and leave to set. Turn out into a fairly deep dish, and cover with the remaining purée.

Serve with softly whipped cream. This is a good way of using a glut of overripe soft fruit in the summer, or frozen fruit such as strawberries which lose their texture when thawed. **Serves 4**

CHEESECAKES and GATEAUX

Cheesecake

6 oz (175 g) **Allinson** 100% Wholewheat Flour, plain
½ teaspoon (2.5 ml) sea salt
3 oz (75 g) vegetable margarine
2 tablespoons (30 ml) soft brown sugar
1 egg yolk
cold water to mix
Filling
1 lb (450 g) curd *or* cottage cheese
1 egg white
4 oz (100 g) soft brown sugar
1½ oz (40 g) sultanas, washed and thoroughly dried

Place the flour and salt in a bowl and rub in the margarine. Mix in the sugar and bind with the egg yolk and water to form a dough. Reserve a little egg yolk for glazing. Roll out two-thirds of the pastry and use to line a greased 7 in (18 cm) sandwich tin. Cut long strips from the remaining pastry.
   Place all the filling ingredients in a bowl and mix well. Pour into the prepared pastry case and arrange the strips of pastry in a lattice pattern on top. Brush the top with beaten egg and bake for 45–50 minutes in a pre-heated oven (375°F, 190°C, Gas Mark 5). Cool in the tin.   **Serves 6–8**

Light Yoghurt Cheesecake

12 digestive biscuits
1 oz (25 g) caster sugar
2 oz (50 g) butter
5 fl oz (150 ml) carton soured cream

3 oz (75 g) cream cheese
¼ pint (150 ml) cold milk
1 sachet **Bird's** Raspberry Yoghurt Whirl

Have ready a 7 in (18 cm) loose-bottomed cake tin. Crush the digestive biscuits and add the sugar, melt the butter and stir into the biscuit mixture. Press the mixture into the base of the cake tin. Whisk together in a basin the milk, soured cream and cream cheese, sprinkle on the Yoghurt Whirl and whisk until smooth and creamy. Spoon immediately over the biscuit base. Chill for at least 30 minutes before serving. Decorate as liked.   **Serves 4–5**

Mocha Cheesecake

12 chocolate digestive biscuits
2 oz (50 g) butter
3 eggs, separated
3 oz (75 g) sugar
4 teaspoons (20 ml) **Maxwell House** Instant Coffee
1 lb (450 g) cream cheese
1 sachet **Bird's** Dream Topping
¼ pint (150 ml) cold milk
1 sachet gelatine
3 tablespoons (45 ml) water

Crush the biscuits, work in the butter and press well into the base of an 8 in (20 cm) loose-bottomed cake tin. Put to chill. Whisk the egg yolks, sugar and coffee until thick. Work in the cream cheese. Make up the Dream Topping as directed and stir lightly into the cheese mixture. Put the gelatine to dissolve in the water over a pan of hot water. Stir thoroughly into the cheese mixture. Whisk the egg whites stiffly then fold into the mixture and turn on to the crumb base. Put to chill and set.
   When ready to serve, ease from the tin and decorate as liked.
Serves 6–8

Bournville

Festive Cheesecake

3 oz (75 g) butter
2 tablespoons (30 ml) **Bournville** cocoa
1 oz (25 g) caster sugar
4 oz (100 g) digestive biscuits
Filling and decoration
8 oz (225 g) cream cheese
small carton natural yoghurt
2 eggs, separated
grated rind of 1 small orange
2 teaspoons (10 ml) honey
½ oz (14 g) gelatine
2 oz (50 g) caster sugar
3 standard **Cadbury's** Flakes
glacé cherries

Mix the melted butter, cocoa, sugar and crushed biscuits together; press into an 8 in (20 cm) round, loose based tin. Blend the cheese, yoghurt, egg yolks, orange rind and honey together. Add the gelatine dissolved in 4 tablespoons (80 ml) water. Whisk egg whites stiffly, fold in sugar and whisk again; fold in cheese mixture with a crushed Flake. Pour on to the biscuit crust; set. Lift out the cheesecake. Decorate with crushed Flake round the edge and halved glacé cherries.

Strongbow Cheesecake

4 oz (100 g) plain chocolate
  digestive biscuits
2 oz (50 g) butter, melted
½ oz (15 g) gelatine
¼ pint (150 ml) **Bulmers**
  Strongbow Cider
8 oz (225 g) cottage cheese
4 oz (100 g) cream cheese
1–2 oz (25–50 g) icing sugar
½ pint (300 ml) double cream
fresh orange slices to decorate

Grease an 8 in (20 cm) spring-clip
or loose-bottomed cake tin. Crush
the biscuits, mix into the melted
butter and press the mixture over
the base of the tin. Dissolve the
gelatine in the warmed cider and
leave to cool but not set.

Sieve the cottage cheese and
cream cheese, stir in the icing
sugar and then add the gelatine
mixture, beating thoroughly.
Whisk half the cream until fairly
thick and fold into the mixture,
pour over the base and leave to set.

To decorate, pipe rosettes of the
remaining cream (whipped) on the
top and add slices of fresh orange.
Serves 6–8

Cadbury's

Hazelnut Meringue Gateau

3 large egg whites
6 oz (150 g) caster sugar
2 oz (50 g) desiccated coconut
3 oz (75 g) hazelnuts
2 large **Cadbury's** Flakes
½ pint (284 ml) whipping
  cream, 3 large **Cadbury's**
  Flakes and 6 whole hazelnuts
  dipped in melted **Bournville**
  Dark Plain Chocolate to
  decorate

Whisk the egg whites until very
stiff then whisk in half the sugar
until as stiff again. Fold in the

remaining sugar with the coconut,
ground hazelnuts and crushed
Flakes. Divide the mixture
between 2 (7 in, 18 cm) shallow,
round cake tins, greased and base
lined, and bake in the oven at
375°F, 190°C, Gas Mark 5, for 25
minutes or until firm to the touch.
Turn out and cool.

Whisk the cream quite stiffly
then sandwich the layers together
with one third of it. Reserving
3 tablespoons (60 ml), spread the
remaining cream over the top and
sides. Cover the sides with 2 of the
Flakes, crushed. Cut the other
Flake in half then divide each piece
into 3 thin lengths; arrange the
pieces on the top. Pipe small swirls
of cream in the centre and between
each piece of Flake. Place a dipped
hazelnut on top of the swirls of
cream.   **Serves 8**

Layered Chock-Block

10 **Cadbury's** Flakes from the
  Family Pack
3 oz (75 g) ginger biscuits
1 oz (25 g) butter
2 tablespoons (40 ml)
  Cadbury's Drinking
  Chocolate
8 fl oz (227 ml) double cream
1 egg white
1 tablespoon (20 ml) brandy
1 teaspoon (5 ml) icing sugar
4 glacé or maraschino cherries,
  halved, to decorate

Lay a double piece of foil the width
of a 1 lb (500 g) loaf tin in the base,
allowing it to protrude at either
end. Halve 6 Flakes lengthwise
and place in the tin with the cut
side uppermost. Crush the
biscuits coarsely then stir in the
melted butter. Dissolve the
drinking chocolate in an equal
amount of hot water and cool.
Whisk the cream quite stiffly, then
the egg white. Fold together,
adding the brandy and sieved
icing sugar. Crush the remaining
Flake and add to half the mixture
with two-thirds of the drinking
chocolate. Pour half this mixture
over the Flakes in the tin, spoon
over the plain mixture, then all the
chocolate. Press the biscuits on
top, levelling the surface. Leave in

the freezer for at least 2 hours until
firm. If the pudding is to be kept
for some time, wrap completely in
foil.

To serve, dip the tin in hot water
just enough to loosen the sides
before turning on to a plate.
Decorate with halved cherries
down the centre.   **Serves 6**

Camp Biscuit Cake

3 tablespoons (45 ml) **Camp**
  Coffee and Chicory Essence
2 tablespoons (30 ml) brandy or
  rum
¼ pint (150 ml) hot water
48 morning coffee biscuits
½ pint (300 ml) double cream,
  lightly whisked and
  sweetened to taste
walnut halves to decorate

Mix the Camp Essence, rum or
brandy and water together. Dip
each biscuit in the coffee mixture
for 1 minute until soft. Arrange on
a serving dish in 6 layers of
8 biscuits, each in two rows of 4,
sandwiching the biscuits together
with half the sweetened cream.
Cover with foil and refrigerate for
12 hours. Just before serving, cover
the biscuit cake with the
remaining whipped cream and
decorate with the walnuts.
Serves 4–6

```
FRANK
COOPER®
```

Apple and Honey Cheesecake

8 oz (227 g) packet gingernut
  biscuits, crushed
2 oz (50 g) butter, melted
8 oz (200 g) cottage cheese
5 oz (142 ml) carton single
  cream
2 tablespoons (30 ml) honey
5 level teaspoons (25 ml)
  powdered gelatine, dissolved

in 3 teaspoons (15 ml) water
6 oz (170 g) jar **Frank Cooper's**
  Apple Sauce
½ level teaspoon (2.5 ml)
  ground cinnamon

Mix together the gingernut
biscuits and the butter and press
into an 8 in (20 cm) flan dish or
loose-bottomed tin. Beat together
the cottage cheese, cream, honey,
gelatine, apple sauce and cinnamon and pour into the gingernut
case. Place in a refrigerator and
chill before serving.   **Serves 6**

Marmalade Cheesecake

2 oz (50 g) butter
4 oz (100 g) digestive biscuits,
  crushed
3 eggs, separated
6 oz (150 g) caster sugar
8 oz (200 g) cream cheese
2 tablespoons (30 ml) lemon
  juice
3 tablespoons (45 ml) **Frank
  Cooper's** Fine Cut 'Oxford'
  Marmalade
½ oz (15 g) gelatine dissolved
  in 3 tablespoons (45 ml)
  water
¼ pint (125 ml) double cream
strips of marmalade rind for
  decoration

Grease and line a loose-bottomed
7 in (18 cm) cake tin.

Melt the butter, stir in the
biscuits and press lightly into the
base of the tin. Beat together the
egg yolks and sugar, add the cream
cheese and beat until smooth. Stir
in the lemon juice, marmalade and
gelatine dissolved in water. Whisk
the egg whites until fairly stiff and
half whip the cream and fold both
into the mixture. Pour into the tin
and leave to set.

Serve decorated with strips of
rind from the marmalade.
Serves 6

Pineapple Cheesecake

8 digestive biscuits, crushed
2 oz (50 g) butter
2 oz (50 g) sugar
1 pineapple jelly
1 tablespoon (15 ml) lemon
  juice
1 lb (450 g) cream cheese
½ pint (300 ml) whipping
  cream
13¼ oz (376 g) can **Del Monte**
  Crushed Pineapple

Melt the butter in a saucepan.
Remove from the heat and stir in
the biscuit crumbs and sugar.
Press the mixture firmly into the
base of an 8 in (20 cm) loose-
bottomed cake tin. Dissolve the
jelly in ½ pint (300 ml) of water and
leave until almost set. Add the
lemon juice. Work the cheese until
soft and stir in the jelly. Lightly
whisk the cream and stir into the
cheese mixture. Drain the pineapple and stir into the cream and
cheese. Pour the mixture on to the
crumb base and leave until set.

Decorate as liked.
Serves 8–10

Orange Surprise Cheesecake

4 oz (100 g) digestive biscuits,
  crushed
2 oz (50 g) butter, melted
Filling
12 oz (350 g) cream cheese
⅓ can **Findus** Orange Juice,
  thawed
4 oz (100 g) castor sugar
Topping
1 oz (25 g) castor sugar
1 level dessertspoon (10 ml)
  cornflour
remainder of the can of Orange
  Juice

Combine the base ingredients and
press into a 7 in (18 cm) pie dish.
Chill. Combine the cheese and
sugar with 2 fl oz (50 ml) of the
orange juice and spread over the
mixture in the dish. For the
topping, gradually add the orange
juice to the cornflour and sugar,
and bring to the boil. Cool before
spreading over the cheesecake.
Decorate as desired.   **Serves 6**

Homepride

Cherry Layer Gateau

3 eggs (size 2)
3 oz (75 g) caster sugar
3 oz (75 g) **Homepride** Self-
  raising Flour
1 tablespoon (15 ml) warm
  water
a little cherry jam, warmed
4 oz (100 g) almonds, chopped
  and toasted
5 oz (142 ml) carton double
  cream, whipped
13½ oz (382 g) jar cherry
  flavour pie-filling

Grease the bottom line an 8 × 12 in
(20 × 30 cm) swiss roll tin. Whisk
the eggs and sugar until thick
enough to leave a trail. Fold in the
flour with a metal spoon and add
the warm water. Pour the mixture
into the prepared tin and bake at
450°F, 230°C, Gas Mark 8, for 10–15
minutes, until well risen and
golden brown. Turn on to a wire
tray and remove the paper. When
cold, cut into 3 equal sized
rectangles. Using a spatula, sandwich the sponge layers together
with jam. Cover the sides with jam
and dip in the chopped nuts, to
coat evenly. Decorate the edges
with rosettes of cream. Spoon
some of the cherry filling into the
centre of the cake. Purée the
remainder and serve as a sauce
with the gateau.

If wished, a little kirsch or
almond essence can be added to
the cream before whipping.

American Country Cheesecake

1½ oz (40 g) butter *or* margarine
1 tablespoon (15 ml) golden syrup
4 oz (100 g) **Kellogg's** Country Store
Filling
6 oz (175 g) cream cheese
½ pint (300 ml) double cream
1 packet **Kellogg's** Rise & Shine Orange
½ pint (300 ml) water
½ oz (15 g) powdered gelatine
2 large oranges
angelica for decoration

Put the butter and golden syrup into a saucepan and heat gently until the butter has melted. Remove from the heat and stir in the Country Store, mixing well. Press into the base of a lightly oiled 8 in (20 cm) loose-based cake tin. Leave in a cool place while pre-paring the filling.

Beat the cream cheese until soft. Gradually stir in the cream and beat or whisk until the mixture thickens. Make up the Rise & Shine with the water. Place 4 tablespoons (60 ml) of the prepared drink in a small bowl and sprinkle on the gelatine. Stand the bowl in a pan of hot water and stir until the gelatine has dissolved. Stir the remaining orange drink into the dissolved gelatine, then gradually stir this into the cream cheese mixture. Remove the peel and pith from one orange and divide into segments, chop and add to the cream cheese mixture. Leave until beginning to set then pour on to the prepared base in the tin. Leave in a cool place until set. Carefully remove the cheesecake from the tin and slide gently on to a serving plate. Decorate with the angelica 'leaves' and the second orange, peeled and cut into segments.

To freeze the cheesecake, do not decorate. Slide the cheesecake on to a baking tray covered with a piece of freezer film. Freeze quickly, then wrap completely in film and overwrap with foil. When required, unwrap and place on a serving plate, cover loosely with a polythene bag and thaw at room temperature for 6–8 hours before decorating as above.
Serves 6–8

Fluffy Lemon Cheesecake

2 oz (50 g) **Kraft** Superfine Margarine
1½ oz (40 g) caster sugar
4 oz (100 g) digestive biscuits, crushed
8 oz (227 g) packet **Kraft** Philadelphia Soft Cheese
3 oz (75 g) caster sugar
2 eggs, separated
5 fl oz (150 ml) carton natural *or* lemon yoghurt
juice and grated rind of 1 lemon
½ oz (15 g) gelatine
⅛ pint (65 ml) water

Melt the margarine in a pan, stir in the sugar and crumbs, combine well and press into base of a 7–8 in (18–20 cm) cake tin with a re-movable base. Chill until firm. Cream the cheese with the sugar until smooth. Gradually add the egg yolks, yoghurt, lemon juice and rind. Sprinkle the gelatine into the water in a small basin and place over a pan of hot water until melted. Cool slightly and beat into the cheese mixture. Whisk the egg whites until stiff and fold carefully into the mixture. Pour the mixture on to the base and put to set in the refrigerator or a cool place.
Serves 6

Chocolate Box

6 oz (150 g) butter
6 oz (150 g) caster sugar
finely grated rind and juice of 1 orange
3 eggs
6 oz (150 g) self-raising flour
1 level teaspoon (5 ml) ground cinnamon
1 packet **Lyons** Melt in the Bag, milk chocolate flavour
½ pint (275 ml) double cream, whipped
11 oz (312 g) can mandarin orange segments, drained

Cream the butter, sugar and orange rind together until light and fluffy. Gradually beat in the eggs, one at a time, adding a little of the flour with each egg after the first to prevent curdling. Fold in the remaining flour, cinnamon and orange juice. Place the mixture in a greased and floured 8 in (20 cm) square tin. Bake in the centre of an oven pre-heated to 350°F, 180°C, Gas Mark 4, for 50–60 minutes until well risen and springy to the touch. Allow to cool in the tin for a few minutes before turning out on to a cooling rack. Prepare the Melt in the Bag according to directions. Draw an 8 in (20 cm) square on greaseproof paper and flood with Melt in the Bag, using a knife to ensure it is spread evenly. Allow to set. Cut into 16 squares. Cover the cake with the cream. Place chocolate squares around the sides of the cake. Decorate with mandarin oranges and piped cream.

To freeze, open freeze the com-plete gateau until the cream has become firm. Put into a polythene bag and, for extra protection, place this in a rigid plastic container or cardboard box. Recommended freezer life is 3 months.

To use, take out of the box and remove from the polythene bag. Leave at room temperature for 4 hours. The surface of the chocolate will appear moist after freezing.
Serves 12

Coffee Cream Gateau

8 eggs
9 oz (250 g) caster sugar
5 oz (150 g) almonds, finely
  chopped
5 oz (150 g) flour

Filling

6 egg yolks
9 oz (250 g) sugar
½ cup very strong black **Lyons**
  Coffee
6 oz (175 g) butter
½ pod vanilla (the inside) *or*
  a few drops vanilla essence

Whisk the egg yolks and sugar
until creamy and add the finely
chopped almonds. Sift the flour
and stir in lightly. Whip the whites
and finally fold them into the cake
mixture. Turn the mixture into a
greased and floured gateau tin and
bake in a moderate oven (350–
360°F, 177–182°C, Gas Mark 4) for
30 minutes. When ready, put the
cake on a wire tray and let cool.

For the filling, beat the egg yolks
and sugar until smooth. Add the
black coffee and put mixture in a
bowl over a pan of boiling water.
Keep stirring until the mixture
thickens. Beat the butter until
smooth and white, and add to
mixture with the vanilla.

When the sponge cake is cold cut
it in half horizontally and spread
half the cream over the bottom
half. Replace the top half and
spread the remaining cream
evenly over the top and sides of the
cake. Decorate with crumbled
chocolate flake, chocolate
vermicelli, chopped almonds or
chocolate beans and whipped
cream if wished.   **Serves 8–10**

Cheesecake Strawberry Crunch

2 oz (50 g) butter
1 oz (25 g) caster sugar
4 oz (100 g) **McVitie's** Digestive
  Biscuits
2 oz (50 g) plain chocolate,
  grated

2 oz (50 g) walnuts, chopped *or*
  crushed very finely

Filling

5 oz (150 g) cream cheese
1 small can condensed milk
5 oz (142 g) carton strawberry
  yoghurt

Topping

1 oz chocolate, grated

Melt the butter in a saucepan and
add the sugar. Remove from the
heat and add the biscuits, chocolate and nuts and mix thoroughly.
Press into an 8 in (20 cm) flan tin,
lined with foil and chill
thoroughly. Beat the cream cheese
and condensed milk together and
then stir in the yoghurt. Pour into
the biscuit shell and leave in the
refrigerator to set.

To serve, sprinkle with grated
chocolate.   **Serves 6**

Chocolate Rum or Brandy Cake

8 oz (225 g) butter
8 oz (225 g) plain cooking
  chocolate
4 oz (100 g) caster sugar
3 eggs
4 oz (100 g) glacé cherries,
  chopped
4 oz (100 g) walnuts, chopped
2 tablespoons (30 ml) rum *or*
  brandy
8 oz (225 g) **McVitie's** Digestive
  Biscuits, broken in pieces
whipped cream and glacé
  cherries to decorate

Place the butter and chocolate in a
saucepan and heat gently until
melted, remove from the heat and
cool slightly. Whisk the sugar and
eggs together, until thick, in a
large mixing bowl. Fold in the
melted chocolate mixture and then
add the remaining ingredients.
Pour into a 2 lb (900 g) loaf tin and
leave in the refrigerator for at least
8 hours or preferably overnight.
Turn out, decorate with the cream
and glacé cherries and serve cut in
slices.

This will freeze well for future
use.   **Serves 8–10**

Creamy American Cheesecake

1 **McVitie's** Lemon Spice Cake
1 oz (25 g) cornflakes, crushed
1 oz (25 g) **McVitie's** Digestive
  Biscuits, crushed
2 oz (50 g) butter
2 oz (50 g) demerara sugar
2 tablespoons (30 ml) golden
  syrup

Filling

8 oz (225 g) full-fat soft cream
  cheese
8 oz (225 g) cottage cheese,
  sieved
5 oz (150 g) caster sugar
1 teaspoon (5 ml) vanilla
  essence
pinch of salt
3 eggs, separated
¼ pint (150 ml) evaporated
  milk
4 fl oz (100 ml) double cream
4 tablespoons (60 ml) plain
  flour
2 teaspoons (10 ml) lemon juice

Pre-heat the oven to 450°F, 230°C,
Gas Mark 8. Rub the cake through
a coarse sieve and mix with the
cornflakes and digestive crumbs.
Melt the butter, demerara sugar
and syrup in a heavy-based pan,
add the cake mixture and mix well.
Using the back of a spoon press on
to the base of a lightly greased 9 in
(23 cm) loose-bottomed, spring-
release cake tin. Chill to set.

Meanwhile, mix the cream
cheese, cottage cheese, sugar,
vanilla, salt and egg yolks
together, beating well until
smooth and creamy. Add the
evaporated milk, cream and flour.
Whisk the egg whites until they
stand in firm peaks and fold into
the cheese mixture with the lemon
juice. Turn this mixture into the
prepared tin and place in the oven.
Immediately reduce the oven
temperature to 350°F, 180°C, Gas
Mark 4. Bake for 45 minutes and
then turn off the oven. Allow the
cheesecake to cool in the oven with
the door slightly ajar. Chill before
serving. Decorate with fresh fruit
in season.   **Serves 10**

Pineapple Freezer Cake

6 oz (175 g) plain chocolate

8 oz (225 g) butter, softened

6 oz (175 g) icing sugar, sieved

3 oz (75 g) crushed pineapple, drained

2 tablespoons (30 ml) golden syrup

12 oz (350 g) **McVitie's** Digestive Biscuits, crushed

whipped cream and pineapple to decorate

Line a 2 lb (900 g) loaf tin with foil. Melt the chocolate in a bowl over a pan of hot water and spread half of this over the base of the tin. Cream 2 oz (50 g) of the butter with the icing sugar in a bowl until light and then add the pineapple. Melt the remaining butter in a saucepan with the golden syrup, remove from the heat, add the biscuits and stir until well coated. Spread half of this mixture over the chocolate, pressing well down. On top of this spread the pineapple cream and then the remainder of the biscuit mixture and on top of that the rest of the chocolate. Refrigerate until set. Turn out on to a serving dish and decorate with the cream and pineapple.

Serve very cold.   **Serves 6**

Nestlé

Cherry Cheesecake

8 oz (225 g) chocolate digestive biscuits, crushed

½ teaspoon (2.5 ml) cinnamon

4 oz (100 g) butter, melted

Filling

1 large can **Nestlés** Sweetened Condensed Milk

8 oz (225 g) cream cheese, softened

6 tablespoons (90 ml) lemon juice

Topping

15 oz (425 g) can cherry pie filling

1 tablespoon (15 ml) brandy (optional)

Mix the crushed biscuit, cinnamon and butter together. Press into an 8 in (20 cm) flan ring on a baking sheet to form a shell and chill well. Gradually beat the Nestlés Milk into the softened cream cheese and then add the lemon juice. Pour into the prepared crumb shell. Allow to set before topping with the cherry pie filling and brandy mixed together. Chill well before serving.
Serves 8–10

Malakoff Gâteau

4 oz (100 g) butter

4 oz (100 g) caster sugar

3 egg yolks

2 level teaspoons (10 ml) **Nescafé** Fine Blend dissolved in 2 teaspoons (10 ml) boiling water

4 oz (100 g) blanched almonds, chopped

5 tablespoons (75 ml) rum

1 small can **Nestlé's** Milk

6 tablespoons (90 ml) cold water

2 packets sponge fingers (30 approximately)

4 oz (113 g) can **Nestlé's** Cream, chilled (see note below)

1 oz (25 g) toasted flaked almonds

Line a 2 lb (900 ml) loaf tin with kitchen foil. Cream the butter and sugar until light and fluffy then beat in the egg yolks thoroughly. Add the Nescafé, almonds, 3 tablespoons (45 ml) of the rum and 3 tablespoons (45 ml) of the Nestlé's Milk and mix well. Mix together the remaining Nestlé's Milk and rum with the water. Place a layer of sponge fingers over the base of the prepared tin. Spoon a little of the rum and milk mixture over and then spread with a little of the coffee mixture. Repeat these layers, finishing with sponge fingers. It may be necessary to cut some of the sponge fingers to fit. Cover with kitchen foil, then place heavy weights evenly on top. Chill in the refrigerator for 2–3 hours.

To serve the gâteau, remove the weights and foil and turn out of the tin. Carefully remove the foil from the sides of the gâteau. Decorate with piped Nestle's Cream and toasted almonds and serve immediately.

Note: To use Nestle's Cream for piping, chill the can in the refrigerator for 2 hours. Open, then turn the can upside down without shaking and pour off the whey. The cream is now ready for piping and no further mixing is required.

Yorkshire Cheese Cake

shortcrust pastry made with 4 oz (100 g) flour

4 oz (100 g) **Primula** Cheese

2 oz (50 g) sugar

1 teaspoon (5 ml) whisky

1 egg

2 oz (50 g) currants

Use the pastry to make a 7 in (18 cm) flan case. Beat the cheese and sugar until creamy, add the whisky and pour in the beaten egg. Mix well and add the currants. Put the mixture into the pastry case and bake in a moderate oven at 350°F, 180°C, Gas Mark 4, for about 20 minutes.   **Serves 4**

SCHWARTZ

Cranberry Cream Dessert

2 oz (57 g) butter

4 oz (113 g) digestive biscuits, roughly crushed

1 teaspoon (5 ml) **Schwartz** Ground Ginger

Filling

6 oz (170 g) full fat cream cheese

3 oz (85 g) caster sugar

1 tablespoon (15 ml) powdered gelatine, dissolved in 4 tablespoons (60 ml) hot water and allowed to cool slightly

½ pint (285 ml) double cream, lightly whipped

12½ oz (350 g) jar **Ocean Spray** Cranberry Sauce
¼ pint (150 ml) double cream, whipped, to decorate (optional)

Melt the butter in a saucepan and stir in the crushed biscuits and ginger. Use to line the base of a greased, loose-bottomed 7 in (18 cm) tin. Soften the cream cheese in a large bowl, stir in caster sugar and prepared gelatine mixture and fold in the cream and cranberry sauce. Spread the mixture on top of the biscuit crumb base and leave in the refrigerator until completely set. Remove the dessert from the tin, spread the remaining cranberry sauce over the top and decorate with cream if desired.

This dessert may be stored for up to 2 days in a refrigerator or up to 2 months in a freezer.
Serves 4–6

Stork

Black Forest Gateau

4 eggs (size 2 *or* 3)
4 oz (125 g) caster sugar
3 oz (75 g) self-raising flour sieved with 1 oz (25 g) cocoa powder
3 oz (75 g) **Stork** Margarine, melted and cooled

Icing
3 oz (75 g) **Stork** Margarine

8 oz (225 g) icing sugar, sieved
1 tablespoon (15 ml) cocoa blended with
2 tablespoons (30 ml) hot water and cooled

Filling and decoration
½ pint (275 ml) double *or* whipping cream
2 oz (50 g) walnuts, chopped
14 oz (396 g) can red cherries, drained
melted chocolate to decorate

Prepare two 8 in (20 cm) sandwich tins by bottom-lining, greasing and flouring. Whisk the eggs and sugar together over a pan of hot water until the mixture is thick enough to leave a trail when the whisk is lifted out. Sift in the flour and fold in carefully with the melted margarine, making sure that all the flour is incorporated. Turn the mixture into the prepared tins and bake in the centre of a moderate oven at 350°F, 180°C, Gas Mark 4, for 35–40 minutes, until the cake springs back when lightly pressed. Turn out and cool. Split each cake in half when cold.

Place all the ingredients for the icing in a mixing bowl and beat with a wooden spoon until well mixed. Whisk the cream until thick and fold in the walnuts and most of the cherries, reserving the rest for decoration. Sandwich together the cake layers alternately with the cream and icing. Spread icing on the top. Pipe rosettes of cream around the edge, decorate with the reserved cherries and drizzle over the melted chocolate. **Serves 8**

Strawberry Cheesecake

4 oz (125 g) digestive biscuits, crushed
2 oz (20 g) **Stork** margarine, melted

Filling
¼ pint (150 ml) milk
4 oz (125 g) caster sugar
1 egg, size 2, separated
rind and juice of 1 lemon
½ oz (15 g) gelatine
2 tablespoons (30 ml) water
6 oz (175 g) cream cheese
6 oz (175 g) cottage cheese
¼ pint (150 ml) double cream
strawberries to decorate

Mix together the biscuits and Stork and press into an 8 in (20 cm) loose-based tin. Chill. Place milk, sugar, egg yolk, rind and juice of lemon in a blender and mix for a few seconds. Pour into a saucepan and cook over a low heat for 5 minutes, stirring continuously. Sprinkle gelatine over cold water, leave to soak and place over a pan of hot water until gelatine is dissolved. Add gelatine to custard. Place cheeses and liquid in blender and mix well together. Whisk the cream until thick and fold into mixture. Whisk the egg white and fold in. Pour over the biscuit base and leave to set in refrigerator. Turn out and decorate with the strawberries.

SWEET PASTRIES

Old English Treacle Tart

6 oz (150 g) self-raising flour,
   sifted
3 oz (75 g) **Atora** Shredded Suet
pinch of salt
1 egg (size 3), beaten
milk to mix
Filling
1 oz (25 g) porridge oats *or* 1 oz
   (25 g) desiccated coconut *or*
   2 oz (50 g) fresh white
   breadcrumbs
8 tablespoons (120 ml) golden
   syrup
rind and juice of 1 lemon
a little egg white and caster
   sugar to glaze

Make the pastry by stirring
together the flour, suet and salt
and mixing to a firm dough with
the beaten egg and milk. Roll out to
¼ in (0.5 cm) thick and use to line
an 8 in (20 cm) flan dish or ring set
on a baking sheet. Prick the pastry
base and bake 'blind', lined with
paper or foil and baking beans.
When baked, remove the foil and
beans and sprinkle in the oat
flakes, coconut or breadcrumbs
and add the syrup. To spoon it
easily, either stand the tin in a pan
of simmering water and spoon out
the syrup when melted, or heat a
tablespoon over a gas flame or in
boiling water and use it to spoon
out the syrup, which will then run
off easily. Sprinkle the lemon juice
and rind over the flan. Using the
pastry trimmings, roll out several
10 in (25 cm) long, thin strips and
make a lattice on the top. Brush the
strips with the egg white and
sprinkle with the castor sugar for a
nice sparkle when baked. Bake at
375°F, 190°C, Gas Mark 5, for 20
minutes until golden.

   Serve warm or cold with cream,
or custard.   **Serves 4–6**

Vintage Marmalade and Whisky Flan

Pastry
4 oz (100 g) flour
pinch of salt
3 oz (75 g) butter
1 level teaspoon (5 ml) caster
   sugar
1 egg yolk
a little cold water
Filling
2 oz (50 g) butter
12 oz (300 g) **Baxters** Vintage
   Marmalade
1 egg, beaten
1 tablespoon (15 ml) Scotch
   whisky liqueur, such as
   Glayva

Sieve the flour and salt into a
mixing bowl and rub in the butter
until the mixture resembles fine
breadcrumbs. Stir in the sugar and
egg yolk and enough cold water to
make a firm dough. Turn out on to
a lightly floured board and knead
lightly until smooth. Roll out and
carefully line a 7 in (18 cm) flan tin
or ring, trimming the edges neatly
and pricking the base with a fork.

   To make the filling, melt the
butter in a saucepan, add the
marmalade and beat lightly until
blended. Add the beaten egg and
liqueur and stir until well mixed,
but do not allow the mixture to
boil. Pour into the flan case and
bake in a pre-heated oven at 425°F,
220°C, Gas Mark 7 for about 10
minutes, then reduce the heat to
350°F, 180°C, Gas Mark 4 and bake
for a further 15 minutes until the
filling is set and the pastry golden
brown.

   Serve with pouring cream to
which a little of the liqueur can be
added to taste.   **Serves 5–6**

Fruity Syrup Tart

4 oz (100 g) **Be-Ro** Self-raising
   Flour
2 oz (50 g) shredded suet
pinch of salt
½ teaspoon (2.5 ml) cinnamon
milk to mix
Filling
4 tablespoons (60 ml) golden
   syrup, warmed
1 oz (25 g) desiccated coconut
2 oz (50 g) sultanas
2 oz (50 g) currants

Mix together the dry pastry
ingredients with sufficient milk to
make a pliable dough. Roll out the
pastry and use to line an 8 in
(20 cm) pie plate. Combine the
filling ingredients and pour over
the pastry. Crimp the edges of the
tart and bake for 20–25 minutes at
400°F, 200°C, Gas Mark 6.

   Serve hot or warm with cream or
custard.   **Serves 4–6**

Black Forest Flan

1½ oz (40 g) plain chocolate
1 pint (568 ml) milk
1½ oz (40 g) **Bird's** Custard
   Powder
1½ oz (40 g) sugar
9 in (23 cm) baked pastry case
13½ oz (375 g) can black
   cherries
1 dessertspoon (10 ml)
   arrowroot
¼ pint (150 ml) double cream,
   whipped

Break the chocolate into a
saucepan with the milk. Bring
slowly to the boil and use to make

the custard as usual. Cover the surface with cling film and leave to cool. Drain the can of black cherries and thicken the syrup by bringing to the boil with the arrowroot. Leave to cool. Pour the chocolate custard into the pastry case and decorate with the whipped cream. Stir the black cherries into the thickened syrup and use to decorate the flan. Chill before serving. **Serves 4–6**

Eccles Cakes

2 sheets **Birds Eye** Puff Pastry, thawed
1 oz (25 g) butter
2 oz (50 g) demerara sugar
4 oz (100 g) currants
1½ oz (40 g) candied peel, finely chopped
½ teaspoon (2.5 ml) nutmeg, freshly grated
beaten egg to bind and glaze
caster sugar

Roll out each pastry sheet thinly and cut two 6 in (15 cm) circles from each. Re-roll the trimmings to make a third circle. Leave in a cool place while preparing the filling. Melt the butter and mix with the remaining filling ingredients. Divide this mixture between the pastry circles. Brush the edges of the pastry with beaten egg and draw them together firmly. Turn each Eccles cake over, shape into a round and flatten down slightly. Score the top 3 times, glaze with beaten egg and sprinkle with caster sugar. Bake in an oven pre-heated to 425°F, 220°C, Gas Mark 7, for about 15–20 minutes or until golden brown.

Sprinkle with extra sugar and serve warm.
Makes 6

Vanilla Cream Slices

2 sheets **Birds Eye** Puff Pastry, thawed
2 oz (50 g) cornflour

½ pint (250 ml) milk
2 egg yolks
1 oz (25 g) sugar
½ teaspoon (2.5 ml) vanilla essence
a little glacé icing
glacé cherries and angelica to decorate

Trim ⅛ in (3 mm) off the pastry sheets to ensure even rising. Do not roll out the sheets but cut into three, lengthwise. Bake in an oven pre-heated to 425°F, 220°C, Gas Mark 7, for about 10 minutes or until well risen and golden brown. Allow to cool. Blend the cornflour with the milk, beat in the egg yolks and sugar and cook over a gentle heat until thick. If the mixture becomes lumpy, beat vigorously until smooth. Stir in the vanilla essence and allow to cool. Cut through the centre of the pastry fingers, spread the custard over one half and sandwich together again. Drizzle the tops with the glacé icing and decorate with the cherries and angelica.
Makes 6

Cookeen

Danish Apple Flan

Pastry
3½ oz (100 g) **Cookeen** Blended Cooking Fat
7 oz (200 g) plain flour, sieved
1 oz (25 g) caster sugar
2 tablespoons (30 ml) cold water
Filling
6 large cooking apples, peeled, cored and sliced
1½ oz (40 g) **Stork** Margarine
4 oz (100 g) wholemeal breadcrumbs
2 oz (50 g) demerara sugar
3 teaspoons (15 ml) cinnamon
2 oz (50 g) flaked almonds
Decoration
¼ pint (150 ml) whipped double cream
flaked almonds, toasted

Rub the Cookeen into the flour until the mixture resembles fine

breadcrumbs. Add sugar. Mix thoroughly. Add water and mix to a firm dough. Knead lightly. Roll out on a lightly floured surface and line the base of an 8 in (20 cm) loose-bottomed cake tin. Bake blind and cool in tin. Stew apples in a small amount of water until a thick purée is obtained. Fry the breadcrumbs in Stork and mix with the sugar and cinnamon. On top of the cooked pastry base in the tin, layer up the stewed apple, then the breadcrumb mixture and flaked almonds. Finish with a topping of breadcrumb mixture. Leave in the refrigerator to chill thoroughly. Remove from the cake tin by pushing up gently from the base.

Decorate with whirls of cream and toasted flaked almonds.
Serves 6

FRANK COOPER®

Cranberry Lattice Tart

4 oz (100 g) plain flour
2 oz (50 g) cornflour
3 oz (75 g) butter
1 teaspoon (5 ml) caster sugar
1 egg yolk
Filling
2 oz (50 g) raisins
2 oz (50 g) currants
2 oz (50 g) sultanas
1 oz (25 g) mixed peel, chopped
1 oz (25 g) walnuts, chopped
6½ oz (185 g) jar **Frank Cooper's** Cranberry Sauce

Sieve together the flour and the cornflour and rub in the butter until the mixture resembles fine breadcrumbs. Add the sugar and egg yolk and mix to a stiff dough. Roll out the pastry and use to line a 7 in (18 cm) flan ring. Mix all the ingredients for the filling together and place in the flan case. Make a lattic design on top of the tart using the pastry trimmings. Bake at 350°F, 180°C, Gas Mark 4 for 20—25 minutes. **Serves 4**

Cranberry Mince Pies

8 oz (200 g) plain flour
4 oz (100 g) cornflour
6 oz (150 g) butter
2 oz (50 g) caster sugar
2 eggs
6½ oz (185 g) jar **Frank Cooper's** Cranberry Sauce
8 oz (200 g) mincemeat
caster sugar to serve

Sieve the flour and cornflour together, rub in the butter and stir in the sugar. Lightly whisk the eggs and stir into the flour to form a firm dough. Knead until smooth. Roll out the pastry and cut into fluted rounds, half with a 3 in (8 cm) cutter and half with a 2 in (5 cm) cutter. Line the bases of patty tins with the larger rounds. Mix together the cranberry sauce and mincemeat and put a teaspoonful (5 ml) in each pastry case. Cover with the smaller circles, damping the edges and sealing well together, snip the tops with scissors and bake in a hot oven (400°F, 200°C, Gas Mark 6) for 15–20 minutes. When cool dredge with caster sugar

▶Dietade

Bermuda Tart

shortcrust pastry to line a 7 in (18 cm) flan tin *or* ring
2–3 oz (50–75 g) **Delicia** Raspberry, Strawberry *or* Apricot Jam
a few flaked almonds (optional)
2 oz (50 g) margarine
1 oz (25 g) **Dietade** Fruit Sugar
4 oz (100 g) desiccated coconut
1 egg, beaten

Line the flan tin or ring with the pastry, spread the jam over the base and sprinkle on the almonds, if used. Heat the margarine and fruit sugar until melted, stir in the coconut and the beaten egg and spread the mixture evenly over the jam. Bake near the top of the oven at 375°F, 190°C, Gas Mark 6 for 30–35 minutes. Cover with greaseproof paper for part of the cooking

time if the coconut begins to get too brown before the flan is set.

Serve hot with custard, or the flan can be served cold.
Serves 4

Christmas Meringue Pie

8 oz (225 g) shortcrust pastry
15 oz (425 g) jar **Elsenham** Mincemeat with Brandy
3 oz (75 g) preserved ginger, chopped
3 oz (75 g) glacé cherries, chopped
3 eggs, separated
6 oz (175 g) caster sugar

Line a 9 in (23 cm) flan ring with the pastry. Fill with aluminium foil and baking beans or rice. Bake in the oven at 400°F, 200°C, Gas Mark 6, for 20 minutes. Remove the foil and beans and bake for a further 15 minutes or until dry and lightly browned. Cool. Meanwhile, mix together the mincemeat, ginger, cherries and egg yolks in a saucepan and heat gently until almost boiling. Cool. Whisk the egg whites until very stiff. Add half the sugar and continue whisking until stiff again. Fold in the remaining sugar. Spoon the mincemeat filling into the pastry case and cover with the meringue, taking care to completely seal the edges. Place in the oven, preheated to 425°F, 220°C, Gas Mark 7, for several minutes until the meringue is browned.

Serve hot or cold. **Serves 6**

GALE'S

Normandy Apple Tart

2 lb (900 g) cooking apples, peeled, cored and sliced
3 tablespoons (45 ml) water
5 tablespoons (75 ml) **Gale's** Clear Honey
grated rind and juice of 1 small lemon
1 oz (25 g) butter
1 teaspoon (5 ml) ground cinnamon
1 tablespoon (15 ml) brandy *or* sherry (optional)
shortcrust pastry made with 6 oz (175 g) flour
3 eating apples

Cook the apples gently with the water in a covered pan until soft. Add 3 tablespoons (45 ml) honey, the grated lemon rind, butter and cinnamon and simmer uncovered until reduced to a thick purée (if wished, stir in 1 tablespoon (15 ml) brandy or sherry). Allow the apple purée to cool.

Roll out the pastry and line an 8 in (20 cm) flan ring. Bake blind, lined with foil and beans, at 400°F, 200°C, Gas Mark 6, for 10–15 minutes. Remove the foil and beans and pour in the apple purée. Core the eating apples but do not peel. Halve them, slice very thinly and arrange on top of the purée. Bake for a further 20 minutes at the same oven temperature. Place 2 tablespoons (30 ml) honey in a pan with the lemon juice and heat gently until the honey dissolves. Brush or spoon over the surface of the tart to give it a shiny glaze.
Serves 8

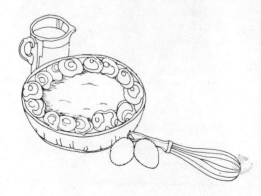

Lemon Curd Tarts with Home-Made Lemon Curd

Lemon Curd
3 eggs, beaten with a fork and strained through a sieve
3 oz (75 g) butter
6 tablespoons (90 ml) **Jif** Lemon Juice
8 oz (225 g) granulated sugar

Put all the ingredients together in the top of a double boiler or a bowl, placed over a pan of hot water. Beat well and stir until thick. Pour into a jar and cool. Cover and store if necessary. Makes just over 1 lb (450 g).

Lemon Curd Tarts
7 oz (200 g) plain flour
pinch of salt
4 oz (100 g) butter
about 7 tablespoons (120 ml) home-made lemon curd

Sift the flour with the salt into a large bowl. Cut the butter into small pieces and add to the flour, then rub in until the mixture resembles breadcrumbs. Add the water gradually and stir to form a dough. Knead lightly for a few seconds until smooth and firm. Leave the pastry in the refrigerator for 15–20 minutes. Roll out the pastry and cut into rounds large enough to fit into 12 tartlet tins and put a teaspoonful (5 ml) of lemon curd into each. Decorate with little pastry cutouts. Bake at 375°F, 190°C, Gas Mark 5 for 10–12 minutes. Serve cool.
Makes 12

Apple Caramel Tart

1½ lb (700 g) cooking apples, peeled, cored and sliced
6 oz (175 g) caster sugar

7½ oz (215 g) packet **Jus-rol** Shortcrust Pastry, thawed
3 eating apples
lemon juice
2 tablespoons (30 ml) water

Stew the cooking apples gently in a covered pan with 1 oz (25 g) of the sugar until soft and puréed. Strain through a fine sieve to remove excess liquid and cool. Roll out the pastry and use to line an 8–9 in (20–23 cm) tart tin or china flan dish. Put the cooled purée into the pastry case. Peel the eating apples, remove the cores using a corer or peeler to keep the apples whole, slice into thin rings and arrange over the purée. Brush with a little lemon juice and sprinkle with 1 oz (25 g) of the sugar. Bake in a pre-heated oven at 400°F, 200°C, Gas Mark 6, for about 35 minutes until golden brown. Leave to cool. Dissolve the remaining sugar in the water, bring to the boil and cook until caramelised. Pour over the top of the tart. Serve the same day while the caramel is crunchy.
Serves 4

Bakewell Tart

7½ oz (215 g) packet **Jus-rol** Shortcrust Pastry, thawed
3 tablespoons (30 ml) raspberry jam
2 oz (50 g) butter
2 oz (50 g) caster sugar
1 egg
1 oz (25 g) self-raising flour
2 oz (50 g) ground almonds
1 tablespoon (15 ml) milk
few drops almond essence

Roll the pastry out to a 10 in (25 cm) square and use to line an 8 in (20 cm) tin or plate. Trim the surplus from the edges. Spread the pastry base with the jam. Cream the butter and sugar together and beat the egg into the mixture. Sift the flour and stir it in with the ground almonds, milk and almond essence. Spread the mixture over the jam. Roll out the pastry scraps and cut them into ½ in (1 cm) strips. Lay these over the tart in a criss-cross design. Seal the ends with a drop of water and then trim

neatly. Bake in a pre-heated oven at 375°F, 190°C, Gas Mark 5, for about 30 minutes or until golden brown.

Serve hot or cold.   **Serves 4**

Chocolate Rum Slice

7½ oz (215 g) packet **Jus-rol** Puff Pastry, thawed
6⅔ fl oz (180 ml) carton double cream
1 level tablespoon (15 ml) caster sugar
1½ tablespoons (20 ml) rum
Glacé icing
4 oz (100 g) icing sugar
3 level teaspoons (15 ml) cocoa powder
1–2 tablespoons (15–30 ml) warm water
½ oz (15 g) block chocolate for decoration

Roll out the pastry evenly into a rectangle 9 × 10 in (23 × 26 cm) and prick very well with a fork. Place on a dampened baking sheet and bake in the centre of the oven, pre-heated to 425°F, 220°C, Gas Mark 7, for 15–20 minutes, until well risen and golden brown. Cool on a rack. When cold cut in half lengthwise. In a bowl whip the double cream and when it begins to thicken add the rum and caster sugar. Continue to whip until fairly firm. Spread the cream evenly over one piece of pastry and place the second piece on the top.

To make the glacé icing, sift the icing sugar and cocoa powder into a bowl and gradually add enough warm water to give a fairly thick consistency. Spoon on to the top of the slice and coarsely grate the block chocolate over the top. Leave to set. Cut the slice with a sharp knife.   **Serves 6**

Kellogg's

Apple Butter Squares

2 oz (50 g) **Kellogg's** Rice
  Krispies, finely crushed
7 oz (200 g) plain flour
½ teaspoon (2.5 ml) salt
6 oz (175 g) butter *or* margarine
1–2 tablespoons (15–30 ml)
  milk
Filling
¼ teaspoon (1.25 ml) ground
  cinnamon
pinch ground nutmeg
2 oz (50 g) granulated sugar
1½ lb (675 g) cooking apples,
  peeled, cored and sliced
1 tablespoon (15 ml) lemon
  juice
Icing
4 oz (100 g) icing sugar
1–2 tablespoons (15–30 ml)
  water

Stir together the cereal, flour and
salt. Rub in the butter or margarine
until the mixture resembles coarse
crumbs and add sufficient milk to
bind. Roll out half the pastry to
cover the base of a 9 in (23 cm)
square cake tin. Mix together the
filling ingredients and arrange on
top. Roll out the remaining pastry
to cover the apples and prick with a
fork in several places. Bake in a
moderately hot oven (375°F, 190°C,
Gas Mark 5) for about 45 minutes,
until the apples are tender and the
pastry golden brown. Meanwhile,
mix the icing sugar with enough
water to make a smooth consistency. Cut the pastry into squares
and drizzle the icing over.
  Serve warm or cold.
Makes 9 squares

Rich Black Cherry Flan

6 oz (150 g) plain flour
3 oz (75 g) butter
1 tablespoon (15 ml) caster
  sugar
1 egg yolk

generous 2 oz (50 g) **Kerrygold**
  Frozen Whipping Cream,
  thawed
Topping
1 lb (400 g) black cherries *or*
  14 oz (350 g) tin cherries
2 tablespoons (30 ml)
  redcurrant jelly
1 glass red wine (2 fl oz,
  115 ml)
grated rind and juice of
  ½ orange
2 teaspoons (10 ml) arrowroot
Filling
4 oz (100 g) **Kerrygold** Frozen
  Cream (¼ pint/5 fl oz
  double cream, thawed)

First prepare the pastry. Sift the
flour into a bowl with a pinch of
salt. Lightly rub the fat into the
flour until it resembles fine
breadcrumbs. Add the sugar. Mix
the egg yolk and cream together
and mix into the flour and butter
mixture with a round-bladed
knife. You may need ½ tablespoon
cold water to bring the dough
together. Knead very lightly until
smooth. Wrap and chill for at least
30 minutes before using.
  Meanwhile prepare the cherry
topping. Stone the cherries, put
into a pan with a tablespoon
(15 ml) of caster sugar. Cover and
set over a low heat until the juice
begins to run. Turn into a bowl.
Pour the wine into a pan and
reduce by half, add the redcurrant
jelly, orange rind and juice and
heat gently until the jelly is melted
then add the cherries and juice and
cook for 3–4 minutes. Mix the
arrowroot with a little cold water,
add 3 tablespoons of the hot cherry
juice, return this mixture to the
pan and re-boil. If using the tinned
cherries, drain, reduce the cherry
juice and wine by half and then
proceed as above. Allow the mixture to cool completely.
  Roll out the pastry, line an 8 in
(20 cm) flan ring and bake blind for
about 15–20 minutes. Allow to cool
on a cooling rack. Lightly whip the
cream, add a little vanilla essence
and sugar and place in the baked
flan case. Spread to the edges and
then spoon the cold cherry mixture
on top.   **Serves 6**

Libby's

Danish Pastries

½ oz (12.5 g) fresh yeast
⅛ pint (75 ml) warm water
8 oz (200 g) plain flour
½ level teaspoon (2.5 ml) salt
1 level tablespoon (15 ml) sugar
1 oz (25 g) lard
1 egg, beaten
5 oz (125 g) butter, soft and
  oblong shaped
29 oz (822 g) can **Libby's** Peach
  Halves, drained, with the
  syrup reserved
flaked almonds, toasted

Blend the yeast with the water.
Mix the dry ingredients and rub in
the lard. Add the yeast and egg,
mix to an elastic dough, cover and
refrigerate for 10 minutes. Roll the
dough to 3 times the size of the
butter and proceed as for puff
pastry. Roll out thinly, cut in 4 in
(10 cm) squares and cut and fold as
for a paper windmill. Place a peach
half in the centre of each pastry. Set
aside to rise for 30–40 minutes.
Bake for about 15 minutes in a pre-
heated oven at 425°F, 220°C, Gas
Mark 7. Whilst hot, glaze liberally
with the fruit syrup boiled to
reduce by half. Top with the
almonds.
Makes 10 pastries

Chocolate Cherry Bakewell

shortcrust pastry made with
  6 oz (150 g) plain flour *or*
  1 packet **Lyons** Short Pastry
  Mix
8 tablespoons (120 ml) cherry
  jam
2 oz (50 g) margarine
2 oz (50 g) caster sugar
1 egg
1 packet **Lyons** Melt in the Bag,
  plain chocolate flavour
2 oz (50 g) self-raising flour

2 oz (50 g) ground almonds

Roll out the pastry to line an 8 in (20 cm) flan ring. Retain the trimmings. Spread the jam evenly over the base of the pastry flan case. Cream the margarine and sugar together until light and fluffy and beat in the egg. Prepare the Melt in the Bag and stir into the creamed mixture with the flour and ground almonds. Spread the chocolate mixture evenly over the jam. Roll out the remaining pastry into a rectangle and cut into ¼ in (0.5 cm) strips. Twist each pastry strip and lay across the chocolate mixture to form a lattice. Bake towards the top of an oven pre-heated to 400°F, 200°C, Gas Mark 6, for 20 minutes. Reduce the oven temperature to 350°F, 180°C, Gas Mark 4 and bake for a further 20 minutes.   **Serves 6**

McVitie's Treacle Tart

shortcrust pastry made with
  6 oz (175 g) flour
½ **McVitie's** Golden Syrup
  Cake *or* ½ **McVitie's** Jamaica
  Ginger Cake
4 oz (100 g) mixed dried fruit
1 dessert apple, peeled, cored
  and grated
grated rind and juice of 1 lemon
4 tablespoons (60 ml) golden
  syrup
2 tablespoons (30 ml) milk

Roll out the pastry on a lightly floured surface and use to line a 9 in (23 cm) pie plate or a shallow flan dish. Reserve any pastry trimmings. Coarsely grate the cake and mix with the dried fruit, apple, lemon rind, lemon juice, golden syrup and milk. Spread over the pastry to within 1 in (2.5 cm) of the edges. Moisten the edges with cold water. Roll out the pastry trimmings and cut into thin strips. Arrange in a criss-cross design over the filling. Place on a baking tray and bake in a moder-

ately hot oven (400°F, 200°C, Gas Mark 6) for about 30–40 minutes, or until the pastry is golden. Serve with fresh single, double or soured cream.   **Serves 6**

Cadbury's Marvel

Tarte a l'Orange

Pastry
3 oz (75 g) wholewheat flour
3 oz (75 g) plain flour
1 tablespoon (15 ml) icing
  sugar
3 oz (75 g) margarine
1 egg, beaten
a little cold water
Filling
1 oz (25 g) cornflour
½ pint (275 ml) liquid **Marvel**
  2 eggs, beaten
3 oz (75 g) soft dark brown
  sugar
2 oranges
Glaze
3 tablespoons (45 ml) apricot
  jam
1 teaspoon (5 ml) Cointreau
  (optional)

Make the pastry by rubbing the fat into the mixed flour and icing sugar. Bind with the beaten egg and a little cold water if necessary. Roll out and line an 8 in (20 cm) flan ring, pricking the base. Chill for 30 minutes. Bake blind for 15 minutes at 400°F, 200°C, Gas Mark 6, then remove the paper and beans and return to the oven for a further few minutes.

Blend the cornflour with a little liquid Marvel then add the eggs, two-thirds of the sugar, the finely grated rind of 1 orange and the remaining Marvel. Cook the custard in the top of a double saucepan, or very gently in a pan, stirring continuously. Do not allow to boil. Cool the thickened custard a little before pouring into the pastry case. Peel and thinly slice both oranges then overlap on top of the custard. Sprinkle with the remaining sugar and return to

the oven for up to 10 minutes until the oranges are beginning to brown. Bring the jam to the boil with 2 tablespoons (30 ml) of water. Stir in the Cointreau and spread the glaze over the oranges.
Serves 5–6

Nestlé

French Apricot Tart

Pâté Sucre
4 oz (100 g) plain flour
pinch of salt
2 oz (50 g) butter
2 oz (50 g) caster sugar
2 egg yolks
Filling
1 tablespoon (15 ml) **Fulcreem
  Co.** Custard Powder
¼ pint (150 ml) milk
6 oz (170 g) can **Nestlé's** Cream
1 tablespoon (15 ml) sugar
few drops of **Crosse &
  Blackwell** Almond Essence
Topping
14.5 oz (410 g) **Libby's** Apricot
  Halves, drained and syrup
  reserved
1 teaspoon (5 ml) arrowroot

Heat the oven to 375°F, 190°C, Gas Mark 5. Place the flour and salt in a bowl, make a well in the centre, add remaining ingredients. Cream these together with the fingertips. Gradually combine the flour with the creamed mixture, form into a ball and refrigerate for 30 minutes. To make the filling, blend custard powder, milk and cream in a saucepan. Bring to the boil, whisking continuously until thickened. Add the sugar and essence. Place an 8 in (20 cm) flan ring on a baking sheet and line with pastry. Bake blind for about 20 minutes. When cool, fill the pastry case with custard and arrange the apricot halves on top. Add the arrowroot to the syrup, bring to the boil, whisking continuously until clear. Use to glaze the tart.   **Serves 6**

Ipswich Almond Pudding

shortcrust pastry made with
   6 oz (175 g) flour
2 oz (50 g) butter
2 oz (50 g) caster sugar
2 eggs
1 small can **Nestlé's** Ideal Milk
2 oz (50 g) ground almonds
grated rind of ½ lemon
1 teaspoon (5 ml) almond
   essence
1 oz (25 g) flaked almonds
6 oz (170 g) can **Nestlé's** Cream

Line a 7 in (18 cm) flan ring with the pastry. In a bowl, cream the butter and sugar. Beat in the eggs, Ideal Milk, ground almonds, lemon rind and essence. Spoon the mixture into the lined flan ring and bake in a pre-heated oven at 425°F, 220°C, Gas Mark 7, for 10 minutes then at 350°F, 180°C, Gas Mark 4, for 45 minutes. Sprinkle with the flaked almonds 15 minutes before the end of baking time.

Serve hot or cold with Nestlé's Cream.   **Serves 6–8**

Tangy Lime Pie

6 oz (150 g) plain flour
3 oz (75 g) margarine, *or* use
   white fat and margarine
   mixed
4 tablespoons (80 ml) **Rose's**
   Lime Juice
1 oz (25 g) cornflour
2 eggs, separated
5 oz (125 g) caster sugar

Rub the margarine into the flour then add just enough water to bind together. Knead lightly, roll out and line an 8 in (20 cm) fluted flan ring placed on a baking tray. Line with foil and bake in a moderately hot oven (400°F, 200°C, Gas Mark 6) for 20 minutes, removing the foil for the last 5 minutes. Lift off the flan ring.

Make the lime juice up to ½ pint (250 ml) with water. Blend the cornflour with a little water then mix into the lime juice in a saucepan. Bring to the boil, stirring continuously until thickened. Take off the heat and beat in the egg yolks and 1 oz (25 g) of the sugar; pour into the pastry case. Stiffly whisk the egg whites then whisk in half the remaining sugar. When standing in peaks, fold in the remaining sugar and pipe or spoon on top of the flan. Gently brown in a very slow oven (300°F, 150°C, Gas Mark 2) for 25 minutes. Serve hot or cold.
Alternatively the meringue may be flashed under the grill or put into a hot oven for about 5 minutes.
Serves 6

Stork

Baklava

12 oz (350 g) puff pastry
Syrup
8 oz (225 g) honey
½ pint (275 ml) water
2 tablespoons (30 ml) orange
   juice
Filling
4 oz (125 g) **Stork** Margarine
1 teaspoon (5 ml) honey
8 oz (225 g) nuts, chopped
2 teaspoons (10 ml) mixed spice
1 teaspoon (5 ml) nutmeg
1½ tablespoons (22 ml) lemon
   juice

Roll out the puff pastry until almost paper thin. Cut into 4 equal-sized oblongs. Place the syrup ingredients in a pan and bring to boiling point. Simmer for about 5 minutes. Cool. Beat Stork margarine and honey together until creamy. Mix together with the remaining filling ingredients. Put a layer of pastry on a board, spread with one third of the filling, cover with pastry, repeat layers, finishing with pastry. Cut into diamond-shaped pieces. Place in refrigerator for 30 minutes. Bake near the top of pre-heated oven

(450°F, 230°C, Gas Mark 8) for 15–20 minutes until crisp and golden. Remove from the oven and pour syrup over the pastries while hot, then place on a cooling tray.

whitworths

Iced Bakewell Tart

flaky pastry made with 4 oz
   (100 g) flour
1 tablespoon (15 ml) apricot
   jam
2 oz (50 g) margarine
2 oz (50 g) **Whitworths** Caster
   Sugar
juice of ½ lemon
4 oz (100 g) **Whitworths**
   Ground Almonds
2 oz (50 g) **Whitworths** Self-
   raising Flour
Decoration
4 oz (100 g) icing sugar
a little cold water to mix
3 **Whitworths** Glacé Cherries,
   halved

Roll out the pastry and use to line an 8 in (20 cm) flan tin. Spread the inside base of the pastry case with the apricot jam. Cream together the margarine and sugar. Add the lemon juice and egg and beat well. Fold the almonds and flour into the creamed mixture. Spread the mixture evenly in the pastry case. Bake for 20–30 minutes at 400°F, 200°C, Gas Mark 6. Leave to cool.

Mix together the icing sugar and water to make an icing of coating consistency. Spread the icing over the Bakewell Tart and decorate with the cherry halves.

CAKES

Cinnamon Honey Cake

4 oz (125 g) vegetable margarine
2 oz (50 g) soft brown sugar
2 tablespoons (30 ml) clear honey
2 eggs, slightly beaten
8 oz (225 g) **Allinson** 81% Farmhouse Flour, self-raising
½ teaspoon (2.5 ml) ground cinnamon
a little milk to mix
blanched almonds (optional)

Cream together the margarine and sugar until soft, then beat in the honey. Add the eggs a little at a time. Sieve the flour and cinnamon and add to the creamed mixture, with a little milk if required to give a soft consistency. Grease an 8 in (20 cm) cake tin and put a few almonds in the base if liked. Pour in the cake mixture and bake in a pre-heated oven (350°F, 180°C, Gas Mark 4) for about 1 hour or until firm to the touch. Turn out and cool on a wire rack.

Farmhouse Fruit Cake

2 oz (50 g) dried apricots, chopped
8 oz (225 g) **Allinson** 100% Wholewheat or 81% Farmhouse Flour, plain
6 oz (175 g) vegetable margarine
6 oz (175 g) brown sugar
3 eggs (size 2)
5 oz (150 g) sultanas, washed and dried thoroughly
2 oz (50 g) mixed peel
½ teaspoon (2.5 ml) baking powder
½ teaspoon (2.5 ml) mixed spice

Simmer the apricots for 10 minutes in a little water. Drain and place with all the other ingredients in a large bowl and mix well until blended. Pour into a greased and lined, deep 7 in (18 cm) cake tin and smooth the top. Bake for 1½–1¾ hours in an oven pre-heated to 325°F, 160°C, Gas Mark 3. Turn out and cool on a wire rack.

Raisin Gingerbread

12 oz (350 g) **Allinson** 100% Wholewheat Flour, plain, sifted with 1½ teaspoons (7.5 ml) baking powder
2 teaspoons (10 ml) ground ginger
6 oz (175 g) raisins, washed and dried thoroughly
6 oz (175 g) clear honey
2 oz (50 g) molasses
6 oz (175 g) vegetable margarine
3 oz (75 g) brown sugar
2 eggs, beaten
1 teaspoon (5 ml) bicarbonate of soda
4 tablespoons (60 ml) milk

Grease and line an 8 in (20 cm) square or 6 × 10 in (15 × 25 cm) baking tin. Sieve the flour and ginger into a bowl and add the raisins. Place the honey, molasses, margarine and sugar in a saucepan and heat gently until the sugar has dissolved. Pour on to the dry ingredients, add the eggs, bicarbonate of soda and milk. Beat well together and pour into the prepared tin. Bake for 1½ hours in a pre-heated oven (325°F, 160°C, Gas Mark 3). Turn out and cool on a wire rack. Cut into squares when cold.

Wholewheat Hot Cross Buns

1 oz (25 g) fresh yeast or ½ oz (15 g) **Allinson** Dried Yeast
1 (25 mg) vitamin C tablet, crushed
1½ oz (45 g) brown sugar
½ pint (250 ml) lukewarm milk
1 lb (450 g) **Allinson** 100% Wholewheat Flour, plain
1 teaspoon (5 ml) sea salt
1½ teaspoons (7.5 ml) mixed spice
½ teaspoon (2.5 ml) cinnamon
2 oz (55 g) vegetable margarine
4 oz (125 g) currants
2 oz (55 g) mixed peel
1 egg, beaten
Glaze
1 large tablespoon (20 ml) sugar
1 large tablespoon (20 ml) water

Mix the yeast and the crushed vitamin C tablet with a little of the sugar and a little of the milk. If using dried yeast leave in a warm place for 10–15 minutes until frothy. Mix the flour, salt and spices in a large bowl, rub in the margarine and add the currants, peel and sugar. Mix well, and tip the beaten egg, yeast mixture and the rest of the milk into the centre. Mix to a soft dough and knead for about 10 minutes or until smooth. Divide the dough into 15 pieces, roll each into a round bun shape and place on a well-greased baking tray. Mark a cross on top either by cutting with a knife or brushing across with a paste of flour and water. Leave the baking tray in a warm place for about 20 minutes.

Meanwhile, heat the oven to 450°F, 230°C, Gas Mark 8. Dissolve the sugar in the water for the glaze and boil for 1 minute. Brush the buns with this just before baking. Bake for 15–20 minutes and repeat the glazing as soon as the buns are removed from the oven.
Makes 15 buns

Alpen®

Brownies

4 oz (100 g) plain chocolate
4 oz (100 g) butter
6 oz (150 g) caster sugar
2 eggs
4 oz (100 g) self-raising flour
2 oz (50 g) **Alpen**
2 oz (50 g) walnuts, chopped
little icing sugar to decorate

Melt the chocolate and butter in a saucepan over a low heat. Remove from the heat and beat in the sugar and eggs. Stir in the sieved flour, the Alpen and the chopped walnuts. Put the mixture into a greased 8 in (20 cm) square tin and bake at 350°F, 180°C, Gas Mark 4, for 30–35 minutes until the top has a dull crust. Cool in the tin then cut into 2 in (5 cm) squares and dust with icing sugar.   **Makes 16**

Appleford

Caribbean Ginger Cake

3 oz (75 g) butter
3 oz (75 g) **Appleford's** Muscovado Raw Sugar
3 tablespoons (45 ml) golden syrup
3 tablespoons (45 ml) **Appleford's** Crude Black Strap Molasses
approximately ¼ pint (150 ml) milk
8 oz (225 g) wholemeal flour, self-raising
1 teaspoon (5 ml) each of mixed spice, ground cinnamon and ground ginger
1 egg, beaten

Melt the butter, sugar, syrup, molasses and milk very slowly together in a saucepan. Sift the flour with the spices and place in a mixing bowl. Add the melted ingredients slowly to the flour and then stir in the egg. Mix well. Line a 1 lb (450 g) loaf tin or 7 in (18 cm)

diameter deep cake tin with greased greaseproof paper and pour in the mixture, which should be quite soft. Bake for 1½ hours in a fairly slow oven, 350°F, 180°C, Gas Mark 4, reducing the heat slightly for the last half hour. Keep in a tin for a day before cutting the cake.

Molasses Layer Cake

Bottom layer
4 oz (100 g) margarine
3 oz (75 g) **Appleford's** Muscovado Raw Brown Sugar
2 eggs
2 tablespoons (30 ml) **Appleford's** Crude Black Strap Molasses
4 oz (100 g) 100% wholemeal flour, self-raising

Top layer
2 oz (50 g) margarine
2 tablespoons (30 ml) **Appleford's** Crude Black Strap Molasses
2 oz (50 g) **Appleford's** Muscovado Raw Brown Sugar
2 oz (50 g) 100% wholemeal flour, self-raising
3 oz (75 g) walnut halves

Lightly grease a 7 × 11 in (18 × 28 cm) shallow swiss roll tin.

To make the bottom layer, beat the margarine and sugar together, then beat in the eggs and molasses and fold in the flour. Pour the mixture into the prepared tin.

To make the top layer, melt the margarine and molasses together in a saucepan, remove from the heat, add the sugar and the flour. Spread over the layer in the tin and decorate with walnut halves in even rows, 2 in (5 cm) apart, so that when the cake is cut into squares, there will be a walnut half on each piece. Bake for 40–45 minutes in a pre-heated oven at 350°F, 180°C, Gas Mark 4.

Rich Chocolate Sandwich Cake

4 oz (100 g) butter *or* margarine
4 oz (100 g) **Appleford's**

Muscovado Raw Brown Sugar
1 tablespoon (15 ml) **Appleford's** Crude Black Strap Molasses
2 eggs, beaten
4 oz (100 g) 81% self-raising flour
2 tablespoons (30 ml) cocoa powder
½ teaspoon (2.5 ml) vanilla essence

Icing
4 oz (100 g) icing sugar, sieved
1 rounded dessertspoon (15 ml) cocoa powder
2 oz (50 g) butter, softened
1 dessertspoon (10 ml) molasses
2–3 drops vanilla essence
a little grated chocolate to decorate

Grease two 7 in (18 cm) diameter shallow sandwich tins and line each with a circle of greased greaseproof paper.

Cream together the butter and sugar until light and fluffy and add the molasses. Gradually add the eggs, beating well after each addition. Fold in the flour, cocoa and vanilla essence. Divide the mixture between the tins, smooth the tops and bake in a pre-heated oven, 350°F, 180°C, Gas Mark 4, for 20–25 minutes, until the cakes have shrunk away from the sides of the tins and spring back when touched lightly in the centre with a fingertip. Turn on to a wire rack to cool.

To make the icing, beat all the ingredients together to make a fairly stiff, smooth consistency. Sandwich the cakes together with half the icing, spreading the remainder over the top. Sprinkle the top with the grated chocolate.

Fruit Cake (with variations)

Basic Recipe
8 oz (200 g) **Be-Ro** Self-raising Flour
pinch of salt
4 oz (100 g) margarine
4 oz (100 g) caster sugar
2 eggs
2 tablespoons (30 ml) milk
6 oz (150 g) mixed dried fruit

Mix the flour and salt and rub in the margarine. Stir in the sugar and fruit. Beat together the eggs and milk. Mix all together to a soft consistency. Place in a greased 6 in (15 cm) cake tin. Bake in a moderate oven at 350°F, 180°C, Gas Mark 4, for about 1¼ hours.

Variations
Omit the mixed dried fruit and substitute as follows:
Lemon and Sultana Cake—Add 6 oz (150 g) sultanas and the grated rind of 1 lemon.
Orange and Spice Cake—Add 1 teaspoon (5 ml) mixed spice and the coarsely grated rind of 1 orange.
Date Cake—Add 3 oz (75 g) chopped dates.
Chocolate Chip Cake—Add 3–4 oz (75–100 g) chocolate, finely chopped *or* chocolate chips.

Milk Chocolate Cake

7 oz (175 g) **Be-Ro** Self-raising Flour
8 oz (200 g) caster sugar
½ teaspoon (2.5 ml) salt
1 oz (25 g) cocoa
4 oz (100 g) margarine
2 eggs, beaten with 5 tablespoons (75 ml) evaporated milk
5 tablespoons (75 ml) water
few drops vanilla essence

Milk Chocolate Icing
2½ oz (60 g) margarine
4 tablespoons (60 ml) cocoa
8 oz (200 g) icing sugar, sieved

3 tablespoons (45 ml) hot milk
1 teaspoon (5 ml) vanilla essence

Sieve the flour, sugar, salt and cocoa and rub in the margarine. Stir in the eggs, essence and liquid and beat well. Grease and flour two 8 in (20 cm) tins (not loose-bottomed as the mixture would run out) and divide the mixture between them. Bake in a moderate oven at 350°F, 180°C, Gas Mark 4, for about 30–35 minutes.

When cold, cover the sandwich with Milk Chocolate Icing made by melting the margarine, blending in the cocoa, then stirring in the icing sugar, milk and essence. Beat until smooth and thick.

Quick and Easy Spice Cake

8 oz (200 g) **Be-Ro** Self-Raising Flour
1½ teaspoons (7.5 ml) mixed spice
3 oz (75 g) caster sugar
2 tablespoons (30 ml) marmalade
2 tablespoons (30 ml) golden syrup
3 tablespoons (45 ml) water
3 oz (75 g) margarine
3 oz (75 g) sultanas
1 egg

Mix the flour and spice. Gently heat the margarine, sugar, syrup, marmalade and water until the margarine has melted, add to the flour and mix well. Stir in the sultanas and beaten egg. Place in a greased 7–8 in (18–20 cm) cake tin and bake in a moderate oven at 350°F, 180°C, Gas Mark 4, for about 1¼ hours, until firm.

Cadbury's

Hideaway Cake

4 oz (125 g) butter
4 oz (125 g) caster *or* soft brown sugar
2 eggs

5 oz (125 g) plain flour, sieved with a pinch of salt
a good 2 oz (60 g) **Cadbury's** Drinking Chocolate
1 level teaspoon (5 ml) baking powder
2 oz (50 g) walnuts, chopped
1 dessertspoon (10 ml) coffee essence *or* 2 teaspoons (10 ml) instant coffee mixed with a little hot water
4 oz (100 g) **Cadbury's** Dairy Milk Chocolate
icing *or* caster sugar to decorate

Cream the butter and sugar together and beat in the eggs gradually. Sieve the dry ingredients together and fold in with the nuts and coffee, making a dropping consistency. Cut each square of chocolate into 4 and fold in evenly. Turn the mixture into a greased and base lined 7½ in (19 cm) sandwich tin at least 1¼ in (3.5 cm) deep, hollowing out the centre slightly. Bake in a pre-heated oven at 350°F, 180°C, Gas Mark 4, for 50 minutes. Turn out and cool. Dust with icing or caster sugar to serve.

Swiss Tarts

4 oz (100 g) softened butter
1 oz (25 g) icing sugar
4 oz (100 g) plain flour
2 tablespoons (40 ml) **Cadbury's** Drinking Chocolate
icing sugar and apricot jam to decorate

Cream the butter well. Beat in the sieved icing sugar then half the flour and the drinking chocolate. Beat really well before adding the remaining dry ingredients. Fill a piping bag with a star vegetable nozzle attached and pipe whirls of the mixture into paper cake cases. Bake in a moderately hot oven (380°F, 190°C, Gas Mark 5) for 30 minutes. Cool, then dust with icing sugar and spoon jam into the centre of each tart.

Place the paper cases in bun tins if available to ensure even shapes. The mixture will not pipe easily if it is too cold. **Makes 8 tarts**

Camp Fudge Shortcake

1 packet chocolate chip biscuits
4 oz (100 g) butter
2 oz (50 g) sugar
2 teaspoons (10 ml) golden
  syrup
2 teaspoons (10 ml) **Camp**
  Coffee and Chicory Essence
walnut halves

Line a round 7 in (18 cm) sandwich tin with greaseproof paper.
Crush the biscuits. Melt the butter
in a saucepan with the sugar and
syrup. Add the Camp Essence and
the biscuits and stir. Press into the
sandwich tin and decorate the top
with walnut halves, pressing them
into the mixture. Chill for 1 hour
before serving.   **Serves 6–8**

Camp Walnut Roll

3 large eggs
4 oz (100 g) caster sugar
3 oz (75 g) self-raising flour
1 tablespoon (15 ml) hot water
1 oz (25 g) butter, melted
Filling
2 oz (50 g) butter
6 oz (150 g) icing sugar
1 tablespoon (15 ml) **Camp**
  Coffee and Chicory Essence
1 tablespoon (15 ml) boiling
  water
4 oz (100 g) walnuts, chopped

Whisk the eggs with the sugar
until thick and creamy. Fold in the
flour and then the hot water and
melted butter. Line a shallow,
oblong tin with greased foil and
pour in the mixture. Bake in a hot
oven at 425°F, 220°C, Gas Mark 7,
for about 8 minutes. Meanwhile,
make the butter cream filling. Beat
the butter until soft and white, add
the icing sugar and Camp Essence
and beat well again. Stir in the
boiling water. Turn the sponge out
of the tin on to a fresh piece of
sugared foil and roll up, with the
sheet of foil inside. Leave for
2 minutes until fairly cool, then

unroll and leave until completely
cold. Spread with the butter
cream, sprinkle with the chopped
walnuts and roll up once again.

CHIVERS

Regency Chocolate Cake

4 oz (100 g) soft margarine
4 oz (100 g) caster sugar
1 oz (25 g) **Bournville** Cocoa
3 tablespoons (45 ml) **Chivers**
  Olde English Marmalade
2 eggs, separated
6 oz (150 g) self-raising flour,
  sieved
1 oz (25 g) ground almonds
4 oz (100 g) **Bournville**
  Chocolate
4 oz (100 g) butter
12 oz (300 g) icing sugar
2–3 tablespoons (30–45 ml)
  milk
crystallised orange slices to
  decorate

Cream the margarine and sugar
together until light. Dissolve the
cocoa in 4 tablespoons (60 ml) of
boiling water and beat into the
mixture with 2 tablespoons
(30 ml) of the marmalade. Add the
egg yolks, fold in the sieved flour
and ground almonds then the
stiffly beaten egg whites. Turn into
an 8 in (20 cm) round, deep cake
tin, greased and base lined, and
bake in an oven set at 325°F, 170°C,
Gas Mark 3, for 1–1¼ hours until
firm to the touch. Turn out and
cool.

Melt the chocolate and butter in
a basin over a pan of hot water,
beat in the icing sugar and enough
milk to make a soft consistency.
Leave to cool then beat again until
light and creamy. Split the cake in
half, spread one half with the rest
of the marmalade and a third of the
chocolate mixture and sandwich
the cakes together. Spread the
remaining mixture around the
sides and over the top of the cake.

Decorate with crystallised
orange slices.

American Cranberry Cake

6 oz (175 g) plain flour
1 level teaspoon (5 ml) baking
  powder
4 oz (100 g) butter
4 oz (100 g) caster sugar
2 eggs, lightly beaten
8 oz (225 g) **Elsenham**
  Cranberry with Burgundy
4 oz (100 g) walnuts, finely
  chopped
strained juice of 1 small orange

Sift the flour and baking powder
on to a plate and set aside. Cream
the butter and sugar until light and
fluffy, then beat in the eggs a little
at a time, beating thoroughly after
each addition. Add the Cranberry
with Burgundy and beat in, then
fold in the flour and nuts along
with the orange juice. Spoon the
mixture into a greased and lined
2 lb (900 g) loaf tin and slightly
hollow out the centre to give the
cooked cake an even top. Place in
the centre of a moderately hot
oven, 375°F, 190°C, Gas Mark 5,
for about 1 hour, or until golden
brown and springy to the touch.
Remove from the oven and allow to
cool a few minutes before turning
out on to a cooling tray.

Farmhouse Bran

Farmhouse Fruit and Almond Cake

4 oz (100 g) **Farmhouse Bran**,
  crushed
3 oz (75 g) caster sugar
4 oz (100 g) almonds, chopped
10 oz (250 g) mixed dried fruit
12 fl oz (350 ml) milk
4 oz (100 g) self-raising flour
halved almonds to decorate
  (optional)

Put the Farmhouse Bran, sugar,
nuts and dried fruit into a basin

and mix together. Stir in the milk and leave to stand for 30 minutes. Sieve in the flour, mixing well, and pour the mixture into a deep, well-greased 6 in (15 cm) cake tin or 2 lb (900 g) loaf tin. Decorate with halved almonds if desired. Bake at 350°F, 180°C, Gas Mark 4 for approximately 1 hour. Turn out and cool.

Basic All-in-One Victoria Sandwich Cake

4 oz (125 g) **Flora** Margarine
4 oz (125 g) caster sugar
2 eggs (size 2 *or* 3)
4 oz (125 g) self-raising flour
   sieved with 1 teaspoon (5 ml)
   baking powder

Filling
2 tablespoons (30 ml) jam
caster *or* icing sugar to dredge

Place all the cake ingredients in a mixing bowl and beat with a wooden spoon until well mixed (2–3 minutes, or 1–2 minutes if using an electric mixer). Divide the mixture between two oiled and bottom-lined 6 in (15 cm) sand-wich tins. Bake on the middle shelf of a pre-heated oven at 325°F, 160°C, Gas Mark 3 for 25–30 minutes. Turn out, remove the paper and cool on a wire tray. When cold, sandwich the cakes together with jam and dredge the top with caster or icing sugar.

GALE'S

Honeyed Greek Meringues

6 egg whites
12 oz (350 ml) caster sugar
Filling
½ pint (284 ml) double cream
2 tablespoons (30 ml) **Gale's** Clear Honey
4 oz (100 g) hazelnuts *or* almonds, chopped

2 teaspoons (10 ml) brandy *or* liqueur (optional)

Whisk the egg whites until very stiff, whisk in 1 teaspoon (5 ml) of sugar for each egg white, then fold in the rest of the sugar. Either pipe or drop teaspoons of the mixture on to a lightly oiled baking tray. Bake for about one hour at 275°F, 140°C, Gas Mark 1. Leave to cool on a wire tray.

Whip the cream until stiff and fold in the honey, nuts and brandy or liqueur if liked. Sandwich the meringues with the cream filling and arrange carefully on a cake tray or glass dish.
Makes 12 medium sized meringues

Spiced Honey Cake

2 oz (50 g) butter *or* margarine
5 oz (150 g) **Gale's** Clear Honey
5 oz (150 g) demerara sugar
10 oz (300 g) plain flour
pinch of salt
1 teaspoon (5 ml) bicarbonate
   of soda
1 teaspoon (5 ml) baking
   powder
1 teaspoon (5 ml) mixed spice
1 teaspoon (5 ml) ground
   cinnamon
1 teaspoon (5 ml) ground
   ginger
4 oz (100 g) mixed peel,
   chopped
1 egg
¼ pint (150 ml) milk
flaked almonds for decoration

Slice the butter into a pan and heat gently until melted. Draw the pan off the heat and stir in the honey and sugar. Allow to cool. Sift the flour, salt, bicarbonate of soda, baking powder, mixed spice, cinnamon and ginger into a bowl and add the peel. Beat the egg and milk together and mix thoroughly with the cooled honey mixture. Add to the flour and beat until smooth. Pour into a greased and base-lined 2 lb (900 g) loaf tin. Scatter the flaked almonds on the top. Bake at 325°F, 170°C, Gas Mark 3 for about 1¼ hours until firm to the touch.

Serve sliced and buttered with coffee or as spicy tea bread.

Chocolate Marmalade Cake

6 oz (175 g) butter
6 oz (175 g) caster sugar
3 large eggs, lightly beaten
6 oz (175 g) self-raising flour,
   sifted
2 tablespoons (30 ml) **Keiller**
   Dundee Orange Marmalade
1 oz (25 g) cocoa powder,
   blended with 1 tablespoon
   (15 ml) boiling water
Filling
2 tablespoons (30 ml) **Keiller**
   Dundee Orange Marmalade
Icing
6 oz (175 g) butter *or* margarine
12 oz (350 g) icing sugar
orange colouring and
   flavouring
2 oz (50 g) biscuits, finely
   crushed
orange and lemon slices for
   decoration

Grease a 7 in (18 cm) round cake tin and line the base with greaseproof paper. Cream the butter and sugar together until light and fluffy. Add the eggs, a little at a time, beating well after each addition. Gently fold in the flour with a metal spoon. Mix the marmalade and blended cocoa powder together and add to the creamed mixture. Pour into the prepared tin. Bake in the centre of the oven, pre-heated to 350°F, 180°C, Gas Mark 4, for 1 hour. Allow to cool on a wire rack then split through the middle and fill with the marmalade.

To make the icing, cream the butter until soft and gradually beat in the sieved icing sugar, adding a few drops of colouring and flavouring. Coat the sides of the cake with some of the icing and roll in the crushed biscuits to decorate. Spread the remaining icing on top of the cake and decorate as desired.

Kellogg's

Delicious Cinnamon Twists

1½ oz (40 g) caster sugar
3 tablespoons (45 ml) warm
   water (37°C, 100°F)
½ oz (15 g) dried yeast
3 oz (75 g) margarine
1 teaspoon (5 ml) salt
1 teaspoon (5 ml) vanilla
   essence
6 tablespoons (90 ml) milk
1 lb 1 oz (500 g) plain flour
3 eggs, lightly beaten
Coating
2 oz (50 g) **Kellogg's** Frosties,
   finely crushed
1½ oz (40 g) almonds,
   blanched and finely chopped
2 oz (50 g) caster sugar
1 teaspoon (5 ml) ground
   cinnamon
2 oz (50 g) butter *or* margarine,
   melted

Put 1 teaspoon (5 ml) of the sugar into a jug with the warm water and stir until the sugar has dissolved. Stir in the yeast and leave until frothy. Put the margarine, salt, vanilla essence and remaining sugar into a large mixing bowl. Heat the milk until almost boiling and pour into the bowl. Stir until the fat has melted. Leave until lukewarm then stir in the yeast mixture, add half the flour and beat until smooth. Gradually add the eggs, beating well after each addition. Add the remaining flour and mix well to form a soft but not sticky dough. Cover lightly and leave in a warm place until doubled in size, about 30 minutes.

   Meanwhile, prepare the coating. Mix together the Frosties, almonds, sugar and cinnamon in a shallow dish. When the dough has risen, turn out on to a lightly floured surface and knead gently. Divide into 16 pieces and, using the fingers, gently roll each to a stick 6 in (15 cm) long. Roll each stick in the melted butter then coat with the Frosties mixture, twisting

each stick slightly into an arc. Place on a baking tray and bake in a moderately hot oven (375°F, 190°C, Gas Mark 5) for about 15 minutes, or until lightly browned. Cool on a wire rack.   **Makes 16**

Fruit Cake with a Difference

1 lb (450 g) mincemeat
12 oz (350 g) mixed dried fruit
2 oz (50 g) mixed peel, chopped
4 oz (100 g) glacé cherries,
   halved
4 oz (100 g) shelled walnuts,
   chopped
8 oz (225 g) **Kellogg's** Corn
   Flakes, crushed
3 eggs, beaten
14 oz (396 g) can sweetened
   condensed milk
1 teaspoon (5 ml) ground
   mixed spice
1 teaspoon (5 ml) baking
   powder

Put all the ingredients into a large bowl and mix thoroughly. Pour the mixture into a greased and lined 8 in (20 cm) round cake tin, and smooth the top. Bake in a cool oven (300°F, 150°C, Gas Mark 2) for 1¾–2 hours, or until a skewer inserted into the centre of the cake comes out clean. Allow to cool for 10 minutes in the tin, then turn out and cool on a wire rack.

Christmas Wreath

8 oz (225 g) self-raising flour
1 teaspoon (5 ml) baking
   powder
3 oz (75 g) butter
2 oz (50 g) soft brown sugar
1 packet **Lyons** Polka Dots
2 oz (50 g) walnuts, chopped
3 tablespoons (45 ml) brandy
1 egg (size 3)
milk to mix and glaze
Glacé icing
6 oz (150 g) icing sugar, sieved

and mixed with 4 teaspoons
   (20 ml) cold water

Sieve the flour and baking powder into a mixing bowl and rub in the butter until the mixture resembles fine breadcrumbs. Stir in the sugar, Polka Dots (reserving a few for decoration) and walnuts. Add the brandy, lightly beaten egg and sufficient milk to form a soft dough. Turn out on to a lightly floured surface and shape the dough into a long roll, approximately 15 in (45 cm) long. Brush the ends of the dough with milk and pinch together to form a ring. Transfer to a lightly greased baking tray and brush with milk. Bake in the centre of a pre-heated oven at 400°F, 200°C, Gas Mark 6, for 25 minutes. Transfer to a wire cooling rack.

   Decorate the cooled Christmas Wreath with the glacé icing and reserved Polka Dots. Christmas Wreath is best eaten fresh but can be made in advance and frozen.

Spicy Lemon Doughnuts

8 oz (227 g) packet **Lyons**
   Doughnut Mix
¼ teaspoon nutmeg, grated
finely grated rind 1 lemon
juice of 1 lemon made up to
   3 fl oz (85 ml) with cold water
deep oil *or* fat for frying
thin lemon glacé icing to
   decorate

Mix together the Doughnut Mix, nutmeg and grated lemon rind. Add the liquid to the dry ingredients and mix with a fork until a dough is formed. Roll out on a lightly floured board to ¼ in (0.5 cm) thickness. Shape the doughnuts using two sizes of pastry cutter. Heat the oil or fat to 375°F, 190°C, or until a piece of dry bread browns in 40 seconds. Do not allow the fat to become smoking hot. Deep fry the doughnuts until golden brown and drain on kitchen paper. Coat the top of each doughnut with a little lemon glacé icing when cooled.

McMocha Brownies

5 oz (150 g) plain chocolate
2 oz (50 g) butter
3 eggs
4 oz (100 g) caster sugar
1 teaspoon (5 ml) vanilla
  essence
4 oz (100 g) self-raising flour
5 **McVitie's** Digestive Biscuits,
  crushed

Icing
1 tablespoon (15 ml) milk
½ oz (15 g) butter
1 teaspoon (5 ml) instant coffee
4 oz (100 g) icing sugar

Melt the chocolate and butter in a
bowl over a pan of hot water. Cool.
In a bowl beat the eggs and sugar
until light and fluffy and then add
the chocolate mixture and vanilla
essence and beat well. Stir in the
flour and biscuit crumbs until
evenly distributed. Turn the mixture into a greased tin, 6½ × 8½ in
(17 × 22 cm). Bake in the oven at
350°F, 180°C, Gas Mark 4, for about
35 minutes until cooked. Insert a
skewer into the middle of the cake;
if it comes out clean then the cake
is done.

In a small saucepan heat the
milk, butter and instant coffee
until the butter has melted.
Remove from the heat and stir in
the icing sugar, beat until smooth
and then spread over the cake.

When cold, cut into squares.
Best eaten on the day that they are
made.   **Makes 16 squares**

Mazola

Date and Walnut Loaf

8 oz (225 g) plain flour
1 level teaspoon (5 ml) baking
  powder
1 level teaspoon (5 ml)
  bicarbonate of soda
4 oz (100 g) soft brown sugar

6 oz (175 g) cooking dates,
  chopped
2 oz (50 g) walnuts, chopped
4 tablespoons (60 ml) **Mazola**
  Pure Corn Oil
1 egg
6 tablespoons (90 ml) milk

Lightly oil and base line a 1½ lb
(675 g) loaf tin. Sieve together the
flour, baking powder and bicarbonate of soda and stir in the
sugar, dates and walnuts. Mix
together the corn oil, egg and milk,
and add to the dry ingredients to
give a soft, dropping consistency.
Turn into the prepared tin and
bake at 350°F, 180°C, Gas Mark 4,
for 1–1¼ hours. Cool on a wire
rack.

The corn oil gives a moist result
and will help bread and cakes to
remain fresh for longer.

Dundee Cake

approx ¼ pint (100 ml) **Mazola**
  Pure Corn Oil
6 oz (175 g) caster *or* soft brown
  sugar
3 eggs
1 lb (450 g) mixed dried fruit
2 oz (50 g) almonds, chopped
2 oz (50 g) glacé cherries,
  chopped
2 oz (50 g) mixed peel, chopped
8 oz (225 g) plain flour
1½ level teaspoons (7.5 ml)
  baking powder
1–2 level teaspoons (5–10 ml)
  mixed spice
2–3 tablespoons (30–45 ml)
  milk
split almonds to decorate

Oil and line the base of an 8 in
(20 cm) round cake tin. Mix
together the corn oil, sugar and
eggs with a wooden spoon. Add
the dried fruit, chopped almonds,
cherries and peel and beat well.
Sieve together the flour, baking
powder and mixed spice and fold
into the mixture. Add sufficient
milk to give a soft, dropping
consistency. Place the mixture in
the cake tin and arrange the split
almonds on top. Bake at 325°F,
170°C, Gas Mark 3, for 2–2¼
hours. Cool slightly in the tin

before turning out and cooling on a
wire rack.

Gingerbread

approx ¼ pint (100 ml) **Mazola**
  Pure Corn Oil
6 oz (175 g) black treacle
2 oz (50 g) golden syrup
¼ pint (150 ml) milk
2 eggs, beaten
8 oz (225 g) plain flour
2 oz (50 g) caster sugar
1 level teaspoon (5 ml) mixed
  spice
1 level teaspoon (5 ml)
  bicarbonate of soda
2 level teaspoons (10 ml)
  ground ginger

Line a 7–8 in (18–20 cm) square
cake tin with oiled greaseproof
paper. Place the corn oil, treacle
and syrup in a saucepan and warm
gently, stirring occasionally.
Remove from the heat and add the
milk and beaten eggs. Sieve
together the flour, caster sugar,
mixed spice, bicarbonate of soda
and ground ginger. Add the treacle
mixture and beat well. Pour into
the prepared tin and bake at 325°F,
170°C, Gas Mark 3, for 1–1¼
hours.
Makes 15–20 squares

Rock Buns

8 oz (225 g) plain flour
3 level teaspoons (15 ml)
  baking powder
pinch salt
4 oz (100 g) caster sugar
1 level teaspoon (5 ml) mixed
  spice
4 oz (100 g) mixed dried fruit
⅛ pint (75 ml) **Mazola** Pure
  Corn Oil
1 egg
3 tablespoons (45 ml) milk

Sieve together the flour, baking
powder, salt, caster sugar and
mixed spice. Stir in the dried fruit.
Mix together the corn oil, egg and
milk and add to the dry ingredients to form a stiff consistency.
Drop in spoonfuls on an oiled
baking sheet. Bake at 425°F, 220°C,
Gas Mark 7, for 10–12 minutes.
Makes 12–14 buns

Nestlé

Caramel Shortcake

4 oz (100 g) margarine *or* butter
2 oz (50 g) caster sugar
6 oz (175 g) self-raising flour
Filling
4 oz (100 g) margarine *or* butter
4 oz (100 g) caster sugar
2 tablespoons (30 ml) golden syrup
1 small can **Nestlé's** Milk
Topping
6 oz (175 g) **Nestlé's** Plain Chocolate

Grease a 7 × 11 in (18 × 28 cm) swiss roll tin. Cream the margarine and sugar together until light and fluffy, sieve the flour and fold into the creamed mixture. Press the mixture evenly over the base of the prepared tin and bake in the centre of the oven, pre-heated to 350°F, 180°C, Gas Mark 4, for 15–20 minutes until golden brown.

To make the filling, place all the ingredients in a saucepan and boil gently for 5–10 minutes, stirring continuously. Spread over the cooked base and allow to cool. Place the chocolate on a plate over a pan of hot water and allow to melt over a low heat. When melted, quickly pour over the caramel and spread evenly. Mark into portions before the chocolate sets firm. **Makes about 32 pieces**

Chocolate Sponge Drops

2 eggs
3 oz (75 g) sugar
2½ oz (65 g) self-raising flour
caster sugar
Filling
2 oz (50 g) butter
1 oz (25 g) icing sugar
2 oz (50 g) **Ovaltine** Drinking Chocolate

Icing
2 oz (50 g) plain chocolate (optional)

Whisk the eggs and sugar until really thick. Sieve the flour and fold into the egg mixture. Either put about 24 teaspoons of the mixture on lightly greased paper on baking tins, or pipe with a plain ½ in (1 cm) nozzle and bag into small blobs. Dust with the caster sugar. Bake for approximately 8–10 minutes in a hot oven, (450°F, 230°C, Gas Mark 8). Remove the cakes from the paper and, when cold, sandwich together with the filling made by creaming the butter and sugar and adding the drinking chocolate.

To ice the cakes, melt the chocolate in a basin over hot water and coat each cake before the chocolate sets.   **Makes 24 cakes**

Ovaltine Fairy Cakes

4 oz (100 g) margarine
4 oz (100 g) sugar
5 oz (150 g) self-raising flour
1 oz (25 g) **Ovaltine**
2 eggs, beaten

Sieve the flour and Ovaltine together on a plate. Cream the margarine and sugar together until soft and light. Add the beaten eggs a spoonful at a time. Lightly fold in half the flour and Ovaltine mixture and add a little milk. Fold in the remaining flour and Ovaltine. Place a large teaspoonful of the mixture into separate greased patty tins or cake cases. Bake in the centre of a hot oven, 375°F, 190°C, Gas Mark 5, for about 20 minutes, until golden brown.

Ovaltine Tea Loaf

8 oz (225 g) self-raising flour
3 oz (75 g) sugar
4 oz (100 g) mixed fruit
2 tablespoons (45 ml) **Ovaltine**
1 cup half milk/half water mixture

Mix all the ingredients together well. Bake in a 2 lb (900 g) loaf tin for 1–1¼ hours at 350°F, 180°C, Gas Mark 4.   **Makes 1 loaf**

Sandwich Cake

3 oz (75 g) self-raising flour
1 oz (25 g) **Ovaltine**
2 eggs
4 oz (100 g) soft margarine
4 oz (100 g) caster sugar
1 teaspoon (5 ml) baking powder
1 tablespoon (15 ml) warm water
Filling
1 teaspoon (5 ml) cornflour
¼ pint (150 ml) milk
2 oz (50 g) soft margarine
2 oz (50 g) caster sugar
¼ teaspoon vanilla essence
caster sugar to decorate

Grease and flour two 7 in (18 cm) sandwich tins. Cream the margarine and sugar together until light and fluffy. Whisk the eggs and gradually beat into the creamed mixture, then lightly fold in the flour and warm water. Divide the mixture between the two tins and bake near the top of the oven at 375°F, 190°C, Gas Mark 5, for 25–30 minutes. Remove from the oven and cool the cakes on a wire rack.

Blend the cornflour with the milk and boil until thick. Leave until cold with a piece of wet greaseproof paper on top to prevent a skin forming. Meanwhile, cream the fat and sugar together until very soft and then gradually add the cold cornflour mixture and beat vigorously until thick. Add the vanilla essence and spread on one of the cakes. Sandwich the cakes together and dust the top with caster sugar.

RY·KING

Crunchy Meringues

2 egg whites
4 oz (100 g) caster sugar
good pinch cinnamon
2 oz (50 g) **Ry-King** Light,
crumbled

Whisk the egg whites stiffly until
they stand in peaks, gradually
whisk in the sugar and cinnamon
then fold in the crumbled Ry-King.
Place spoonfuls of the mixture on a
baking sheet lined with silicone
paper and place in the oven at
200°F, 100°C, Gas Mark ¼, to dry
out for 1½–2 hours.

No Bake Chocolate Cake

4 oz (100 g) margarine
3 oz (75 g) sugar
3 oz (75 g) chocolate
3 tablespoons (45 ml) honey
14 slices **Ry-King** Brown Rye,
well crumbled
2 oz (50 g) raisins *or* dates,
chopped
6 oz (150 g) chocolate (optional)

Melt together the margarine,
chocolate, sugar and honey, stir in
the Ry-King crumbs and dates.
Press the mixture into a 7 in (18 cm)
square tin and chill to set. If
desired, top with melted chocolate
and allow to set before serving.
Cut into squares to serve.

SCHWARTZ

Mandarin and Gingerbread Ring

6 oz (170 g) self-raising flour
2 teaspoons (10 ml) **Schwartz**
Ground Ginger
1 teaspoon (5 ml) **Schwartz**
Mixed Spice
2 oz (57 g) sultanas
3 oz (85 g) butter
4 oz (113 g) golden syrup
2 oz (57 g) caster sugar

1 tablespoon (15 ml) thin-cut
orange marmalade
6 tablespoons (90 ml) milk
1 egg (size 3), beaten
Topping
11 oz (312 g) tin mandarin
oranges
4 oz (113 g) icing sugar

Thoroughly grease and flour a 9 in
(23 cm) ring mould cake tin. Sieve
the flour, ginger and mixed spice
together into a mixing bowl. Stir in
the sultanas. Melt the butter,
syrup, sugar and marmalade in a
pan over a low heat. Make a well in
the centre of the dry ingredients
and mix in the melted mixture. Stir
in the milk and beaten eggs. Pour
the mixture into the prepared tin
and cook in a pre-heated oven at
325°F, 160°C, Gas Mark 3, for
45 minutes–1 hour until the cake
is well risen and firm to the touch.
Allow the cake to cool slightly in
the tin before easing the cake
edges away from the side of the tin
with a knife and turning out on to a
cooling rack. Leave until cold.

Drain the mandarin oranges and
reserve the juice. Arrange the
mandarin segments around the
top of the cake. Sift the icing sugar
into a bowl and mix with enough
mandarin juice to form a coating-
consistency icing, which when
poured over the oranges will coat
the top of the mandarins and run
down sides of the cake forming a
decorative effect. Allow the icing
to set before transferring to a
serving plate.

The decorated cake may be
stored in an airtight container for
up to 1 week or the undecorated
cake in a freezer for up to 4
months.

Schwartz Chocolate Log

3 eggs (size 3)
3 oz (85 g) light brown sugar
3 oz (85 g) plain flour
2 teaspoons (10 ml) **Schwartz**
Ground Cinnamon
1 tablespoon (15 ml) warm
water
Filling and icing
8 oz (227 g) butter
1 lb (454 g) icing sugar, sifted
2 tablespoons (30 ml) cocoa
powder
2 tablespoons (30 ml) milk
a little icing sugar for dusting

Grease and line a 7 × 11 in
(18 × 28 cm) swiss roll tin with
greaseproof paper. Whisk the eggs
and sugar together until light and
creamy and a spoonful of the
mixture, when lifted with the
whisk, leaves a trail. Sift the flour
and cinnamon together and gently
fold into the whisked mixture.
Carefully fold in the water and
pour the mixture into the prepared
tin. Cook for 15–20 minutes in the
oven, pre-heated to 375°F, 190°C,
Gas Mark 5, until well risen and
firm to the touch. While still hot,
turn the cake on to a sheet of
greaseproof paper. Place another
sheet of greaseproof paper over the
cake and roll the cake up tightly.
Leave the cake rolled in the paper
until completely cold.

Meanwhile, to make the filling,
cream the butter, sifted icing sugar
and cocoa powder together. Add
the milk and mix well. Carefully
unroll the cake and remove the
paper. Spread a thin covering of
the filling over the inside of the
cake and re-roll. Spread a very thin
layer of filling on to the cake sides
and pipe the remaining filling to
completely cover the cake to make
a 'log' effect, or simply spread all
the remaining filling over the cake
and fork over to form a pattern.
Dust with the icing sugar, decorate
as desired and carefully transfer to
a serving plate.

The cake, with filling and icing,
may be stored in an airtight container for up to 3 days or in a
freezer for up to 2 months. Alternatively the cake and filling can be
frozen separately.

Spicy Date and Almond Fruit Cake

8 oz (227 g) butter
6 oz (170 g) dark brown sugar
3 tablespoons (45 ml) black treacle
4 eggs (size 3), beaten
12 oz (340 g) self-raising flour
2 teaspoons (10 ml) **Schwartz** Ground Nutmeg
2 teaspoons (10 ml) **Schwartz** Ground Cinnamon
2 teaspoons (10 ml) **Schwartz** Ground Ginger
2 oz (57 g) blanched almonds, finely chopped
8 oz (227 g) pitted dates, roughly chopped
12 oz (340 g) sultanas
3 tablespoons (45 ml) dark rum

Grease and line an 8 in (20 cm) square cake tin with a double layer of greaseproof paper. Cream the butter and sugar together. Stir in the treacle. Beat in the eggs one at a time, adding a spoonful of the flour, sifted with the spices, with each one. Mix in the remaining flour mixture followed by the almonds, dates, sultanas and rum. Spoon the mixture into the cake tin. Hollow out the centre of the mixture slightly and cook in the oven pre-heated to 300°F, 150°C, Gas Mark 2, for approximately 2 hours or until the cake is risen and firm to the touch.

Decorate the cake in the conventional way using marzipan and royal icing, or serve dredged with caster sugar. The cake may be stored for up to 2 weeks in an airtight container or for up to 4 months in a freezer.

Peppermint Squares

6 oz (175 g) butter *or* hard margarine
6 oz (175 g) soft brown sugar
2 eggs
5 oz (150 g) self-raising flour
pinch of salt
1 oz (25 g) **Bournville** cocoa
3 tablespoons (45 ml) **Schweppes** Peppermint Cordial
4 oz (100 g) caster sugar
3 tablespoons (45 ml) water

Soften the butter, beat in the brown sugar and then the eggs. Sieve the flour with a pinch of salt and the cocoa and fold into the mixture. Place in a greased 9½ × 13½ in (24 × 34 cm) swiss roll tin and level the surface. Bake in a moderate oven at 350°F, 180°C, Gas Mark 4, for about 30–40 minutes. When cooked, the surface should be soft, but set. Mix the peppermint cordial and sugar with the water to a smooth paste. Remove the cake from the oven and immediately spread the peppermint paste over the top. When cold, cut into squares.
Makes about 24 squares

Honey and Cinnamon Doughnuts

12 oz (350 g) self-raising flour
¼ level teaspoon salt
½ level teaspoon (2.5 ml) baking powder
½ level teaspoon (2.5 ml) cinnamon
2 oz (50 g) caster sugar
1 tablespoon (15 ml) honey
4 tablespoons (60 ml) **Spry** Crisp 'n Dry
7 tablespoons (100 ml) milk
1 large egg, beaten
Spry Crisp 'n Dry for deep frying
caster sugar for dredging

Sieve the dry ingredients into a large bowl and add the sugar. Beat together the honey, Crisp 'n Dry, milk and egg and add to the dry ingredients to form a soft dough. Knead lightly on a floured surface and roll out to ½ in (1 cm) thickness. Cut into rounds with a 2½ in (7 cm) plain cutter and remove the centres with a 1 in (2.5 cm) cutter. Re-roll and cut out more rings. Heat the Crisp 'n Dry to 360°F (185°C). Fry the doughnuts, a few at a time, for 2–3 minutes. Drain well on kitchen paper and dredge with caster sugar.

Serve warm or cold.
Makes 14–16 doughnuts

Stork

Carrot Cake

3 eggs (size 2) separated
5 oz (150 g) soft brown sugar
8 oz (225 g) carrots, peeled and grated
2 oz (50 g) ground almonds (optional)
3 oz (75 g) flaked almonds
rind of 1 lemon
2 oz (50 g) wholewheat flour sieved with
½ teaspoon (2.5 ml) baking powder
1 oz (25 g) **Stork** Margarine
Praline
1 oz (25 g) caster sugar
1 oz (25 g) almonds
Icing
8 oz (225 g) icing sugar, sieved
3 oz (75 g) **Stork** Margarine
1–2 tablespoons (15–30 ml) milk

Whisk the egg yolks and sugar until thick and creamy. Stir in the carrots, almonds and lemon rind and fold in the flour. Whisk the egg whites until stiff and carefully fold into the mixture. Turn into a greased and bottom-lined 8 in (20 cm) cake tin and bake in a pre-heated oven at 350°F, 180°C, Gas Mark 4, for 40–45 minutes. Turn out on to a wire tray and cool. Split in half when cold. To make the praline, place the sugar and almonds in a heavy-based saucepan and heat gently, stirring occasionally, until the sugar has melted and caramelised. Coat the almonds and pour on to waxed paper. Leave until set and cool. Place in a polythene bag and crush with a rolling pin. To make the icing, beat together the icing sugar, margarine and milk until creamy and add the praline. Place one-third of the icing in a piping bag with a star nozzle. Use the remainder to sandwich the cake together. Pipe the icing around the edge of the cake and dredge with icing sugar. Cut into wedges to serve.

TREX

Parkin

8 oz (227 g) **Trex** Pure Vegetable Fat
6 oz (170 g) sugar
8 oz (227 g) golden syrup
3 eggs
1½ oz (40 g) plain flour
14 oz (400 g) fine oatmeal
1 teaspoon (5 ml) mixed spice
1 teaspoon (5 ml) ground ginger
1 teaspoon (5 ml) baking powder

Heat the Trex, sugar and syrup in a saucepan over a low heat until the fat has melted and the ingredients are blended well together. Remove from the heat and add the beaten eggs gradually then fold in all the other ingredients and mix well. Pour into a well-greased 10 in (25 cm) square cake tin and bake for 1¼ hours at 300°F, 150°C, Gas Mark 2.

whitworths

Date and Raisin Cake

6 oz (150 g) **Whitworths** Plain Flour
½ teaspoon (2.5 ml) baking powder
pinch of salt
4 oz (100 g) margarine
4 oz (100 g) **Whitworths** Caster Sugar
2 eggs
1 tablespoon (15 ml) milk
6 oz (150 g) **Whitworths** Seedless Raisins
4 oz (100 g) **Whitworths** Chopped Dates
3 oz (75 g) **Whitworths** Glacé Cherries, halved
2 oz (50 g) **Whitworths** Walnuts, chopped

Sift the flour, baking powder and salt into a bowl. Cream together the margarine and sugar until light and fluffy. Beat in the eggs. Stir in the milk, fruit and nuts and fold in the flour. Turn into a greased and lined 7 in (18 cm) round cake tin and bake for about 2 hours at 300°F, 150°C, Gas Mark 2.

Sultana Tea Loaf

12 oz (350 g) **Whitworths** Sultanas
4 oz (100 g) **Whitworths** Demerara Sugar
¼ pint (125 ml) strong tea
3 tablespoons (45 ml) sherry *or* brandy
8 oz (225 g) **Whitworths** Self-raising Flour
1 egg, beaten
2 oz (50 g) **Whitworths** Walnuts, chopped
grated rind of ½ lemon

Put the sultanas and sugar into a bowl. Pour over the cold tea and sherry or brandy and leave to stand overnight. Next day, add the remaining ingredients and beat well. Turn into a greased loaf tin 4 × 7 in (11 × 18 cm) and bake for about 1¼ hours at 350°F, 180°C, Gas Mark 4.

BISCUITS

Flakey Bars

4 oz (125 g) butter
4 oz (125 g) brown sugar
3 dessertspoons (30 ml) honey
4 oz (125 g) **Allinson** Bran
  Muesli
4 oz (125 g) peanuts
4 oz (125 g) desiccated *or* grated
  fresh coconut

Put the butter, sugar and honey
into a saucepan, bring to the boil
and simmer for 5 minutes. Remove
from the heat and add the muesli,
nuts and coconut, mixing well.
Press into a greased swiss roll tin
and mark into bars. Chill in the
refrigerator until set.
Makes 16 pieces

Garibaldi Biscuits

½ oz (15 g) butter *or* vegetable
  margarine
2 oz (50 g) **Allinson** 100%
  Wholewheat Flour, plain
1 tablespoon (15 ml) brown
  sugar
water to mix
1 oz (25 g) currants

Rub the fat into the flour, add the
sugar and enough water to make a
workable dough. Roll out thinly
into a rectangle. Trim the edges
and cut in half. Spread the currants
evenly over one half, place the
other half on top and lightly roll
out again. Cut into about 15 small
squares or rectangles and bake for
15 minutes in a pre-heated oven,
350°F, 180°C, Gas Mark 4.
  This is a plain dough biscuit—it
can be made richer by doubling
the quantity of fat used.
Makes about 15 biscuits

Chocolate Chip Cookies

3 oz (75 g) margarine
3 oz (75 g) brown sugar
1 egg
few drops vanilla essence
6 oz (150 g) **Be-Ro** Self-raising
  Flour
pinch of salt
4 oz (100 g) plain chocolate,
  chopped *or* 4 oz (100 g)
  chocolate chips

Cream the margarine and sugar,
beat in the egg and essence and stir
in the flour, salt and chocolate.
Place in small spoonfuls on
greased baking trays and bake in a
moderate oven at 350°F, 180°C, Gas
Mark 4, for about 10–15
minutes.

Nut Cookies

4 oz (100 g) butter *or* margarine
4 oz (100 g) demerara sugar
1 egg, beaten
6 oz (175 g) **Be-Ro** Self-raising
  Flour
3 oz (75 g) walnuts, chopped

Cream the butter with the sugar
and beat in the egg gradually. Stir
in the flour and chopped nuts,
shape into a long roll, wrap in
aluminium foil and put into a cool
place, ideally a refrigerator. Leave
for several hours. Grease two
baking trays, cut the roll into thin
slices and place the biscuits,
widely spaced, on the trays. Bake
for 10–12 minutes at 400°F, 200°C,
Gas Mark 6.

Oatmeal Biscuits

5 oz (125 g) **Be-Ro** Self-raising
  Flour
5 oz (125 g) oatmeal

pinch of salt
3 oz (75 g) sugar
3 oz (75 g) margarine
milk to mix

Mix the dry ingredients, rub in the
margarine and add sufficient milk
to make a stiff dough. Roll out
thinly and cut into rounds. Place
on greased baking trays and bake
in a moderate oven at 350°F, 180°C,
Gas Mark 4, for about 15 minutes.

Bran Biscuits

2 oz (50 g) margarine
4 oz (100 g) wholewheat flour,
  plain
1 egg, beaten
pinch salt
1 oz (25 g) sugar
2 oz (50 g) **Bran Fare**
1 heaped teaspoon (10 ml)
  baking powder

Cream the fat and sugar and add
the beaten egg. Mix in the sifted
flour, baking powder, salt and
Bran Fare. Knead into a dough.
Roll out to ¼ in (0.5 cm) thick and
cut into rounds or squares. Place
on a greased baking tray and bake
in the oven at 375°F, 190°C, Gas
Mark 5, for 20 minutes or until
crisp.   **Makes 24 biscuits**

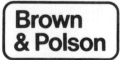

Chocolate Shortbread

4 oz (100 g) butter
2 oz (50 g) caster sugar
5 oz (150 g) plain flour
1 packet **Brown & Polson**
  Chocolate Blancmange
  Powder

whipped cream and fresh *or* canned fruit to decorate

Cream together the butter and sugar until light and creamy. Sift together the flour and blancmange powder and gradually work into the creamed mixture. Knead until smooth and shape into a round on a baking sheet. Prick with a fork and mark into wedges. Bake at 325°F, 170°C, Gas Mark 3, for 40 minutes. Cut into wedges and allow to cool. Top with whipped cream and fresh or canned fruit when cold.

Cadbury's

Chocolate Crisps

6 oz (150 g) butter *or* hard
  margarine
3 oz (75 g) caster sugar
2 tablespoons (40 ml)
  Cadbury's Drinking
  Chocolate
5 oz (125 g) plain flour
2 oz (50 g) cornflakes
few drops vanilla essence

Cream the fat and sugar until light in colour. Mix in the remaining ingredients, crushing the corn-flakes a little. Place teaspoons of the mixture on to greased baking trays, allowing room to spread. Bake at 350°F, 180°C, Gas Mark 4, for 20 minutes. Cool a little on the tray before lifting off. Store in an airtight container.
Makes about 24

Cottage Cookies

4 oz (100 g) margarine
4 oz (100 g) caster sugar
2 eggs
7 oz (175 g) self-raising flour,
  sieved
1 oz (25 g) **Cadbury's** Drinking
  Chocolate
2 tablespoons (30 ml) **Chivers**
  Olde English Marmalade
2 oz (50 g) porridge oats
marmalade peel to decorate

Cream the margarine and sugar

well and beat in the eggs. Fold in the sieved flour and drinking chocolate and add the marmalade. Roll teaspoons of the mixture in the oats and place on a greased baking tray. Bake at 400°F, 200°C, Gas Mark 6, for about 15 minutes. Decorate with pieces of marmalade peel when cold.
Makes about 30 cookies

Fork Biscuits

6 oz (150 g) butter
1 oz (25 g) icing sugar
4 oz (100 g) plain flour
2 oz (50 g) cornflour
1 oz (25 g) **Cadbury's** Drinking
  Chocolate
½ teaspoon (2.5 ml) vanilla
  essence
sugar to decorate

Cream the butter and sugar until light in colour. Beat in the sieved dry ingredients and vanilla essence. Divide into 20 pieces and roll each into a walnut-sized ball. Space apart on lightly greased baking trays then mark each one with a wet fork. Bake in a moderately hot oven (380°F, 190°C, Gas Mark 5) for about 12 minutes. Dust with sugar and cool.
Makes 20 biscuits

Farmhouse Bran

Farmhouse Bran Flapjacks

5 oz (125 g) butter
1 level tablespoon (15 ml)
  honey
2 oz (50 g) dark brown sugar
2 oz (50 g) **Farmhouse Bran**,
  crushed into fine, even
  crumbs
4 oz (100 g) **Alpen**
4 oz (100 g) porridge oats
2 oz (50 g) chopped nuts

Grease and line a tin 7 × 11 in (18 × 28 cm) or 8 in (20 cm) square. Melt the butter in a saucepan, add the honey and brown sugar and stir until melted.

Add the Farmhouse Bran, Alpen, porridge oats and nuts and stir until well incorporated. Spread evenly in the prepared tin and bake for approximately 30 minutes in the oven set at 300°F, 150°C, Gas Mark 2. Mark into fingers while still hot and leave in the tin until cold. When cold carefully remove the paper and serve.
Makes 8–10 flapjacks

Cherry and Walnut Cookies

4 oz (125 g) **Flora** Margarine
4 oz (125 g) caster sugar
5 oz (150 g) self-raising flour,
  sieved
pinch of salt
1 oz (25 g) walnuts, chopped
1 oz (25 g) glacé cherries,
  chopped
½ teaspoon (2.5 ml) vanilla
  essence

Place the margarine and sugar in a bowl and beat with a wooden spoon until light and creamy. Add the remaining ingredients and stir until thoroughly mixed. Place small spoonfuls of the mixture well apart on a baking sheet lightly greased with Flora oil and press each out into a flat round. Bake in a pre-heated oven at 375°F, 190°C, Gas Mark 5, for about 15 minutes until pale golden. Leave to cool on the baking sheet for a few minutes before removing to a wire rack.
Makes approximately 20 cookies

Kellogg's

Crunchy Florentines

2 oz (50 g) butter or margarine
1 tablespoon (15 ml) honey
2 oz (50 g) stoned dates,
   chopped
2 oz (50 g) seedless raisins
2 oz (50 g) glacé cherries,
   chopped
1 tablespoon (15 ml) blanched
   almonds, chopped
2 oz (50 g) **Kellogg's** Rice
   Krispies

Topping
6 oz (175 g) plain chocolate
2 tablespoons (30 ml) milk

Melt the butter with the honey.
Add the dates and cook for
1 minute, stirring all the time.
Remove from the heat and stir in
the raisins, cherries, almonds and
Rice Krispies. Turn into a shallow,
buttered, 7 in (18 cm) square tin
and press down firmly. Place the
chocolate and milk in a basin over
a pan of hot water and heat gently,
stirring frequently until the
chocolate has melted. Pour over
the florentines and spread evenly.
Leave until set. Cut into squares or
fingers.   **Makes about 12**

Dotty Cookies

9 oz (250 g) plain flour
½ teaspoon (2.5 ml)
   bicarbonate of soda
½ teaspoon (2.5 ml) salt
8 oz (225 g) butter _or_ margarine
8 oz (225 g) castor sugar
2 eggs
1 teaspoon (5 ml) vanilla
   essence
1½ oz (40 g) **Kellogg's** Frosties,
   crushed
6 oz (175 g) chocolate dots,
   melted

Stir together the flour, soda and
salt. In a large mixing bowl beat
the butter with the sugar until pale
and fluffy. Beat in the eggs and
vanilla essence. Add the flour then

stir in the Frosties. Drizzle melted
chocolate over the mixture and
swirl through gently with the
point of a knife. Drop tablespoonfuls on to greased baking
trays and bake in a moderate oven
(350°F, 180°C, Gas Mark 4) for
about 12 minutes, until lightly
browned. Cool on wire racks.
Makes about 60

Macaroons

2 egg whites
¼ teaspoon cream of tartar
½ teaspoon (2.5 ml) vanilla
   essence
5 oz (150 g) caster sugar
2 oz (50 g) shelled walnuts _or_
   pecan nuts, chopped
1½ oz (40 g) desiccated coconut
1 oz (25 g) **Kellogg's** Corn
   Flakes

Whisk the egg whites until stiff but
not dry. Stir in the cream of tartar
and vanilla. Gradually add the
sugar, whisking until stiff and
glossy. Fold in the nuts, coconut
and Corn Flakes. Drop rounded
measuring tablespoonfuls of the
mixture on to well greased baking
trays and bake in a moderate oven
(160°C, 325°F, Gas Mark 3) for 15–
20 minutes. Remove immediately
and cool on a wire rack.
Makes about 18

Choc 'n' Cherry Shortbread

4 oz (100 g) butter
2 oz (50 g) caster sugar
6 oz (150 g) plain flour
½ packet **Lyons** Polka Dots
1 oz (25 g) glacé cherries,
   quartered

Cream the butter and sugar until
light and fluffy. Gradually fold in
the flour, Polka Dots and quartered
cherries. Divide the mixture
between two 7 in (18 cm) lightly
greased sandwich tins, pressing
the mixture down firmly. Bake

near the top of the oven pre-heated
to 325°F, 160°C, Gas Mark 3, for 25
minutes. Cut each shortbread into
8 and leave to cool in the tins.
Makes 16 biscuits

Choc 'n' Mallow Shortbread

6 oz (150 g) plain flour
2 oz (50 g) caster sugar
4 oz (100 g) butter
4 oz (100 g) marshmallows
1 packet **Lyons** Melt in the Bag,
   milk chocolate flavour

Lightly grease a 7 in (18 cm) loose-
bottomed cake tin. Mix the flour
and sugar together and rub in the
butter until a soft dough is formed.
Press the shortbread evenly into
the cake tin. Bake in the centre of
an oven, pre-heated to 350°F,
180°C, Gas Mark 4, for 40 minutes.

   While the cake is in the oven, cut
the marshmallows into two around
the middles, using wetted
scissors. Immediately the shortbread is baked, arrange these, cut
side down, to cover the surface.
Prepare the Melt in the Bag and
drizzle over the marshmallows.
Allow to cool and the chocolate to
set before removing from the tin.

   Best eaten on day of baking and
not suitable for freezing.
Serves 6

Lazy Lemon Cookies

10 oz (283 g) packet **Lyons**
   Short Pastry Mix
4 oz (100 g) caster sugar
1 packet **Lyons** Polka Dots
finely grated rind and juice of
   2 lemons
1 large egg, beaten
caster sugar to decorate

Place the pastry mix, sugar, Polka
Dots and lemon rind in a mixing
bowl and gradually add the egg
and sufficient lemon juice to form a
soft dough. Roll out on a lightly
floured board to ¼ in (0.5 cm)
thickness. Cut into 2½ in (7 cm)
rounds and place on lightly
greased baking sheets. Chill for 10
minutes. Bake near the top of the
oven, pre-heated to 400°F, 200°C,

Gas Mark 6, for 15 minutes. Allow to cool for 1 minute before removing from the baking sheets. Sprinkle with a little caster sugar. **Makes 24 biscuits**

Mazola

Cheese Straws

6 oz (175 g) plain flour
¼ level teaspoon salt
3 oz (75 g) cheese, finely grated
⅛ pint (75 ml) **Mazola** Pure Corn Oil
2 tablespoons (30 ml) water

Sieve together the flour and salt and stir in the cheese. Mix together the corn oil and water, add to the dry ingredients and mix to form a stiff dough. Roll out on a lightly floured board to ¼ in (0.5 cm) thickness. Cut into straws approximately 3 × ½ in (8 × 1 cm) and place on lightly oiled baking sheets. Bake at 400°F, 200°C, Gas Mark 6, for 10–12 minutes.
Makes about 20 straws

Lemon Sugar Cookies

8 oz (225 g) plain flour
½ level teaspoon (2.5 ml) baking powder
pinch salt
pinch ground nutmeg
4 oz (100 g) caster sugar
approx ¼ pint (100 ml) **Mazola** Pure Corn Oil
1 egg
grated rind of 1 lemon
granulated sugar

Sieve together the flour, baking powder, salt, nutmeg and caster sugar. Mix together the corn oil, egg and lemon rind and add to the dry ingredients. Mix well and divide the mixture into balls approx ¾ in (2 cm) in diameter. Flatten each ball, dip the top in granulated sugar and place, sugar side up, on oiled baking sheets. Criss-cross the biscuits with the prongs of a fork and bake at 375°F, 190°C, Gas Mark 5, for 10–15

minutes until pale gold in colour. Cool on a wire rack.
Makes 25–30 cookies

Chocolate Macaroons

3 egg whites
3 oz (75 g) **Ovaltine** Drinking Chocolate
3 oz (75 g) ground almonds
2–3 oz (50–75 g) sugar (depending on sweetness desired)
1½ oz (40 g) fine semolina *or* ground rice
rice paper

Whisk egg whites lightly. Do not allow to become too stiff. Add the other ingredients to the egg whites. Roll into small balls and put on rice paper on baking trays, allowing room to spread. Bake for approximately 20 minutes in the centre of a moderate oven (375°F, 190°C, Gas Mark 4). When nearly cold, remove from the tin and tear or cut round rice paper.

SCHWARTZ

Christmas Macaroons

1 egg white (size 3)
2 oz (57 g) ground almonds
2 oz (57 g) caster sugar
½ teaspoon (2.5 ml) **Schwartz** Ground Cinnamon
a few almond flakes

Line 2 baking trays with rice paper. Whisk the egg white until stiff, and fold in the ground almonds, sugar and cinnamon. Place teaspoonfuls of the mixture on to the baking trays. Decorate each with a split almond and cook in a pre-heated oven for 15–20 minutes at 350°F, 180°C, Gas Mark 4, until firm to the touch and crisp. Remove from the trays when cold and trim away the rice paper from the macaroon edges before serving.
Makes about 12 macaroons

Stork

Derbyshire Flapjacks

8 oz (225 g) **Stork** Margarine
1 tablespoon (15 ml) golden syrup
10 oz (275 g) sugar
4 oz (100 g) rolled oats
4 oz (100 g) coconut
6 oz (175 g) plain flour
½ teaspoon (2.5 ml) bicarbonate of soda
1 teaspoon (5 ml) vanilla essence

Melt the margarine and syrup in a large pan. Add the rest of the ingredients and stir until well mixed. Divide the mixture into 2 lined and greased baking tins 7 × 10 in (18 × 25 cm). Bake in the centre of a pre-heated oven (375°F, 190°C, Gas Mark 5) for 25 minutes. This mixture rises and then falls in the middle. Allow to cool for 5–10 minutes before cutting into squares.

whitworths

Walnut Butter Cookies

6 oz (150 g) **Whitworths** Soft Brown (Light Golden) Sugar
4 oz (100 g) butter
1 egg
2 oz (50 g) **Whitworths** Walnuts, finely chopped
8 oz (225 g) **Whitworths** Self-raising Flour
pinch of salt
few drops of vanilla essence

Cream together sugar and butter. Beat in the egg and walnuts. Work in the flour, salt and vanilla essence and knead to a smooth dough. Roll pieces of dough into balls, place well apart on greased baking trays and flatten them with a fork. Bake for 15–20 minutes at 350°F, 180°C, Gas Mark 4.

Makes about 30

BREADS

Banana Bread

8 oz (225 g) **Allinson** 100%
　Wholewheat Flour, plain *or*
　81% Farmhouse Flour, plain
3 teaspoons (15 ml) baking
　powder
2 oz (50 g) margarine
1 egg, beaten
2 oz (50 g) brown sugar
grated rind of 1 lemon
3 medium bananas, mashed
a little milk to mix

Sieve the flour with the baking
powder, rub in the margarine and
add the beaten egg, sugar, lemon
rind and bananas. Mix thoroughly,
adding enough milk to give a soft
consistency. Pour into a greased
and floured 1 lb (450 g) loaf tin and
bake in the centre of the oven at
350°F, 180°C, Gas Mark 4, for 45
minutes.

Fruity Tea Bread

1 teaspoon (5 ml) brown sugar
¼ pint (150 ml) warm water
1½ teaspoons (7.5 ml) **Allinson**
　Dried Yeast
1 lb (450 g) **Allinson** 100%
　Wholewheat Flour, plain
2 teaspoons (10 ml) salt
1 oz (25 g) vegetable margarine
1 tablespoon (15 ml) honey,
　made up to ¼ pint (150 ml)
　with warm milk
4 oz (125 g) seedless raisins,
　washed and dried thoroughly
4 oz (125 g) currants, washed
　and dried thoroughly
4 oz (125 g) mixed peel
honey to glaze

Dissolve the sugar in ¼ pint
(150 ml) warm (104°F, 43.4°C)
water, sprinkle the yeast on top
and leave until frothy—about
10 minutes.

Mix the flour and salt, rub in the
margarine and blend in the liquid
all at once. Work to a dough by
squeezing with the fingers until it
leaves the bowl clean. Turn on to a
lightly floured board and knead
until the dough feels smooth and
elastic (about 5 minutes). Put the
dough in a lightly greased
polythene bag, loosely tied, or in a
saucepan with a lid and leave to
rise until the dough doubles its
size and springs back when lightly
pressed with a floured finger. Turn
the dough on to a board and work
in the fruit. Divide the dough in
two, flatten each piece and roll up
like a swiss roll to fit two greased
1 lb (450 g) loaf tins. Place the tins
in polythene bags and leave to rise
until the dough reaches the top of
the tins, or springs back when
lightly pressed. Bake on the
middle shelf of a pre-heated oven
(375°F, 190°C, Gas Mark 5) for
30–40 minutes. Brush the tops of
the hot loaves with a wet brush
dipped in honey to glaze. Cool on a
wire tray.　**Makes 2 loaves**

Potato Bread

1 lb (450 g) potatoes, peeled
　and chopped
1 oz (25 g) vegetable margarine
2 teaspoons (10 ml) salt
3–4 oz (75–100 g) **Allinson** 81%
　Farmhouse Flour, plain
2 teaspoons (10 ml) baking
　powder

Boil the potatoes, drain and mash
them with the margarine and salt.
Cool slightly and then work in the
flour, sieved with the baking
powder. Knead the dough lightly
on a floured board and divide the
mixture into four.

Roll each quarter into a round
(approximately 6 in (15 cm) across)
and divide each round into four
triangular shapes. Cook in a hot,
greased frying pan until brown on
both sides and serve hot.

Soda Bread

10 oz (275 g) **Allinson** 100%
　Wholewheat Flour, plain
1 teaspoon (5 ml) sea salt
½ teaspoon (2.5 ml)
　bicarbonate of soda
1 teaspoon (5 ml) baking
　powder
just under ½ pint (300 ml) sour
　milk to mix

Place all the ingredients in a bowl
and mix to a soft dough. Shape into
a large, round scone, place on a
baking sheet and divide into
sections by scoring deeply with a
knife. Bake for 20–30 minutes in a
pre-heated oven (425°F, 220°C,
Gas Mark 7).

Milk left at room temperature for
several days will go sour of its own
accord, or the process can be
accelerated by stirring in a teaspoonful of lemon juice.
Makes 1 loaf

Wholewheat Bran Bread

1 teaspoon (5 ml) clear honey
1 (25 mg) vitamin C tablet,
　crushed
½ oz (15 g) **Allinson** Dried
　Yeast
1¼ pints (700 ml) lukewarm
　water
2 lb (900 g) **Allinson** 100%
　Wholewheat Flour, plain
3 oz (75 g) **Allinson** Bran Plus
2 teaspoons (10 ml) sea salt
2 teaspoons (10 ml) vegetable
　oil

Dissolve the honey, vitamin C
tablet and yeast in half a cup of the
measured water. Leave the
mixture in a warm place for 10–15
minutes until frothy. Mix the flour,
bran and salt, add the yeast
mixture, oil and remaining
lukewarm water and mix well.
Knead on a floured board for about
10 minutes, until smooth. A little
extra flour may be needed.

Warm and grease three 1 lb

(450 g) loaf tins and divide the dough into 3 pieces. Knead each piece into a cylindrical shape and place in the tins. Cover with polythene and leave to rise in a warm place for about 40 minutes or until the dough has doubled in bulk. Bran bread may take longer and rise less than ordinary bread. Pre-heat the oven to 475°F, 240°C, Gas Mark 9 and bake the bread at this temperature for 10 minutes then lower the heat to 425°F, 220°C, Gas Mark 7 for a further 20–25 minutes. Turn out and cool on a wire tray. **Makes 3 loaves**

Wholewheat Bread

1 oz (25 g) **Allinson** Dried Yeast
 or 2 oz (50 g) fresh yeast
1 (50 mg) vitamin C tablet,
 crushed
1 tablespoon (15 ml) brown
 sugar
1 oz (25 g) vegetable margarine
3 lb (1.5 kg) **Allinson** 100%
 Wholewheat Flour, plain
1 tablespoon (15 ml) salt
1½ pints (900 ml) warm water,
 made by mixing 1 pint
 (600 ml) cold water with
 ½ pint (300 ml) boiling water

If using dried yeast, place it with the crushed vitamin C tablet and 1 teaspoon (5 ml) of the sugar in a small bowl. Add ½ pint (300 ml) of the warm water and whisk together with a fork. Leave in a warm place for 10–15 minutes, until frothy. If using fresh yeast, mix with the water and sugar as above, crush in the Vitamin C tablet and go on to the next stage immediately.

Take a cupful of flour out of the bag and tip the rest of the flour,

sugar, salt, margarine and water into a large bowl. Add the yeast mixture and stir well together. Sprinkle some flour from the cup on to a clean work top and rub the hands with the flour. Turn the bread dough on to the work top and knead for 10 minutes. Use the rest of the flour from the cup to stop the dough sticking. The dough will become smooth and elastic. Divide into 4 to shape into loaves.

To make four 1 lb (450 g) tin loaves, flatten each piece of dough into a rectangle as wide as the tin, fold into three and place in the greased tins with the fold at the bottom. This helps to give the loaf a good shape. Cover the tin loosely with greased polythene and leave in a warm (not hot) place to rise. Allow to prove for 45–60 minutes. Turn the oven to 450°F, 230°C, Gas Mark 8, after 30 minutes, as the loaves must go into a thoroughly heated oven. After proving, remove the covering from the loaves. The dough should have risen to about ½ in (1 cm) above the sides of the tins. Do not be tempted to let it rise more, or it may collapse in the oven. If it hasn't risen enough, leave for a further 10 minutes. Bake the loaves in the hot oven for 15 minutes, then for 20 minutes more at 400°F, 200°C, Gas Mark 6. The loaves should sound hollow when the bases are tapped with the knuckles. Turn out of the tins to cool on a wire rack.
Makes four 1 lb (450 g) loaves

Banana Tea Bread

8 oz (200 g) **Be-Ro** Self-raising
 Flour
¼ teaspoon bicarbonate of
 soda
½ teaspoon (2.5 ml) salt
3 oz (75 g) butter
6 oz (175 g) caster sugar
2 eggs, beaten
1 lb (450 g) bananas, mashed
4 oz (100 g) walnuts, chopped

Mix together the flour, bicarbonate of soda and salt. Cream the butter and sugar until pale and fluffy and add the eggs a little at a time, alternately with the flour. Stir in the remaining flour, bananas and walnuts. Place in a greased and lined loaf tin 5 × 8 in (13 × 20 cm). Bake for 1¼ hours at 350°F, 180°C, Gas Mark 4. Cool on a wire rack and keep for 24 hours before serving.

Emergency Bread

1 lb (400 g) **Be-Ro** Self-raising
 Flour
1 teaspoon (5 ml) salt
2 oz (50 g) lard (optional)
½ pint (250 ml) milk

Mix the flour and salt and rub in the lard, if used. Add the milk and mix to a dough. Shape lightly and place in a greased 7 in (18 cm) cake tin. Bake in a moderate oven at 350°F, 180°C, Gas Mark 4, for about 1 hour.

Sultana Malt Loaf

12 oz (330 g) **Be-Ro** Self-raising
 Flour
pinch salt
2 oz (50 g) caster sugar
4 oz (100 g) sultanas
4 tablespoons (60 ml) malt
 extract
2 oz (50 g) margarine
2 eggs
scant ¼ pint (125 ml) milk

Grease a 2 lb (900 g) loaf tin and line the base with greaseproof paper. Mix the flour, salt, sugar and sultanas. Warm the malt and margarine gently and when the margarine has melted, add to the dry ingredients, gradually mixing in the egg and milk to make a soft dough. Spread evenly into the tin and bake for approximately 1 hour 10 minutes at 325°F, 160°C, Gas Mark 3.

Bran Muffins

4 oz (125 g) wholemeal flour
2 teaspoons (10 ml) baking
   powder
½ teaspoon (2.5 ml) salt
3 oz (75 g) bran
1 tablespoon (15 ml)
   wheatgerm
1½ oz (40 g) soft brown sugar
1 egg (size 4)
½ pint (275 ml) skimmed milk
4 tablespoons (60 ml) **Flora** Oil

Brush 12 deep bun tins with Flora
oil. Place the dry ingredients in a
bowl. Beat the egg in a basin with
the milk and oil. Add to the dry
ingredients and mix together. Fill
each bun tin with the mixture and
bake in a hot oven at 400°F, 200°C,
Gas Mark 6, for 25–30 minutes.
Serve warm, spread with Flora
margarine and with honey or
marmalade if desired.
Makes 12

Homepride

Harvest Gold Bread

Basic Dough
1½ lb (750 g) **Homepride
   Harvest Gold** White Strong
   Plain Flour
½ oz (15 g) salt
½ oz (15 g) lard
1 sachet **Homepride Harvest
   Gold** Yeast
¾ pint (400 ml) warm water

In a large bowl, combine the flour
and salt and, using the fingertips,
rub in the fat. Empty the contents
of the yeast sachet into the flour
mixture, stirring thoroughly. (NB
Unlike fresh or other dried yeast,
this yeast must NOT be reconstituted before use). Add the liquid
to the flour and beat together to
form a firm dough. Turn the dough
on to a lightly floured surface and
knead by folding the dough

towards you, then pushing it away
with the palm of the hand, until
firm and elastic—about 10
minutes. Shape into a ball and
place in a large bowl covered with
lightly oiled polythene. Leave to
rise until double in size and
springy to the touch—1 hour in a
warm place or 1½–2 hours at
average room temperature.
Uncover, knock back and knead.
Shape as desired.

Cover with lightly oiled polythene and leave to rise again until
double in size. Glaze (see below) if
desired and bake at 450°F, 230°C,
Gas Mark 8 for 30–40 minutes.
When the bread is cooked it should
sound hollow when tapped on the
base. Cool on a wire tray.
Glazes and Toppings
For a softer top, sprinkle the risen
loaf with flour before baking. Milk
can be used to glaze but beaten egg
mixed with a little water will give
a shiny crust. Use a glaze when
sprinkling with poppy seeds,
sesame seeds, chopped nuts,
cracked wheat, oatmeal or caraway
seeds.
*To Make Harvest Gold Brown
Wheatmeal and Wholewheat Bread*
Follow the basic recipe using
Brown Wheatmeal or Wholewheat
flour. In the case of wholewheat,
increase the liquid to 500 ml when
making up the metric recipe.

Wheatmeal, Honey and Nut Cottage Loaf

half quantity basic dough using
   Homepride Harvest Gold
   Brown Wheatmeal Flour (see
   above)
2 tablespoons (30 ml) clear
   honey
4 tablespoons (60 ml) chopped
   mixed nuts

Use half quantity of dough. Use
two-thirds of the dough to make a
large round and place on a lightly
greased baking sheet. Similarly
shape the remaining dough and
place on top of the larger round.
Using the floured handle of a
wooden spoon, pierce through the
centre of the two rounds, joining
them together. Cover the loaf with
oiled polythene and leave to

double in size in a warm place.
Uncover the dough, dribble the
honey evenly all over and sprinkle
with the nuts. Bake at 450°F, 230°C,
Gas Mark 8, for 30–35 minutes.
Cool on a wire tray.

Serve sliced with butter or cream
cheese and preserves.

Kellogg's

Bran Fruit Loaf

4 oz (100 g) **Kellogg's** All-Bran
   or Bran Buds
5 oz (150 g) caster sugar
10 oz (275 g) mixed dried fruit
½ pint (300 ml) milk
4 oz (100 g) self-raising flour

Put the All-Bran, sugar and dried
fruit into a bowl and mix well
together. Stir in the milk and leave
to stand for 30 minutes. Sift in the
flour, mixing well, and pour the
mixture into a well-greased 2 lb
(900 g) loaf tin. Bake in a moderate
oven (350°F, 180°C, Gas Mark 4,)
for about 1 hour. Turn out of tin
and allow to cool.

To serve, cut into slices and, if
liked, spread with butter.
Makes 1 loaf

Golden Brunch Bread

2 oz (50 g) **Kellogg's** All-Bran *or*
   Bran Buds
¼ pint (150 ml) milk
4 oz (100 g) butter, softened
4 oz (100 g) soft brown sugar
2 eggs, lightly beaten
4 oz (100 g) self-raising flour
4 oz (100 g) dried apricots,
   soaked overnight and
   chopped
2 oz (50 g) shelled walnuts,
   chopped

Put the All-Bran into a bowl with
the milk and leave until the milk is
absorbed. Cream the butter and
sugar together. Gradually beat in
the eggs. Fold in the flour and stir
in the apricots and walnuts with
the All-Bran mixture. Pour into a
greased and base-lined 1 lb (450 g)
loaf tin and bake in a moderate

oven (350°F, 180°C, Gas Mark 4) for 1–1¼ hours.

Serve warm or cold, sliced, with butter. The bread keeps moist for up to 10 days if wrapped in foil. **Makes 1 loaf**

Treacle Bread

5 oz (150 g) self-raising flour
1 teaspoon (5 ml) baking powder
½ teaspoon (2.5 ml) salt
½ teaspoon (2.5 ml) ground cinnamon
1 egg
3 oz (75 g) **Kellogg's** All-Bran *or* Bran Buds
3 oz (75 g) seedless raisins
1 oz (25 g) lard
4 tablespoons (60 ml) treacle
8 fl oz (225 ml) very hot water

Sift together the dry ingredients. In a large bowl beat the egg. Mix in the All-Bran, raisins, lard and treacle. Add the water, stirring to melt the fat. Fold in the flour mixture and pour into a greased 2 lb (900 g) loaf tin. Bake in a moderate oven (350°F, 180°C, Gas Mark 4) for 45 minutes. Remove from the tin and cool slightly.

Serve warm, or cool completely, wrap in foil and serve the following day.   **Makes 1 loaf**

Vegetable Bran Bread

1 oz (25 g) butter *or* margarine
4 oz (100 g) onions, peeled and finely chopped
4 oz (100 g) carrots, peeled and grated
4 oz (100 g) **Kellogg's** All-Bran *or* Bran Buds
¼ pint (150 ml) milk
1 teaspoon (5 ml) sugar
¼ pint (150 ml) warm water (37°C, 100°F)
½ oz (15 g) dried yeast
12 oz (350 g) plain flour
2 teaspoons (10 ml) salt

Melt the butter in a small saucepan. Add the onion and carrot and cook gently, covered, until tender but not brown. Allow to cool. Put the All-Bran and milk into a mixing bowl and leave until softened. Dissolve the sugar in the water, stir in the yeast and allow to stand until the yeast is frothy. Stir in the All-Bran mixture. Sift the flour and salt together and add to the All-Bran mixture with the cooled carrot and onion. Mix to a firm dough then knead for about 5 minutes, until the dough is elastic. Place in a greased 2 lb (900 g) loaf tin and cover with greased polythene. Leave in a warm place until the dough has risen to the top of the tin, about 40 minutes.

Bake the loaf in a hot oven (425°F, 220°C, Gas Mark 7) for 10 minutes, then reduce to moderately hot (400°F, 200°C, Gas Mark 6) for a further 30–40 minutes. Cover lightly with foil during the last 10 minutes cooking if the loaf is browning to much on top. Turn out and cool on a wire rack.

Use to make open sandwiches. **Makes 1 loaf**

Mazola

Mazola Bread

½ pint (300 ml) lukewarm water
1 level teaspoon (5 ml) sugar
½ oz (15 g) dried yeast (if using fresh yeast, use double the quantity)
2 tablespoons (30 ml) **Mazola** Pure Corn Oil
1 lb (450 g) strong plain flour
2 level teaspoons (10 ml) salt

Mix together the water, sugar and yeast and leave in a warm place until frothy. Stir the corn oil into the yeast mixture. Sieve together the flour and salt, add the liquid ingredients and mix to form a dough. Turn on to a lightly floured board and knead until smooth. Place the dough back in the bowl, cover and leave in a warm place until doubled in size (approximately 1–1½ hours). Turn out and knead again until smooth. Shape into a loaf or rolls and place in an oiled tin or on oiled baking sheets.

Cover and leave in a warm place until doubled in size. Bake at 425°F, 220°C, Gas Mark 7, for 20–25 minutes for rolls and 30–40 minutes for a loaf
Makes 1 loaf or 8–10 rolls

Nestlé

Pineapple Nut Bread

½ oz (15 g) cooking fat
6 oz (175 g) caster sugar
1 egg
10 oz (283 g) can crushed pineapple
1 small can **Nestlé's** Ideal Milk
1 tablespoon (15 ml) lemon juice
1 oz (50 g) walnuts, chopped
12 oz (350 g) plain flour
4 level teaspoons (20 ml) baking powder
½ level teaspoon (2.5 ml) bicarbonate of soda
1 level teaspoon (5 ml) salt
½ level teaspoon (2.5 ml) ground cinnamon

Beat the fat and sugar together until creamy then add the egg and beat well. Stir in the pineapple, milk, lemon juice and nuts. Sift the dry ingredients together and fold in lightly. Turn into a greased 2 lb (900 g) loaf tin and bake at 375°F, 190°C, Gas Mark 5, for 1 hour. Cool for 5 minutes in the tin before turning out on to a cooling tray.

This bread is better kept and cut on the second day. Serve cut into thick slices spread with butter.

Cheese Loaf

8 oz (225 g) self-raising flour
½ level teaspoon (2.5 ml)
    mustard powder
salt and pepper
3 oz (75 g) margarine
1 Red **Oxo** Cube, crumbled
4 oz (100 g) Cheddar cheese,
    grated
4 rashers bacon, with rinds
    removed, chopped
1 egg, beaten
8 tablespoons (120 ml) milk
butter to serve

Sieve the flour, mustard powder
and seasoning into a basin and rub
in the margarine. Add the Oxo
cubes, cheese and bacon and mix
well. Add the egg and milk and
mix to a soft dough. Place the
dough in a greased 1 lb (450 g) loaf
tin and bake in the oven at 375°F,
190°C, Gas Mark 5, for about
50 minutes. Leave in the tin until
quite cold.

Serve sliced, with butter.

Herby Bread

8 oz (225 g) each of brown and
    white plain flours
1 teaspoon (5 ml) salt
1 teaspoon (5 ml) sugar
1 teaspoon (5 ml) mixed herbs
½ oz (15 g) **Stork** Margarine
½ oz (15 g) fresh yeast
½ pint (275 ml) water, heated
    to blood heat

Topping
½ oz (15 g) **Stork** Margarine,
    melted
¼ teaspoon mixed herbs

Mix the flours, salt, sugar and
herbs together in a bowl, and rub
in the margarine. Blend the yeast
in the water and add all at once.
Beat well to form a soft, scone-like
dough that leaves the bowl clean.
Knead thoroughly on a lightly-
floured surface. Take out 4 (3 oz,
75 g) pieces and roll each piece into
a ball. Place the rolls in a row in a
greased 1 lb (450 g) loaf tin. Brush
the top of the loaf with the melted
margarine and sprinkle with the
mixed herbs. Place in a lightly-
oiled polythene bag and allow to
rise until the dough reaches just
above the top of the tin. Use the
remaining dough to make 6 individual rolls and prove until
doubled in size. Bake on the
middle shelf of a pre-heated oven
at 450°F, 230°C, Gas Mark 8, for
about 30 minutes until the
underneath sounds hollow when
tapped with the knuckles.
Makes 1 loaf and 6 rolls

Poppy Seed Rolls

1 oz (25 g) fresh yeast
15 fl oz (425 ml) warm water
1 (25 mg) tablet ascorbic acid
1½ lb (675 g) strong plain flour
½ oz (15 g) salt
1 teaspoon (5 ml) sugar
½ oz (15 g) **Stork** Margarine
beaten egg, to glaze
poppy seeds to decorate

Blend the yeast with the water and
crush the ascorbic acid tablet in the
yeast liquid. Sieve together the
flour, salt and sugar and rub in the
margarine. Mix in the liquid and
beat until the dough leaves the
sides of the bowl clean. Turn out

on to a floured surface and knead
until smooth and elastic. Shape
into rolls, 2 oz (50 g) in weight.
Place on a greased baking sheet
and cover with lightly oiled
polythene. Leave to rise until
double in size (approximately
25–30 minutes). Brush with the
beaten egg and sprinkle with the
poppy seeds. Bake in a pre-heated
oven at 450°F, 230°C, Gas Mark 8,
for 15–20 minutes.

whitworths

Wholemeal Fig Loaf

4 oz (125 g) plain flour
4 oz (125 g) wholemeal flour
1 dessertspoon (10 ml) baking
    powder
2 oz (50 g) margarine
8 oz (225 g) **Whitworth** Figs,
    with stalks removed,
    chopped
1 egg
2 tablespoons (30 ml) golden
    syrup
4 fl oz (100 ml) milk

Grease and line a 2 lb (900 g) loaf
tin. Pre-heat oven to 375°F, 190°C,
Gas Mark 5. Place the flours and
baking powder in a mixing bowl.
Add the margarine and rub in until
the mixture resembles fine breadcrumbs. Stir in the figs. Lightly
beat the egg and combine with the
syrup and milk. Pour over the dry
mixture and mix thoroughly. Turn
into the prepared tin and bake in
the centre of the pre-heated oven
for 1 hour. Allow to cool in the tin.

Serve sliced and buttered.

CALORIE COUNTED RECIPES

Cheese and Parsnip Roast

2 lb (900 g) parsnips, peeled and sliced
pinch sea salt *or* celery salt
1½ oz (40 g) vegetable margarine
2 oz (50 g) breadcrumbs made from **Allinson** Wholewheat Bread
8 oz (225 g) Cheshire cheese, grated

Cook the parsnips in a little water with a pinch of sea salt or celery salt until tender. Mash with the margarine and add the breadcrumbs and cheese. Put in a greased, ovenproof dish and bake for about 20 minutes at 350°F, 180°C, Gas Mark 4, until brown.
Serves 4 (approx. 400 Calories per portion)

Corned Beef, Beetroot and Orange Salad

2 medium oranges
8 oz (225 g) cooked beetroot, coarsely grated
2 tablespoons (30 ml) salad oil
1 tablespoon (15 ml) vinegar
1 teaspoon (5 ml) sugar *or* artificial sweetener
6 oz (175 g) bean sprouts, washed and drained
salt and pepper
12 oz (340 g) can **Armour** Corned Beef
watercress to garnish

Peel the oranges, removing all pith and catching as much juice as possible in a bowl. Separate the orange segments and halve them. Mix the orange juice and segments with the beetroot, oil, vinegar, sugar, bean sprouts, salt and pepper to taste. Cut the corned beef into strips and mix lightly into the salad. Serve in a bowl, garnished with the watercress.
Serves 4–6 (approx. 230–350 Calories per portion)

Corned Beef Florence

15 oz (415 g) can spinach purée *or* 1 lb (500 g) frozen spinach, cooked and well drained
salt and pepper
good pinch grated nutmeg
12 oz (340 g) can **Armour** Corned Beef, thinly sliced
2 teaspoons (10 ml) French mustard
2 oz (50 g) Edam cheese, grated

Mix the spinach with the salt, pepper and nutmeg. Spread the corned beef slices with mustard. Fill a buttered, 2 pint (1.2 litre) ovenproof pie dish with layers of spinach, corned beef slices and cheese, finishing with corned beef and cheese. Bake towards the top of the oven pre-heated to 400°F, 200°C, Gas Mark 6, for 20–25 minutes.

Serve hot with grilled mushrooms or tomatoes.
Serves 4–6 (approx. 190–290 Calories per serving)

Potato Waffles for Slimmers

Grilled or baked, each **Birds Eye** Potato Waffle contains only 130 calories. Here are 2 slimming recipes using the waffles.

1. On a waffle place a grilled Birds Eye beefburger topped with 1 dessertspoon (10 ml) low calorie dressing or 1 tablespoon (15 ml) cottage cheese into which you could mix crushed garlic, onion, chopped tomato or cucumber.
Serves 1 (approx. 290 Calories per portion)
2. Make a hot, spicy vegetable topping by simmering sliced courgettes, chopped onion, green pepper, tomatoes and sweetcorn in a little water with garlic, chilli powder, salt and black pepper until the vegetables are tender and the liquid reduced. Spoon on to a grilled waffle. **Serves 1** (approx. 150 Calories per portion)

Chicken and Grape Salad

1 lb (450 g) cooked chicken
1 lettuce
¼ pint (150 ml) low-fat natural yoghurt
¼ pint (150 ml) stock made with ½ a Chicken Cube from **Bovril**
salt and pepper
pinch of curry powder
4 oz (100 g) white grapes
1 oz (25 g) flaked almonds

Cut the chicken into neat pieces and arrange on a bed of lettuce leaves. Mix the yoghurt and cold stock and season with salt, pepper and curry powder. Halve the grapes and remove the pips or leave whole if seedless, and stir into the yoghurt. Pour over the chicken and chill. Spread the almonds on a baking tray and grill until golden. Sprinkle on the salad just before serving. **Serves 4** (approx. 300 Calories per serving)

Energen

Chopped Liver

6 oz (150 g) chicken livers
1 medium onion, peeled and
 finely chopped
2 eggs, hard-boiled
1 oz (25 g) butter
pinch mixed spice
salt and pepper
8 **Energen** Crispbreads
chopped parsley to garnish

Fry the chicken livers and half the
onion in the butter until well
cooked and browned. Set aside to
cool. Finely chop or mince the
livers and eggs. Mix together with
the remaining onion. Season well
with mixed spice, salt and pepper.
Divide into 8 and serve on Energen
Crispbreads. Sprinkle with
parsley to garnish.   **Serves 8**
(approx. 236 Calories per portion)

Mulligatawny Soup

1 large onion, peeled and finely
 chopped
1 tablespoon (15 ml) oil
1 teaspoon (5 ml) curry powder
1 small green pepper, de-
 seeded and chopped
1 apple, peeled and grated
1 carrot, peeled and grated
2 sticks celery, chopped
14 oz (397 g) can tomatoes
1½ pints (750 ml) beef stock
1 tablespoon (15 ml) **Energen**
 Low-Calorie Orange
 Marmalade
salt and pepper

Fry the onion gently in the oil until
transparent. Add the curry powder
and cook for 1 minute. Add the
apple and remaining vegetables
and fry gently for 5 minutes, then
add the beef stock and marmalade.
Bring to the boil and simmer for
30 minutes. Blend in a liquidiser
until smooth and season with salt
and pepper.   **Serves 6**
(approx. 81 Calories per 5 fl oz
(175 ml) portion)

Oriental Fish

1 small onion, peeled and
 chopped
1 oz (25 g) root ginger, peeled
 and chopped
1 teaspoon (5 ml) oil
1 teaspoon (5 ml) curry powder
¼ pint (125 ml) water
1 teaspoon (5 ml) **Energen**
 Low-Calorie Lemon
 Marmalade
10 oz (250 g) cod fillet

Fry the onion and ginger gently in
the oil. Add the curry powder and
cook for 1 minute. Add the water
and marmalade and pour over the
fish. Bake for 20 minutes at 350°F,
180°C, Gas Mark 4.   **Serves 2**
(approx. 300 Calories per portion)

Pot Roasted Chicken

1 small onion, peeled and finely
 chopped
1 rasher streaky bacon, with
 rind removed, chopped
1 stick celery, finely chopped
2 oz (50 g) button mushrooms,
 washed and finely chopped
1 **Energen** Starch-Reduced Roll,
 finely crumbled
½ teaspoon (2.5 ml) thyme
½ teaspoon (2.5 ml) rosemary
salt and pepper
3 lb (1.4 kg) roasting chicken
½ pint (250 ml) chicken stock

Combine the onion, bacon, celery,
mushrooms, crumbs, herbs and
seasonings. Stuff the mixture into
the neck and cavity of the chicken.
Place the bird in a pot roasting tin,
pour the stock round it, cover and
bake at 325°F, 160°C, Gas Mark 3,
for 2 hours.   **Serves 6** (approx.
252 Calories per portion)

Apple and Blackcurrant Fluff

1 lb (400 g) cooking apples,
 peeled, cored and sliced
2 fl oz (50 ml) water
Energen Sweet'n Low
 Sweetener to taste
2 egg whites

2 tablespoons (30 ml) **Energen**
 Low-Calorie Blackcurrant
 Jam

Cook the apples in the water with
the sweetener until a thick pulp.
Leave aside to cool. Whisk the egg
whites until stiff and fold gently
into the apple purée. Heap into
4 individual sundae glasses or one
large bowl and swirl the blackcurrant jam on top.   **Serves 4**
(approx. 62 Calories per portion)

Pineapple Crush

14 oz (396 g) can crushed
 pineapple in low-calorie
 syrup
11½ fl oz (327 ml) **Energen**
 One-Cal Orangeade
2 egg whites

Combine the pineapple and One-
Cal and pour into a freezer tray.
Freeze until half frozen. Whisk the
egg whites until stiff. Turn the
half-frozen mixture into a bowl
and fold in the egg whites. Return
the mixture to the freezer, until
firm.   **Serves 6** (approx. 82
Calories per portion)

Iced Tea Cocktail

¼ pint (125 ml) cold tea
11½ fl oz (327 ml) can **Energen**
 One-Cal Lemonade
2 (11½ fl oz, 327 ml) cans
 Energen One-Cal Orangeade
slices of cucumber, apple,
 orange and sprigs of mint to
 decorate

Mix together the tea and One-Cal
in a tall jug. Pour into glasses, top
up with ice and decorate with the
cucumber, apple, orange and
mint.   **Serves 6** (approx. 4
Calories per portion)

St Clement's Fizz

7 fl oz (178 ml) can frozen
   orange juice (unsweetened)
11½ fl oz (327 ml) can **Energen**
   One-Cal Lemonade
slices of orange and lemon
ice to serve

Reconstitute the frozen orange
juice in a tall jug as directed on the
package. Add the One-Cal
Lemonade and orange and lemon
slices and pour into tall glasses
topped up with ice.   **Serves 6–8**
(approx. 10 Calories per portion)

Breakfast Sunshine

4 tablespoons (60 ml) rolled
   oats
1 banana, sliced
1 orange, segmented
2 oz (50 g) sultanas
1 oz (25 g) almonds, chopped
½ oz (10 g) sunflower seeds
   (optional)
1 tablespoon (15 ml) honey
1 teaspoon (5 ml) **Flora** Oil
skimmed milk

Mix all the dry ingredients
together with the honey and oil
and serve with the skimmed
milk.   **Serves 2** (approx. 350
Calories per serving)

Mackerel Pizza

1½ oz (40 g) **Flora** Margarine
2 oz (50 g) wholemeal flour
2 oz (50 g) plain flour, sieved
½ teaspoon (2.5 ml) baking
   powder
½ teaspoon (2.5 ml) salt
½ teaspoon (2.5 ml) mixed
   herbs
1 egg
1 tablespoon (15 ml) milk
1 onion, peeled and chopped
3 oz (75 g) mushrooms, washed
   and chopped
7½ oz (210 g) can tomatoes,
   drained

7½ oz (210 g) can mackerel,
   drained and flaked
pinch of oregano
3 oz (75 g) Edam cheese, grated
sliced green olives to garnish

Place 1 oz (25 g) of the margarine,
the flour, baking powder, salt,
mixed herbs, egg and milk in a
mixing bowl and thoroughly mix
together. Turn on to a floured
surface and knead lightly. Shape
into a flat round 8–9 in (20–22 cm)
in diameter and place on a baking
sheet. Melt the remaining margarine and sauté the onion and
mushrooms. Add the tomatoes,
mackerel and oregano and spread
the mixture over the scone base.
Sprinkle over the cheese and
garnish with the sliced olives.
Bake in the oven pre-heated to
400°F, 200°C, Gas Mark 6, for
20–25 minutes.

   Serve hot or cold, with a green
salad.   **Serves 4** (approx. 375
Calories per portion)

Plaice and Orange Bake

1 small orange, peeled
1 small green pepper, de-
   seeded and halved
4 oz (125 g) cottage cheese
black pepper
4 fillets of plaice, each approx
   3 oz (75 g) in weight, skinned
½ oz (15 g) **Flora** Margarine
rind and juice of 1 orange
parsley to garnish

Chop half the orange and half the
pepper and slice the remainder of
each for the garnish. Combine
together the chopped orange,
green pepper, cottage cheese and
black pepper, divide between the
plaice fillets and roll up. Place
together in a casserole and dot
with the margarine. Pour over the
orange juice and rind, cover and
cook in the centre of the oven, pre-
heated to 375°F, 190°C, Gas Mark 5,
for 40 minutes. Decorate with the
orange and pepper slices and the
parsley.

   Serve with green beans and new
potatoes.   **Serves 2** (approx. 295
Calories per serving)

Lamb Kebabs with Savoury Sauce

12 oz (350 g) leg lamb with
   surplus fat removed, cut into
   1½ in (4 cm) cubes
4 small tomatoes, halved
4 oz (125 g) button mushrooms,
   washed
1 green pepper, de-seeded and
   cut into 1 in (2.5 cm) squares
8 bay leaves (optional)
Flora Oil for brushing
Sauce
1 oz (25 g) **Flora** Margarine
1 onion, peeled and finely
   chopped
14 oz (376 g) can tomatoes,
   chopped
1 oz (25 g) flour blended with a
   little juice from tomatoes
¼ pint (150 ml) cider
½ pint (275 ml) water
1 beef stock cube
1 tablespoon (15 ml) sugar
2 tablespoons (30 ml) vinegar
1 teaspoon (5 ml)
   Worcestershire sauce

Arrange the lamb, tomatoes,
mushrooms, pepper and bay
leaves on 4 long or 8 short skewers.
Brush with oil and place under a
pre-heated grill for 10–12 minutes,
turning and brushing regularly.
Suggested accompaniments:
boiled rice and mixed salad.

   To make the sauce, melt the
margarine and sauté the onion for
10 minutes. Remove from the heat
and add the remaining ingredients. Bring to the boil and
simmer for 20 minutes. Serve with
the kebabs.

   The sauce is also suitable for
serving with other meat and
vegetable dishes.   **Serves 4**
(approx. 440 Calories per serving)

Tomato and Cucumber Flan

2 oz (50 g) wholewheat flour mixed with 2 oz (50 g) plain flour
2 oz (50 g) **Flora** Margarine
1 tablespoon (15 ml) water
Filling
1 oz (25 g) **Flora** Margarine
1 onion, peeled and sliced
1 oz (25 g) flour
7 fl oz (200 ml) skimmed milk
3 tomatoes, skinned and sliced
3 in (8 cm) length cucumber, peeled and sliced
½ teaspoon (2.5 ml) oregano
salt and black pepper
3 oz (75 g) Edam cheese, grated
sliced tomato and parsley sprigs to garnish

Rub the margarine into the mixed flours until the mixture resembles fine breadcrumbs. Add the water and mix to a firm dough. Roll out and use to line a 7 in (18 cm) flan ring. Bake blind in a hot oven at 400°F, 200°C, Gas Mark 6, for 15–20 minutes

To make the filling, melt the margarine and sauté the onion until soft. Add the flour and cook for 1 minute. Gradually add the skimmed milk, stirring continuously, and bring to the boil. Cook for 1–2 minutes. Add the tomatoes and cucumber and cook for a further 3–5 minutes. Add the herbs and seasoning and 2 oz (50 g) of the cheese. Pour into the baked flan case, sprinkle over the remaining cheese and return to the oven until the cheese has melted.

Garnish with the sliced tomato and parsley sprigs. Serve hot.
Serves 4 (approx. 335 Calories per serving)

Melon, Grape and Grapefruit Cocktail

1¼ lb (575 g) melon
4 oz (125 g) grapes
1 grapefruit
2 tablespoons (30 ml) fresh orange juice
2 tablespoons (30 ml) lemon juice
½ teaspoon (2.5 ml) **Hermesetas** Liquid Sweetener
4 sprigs mint (optional)

Cut the skin away from the melon and discard. Cut the flesh into ½ in (1 cm) pieces. Halve and de-seed the grapes. Cut the peel and pith off the grapefruit using a small serrated knife and then cut out the segments. Work on a plate to catch any juice that escapes and mix this with the orange juice, lemon juice and Hermesetas Liquid Sweetener. Place the grapefruit in the bottom of a basin and put the grapes and melon on top. Pour over the juices, cover with clear food wrap and chill for at least 1 hour.

Just before serving mix all the fruits together and divide between 4 sundae glasses. Pour over the juice and decorate with the mint sprigs. **Serves 4** (approx. 50 Calories per serving)

Mushroom Marinade

8 oz (225 g) button mushrooms
½ teaspoon (2.5 ml) **Hermesetas** Liquid Sweetener
3 fl oz (75 ml) white wine *or* cider vinegar
2 fl oz (50 ml) water
1 clove garlic, crushed
½ level teaspoon (2.5 ml) mustard powder
1 teaspoon (5 ml) Worcestershire sauce
1 level tablespoon (15 ml) tomato purée
¼ level teaspoon mixed dried herbs
salt and pepper
1 rounded tablespoon (30 ml) parsley, chopped

Slice the mushrooms and place in a bowl. Mix together the Hermesetas Liquid Sweetener, vinegar, water, crushed garlic, mustard powder, Worcestershire sauce, tomato purée and herbs.

Pour over the mushrooms and season with salt and pepper. Cover with clear food wrap and leave in the refrigerator or a cool place to marinade overnight. Turn the mushrooms over in the juices once or twice while marinading.

Drain off the excess liquid and discard. Empty the mushrooms into a serving dish and sprinkle with chopped parsley.

Can be served as a starter or as a salad to accompany meat or fish. **Serves 4** (approx. 10 Calories per portion)

Chilled Summer Soup

2 (5 oz, 142 g) cartons natural yoghurt
½ pint (275 ml) tomato juice
grated rind and juice of ½ lemon
1 teaspoon (5 ml) Worcestershire sauce
¼ teaspoon **Hermesetas** Liquid Sweetener
salt and pepper
¼ cucumber, peeled and diced
1 small onion, peeled and finely chopped
½ green pepper, de-seeded and diced

Whisk together the yoghurt, tomato juice, lemon rind and juice, Worcestershire sauce and Hermesetas Liquid Sweetener. Season to taste with salt and pepper. Add the cucumber, pepper and onion to the soup and chill well before serving. **Serves 4** (approx. 65 Calories per portion)

Courgette and Carrot Soup

8 oz (225 g) courgettes
8 oz (225 g) carrots, peeled and sliced
1 oz (25 g) onion, peeled and chopped
1 pint (575 ml) beef stock
1 bay leaf
1 level tablespoon (15 ml) tomato purée
salt and pepper

¼ teaspoon **Hermesetas** Liquid Sweetener

3 tablespoons (45 ml) natural yoghurt

Trim the ends off the courgettes and slice them. Place all the vegetables in a saucepan with the stock, bay leaf and tomato purée. Season with salt and pepper. Bring to the boil, cover the pan and simmer gently for 30 minutes. Remove the bay leaf. Purée in a liquidiser or rub through a sieve. Return to the pan and reheat. Stir in the Hermesetas Liquid Sweetener and yoghurt and serve.
Serves 4 (approx. 40 Calories per portion)

Sweet and Sour Cabbage

1 lb (450 g) green cabbage, shredded
1 small onion, peeled and chopped
2 oz (50 g) streaky bacon rashers, chopped
¼ oz (7 g) butter
1 eating apple, peeled, cored and diced
½ teaspoon (2.5 ml) caraway seeds
1 tablespoon (15 ml) wine vinegar
2 tablespoons (30 ml) water
salt and pepper
¼ teaspoon **Hermesetas** Liquid Sweetener

Cook the onion and bacon in the butter in a large saucepan until the onion is soft and the bacon fat is transparent. Add the cabbage and the apple, with the caraway seeds, vinegar, water and salt and pepper. Cover and cook over a moderate heat until the cabbage is soft and nearly all the moisture has evaporated. Stir in the Hermesetas Liquid Sweetener and serve.
Serves 4 (approx. 110 Calories per portion)

Barbecue Sauce

2 sticks celery, chopped
1 small onion, peeled and chopped
14 oz (397 g) can tomatoes
1 level teaspoon (5 ml) English mustard
1 teaspoon (5 ml) Worcestershire sauce
pinch mixed herbs
juice 1 lemon
2 fl oz (50 g) vinegar
salt and pepper
¼ teaspoon **Hermesetas** Liquid Sweetener

Place the celery and onion in a saucepan with all the ingredients, except the Hermesetas Liquid Sweetener. Cover the pan, bring to the boil and simmer gently for 10–15 minutes, or until the vegetables are tender. Purée in a liquidiser, or rub through a sieve. Sweeten with Hermesetas Liquid Sweetener and serve with grilled meat or fish.
Serves 4 (approx. 20 Calories per portion)

Tomato Sauce

1 medium onion, peeled and chopped
1 small red *or* green pepper, de-seeded and diced
1 lb 3 oz (539 g) can tomatoes
½ level teaspoon (2.5 ml) dried basil
1 bay leaf
1 tablespoon (15 ml) lemon juice
garlic salt
black pepper
¼ teaspoon **Hermesetas** Liquid Sweetener

Place the onion, pepper, tomatoes and their juice, basil, bay leaf and lemon juice in a saucepan, cover the pan and simmer for about 25 minutes. Remove and discard the bay leaf. Purée the sauce in a liquidiser or rub through a sieve. Return to the pan and reheat. Stir in the Hermesetas Liquid Sweetener and serve.

Serve with chicken, hamburgers, chops or pasta.
Serves 4 (approx. 25 Calories per portion)

Apple and Bran Crunch

1 medium eating apple
5 oz (142 g) carton natural yoghurt
1 level tablespoon (15 ml) bran breakfast cereal
¼ teaspoon **Hermesetas** Liquid Sweetener
1 level teaspoon (5 ml) chopped walnuts

Core and dice the apple but do not peel it. Mix with the yoghurt, bran cereal, Hermesetas Liquid and chopped walnuts. **Serves 1** (approx. 165 Calories per portion)

Blackberry Ice

1 lb 2 oz (500 g) blackberries
2 tablespoons (30 ml) water
4 tablespoons (60 ml) single cream
1 teaspoon (5 ml) **Hermesetas** Liquid Sweetener
2 egg whites

Place 1 lb (450 g) of the black-berries in a saucepan with the water. Cover and cook gently until soft. Rub through a sieve and discard the seeds. Leave to cool. Add the cream and Hermesetas Liquid Sweetener and pour into a shallow container. Cover with a piece of foil and freeze until mushy. Turn out into a basin and whisk. Whisk the egg whites until stiff and fold into the ice. Return to the freezer and freeze until firm.

Remove from the freezer and place in the refrigerator for 20 minutes before serving. Scoop or spoon into glasses and decorate with the extra blackberries.
Serves 4 (approx. 75 Calories per portion)

Hazel Nut Pavlova

3 large egg whites
1 level teaspoon (5 ml) cream of tartar
3 level tablespoons (45 ml) powdered skimmed milk
¾ teaspoon (3.75 ml) **Hermesetas** Liquid Sweetener
2 oz (50 g) ground hazel nuts

Topping
5 oz (142 g) carton natural yoghurt
8 oz (225 g) raspberries, fresh *or* frozen
¼ teaspoon **Hermesetas** Liquid Sweetener

Whisk the egg whites lightly. Add the cream of tartar and continue whisking until stiff and standing in peaks. Whisk in the powdered skimmed milk, a tablespoon at a time, and then whisk in ¾ teaspoon (3.75 ml) Hermesetas Liquid Sweetener. Fold in the ground hazel nuts using a metal spoon. Draw a 7 in (18 cm) circle on a piece of non-stick paper and place it on a baking tray. Spread the meringue in the circle and cook in the oven at 300°F, 150°C, Gas Mark 2, for about 30 minutes. Leave to cool. Carefully remove to a serving plate, using a fish slice.

Mix together the yoghurt, most of the raspberries and the Hermesetas Liquid. Pile the mixture on to the meringue base and decorate with the remaining raspberries. **Serves 6** (approx. 75 Calories per portion)

Souffle Omelette with Orange Filling

2 medium oranges
¼ teaspoon **Hermesetas** Liquid Sweetener
4 eggs (size 3)
2 tablespoons (30 ml) water
2–3 drops vanilla essence
¼ oz (7 g) butter

Grate the rind of half of 1 orange and set aside. Using a sharp knife cut away the peel and pith from the oranges and slice them. Separate the eggs and beat the yolks with water, vanilla essence and

Hermesetas Liquid until well blended. Whisk the whites until stiff and fold into the yolk mixture. Melt the butter in a large omelette pan and swirl around, until the surface of the pan is completely coated. Pour in the egg mixture and cook over a moderate heat, without stirring, until well risen and golden brown underneath. Place under a pre-heated grill to brown the top. Make a cut down the centre, through half the thickness of the omelette, to ease folding. Place the orange on one half. Fold over and slide on to a warm plate. Sprinkle the reserved grated rind on top. Cut into 4 and serve immediately. **Serves 4** (approx. 110 Calories per portion)

Fruit 'n' Spice Teabread

2 oz (50 g) butter *or* margarine
grated rind and juice of 1 lemon
1 egg (size 3)
4 oz (125 g) unsweetened stewed apple
3 teaspoons (15 ml) **Hermesetas** Liquid Sweetener
8 oz (225 g) self-raising flour
1 level teaspoon (5 ml) ground allspice
pinch salt
2 oz (50 g) sultanas
1 oz (25 g) walnuts, chopped

Grease and line a 1 lb (450 g) loaf tin. Cream the butter with the lemon rind until soft. Beat in the egg and then stir in the stewed apple and Hermesetas Liquid Sweetener. Sift together the flour, allspice and salt and stir into the mixture with the sultanas and walnuts. Put into the prepared tin and bake for 1 hour at 350°F, 180°C, Gas Mark 4. Cool on a wire rack. Serve sliced plain.
Makes 10 slices (approx. 160 Calories per portion)

Plain Buns

2 oz (50 g) butter *or* margarine
4 oz (125 g) self-raising flour
pinch salt
2 level tablespoons (30 ml) **Hermesetas** Sprinkle Sweet
1 egg (size 2), beaten
2 tablespoons (30 ml) skimmed milk

Rub the fat into the flour until it resembles fine breadcrumbs. Stir in the Sprinkle Sweet. Make a well in the centre, pour in the egg and milk and mix to form a stiff consistency. Divide between paper cake cases and bake at 375°F, 190°C, Gas Mark 5, for 15–20 minutes. **Makes 10** (approx. 90 Calories each)
Variations
Fruit Buns Add 1 oz (25 g) dried fruit with the Sprinkle Sweet (approx. 160 Calories each).
Coconut Buns Replace 1 oz (25 g) flour with 1 oz (25 g) desiccated coconut and add with the Sprinkle Sweet (approx. 170 Calories each).
Chocolate Buns Replace ½ oz (15 g) of the flour with ½ oz (15 g) cocoa and add ¼ teaspoon vanilla essence with the egg and milk (approx. 104 Calories each).
Orange Buns Add 1 level teaspoon (5 ml) grated orange rind and replace 1 tablespoon (15 ml) of the skimmed milk with orange juice (approx 90. Calories each).

Mint Julep

6 mint leaves
2 fl oz (50 ml) whisky
¼ teaspoon **Hermesetas** Liquid Sweetener
ice
1 slice lemon
2 sprigs mint to decorate

Shred the mint leaves and divide between two cocktail glasses. Add the whisky and Hermesetas Liquid Sweetener and leave to stand for 10 minutes. Add some ice to each glass and float half a lemon slice on top. Decorate with the sprigs of mint. **Serves 2** (approx. 50 Calories per portion)

Knorr

Beef and Herb Stew

1½ lb (600 g) chuck *or* shoulder steak
2 onions, peeled and thinly sliced

4 tomatoes, skinned and
  chopped
large pinch oregano
large pinch basil
large pinch thyme
salt and pepper
½ pint (250 ml) **Knorr** beef
  stock

Mix the spices and seasoning
together. Sprinkle all over the
meat. Put the meat into a saucepan
together with the onions, tomatoes
and stock. Cover tightly and
simmer for 1¼ hours. Remove the
lid and continue to simmer for a
further 15 minutes to reduce the
liquid.
  Serve with potatoes and fresh
vegetables. **Serves 4** (approx.
320 calories per portion)

Boiled Beef and Onions

1½ lb (675 g) salted silverside
  beef
1½ pints (900 ml) **Knorr** beef
  stock
3 onion, peeled and left whole
12 peppercorns
1 bay leaf

Soak the meat in cold water
overnight. Drain and put into a
large saucepan. Cover with the
stock and add the onions,
peppercorns and bay leaf. Cover
and simmer for about 2 hours or
until the meat is tender.
Serves 4 (approx. 310 Calories per
portion)

Slimmer's Beef Casserole

2 tablespoons (30 ml) oil
1 large onion, peeled and sliced
2 sticks celery, sliced
1 lb (400 g) topside, cut into
  1 in (2.5 cm) cubes
2 tablespoons (30 ml)
  Worcestershire sauce
½ pint (250 ml) **Knorr** beef
  stock
8 oz (200 g) carrots, peeled and
  quartered
4 oz (100 g) button mushrooms,
  washed
salt and pepper

Heat the oil in a large flameproof
dish and gently fry the onion and
celery until soft, about 5 minutes.
Add the beef and fry for a further
10 minutes, until brown all over.
Add the remaining ingredients,
except the mushrooms. Cover and
cook at 325°F, 170°C, Gas Mark 3,
for 1½ hours. Add the mushrooms
and cook for a further 30 minutes
at the same temperature. Check
the seasoning and serve.
Serves 4 (approx. 325 calories per
portion)

Clear Brown Soup

1½ pints (900 ml) water
4 teaspoons (20 ml) **Marmite**
2 bay leaves
½ teaspoon (2.5 ml) dried
  marjoram
pinch of dried thyme
1 medium carrot, peeled and
  thickly sliced
1 medium onion, peeled and
  thickly sliced
1 tablespoon (15 ml) dry sherry
2 teaspoons (10 ml) lemon juice
salt and pepper
lemon slices and chopped
  chives for garnish

Put the water, Marmite, herbs,
carrot and onion into a saucepan.
Bring slowly to the boil and then
lower the heat and cover. Simmer
gently for 1 hour. Strain and return
to the saucepan. Add the sherry
and lemon juice and season to taste
with salt and pepper. Reheat
without boiling. Serve garnished
with lemon slices and chopped
chives. **Serves 4** (approx. 14
calories per serving)

Cadbury's
Marvel

Summer Soup

1 large cucumber
1 onion, peeled and chopped
few sprigs of fresh mint *or*
  chopped chives

1 pint (550 ml) chicken stock
2 oz (50 g) **Marvel** made up to
  ½ pint (275 ml) with water
1 teaspoon (5 ml) lemon juice
green food colouring
¼ pint (150 ml) natural yoghurt
  (optional)

Cut off a few thin slices of cucumber for the garnish, and peel and
chop the remainder. Place the
cucumber and onion with most of
the mint, stock and seasoning in a
saucepan. Bring to the boil and
simmer with the lid on for about
15 minutes until tender. Blend
until smooth and then cool. Later,
stir in the dissolved Marvel and
lemon juice. Add a little colouring
and adjust seasoning. Serve
chilled, garnished with cucumber
slices and mint sprigs.
  For extra sharpness, add ¼ pint
(150 ml) natural yoghurt.
Serves 4 (approx. 69 Calories per
portion; 90 Calories with yoghurt)

Lamb Bake

just over 1 lb (500 g) root
  vegetables
8 oz (225 g) cooked lean lamb
1 onion
¼ pint (150 ml) beef stock
1 tablespoon (20 ml) tomato
  purée *or* ketchup
1 teaspoon (5 ml) any piquant
  sauce
1 teaspoon (5 ml) dried oregano
2 oz (50 g) dry **Marvel**
1 egg
3 oz (75 g) Edam cheese, grated
grated nutmeg (optional)

Prepare the vegetables, using only
a few potatoes, and par-boil.
Mince the lamb and onion. Add
the stock, sauces, oregano and
seasoning. Slice the vegetables
thinly then layer them in a 3 pint
(1.6 litre) ovenproof dish with the
meat mixture in between. Beat the
Marvel and egg with ½ pint
(275 ml) of the vegetable water.
Add the cheese and seasoning and
pour into the dish. Sprinkle with
grated nutmeg if available. Bake in
a moderate oven (350°F, 180°C, Gas
Mark 4) for about 45 minutes.
Serves 4–5 (approx. 225–282
Calories per portion)

Surprise Meat Slice

¾ lb (325 g) lean mince
2 oz (50 g) dry **Marvel**
small can tomatoes
1 oz (25 g) brown breadcrumbs
1 teaspoon (5 ml) dried mixed
    herbs
1 teaspoon (5 ml) prepared
    mustard
1 teaspoon (5 ml) salt
freshly ground pepper
2 hard-boiled eggs

Mix all the ingredients together in a bowl, except the eggs. Lightly grease a 1 lb (500 g) loaf tin (preferably non-stick) and press half the mixture into the tin, then lay the eggs along the centre. Press the remaining mixture on top. Cover the tin with a butter paper or foil, place in a roasting tin half filled with warm water and cook in a moderate oven, (350°F, 180°C, Gas Mark 4) for 2 hours. The meat should be thoroughly cooked. Leave overnight before slicing. Serve with a salad. **Serves 4–6** (approx. 192–287 Calories per portion)

Cauliflower Bake

1 lb (450 g) cauliflower
3 tomatoes, skinned and
    chopped
1 oz (25 g) dry **Marvel**
1 oz (25 g) low-fat spread
1 oz (25 g) flour
2 oz (50 g) Edam cheese, grated
2 eggs, separated

Break up the cauliflower and cook in boiling, salted water for up to 10 minutes so that it is still crisp. Drain, reserving the cooking liquid. Make up the Marvel to ½ pint (300 ml) with the cooking liquid and make a sauce with the low-fat spread, flour and Marvel. Add half the cheese and, when cooled a little, the egg yolks, then the whisked egg whites. Layer the vegetables and sauce in a 2½ pint (1.5 litre) ovenproof dish and sprinkle with the remaining cheese. Cook in a fairly hot oven (400°F, 200°C, Gas Mark 6) for 30–40 minutes until risen and golden brown. The top should be

set. Serve immediately.
Serves 4–6 (approx. 102–154 Calories per portion.)

Low Calorie Topping

2 oz (50 g) **Marvel**
ice cold water
2 teaspoons (10 ml) lemon juice
artificial sweetener
vanilla essence

Make up the Marvel to ¼ pint (150 ml) with the iced water then mix with lemon juice, sweetener and essence to taste. Whisk hard with a rotary or electric whisk until stiff. Serve with fresh fruit salad or use as required. The topping may be made up to 30 minutes before it is to be used.
Makes ¼ pint (approx. 200 Calories)

Marvel Low-fat Yoghurt

8 heaped tablespoons (320 ml)
    dry **Marvel**
1–2 tablespoons (15–30 ml)
    fresh commercial natural
    yoghurt
1 pint (600 ml) water

Sterilise all equipment to be used, before beginning. Boil the water and pour into a bowl. Cover and leave to cool for about two hours; the ideal temperature is 140°F, 40°C, if a thermometer is available. Whisk the Marvel and yoghurt into the water and when smooth, pour into a warm, wide-necked flask or a yogurt maker, previously sterilised. Seal or cover and leave undisturbed overnight. Keep some of the yoghurt to start the next batch. Revert to commercially produced yoghurt occasionally.

   Sweet and savoury flavourings can be added but try to make these low in calories. Some examples are finely grated orange rind, instant coffee, crisp lean bacon, chopped onion, tomato or cucumber.
Makes 1 pint (550 ml) (approx. 420 Calories)

Pink Crush

1½ pints (900 ml) liquid
    Marvel

4 oz (100 g) strawberry ice
    cream
4 oz (100 g) fresh *or* frozen
    strawberries
pink food colouring

Blend all the ingredients together, making a really frothy drink. Divide between 6 glasses and decorate with pieces of fresh or frozen strawberry.   **Serves 6** (approx. 82 Calories per portion)

Outline

Golden Vegetable Soup

4 oz (100 g) carrots, peeled and
    finely diced
4 oz (100 g) parsnips, peeled
    and finely diced
4 oz (100 g) swede, peeled and
    finely diced
8 oz (225 g) leeks, cleaned and
    sliced
2 sticks celery, chopped
1 oz (25 g) **Outline** Low Fat
    Spread
2 oz (50 g) red lentils
1 pint (575 ml) chicken stock
salt and pepper

Melt the Outline over a low heat and gently fry the vegetables for 5 minutes. Add the lentils, stock and seasoning. Bring to the boil and simmer for 35–40 minutes.
Serves 4 (approx. 121 Calories per portion)

Onion and Tomato Soup

1 oz (25 g) **Outline** Low Fat
    Spread
12 oz (350 g) onions, peeled
    and cut into rings
1½ pints (850 ml) beef stock
1 teaspoon (5 ml) Marmite
2 tablespoons (30 ml) tomato
    purée
salt and pepper

Gently melt the Outline and sauté the onions for 12–15 minutes until brown. Add the remaining ingredients and simmer for 25–30 minutes.   **Serves 4** (approx. 68 Calories per portion)

Spicy Crab Soup

2 oz (50 g) **Outline** Low Fat
  Spread
1 onion, peeled and chopped
1 stick celery, chopped
1 dessertspoon (10 ml) curry
  powder
½ teaspoon (2.5 ml) mustard
  powder
1 clove garlic, crushed
large pinch chervil
2 oz (50 g) flour
¾ pint (425 ml) skimmed milk
½ glass dry white wine
  (optional)
½ glass tarragon vinegar
½ pint (275 ml) fish *or* chicken
  stock
2 tablespoons (30 ml)
  Worcestershire sauce
8 oz (225 g) white crabmeat
2 bay leaves

Melt the Outline in a saucepan and
stir in the onion, celery, curry
powder, mustard, garlic and
chervil. Cook for 2 minutes and
then blend in the flour to form a
paste. Remove from the heat. Pour
in the milk, stirring continuously
until a smooth cream is formed.
Pour in the white wine if used, the
vinegar, stock and Worcestershire
sauce and stir in the crabmeat.
Add the bay leaves. Season lightly
and cook over a low heat for
15 minutes. Remove the bay
leaves, adjust the seasoning and
serve. **Serves 4** (approx. 215
Calories per portion)

Chicken Liver Paté

1 oz (25 g) **Outline** Low Fat
  Spread
½ small onion, peeled and
  finely chopped
8 oz (225 g) chicken livers
1 tablespoon (15 ml) red wine
½ oz (15 g) flour
4 oz (125 g) curd cheese
pinch ground bay leaf
salt and freshly ground black
  pepper

Melt the Outline in a pan and sauté
the onion until tender but not
brown. Add the chicken livers and
cook for about 5 minutes. Add the

flour and wine and cook for a further 2 minutes. Place this mixture
together with the curd cheese,
ground bay leaf, salt and pepper
into a liquidiser and blend until
smooth. Pour into a dish and chill
in the refrigerator. **Serves 4**
(approx. 160 Calories per portion)

Chicken and Cucumber with Rice

4 oz (125 g) rice
4 oz (125 g) mixed vegetables,
  cooked
½ red pepper, de-seeded and
  chopped
1 oz (25 g) **Outline** Low Fat
  Spread
1 oz (25 g) plain flour
¾ pint (425 ml) chicken stock
1 lb (450 g) cooked chicken,
  chopped
½ cucumber, diced
salt and freshly ground black
  pepper

Cook the rice in boiling, salted
water for 10–15 minutes. Drain.
Add the vegetables and red pepper
and reheat. Place the Outline, flour
and stock in a pan over moderate
heat and bring to the boil, stirring
continuously. Cook for 2–3
minutes until thickened and
smooth. Add the chicken, cucumber and seasoning to taste. Reheat.
  Serve the chicken and cucumber
on a bed of rice mixture.
Serves 4 (approx. 360 Calories per
portion)

Kidney and Rice

1 oz (25 g) **Outline** Low Fat
  Spread
1 onion, peeled and chopped
8 lambs' kidneys, skinned,
  cored, cut into 4 and tossed in
  1 oz (25 g) seasoned flour
1 clove garlic, crushed with a
  little salt
¼ pint (125 ml) chicken stock
6½ oz (190 g) can pimentos
½ teaspoon (2.5 ml) thyme
4 oz (100 g) mushrooms
8 oz (225 g) patna rice

Melt the Outline gently in a large
pan and fry the onion for 2–3

minutes. Add the kidney and garlic and fry until well sealed and
brown. Add the remaining ingredients and simmer for 15 minutes.
  Cook the rice in a saucepan of
boiling, salted water for 10–12
minutes. Drain the rice, pour hot
water through and place in a
border around a serving dish. Pour
the tomato and kidney sauce into
the centre of the dish. **Serves 4**
(approx. 377 calories per portion)

Cheesy Pizzas

Scone Base
1 oz (25 g) **Outline** Low Fat
  Spread
4 oz (100 g) self-raising flour
½ teaspoon (2.5 ml) baking
  powder
½ teaspoon (2.5 ml) salt
½ teaspoon (2.5 ml) mixed
  herbs
1 egg (size 5)
1 tablespoon (15 ml) skimmed
  milk

Topping
½ oz (15 g) **Outline** Low Fat
  Spread
1 small onion, peeled and
  chopped
4 oz (100 g) mushrooms, sliced
8 oz (225 g) can tomatoes
3 oz (75 g) Edam cheese, grated
salt and pepper
1 teaspoon (5 ml) oregano
4 anchovies, halved
1 oz (25 g) black olives, halved
  and stoned

Place all the ingredients for the
scone base in a mixing bowl and
mix with a wooden spoon to form a
soft dough. Knead lightly on a
floured surface, divide into four
and with floured fingers form each
into a 5 in (13 cm) round. Melt the
Outline and gently sauté the onion
for 5 minutes. Add the mushrooms
and cook for a further 3 minutes.
Stir in the tomatoes, cheese and
seasoning. Divide between the
scone bases and decorate with
anchovies and halved olives. Bake
on the second from the top shelf of
a pre-heated oven at 400°F, 200°C,
Gas Mark 6 for 20 minutes.
Makes 4 individual pizzas
(approx. 240 Calories per portion)

Lemon Delight Pudding

2 oz (50 g) **Outline** Low Fat
    Spread
2 oz (50 g) **Slimcea** sugar
2 eggs (size 2) separated
finely grated rind and juice of
    1 large lemon
1 oz (25 g) self-raising flour
¼ pint (150 ml) skimmed milk

Beat together the Outline and
Slimcea sugar. Add the egg yolks
and beat until smooth. Grate the
lemon rind into the flour. Add the
lemon juice to the Outline and egg
mixture, then stir in the flour and
gradually add the milk. Finally fold
in the stiffly beaten egg whites and
pour into a 1½ pint (900 ml) pie
dish. Place this dish in a deep
baking tin two-thirds full of water.
Bake in the oven on the middle
shelf at 350°F, 180°C, Gas Mark 4,
for 30–35 minutes until pale
golden in colour.

When cooked this pudding
separates out into a light spongy
top with a sauce underneath. Can
be eaten hot or cold.   **Serves 4**
(approx. 180 Calories per portion)

Fruity Crumble

1 orange, peeled and diced
1 banana, sliced
2 pears, cored and diced
4 tablespoons (60 ml) water
1 oz (25 g) caster sugar
2 oz (50 g) wholemeal flour
¼ teaspoon cinnamon
1 oz (25 g) **Outline** Low Fat
    Spread
1 tablespoon (15 ml) demerara
    sugar

Mix the fruit together with the
water and caster sugar and pour
into a shallow, ovenproof dish. Sift
the flour and cinnamon into a bowl
and rub in the Outline. Spoon over
the fruit mixture and sprinkle with
the demerara sugar. Bake for
20 minutes in an oven pre-heated
to 375°F, 190°C, Gas Mark 5, until
the topping is crisp.   **Serves 4**
(approx. 176 Calories per portion)

Orange Rice Pudding

2 oz (50 g) pudding rice
1 pint (575 ml) skimmed milk
rind of 1 orange
pinch of nutmeg
½ oz (15 g) **Outline** Low Fat
    Spread
2 egg whites
2 oz (50 g) caster sugar

Place all the ingredients, except the
egg whites and sugar, in a
saucepan and cook over a very low
heat for 1½–2 hours, stirring
occasionally. When the rice is
tender, place in a serving dish.
Whisk the egg whites to a soft
peak, fold in the sugar and spread
or pipe over the rice. Place under a
hot grill until lightly browned and
serve immediately.   **Serves 4**
(approx. 177 Calories per serving)

Slimmer's Orange Cheesecake

¾ oz (20 g) **Outline** Low Fat
    Spread
4 digestive biscuits, crushed
Filling
8 oz (225 g) curd cheese
finely grated rind of ½ orange
juice of 1 orange and
    3 tablespoons (45 ml) orange
    juice
1½ tablespoons (25 ml) water
¼ oz (6 g) gelatine
½ packet **Birds** Dream Topping
⅛ pint (75 ml) skimmed milk
1 egg white
1 small tin mandarin oranges,
    drained, to decorate

Melt the Outline and add the
crushed biscuits. Mix well then
press into a 7 in (18 cm) loose-
based flan tin and chill. Place the
curd cheese in a bowl together
with the orange rind and juice and
beat until smooth. Place the
gelatine and water in a small bowl
over a pan of hot water until the
gelatine has dissolved. When cool
add to the cheese mixture. Make
up the Dream Topping with the
skimmed milk as directed on the
packet, then fold into the cheese
mixture. Whisk the egg white until
stiff and fold into the mixture,
pour over the biscuit base and
leave to set in the refrigerator.
When set, remove from the tin and
decorate with the mandarin
oranges.   **Serves 8** (approx. 110
Calories per serving)

RYVITA

Baked Tomatoes

8 large tomatoes
1 **Ryvita**, crumbled
8 oz (225 g) cooked lean lamb *or*
    chicken, minced *or* finely
    chopped
4 oz (100 g) cottage cheese
2 tablespoons (30 ml) chives *or*
    spring onions, chopped
salt and pepper
garlic salt (optional)

Cut the tops off the tomatoes and
carefully scoop out the seeds. In a
bowl mix the Ryvita, lamb, cottage
cheese and chives, and season well
with salt, pepper and garlic salt.
Add sufficient tomato pulp to bind
the ingredients together. Spoon
the mixture into the tomato shells
and replace the lids. Place in an
ovenproof dish and cook at 375°F,
190°C, Gas Mark 5, for about
30 minutes. These tomatoes can be
served uncooked, if preferred.
Serves 4 (approx. 200 Calories per
portion)

Beans Provençal

1½ lb (675 g) French beans,
    fresh *or* frozen
½ oz (15 g) butter
½ lb (225 g) onions, peeled and
    chopped
1–2 cloves garlic, crushed
    (optional)
14 oz (396 g) can peeled
    tomatoes
salt and pepper
6 oz (175 g) Dutch cheese,
    grated
1 **Ryvita**, crumbled

Cook the beans in boiling, salted
water then drain. Place in a
shallow, ovenproof casserole. Melt
the butter in a pan and fry the

onions and garlic gently until they begin to brown. Stir in the tomatoes, salt and pepper and simmer for 10 minutes. Pour over the beans and cover with the grated cheese and crumbled Ryvita. Cook at 400°F, 200°C, Gas Mark 6, for 20–25 minutes, then brown under the grill before serving.
Serves 4 (approx. 215 Calories per portion)

Cauliflower and Mushroom Polonaise

1½ lb (675 g) cauliflower, cut into sprigs
8 oz (225 g) carrots, peeled and diced
4 oz (100 g) button mushrooms, washed and chopped
¾ oz (20 g) butter
1 tablespoon (15 ml) flour
¼ pint (150 ml) milk
2 (5 oz, 142 ml) cartons natural yoghurt
salt and pepper
4 oz (100 g) Cheddar cheese, finely grated
1 **Ryvita**, crumbled
paprika pepper

Cook the cauliflower and carrots until tender. Drain, place in a serving dish and keep warm. Fry the mushrooms in butter until soft, then stir in the flour. Add the milk, bring to the boil and cook for 1 minute. Stir in the yoghurt and reheat to just below boiling point. Season well. Stir in the cheese and pour over the cauliflower. Sprinkle with the Ryvita and paprika.
Serves 4 (approx. 300 Calories per portion)

Chicken Cruncher

6 oz (175 g) cooked chicken, diced
2 tablespoons (30 ml) tomato chutney
2 large spring onions, chopped or 2 tablespoons (30 ml) chives, chopped
4 oz (100 g) celery, chopped
2 oz (50 g) Cheddar cheese, grated
4 **Ryvita**, lightly buttered

Combine the chicken, chutney, onion, celery and cheese. Spoon carefully onto the Ryvita.
Serve with coleslaw.
Serves 4 (approx. 200 Calories per portion)

Prawn Toasties

4 oz (100 g) peeled prawns
12 oz (350 g) cottage cheese
2 spring onions, chopped
4 **Ryvita**, lightly buttered
a little made mustard
4 tomatoes, sliced
a few whole prawns and watercress sprigs to garnish

Combine the peeled prawns, cottage cheese and onions. Spread the Ryvita lightly with mustard then cover with the sliced tomatoes. Place the Ryvita on a grill rack and spoon the prawn mixture on top. Grill slowly for about 5 minutes until tinged brown. Garnish with whole prawns and watercress and serve with a salad of cucumber, tomatoes and watercress.   **Serves 4** (approx. 170 Calories per portion)

Cool Refresher

1 cucumber, peeled and cut into small dice
salt and black pepper
½ honeydew melon
6 firm tomatoes, skinned, de-seeded and roughly chopped
2 sticks celery, washed and chopped
8.5 fl oz (241 ml) bottle **Schweppes** Slimline Sparkling Orange
2 teaspoons (10 ml) salad oil
1 teaspoon (5 ml) mixed fresh herbs, chopped, to garnish

Sprinkle the cucumber with salt and black pepper and leave to stand for about 30 minutes. Remove the seeds from the melon and scoop out the flesh in small balls. Whisk the Slimline Orange

and the oil together and season well. Rinse the cucumber and drain, then toss in the dressing with the melon, tomato and celery. Chill for an hour. Divide between 6 individual dishes or put into a large serving dish and sprinkle with the chopped herbs.
Serves 6 (approx. 49 Calories per portion)

Speedy Pork

1 lb (450 g) lean pork, cut into thin strips
1 large onion, thinly sliced
2 tablespoons (30 ml) vegetable oil
8.5 fl oz (241 ml) bottle **Schweppes** Slimline Sparkling Orange
8.5 fl oz (241 ml) bottle **Schweppes** Slimline American Ginger Ale
1 oz (25 g) cornflour, mixed with a little water
salt and pepper
2 sticks celery, chopped
flaked almonds to garnish
cooked green beans or crisp cabbage to serve

Fry the pork with the onion in the oil for about 5 minutes. Stir in the Sparkling Orange and half the American Ginger Ale. Stir in the blended cornflour and bring to the boil, season to taste. Simmer for about 20 minutes until the meat is cooked. Add the chopped celery and cook briefly, so that it remains crisp.

Serve with the flaked almonds sprinkled over, in a ring of green beans or crisp cabbage.
Serves 4 (approx. 266 Calories per portion)

Apple Posset

1½ lb (750 g) cooking apples, peeled, cored and sliced
8.5 fl oz (241 ml) bottle **Schweppes** Slimline Lemonade
1 tablespoon (15 ml) caster sugar *or* artificial sweetener
1 teaspoon (5 ml) ground cinnamon
1 rounded tablespoon (30 ml) cornflour
green *or* red food colouring
4 tablespoons (80 ml) low fat natural yoghurt

Simmer the apples in a covered saucepan with the lemonade, sugar or artificial sweetener and cinnamon until soft. Sieve or liquidise to obtain a purée then return to the rinsed pan. Mix the cornflour with a little cold water, add to the purée and bring to the boil, stirring continuously. Add a little food colouring if liked. When cool, divide between individual dishes and swirl yoghurt into each. Chill well before serving. **Serves 4** (approx. 125 Calories per portion)

Fruit Jellies

¼ pint (150 ml) water
½ oz (15 g) gelatine
1 lemon
3 tablespoons (45 ml) caster sugar
2 (8.5 fl oz, 241 ml) bottles **Schweppes** Slimline American Ginger Ale
2 oranges
4 oz (100 g) grapes

Put the water into a small saucepan, sprinkle in the gelatine and add the thinly pared lemon rind. Heat slowly, stirring occasionally, until the gelatine has dissolved. Add the sugar and stir until this has dissolved. Leave to cool for 10 minutes then stir in the lemon juice and the ginger ale. Strain the liquid into a bowl and leave in a cool place until on the point of setting. Meanwhile, segment the oranges, cutting each in half, and remove the seeds from the grapes. Fold the fruit into the jelly and spoon into individual glasses. Leave to set completely before serving. **Serves 4** (approx. 98 Calories per portion)

Cider Bowl

2 (8.5 fl oz, 241 ml) bottles **Schweppes** Slimline Sparkling Orange
2 (8.5 fl oz, 241 ml) bottles **Schweppes** Slimline Bitter Lemon
½ pint (275 ml) dry cider
8.5 fl oz (241 ml) bottle **Schweppes** Slimline Tonic *or* Lemonade
tangerines *or* ½ oranges studded with cloves

Chill the orange and bitter lemon and pour into a large bowl. Add the cider and tonic or lemonade. Decorate with the tangerines or oranges. **Serves 4** (approx. 178 Calories in total)

Slim Fizz

Schweppes Slimline Sparkling Orange
Schweppes Slimline Bitter Lemon
1 teaspoon (5 ml) rum essence
ice cubes
lemon peel to decorate

Fill a glass ²/₃ full with the orange and top up with the bitter lemon. Add the rum essence and ice cubes and decorate the top of the glass with a strip of lemon peel. **Serves 1** (approx. 9 Calories per glass)

Slimmer's Party Punch

1 glass unsweetened grape *or* apple juice
2 glasses dry white wine
2 (8.5 fl oz, 241 ml) **Schweppes** Slimline Sparkling Orange
2 (8.5 fl oz, 241 ml) **Schweppes** Slimline Tonic Water
2 measures white rum
thin slices fruit and cucumber, ice cubes and sprigs of mint

Pour all the liquid ingredients into a large bowl and chill until required. To serve, garnish with the fruit, cucumber, ice cubes and mint sprigs. Do not use too much cucumber, as this has a very distinctive flavour. (approx. 178 Calories in total)

Spiced Shandy

crushed ice
2 tablespoons (30 ml) **Schweppes** Ginger Cordial
8.5 fl oz (241 ml) bottle **Schweppes** Slimline Shandy
slices of orange to decorate

Half fill two glasses with crushed ice. Add 1 tablespoon (15 ml) ginger cordial to each then divide the bottle of shandy between them. Decorate with a slice of orange on the rim of each glass. **Serves 2** (approx. 33 Calories per glass)

slimcea

Cream of Leek and Courgette Soup

4 medium leeks
8 oz (225 g) courgettes
1 pint (568 ml) **Slimcea** Light Milk
salt and pepper
parsley, chopped

Wash the leeks and courgettes, trim off ends and slice. Place these in a medium-sized saucepan with the milk and bring to the boil. Season and then simmer for 20 minutes until the vegetables are soft. Purée in a blender or pass through a sieve and reheat.

Serve with chopped parsley. **Serves 4** (approx. 100 Calories per portion)

Fish Caper

12 oz (350 g) coley fillet
¾ pint (450 ml) **Slimcea** Light Milk
1 bay leaf
2 oz (50 g) noodles
salt and pepper
2 level tablespoons (30 ml) cornflour

1 level tablespoon (15 ml)
  capers
4 gherkins, sliced
4 teaspoons (20 ml) parsley,
  chopped
4 oz (100 g) cheese, grated

Place the coley, milk and bay leaf in a frying pan and poach for 10 minutes. Strain and reserve the juice. Discard the bay leaf. Flake the fish, discarding all the skin and bones. Cook the noodles in salted water in the usual way. Blend the cornflour with a little water to form a smooth, thin paste. Pour the milk into the frying pan, heat to simmering and gradually stir in the cornflour paste. Bring slowly to the boil then simmer for 1–2 minutes. Stir the flaked fish, capers, gherkins, parsley and half the grated cheese into the sauce. Turn the mixture into a 1¾ pint (1 litre) serving dish. Arrange the noodles on top and sprinkle over the remaining grated cheese. Place under a hot grill until bubbling and golden brown. **Serves 4** (approx. 250 Calories per portion)

Savoury Pancakes

4 oz (100 g) plain flour
salt
1 egg
½ pint (300 ml) **Slimcea** Light
  Milk
8 oz (227 g) carton cottage
  cheese
4 oz (100 g) lean ham, chopped
freshly ground black pepper

Beat the eggs and milk together and add gradually to the flour, with a pinch of salt, in a mixing bowl to form a batter. Make 12 small pancakes from this and keep them warm. Mix the cottage cheese, ham, salt and pepper together and use to fill the rolled up pancakes. **Serves 4** (approx. 95 Calories per pancake)

Baked Egg Custard

1 pint (568 ml) **Slimcea** Light
  Milk
4 eggs
4 level teaspoons (20 ml) sugar
whole nutmeg

Warm the milk in a saucepan but do not allow to boil. Whisk the eggs and sugar lightly in a basin. Pour on the warm milk, stirring all the time. Strain the mixture through a nylon sieve into a lightly greased 1½ pint (900 ml) ovenproof dish. Finely grate over a little nutmeg. Stand the dish in a shallow roasting tin containing 1 in (2.5 cm) of water. This helps to ensure the custard does not curdle or separate through overheating. Bake in the oven at 325°F, 170°C, Gas Mark 3, for about 45 minutes, or until set and firm to the touch.

  May be served hot or cold.
Serves 4 (approx. 110 Calories per portion)

Orange Sherbet

2 oranges
½ pint (300 ml) water
1 level teaspoon (5 ml) **Slimcea**
  Sweet 'n Slim Granulated
  Sugar
1 pint (600 ml) unsweetened
  canned orange juice
juice of 1 lemon

Pare the rinds from the oranges free of all traces of white pith and put in a saucepan with the water. Boil for 10 minutes then strain. Add the Slimcea sugar to the strained liquid with the orange and lemon juices. Strain, chill and freeze in the freezing compartment of the refrigerator or in the freezer until firm but not hard.
Serves 4 (approx. 75 Calories per portion)

Raspberry Mousse

4 oz (100 g) fresh raspberries
1 egg white
1½ level teaspoons (7.5 ml)
  Slimcea Sweet 'n Slim
  Granulated Sugar

Crush the raspberries through a sieve, or liquidise. Add the Slimcea sugar. Whisk one egg white until stiff and fold into the raspberry purée. Pile into a small dish to serve. **Serves 1** (approx. 42 Calories per portion)

Tutti-Frutti Ice Cream

8 fl oz (225 ml) **Slimcea** Light
  Milk
3.1 oz (88 g) 2 sachet packet
  Dream Topping
1 oz (25 g) glacé cherries,
  chopped
1 tablespoon (15 ml) cut mixed
  peel, finely chopped
1 in (2.5 cm) strip angelica,
  finely sliced
2 dried apricots, finely
  chopped
large pinch ground cinnamon

Use the measured amount of Light Milk to make up the sachets of Dream Topping as directed on the packet. Fold in the dried fruit mixture and cinnamon. Turn into a rigid container and freeze until firm. Serve spooned into glasses.

  If preferred, pour the mixture into individual soufflé dishes and freeze. Serve in the dishes.
Serves 4 (approx. 130 Calories per portion)

Fresh Apple Drink

1½ lb (675 g) cooking apples
pared rind of 1 lemon
1½ pints (900 ml) boiling water
1 oz (25 g) **Slimcea** Sweet 'n
  Slim Granulated Sugar
apple slices to serve

Wash the apples and cut into wafer-thin slices, including the peels and cores. Put them into a heatproof bowl with the lemon rind. Pour the boiling water over the apple and cover the bowl. Leave until completely cold. Strain the liquid, add the Slimcea sugar and stir until dissolved. This drink keeps for up to 5 days.

  Serve with apple slices floating on top.
Makes 1½ pints (approx. 200 Calories total)

BEVERAGES

Bran Drink

1 tablespoon (15 ml) **Allinson**
   Bran Plus
1 oz (25 g) cottage cheese
¼ pint (150 ml) tomato juice

Mix all the ingredients in a
liquidiser. Serve cold as a starter to
a meal.   **Serves 2**

Toffee Tumbler

½ pint (300 ml) cold milk
2 teaspoons (10 ml) **Bird's**
   Toffee Instant Whip
1 scoop vanilla ice cream
8 Maltesers
Maltesers to decorate (optional)

Put all the ingredients into a
liquidiser and blend until all the
Maltesers have been crushed. Pour
into glasses. If liked, decorate with
more Maltesers.   **Serves 2**

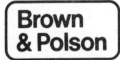

Hot Noggin

2 pints (1.2 litres) milk
1 packet **Brown & Polson**
   Chocolate Blancmange
   Powder
1–2 tablespoons (15–30 ml)
   brown sugar
1–2 tablespoons (15–30 ml)
   brandy *or* sherry (optional)
8 marshmallows

Pour the milk into a small
saucepan and sprinkle over the
blancmange powder and sugar.
Bring to the boil, whisking

continuously, and simmer for 1–
2 minutes. Stir in the brandy or
sherry. Pour into 4 mugs and float
2 marshmallows on top of each
mug.   **Serves 4**

Cream Sherry Pomagne

1 bottle **Bulmers** Sweet
   Pomagne
1 wine glass cherry brandy
1 tablespoon (15 ml) cherry
   ripple ice cream to each glass
glacé or maraschino cherries to
   decorate

Mix together the Pomagne and
cherry brandy and chill. Pour into
large glasses, top with the ice
cream and decorate with
cherries.

Grape and Apple Delight

1 bottle **Bulmers** Grape Juice
1 bottle **Bulmers** Apple Juice
1 small bottle soda water
2 oz (50 g) sugar
¼ pint (150 ml) water
juice of 2 lemons
1 banana, sliced
4 oz (100 g) grapes, with skins
   and seeds removed
slices of lemon and glacé *or*
   maraschino cherries to
   decorate

Chill the grape and apple juices
and soda water. Boil the sugar and
water together, add the lemon
juice and chill. Mix all together,
except the soda water, when
thoroughly chilled. Put slices of
banana and prepared grapes into
glasses, pour juice mixture onto
these and top up with soda water.
Decorate with slices of lemon and
cherries.

Mulled Cider Cup

2 oranges
2 lemons
cloves
1 bottle **Bulmers** Special
   Reserve Fine Dry Cider
½ bottle sherry
1 glass brandy
1–2 sticks cinnamon

Stick 1 orange and 1 lemon with
cloves. Slice the remaining orange
and lemon. Put the cider, sherry
brandy, cinnamon, whole and
sliced fruit into a large saucepan.
Gently heat until simmering point
(do not allow to boil). Simmer for
about 2 minutes then remove the
cinnamon sticks. Pour into a jug or
bowl to serve.
   Serve hot with fruit slices. It is
advisable to put a metal spoon into
the jug or bowl when pouring in
the hot cup to prevent cracking.

Special Reserve Cup

1 orange
2 lemons
¼ pint (150 ml) water
3 oz (75 g) sugar
ice cubes
1 bottle **Bulmers** Special
   Reserve Cider
wine glass of brandy
cucumber slices, mint and
   orange slices to decorate

Pare the rinds from the orange and
lemons very thinly and squeeze
out the juice. Simmer the rinds in
the water for about 5 minutes and
add the sugar. Strain and allow to
cool. Blend with the fruit juices.
Put the ice into a bowl or jug, add
the fruit syrup, cider and brandy
and stir gently. Decorate with
cucumber, mint and orange
slices.

Cadbury's

Banana Shake

4 tablespoons (80 ml)
  Cadbury's Drinking
  Chocolate
1 pint (550 ml) milk
2 ripe bananas
vanilla ice cream
4 small **Cadbury's** Flakes

Mix the drinking chocolate with a
little boiling water then pour into a
liquidiser with the cold milk,
bananas and a scoop of ice cream.
Blend until smooth and frothy.
Pour into 4 glasses or mugs and
top each with a scoop of ice cream
and a Flake.   **Serves 4**

Chocolate Noggin

1 ripe banana
2 tablespoons (40 ml) natural
  yoghurt
½ pint (275 ml) cold milk
2 tablespoons (40 ml)
  Cadbury's Drinking
  Chocolate
4 tablespoons (80 ml)
  Schweppes Peppermint
  Cordial

Blend all the ingredients together
in a liquidiser until frothy and
quite thick.   **Serves 3**

After Dinner Camp

Camp Highland Warmer
2 teaspoons (10 ml) **Camp**
  Coffee and Chicory Essence
5 tablespoons (75 ml) hot water
1 tablespoon (15 ml) Scotch *or*
  Irish whisky
cream
sugar to taste
Camp Russian
2 teaspoons (10 ml) **Camp**
  Coffee and Chicory Essence

5 tablespoons (75 ml) hot water
1 tablespoon (15 ml) vodka
cream
sugar to taste
Camp Caribbean
2 teaspoons (10 ml) **Camp**
  Coffee and Chicory Essence
5 tablespoons (75 ml) hot water
1 tablespoon (15 ml) rum
cream
sugar to taste
Camp Parisian
1 teaspoon (5 ml) **Camp** Coffee
  and Chicory Essence
5 tablespoons (75 ml) hot water
1 tablespoon (15 ml) brandy
cream
sugar to taste
Camp Orange
1 teaspoon (5 ml) **Camp** Coffee
  and Chicory Essence
5 tablespoons (75 ml) hot water
1 tablespoon (15 ml) Cointreau
cream
sugar to taste

Pour the spirits first, then add the
sugar, Camp Essence and hot
water and stir. Pour the cream over
the back of a warm spoon on to the
coffee and it will settle on the
top.   **Each recipe serves 1**

Caribbean Iced Coffee

1 tablespoon (15 ml) **Camp**
  Chicory and Coffee Essence
2 teaspoons (10 ml) dark rum
½ pint (300 ml) ice cold milk
Topping: (optional)
1 tablespoon (15 ml) whipped
  cream
a little **Schwartz** Ground
  Cinnamon
or
approx 1 tablespoon (15 ml)
  vanilla ice cream
a little **Camp** Chicory and
  Coffee Essence
2 **Schwartz** Whole Cinnamon
  Sticks

Pour the Camp Essence and the
rum into a glass, add the milk and
stir well until thoroughly
combined. Either top the drink
with whipped cream and a
sprinkling of ground cinnamon or

with ice cream and a swirl of Camp
Essence, with 2 whole cinnamon
sticks protruding.
Makes ½ pint

Carnation.

Coffee Milk Shake

1 tablespoon (15 ml) instant
  coffee
3 tablespoons (45 ml) icing
  sugar
2 tablespoons (30 ml) boiling
  water
²/₃ large can **Carnation**
  Evaporated Milk
vanilla ice cream
1 oz (25 g) walnuts, chopped

Dissolve the instant coffee and
icing sugar in the boiling water.
Add the Carnation milk made up
to 1 pint (600 ml) with cold water
and whisk until thoroughly
blended. Chill before serving.
Pour into glasses and top each with
a spoonful of vanilla ice cream and
chopped walnuts.
**Makes approximately 1 pint
(600 ml)**

Hot Minty Chocolate

1 small can **Carnation**
  Evaporated Milk
8 chocolate coated peppermint
  creams

Make the Carnation milk up to
¾ pint (450 ml) with water and
heat gently over a moderate heat
but do not boil. Roughly chop the
peppermint creams and whisk
them into the hot Carnation until
they have completely dissolved.
Serve at once.
**Makes approximately 1 pint
(600 ml)**

DUBONNET

Dubonnet Punch

14½ oz (410 g) can fruit cocktail
5 tablespoons (75 ml) brandy
75 cl bottle **Dubonnet**
2 (11.5 fl oz, 326 ml) cans
    Schweppes Lemonade
orange and lemon slices
ice cubes to serve

Steep the contents of the can of
fruit cocktail in the brandy in a
bowl for several hours. Add the
Dubonnet and lemonade. Float the
orange and lemon slices on the
surface, add the ice cubes and
serve.   **Serves 10**

GALE'S

Honeyed Hot Orange

6 oranges
4 tablespoons (60 ml) lemon
    juice
½ pint (300 ml) water
¼ pint (150 ml) **Gale's** Clear
    Honey
a few cloves

Squeeze the juice from five of the
oranges and add the lemon juice.
Add the water and sweeten with
the honey. Heat until almost
boiling and pour into mugs. Slice
the remaining orange and press
one or two cloves into the centre of
each slice. Float an orange slice on
the top of each mug.   **Serves 4**

Mulled Wine

1 bottle red wine
3 tablespoons (45 ml) **Gale's**
    Clear Honey
1 orange, studded with cloves
1 pint (600 ml) boiling water
1 miniature bottle brandy
good pinch ground cinnamon

Heat the wine, honey and
cinnamon with the orange and stir
well. Add the boiling water and

just before serving stir in the
brandy. It is not necessary to use
an expensive wine for this recipe.

Kellogg's

Breakfast Nog

1 packet **Kellogg's** Rise & Shine
    Orange
1 pint (600 ml) water
2 eggs, beaten

Make up the Rise & Shine with the
water. Heat until almost boiling
then quickly pour on to the beaten
eggs, whisking. Serve immediately.   **Serves 2**

Honey and Banana Breakfast Drink

2 bananas
1 packet **Kellogg's** Rise & Shine
    Orange
2 teaspoons (10 ml) honey
½ teaspoon (2.5 ml) ground
    cinnamon
1 pint (568 ml) cold milk

Mash the bananas in a bowl. Add
the Rise & Shine, honey and
cinnamon and gradually whisk in
the milk.
    Pour into individual glasses to
serve.   **Serves 2–4**

Icy Blackcurrant Surprise

1 packet **Kellogg's** Rise & Shine
    Blackcurrant
1 pint (600 ml) lemonade
1 individual block vanilla ice
    cream

Put all the ingredients into a large
jug and whisk together until
thoroughly blended.
    Pour into tall glasses to serve.
Serves 2–4

Lemon Balalaika

1 packet **Kellogg's** Rise & Shine
    Lemon
1 miniature bottle *or* 2
    measures Cointreau

2 miniature bottles *or*
    4 measures vodka
crushed ice
8 orange slices

Make up the Rise & Shine according to the packet instructions.
Mix together the lemon drink,
Cointreau and vodka and shake or
whisk well together.
    Pour over the ice into four
glasses and serve with the orange
slices.   **Serves 4**

Spicy Hot Tea Punch

2 pints (1.2 litres) water
½ pint (300 ml) **Kellogg's** Rise
    & Shine Orange (made up)
¼ pint (150 ml) **Kellogg's** Rise
    & Shine Lemon (made up)
4 oz (100 g) caster sugar
2 teaspoons (10 ml) whole
    cloves
1 cinnamon stick
1 teaspoon (5 ml) whole
    allspice
2 tea bags

Put all the ingredients except the
tea bags into a large saucepan and
bring to the boil. Reduce the heat
and simmer for 5 minutes.
Remove from the heat, add the tea
bags and allow to infuse for
5 minutes. Discard the tea bags
and spices and serve hot.
Serves 8–10

Ginger Glow

6 cloves
piece of cinnamon stick
1 orange, thinly peeled
1 lemon, thinly peeled
1 pint (550 ml) water
1 bottle red wine
⅓ pint (170 ml) brandy
¼ pint (125 ml) concentrated
    Kia-Ora Orange Drink
2 heaped tablespoons (80 ml)
    caster sugar
¼ pint (125 ml) **Schweppes**
    Ginger Cordial

Put the cloves, cinnamon stick and the thinly peeled rinds of the lemon and orange into a saucepan with the water, bring to the boil, simmer for 10 minutes then strain. Add the red wine, brandy, orange drink, sugar and ginger cordial. Heat gently until almost boiling, but do not allow to boil. Stir all the time.

Serve hot in small punch cups or glasses. **Serves 6–8**

Spicy Mulled Punch

1 pint (550 ml) cider
¼ pint (125 ml) concentrated **Kia-Ora** Orange Drink
4 oz (100 g) soft brown sugar
piece of cinnamon stick
1 pint (550 ml) water
1 orange
1 pint (550 ml) strong tea
¼ pint (125 ml) brandy

Heat the cider, orange drink, sugar, cinnamon stick and water in a large saucepan. Add the thinly peeled rind of the orange, cut into narrow strips, and the orange flesh in chunks. Infuse for a few hours. Add the tea and brandy and reheat gently. Serve hot in special glasses or put a metal spoon into each glass and add the hot liquid gradually to avoid breaking the glass.
Serves 10

Ashbourne Fizz

1 large bottle sparkling **Ashbourne** Water
41¾ fl oz (1.8 litre) can **Libby's** Unsweetened Orange Juice
dash of Angostura Bitters
orange slices
mint sprigs
brandy *or* rum (optional)

Combine the Ashbourne water, orange juice and bitters together in a large jug. Add the orange slices and chill. Pour into glasses and garnish with the mint sprigs.

If alcohol is used, place one measure in each glass and top up with Ashbourne Fizz. **Serves 6–8**

Créole Café Brulôt

2 cups strong, freshly prepared, **Lyons** Coffee
½ cup brandy
1 whole orange peel cut in a spiral
1 whole lemon peel cut in a spiral
3 in (8 cm) cinnamon stick
12 whole cloves
2 in (5 cm) vanilla pod
4 cubes sugar

Place all the spices and fruit peels, together with the brandy, in a saucepan and heat slowly. Warm a ladle, by putting it under hot water, and scoop up one ladle full of liquid from the saucepan. Place the sugar lumps in the ladle and set alight. Gently pour the flaming spirit back into the pan. Add the strong, hot coffee and allow to infuse for about 3 minutes.

To serve, pour through a strainer into small coffee cups.
Serves 4–6

Continental Iced Coffee

2 tablespoons (30 ml) **Nescafé** Blend 37
2 tablespoons (30 ml) boiling water
4 heaped teaspoons (40 ml) Chocolate **Nesquik**
2 level tablespoons (30 ml) caster sugar
1 small can **Nestlé's** Ideal Milk
Nestlé's Cream for serving
Nescafé Blend 37 granules for serving

Dissolve the Nescafé in the boiling water and make up to 1 pint (600 ml) with cold water. Whisk in the Nesquik, sugar and Ideal Milk. Chill well, then serve in tall glasses topped with a teaspoon of Nestlé's Cream and a sprinkling of coffee granules. **Serves 3**

Nescafé on the Rocks

3 fl oz (90 ml) chilled milk
6 fl oz (180 ml) iced water
3 teaspoons (45 ml) **Nescafé**
2 teaspoons (30 ml) sugar (icing sugar is best)

Measure the ingredients into a shaker or large, screw-topped jar and shake vigorously for 5 seconds. Pour into a tall glass and serve with plenty of ice.
Serves 1

Strawberry Mallow

1 pint (600 ml) milk
6 rounded teaspoons (50 ml) Strawberry **Nesquik**
6 marshmallows
Milo for sprinkling

Bring the milk to the boil and pour into 3 mugs or heatproof glasses. Stir 2 teaspoons (20 ml) of Nesquik into each mug; top with two lightly toasted marshmallows and sprinkle with the Milo.
Serves 3

Crusha Coolers

3 capfuls *or* 3 teaspoons **Rayner's Crusha** Milk Shake Syrup for each person
½ pint (300 ml) milk for each person
lightly beaten egg white and caster sugar to decorate each glass

Put the lightly beaten egg white on a saucer and the castor sugar on a piece of paper. Dip the rim of a tall glass in the egg white and then into the sugar, flicking the sugar up with the edge of the paper so that it clings to the egg white. Turn the glass upright and leave to dry.

Put the Crusha into a prepared glass and add the milk. No need to shake or stir if the milk is added reasonably quickly. **Serves 3–4**

Portuguese Wine Cup

1 bottle Portuguese white
  wine, chilled
1 bottle Portuguese rosé wine,
  chilled
3 tablespoons (45 ml) **Rayner's
  Crusha** Strawberry Milk
  Shake Syrup
6 tablespoons (90 ml) brandy
1 bottle lemonade, chilled

Mix the wines with the Crusha and
brandy. Add the lemonade and
serve at once.   **Serves 8**

Super Shakers

²/₃ glass of milk
1 portion ice cream
1–1½ tablespoons (15–20 ml)
  Rayner's Crusha Milk Shake
  Syrup

Place the milk, ice cream and
Crusha in a bowl, whisk and pour
into a glass.   **Serves 1**

Children's Party Punch

8 oz (225 g) white sugar
1 pint (550 ml) water
1¾ pints (1 litre) grapefruit
  juice
1¾ pints (1 litre) orange juice
¾ pint (400 ml) **Rose's** Lime
  Juice Cordial
1¾ pints (1 litre) **Schweppes**
  Ginger Ale
ice cubes and slices of fruit to
  serve

Dissolve the sugar in the water
over a gentle heat and, when quite
clear, boil for no more than
2 minutes. Leave the syrup to cool.
Make up the punch in a large bowl
or jug by combining the cooled
sugar syrup with the grapefruit
and orange juices. Stir in the lime
juice cordial and add the ginger
ale. Add slices of fruit and ice
cubes just before serving.
Serves 12

Dean's Gate

crushed ice
1 sherry glass white rum
½ sherry glass **Rose's** Lime
  Juice Cordial
½ sherry glass Drambuie
twists of orange peel to decorate

Half fill a small glass jug with the
crushed ice. Measure in the liquids
and leave to chill thoroughly
before straining into glasses. Do
not allow the ice to melt. Decorate
with the orange peel twists.
Serves 2–3

Lime on the Rocks

2 tablespoons (40 ml) **Rose's**
  Lime Juice Cordial
2 tablespoons (40 ml) fresh
  lemon juice
1 heaped teaspoon (10 ml) icing
  sugar
1 teaspoon (5 ml) egg white
ice cubes
Schweppes Soda Water
slices of lime to serve

Put the lime juice cordial and
lemon juice into a screw-topped jar
or cocktail shaker. Add the icing
sugar and egg white and shake
vigorously until thoroughly
mixed. Pile ice cubes into 3 small
cocktail glasses, divide the lime
mixture between them then add a
dash of soda water to each.
Decorate each glass with slice of
lime and serve immediately.
Serves 3

ROWNTREE'S

Strawberry Cider Punch

2 packets **Rowntree's**
  Strawberry Jelly
3 pints (2 litres) cider, well
  chilled
½ pint (300 ml) lemon juice
2 bottles (1 litre size) lemonade
ice cubes, slices of apple and
  fresh *or* frozen strawberries

Make up the strawberry jellies as
directed on the pack. When cool,
pour into a large punch bowl and

add the other ingredients. Mix
well, add plenty of ice cubes and
decorate with the slices of apple
and fresh or frozen strawberries.

SCHWARTZ

Fruity Spiced Punch

1 pint (550 ml) sweetened
  orange juice
1 pint (550 ml) strong still cider
¼ pint (150 ml) water
½ teaspoon (2.5 ml) **Schwartz**
  Ground Ginger
½ teaspoon (2.5 ml) **Schwartz**
  Mixed Spice
1 orange, sliced
1 apple, sliced

Place the orange juice, cider, water
and spices in a saucepan. Bring the
mixture to the boil, then simmer
gently over a low heat for about
5 minutes. Pour into glasses and
add slices of orange and apple to
the warm punch before serving.
Makes 2½ pints (1.5 litres)

Potent Party Punch

1 bottle red wine
1 pint (550 ml) medium sweet
  cider
3 tablespoons (45 ml) honey,
  plus extra to taste if required
3 heaped teaspoons (30 ml)
  Schwartz Whole Allspice
2 **Schwartz** Cinnamon Sticks,
  roughly broken
2 tablespoons (30 ml) dark rum
apple and orange slices to
  decorate

Place the wine, cider, honey, allspice and cinnamon in a saucepan.
Heat gently at just below boiling
point for about 10 minutes. Add
the rum and adjust the sweetness
to taste by adding a little more
honey if required. Strain the
punch through a sieve, discarding
the spices. Add the slices of fruit to
decorate and serve warm in
warmed glasses.
Makes about 2¼ pints (1.3 litres)

Brandy Buster

1 measure brandy
½ measure orange Curaçao
ice cubes
Schweppes American Ginger
   Ale
lemon peel to decorate

Pour the brandy and orange
Curaçao into a large tumbler. Add
some ice cubes, top up with the
American ginger ale and stir.
Decorate with the lemon peel.
Serves 1

Cool Dew

1 measure vodka
½ measure Cointreau
Schweppes Tonic Water
ice cubes
slice of lemon

Add the vodka to the Cointreau
and top up with Schweppes Tonic
Water. Add ice and a slice of lemon
and stir.   **Serves 1**

Devilled Tomato Cocktail

2 teaspoons (10 ml) white wine
   vinegar
dash of Worcestershire sauce
4 fl oz (114 ml) **Schweppes**
   Tomato Juice Cocktail
slice of cucumber and 2 stuffed
   olives to decorate

Stir the vinegar and Worcestershire sauce into the Tomato Juice
Cocktail and chill well. Serve
decorated with a slice of cucumber
and 2 stuffed olives on a cocktail
stick.   **Serves 1**

Hot Toddy

1 measure whisky
1 tablespoon (20 ml)
   Schweppes Ginger Cordial
1 tablespoon (20 ml) clear
   honey
juice of ½ a lemon
boiling water

Place the whisky, ginger cordial,
honey and lemon juice in a mug or
heatproof glass. Fill up with
boiling water, stirring well.
Serves 1

Party Warmer

1 bottle inexpensive red wine
1 pint (550 ml) apple juice
½ pint (275 ml) **Schweppes**
   Ginger Cordial
8 cloves
1 stick cinnamon
2 lemons
2 oz (50 g) caster sugar
1 measure brandy

Empty the wine, apple juice and
ginger cordial into a saucepan.
Add the cloves and the cinnamon
stick broken in half. Reserve a few
slices of lemon, grate a little lemon
rind and add all the juice. Cover
the pan and heat for an hour but on
no account allow to boil. Lift out
the cinnamon and any cloves that
can be seen, add the sugar, brandy
and lemon slices and serve in small
amounts in heatproof mugs or
glasses.

   It is easy to increase the amount
for a larger number of people but it
is essential to warm the liquid for
the given length of time so that the
flavour develops.   **Serves 6–8**

Sunny Zip

3 dessertspoons (40 ml)
   Schweppes Ginger Cordial
1 bottle 7UP
slice of orange to decorate

Measure the ginger cordial into a
tall glass and pour the 7UP on top.
Decorate with the slice of
orange.   **Serves 1**

Tropical Quencher

fresh orange juice
Schweppes Lime Flavoured
   Cordial
lemon juice
Pepsi-Cola
ice cubes
slices or orange and lemon

Measure equal amounts of fresh
orange juice to lime flavoured
cordial into glasses or a jug. Add
half quantity of lemon juice and
top up with the chilled Pepsi-Cola
and ice cubes, adding slices or
orange and lemon if liked.

Ginger Tea Toddy

1 pint (550 ml) **Typhoo** Tea
½ pint (275 ml) **Schweppes**
   Ginger Cordial
½ pint (275 ml) cider
2 oz (50 g) caster sugar
6 cloves
4 tablespoons (80 ml) whisky
1 orange, sliced

Place all the ingredients in a
saucepan and bring to the boil.
Simmer for about 5 minutes. Serve
hot in mugs.   **Serves 6**

Lime Tea

2 **Ty-Phoo** Fresh Brew Tea Bags
1 pint (550 ml) boiling water
1 tablespoon (20 ml) sugar
¼ pint (125 ml) **Rose's** Lime
   Juice Cordial
slices of lime to serve

Place the tea bags in a warm jug
and pour on the boiling water.
Leave to brew for a short while to
the required strength then remove
the bags. Stir in the sugar and lime
juice cordial. Serve in heatproof
glasses with thin slices of lime
floating on top.

   Lime Tea is also most refreshing
served chilled on a warm day.
Serves 3–4

245

Chocolate Mandarin Whizz

11 oz (312 g) can **John West** Mandarin Oranges in Light Syrup
5 oz (142 ml) carton natural yoghurt
2 eggs
2 teaspoons (10 ml) drinking chocolate *or* malted milk powder

Put all the ingredients into a liquidiser and blend until smooth. Pour into glasses and serve immediately.
Makes 4 small servings

Honey Wheat Grapefruit Dip

19 oz (539 g) can **John West** Grapefruit Segments in Natural Juice
3 tablespoons (45 ml) wheatgerm
4–5 tablespoons (60–75 ml) honey
¼ pint (125 ml) milk
2 scoops ice cream

Put the grapefruit segments, juice from the can, wheatgerm and honey into a liquidiser and blend until smooth. Leave for about 10 minutes for the wheatgerm to soften, then add the milk and blend until frothy. Pour into glasses and serve topped with ice cream.   **Serves 4–6**

Pineapple Jogger

15½ oz (439 g) can **John West** Pineapple Rings in Natural Juice
5 oz (125 ml) carton natural yoghurt
4 tablespoons (60 ml) rosehip syrup
½ pint (250 ml) milk

Put the pineapple rings, juice from the can, yoghurt and rosehip syrup into a liquidiser and blend until smooth. Add the milk and blend until frothy. Pour into glasses and serve.   **Serves 4**

Tomato Taster

14 oz (397 g) can **John West** Tomatoes
juice of 1 large orange
1 medium carrot, peeled and chopped
1 stick celery, chopped
1 in (2.5 cm) piece of cucumber, peeled and chopped
salt and pepper
few drops Worcestershire sauce

Put all the ingredients in a liquidiser goblet and blend until smooth. Rub through a coarse strainer, pour into glasses and serve.   **Serves 3–4**

BRAND NAME INDEX

RECIPE INDEX